Wayne O. McCready is Professor of Western Religions and Director of the Calgary Institute for the Humanities at the University of Calgary and the author of numerous articles on Second Temple Jewish literature.

Adele Reinhartz is Associate Vice President for Research and Professor of Classics and Religious Studies at the University of Ottawa and the author of *"Why Ask My Name?" Anonymity and Identity in Biblical Narrative* (1998), *Befriending the Beloved Disciple: A Jewish Reading of the Gospel of John* (2001), *Scripture on the Silver Screen* (2003), and *Jesus of Hollywood* (2006).

Common
Judaism

Common Judaism

Explorations in
Second-Temple Judaism

Edited by Wayne O. McCready and Adele Reinhartz

Minneapolis
Fortress Press

COMMON JUDAISM
Explorations in Second-Temple Judaism

Scripture quotations are from the New Revised Standard Version Bible, copyright © 1989 by the Division of Christian Education of the National Council of the Churches of Christ in the USA. Used by permission. All rights reserved.

Cover images: Scale model of Jerusalem, photo © Erich Lessing / Art Resource, NY. Hebrew Bible text photo © IStockphoto.com / Boris Katsman.
Cover design: John Goodman
Book design: Jessica A. Puckett

Library of Congress Cataloging-in-Publication Data

Common Judaism : explorations in Second-Temple Judaism / Wayne O. McCready and Adele Reinhartz, eds.
    p. cm.
  Includes indexes.
  ISBN 978-0-8006-6299-8 (alk. paper)
  1. Judaism—History. I. McCready, Wayne O., 1947– II. Reinhartz, Adele, 1953– III. Title.

  BM155.3.C66 2008
  296.09'014—dc22

                                                        2008022280

The paper used in this publication meets the minimum requirements of American National Standard for Information Sciences—Permanence of Paper for Printed Library Materials, ANSI Z329.48-1984.

Manufactured in the U.S.A.

12   11   10   09   08   1   2   3   4   5   6   7   8   9   10

Dedicated to Ed Parish Sanders, our esteemed and wise teacher, who taught us knowledge, sought to find pleasing words, and wrote words of truth plainly (Ecclesiastes 12:9-10)

CONTENTS

Contributors

David Amit is Senior Archaeologist for the Israel Antiquities Authority, Jerusalem, Israel.

Albert I. Baumgarten is Professor in the Department of Jewish History at Bar Ilan University, Ramat Gan, Israel.

Susan Haber (deceased) was a doctoral student in the Department of Religious Studies at McMaster University, Hamilton, Ontario.

Lee I. Levine is Professor of Jewish History and the Rev. Moses Bernard Lauterman Family Chair in Classical Archaeology at the Institute of Archaeology, Hebrew University of Jerusalem, Israel.

Wayne O. McCready is Professor in the Department of Religious Studies and Director of the Calgary Institute for the Humanities at the University of Calgary, Calgary, Alberta, Canada.

David M. Miller is Assistant Professor of New Testament at Briercrest College and Seminary in Caronport, Saskatchewan, Canada.

Anne Moore is Senior Instructor in the Department of Religious Studies at the University of Calgary, Calgary, Alberta, Canada.

Tessa Rajak is Professor of Ancient History in the Department of Classics at the University of Reading, Reading, United Kingdom.

Adele Reinhartz is Professor in the Department of Classics and Religious Studies at the University of Ottawa, Ottawa, Ontario, Canada.

Anders Runesson is Associate Professor in the Department of Religious Studies at McMaster University, Hamilton, Ontario, Canada.

E. P. Sanders is Arts and Sciences Professor of Religion Emeritus in the Department of Religion at Duke University, Durham, North Carolina.

Seth Schwartz is Professor of History at Jewish Theological Seminary, New York, New York.

Ian W. Scott is Assistant Professor of New Testament at Tyndale Seminary, Toronto, Ontario, Canada.

Eliezer Segal is Professor in the Department of Religious Studies at the University of Calgary, Calgary, Alberta, Canada.

Cecilia Wassen is Assistant Professor in the Department of Religious Studies at Uppsala University, Uppsala, Sweden.

Boaz Zissu is Senior Lecturer in the Department of Land of Israel Studies and Archaeology at Bar Ilan University, Ramat Gan, Israel.

Acknowledgments

This book would not have been possible without the help of some key individuals and organizations. The workshop at which the papers were first presented and the ideas developed was generously funded by the Social Sciences and Humanities Research Council of Canada, with additional support from the Department of Religious Studies and the Faculty of Humanities at the University of Calgary and the Department of Religious Studies at McMaster University. The workshop was graciously hosted by the Calgary Institute for the Humanities at the University of Calgary. We are particularly grateful for the assistance of Denise Hamel, administrator of the Humanities Institute, for overseeing the practical arrangements for the workshop and communicating with the contributors throughout the process of book preparation. The Institute and University of Ottawa funded two meetings between the coeditors in Calgary, during which we were able to plan the book's themes and structures and outline the introduction and conclusion. Steven Scott, a Ph.D. candidate at the University of Ottawa, acted as research assistant; he formatted the essays in conformity with Fortress guidelines, prepared the bibliography, and assisted with the copyediting and final proofreading. Albert Baumgarten helped us to shape the vision for the workshop and provided valuable editorial advice particularly on the introductory and concluding chapters. Our appreciation is also offered to the editorial and production staff of Fortress Press for working with us to bring this project to fruition.

Finally, we wish to thank Ed Sanders for his active participation in this entire project. Not only did he engage with all of the papers during the conference, but he prepared detailed comments on each one, which the writers found invaluable in the process of revising their papers for publication. While this book is not a Festschrift in the usual sense, we hope that by engaging so seriously with Ed's work we have acknowledged one small part of the debt that we personally owe him for his role as our teacher and mentor and that the field of studies in first-century Judaism owes him for his monumental contribution.

.

Introduction

1. Common Judaism and Diversity within Judaism

Wayne O. McCready and Adele Reinhartz

In *Judaism: Practice and Belief, 63 BCE–66 CE* (Philadelphia: Trinity Press International, 1992), E. P. Sanders argued that, notwithstanding the well-known diversity of first-century Judaism, the ordinary people practiced a common Judaism centered on temple, synagogue, and home. In Sanders's words, ordinary people "worked at their jobs, they believed the Bible, they carried out the small routines and celebrations of the religion, they prayed every day, thanked God for his blessings, and on the Sabbath went to the synagogue, asked teachers questions, and listened respectfully."[1]

In the sixteen years since the publication of Sanders's book, the idea that there existed a common Judaism that transcended the well-known parties and sects has become widely accepted, at the same time as scholars continue to explore the diverse forms of first-century Judaism. This collection of essays builds on Sanders's insights in order to explore both the consistency and the variety within first-century Judaism in Judea and in the Diaspora. Most of the essays were presented in preliminary form at a workshop held under the auspices of the Calgary Institute for the Humanities, University of Calgary, May 15–17, 2005. The Social Sciences and Humanities Research Council of Canada generously funded the workshop.

Two main questions guide the book. First, is it possible to describe more precisely the interplay between common Judaism and Jewish diversity in the first century? Second, does the common Judaism that Sanders described so convincingly extend beyond Judea to other areas of Roman Palestine and the Diaspora? In addressing these questions, the essays examine the variety of evidence of first-century Judaism, both literary and material. While the overall approach is historical-critical, the essays also draw on other

1

methodological approaches including literary and social-scientific criticism. The result is both a tribute to the impact of Sanders's theory about common Judaism and an original contribution to our understanding of first-century Judaism in all its diversity.

Common Judaism

At first glance, common Judaism seems to be a simple and uncontroversial concept. It acknowledges the deep differences among known groups that fell within the spectrum of Judaism in the Second Temple period, including the Pharisees, the Sadducees, and the Essenes. But it asserts that there nevertheless existed a common core of practice and belief that characterized Jews qua Jews, whether they were affiliated with a group or not. This common core would have been recognized as "Jewish" by Jews and Gentiles alike.

But the term "common Judaism" in fact makes a twofold and therefore more complex claim. In the first instance, the term signifies the beliefs and practices of the vast majority of Jews in the Second Temple period who did not belong to the major parties or sects and therefore did not engage in the practices or hold the beliefs that differentiated one group from another. In other words, common Judaism reflects the lives of the common Jews, those who were often referred to as the 'ammê hā-āreṣ as well as the ordinary priests, as distinct from "the powerful," including the chief priests as well as the Pharisees, Sadducees, and Essenes.[2] This understanding emphasizes the distinction between the ordinary people on the one hand and the powerful people on the other. Further, it suggests that the common people were not as unconcerned with their lives as Jews as some of the primary sources made them out to be. Sanders, following Morton Smith, points out that one of the features of a Scripture-based religion is that texts deemed Scripture cannot be the property of the elite only. In Second Temple Judaism, Scripture was accessible to laypeople who encountered it regularly in the synagogue. Thus, we must at least consider the possibility that ordinary people were responsible for knowing and observing the law in their private lives. Smith notes, for example, that in the Second Temple period, laypeople claimed to be better informed about purity laws than the temple priesthood, on the basis of both knowledge and interpretation of Scripture.[3]

The term also had a broader referent, however: not only those aspects of Judaism that were held in common by the ordinary people and the ordinary priests, but also those that would have been followed by Pharisees, Sadducees, Essenes, and other special groups alongside their own specific practices. As Sanders notes in the chapter included in the present volume, there are four elements that Jews held in common: (1) they believed in and worshiped the God of Israel; (2) they accepted the Hebrew Bible (often in translation) as revealing God's will; (3) consequently they observed most aspects of the Mosaic law; and (4) they identified themselves with the history and fate of the Jewish people.[4] Practice was centered on three physical locales: the temple, the synagogue, and the home.

Sanders's 1992 book addresses primarily the first sense of common Judaism, although the second sense is also adumbrated at numerous points. The focus on the practices and beliefs of the common people rather than of the elite was a powerful response to two major trends in scholarship on this period. One was the emphasis on the Pharisees as the originators and/or transmitters of the theological and legal traditions that later became normative Judaism. The second was the tendency of scholars to focus on what was distinctive about the sects and parties mentioned in our extant sources, to the point of referring to them as distinctive "Judaisms" rather than as diverse, divergent, and sometimes antagonistic Jewish groups. Also a factor, at least among scholars interested in the place of nascent Christianity within the Jewish spectrum, was the relationship of the Jesus movement, including its Pauline manifestation, to the rest of Jewish society, particularly as the movement forged its theology and opened up membership to Gentiles without requiring conversion to Judaism.

Although Sanders's immediate focus was on the lives of the ordinary people as distinct from the elite, he recognized that the practices and beliefs associated with the common people were by no means rejected by the Pharisees, Sadducees, Essenes, and the more powerful priests. They too observed the pilgrimage festivals, believed the Torah to be divinely given, and were intensely involved with the temple, the synagogue, and the home as the loci for religious activity; this common Judaism then served as a point of departure for the specific practices of particular groups.

The comprehensive understanding of common Judaism, a consistent thread throughout the book, has come increasingly to the fore in Sanders's subsequent writings on this topic. In the essay included in the present volume, Sanders expresses this understanding vividly in the form of a question: "If in (let us say) 60 C.E. a Jew from Italy, one from Egypt, one from Mesopotamia, and one from Jerusalem sat together for Passover, would each recognize what the other was doing? If they talked about the Jewish people and the law of Moses, would they find common ground?" In his view, the answer is yes.

While Sanders's *Judaism: Practice and Belief* was not a polemical work, it did indirectly comment on the tendency of scholars to focus on the religious elites whose views are reflected in the extant sources and are often interpreted as both descriptive and prescriptive with regard to both practice and belief. In this sense, it anticipated the current interest in social history and, more precisely, in "lived religion," which studies religion not as it is preached from the pulpit or enshrined in learned theological tomes, but as it is practiced by the common people, as it influences their daily lives, informs their decisions in matters large and small, and structures their days, weeks, months, and years.[5]

The Impact of "Common Judaism"

Judaism: Practice and Belief had a major impact on the study of Second Temple Judaism, not only because of the power of the hypothesis and the arguments in its favor, but also because of the compelling way in which the book described the experience of ordinary

Jews during this period. Every student of Second Temple Judaism and, indeed, of the Gospels knows that Jewish males were enjoined to make pilgrimage to the temple to offer sacrifices for the festivals of Tabernacles, Passover, and Weeks. For many readers, however, it was Sanders's detailed description that made them truly reflect on what the experience may have been like. His ability to piece together information from disparate sources in order to provide the detailed description of common Jewish life made readers recognize the significance that this common Judaism would have had for ordinary people. It is no exaggeration to say that since the publication of this book, virtually every scholar who tries to make sense of the variety and diversity of evidence for Judaism in this period addresses Sanders's theory and situates his or her work in the context of Sanders's theory of common Judaism.

This is not to say, of course, that all agree with Sanders's formulation or his arguments. Some scholars suggest that common Judaism is a category that may have been meaningful primarily to Gentile authors, who viewed Judaism from the outside. They argue that insiders, however, would have been far more aware of the practices and beliefs that distinguished "their" group than of the practices and beliefs held in common with other Jews.[6] Objections have also been raised with regard to the relatively minor role that Pharisaism plays in Sanders's understanding of Second Temple Judaism and in the determination of what actually constituted common Judaism.[7] Some raise the methodological question of how sources from different geographical areas and time periods should be used in describing the common Judaism of the Second Temple period.[8] Others call the identification of a common Judaism an exercise in essentialism and argue that the concept fails to do justice to the diversity of and variety within Second Temple Judaism.[9]

These comments do not undermine Sanders's thesis so much as draw out its implications for a number of the major issues in the study of Second Temple Judaism. It is demonstrable that outsiders may be less aware of or sensitive to internal differences than insiders, but this does not by any means constitute an argument against common Judaism. As Sanders explains in the essay included in the present volume, both Jews and Gentiles viewed certain beliefs and practices as characteristic of Jews as a nation, both in Judea and in the Diaspora.[10] The role and relative importance of the Pharisees continue to be a matter of debate. Certainly the Pharisees loom large for Josephus, the New Testament, and rabbinic sources, yet it is difficult to judge whether their prominence in these sources reflects their actual status and authority in Jewish society or corresponds to the ways in which they were perceived by ordinary Jews in the Second Temple period. Lester L. Grabbe is, of course, correct that sources from different eras must be used carefully, a principle with which all would agree and to which Sanders, like many scholars, adheres scrupulously. The fact that interpretations differ does not signify a methodological problem. The charge of essentialism is one that Sanders himself addresses in the essay included in the present volume. Even scholars who focus their attention primarily on the diversity of Second Temple Judaism either explicitly or implicitly acknowledge some level of commonality on the basis of which certain groups warrant the label "Jewish" in the first place.[11] Similarly, treatments of the "parting of the ways" between Judaism and Christianity must make some assumptions regarding the nature of the "Judaism" from which Christianity may or may not have parted.[12]

These considerations, therefore, do not detract from the overall thesis that there existed a common Judaism that comprised the practices and beliefs of ordinary Jews and was shared also by the sects and parties for which we have some evidence. On the contrary. The emphasis on what was held in common provides an important corrective. It reminds us that within the diversity that certainly characterized Second Temple Judaism, there nevertheless existed an area of common ground great enough to warrant the singular "Judaism." At the same time, it does not ignore the fact that at least two of these groups, the Essenes and the Jesus movement, were in the process of challenging some of the elements of common Judaism such that they might eventually have defined themselves as being outside of Judaism altogether.

Finally, Sanders's exposition invites us to view our extant sources in a new light. In particular, we are challenged to reconsider the role of the temple and the sacrificial cult and to attempt to unravel the relative weight that the institutions of temple, synagogue, and Torah would have had in the lives of ordinary Jews in the Second Temple period. One cannot deny the importance of the temple cult and the sacrificial system, but what impact would they have had on Jews for whom regular pilgrimage was a physical and economic hardship? How much Torah did the ordinary person know, and what was the relationship between knowledge and practice? Would the ordinary person have encountered Torah directly, or as mediated through experts? What might this issue tell us about literacy among Jews in the Second Temple period?[13]

Common Judaism Explored

The present volume provides a set of responses to Sanders's invitation to rethink Second Temple Judaism. It focuses primarily on the lived experience of Jews in Palestine and the Diaspora. For this reason, the essays rely primarily on the more expansive definition of common Judaism, as pertaining to the elements that Jews of all groups or none would have practiced and believed, though, as we shall see, the diversity within Judaism is by no means ignored. The hypothesis developed throughout the book is that Second Temple Judaism was engaged in a productive tension between diversity on the one hand and common practice and belief on the other. This productive and creative tension was negotiated in deliberate acts of piety, such as liturgy, purity rituals, and pilgrimage, and was played out in the context of Hellenism that by the first century was deeply ingrained in Jewish life in both Palestine and the Diaspora.

A major concern of the essays in this volume is the presence of common Judaism in the Diaspora. This question has two dimensions. First, is there a lived form of Judaism with practices and beliefs that would have been held in common throughout the diverse regions of the Diaspora? Second, were the practices and beliefs the same as those we can identify for Palestinian Judaism in the Second Temple period? Sanders's book already engages with Hellenism, considers its role in the development of common Judaism, and anticipates an affirmative answer to both questions. This volume will address this position in more detail to help discern the areas of both commonality and difference within Diaspora Judaism on the one hand and between Diaspora and Palestinian Judaism on the other.

Part 1: Common Judaism in Its Local Settings

The first group of essays considers *common Judaism in its local settings*. Sanders's book dealt with the Jerusalem temple and priests, as well as with who controlled what in regard to this central religious institution of Second Temple Judaism. The first section of *Common Judaism: Explorations in Second-Temple Judaism* extends this focus to an examination of synagogues, *mikwa'ot*, and matters of purity in the land of Israel and in the Roman Diaspora. These topics reframe the institutional considerations from *Practice and Belief* while retaining Sanders's emphasis on the religiosity of the common people. Both literary and material evidence is of importance in exploring these issues.

Alongside the centralized sacrificial cult that took place in the precinct of the Jerusalem temple, Second Temple Jewish practice and belief were manifested locally in a variety of institutions. The chapters in this section draw on the results of archaeological investigation to focus on two of the most important: the synagogue and the ritual bath. While these institutions are local, they are also pervasive: it is likely that every Jewish locality, whether in Palestine or in the Diaspora, had a synagogue and one or more ritual baths. For this reason, they are also eminently useful in investigating the question of whether a common Judaism extended beyond the borders of Palestine to include also the Roman Diaspora.

Lee I. Levine's study, "'Common Judaism': The Contribution of the Ancient Synagogue," begins by examining the dynamics of common Judaism against its variety and diversity in late antiquity (third through seventh centuries), for which there is considerable data. Levine then turns to less amply documented first- and second-century c.e. materials to attempt the same kind of comparison. Much of the variety that he finds in both early and late antiquity can be explained by the local context of each synagogue building and the influence of the immediate social and religious surroundings. Common elements, however, raise fascinating, if difficult, questions regarding the reasons for (or causes of) the similarities. How and why did it happen that Jews in far-flung communities adopted the same practices? Was it due to a shared heritage or to dictates of a centralized authority, or were there active channels of communication among the various communities throughout the Roman world?

Boaz Zissu and David Amit focus on the second common institution, the ritual bath, and its role in Jewish society. Their chapter, "Common Judaism, Common Purity, and the Second Temple Period Judean *Miqwa'ot* (Ritual Immersion Baths)," focuses primarily on

Palestinian Judaism. Zissu and Amit consider ritual baths as evidence for Jewish settlement patterns in the Second Temple period, and for the details of village life. The ubiquity of ritual baths and their growing numbers through the Second Temple and rabbinic periods point to the centrality and widespread practice of purity laws in these periods.

The strong association between the ancient synagogue and water raises the question of whether ritual purity—associated primarily with the central temple and the sacrificial service—was also attached to this local institution. This is the question addressed by Susan Haber's chapter, "Common Judaism, Common Synagogue? Purity, Holiness and Sacred Space at the Turn of the Common Era." Haber points out the strong evidence linking synagogues and water. Synagogues were often located in coastal regions, or they had adjacent water facilities, such as ritual baths (*mikwāʾot*) and basins. This proximity to both natural and constructed sources of water implies an association between purity practices and the synagogue and also suggests that the concern about impurity extended well beyond the sacred precincts of the Jerusalem temple.

Taken together, the articles demonstrate the relevance of the archaeological record for illuminating the creative dynamic of common practices and beliefs expressed in the diversity that characterized Jewish communities in Palestine and the Diaspora.

Part 2: Common Judaism/Partisan Judaism

The second group of essays looks specifically at the intersection between common Judaism and partisan Judaism, that is, between the lived religion of the ordinary people and the major sects and parties. One of the challenges of the hypothesis of a common Judaism lies in its ability to address diversity within Judaism as well as the common elements of Jewish practice and religious life. These essays tackle this question directly, with regard to the main sects and parties that are known to us from the writings of Josephus and archaeological finds such as the Dead Sea Scrolls.

Sanders's emphasis on the practices and beliefs of the ordinary people shifted scholarly focus away from the concentration on the Pharisees, Sadducees, and Essenes that had characterized the field before the publication of his book. Albert I. Baumgarten's essay, "Pharisaic Authority: Prophecy and Power (*Antiquities* 17.41–45)," takes as its starting point Sanders's argument that although the Pharisees did not control ancient Jewish life, they did exercise authority. His contextual analysis of *Ant.* 17.41–45 places the story about the role of the Pharisees in Herod's court in the context of ancient discussions about religious leaders and their claims to foreknowledge. He proposes that the Pharisees achieved and justified their leadership roles by means that were linked to the nature of charisma of holy men in antiquity.

Anders Runesson, in "From Where? To What? Common Judaism, Pharisees, and the Changing Socioreligious Location of the Matthean Community," also focuses on the Pharisees, but this time in relationship to proto-Christianity, in particular, the Matthean community. He points out that any attempt to solve the problem of Matthew's relationship to Jewish religion and society—a question that is part of the larger problem of the so-called parting(s) of the ways between Judaism and Christianity—must begin by asking, Which Judaism and which Jewish society? Equally important is the definition of the institutional framework within which groups and individuals interacted and how it provided a context for the choices made. By considering religious type, ethnic identity, and institutional belonging as analytical categories, this chapter proposes that the emerging Matthean community recently had parted ways with the larger Pharisaic community, but not with Jewish society and religion. Furthermore, Runesson argues that the Mattheans were deeply involved in public Jewish institutional life in the last decades of the first century c.e. In other words, Mattheans still participated in common Judaism despite their separation from Pharisaism.

Whereas the earlier chapters in this section examined the relationships between and among various Second Temple Jewish groups, Cecilia Wassen's contribution, "What Do the Angels Have against the Blind and the Deaf? Rules of Exclusion in the Dead Sea Scrolls," looks at inclusion and exclusion within one such group, the Qumran community. Three of the sectarian documents from the Dead Sea Scrolls contain lists that exclude certain categories of people, particularly the physically disabled, from participating in specific activities. The three texts—the *Damascus Document* (CD XV/4QDa 8 i 6–9), the *Rule of the Congregation* (1QSa II 3–9) and the *War Scroll* (1QM VII 3–6)—offer the same rationale for these exclusions: the presence of holy angels. Underlying this rationale is the belief that it was demons who caused these physical or other disabilities; those affected by this demonic activity could not appear in the presence of the angels. The study points to a broad and common Jewish worldview in the late Second Temple period that understood demons as malignant and active forces that caused various kinds of suffering among people. The exclusion rules in the Dead Sea Scrolls fit within a common worldview that sought to protect sacred spheres against demonic influence.

Like Wassen's study, Anne Moore's chapter, "The Search for the Common Judaic Understanding of God's Kingship," focuses on a single, common, and broadly shared idea—in this case, the belief in divine sovereignty. This chapter draws on insights provided by cognitive linguistics and literary analysis to investigate the metaphor "God is king" in the Hebrew Bible and selected texts from the Second Temple period. Moore's proposal is that the metaphor of kingdom of God accommodated a range of meanings in diverse religious settings. In this sense, the metaphor mirrors the relationship between commonality and diversity that is evident in Second Temple Judaism more broadly.

These essays demonstrate the complex relationship between common and partisan Judaism. As Wassen and Moore show, certain beliefs as well as metaphorical expressions were so widespread that they provided a conceptual basis that allowed individuals and groups to experiment with new and innovative ways of understanding their religiosity while remaining solidly within common Judaism. Baumgarten and Runesson identify the Pharisees as one substantial force in Second Temple Judaism that jockeyed with other groups for influence and power. The activities of these groups reflected and, indeed, engendered inner-Jewish conflicts and controversies. Yet these conflicts were located in a context in which the diversity of opinion and practice was framed by a larger common confidence that this religion had the capacity to accommodate controversy.

Part 3: Common Judaism and Hellenism

The final group of essays focuses on the Hellenistic and Roman contexts of common Judaism. Sanders has commented on the importance of viewing common Judaism in its broader social, political, and cultural context. These essays examine the impact of that context—in particular, the Hellenism that had become deeply ingrained in Jewish thought and practice—on common Judaism as well as on the elements that distinguished Jewish groups from one another.

While it can be tempting to distinguish between a "purely Jewish" Palestine and a "highly Hellenized" Diaspora, it has long been recognized that Hellenism was a powerful social, cultural, and linguistic force throughout the Jewish world in the Second Temple period. The essays in this section explore some aspects of this Hellenistic context and consider its impact on the question of common Judaism.

Tessa Rajak's chapter, "'Torah Shall Go Forth from Zion': Common Judaism and the Greek Bible," focuses on one major area shared by all Jews in the period—the text of Scripture itself, whether in Hebrew or in Greek. The importance of a common biblical text for the possibility of a common Judaism cannot be overestimated; after all, Jewish communities were text-based societies. The uses they made of the texts, and the relation of text to life, were not, however, always the same. Indeed, there was a spectrum of textuality within different types of communities including the early Christian groups. Rajak examines specifically the role of the Greek Bible in the construction of Jewish identity in the Diaspora.

In his chapter entitled "Aristeas or Haggadah: Talmudic Legend and the Greek Bible in Palestinian Judaism," Eliezer Segal considers the legends surrounding the composition of the Greek Bible. He examines the rabbinic tale about textual emendations that were supposedly introduced by the translators of the Septuagint. A literary analysis of the tradition, on its own terms, in light of theological concerns during the Talmudic era—and in the context of recent discoveries of Greek Bible fragments in the Dead Sea Scrolls—indicates that the story has little credibility as a history of the Septuagint. However, the investigation enriches our appreciation of the place of the Greek Bible in the common Judaism of ancient Palestine.

The next two chapters, like Baumgarten's essay in part 2, focus on Josephus, the first-century Jewish historian. Josephus's extensive treatises are our best source for Second Temple Judaism, its political social composition and dynamics, and its major events, particularly in the period immediately preceding the first Jewish revolt.

David Miller's chapter, "Whom Do You Follow? The Jewish *Politeia* and the Maccabean Background of Josephus's Sign Prophets," argues that Josephus expresses his views on the submission of Judea to Rome through his portrayal of the "signs prophets" in the context of his views on Hellenization and against the background of the Maccabean revolt.

Seth Schwartz's article, "Memory in Josephus and the Culture of the Jews in the First Century," discusses the culture of memorialization in first-century Judea. It has recently been argued that Roman culture of the early empire was unusually concerned with memorialization. The tombs of the citizenry and writing that decorated them, such as the dedicatory and honorary inscriptions posted in temples and marketplaces, all reflect efforts by citizens, and the communities that they supported, to mark their place in an alarmingly unstable world. In this study, Schwartz considers where the Jews of Palestine fit in this regard. Did they participate in the general early imperial culture of memorialization, or did they reject it?

Ian W. Scott, in "Epistemology and Social Conflict in *Jubilees* and *Aristeas*," probes the attitudes toward religious knowing in these two Hellenistic Jewish texts. On the one hand, texts such as *Jubilees* and the *Community Rule* in the Dead Sea Scrolls treat religious knowing primarily as a moral matter. Knowledge is "given" in revelation, and a failure to respond to this revelation is treated as morally culpable. Other texts, such as *Pseudo-Aristeas*, place comparatively more emphasis on intellectual hurdles faced by human beings in their knowledge of God and understand that revelation is recognized as such by intellectual inquiry. In some instances, such rationalistic texts even imply that human reason will, when followed consistently, lead to the same ideas that God gave through revelation to Israel. When attitudes toward non-Jews are investigated, an increased emphasis on an intellectual quest for knowledge tends to reflect an increased openness to, and sympathy for, Gentiles. These latter texts reflect optimism about the human intellect; however, their ideas were part of the politically fraught process of Hellenization whereby the Greek traditions of virtue and piety are understood as dominant and transparently rational.

From these chapters, it is clear that Palestinian and Diaspora Judaism were both involved in an ongoing and complex relationship with (and often against) the Hellenistic cultural environment and Roman political context. In both its Hebrew and Greek versions, the Bible was considered the sacred foundation of Judaism and in that sense the property and focus of common Judaism transcended geographical boundaries.

The book contains contributions from sixteen scholars, yet it is also a unified whole. This unity is achieved by means of its theme and its focus on a common set of questions. This introduction and the concluding chapter are intended to clarify how the essays fit into the theme and what they contribute to the overall argument. Sanders's essay provides his own reflections on the theme of common Judaism fifteen years after the publication of *Judaism: Practice and Belief.*

2. Common Judaism Explored

E. P. Sanders

The principal aim of this chapter is to explain the origin of the phrase "common Judaism," which I employed in *Judaism: Practice and Belief*;[1] consequently most of what follows is autobiographical in nature, dealing chronologically with the stages of my own study of Judaism and focusing especially on how my thinking has been shaped by reaction to the work of others.[2] In the penultimate section, however, I restate one of the several arguments that allows us to say that in the ancient world there was an entity best called "Judaism," and I illustrate the sorts of practices and beliefs that were common or typical (though not uniform or normative). This section is especially indebted to discussion with Albert Baumgarten. The conclusion discusses some of the issues that arise when one attempts to summarize a complicated religion.

Steps toward "Common Judaism"

1. I am a New Testament scholar, and my understanding of nascent Christianity helped form my early views of Judaism. At least since 1934, historians of early Christianity have known that Christian "orthodoxy" emerged slowly and painfully from a situation of competing versions of the new religion.[3] One sees ferocious controversies over the right shape of the movement in the letters of Paul, which are the earliest surviving Christian documents, and especially in Galatians and 2 Corinthians 10–13. Scholars have universally regarded the competing factions as subgroups within a larger movement, and this still seems to me to be the correct way to look at them.

When I turned to the study of Judaism I saw it in the same way. Everybody knew about Josephus's three (or four) parties or sects,[4] and at the time (the early to mid-1960s) the world was still buzzing over the new discovery that proved the diversity of

Judaism—the Dead Sea Scrolls. Christian scholars showed some desire to divide Jewish groups into competing theological camps, and consequently some of them saw different subgroups at Qumran. The party or parties responsible for the *Hodayot* (1QH) believed in grace, while those responsible for the *Community Rule* (1QS) believed in works, and so on.[5] Such distinctions seemed to me to be only differences of emphasis that varied with the genre of the literature, and in any case everyone knew that dogma did not play the role in Judaism that it did in Christianity. So I, with most, simply saw variety within a single large entity, Judaism, very clearly exemplified.

2. When I decided to write a study comparing Judaism and Christianity in the first century, I knew that I faced a difficult conceptual problem. How can one compare two large, variegated entities with each other? I reduced the problem by deciding to concentrate on Paul's letters on the Christian side, but this by no means eliminated the difficulty. Was there an entity called "Judaism"? As I just observed, I assumed that there was. Nevertheless, I was concerned that variety might have been so great that one could not find a significant way to compare Paul with ancient Judaism as a whole. After carrying this question around with me for a few years and considering diverse topics but finding them lacking, I saw a solution: enlarge the categories; think about the most elementary and basic of all questions about a religion, namely, how one enters and how one remains in good standing. So I decided to ask whether, in surviving bodies of literature, one can find substantial agreement about how people became Jewish and how they maintained their status ("getting in and staying in").[6] As far as I can now discover, I did not use the term "common denominator" in *Paul and Palestinian Judaism* (though it does appear elsewhere),[7] but that is how I thought: granting a lot of variety, was there a *basic* and *common* understanding of becoming and remaining Jewish?[8] The difficulty was to find generalizations that actually applied and that were neither trivial nor misleading.

People need generalizations, and historians often use them. I objected to those that were in most frequent use in defining Judaism and Christianity by Christian scholars, who often drew a contrast between a religion of law, or of legalism, and a religion of love and grace. This seemed to me to be wrong on both sides: Judaism is based on love and grace, as well as on the law, and the letters of Paul do not lack "legalistic" passages, in which judgment is according to works (for example, Rom 2:12-16; 1 Cor 11:27-32; 2 Cor 5:10). A lot of smaller comparisons could be done that would not replace that large but erroneous comparison, legalism *versus* grace: one could, for example, compare Philo and Paul, or Philo and John, or various Jewish and Christian documents on individual points, such as the Sabbath or monotheism. Such comparisons would leave the main, misleading comparison untouched. So I needed some way to generalize that would be truer and better, but that would be roughly equally encompassing.

As most readers of this essay know, I concluded that this could be done: that there was enough agreement among diverse bodies of Jewish literature on a very big question that one could speak of Judaism—more precisely, Palestinian Judaism—in a way that was fair, generally accurate, sufficiently encompassing, and nontrivial.[9] The agreement depends on two figures: Abraham and Moses. God chose Abraham and his descendants, and later he gave them the law, obedience to which was required of the elect. The common understanding, then, was that Jews were Jews because God chose them and that they could remain in good standing by obeying the law. In *Paul and Palestinian Judaism*, I called this understanding "covenantal nomism." Legal obedience was founded not on the (entirely hypothetical) principle that each individual must earn salvation by compiling merits, but rather on the (well-supported) principle that this is what God, who chose the people, specified as the way they should live.

In this essay, I do not wish to defend this proposal except on one point: whether or not it is trivial.[10] In the course of numerous criticisms, Jacob Neusner wrote that my "pattern of religion" would be recognized by anyone who is familiar with Jewish liturgy.[11] Thus, if covenantal nomism is true as a description of the underlying or basic pattern of diverse forms of Judaism, it may be simply self-evident.[12] If one looks at the reactions to the book, however, it will readily be seen that in the context of New Testament scholarship it was not a trivial result. *Paul and Palestinian Judaism* resulted in a long pause in the Christian assertions that Judaism was a legalistic religion of works-righteousness, though now some scholars wish to resurrect the old depiction of Jewish legalism under the rubric "merit theology."[13] So, in some circles at least, the issue still lives, and it is still important.

3. In his centennial lecture to the Society of Biblical Literature in 1978, Jonathan Z. Smith illustrated the difficulties of comparing religions by asking: "In what respects is it interesting to compare and contrast the walnut and the praline? Shall they be compared with respect to color, or texture, or taste?"[14] A walnut tree has many characteristics. One cannot say that one of these characteristics is more essential to its walnutness than another. Similarly, Smith argued, an ancient Jew had many characteristics. It is misleading to try to find a Jewish essence. Though I had argued against the usefulness of "reduced essences" (such as "grace") in defining religions,[15] Smith regarded me as someone who sought the *essence* of Judaism. I supposed on reflection that I did believe in *a basic understanding of being Jewish*. Would I regard someone who rejected both covenant and law as Jewish if that person claimed to be Jewish? Such a person would fall outside my "common denominator" and thus outside Palestinian Judaism as I defined it. At the time, I did not have a clear view of how I would relate essence to identity or to identity markers, or how to relate these things to my "common denominator," covenantal nomism. Covenantal nomism is what I found as the underlying *theology* in Jewish *literature*, and when Smith's lecture led me to pose to myself the questions of how a theology relates to the essence of an entity and to the identity of groups and individuals, I found myself puzzled. This would turn out to be a useful puzzlement.

The question of *essentialism* still bothers me, because I do not want to be the distiller of an essence, but only a describer of a religion; for this reason, I shall return to the topic at the conclusion of this essay. We shall also see below that I would later find Jonathan Smith's appeal to taxonomy to be extremely useful in understanding Judaism.[16]

4. *Paul and Palestinian Judaism* was completed in 1975 and published in 1977. I shall very briefly mention the McMaster University project on normative self-definition in Judaism and Christianity (1976–1981). The question was why, when, and how Jewish and Christian groups decided to try to achieve normative self-definition, which got us into issues of identity and identity markers. The three principal planners were Ben Meyer, Albert Baumgarten, and myself. At an early point, Gérard Vallée joined us, and when the project began we added Alan Mendelson and Benno Przybylski.[17] The project sponsored various conferences. At the conference on Judaism, Larry Schiffman, who later wrote on Jewish identity,[18] was one of the participants. In terms of the present topic, two of the most obvious assumptions of the project were (a) that there was an entity, "Judaism," that consisted of diverse viewpoints and practices and (b) that at some point some people within this large Judaism wanted to create a greater degree of uniformity—*normative* self-definition.[19] Speaking only for myself, I would say that my opening assumption of diversity within an overarching unity survived the research project intact.

5. This large assumption of diversity within unity—which, I believe, many people shared—was challenged by Jacob Neusner. Neusner's views are difficult to discuss, partly because he has published so much, partly because he has sometimes published criticisms of his own earlier views. I am a very long way from having mastered the entire Neusner corpus, and here I shall focus on a few items. In the early and mid-1980s he published books and essays that took an extreme stance on unity and diversity. There was little unity, and the diversity amounted to a substantial degree of isolation: there were various Judaisms, each having very little—or, as he sometimes said, "nothing"—to do with another. The Mishnah, he wrote, "exhaustively express[es] a complete system—the fit of the world view and way of life—fantasized by its framers."[20] Most Jews, represented by *4 Ezra* and *2 Baruch*, thought historically and hoped for a coming redemption. But this view is "utterly unrelated" to the message of the Mishnah.[21] The most amazing sentences that I remember reading from this period are these:

> Each of the diverse systems produced by Jews in ancient times constituted a world-view and way for life for a circumscribed social group. While these various Judaic systems drew upon a common Scripture and referred to some of the same themes, they sufficiently differed from one another to be regarded as essentially distinct social-religious constructions.[22]

In his work during this period, Neusner tended to equate a literary document with a worldview and linked the two to an exclusive social group. When this is combined with the opinion that each document "exhaustively" presents a complete system—everything that its "framers" believed and thought important—we are led to suppose that there was a different Judaism for each document or virtually each document.

This rhetoric was attractive to many people. The word "Judaisms" came into widespread use. I once had a couple of conversations with a specialist in the Dead Sea Scrolls in which he kept insisting that the *Covenant of Damascus* contains a "complete system," which meant that he could study it in isolation from everything else and find in it an entire Judaism. I finally showed him a little list of things not in the *Covenant of Damascus*, but necessary to have in a whole system, but I don't think that it made much of an impression. The equation (document = complete system or worldview = a distinct social entity) seemed to me to be wrong at every point, and I hardly knew how to begin criticism of such profound errors (as I took them to be). I thought that my "common denominator" was truer to the evidence than Neusner's "essentially distinct social-religious constructions," but I did not at first see how to test his proposal and describe the results.

Before leaving this point, I should add that in his book *Messiah in Context* Neusner stated that his ideas were actually more complex than the simple equation, document = worldview = distinct social group. He wrote that in describing three "distinct types of holy men we know as priests, scribes, and messiahs," as well as their "definitive activities" ("cult, school and government offices and (ordinarily) battlefield"), he was following a scientific principle. He had first to describe the three complete systems separately before bringing them together.[23] After noting that all three were combined at Qumran, he added a potentially major qualification: "None of the symbolic systems at hand, with their associated modes of piety, faith, and religious imagination, ever existed as we treat them here: pure and unalloyed, ideal types awaiting description and interpretation."[24] If these qualifications had shaped the rest of the book, and if he had then revised *Judaism: The Evidence of the Mishnah* to agree with them, all would have been well. But he did not. A few pages later, he wrote that it was the destruction of the temple in 70 c.e. that "joined priest, sage, and messianist. . . . The three definitive components were then bonded."[25]

One of the problems with this formula was that his earlier publications on the Mishnah—a composite document that was finished much later than 70 c.e.—had already excluded some of the major aspects of the worldview of the messianists, including especially history. Thus, the claim in *Messiah in Context* (1983) that the three religious types "bonded" in the year 70 seems to have been an afterthought that had no effect on the four principal books and several essays that constitute Neusner's major publications on the existence of various Judaisms.[26]

While he may in fact have been working all along with a more complicated view than he expressed in these books and articles, I have knowledge only of what he published. Except for a few sentences, what he wrote on Judaism and Judaisms during this period had the effect of denying commonality to Jews and thus denying the existence of an entity that we could call "Judaism."

The publications that I have principally in mind, which appeared from 1981 to 1985, inspired me to write an essay on the philosophy of the Mishnah, which was fun but probably ineffective.[27] At about this time, the thought occurred to me that these publications could best be answered by considering specific cases. If in (let us say) 60 C.E. a Jew from Italy, one from Egypt, one from Mesopotamia, and one from Jerusalem sat together for Passover, would each recognize what the other was doing? If they talked about the Jewish people and the law of Moses, would they find common ground? I thought that the answer would be yes and that I could make a small contribution to the subject, making use of the literature with which I was acquainted. I further thought that the Greek and Roman authors who commented on Jews and Judaism, and who were so masterfully collected by Menahem Stern, would in general recognize that all these people belonged to one entity.[28] Greeks and Romans seem to have lumped Jews together. Did not Jews do the same? I thought that they did.[29]

6. As I have explained elsewhere, in the middle to late 1980s I had long wanted to explore pious practices in Palestine and the Greek-speaking Diaspora.[30] I had begun these studies before I wrote the essay on Neusner's philosophy of the Mishnah. As I related the issues of pious practices with which I was concerned to Neusner's theory of separate social groups, each with its own Judaism, I happily remembered the essays of one of the great heroes of my life, Morton Smith. In an article titled "Palestinian Judaism in the First Century," which first appeared in 1956, he had written the following sentences:

> There is no doubt that the picture of Judaism derived from the Roman imperial inscriptions and from the remarks of classical authors agrees in its main outlines with the picture derived from Rabbinic literature.
>
> The average Palestinian Jew of the first century was probably the 'am ha'arets, any member of the class which made up the "people of the land," a Biblical phrase probably used to mean hoi polloi. . . . The members of this majority were not without religion.
>
> If there was any such thing, then, as an "orthodox Judaism," it must have been that which is now almost unknown to us, the religion of the average "people of the land."[31]

In another article Smith had written:

> Down to the fall of the Temple, the normative Judaism of Palestine is that compromise of which the three principal elements are the Pentateuch, the Temple, and the 'amme ha'arets, the ordinary Jews who were not members of any sect.[32]

These words seemed totally convincing to me, for the good and simple reason that they corresponded to the evidence. And so I did what I could to reconstruct the Judaism of the common people, paying some attention, of course, to the famous parties but trying to focus on the Pentateuch, the temple, and the ordinary people. I could not use the words "orthodox" or "normative," since both imply control, and I thought that there was relatively little control over what ordinary people did and thought (apart from their activities in the temple). The only term I could think of for Smith's Judaism was "common Judaism."

7. And so I wrote *Judaism: Practice and Belief* (1992, corrected ed. 1994). It is based mostly on the Bible and Josephus, making liberal use of points gained from Philo's *Special Laws*, rabbinic literature, the Dead Sea Scrolls, and some of the Apocrypha and Pseudepigrapha, with some supporting evidence from pagan authors and the New Testament. I assumed—and argued—that people did not necessarily do what rabbinic literature says that they ought to do, and the emphasis on the Bible and Josephus kept me (I hope) from following the rabbis slavishly.

I do not know to what degree this should be judged a successful effort to describe the religion of the ordinary people. My consolation is that at least I tried to find the religion that Morton Smith said was "almost unknown to us." Certainly I could have included more topics, and there must be a good number of errors, since the subjects are so numerous and varied. The chief fault of which I am aware is that I did not do enough to fit Jewish practices into the wider world. If I were to redo the work today, I would include sections on the Jewish temple, sacrifices, and purifications in light of pagan practices, since a lot of points are common not just to Jews but to the ancient world in general. I am confident, however, that the major point—which I owe to Morton Smith—is correct and that one should seek common Judaism principally among the ordinary people.

I should add here three brief comments about the relationship between "covenantal nomism" and "common Judaism": (1) In *Paul and Palestinian Judaism*, "covenantal nomism" rests to an appreciable degree on an argument about the *presuppositions* that underlie ancient Jewish literature.[33] "Common Judaism" results from a study that is similar to a topographical survey in archaeology. One can turn the pages of Jewish literature and find the topics. One can also, as Shaye Cohen has emphasized, turn the pages of Greek and Latin literature on Jews and find the very same topics.[34] Therefore, common Judaism is easy to verify. (2) Covenantal nomism is a *theology*, whereas common Judaism emphasizes practices but includes beliefs. (3) Since the election and the law are among the common beliefs, common Judaism includes covenantal nomism. Though I still regard the argument about presuppositions in *Paul and Palestinian Judaism* as valid and convincing, it would have been easier to argue first in favor of common Judaism and then in favor of covenantal nomism—if only I had thought of it in 1968 or thereabouts.

8. I do not have a theoretical way of stating the relationship between unity and diversity, but I did make one effort after publication of *Judaism: Practice and Belief*. This

was inspired in part by Jonathan Smith's lecture, to which I referred above, that included comments on the walnut tree. I decided to try to parallel social groups to groups in nature. I shall here quote a few paragraphs from an essay titled "The Dead Sea Sect and Other Jews: Commonalities, Overlaps, Differences."[35] One of the virtues of these paragraphs is that they conclude—at last!—my efforts to respond to the writings of Jacob Neusner to which I referred above (except, of course, for the present essay).

> I imagine groups in human society as being in some ways like groups in nature.[36] To simplify, life-forms are divided into two kingdoms, animal and vegetable; animals are chordata or not; chordata are vertebrate or not; vertebrate animals are subdivided into mammals, birds, reptiles, amphibians and fish; some mammals are primates, some primates are homidae, and so on. At each stage, there are both common and distinguishing characteristics of each group.
>
> In the ancient world . . . , we find Jews and non-Jews. Both were humans, and both were ancient, which means that they were all alike in numerous ways. Our ability to say that some ancient people but not others were Jews, however, indicates that there were some distinguishing characteristics.
>
> The question of common and distinctive characteristics . . . , which is frequently complicated in botany and biology, becomes even more complex when we consider human social groupings. There will sometimes be no one decisive feature that places people in one group or sub-group rather than another. We cannot say that all Jews were monotheists, that all Jews observed the Sabbath, that all Jews avoided pork, or that all male Jews were circumcised. In the ancient world, *most* people whom we can identify as Jews were monotheists; most observed the Sabbath in one way or other; most would not consume pork, shellfish or blood; and most Jewish males were circumcised. These were extremely *frequent* characteristics, but we could not insist on a single one of them as a completely definitive distinguishing mark. Who were Jews? In general, they were people who were born of a Jewish mother or who converted to Judaism. Another general way of defining ancient Jews fixes on perception: Jews were people who regarded themselves as Jewish and who were so regarded by other people.
>
> The vast majority of Jews in the ancient world had these characteristics: (1) they believed in and worshipped the God of Israel; (2) they accepted the Hebrew Bible (often in translation) as revealing his will; (3) consequently they observed most aspects[37] of the Mosaic law; (4) they identified themselves with the history and fate of the Jewish people.

Jews sometimes formed sub-groups. Clubs and societies were a strongly marked feature of the ancient world. In fact, the voluntary formation of relatively small groups is a general human characteristic, and there may be an evolutionary explanation of this tendency.[38] In any case, Jews shared it. Voluntary groups necessarily have a good number of the characteristics of the surrounding society: they cannot be entirely unique. Even when they are deliberately counter-cultural societies, they still share characteristics with the larger whole of which they are a part.[39] American hippies were, and American militia are strongly American. No matter how radical they intend to be, people cannot escape the circumstances that fashion them.

It follows that in the Graeco-Roman period Jewish sub-groups were Jewish. They shared enough of the common Jewish identity markers . . . that a learned and perceptive student in the ancient world, had he or she found the writings of a Jewish sub-group, would have been able to recognize it as Jewish.

Thus, diversity and the creation of subgroups do not necessarily destroy unity. The Pharisees, the Sadducees, the Essenes, the members of the "fourth philosophy," the common people, and Hellenistic Jewish philosophers such as Philo all disagreed on lots of points. They all belonged, however, to Judaism. Where most of them agree is where we find "common Judaism."

Common Judaism: Some Examples

I shall now briefly present a little of the evidence that points toward "common Judaism." Most of the argument that appears in *Judaism: Practice and Belief* depends on citing passages from diverse sources that agree on a certain observance (such as circumcision of males) or belief (such as God's election of Israel). There is also overwhelming evidence, which is scattered through the pages of *Judaism: Practice and Belief*, that Jews throughout the Roman Empire constituted a *single social group*. Outsiders could identify Jews as *Jews*, and Jews saw themselves as constituting *a* distinctive group—not several different groups. This means that Jews had identifiable characteristics. They were distinctive in part because of observances, in part because of belief. I wish to summarize some of the evidence that points toward a single (though diverse) group—not a lot of Judaisms, but a common Judaism.

1. Both Julius Caesar and Augustus offered various advantages or concessions to Jews throughout the empire, and the cities of the empire hastened to confirm these rights. There are two substantial passages in Josephus that describe the conferral or confirmation of Jewish rights: *Ant.* 14.213–64 (relating to the time of Julius Caesar and the period after his death) and *Ant.* 16.160–73 (the period of Augustus, though some of Josephus's material

in this section is earlier).[40] I shall single out four of the main rights: assembly, the Sabbath, the Jews' ancestral food, and the contribution of money to the temple. From these we may infer that pagans identified Jews as people who needed to meet together (one assumes in synagogues), who wished not to work or appear in court on Saturdays, who preferred not to eat certain foods, and who desired to support the temple in Jerusalem.[41]

Jews saw themselves in the same way: they clamored for these rights. Provincial officials or city councils sometimes denied Jewish requests or overturned traditional rights, and so the Caesar of the day, or one of his agents, had to step in. For example: while Herod the Great and his courtier, Nicolaus of Damascus, were in Ionia, the local Jews complained to them that they were being prohibited from obeying their own laws, particularly those relating to the Sabbath and the contribution of money to Jerusalem. Herod and Nicolaus supported them. Marcus Vipsanius Agrippa (Augustus's right-hand man), because of Herod's goodwill and friendship, upheld the appeal and confirmed (or restored) the rights of Ionian Jews (*Ant.* 16.27–65). Herod's intervention in Asia Minor provides extremely clear evidence of the common interests of Jews throughout the Roman Empire.

These observances (Sabbath, kosher food, and so on) imply basic beliefs: the Jews follow their own God and believe that he requires them to live in a certain way. That is, their God is the one true God, and Jews have a special relationship with him. His will is found in the Bible.

2. The collection of money for Jerusalem deserves emphasis. It appears that most Jews in the Roman Empire, and in Mesopotamia as well, were loyal to the temple and supported it. Payment of the temple tax from both the western and the eastern Diaspora is well attested in Josephus and Philo.[42] Payment is taken for granted in Matt 17:24. Cicero objected to the right of Jews to export money from their local provinces and supported the governors who confiscated the funds or forbade their export.[43] According to Josephus, the temple was occasionally plundered—which indicates that it contained a lot of wealth.[44] Probably most of it came from Diaspora Jews, both in Mesopotamia and in the Roman Empire.[45] Both Gentiles and Jews saw support of the Jerusalem temple as an identifying mark of Jews. The strongest proof of the connection between the *temple* and *Jewish identity* is the fact that after the first revolt (66–73 c.e.) the temple tax was collected and sent to Rome for other purposes.[46] The Jews were a distinct body of people in the Roman Empire, and all Jews in the empire were identified and taxed after the revolt in Palestine.

The practice of collecting money and sending it to the temple in Jerusalem implies, again, beliefs: that the worship of the true God was conducted there and that the biblical requirement of the temple tax should be observed.[47]

3. One of the principal Jewish rights in the Diaspora was that they were not required to worship the city gods, despite Gentile pressure.[48] This again points to a belief: that the

Jewish God was the only true God. Both Jews and Gentiles recognized this as a defining characteristic of Jews.

4. Circumcision of sons is commanded in the Bible and is a main feature in the story of the Hasmonean revolt. Jews and Greeks agreed that Jewish males were circumcised.[49] Circumcision is commanded in the Bible (Genesis 17), and Jews believed that they should obey.

This correspondence between Jewish and Greco-Roman views of Jewish practices proves that there were common observances. A sociologist might stop with observable customs: Jews were people who followed some or all of the practices just listed (plus others that can be established in various ways: the list above is not exhaustive). But a lot of Jewish literature offers *motives*, and I think that we should go beyond a list of practices. Jewish observance of the law was based on the view that God ordained it. Moreover, Jews were monotheists: their God was the only true God. This belief, coupled with the view that they should follow God's law, shows that they thought of themselves as having a special relationship with God. He had a covenant with them, and he had chosen them to obey him.

Consequently, to this list of common observances,[50] I would add three major beliefs: monotheism, election, and the divine origin of the law. Thus, I regard "covenantal nomism" (the election plus the law) as part of "common Judaism."[51]

Conclusion: Basic Elements, Cores, and Essences

If I were asked the classic question whether Philo and R. Aqiba would have understood each other, I would say that they would. I assume that they would have disagreed about exegetical techniques and other items, but that if one could have visited the other at Passover, they would have agreed on what they were doing and why—on practice and belief. I would also respond affirmatively to my earlier question, whether or not at Passover Jews from Italy, Egypt, Mesopotamia, and Jerusalem would have understood one another's Passover observance. For the most part, all Jews understood "common Judaism," as did a lot of Gentiles.

Was common Judaism "essential"? It appears to me that it was essential to Judaism as a whole and to most individual Jews. That does not mean that it was *uniform* in the life of every Jew, much less that it was in some way *enforced*—except by local public opinion: I do not think that in the period I have studied normative Judaism had emerged. Without *common or shared identity*, however, Judaism might have broken up into Neusner's separate Judaisms, and many more Jews would have assimilated themselves to common Mediterranean life.

But could individual people be Jews while omitting, say, half or even three-fourths of the common, typical practices and beliefs? I would say yes, if they counted themselves

Jewish and if other people saw them as Jewish. A person who gave up all of the typical practices, it would seem to me, would merge into the Gentile world. Legally, a "son of Israel" might still be a Jew by birth; but socially, a total apostate would have removed himself or herself from the collective entity Judaism.

Have I proposed an "essentialist" definition of Judaism? It is at least sometimes instructive to discuss terminology, and I think that this is one of the times, partly because some people use the word "essence" in discussing my work,[52] but mostly because the use of brief descriptions and summaries in defining complicated movements deserves a few more lines. To recall an earlier observation: we all need brief depictions, and we shall all continue to employ them. They are useful in discussion of religions, political parties, systems of government—all sorts of things. If every time we wanted to say something about "democracy," for example, we had to say that there are several democracies, and then give an account of the diverse legislative or parliamentary systems in the more-or-less democratic nations, we would have to refer to an encyclopedia every time we wanted to say anything about democracy as an "ism," and it might be hard to see the elements that are common to the democracies.

The question of whether it is useful to search for an "essence" depends, I suppose, on how one understands the word. I continue to think of an *essence* as either an *inner quality* or an *abstract* word or phrase of the sort that cannot be historically evaluated. Examples of qualities that are sometimes held to be the essence of a religion are *love*, *faith*, and *grace*. As examples of abstract phrases, I offer "the fatherhood of God and the brotherhood of man" (which was common before the women's movement) and Adolf von Harnack's "eternal life in the midst of time" in his work *Das Wesen des Christentums*, which might be translated "the essence of Christianity" (see below).[53] Essences like these are beyond historical research and so cannot aid historical understanding—however useful they may be homiletically.

Take *love*, for example. We can to some degree study by historical means the way in which Jews and Christians *treated* both insiders and outsiders. Would a strong record of charitable acts prove that love is the essence of either religion? Not precisely, since there might be other explanations of charity (such as enlightened self-interest or the need to curry favor), and in any case we could not prove that charitable acts were performed by all people who claimed to be Jewish or Christian. If love were the one and only essence of a religion, a lot of people who claimed membership would be found not to behave in accordance with the essence. The essence, then, would turn out to be theoretical, and we would have a theoretical religion, not a historical one.

This may become a little clearer if we return to von Harnack.[54] There was a debate in Germany about the usefulness of the Apostles' Creed in worship. Von Harnack was of the view that it was outmoded. But would anything replace it if it were dropped? It was in that context that von Harnack gave the lectures that became the book *Das Wesen des Christentums*, which was translated into English as *What Is Christianity?* Professor Hillerbrand suggested to me that the best translation of *Wesen* in this context is not "essence" but "core." The bare core, "eternal life in time," was supplemented in von Harnack's lectures by appeal to some of the basic teachings of Jesus, which would combine with the core idea to produce a conception of Christianity that was more relevant than an ancient creed that listed dogmas.

Von Harnack—arguably the greatest historian of Christianity—did not propose that "eternal life in the midst of time" could be proved to be the inner guiding principle in each version of Christianity throughout history. The aim, rather, was to find a theological statement that was appropriate to Christianity and that could be used to lead parishioners toward the *right sort* of Christianity, one that was simple, sensible, humane, and not burdened with antique metaphysical dogmas.

Thus, I regard von Harnack's "core" as theological and homiletical, not historical. In terms of *history*, it might well be an item on a list of frequently held Christian beliefs. One might argue that it is central to *true* Christianity—a theological position—without seeing it as having shaped all or even most forms of Christianity historically.

I shall give a final example of the difference between a "common characteristic" and an "essence." I believe it to be true that, on average, ancient Jews were *loyal* to the Jewish people and to the God of Israel, but I do not know whether they all *loved* God or one another. In modern speech, "love" is an *inner* quality, and it cannot be supported by historical evidence the way loyalty can be. We can prove widespread loyalty by the number of instances in which ancient Jews were willing to fight and die for their ancestral traditions and were also willing to suffer difficulty, discomfort, and discrimination as they struggled to maintain them.

In my own view, I have been in quest of historically ascertainable characteristics of a religion, which I distinguish from an essence. One of the things that I like about "covenantal nomism" as a theological lowest common denominator is that it has a lot of content. It actually depends on the idea of *loyalty*. It is as theological as von Harnack's "core" of Christianity, but it is much better suited to historical proof, because loyalty to the people of Israel and to the law can be supported by evidence. "Common Judaism," of course, puts more meat on those bones and is more obviously descriptive.

Thus, I do not think that I know what the essence of Judaism was. I think that there were *basic* and *common* observances and beliefs that served to identify some people as Jews in the ancient world and that gave the group a firm identity. The theology that held these practices and beliefs together was the underlying faith that the God of Israel is the one true God of the world and that his will is found in the Hebrew Scripture (or in its Greek translation). This Scripture includes the history of God's dealing with his people, including the election of Abraham, the exodus from Egypt, and the giving of the law to Moses on Mount Sinai. The Bible is the basis of common Judaism (though just which parts of it each group of people observed, and precisely how they observed those parts, varied).

Part One

Common Judaism
in Its Local Settings

3. "Common Judaism": The Contribution of the Ancient Synagogue

Lee I. Levine

Unity versus diversity has been an issue of prime concern in the study of Judaism over the past half century. Until the mid-twentieth century, the *communis opinio* held that there was one normative Judaism, beginning with the biblical period, extending through the Talmudic sages of antiquity and the rabbinic authorities of the Middle Ages, and subsequently codified in the sixteenth-century *Shulhan Arukh*. This traditional Jewish view was articulated in the opening chapter of *Pirqei Avot*, discussed in medieval historiography (for example, *Sefer Ha-Qabbalah* of Abraham ibn Daud), and later adopted as axiomatic by early modern Jewish historians. In 1927, this concept was given wider academic legitimacy with George F. Moore's assertion that a normative Judaism, "which most truly represented the historical character and spirit of the religion . . . and accomplished the unification of Judaism," existed in antiquity.[1]

The 1950s witnessed the first major challenges to this point of view. First, the Dead Sea Scrolls, discovered in 1947, provided evidence for a radically different system of beliefs and practices within Second Temple Judaism from what had been known beforehand. Second, Erwin R. Goodenough's magnum opus on Jewish art, while focusing on late antiquity, raised a fundamental question regarding rabbinic control of and influence on Jewish life.[2] Third, Morton Smith's provocative and stimulating essay on Palestinian Judaism in the first century argued for extensive Hellenization among Jewish religious sects and concluded that no one group, Pharisees included, dominated Jewish life at the time.[3] Finally, Jacob Neusner posited an extreme position that negated any sort of normative Judaism in antiquity; he introduced the term "Judaisms" into

27

scholarly discourse, not only with respect to the pre-70 period but also with regard to late antiquity; and even viewed the different midrashic collections in rabbinic literature as each reflecting a variant form of Judaism.[4]

E. P. Sanders provided a bridge between these polarized positions by proposing a more nuanced understanding of ancient Judaism. First, he suggested that the diverse Jewish groups in the Greco-Roman period shared fundamental theological beliefs. He then made the same kind of claim with regard to common Jewish practices by focusing on such matters as food and purity laws, the variety of Temple offerings (from tithes to sacrifices), worship, Sabbath, circumcision, and leadership groups (Pharisees, scribes, priests, and teachers).[5] Without denying that "Judaism . . . was dynamic and diverse," Sanders highlighted common features that bound together first-century Jewish groups.[6]

In what follows, I will suggest that one fruitful area for gauging the extent and degree of a common Judaism is the ancient synagogue. This Jewish communal institution par excellence makes a unique contribution to the issue at hand, in part because of its ubiquity throughout the ancient Jewish world. Both in Roman-Byzantine Palestine and in the Diaspora, the synagogue figured prominently in all areas of communal life.[7] It provides a communal perspective stretching over centuries, as well as an abundance of material from a wide range of urban and rural locales. Synagogue-related material thus serves as a basis for establishing points of consensus and diversity.

We will focus first on late antiquity (third/fourth through seventh centuries) since this period has yielded especially rich evidence for both Palestine and the Diaspora. After examining the dynamics of common Judaism against its variety and diversity at this time, we will then turn to the first century C.E. and attempt, *mutatis mutandis*, the same kind of comparison.

The Synagogue in Late Antiquity: Between Diversity and Commonality

Late antiquity has left an abundance of archaeological material pertaining to the synagogue in comparison with earlier periods. In the Diaspora, thirteen buildings have been securely identified as synagogues, while nine additional sites are somewhat less certain. Also extant are hundreds of inscriptions, mostly dedicatory, from synagogue buildings and numerous others from funerary contexts that refer to the association of the interred with a synagogue. Even more archaeological evidence has been found for Roman-Byzantine Palestine.[8] To date, more than one hundred synagogues have been so identified, as well as some two hundred inscriptions—almost two-thirds in Hebrew or Aramaic and the remainder in Greek. A score of amulets have been found in synagogue contexts, as well as dozens of mosaic floors, some remarkably well preserved.

Literary remains relating to the synagogue of late antiquity are scattered among the writings of Byzantine authors (for example, *Scriptores Historiae Augustae*), church fathers

(Epiphanius, John Chrysostom), the Theodosian Code, and Justinian's *Novellae*. The preponderance of literary material, however, derives from rabbinic sources. More than four hundred pericopes explicitly refer to the synagogue from a historical, communal, or liturgical perspective; many hundreds, if not thousands, mention liturgical activities, most of which undoubtedly took place within the confines of this institution (even if the synagogue is not explicitly mentioned in the pericopes themselves). Other Jewish texts relating to synagogue matters include the mystical Hekhalot writings, *targumim*, *piyyutim*, and halakhic material, such as the list of variant practices in Palestine and Babylonia.[9]

What can be learned from these sources regarding the question of a common Judaism? The synagogues' plans, architecture, art, and inscriptions exhibit extraordinary diversity: no two buildings are identical. In the Diaspora, for example, Sardis is a far cry from Dura Europos, as is Ostia from Stobi, while in Byzantine Palestine, despite geographical proximity, Capernaum is worlds apart from Ḥammat Tiberias, as is Reḥov from Bet Alpha and Jericho from Naʿaran. The same diversity holds true for a Galilean synagogue as against a Judean one, for a Palestinian community as against a Diaspora one, or for a Greek-speaking environment as opposed to an Aramaic or even Latin one. Morton Smith has summed up this variety as follows:

> But the different parts of the country (that is, Palestine—L.L.) were so different, such gulfs of feeling and practice separated Idumea, Judea, Caesarea, and Galilee, that even on this level there was probably no more agreement between them than between any one of them and a similar area in the Diaspora.[10]

A striking example of this diversity among synagogues is evident in the Bet Shean area, where we know of five contemporaneous synagogue buildings that functioned in the sixth century: Bet Shean A, just north of the city wall; Bet Shean B near the southwestern city gate; Bet Alpha to the west; Maʿoz Ḥayyim to the east; and Reḥov to the south. To date, no other urban setting boasts such a concentration of remains that have both geographical and chronological propinquity. Yet these synagogues are remarkably different from one another in terms of their architecture, art, and inscriptions (that is, language and culture).[11]

Synagogue art also exhibits a range of representations and a variety of interpretations. Some examples reflect the differences between urban and rural settings or between chronological periods. The depiction of Helios in fourth-century Tiberias most likely reflects a set of beliefs and associations different from those evoked in rural Naʿaran or Bet Alpha of the sixth century. Artistic representations of the Temple's facade, the Torah shrine, or various Jewish symbols probably did not carry the same meaning in third-century Dura Europos as they did in fourth-century Tiberias, fifth-century Sepphoris, or sixth-century Bet Alpha. Noting what he calls the polyvalent dimension in Roman and Byzantine art, Jaś Elsner claims, "People relate to works of art in different ways, depending upon different contexts and at different times."[12] Henry Maguire articulates a similar view in his discussions of plant and animal portrayals in Byzantine Christian contexts:

> Most of the images from natural history that appear in early Byzantine art were not like modern traffic signs, with necessarily fixed and invariable messages, but . . . were more akin to metaphors. The meanings of any given image, an eagle, for example, or a fish, could be nuanced or even completely altered according to the context provided by a given work of art, just as works in a language can change their meanings in different situations. Also like words in a language, the images employed by artists could change their meanings over the course of time.[13]

One reason for this diversity is that Jewish life in late antiquity was characterized by an extensive and pervasive communal autonomy under the control of local leaders or the community at large and was not beholden to any supralocal body or institution.[14] This was not a new phenomenon; a number of third- to fourth-century sources point clearly to local control over various aspects of the synagogue.[15]

Since local needs and preferences of the synagogue community were crucial factors in determining synagogue policy, so too was the choice of artistic motifs. Why did some communities make use of figural art and others did not? Why do biblical scenes and personalities appear only in certain locales? Why did one synagogue depict Helios in all his pagan glory (Ḥammat Tiberias), another substitute the sun for the anthropomorphic figure (Sepphoris), and still another record the names of the zodiac signs epigraphically, without any pictorial representation ('En Gedi)? In most cases, any answers to the above queries must be speculative. With the exception of fourth-century Ḥammat Tiberias and Bet She'arim of the third to fifth centuries, no literary sources illuminate the immediate social, communal, or cultural contexts or shed light on the considerations that might have led to these different artistic choices.[16]

The diversity among synagogues in late antiquity extends also to liturgy. For example, consider the following.

Torah reading. At least four (perhaps five) different systems of the Torah-reading cycle are documented for Byzantine Palestine, from reading the entire Torah in one year (the Babylonian system) to reading it over a period of three to three and a half years (the "triennial" cycle, that is, dividing the Torah reading over 141, 154, 167, and possibly even 175 weeks).[17]

Haftarah (weekly reading from the Prophets). Some synagogues required twenty-one verses,[18] but there also appears to have been a custom of reading only three verses. Tractate *Soferim* mentions at least four different practices: "When are these rules applicable? When there is no translation or homily. But if there is a translator or a preacher, then the *maftir* [the person chanting the *haftarah*] reads three, five, or seven verses [instead of twenty-one] in the Prophets, and that is sufficient" (13, 15; Higger, 250–251).

Piyyut (liturgical poetry). It is generally agreed that the *piyyut* made its first appearance in synagogue liturgy only in late antiquity, but many unresolved issues remain: How many synagogues incorporated this genre into their Sabbath liturgy? How often would a *piyyut* be recited in any given place? And how did the ordinary Jew understand these sophisticated and complex Hebrew poetic compositions when the lingua franca of the community was primarily Aramaic or Greek (or perhaps both)?[19] While thousands of *piyyutim* from late antiquity have already been identified, it is still not clear how widespread a phenomenon this was, and if, in fact, there might have been different concurrent practices.

Common Judaism in Late Antiquity

Alongside this oft-bewildering diversity in the practices associated with the ancient synagogue in late antiquity, there were significant elements of unity and commonality. First and foremost, as already noted, the synagogue was the quintessential Jewish communal institution everywhere. It was created in response to a community's need for a central institution that provided a range of services and offered a communal identity. The practice of referring to the synagogue as a *bet 'am* ("house of [the] people")—to the chagrin of some rabbis—clearly indicates the nature of the institution (*b. Šabb.* 32a).

Moreover, at some point in the third and fourth centuries, the synagogue began to assume an enhanced religious character. Evidence can be found in numerous inscriptions, from both the Diaspora and Palestine, that refer to the synagogue as a "holy place" (*'atra qadishah* or *hagios topos*) and to the community as a "holy congregation" (*qehillah qedoshah*) or a "holy *havurah*," or association (*havurtah qadishah*). References to a "holy place" appear in synagogues throughout Byzantine Palestine, in Ḥammat Tiberias (twice), Naʿaran (four times), Kefar Ḥananiah, Ashkelon, and Gaza, and to "the most holy [place]" also in Gaza and Gerasa (fig. 1).[20] Inscriptions from Bet Shean, Jericho, and Susiya mention a holy congregation or community.[21] The term "the language of the

Fig. 1. Aramaic inscription in the Ḥammat Tiberias synagogue mosaic referring to the synagogue as a "holy place."

holy house" (*lishan bet qudisha'*) occurs frequently in *Targum Pseudo-Jonathan* and seems to refer to the language used in the synagogue setting,[22] while in the same *targum* to Lev 26:1, this term almost assuredly refers to the synagogue as a holy place and sanctuary.

The holy status of the synagogue in the Byzantine period is expressed also in imperial legislation. Valentinian I (ca. 370 C.E.) referred to the synagogue as a *religionum loca* when prohibiting soldiers from seizing quarters there.[23] Such a status likewise is assumed—though not explicitly stated—in other edicts issued over the next half century that aimed at protecting synagogues from violence.

Explanations for this new religious prominence have engaged scholars. Increased sanctity may have been due to the desire for religious continuity following the destruction of the Jerusalem Temple, when the synagogue began to incorporate more and more religious practices and symbols, including those associated with the Temple. Evidence for this process in the period immediately after the destruction is poorly documented, however. Perhaps a holy status evolved quite naturally over time, although, again, there is little data to support this claim. Similarly, it is difficult to assess whether actions such as the introduction of Torah scrolls into the synagogue's main hall or the gradual institutionalization of communal prayer were the cause or the consequence of increased synagogue sanctity.

We have suggested elsewhere that external factors also may have played a role in this process. Evidence points to increased sacrality in late antiquity in both pagan and Christian settings, including matters of worship. "Holiness" as a religious category was becoming a major factor in many religious circles.[24] The Jews of Palestine were undoubtedly aware of the intensive Christian interest in holy places, beginning with Constantine's building of churches in and around Jerusalem, while Jews in the Diaspora probably witnessed the emphasis on the sacred, and even the *imitatio templum*, in the construction of local churches. It is possible that Jews responded to Christianity's new prominence and its hostile attitude toward Judaism by endowing their central religious institution, the synagogue, with an aura of sanctity. Thus, the prominence of artistic religious themes in synagogue settings, occurring now for the first time, may also have served a similar function (see below). Such contextual factors would seem to have contributed significantly to the creation of a sacred dimension in the Byzantine synagogue and to its transformation into what one rabbi referred to as a "diminished temple" (*miqdash me'at*) (*b. Meg.* 29a).[25]

We now turn to other developments within the late antique synagogue that underscore the commonality, albeit in varying degrees, shared by Jewish communities.

1. Jerusalem Orientation[26]

The synagogue's orientation toward Jerusalem undoubtedly reflects a profound change in the Jewish community of late antiquity. On one level, such orientation was a powerful statement of religious and ethnic particularism. No longer was the main communal institution a neutral gathering place, as were the first-century Judean synagogue buildings (see below), but rather it represented in a very physical way, via its orientation, an attachment to Jerusalem and its Temple. The synagogue as a physical structure now began to embody historical memories and, perhaps, hopes (messianic and other) for the future, together with its communal centrality in the present.

There can be little question that the increasingly religious dimension of the synagogue was a major factor in making the issue of orientation so pronounced in synagogue architecture of late antiquity. The Jews now began to imitate the widespread practice of a fixed orientation that had been customary in pagan settings and was now true of churches as well. For the most part, these latter sanctuaries faced east, as did the Tabernacle and both Jerusalem Temples for well over one thousand years. The Jews in late Roman and Byzantine Palestine, from the Galilee to southern Judea, as well as in the Diaspora, adopted a very different practice.[27] While possibly influenced by an earlier Jewish tradition of praying toward Jerusalem,[28] the communities may have instituted this unique orientation out of a demonstrative rejection of pagan practice or owing to a deeply felt religious and ethnic identification with the city and its Temple.

2. Torah Shrine

The Jerusalem orientation of synagogue buildings was further emphasized by the almost universal practice of placing a platform, niche, or apse for the Torah shrine against the Jerusalem-oriented wall.[29] In the Galilean-type synagogue, such a podium was generally located between the entrance portals facing Jerusalem, either on one or both sides of

the main entrance (for example, Gush Ḥalav, Nevoraya, and Merot). In other types of buildings, the platform was situated in the center of the wall facing Jerusalem (as at Reḥov and Khirbet Shemaʿ), while in Susiya there seem to have been two such podiums.

The Jerusalem orientation was even more pronounced in synagogues that adopted a Christian basilica plan— incorporating a niche or apse along the wall facing Jerusalem and an entrance, atrium, and narthex on the opposite side. Architecturally, these plans guided synagogue congregants to face in the direction of Jerusalem, which was also

Fig. 2. Torah shrine in the form of a niche in the western wall of the Dura Europos synagogue.

the direction of the prayer leader, Torah reader, or preacher who was positioned in or near the apse (or niche). Diaspora Jewry followed this pattern as well, as is clearly evidenced in the Dura synagogue (fig. 2).

The *bima* or apse found in most synagogues was not simply an architectural addition. It provided the Torah shrine with a permanent and prominent status within the hall. Second Temple synagogues had no such arrangement (see below), as the Torah scroll(s) were kept elsewhere and were introduced into the assembly hall only at an appointed time. This practice began to change in the latter part of the Roman period, and by late antiquity the presence of a Torah shrine was the norm as well as an important component in further enhancing the religious ambience of the synagogue's main hall. Considerable diversity remained, however, in the way each community expressed the policy of a Torah-oriented interior.

3. The Emergence of a Vibrant Jewish Art

Jewish art underwent a major revolution in late antiquity. For some fifteen hundred years, art produced and used by Jews had consisted primarily of a very limited number of motifs drawn from surrounding cultures; specifically Jewish depictions or symbols were almost nonexistent. Only in late antiquity did a symbolic dimension crystallize on a massive scale in Roman and Christian art, and among Jews as well, and this art may be categorized as follows.

Jewish symbols. The most widespread expression of Jewish collective memory is through the use of Jewish symbols appearing at the overwhelming majority of Jewish archaeological sites. The menorah, shofar, lulav, ethrog, and incense shovel (the last-noted appearing only in Israel) are widely represented. Moreover, the above symbols are often depicted flanking a facade that has been interpreted as that of either the Temple, a Torah shrine, or both.[30] While these symbols might appear individually, they are often clustered together in various combinations.

The menorah is by far the most ubiquitous Jewish symbol. It appears over a thousand times in late antique art, on stone moldings, clay lamps, mosaic floors, and glass vessels.[31] *Menorot* are prominent in Palestinian synagogues and often appear together with other Jewish symbols; in many cases, the Torah shrine or Temple facade is depicted in the center and is flanked by two large and often lavishly ornamented *menorot*, for example, Ḥammat Tiberias, Sepphoris, Bet Alpha, Bet Shean, Naʿaran, and Susiya (fig. 3). Fragments of three-dimensional *menorot* have been found in the synagogues at Merot, Tiberias, ʿEn Gedi, Ḥorvat Rimmon, Eshtemoa, Susiya, and Maʿon (Judea). Such *menorot* were not only ornamental but also served as a source of light in the synagogue hall.

Biblical scenes and figures. Biblical scenes were much rarer than Jewish symbols. The stunning walls of the third-century Dura Europos synagogue preserve some thirty panels of biblical narrative (originally there were double that number). But, absent new finds, Dura may well have been *sui generis* among ancient synagogues. In the seventy-six

Fig. 3. Southern panel in the Ḥammat Tiberias synagogue mosaic displaying a range of Jewish symbols.

years since this building was first discovered in 1932, no other synagogue even begins to approximate its artistic grandeur. The only other synagogue in the Diaspora that clearly displays a biblical scene is the building in Gerasa (Jordan) exhibiting a scene of the Noah story, including the names of two of his sons.[32]

Synagogue remains in Byzantine Palestine are more rewarding in this regard. An *ʿAqedah* scene appears in Bet Alpha and Sepphoris (partly destroyed); a representation of David is in Gaza and perhaps Merot; one of Daniel is in Naʿaran, Susiya, and arguably in ʿEn Samsam (the Golan). In Sepphoris, an almost totally destroyed depiction of Aaron at the altar (only his name and the extremity of his garment remain) is surrounded by sacrificial animals, other offerings (oil, flour), trumpets, and three more substantial artifacts: the showbread table, a first-fruits basket, and a water basin (fig. 4).[33]

The Zodiac and Helios. The most surprising artistic find in ancient synagogues is the zodiac with Helios, appearing in the mosaic floors of no fewer than six late antique Palestinian synagogues. These buildings span the length and breadth of the country (Ḥammat Tiberias, Sepphoris, Ḥuseifa, Bet Alpha, Naʿaran, and Susiya [fig. 5]) and range in date from the fourth century to the sixth.[34] In all cases, the overall plan of the zodiac is a large square containing two concentric circles. The innermost circle depicts Helios (with the exception of Sepphoris, where the sun appears instead). The outer circle depicts the zodiac signs; each appears in one of the twelve radial sections. Outside these circles are the busts of four figures representing the four seasons, each bearing the relevant seasonal symbols.

Closer investigation reveals a rich and diverse iconography in the details. No two representations are identical. Helios appears with all his accoutrements in Ḥammat Tiberias, but is quite stylized and simplified in Bet Alpha; he is replaced by the sun in Sepphoris.[35] The zodiac signs might stand with their heads toward the central circle or,

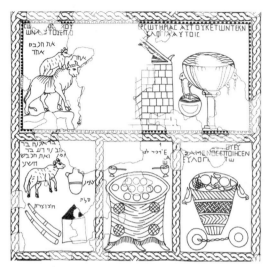

Fig. 4 (top). *Registers in the Sepphoris synagogue mosaic depicting Tabernacle/ Temple-related objects. Courtesy of the Sepphoris Excavations, the Hebrew University of Jerusalem. Fig. 5* (bottom). *Central panel in the Bet Alpha synagogue mosaic displaying Helios, the zodiac signs, and the four seasons.*

just the opposite, with their feet in that direction. The representation at Sepphoris appears to be an attempt to synthesize the zodiacal and calendrical (that is, allegories of the months) cycles into one system.[36]

The zodiac, and the sun god Helios, borrowed from patently pagan models, were placed quite prominently in the center of each and every mosaic floor. While the scene was clearly meaningful, there is no consensus on what it signified for a Jewish community or why it was so popular. Suggested meanings include the God of Israel; the archangel mentioned in *Sefer Ha-Razim*; a symbol of God's power as Creator of the universe or Master of nature and history; the importance of the Jewish calendar (which includes days, months, and seasons); the symbol of God's covenant with Israel; astrological ramifications; and a mere decorative element.

Interestingly, this motif always appears in conjunction with a panel containing well-known Jewish ritual symbols (for example, the menorah and the lulav), and at times with depictions of clearly religious significance (the *'Aqedah*, the Tabernacle sacrifices, and other offerings). The Helios-zodiac motif may have been intended either to supplement or to balance the panel of religious objects, but this is mere speculation.[37]

Monumental rural synagogues. A striking feature in many synagogues of the fifth and sixth centuries in comparison with earlier synagogues is their large size (fig. 6). This is particularly true in rural areas, such as the Upper Galilee, the Golan, and southern

Judea.[38] This development parallels that of rural church buildings in many of these same areas during approximately the same period.[39] This phenomenon may have been due, in part, to an economic upswing. Among Jews, it also may have reflected a response to the spread of Christianity and its claims of superiority to Judaism. Jewish monumental buildings may have presented a reaffirmation of the Jews' own loyalties and pride, and an assertion of their own unique identity. The size and other features of the synagogue also may have reflected a common Judaism that crystallized in no small measure in response to the challenges and opportunities prompted by contemporary Christianity.[40]

Given the dispersion of the Jewish population throughout the Byzantine world, especially in the Diaspora, and the relative paucity of sources, it is extremely difficult to determine how the above-noted common developments took form, who initiated them, how they spread throughout the Jewish world, and whether they were imposed or spontaneously absorbed. Theoretically, at least three explanations are possible.

1. A central authority was involved in the creation and diffusion of these changes. The only office that might have functioned in such a capacity would have been the Patriarchate, which flourished throughout the Jewish world from the third to early fifth centuries C.E.[41] While evidence of patriarchal control and involvement in various aspects of synagogue life (for example, administration, taxes) exists, it is not known whether it extended to synagogue architecture and decoration. Since the Patriarchate disappeared in the early fifth century, it could not have influenced synagogue practice in the later fifth to seventh centuries.

2. These changes were part of the shared heritage of Jewish communities for generations and emerged spontaneously in late antiquity. Since we have no evidence for the above changes in an earlier era, this option remains entirely speculative.

Fig 6. Proposed reconstruction of the monumental Capernaum synagogue dating to the fifth century C.E.

3. These developments originated in some unknown place(s) in the Byzantine era and attest to the remarkable communication system among Jewish communities at that time. Once again, there is no evidence to substantiate (or, for that matter, to refute) such an assertion.

Given the paucity of evidence, it is not possible to draw any firm conclusions.

The First-Century Synagogue

There is far less information available for the first-century synagogue than for the institution in late antiquity. But the extant evidence suggests that in the Second Temple period, the synagogue as a building and as an institution was far less developed, especially in the religious sphere.

One of the main historical sources for the pre-70 era is the work of Josephus, who notes the existence of synagogues in Judea in the context of his political narrative of the first century. At both Dor and Caesarea, the synagogue became a center of controversy during the political struggles between Jews and pagans; in Tiberias, the synagogue (here called *proseuchē*, lit., "house of prayer") was the place where the Jewish community met to deliberate at the outset of the revolt in 66–67 c.e. Josephus also cites a series of Roman documents affecting Jewish communities in the Diaspora, particularly in Asia Minor. The rights accorded the Jews under Roman rule are clearly articulated in these *privilegia*, some of which make explicit reference to the synagogue or, more often, mention activities and functions that most likely took place in the synagogue.

Philo makes only a few passing references to the synagogue or *proseuchē*. In describing the pogroms of 38 c.e., he notes the existence of Alexandrian synagogues, and particularly one monumental and lavishly ornamented building. On several occasions, he mentions the Sabbath-morning Torah-reading ritual, as well as the worship settings and practices of the Therapeutae and Essenes.

The Gospels recount Jesus' activity in Galilean synagogues (for example, Matt 4:23; Mark 1:21–28; John 6:59), and Luke is especially expansive in his opening account of Jesus' preaching in Nazareth (Luke 4:15–38). Acts refers to synagogues in Jerusalem and in regions of Asia Minor and Greece (for example, 6:9; 13:5, 14; 14:1; 17:1).

A number of rabbinic traditions refer to pre-70 synagogues. The Tosefta, for example, extensively describes a first-century Alexandrian synagogue (*t. Sukk.* 4, 5; Lieberman, 1974, 273). However, many of the rabbinic sources, including the Babylonian Talmud and most midrashic compilations, are quite late and thus of questionable historical value for the first century.

Pre-70 archaeological material is scanty but of cardinal importance. Remains of at least six synagogue buildings are attested—five in the province of Judea (Gamla, Masada, Herodium, Modi'in, and Qiryat Sefer [fig. 7])[42] and one (perhaps two) in the Diaspora (Delos and arguably Ostia). It is the inscriptions, however, that provide the bulk of

Fig 7. Proposed reconstruction of the first-century Qiryat Sefer synagogue. Courtesy of Yitzhak Magen.

archaeological evidence from this period. The Theodotus inscription from Jerusalem, that of Julia Severa from Acmonia in Asia Minor, a number of catacomb inscriptions from Rome, three synagogue inscriptions from Berenice (Cyrene), five from Delos, six from the Bosphorus, and sixteen (or parts thereof) from Egypt (including papyrological evidence) offer a varied and far-ranging picture of the institution in the first century c.e.

The Common Dimension of the Late Second Temple Synagogue

First-century Judean synagogues have a number of features in common.[43] Their layout tends to be rectangular with benches lining all four sides. Some have columns and there is usually a *miqveh* close by. The hall functioned primarily as a gathering place. This plan may have been influenced by the Hellenistic council hall (the *bouleutērion* or *ekklesiastērion*), the Alexandrian civic building, or the temple *pronaos* such as that at Dura.[44]

In contrast to synagogue buildings from late antiquity, Judean synagogues do not have an orientation to Jerusalem, nor do they contain religious symbols, a Torah shrine, Jewish art (symbols or biblical), or inscriptions. In short, they have no visual or concrete elements of sanctity. The fact that a *miqveh* is often found near a synagogue may be related more to convenience than to sanctity.

Common to Jewish communities throughout the Second Temple period in both Judea and the Diaspora was the synagogue's role as a central gathering place. Josephus mentions that at both Dor and Caesarea, the synagogue—the hub of the local Jewish populations—became a target of anti-Jewish activity. Furthermore, the events in Tiberias emphasize unequivocally the pivotal role that the local *proseuchē* played as a setting for communal deliberations at the outbreak of the revolt.[45] Evidence for the synagogue's preeminence in the Diaspora is more abundant.[46] The Egyptian *proseuchē* was often dedicated to the king and queen of Egypt. The Cyrene synagogue (referred to as an amphitheater) served not only as a regular meeting place for the congregation; it also was a place where important awards were announced, presented, and memorialized. Bosphoran synagogues often served as the site of legal transactions such as the manumission of slaves. The prominent Roman matron from Asia Minor, Julia Severa, donated a synagogue building to the local Jewish community. The importance of the synagogue is articulated also in the edicts cited by Josephus regarding Diaspora communities, for example, the decree of the Sardians:

> This decree was made by the senate and people, upon the representation of the praetors. Now the senate and people have decreed to permit them to assemble together on the days formerly appointed, and to act according to their own laws; and that such a place be set apart for them by the praetors, for the building and inhabiting the same, as they shall esteem fit for that purpose; and that those that take care of the provision for the city, shall take care that such sorts of food as they esteem fit for their eating may be imported into the city. (*Ant.* 14.259–61)

The synagogue's centrality was recognized by the non-Jewish world. As noted, hostility of pagans toward Jews was often expressed through violent attacks on local synagogues, as at Dor, Caesarea, and Alexandria.[47] In contrast, honor or support for the Jewish community was expressed in the context of the local synagogue. Seleucid rulers are reported as donating spoils from the Jerusalem Temple to a synagogue in Antioch (*J. W.* 7.44), and the many privileges enjoyed by Jewish communities throughout the Diaspora were at times linked, directly or indirectly, to this institution.

Jewish communities, for their part, often chose to honor kings and emperors in their synagogues. Egyptian *proseuchai* were dedicated to Ptolemaic rulers, and an Alexandrian synagogue displayed tributes to the emperor. Some Jews in Rome named their synagogues after Augustus and his viceroy, Agrippa; the Berenice (Cyrene) community honored a Roman official at regular meetings in its synagogue/amphitheater. The benefactions of the pagan noblewoman Julia Severa were noted in the synagogue on what was undoubtedly a prominently placed plaque.[48]

These various activities are documented for synagogues and *proseuchai* throughout the Roman Empire, suggesting that these two institutions played similar roles at this time and fulfilled needs—be they of an economic, social, political, or religious nature— that existed among all Jewish communities, both in Judea and the Diaspora.

A degree of commonality among first-century synagogues is likewise evident in the leadership positions of this institution. While information in this regard is severely limited, evidence points to the priest and the *archisynagōgos* as the most prominent positions in the first century. The Theodotus inscription from first-century Jerusalem refers to its donor Theodotus as both a priest and *archisynagōgos*.[49] Philo refers to priests in Egyptian synagogues who instructed the congregation during Sabbath-day meetings (*Hypoth.* 7, 13), and an earlier instance of priestly leadership in Egypt may be reflected in 3 Macc

7:13. One of the Berenice inscriptions mentions a priest, Cartisthenes son of Archias, at the head of a list of donors who were not community officers.[50] The centrality of priests at Qumran generally is well known, especially with regard to the ritual of prayer and study.

The title *archisynagōgos* is well documented in the literary and epigraphical material, particularly with regard to the post-70 era in both urban and rural communities, in Judea and the Diaspora.[51] In addition to the Theodotus inscription, the term appears in Luke 13:14 with regard to the Galilee and in Acts 13:14–15 with regard to Pisidia, in the Julia Severa inscription from Acmonia, and in an inscription from Egypt that possibly dates from the first century.[52]

That the fundamental religious activity in all synagogues centered around the Torah-reading liturgy is explicit in almost every type of source from the Second Temple period in Judea and in the Diaspora—in cities and in villages. The following sources clearly make this point.

Josephus:

> He [Moses] appointed the Law to be the most excellent and necessary form of instruction, ordaining, not that it should be heard once for all or twice or on several occasions, but that every week men should desert their other occupations and assemble to listen to the Law and to obtain a thorough and accurate knowledge of it, a practice which all other legislators seem to have neglected. (*Ag. Ap.* 2.175)

Philo:

> He [Augustus] knew therefore that they have houses of prayer [*proseuchē*] and meet together in them, particularly on the sacred Sabbaths when they receive as a body training in their ancestral philosophy. (*Leg.* 156)

> He [Moses] required them to assemble in the same place on these seventh days and, sitting together in a respectful and orderly manner, hear the laws read so that none should be ignorant of them. (*Hypoth.* 7.12)[53]

New Testament:

> When he came to Nazareth, where he had been brought up, he went to the synagogue on the Sabbath day, as his custom was. He stood up to read and the scroll of the prophet Isaiah was given to him. He unrolled the scroll and found the place where it was written . . . (Luke 4:16–17)

> But they went on from Perga and came to Antioch in Pisidia. And on the Sabbath day they went into the synagogue and sat down. After the reading

of the law and the prophets, the officials of the synagogue sent them a message, saying. . . . (Acts 13:14–15)

For in every city, for generations past, Moses has had those who proclaim him, for he has been read aloud every Sabbath in the synagogues. (Acts 15:21)

Rabbinic literature:

And a wooden *bima* was to be found in the center [of the hall, referring to an Alexandrian synagogue], and the *ḥazzan* of the synagogue would stand in the corner [of the *bima*] with kerchiefs in his hand. When one came and took hold of the scroll to read [a section from the Torah], he [the *ḥazzan*] would wave the kerchiefs and all the people would answer "Amen" for each blessing. He would [again] wave the kerchiefs and all the people would respond "Amen." (*t. Sukk.* 4, 6; Lieberman 1974, 273)

Archaeological evidence also affirms the primacy of Torah reading in synagogues:

Theodotos, son of Vettenos, priest and *archisynagōgos*, son of an *archisynagōgos* and grandson of an *archisynagōgos*, built the synagogue for reading the law and studying the commandments.[54]

There is no doubt that by the first century C.E., Torah reading had become the core of Jewish synagogue worship. Several related liturgical features—that are not as well attested—accompanied it. Both the Gospel of Luke (4:17–19) and the book of Acts (13:14–15), for example, refer to readings from the Prophets and to sermons that followed the scriptural reading. Philo notes more serious study and instruction.[55] Later rabbinic literature mentions the *targum* (that is, the translation of the Hebrew Scriptures into the vernacular).[56]

Thus, the evidence shows that by the first century, a weekly ceremony featuring communal reading and study of sacred texts was a universal Jewish practice. Indeed, this type of liturgy was unique in the ancient world; no such form of worship—the recitation and study of a sacred text by an entire community on a regular basis—was known in the pagan world (certain mystery cults in the Hellenistic-Roman world produced sacred texts that were read to initiates on occasion).[57] The self-laudatory tone of the Jewish sources may indeed reflect their authors' agenda to trumpet this form of worship, which set the Jewish community apart from the surrounding cultures.[58]

The origins of this common liturgical practice are almost impossible to discern. Some have traced the institution of Torah reading to the circle of Ezra and Nehemiah, a Persian initiative, the Pharisees, the *ma'amadot* connected to the priestly courses, or Temple practice; others have viewed it as a reaction to a perceived Samaritan challenge or to Hellenism, or simply as a natural development of public readings with roots in the

First Temple era.[59] There is, unfortunately, no basis on which to determine who or what was responsible for such an innovation, when precisely it developed, or how it evolved in its early stages.

Diversity in First-Century Synagogues

Together with this significant degree of common Judaism in first-century synagogues, there were also varying degrees of diversity between them. One example concerns the phenomenon of regular communal public prayer. The widespread Diaspora use of the term *proseuchē* (house of prayer) as against the primarily Judaean term *synagōgē* (house of assembly) suggests a substantive difference in liturgy. All Second Temple sources relating to Judea do not include communal prayer as a component of synagogue liturgy.[60] It therefore seems that so long as the Temple still stood, most (if not all) Judean communities limited their liturgical expression to the cluster of activities that accompanied the Torah-reading ceremony.

Outside of Judea—far from the psychological, physical, and political shadow of the Temple, and perhaps stimulated (or challenged) by their surroundings—many Jewish communities developed some sort of communal prayer about which we know virtually nothing. However, this component appears to have been so crucial that they named their communal institution accordingly.[61] There were many Diaspora communities, however, that did not use the term *proseuchē* but preferred *synagōgē* or some other appellation.[62] The evidence suggests that prayer did not play a central role in most synagogue settings at this time.

In addition to public prayer, there were other differences between first-century synagogues, especially between those in Judea and those in the Diaspora. Some Diaspora synagogues in the first century c.e. had a recognizable religious dimension.[63] For example, the Jerusalem Temple vessels were deposited in Antioch—having been appropriated earlier by Antiochus IV during the period of his persecutions. It is in relation to this synagogue that Josephus uses the word *hierōn* ("holy place") (*J. W.* 7.44–45). A number of Egyptian inscriptions specifically refer to "the holy" or "the holy place,"[64] and another inscription, more indirectly, associates the institution with "the Most High God" or "God the Highest."[65] The sanctity of one *proseuchē* was expressed as follows:

> On the orders of the queen and king, in place of the previous plaque about the dedication of the *proseuchē*, let what is written below be written up: King Ptolemy Euergetes [proclaimed] the *proseuchē* inviolate [*asylon*]. The queen and king gave the order.[66]

The plaque, dated by most scholars to the latter part of the second century b.c.e., attests to the holy status enjoyed by this Egyptian *proseuchē* in the Ptolemaic period.

A papyrus from Alexandrou-Nesos in the Fayyum, dated to 218 B.C.E., states that a Jew named Dorotheus was accused of stealing a cloak. He took refuge in a *proseuchē* (for purposes of asylum?). Only after the intervention of a third party did Dorotheus agree to leave the cloak with the *nakōros* (attendant) of the synagogue until his final adjudication.[67] Yet another, if less direct, indication of an Egyptian synagogue's sanctity is the use of terms such as *temenos* and *tōn hierōn perībolon* for "sacred precinct" in connection with a *proseuchē*.[68] Moreover, a second-century papyrus describes a plot of land attached to a *proseuchē* in Arsinoe-Crocodilopolis as a "sacred grove" or "sacred garden" (*hierān parādeisou*).[69] Philo, too, alludes to the sacredness and inviolability of *proseuchai* on a number of occasions.[70] These examples clearly imply that in some Egyptian locales the *proseuchē* was accorded a degree of sanctity.

Finally, the use of the term *proseuchē* itself may also indicate a degree of holiness. The references in Roman edicts to sacred meals, sacred books, and sacred funds are all presumably to be associated with this institution. It is not clear, however, how much the presence of these objects or activities in the building, or even the name *proseuchē* itself, may actually reflect or contribute to the sanctity of the place.

Judean synagogues are rarely, if ever, accorded the holiness that is associated with Diaspora *proseuchē*. From an archaeological perspective, the five buildings discovered in Judea thus far show no signs of sanctity; there is no marked orientation, no art, and no epigraphical evidence. That there was a religious component in their weekly agenda is almost certain (see above), but how it affected the overall profile of the building is unknown. Moreover, as noted, the presence of *miqva'ot* near a number of first-century Judean synagogues tells us little about synagogue sanctity. In the first place, a *miqveh* had nothing inherently to do with synagogue worship; as noted, it was probably placed near this local communal building for accessibility and convenience, and nothing more. Second, even if one wishes to view the location of the *miqveh* as significant, it should be remembered that half of the Judean synagogues were located in places inhabited by populations with high religious motivation (Masada, Herodium, and Gamla); it is far from clear how reflective they were of society as a whole. The same holds true regarding Philo's attribution of sanctity to Essene synagogues in Judea (*Good Person* 81). Even if the accuracy of this characterization is admitted (as against an assumption that it is only the projection of a Diaspora writer), it might rightly be claimed that in this respect, as in many others, the Essenes did not reflect the more general Judean practice.

It is thus clear that while the element of sanctity indeed played a role in some Diaspora synagogues, this was rarely, if ever, the case in contemporary Judean synagogues. As in the case of prayer, it was undoubtedly the social and religious contexts of Diaspora communities that contributed significantly to this development.

Diversity in the first-century synagogue is evident among Diaspora synagogues themselves, particularly in the epigraphical evidence. Some inscriptions are major communal documents (Berenice) or shorter manumission contracts (Bosphorus).

Others are brief statements of individual (Delos, Acmonia, Egypt) or communal (Egypt) benefactions, while still others are epitaphs noting synagogue affiliation (Rome).[71] Each of these inscriptions reflects a particular local reality and deals with the challenges and issues that confronted specific communities. All, however, attest to the attempts of Jewish communities to negotiate between the desire to maintain their Jewish identity on the one hand and to integrate fully into their surroundings on the other.

Another reason for this diversity stems from the fact that the Jews who established these early Diaspora communities in the Hellenistic and Roman periods had no set models for what a Jewish community facility should look like or how it should function. Furthermore, in the Diaspora at least, powerful social and cultural forces impacted each community and resulted in adoption of the patterns of the surrounding culture. Years ago, A. Thomas Kraabel called attention to this phenomenon. With the passage of time as well as new discoveries and studies, this perception is only reinforced.[72] The names used by members of a community often imitated those generally in vogue on the local scene, as in Cyrene. Indeed, the organization and operation of the Jewish *politeuma* in Berenice may well have derived, in part at least, from Cyrenian models.[73] The type of building used by Delian Jews bore similarities to other buildings on that island, while the manumission decrees from Bosphorus with their formulary components are well known in that particular region.

Several studies that have focused on the Egyptian synagogue further confirm this perception. They highlight the many links between the Jewish *proseuchē* on the one hand and the surrounding Greco-Egyptian culture on the other. Such parallels include dedications on behalf of the ruling family, the *proseuchē*'s status as a place of asylum, the names and functions of synagogue officials, and various architectural components.[74]

Conclusion

The prism of the ancient synagogue, both in its late Second Temple and late antique varieties, reveals a delicate balance—or, better, a tension—between common and shared Jewish values and modes of expression on the one hand and the unique and diverse proclivities of each community as it strove to negotiate its way in non-Jewish societies on the other. Both factors were always present. How they were combined was a decision that rested squarely on the shoulders of each community.

The perspective of the ancient synagogue offers an insight into what communities preferred and desired, rather than what some leader(s) wished to project or impose on the communities. The synagogue was first and foremost an institution of the people— what may be termed an expression of the people's Judaism. Thus, in the second century C.E., for example, many Jews viewed the synagogue primarily as a community center and not as a sacred religious institution, even though the sages (or some of them at least) preferred the latter option (*b. Šabb.* 32a; *t. Meg.* 2, 18 [Lieberman, 353]).

Fig. 8. Helios in the Ḥammat Tiberias synagogue mosaic. The figure is holding a globe and staff (or whip).

Throughout late antiquity, Jews regularly replicated the seven-branched menorah even though an early rabbinic tradition, often quoted in the Babylonian Talmud, objected to this practice (*b. Roš Haš.* 24a–b and parallels). In the fourth-century Ḥammat Tiberias synagogue, a daring portrayal of Helios was displayed together with several associated symbols that had been strictly forbidden by the Mishnah 150 years earlier (*m. 'Abod. Zar.* 3, 1; fig. 8). Indeed, several Palestinian *amoraim* decided to remain silent in light of the popularity of figural art among the people—even though they clearly found their position uncomfortable and problematic (*y. 'Abod. Zar.* 3, 3, 42d).

A common Judaism existed among Jewish communities throughout the Roman Empire. It was common in the sense that it was widespread and in the sense that it was an expression of the people rather than the dictate of an authority. Indeed, one of the major contributions of archaeology has been to reveal remains of a wide spectrum of Jewish communities that have been ignored, and certainly never fully documented, in the literary sources.

Through the archaeological lens, we perceive how Jewish society operated on the local level throughout antiquity. Popular will was often expressed in different ways and through channels different from those of the more official or elitist circles. Such a reality might be described as an example of *vox populi vox dei*. Although various Jewish elites might have regarded such a statement with reservation, if not outright rejection, such a reality was clearly at work within the Jewish body politic in antiquity.

4. Common Judaism, Common Purity, and the Second Temple Period Judean *Miqwa'ot* (Ritual Immersion Baths)

Boaz Zissu and David Amit

J ewish ritual baths played a significant role in Jewish life and culture throughout Jewish history. In Tractate *Miqwa'ot*, the Mishnah sets forth the laws of ritual baths in great detail. These laws are quite numerous and include technical terms and arrangements that are sometimes difficult to interpret and reconstruct. Nevertheless, it seems quite certain that in order to be acceptable, ritual baths had to fulfill four basic conditions:

(1) The installation must be integral with the ground.

(2) The minimum amount of water required for purification must be 40 *seahs* (between 500 and 1,000 liters).

(3) This water must be rain- or springwater that flowed into the bath by itself and was not "drawn"—transferred from elsewhere by means of a receptacle.

(4) The bath must be deep and large enough to immerse easily the entire human body at one time.

Accordingly, a ritual bath was almost always a deep rock-hewn pool of water. Its steps were stretched lengthwise, leading conveniently from the top edge to the floor, and its sides and bottom were coated with waterproof plaster to prevent penetration of water. Sometimes, but not always, the ritual bath was sheltered by a roof.

Careful observance of the laws of purity was originally connected with temple ritual and the priests who served in the temple. Over time, however, the practice spread to all Jews and came to be linked with precepts that had little to do with temple practice.[1] The study of the written sources and systematic examination and analysis of the archaeological data lead us to conclude that the observance of ritual purity had an important part in the daily schedule of Jews of all social classes during the late Second Temple period. Jews were aware of ritual purity issues during their day-to-day life, while growing crops, preparing food, and celebrating holidays and religious festivals, especially the pilgrimage to the Holy City of Jerusalem, and most of all while entering the temple courts. The high level of ritual observance is represented by this common rock-cut relic —the ritual immersion bath— which exemplifies its centrality within the Jewish society of the Second Temple period.

We believe that the widespread distribution of these supports the idea of a "common Judaism" while showing the compatibility of the literary and archaeological evidence. It seems that the rabbinic and other literary sources may in fact contain more historical information than we are sometimes willing to acknowledge.

History of Research

In 1990 and 1992, E. P. Sanders published his essential studies on Second Temple period Judaism.[2] In this innovative research he argued for the existence of a "common Judaism" in the Second Temple period that included the observance of the ritual purity laws and the use of the *miqweh* as a means to achieve and maintain ritual purity. Sanders's work drew on both written sources and archaeological evidence. Interestingly, his research was accomplished in the 1980s when few ritual baths were uncovered and identified as such; of those that were known, information about only a small number was made available to scholars through preliminary publications.

The first ritual bath was identified by Yigael Yadin in the excavations of Masada in 1963–1965. Archaeologists and other scholars began to comprehend the scope and significance of these structures only in the 1970s, during the large-scale excavations in Jerusalem, directed by Nahman Avigad in the Upper City and by Benjamin Mazar at the foot of the Temple Mount. The data became widely available during the 1980s, primarily through the work of Ronny Reich.[3] The study of the ritual baths as a distinct archaeological "institution" has developed mainly from 1990 onward, following Reich's doctoral dissertation entitled "Miqva/ot (Jewish Ritual Immersion Baths) in Eretz Israel in the Second Temple and Mishna and Talmud Periods" (in Hebrew; Hebrew University, Jerusalem, 1990).

Reich's dissertation was an archaeological treatment of approximately three hundred ritual baths, from their archaeological perspective. Ninety percent of the baths discussed by Reich were from the Second Temple period; the remainder were from the Mishnaic and Talmudic periods. Most of them were found in Second Temple period Jerusalem. In Judea and Benjamin, Reich counted twenty-two settlements and fortresses in which ritual baths have been found. The identification of additional ritual baths in subsequent excavations and surveys has been based on Reich's groundbreaking work.

The master's thesis of David Amit presented thirty-five "new" ritual baths in the Hebron Hills that strikingly resemble those in Jerusalem. Amit also compiled data on sixty-four ritual baths elsewhere in the country that were not included in Reich's corpus.[4] Most of these baths have been dated to the Second Temple period. To understand the pace of discoveries and the development of research on ritual baths, one must note that in 1990 the only ritual baths known south of Ramat Rahel were those in Herodium. By 1996, thirty-five installations in the area were known.

Boaz Zissu's 2001 doctoral dissertation, "Rural Settlement in the Judaean Hills and Foothills from the Late Second Temple Period to the Bar Kokhba Revolt," detailed the results of his surveys and excavations in the field, mainly in the environs of Jerusalem, and built on the work of Sanders, Reich, and Amit. This research included a systematic review of old published and unpublished archaeological reports. The examination led to the discovery of additional ritual baths that had been mistakenly identified as graves, cisterns, silos, and the like (fig. 1).

Since 1997 the number of ritual baths known in the area south of Jerusalem (Hebron Hills) has doubled, and it now stands at about seventy. Altogether, Zissu's study from 2001 included information on approximately 220 ritual baths at about 130 sites in the Judean hills and foothills as well as in the Land of Benjamin.

Based on the archaeological studies and the halakhic sources, Eyal Regev attempted to link the various types of ritual baths from the Second Temple period to specific Jewish groups and parties.[5] Fresh discussions, mostly focusing on bath preparation techniques, were provided by Asher Grossberg.[6] Yoel Elitzur approached the issue of hand purification basins uncovered at Masada.[7]

The excavations carried out in Second Temple period Jerusalem proved that ritual baths were an essential component of private urban homes belonging to Jews from all social classes, from the poor to the wealthy. The excavations and surveys of the rural parts of Judea show a similar picture. The earliest *miqwa'ot* excavated by archaeologists were dated to the second half of the second century B.C.E. From that period on, the ritual baths have been found in every farm, estate, or village. It is therefore clear that *miqwa'ot* were an integral component in the life of the Jewish community until the destruction of Jerusalem and its temple in 70 C.E., and even afterward, until the devastation of the surrounding region at the end of the Bar Kokhba revolt (135 C.E.).[8]

These baths serve as indicators of the Jewish settlement patterns in the country in the period under discussion. Discovery of the baths, frequently beneath Christian-Byzantine remains, helps to identify earlier Jewish villages not mentioned in any historical source.

In Jewish rural settlements, one to seven ritual baths have been found per village. This variety raises the question of why some places needed more baths than others; it is not known whether this uneven distribution reflects demographic or other factors. Interestingly, there were also ritual baths outside settlements: near roads, for example, perhaps for the use of Jewish pilgrims; within wine and oil presses, so that wine and oil could be produced in purity; and near cemeteries, to allow for purification after contact with the dead. Ritual baths were hewn in royal desert fortresses and in fortresses built and maintained by the Hasmoneans and by Herod in the settled part of the country. The

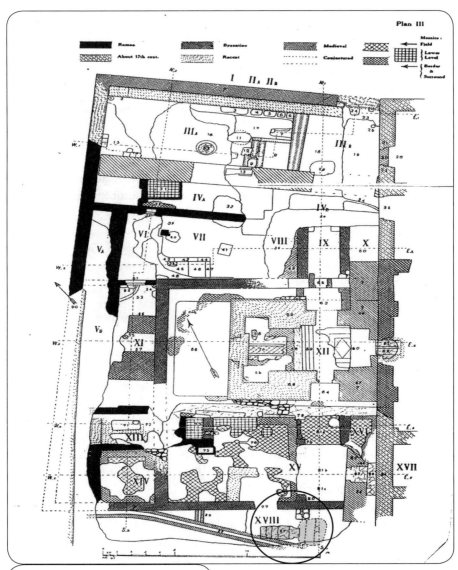

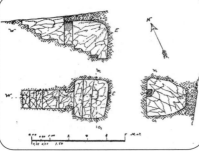

Fig. 1a (above). *General plan of 1941 Franciscan excavations underneath St. John's Church, 'En Karem (Judean Hills). The plan shows several superimposed archaeological strata, postdating the Early Roman period. The ritual bath, dated to the Early Roman period, is circled. Fig. 1b* (left). *Detailed plan and section of that typical ritual bath published as an ancient tomb or underground storage chamber (after Saller 1946: 64–77, pl. 5:1).*[9]

fact that these baths were so widespread and are found in a variety of locations supports Sanders's view that ritual purity was a central feature of common Judaism.

The present chapter attempts to classify the ritual baths from the late Second Temple period and the Bar Kokhba revolt by their functions, emphasizing their archaeological contexts.

Classification of the Ritual Baths by Their Function

The causes of impurity can be classified according to their level of severity, from a seminal emission, which is the least severe, to contact with a corpse, which is the most severe. Accordingly, there is also a hierarchy of purification methods.[10] Because almost all types of impurity are countered by immersion in a ritual bath on its own or alongside other measures, such installations had to be everywhere and had to be adapted to specific conditions, in terms of context, geographical location, size, and architectural features.

Based on the overall finds of ritual immersion baths in the Judean hills and foothills, we will now discuss the main types of ritual baths from a functional perspective.[11]

1. In-Settlement Ritual Immersion Baths: Domestic Baths

Immersion for purification purposes was a routine part of Jewish life, as Jews encountered various causes of impurity on a daily basis. Ritual baths were therefore present throughout Jewish residential quarters in the Second Temple period. Whereas in urban areas, such as in the Upper City of Jerusalem, the bath was an integral part of the house itself, located in its basement through a combination of rock-cutting and building methods, in rural areas relatively few baths were located inside houses. Rather, rural baths were most often installed next to the houses, taking advantage of the ground conditions, topography, rock structure, and availability of open space around the homes. This is particularly evident with respect to ritual baths found in the Judean countryside, which were entirely hewn out of the local limestone, including the ceilings; they usually had no need of additional construction. These *miqwa'ot* were located on the slope beneath the homes so that rainwater could drain into them readily.

Interestingly, most of the baths belonging to this group are conventional in their layout. They do not have separation arrangements, associated baths, or an *otsar* (water storage tank).[12] In many of the examined cases, a water cistern was hewn in close proximity to the bath, without any visible connection between the two installations.[13]

Domestic *miqwa'ot* are found in every type of building inhabited by Jews. At the top of the list stands the type defined by Ehud Netzer as "bath-houses in the Judeo-Hellenistic style." These installations replace the typical cold room (*frigidarium*) and are incorporated in Roman-style heated bathhouses.[14] They were discovered in the Hasmonean winter palaces at Jericho,[15] in the nucleus of Masada's western palace, adjacent to the storeroom complex at Masada, at lower Cypros baths,[16] at Upper and Lower Herodium,[17] at Jerusalem,[18] and at Gezer.[19]

Representative examples of this type of domestic *miqweh* are the excavated baths at the villages of Kiryat Sefer,[20] Horvat 'Ethri (fig. 2),[21] and Nahal Yarmut,[22] and at the site of H. Burnat (South), recently excavated by Amit, where the ritual baths were carved in rooms or in the courtyards located within the residential areas. These examples are outstanding, because the ancient remains were unaltered by later, superimposing settlements. One such example is the bath at Horvat Hillel, where the Byzantine settlement changed the original plan of the site. The archaeological excavation uncovered the stratigraphic relation between the remains of Second Temple period dwellings and the bath located beneath them.[23] At the bottom of the list we can find baths integrated in humble dwellings of remote farmyards, such as the one uncovered by Yitzhak Magen at Qalandia, building F.[24]

2. In-Settlement Ritual Immersion Baths: Public Baths

At some sites, as Horvat 'Ethri (fig. 2),[25] H. Rimmon,[26] and the recently excavated "Nesher Ramleh" and H. Burnat (South) sites, additional larger *miqwaʾot* were carved down the slope, at some distance from the residential quarters, which incorporated typical baths of smaller size. These public baths were likely rock-cut at the community's initiative for "special emergencies." During the rainy season they collected the surplus runoff water that was not caught in the private cisterns and baths situated within the settlement. The water was apparently kept during the long dry season. In years when the summer was longer than usual, the large-sized baths were open for the use of the whole community, especially for "ritual emergencies," until the beginning of the rainy season.

Although they are located within the settlement, most of the baths at Kh. Qumran are markedly different from other domestic baths found in other parts of the country.[27] The exceptional size of these installations, their number, and their careful means of separation suggest their special use for quick immersion of a large number of people in the dry desert environment.[28] Just as this site is unique and exceptional, its ritual baths are unusual and were apparently adapted to the special needs of the sect members who lived there. The generous dimensions of the baths at Kh. Qumran make them comparable to the public baths mentioned above. Both answered to the same necessity: the collection and storage of large amounts of water for the immersion of a large group of people in a brief period of time.

3. In-Settlement Ritual Immersion Baths:
Public Baths Situated Near Synagogues

In 1995, Reich pointed out that *miqwaʾot* were detected near the buildings identified as synagogues from the Second Temple period at Gamla, Masada, and Herodium.[29] During the last decade, archaeologists uncovered three "new" public buildings, all identified as

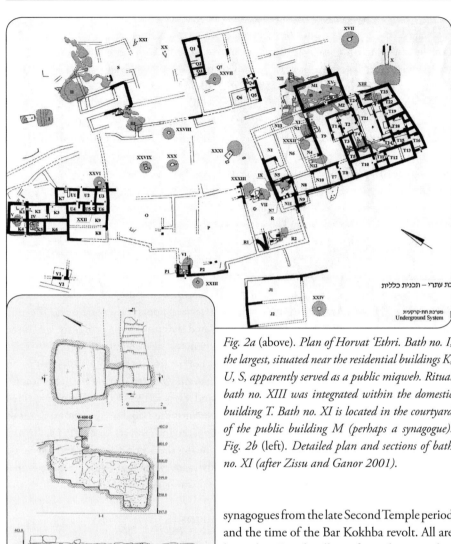

Fig. 2a (above). *Plan of Horvat 'Ethri. Bath no. I, the largest, situated near the residential buildings K, U, S, apparently served as a public miqweh. Ritual bath no. XIII was integrated within the domestic building T. Bath no. XI is located in the courtyard of the public building M (perhaps a synagogue). Fig. 2b* (left). *Detailed plan and sections of bath no. XI (after Zissu and Ganor 2001).*

synagogues from the late Second Temple period and the time of the Bar Kokhba revolt. All are located in Jewish villages from this period at Qiryat Sefer,[30] Horvat 'Ethri (fig. 2),[31] and Kh. Umm el-'Amdan.[32] A ritual immersion bath was detected in close proximity to each of these buildings. A building regarded by its excavator as a synagogue with a well-preserved bath nearby was discovered at the Hasmonean winter palace at Jericho.[33]

Reich discussed the water installations mentioned in the Theodotus inscription from a synagogue in the City of David. This synagogue inscription was found in a cistern, at or near its original location.[34] Two typical ritual baths that may also have belonged to this synagogue were excavated nearby.[35]

The association between the synagogue building and the ritual bath is not easy to explain, since, according to rabbinic law, purity issues have no effect on entry into the synagogue or participation in communal worship. Reich suggested that some activities that took place in the synagogue, such as the holding of sacred meals and the handling of the sacred Scriptures, required a certain degree of purity. Lee I. Levine presented the evidence for water basins in synagogues' *atria*—probably used for the washing of hands and feet (*t. Ber.* 14:2; *y. Meg.*14:1), stressing that in the ancient world ablutions were performed before engaging in sacred worship. Levine suggests that the association between the ritual bath and the synagogue, two important Jewish community institutions, was largely functional and pragmatic, rather than related to synagogue requirements as such.[36] The *miqweh* was a service provided by the synagogue to its community and guests, as we can infer from the Theodotus inscription.

A similar opinion is expressed by Amit in his discussion of the *miqwa'ot* of Gamla.[37] He suggests that the *miqweh* near the synagogue was intended to fulfill the needs of guests or of those of the community who either had no *miqweh* at home or whose home *miqweh* had dried up. The drying up of domestic *miqwa'ot* at the end of the summer of dry years in the climatic conditions of Eretz-Israel was apparently widespread. Belated rains, also a common phenomenon, only aggravated the situation. Apparently, this is the reason that there were public *miqwa'ot* in settlements as mentioned above.

Interestingly, hints about a more integral connection between ritual purity and prayers can be found in the Book of Judith, apparently written during the early Second Temple period: Judith bathed before praying and then returned to the camp purified (Jdt 12:6-9). References in the much later Tosefta and the Babylonian Talmud point to the existence of certain traditions relating immersion and prayers (*t. Ber.* 2:13; *b.Šabb.* 128b). Recently Jonathan Adler suggested that during the Second Temple and Mishnaic periods, a rabbinical enactment required individuals who had experienced seminal emission to immerse in the *miqweh* prior to Torah study and prayer.[38]

4. Ritual Baths and Agricultural Installations

The connection between ritual baths and agricultural production installations, especially wine presses and olive presses, is clear from both archaeological finds and halakhic sources.[39] In several places, ritual baths were found immediately next to wine or olive presses, even when the nearby settlement had domestic baths, as in Qalandya.[40]

In the Hebron Hills, we found some clear examples of such baths,related to wine presses: The ritual bath at the entrance to Kefar Etzion was associated with a wine press. It was carved out as part of the wine-press compound, so close to the collection pit that in secondary use in the Byzantine period it actually became the collection pit and the previous one was turned into a sedimentation pit.[41] The other examples were discovered in surveys at Giv'at Hish (Gush 'Etzion) and Mar Elias (fig. 3, situated between Ramat Rahel and Beit Lehem).[42] Such connection exists also in other parts

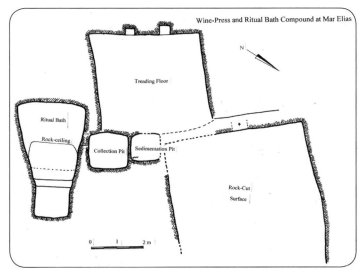

Fig. 3. Plan of ritual bath adjacent to wine press at Mar Elias (situated between Ramat Rahel and Beit Lehem; drawing by B. Zissu).

of the country, for example, at Tel Megiddo.[43] In addition to the examples presented by Reich, these installations illustrate the problems described in the Mishnah, for example: "If wine or olive sap fell therein [into the ritual bath] . . . none may immerse therein" (*m. Miqw.* 7:4).

The presence of ritual baths in proximity to wine and olive presses testifies to the extreme care taken during the production of wine and oil, which entailed conversion of fruit into liquid—*mashkin* in halakhic terminology; as a result of this conversion, the product could become impure and could then easily defile other foods and drinks (*m. Makš.* 1:1; 6:4). Wine was manufactured in a state of ritual purity: "If an Israelite was preparing [his wine] in [conditions of] uncleanness, none may help him to tread the winepress or to gather grapes" (*m. 'Abod. Zar.* 4:9).

In order to be completely sure that wine and olive oil were produced in purity, the vineyard owner installed a ritual bath next to the wine press or olive press and was concerned to purify his workers as soon as they arrived to produce the wine or oil, instead of relying on their immersion at home before beginning their workday. These examples may illustrate the mishnaic passage: "If workers in the olive-press and grape-gatherers are brought to the cavern, that suffices. So R. Meir. R. Jose says: One must need stand over them until they immerse" (*m. Tehar.* 10:3).

This greatly reduced the likelihood that the product would become impure. Reich also pointed out the relationship between these ritual baths and the priestly gifts, as the priest had to be pure to receive them: "From what time in the evening may the Shema be recited? From the time when the priests enter [the temple] to eat of their Heave-offering until the end of the first watch" (*m. Ber.* 1:1).[44]

The proximity of the *miqweh* to an olive or wine press implies that people were pure enough after immersion (and before nightfall) to handle grapes and olives. But the biblical purity laws (for example, Lev 11:39-40; 15:5, 11, 16, 18, 20, 22-23, 27; Num 19:8, 10, 19, 21-22) require a certain period of time to pass between immersion and actual purification, which can take place only after sunset.[45] Therefore, an impure worker who immersed in the bath situated near the agricultural installation could not immediately start his duties, but had to wait at least until sunset (the end of his working day?).Therefore, the fact that the bath is located within the agricultural installation cannot entirely solve the heave-offering's purity concern.

Sometimes baths located outside settlements raise problems of identification. The well-preserved bath surveyed at Shmurat Shayarot is situated near a wine press and other agricultural features, but it is also close to an ancient ascent to Jerusalem, which makes its exact attribution difficult.[46] The waters of the spring at 'En Bikurah (Judean Hills) flow through an underground tunnel into a large pool with steps extending along its entire width—actually a *miqweh*. From there, the waters irrigate the adjacent agricultural plots. No ancient settlement or agricultural installations are visible today, but the location of the pool hints at the ancient use of the spring for purification purposes.

The most impressive examples of ritual baths located within olive-press caves were uncovered at Ahuzat Hazan (fig. 4),[47] at Khirbet Marah el-Juma (Nabi Daniyal),[48] and at Gamla in the Golan.[49] These baths were carved out inside the cave among the other auxiliary installations. In the case of Qiryat Sefer, the immersion bath was located near the entrance to a room that housed the olive press.[50] Similar examples are known from other sites in the Land of Benjamin, such as Kh. Nisya and Pisgat Ze'ev, and from Samaritan sites in Samaria, such as Qedumim and El-Khirbe.[51]

The ritual baths adjacent to agricultural installations are characterized by their relatively small size; this is conspicuous in the Hebron Hills, where the ritual baths of other types are particularly

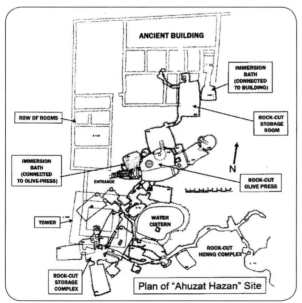

Fig. 4. Plan of ritual bath located within an olive-press cave at Ahuzat Hazan (courtesy of A. Kloner, after Kloner and Tepper 1987: 115–27).

large. A small bath was sufficient, and there was no need to worry about the accumulation of dirt in the water, because few people used the bath and even they used it only during a fairly short period of the year—during the olive or grape seasons.

5. Ritual Baths for Use by Pilgrims

Ritual baths for pilgrims were uncovered for the first time in the immediate vicinity of the Temple Mount in Jerusalem.[52] Reich was the first to discuss them in their proper setting.[53] Their location and concentration make sense in light of the large number of pilgrims who had to enter the Temple Mount in a state of purity.[54] Recently Reich and Ely Shukron uncovered impressive remains of the Siloam Pool from the Second Temple period.[55] The excavators reported that its broad steps are characteristic of a *miqweh*, and it probably served as an enormous bath for the use of pilgrims. This is most probably the Pool of Siloam mentioned in connection with Jesus' cure of the blind man (John 9:7). The Pool of Bethesda, located north of the temple, was apparently another monumental immersion pool, intended to serve large numbers of pilgrims.[56]

However, tannaitic sources also mention ritual baths outside the city, on the pilgrims' way to Jerusalem. Thus, the Mishnah (*m. Šeqal.* 1:1) says: "On the 15th thereof [of the month of Adar] they read the Megillah [of Esther] in walled cities and repair the paths and roads and pools of water [*miqwa'ot*] and perform all public needs and mark the graves."

The Tosefta (*t. Šeqal.* 1:2) explains: "On the fifteenth [of the month of Adar], the emissaries of the court go out and dig ditches and caves and repair the ritual baths and the aqueduct. Every ritual bath that contains forty seahs is fit for use; for one that does not contain forty seahs, one extends the aqueduct to it and fills it to a total of forty seahs so that it will be fit for use."

The Babylonian Talmud (*b. Mo'ed Qat.* 5a) presents a similar *baraitha*: "They go out to clear the thorns from the roads, to repair the streets and roads, and to measure the ritual baths. Into any ritual bath that does not have forty seahs, one pours forty seahs."

These statements by the rabbis are illustrated by the pair of large ritual baths at Allon Shevut, which were located alongside the twelfth milestone marker on the main Jerusalem–Hebron road.[57] The dimensions of these baths, especially the eastern one—an enormous *miqweh* with a capacity of around 250 cubic meters—together with the meticulous means of separation by two parallel hewn staircases, enabled a large group of people to enter and exit the bath rapidly in a "conveyor" fashion. Moreover, we suggest that the smaller, western bath was used first, while the larger, eastern one served as its reservoir and was kept as a *miqweh* for "emergencies" such as when the water of the western bath turned out to be unsuitable for use. Similar arrangements of pairs of *miqwa'ot* for public use were found at the "Tombs of the Kings" in Jerusalem and at Kh. Qumran. Similar features were noticed also in private contexts. The location near the main road, far from any settlement, together with the huge size of these baths and the means of separation, reinforces the hypothesis that they were intended for the immersion of pilgrims a few hours before they entered Jerusalem.

The bath at Bir Ijda near Hebron (fig. 5), whose dimensions resemble those of the previously mentioned bath but are even more impressive, seems to be related to the pilgrims' route as well.[58] Here another significant factor comes into play—the proximity to the Cave of Machpelah—which will be discussed below with the final category of baths.

The group of immersion baths with separate paths was identified in Jerusalem and discussed by Reich.[59] This feature—double opening and separate paths— also characterizes an impressive group of baths found at various rural locations in the northern Hebron Hills, the region situated to the south of Jerusalem.[60]

These baths, all dating from the Second Temple period, have special arrangements designed to ensure problem-free immersion: a narrow and low partition along the length of the staircase leading down into the bath, or a pair of openings at the entrance to the immersion room. In a few cases, both arrangements were found. The effect was to create two separate access paths: one leading to the bath, to be used by people who were still impure, and the other for those leaving after having been immersed and made pure. The idea was to prevent contact between pure and impure people.

This unique group of baths elucidates the statement in the Mishnah regarding the impurity of utensils: "All utensils found in Jerusalem on the path down to the place of immersion must be deemed unclean; but [if they are found] on the path back they may be deemed clean; for the path by which they are taken down is not the same as that by which they are brought back" (*m. Šeqal.* 8:2). It also elucidates Rashi's statement in his commentary on the Talmud (*b. Pesaḥ.* 19b, *incipit* "Even though"): "They would go down to the place of immersion by one path and come up by a different path."

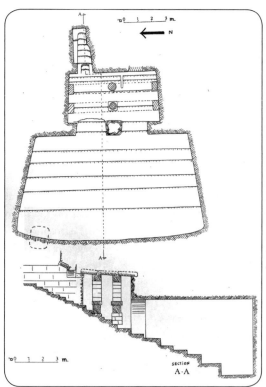

Fig. 5. Plan and sections of bath at Bir Ijda near Hebron, whose outstanding dimensions hint at its relation to the pilgrims' route (after Amit 1996).

This type of bath also illustrates similar passages in two external sources discussed by Saul Lieberman.[61] One of them is an apocryphal Gospel in a fragmentary papyrus discovered at Oxyrhynchus in Upper Egypt. The source presents a dialogue between Jesus and the high priest. When asked by the high priest about permission to be within the sanctified area when he was impure, Jesus responded by asking if the high priest himself was pure. The priest replied: "I am pure; I bathed (immersed) in the ritual bath of David, and I descended by one ladder and ascended by another ladder."

Another source is a description of the Temple Mount by Aristeas (in his letter to Philocrates), in which he says: "There are steps too which lead up to the cross roads, and some people are always going up, and others down, and they keep as far apart from each other as possible on the road because of those who are bound by the rules of purity, lest they should touch anything which is unlawful."[62] Lieberman and Reich both argue that Aristeas was referring to ritual baths, although he did not mention immersion explicitly.[63] Nevertheless, baths with a separation between the entrance and exit—whether a double staircase or a double opening, or even both—are a fairly large minority. Clearly, the effort put into the rock-cutting and building of these architectural features, which ensured separate paths for the pure and the impure, stemmed from greater-than-usual meticulousness in the laws of purity and impurity during immersion of large groups of pilgrims.

The two typical examples discussed above, Allon Shevut and Bir Ijda, represent a phenomenon that most probably existed along the main roads to the city. The bath at Horvat Metzad, situated next to the main road from Emmaus to Jerusalem, can perhaps be included in this category, although it is incorporated within the architectural compound of a Second Temple period road station.[64]

6. Ritual Baths Near Graves

Rabbinic literature contains no reference to ritual baths next to graves, and such a location would seem to be incompatible with rabbinic thought. It is rather surprising, therefore, to find ritual baths in several places integrated in courtyards of Jewish burial complexes or hewn near concentrations of burial caves in Jerusalem and Judea. Amos Kloner and Zissu recorded six instances of ritual baths located near burial caves within the Jerusalem Necropolis.[65] The most impressive example is the pair of ritual baths (initially identified as reservoirs) found at the "Tombs of the Kings" (figs. 6, 7), at the bottom of the monumental stairway leading to the courtyard.[66]

In this context, Reich discussed the large ritual bath discovered at Herodium, at the western end of the course along the lower palace and near the monumental building. If we accept the suggestion of the excavator, Ehud Netzer, that Herod's tomb should be located here and that the course was designed as part of the royal burial compound, the ritual bath—which is also monumental in its design—fits in well with this architectural complex.[67]

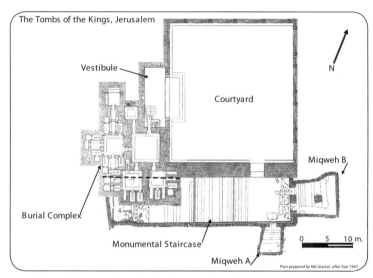

The Tombs of the Kings, Jerusalem

Vestibule

Courtyard

N

Miqweh B

Burial Complex

Monumental Staircase

Miqweh A

0   5   10 m.

Plan prepared by Nili Graicer, after Kon 1947

Fig. 6. General plan of the "Tombs of the Kings" complex, Jerusalem. Note pair of ritual baths located at the bottom of the monumental stairway (drawing by N. Graicer, after Kon 1947: 28–38).

A similar relationship between a monumental tomb and an adjacent monumental ritual bath, although not in a single architectural complex, is found between the Cave of Machpelah, which was enclosed in the Second Temple period within a huge, impressive compound, and the enormous ritual bath of Bir Ijda.[68] This bath served pilgrims who made the way from the burial place of the biblical patriarchs and matriarchs. Together, these cases corroborate the link between graves and ritual baths.

Another impressive example is the monumental courtyard of Tomb H at Jericho (the "Goliath Family Tomb"), which included a ritual bath with an *otsar*—a water storage tank.[69]

Recently, two instances of ritual baths related to burial caves from the late first to early second centuries c.e. were uncovered by Amit. One was found at H. Zichrin on the western slopes of Samaria and the other at Kh. Dar 'Asi on the western slopes of the Judean hills, above Ayalon Valley.[70]

The Qumran literature contains several references to a connection between graves and ritual baths. A halakhic-liturgical text known as 4Q414, which has survived only in part and has been published by Esther Eshel, indicates that a person made impure through contact with the dead must immerse for the sake of purification on the first day, that is, immediately after the burial, and on the third and seventh days.[71] Parallels to this can be found in a similarly worded composition (4Q512) and in the *Temple Scroll*. These writings thus represent a halakhic tradition apparently opposed to the rabbinic tradition, which states that a person who has become impure through contact with the dead immerses only on the seventh day.

Fig. 7. "Tombs of the Kings," Jerusalem. a (top). *Monumental stairway, looking west. b* (center). *Entrances to pair of ritual baths, looking east. c* (bottom). *Photo of interior of Miqweh B, looking east (photos by A. Graicer).*

In the light of this information, Eshel concluded that the baths located near graves should be attributed to a population that followed the halakhic tradition expressed in these writings, since according to Pharisaic halakhah there is no apparent reason for building a ritual bath in a cemetery. Ze'ev and Chanah Safrai pointed to some instances in the Jerusalem Talmud where a place of purity is apparently connected to a cemetery.[72]

Although the new halakhic and archaeological information advances our understanding of the complex relationship between ritual baths and graveyards,[73] we probably should not rush to extrapolate directly from the halakhic sources cited to all such baths. Here, too, the picture may be more complex than it appears, and only future discoveries—archaeological and textual—will fill in what is now missing.

Conclusion

We have shown that the archaeological evidence attests to a wide variety of ritual baths in the Second Temple period, and to their different environmental and functional contexts. A ritual bath designed for the residents of a private farmstead will differ from a public bath on the road to Jerusalem, which is designed to serve many people simultaneously. It will also differ from a bath associated with a wine press or olive press, which serves only a few laborers who have to purify themselves before processing the agricultural produce. The wide distribution of ritual baths reinforces Sanders's assertion that the purity laws were generally obeyed by the Jewish population.[74]

These are only a few examples of the wide variety of ritual baths that are increasingly being discovered in the rural areas of Judea. This variety far surpasses that of the baths of Jerusalem, most of which are located in urban residential areas. Like synagogues, ritual baths are structures unique to the Jewish community and are therefore a clear indication that a site is Jewish, even without any additional information, such as literary sources or inscriptions. In the absence of a historical source giving a detailed description of the rural areas of Judea, archaeological remains are a crucial source for our understanding of this area in the Second Temple period. It is therefore important to gather every available piece of archaeological information, using the ritual baths as a characteristic feature, which assists the reconstruction of the overall picture of settlement in the Judean hills and foothills in the period under discussion.

5. Common Judaism, Common Synagogue? Purity, Holiness, and Sacred Space at the Turn of the Common Era

Susan Haber

In his seminal work *Judaism: Practice and Belief*, E. P. Sanders looks beyond the factional disputes of Judaism at the turn of the Common Era to consider the theology and praxis of the majority of Jews in Palestine and the Diaspora.[1] While acknowledging the diversity of opinion regarding the interpretation of the law, he argues for a common Judaism: basic tenets and practices that were agreed upon by the various parties and the Jewish populace as a whole. According to Sanders, the synagogue was a major locus of Jewish life and worship in the first century.[2] It was the place where Jews assembled on the Sabbath to hear the recitation of Torah and the exposition of its law.

The majority of scholars agree that the first-century synagogue was a central institution in every Jewish community and that it accommodated a variety of liturgical and communal functions.[3] Within this broader position, however, there is no consensus regarding various aspects of the study of the synagogue.[4] One area of disagreement concerns the holiness of the synagogue.[5] Archaeological evidence indicates that synagogues were often located in coastal regions or had water facilities such as *miqwaʾot*, cisterns, or basins constructed adjacent to them. Scholars disagree, however, on whether this close proximity to water indicates a connection between purity practices

---

Editors' note: Susan Haber passed away in July 2006, some months after completing the final version of this paper.

and the synagogue. Some believe that locating synagogues near water reflected a practice whereby Jews entering their places of worship performed some sort of ritual purification that was similar to that required at the entrances of Greco-Roman temples. Others argue that proximity was due to convenience; Jews made use of purification facilities regularly, and they attended synagogue regularly, but this does not mean that purification was required before entering the synagogue.

The present chapter examines the relationship between purity and the synagogue at the turn of the Common Era as it relates to the sacred. Two questions lie at the heart of this investigation. First, did Jews perform ritual ablutions in order to purify themselves before entering the synagogue—that is, did they immerse their bodies, wash their hands, or sprinkle themselves with water? The answer to this question leads directly to the second question: Did they regard the synagogue as a sacred realm?

Two methodological issues are pertinent to this investigation. The first is a matter of definition: what exactly do we mean when we use the term "synagogue"? Here I follow Anders Runesson, who distinguishes four separate aspects of the synagogue: institutional, liturgical, nonliturgical, and spatial.[6] My concern is primarily with the liturgical aspects of the synagogue, that is, the activities that are usually categorized as "religious." In addition, consideration will be given to certain spatial aspects of the place in which these liturgical activities took place. A second methodological concern is the issue of unity and diversity. The ancient synagogue may have held a significant place in common Judaism, but the institution was not a monolithic entity, nor should it be treated as such. In order to account for geographic differences in practice, synagogues in the land of Israel will be considered separately from those existing in the Diaspora.

I begin with an investigation of the ancient concepts of purity and holiness and their perceived relationship. I then examine the relationship between purity and the synagogue, first in the land of Israel and subsequently in the Diaspora. Finally, I consider the notion of the early synagogue as a sacred realm, in order to demonstrate that certain purity practices related to the synagogue point to its sanctity but that the nature of this perceived holiness varies with location.

Purity and Holiness

Purity and holiness were prominent features of Jewish life in the late Second Temple period. Distinctions between pure and impure, holy and common applied to people, objects, space, and time. Not only were these categories fundamental to the social structure of Jewish society, but they also influenced a variety of interactions, as it was a basic tenet of the law that impurity could not come in contact with the sacred.

Jonathan Klawans distinguishes two types of impurity: ritual defilement, a contagion that temporarily excludes the individual from participating in temple rituals; and the more permanent, moral defilement caused by sin, a form of impurity that is not related to temple worship.[7] Ritual impurities include those that arise from childbirth (Lev 12:1-8), scale disease (Lev 13:1—14:32), genital discharges (Lev 15:1-33), the carcasses of certain impure animals (Lev 11:1-47), and human corpses (Num 19:10-22). Ritual impurity is also encountered as a by-product of purificatory procedures (for example, Lev 16:28; Num 19:8). According to Klawans, there are three distinctive characteristics of ritual impurity. First, the sources of ritual impurity are natural, usually unavoidable, and sometimes even desirable. They include birth, death, sex, disease, and other circumstances that reflect the conditions of normal life. Second, there are no prohibitions against contracting these impurities, nor are they considered sinful. The consequence of ritual impurity is relatively minor in that it precludes entrance to the sanctuary and other forms of contact with the sacred. Third, ritual impurity conveys an impermanent contagion through contact with other individuals or objects. It should be emphasized, however, that both primary and secondary forms of ritual impurity may be alleviated through purificatory procedures. Thus, even long-lasting impurities are considered impermanent.

Unlike ritual impurity, moral impurity results from immoral acts, including sexual sins (for example, Lev 18:24-30), idolatry (for example, Lev 19:31; 20:1-3), and bloodshed (for example, Num 35:33-34).[8] These sinful actions are often referred to as *to'evot*, or abominations. The impurity that arises from such sin is a moral defilement, which pollutes the sinner (Lev 18:24), the land (Lev 18:25; Ezek 36:17), and God's sanctuary (Lev 20:3; Ezek 5:11). Although this form of impurity is not contagious, it is considered permanent and therefore may not be ameliorated through rites of purification.[9] Sinners are thus forced to live out their lives in a degraded state or suffer capital punishment. The land upon which grave sin is committed is likewise subject to permanent degradation, which may result in the expulsion of its inhabitants.

The purity laws were widely observed in both the land of Israel and the Diaspora.[10] In the land of Israel, purification required the "immersion" of the whole body in water from a natural source: the sea, a spring, a river, or a *miqweh* in which rainwater, springwater, or runoff was collected by a direct flow.[11] In the Diaspora, ritual ablutions took the form of sprinkling, splashing, or hand washing.[12] Jews everywhere performed these purificatory rites whether or not they approached the sacred precincts of the Jerusalem temple.[13]

Two factors help to explain this widespread practice. First, Jews of the first century believed that the biblical laws, including the purity laws, were divine in origin and hence were a requirement. Their concern was not whether to keep the law but how to do so within their own social and cultural context. Second, according to the law, only those who were in a state of purity could have contact with the sacred. Such holiness was associated not only with the temple but also with the biblical scrolls that were read on the Sabbath, and perhaps even the synagogue in which the Torah was read and studied. Jews purified themselves so that they could draw near to that which was holy.

The concept of holiness implies separation, specifically, separation from the profane.[14] In the first century, ideas of holiness and separation are most apparent in the hierarchical structure of the Jerusalem temple, where access to the various levels of holy space is limited to various groups of individuals according to their level of sanctity.[15] Thus, female Israelites are allowed only as far as the court of the women, while their male counterparts, who occupy a higher place on the continuum from profane to holy, may enter the courtyard of the sacrificial altar.[16] The priests, being even holier, minister in the adytum, where the incense altar is situated, and the high priest, the holiest of God's people, gains access to the innermost shrine, but only once a year on the Day of Atonement.

The relationship between holy/common and pure/impure is complex in that it concerns two separate but related continuums. What is certain is that in the first century Jews recognized that an individual or object was subject to four possible states: holy, common, pure, and impure. The dynamic between these states has been best illustrated by Jacob Milgrom:[17]

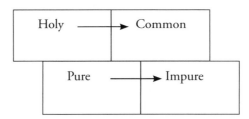

In this diagram the common is contiguous to the realms of both the pure and impure, but the holy is adjacent only to the pure. The categories of holy and impure are antagonistic; they never come in contact with each other.

The relationship between the concept of holiness and that of purity is significant to the discussion of the synagogue as a sacred realm. If Jews in the first century regarded synagogues as sacred spaces, they would have been careful to separate them from all sources of impurity, and therefore to locate them in "pure" locations and provide facilities for ritual ablutions to ensure the ritual purity of all who entered.

Purity and the Synagogue in the Land of Israel

In the land of Israel, synagogues dating to the Second Temple period have been identified at Jericho, Gamla, Masada, Herodium, Qiryat Sefer, and Modi'in.[18] While none of these buildings is located near a natural body of water, the buildings at Jericho, Masada, and Herodium have *miqwa'ot* associated with them. Moreover, *miqwa'ot* have been found at Qumran as well as in the villages of Modi'in and Qiryat Sefer, albeit in locations that do not suggest any spatial connection to a synagogue.[19] Finally, the Theodotus inscription attests to the existence of a first-century synagogue in Jerusalem that had water facilities associated with it.[20]

A brief survey of the archaeological evidence will help to indicate whether the proximity of *miqwa'ot* to synagogues was intended to facilitate purification rites connected with synagogue attendance. The recently excavated synagogue in Jericho is located just outside the compound of the Hasmonean winter palace and is related to a row of houses to the east.[21] The hall, dated to the second phase of construction (70 B.C.E.), measured 16.2 x 11.1 meters and would have seated approximately 125 people.[22] It was bisected by a water channel that originated at a conduit to the north of the hall and terminated at the *miqweh* to the south. A basin located in the northern aisle of the synagogue was also attached to the channel and was likely used for ritual washing of the hands.

The synagogue at Gamla was a public village assembly hall, centrally located near the city gate.[23] The interior of the building (20 x 16 m.) was lined with two to four rows of benches, which would have seated some 340 people.[24] Significantly, there is a water channel from an aqueduct outside the city that penetrates the northeast wall of the building and ends in a small basin in the northern corner of the synagogue. It is likely that this basin was used for hand washing.[25] A *miqweh* dating to the period of the first Jewish revolt (66–67 C.E.) is located about ten meters to the southwest of the building.[26] The presence of three other ritual baths in Gamla indicates a particular concern for purity in this town.[27]

At Masada, the building identified as a synagogue is dated to the time of Herod (37–4 B.C.E.).[28] The building was converted into an assembly hall during the occupation of the Jewish rebels between 66 and 74 C.E. The large hall (12 x 15 m.) was lined with one to four rows of benches, which would have seated 250 people. Its identification as a synagogue is confirmed by the discovery of fragments from the books of Deuteronomy and Ezekiel found in the adjoining room. There is also a *miqweh* located fifteen meters north of the synagogue, which was apparently built by the rebels. In addition, three other *miqwa'ot*, dating to the first Jewish rebellion, are scattered throughout the complex.

Like the synagogue at Masada, the assembly hall at Herodium was also converted from a preexisting structure.[29] In the first phase of the building, the hall served as a triclinium in Herod's fortress palace. It was only during the occupation of the rebels during the first Jewish revolt that the hall was converted into a synagogue. The Herodium synagogue (10.5 x 15 m.) was similar in size to the synagogue at Masada, seating approximately 250 people.[30] Just outside the hall was a *miqweh*, which abutted the eastern wall of the synagogue.[31] In addition, a storage pool and an adjacent bathtub were nearby, from the same phase.

The discovery of several *miqwa'ot* at Qumran also warrants our consideration, especially since the purificatory rites of the Qumran community were related to liturgical activities that were often associated with a synagogue. According to Jodi Magness, *miqwa'ot* are found in areas in which purity was required, as well as those areas in which impurity was incurred. It is therefore not surprising to find a large *miqweh* (loci 56–58) near the entrance to the communal assembly hall (locus 77), which was used for dining. While there are no archaeological remains from Qumran to establish the presence of a synagogue, it is likely that locus 77 was also used for this purpose.[32] Runesson contends that the activities that took place in this room were likely those described in 1QS VI 2–5, which included eating, praying, and deliberating together in a fashion that is reminiscent of Hellenistic associations. Moreover, the *yaḥad* referred to in 1QS may well have been a religious association that was organized much like the synagogue communities of the Diaspora.[33]

The association of water facilities with a synagogue is attested also in the Theodotus inscription:

> Theodotus, the son of Vettenos, priest and archisynagogos, son of an archisynagogos and grandson of an archisynagogos, built the assembly hall [synagogue, *synagōgē* for the reading of the Law and for the teaching of the commandments, and the guest room, the chambers, and the water fittings, as an inn for those in need from foreign parts, [the synagogue] which his fathers founded with the elders and Simonides.[34]

John S. Kloppenborg argues that while the first portion of the inscription describes various portions of the building, the final relative clause treats all of these components collectively, as being part of the synagogue.[35] Thus, in addition to an assembly hall, this synagogue had several rooms for lodgers as well as some sort of water facilities. It is unclear whether these water facilities were used for ritual purposes or to meet other needs of the visitors. Given that the synagogue was founded by a priestly family, however, we might speculate that these facilities included a *miqweh* along with other facilities for drinking and washing.

The archaeological and epigraphic evidence points to two types of ritual ablution associated with synagogues in the land of Israel, namely, ritual hand washing and full immersion. The water basins found inside the assembly halls at Jericho and Gamla suggest that the rituals performed in the synagogue, such as the handling of Torah scrolls, required ritual hand washing.[36] It is less certain that full immersion was also associated with synagogue rituals. Donald D. Binder argues that the presence of *miqwa'ot* in proximity to Second Temple period synagogues is an indication that purity requirements were connected with the synagogue in much the same way as they were associated with the temple. Such a view, however, is problematic. First, priestly law attests to the fact that an individual could not enter the temple in a state of ritual impurity (Lev 15:31). This biblical prohibition is alluded to throughout the Second Temple literature, yet none of the sources describe a similar ruling pertaining to the synagogue.[37] Second, it is difficult from a logistic perspective to envision how one synagogue *miqweh* could accommodate a large group of people all intending to immerse prior to an assembly in the synagogue. At their maximum capacity, the synagogues under consideration could seat hundreds of people. Yet the *miqwa'ot* associated with them were relatively small and therefore clearly intended only for individual immersion.[38] If we estimate that it would take one minute for an individual to enter the *miqweh*, immerse, and emerge, a crowd of 120 people would require some two hours to complete their purification. Given that synagogue worship was a communal rather than an individual act, this scenario is hardly feasible.

More likely, the association of water facilities with the central Jewish institution was a matter of practicality. The public *miqweh* would have been built at the communal center in order to facilitate the observance of Jewish purity practices within the community, in the same way the synagogues were built to facilitate the communal reading and study of the Torah. Thus, members of the community would have used the *miqweh* at the appropriate times in order to maintain their ritual purity on a regular basis. They would have also assembled in the synagogue on the Sabbath, as well as on other occasions, but they probably would not have routinely used the *miqweh* before entering. It is likely that only those who had direct contact with the Torah scrolls would have been required to perform ritual ablutions in connection with synagogue rituals. These individuals would have utilized water basins for the washing of their hands.

Purity and the Synagogue in the Diaspora

The archaeological remains of two Diaspora buildings have been securely identified as synagogues dated to the Second Temple period: the Ostia synagogue and the synagogue on the island of Delos.[39] Both synagogues are located on the seashore, and both have human-made water facilities adjacent to the building. It is often assumed that the proximity of these synagogues to water is associated with purity practices. Yet the existence of both natural and human-made water facilities is somewhat perplexing, since either one or the other would have sufficed to meet any purity requirements associated with the synagogue.

Purity and the Location of the Synagogue

The synagogue on Delos, dated to the second century B.C.E., is the earliest known structure of its kind in either the Diaspora or the land of Israel. It is situated directly on the shore of what was the eastern side of the city, at some distance from the city center and its residential buildings, sanctuaries, and public places.[40] Similarly, the synagogue at Ostia, dated to the first century C.E., stood outside the city walls near the ancient seashore.[41] The epigraphic and literary evidence suggests that synagogues were often to be found in proximity to water (the sea or a river) and at a distance from the city center. A second century B.C.E. land survey from Arsinoe in Egypt, written on papyrus, indicates that a synagogue was located on the outskirts of the town and was situated by a canal.[42] Josephus mentions a decree of the citizens of Halicarnassus that permitted the Jews to build synagogues or houses of prayer near the sea in accordance with their ancestral customs: "To the effect that their sacred services to God and their customary festivals and religious gatherings shall be carried on, we have decreed that those Jewish men and women who so wish may observe their Sabbaths and perform their sacred rites in accordance with the Jewish laws, and may build places of prayer near the sea in accordance with their native custom" (*Ant.* 14.258).[43] Finally, Acts 16:13 indicates that Paul and his companions went outside the gates of Philippi to the riverside to look for the synagogue: "On the sabbath day we went outside the gate by the river, where we supposed there was a place of prayer; and we sat down and spoke to the women who had gathered there." It is quite evident from this passage that Paul expected to find the synagogue outside the city, by the river. Though these sources mention only proximity to water, such locations would often perforce be at the periphery of the city.

Ismar Elbogen correctly points out, however, that synagogues in the Diaspora were not always located beside a source of water. Moreover, there are no halakhic rulings pertaining to building synagogues near water, either in the land of Israel or in the Diaspora. For Elbogen the significance of the passage in Acts is not that Paul expects to find the synagogue by the riverside, but that he presumes that it is outside the city gate. He writes: "The Jews avoided worshipping inside cities that contained pagan sanctuaries; only if special Jewish quarters existed, as in Alexandria, were synagogues established in them."[44]

If Elbogen is correct, then the location of Diaspora synagogues outside the city gate reflects a concern not with a ritual impurity that requires ablutions but with a moral impurity that cannot be washed away. Synagogues—devoted to the worship of the one God—could not be built on land that was considered polluted by idolatry. Philo's description of the events that occurred after the Jews of Alexandria heard about the arrest of their enemy supports this conclusion:

> All night long they continued to sing hymns and songs of praise and at dawn pouring out through the gates, they made their way to the parts of the beach near at hand, since their meeting-houses [*proseuchas*] had been taken from them, *k'an tō katharōtatō stantes* they cried out with one accord "Most Mighty King of mortals and immortals." (*Flacc.* 122–23)

F. H. Colson translates the phrase *k'an tō katharōtatō stantes* as "and standing in the most open place."[45] An alternative translation is offered by Runesson, who suggests that in the Jewish context of this passage it would be more accurate to retain the basic meaning of the term *katharos*, which is "clean" or "pure." One might suggest, however, an even more nuanced reading of the text, in which the term *katharos* is understood in a moral sense as being free from pollution.[46] In the context of Philo's narrative, the Jews of Alexandria sought a "pure" place to worship God, because their city had been polluted by immorality. Not only had their synagogues been taken from them and the Jewish quarters destroyed, but many of the Jews had been tortured and murdered. The blood of innocent people polluted Alexandria, both literally and morally.

In the passage from Philo, the Jews go to a place outside the city—a place that replaces their destroyed synagogues. It is there that they pray in a location that is not defiled by moral pollution. The issue of concern is the status of the land as it pertains to the two continuums of holy/profane and pure/impure. In contrast to the land of Israel, which is considered holy, Gentile lands are regarded as profane, but not necessarily impure. The purity or impurity of a Gentile land depends on the activities of the inhabitants. Thus, the Alexandrian Jews could gather on the beach outside of Alexandria to pray, on land that was considered profane but pure.

In summary, the location of the Diaspora synagogue in proximity to natural sources of water coincides with its position at the periphery of the non-Jewish city. It is probable that Jews built their synagogues outside the city because they considered the land "pure"—that is, unpolluted by the moral impurity associated with idolatrous practices and other sins. The fact that these locations are often near natural sources of water has no implication with respect to moral impurity.[47] It is possible, however, that the water was used for ritual ablutions prior to prayer or the handling of the Torah.

Purity and the Association of Water Facilities with the Synagogue

From the second century B.C.E. until late antiquity, Diaspora synagogues shared one common feature: the presence of a cistern, water basin, or fountain at the entrance area.[48] Most frequently, a water basin was placed in the center of the atrium, just outside the main entrance of the building, in the hall, or in the narthex that led from the street to the sanctuary.[49] Installations of this type were found in a number of synagogues in the Diaspora, including the synagogues of Delos and Ostia.[50]

The water installations associated with the synagogue on Delos include three water basins and a cistern.[51] Fragments from one of the basins are presently located between two benches near what was purportedly the main entrance of the building. A second was found in a room inside the building, and a third in the cistern. It is most probable that these marble basins held water for ritual ablutions.[52] There has been some speculation that the cistern inside the synagogue may have been used for ritual bathing, especially since it allowed for human access.[53] If this were the case, it would be among the earliest known *miqwa'ot* in the world, the earliest associated with a synagogue, and the only ancient *miqweh* discovered outside the land of Israel. Yet the architecture of the Delian water reservoir does not conform to that of *miqwa'ot* of the same period found in the land of Israel. Moreover, its proximity to the sea, which could have served the same purpose as a *miqweh*, makes this identification questionable. In all likelihood, the water from the cistern was used for daily activities such as drinking, cooking, washing, and cleaning.[54]

The earliest plan of the synagogue at Ostia included a well and a shallow cistern that stood to the right of the main entrance.[55] It also had other features that were shared by the guilds of Ostia, including an assembly room and a triclinium.[56] It is likely that the well and the cistern served a function in the synagogue similar to their functions in other Ostian guilds, including both ritual and nonritual purposes. During the first renovation of the synagogue, a basin was constructed in the area to the right just inside the entrance to the eastern main door.[57] The basin holds a large amount of water, some four times the amount that would be required for a *miqweh* constructed according to rabbinic requirements. Yet the form of the basin differs significantly from a traditional *miqweh* in that it is very large and shallow rather than narrow and deep. Moreover, it was probably filled with water that had been drawn from the well rather than by direct access. Runesson concludes that the basin was used for ritual washing and suggests that its shallowness may imply washing of the hands and feet.

The archaeological evidence suggests that ritual ablutions were associated with synagogues in the Diaspora and that these purification procedures did not involve immersion in a *miqweh*.[58] It is not clear, however, how this ritual ablution was performed. The literary sources attest to the relationship between hand washing and synagogue activities. The *Sibylline Oracles* indicate that Jews washed their hands before praying (3.591–93). Similarly, Josephus indicates that the elders who translated the law from Hebrew into Greek washed their hands before handling the sacred Scripture (*Ant.* 12.106). A parallel account in the *Letter of Aristeas* is particularly informative:

> Following the custom of all the Jews, they washed their hands in the sea in the course of their prayers to God, and then proceeded to the reading and explication of each point. I asked this question: "What is their purpose in washing their hands while saying their prayers?" They explained that it is evidence that they have done no evil, for all activity takes place by means of the hands. (305–6)

In this passage, hand washing is associated with both prayer and the handling of Scripture. The purported reason for hand washing, however, is not ritual purification but moral purity. In this passage, there is an overlap between the two categories of ritual and moral impurity. Because sin is regarded as being ritually defiling, it may be removed by washing one's hands.

It is also possible that Jews purified themselves by sprinkling with water. Philo attests to the practice of splashing or sprinkling oneself after sexual relations (*Spec.* 3.63) and to a combination of sprinkling and bathing in order to remove corpse impurity (*Spec.* 3.205; cf. 1.261). The practice of purification by sprinkling with water is widely attested in the Greco-Roman world.[59] At the entrances to Greek temples there were vessels containing water (*perippantēria*, "sprinkling basins"). Prior to entering, the worshipers would dip their hands into the vessel and sprinkle themselves with water.[60] Since only the pure could be admitted to the sanctuary, everyone was required to make use of the water basin in order to achieve a state of purity necessary for approaching the gods. This all-purpose purification rite ensured that no one would defile the temple with *miasma*, a pollution that came from natural sources such as sexual intercourse, birth, and death, as well as from guilt or sin.

Whether Jews washed their hands or sprinkled themselves with water, it is probable that the water facilities located at the entrance to the Diaspora synagogue were intended for the use of all who entered. Like their Greek neighbors, Jews in the Diaspora would have purified themselves prior to entering the buildings in which they worshiped. In so doing, they would not have necessarily differentiated between the categories of ritual and moral impurity. Rather, it is likely that within the larger cultural context in which Jews of the Diaspora lived, such distinctions became blurred.

Purity, Holiness, and the Synagogue

At the turn of the Common Era, as we have seen, the relationship between purity and the synagogue varied with geographic location and cultural context. These regional variances in practice are significant to the discussion of the synagogue as a sacred realm. In the Diaspora, there was a close association between purity and the synagogue. Living among other peoples, Jews made every attempt to isolate their synagogues from the pollution caused by idolatry and other egregious sins. In addition, they adopted the practice of performing ritual ablutions involving hand washing or sprinkling prior to entering the synagogue. This concern with impurity indicates that Jews living in the Diaspora at the turn of the Common Era probably regarded the synagogue building as sacred.

The terminology used to refer to synagogues in the Diaspora attests to the apparent sanctity of the institution. The most common term, *proseuchē*, is used in inscriptions from Egypt dated as early as the third century B.C.E. to refer to Jewish institutions that had "temple-status," as indicated by their honorific dedications to rulers and the right of asylum.[61] The reference to a *proseuchē* also occurs in conjunction with other terms to denote a sacred precinct.[62] Additionally, a second-century papyrus describes a plot of land associated with a *proseuchē* in Arsinoe-Crocodilopolis as a sacred grove.[63] All of these usages seem to imply that the synagogue building was regarded as sacred from an early period.

The textual evidence indicates that in the first century C.E. the Diaspora synagogue was still considered to be a sacred edifice. Philo, for example, almost always uses the term *proseuchē* to refer to the synagogue and employs terms such as *temenos*, *hieros*, and *hieroi periboloi* to indicate the sanctity of the institution (for example, *Legat.* 137; *Flacc.* 48, *Spec.* 3.171). Similarly, Josephus uses the term *hieron* in reference to a synagogue on at least five occasions. Most interesting is his description of the synagogue in Antioch, to which the successors of Antiochus IV restored the votive offerings previously plundered from the Jerusalem temple (*J. W.* 7.44–45). What is significant here is that the synagogue was considered a suitable place to house these brass ornaments and gifts. Clearly, Josephus's use of the term *to hieron* indicates that the Antiochian synagogue was regarded as a consecrated edifice.[64]

The sanctity of the Diaspora synagogue is derived from its liturgical and spatial aspects. In this respect, the synagogue is similar to the Greco-Roman temple and the association building. For our purposes, it is noteworthy that all three types of buildings are places in which worship takes place and all have water basins located at their entrances. The significance of these water facilities is explained by the Greek scholar Pollux (second century C.E.): "The area inside of the *perippantēria* is possessed by the gods, sacred, consecrated, and inviolable while that outside is open to ordinary use" (1.8).[65] In the Greco-Roman world, access to sacred space required purification. Just as the Gentile approaching the shrine of a deity was required to sprinkle him- or herself with water, so too did the Jew entering the Diaspora synagogue perform ritual ablutions.

This direct correlation between ritual ablutions and entrance to the synagogue has no parallel in the land of Israel. The proximity of the *miqweh* to the synagogue cannot be taken as conclusive evidence that the synagogue was considered sacred, since Jews probably maintained a certain level of ritual purity regardless of their intention to participate in communal gatherings. One possible exception may be found at Qumran, where there are *miqwa'ot* in proximity to locus 77, the room most likely to have been used as a synagogue. Yet even here it is difficult to determine the extent to which purity practices were specifically related to worship. Finally, we must consider that water basins associated with the synagogue were located not at the entrance to the building but inside the assembly hall. Thus, these basins could not have been used for purification purposes prior to entering the building.

If material remains are inconclusive, there is some literary evidence to support this claim to holiness. In Philo's detailed account of the Essene community, it is in the sacred spots (*hierous*) that they called synagogues (*synagōgai*) that the Essenes gathered on the Sabbath for the reading and expounding of the Torah (*Prob.* 81–82). It could be argued that Philo is evaluating the Essene synagogues on the basis of his experience with Egyptian synagogues, imposing the holiness from one context on the other. Philo's use of terminology, however, suggests that he is differentiating between the *proseuchē* of Egypt and the *synagōgē* of this community. Additionally, his extensive description of the Essenes points to the likelihood that he had genuine knowledge of the sanctity of the Essene synagogues.

Philo's reference to the holiness of the Essene synagogues is also supported by evidence from the Qumran literature. Liturgical texts, such as the *Songs of the Sabbath Sacrifice*, 4QBerakhot and 4QDaily Prayers, indicate that the worshipers regarded themselves as a sacred assembly and that the angels were envisioned as joining with the community in prayer.[66] This evidence is local-specific, however, and relates to a nonpublic synagogue.

While there is uncertainty pertaining to the sanctity of the early synagogue, it is generally assumed that by late antiquity Jews living in the land of Israel regarded their synagogues as sacred. According to Steven Fine, after the destruction of the Jerusalem temple in 70 C.E., the importance of the synagogue was expressed "through an ever-increasing attribution of sanctity."[67] In his view, one of the sources of this holiness was the Torah scrolls. Fine is undoubtedly correct in suggesting that the sanctity of the synagogue was at least partially derived from the presence of the Torah. What is problematic, however, is his insistence that the transfer of this holiness is triggered by a single historical event, even one as traumatic as the destruction of the temple.

More fruitful, in my view, is evidence concerning the relationship between the Torah and the synagogue. Scholars agree that the public reading and studying of the Torah was the central liturgical function of the synagogue from its origins.[68] At some point during the liturgical development of the synagogue, the Torah became more than sacred Scripture and the scrolls themselves were perceived to be sacred objects in their own right. Evidence for the beginning of the ritualization of the Torah scroll can be traced to the Persian period, when the Torah reading took place at the city gate. This rite, described in Neh 8:1-12, was characterized by a distinct reverence for the Torah. As the Torah scroll was opened in the sight of the people, they changed their posture to a standing position (v. 5). The priest then offered a blessing, to which the people responded in agreement ("Amen, amen") with uplifted hands. Finally, the people prostrated themselves, praying before the Lord (v. 6). Only after the completion of these rituals was the Torah scroll read (vv. 7-8).

The rituals that preceded the reading of Torah served to ritualize the scroll itself by lending sanctity to the very act of unfurling it. Eventually, it was no longer just the text that was considered holy but also the physical scrolls that contained the Scripture. The Jews came to perceive the Torah scrolls as sacred ritual objects in much the same way as Gentiles viewed their idols.[69] By the late Second Temple period, these scrolls were protected by laws governing ritual purity. This attribution of holiness to the scrolls is substantiated by the presence of water basins inside synagogues in the land of Israel. As previously indicated, these basins were likely associated with the handling of the Torah scrolls by the leader of the assembly. This evidence strongly suggests that it is the growing sanctity of the Torah scroll and not the destruction of the temple in 70 C.E. that caused the sacralization of the synagogue.

In the context of a worldview in which space was divided into categories of sacred and profane, the sanctity of the synagogue would not have had the sacred status of the holy of holies, the perceived dwelling place of God. Yet neither would it have been regarded as entirely common, for it was within the synagogue that the sacred Scripture was read and studied. It is likely that for some groups, such as Philo's Essenes and the sacred assemblies described in the Qumran literature, there was a highly developed perception of sanctity associated with the synagogue. For other groups, however, any sanctity associated with the synagogue would probably have been less palpable. As a sacred object, the Torah scroll may have been perceived as importing sanctity to either the building or the assembly that gathered together on the Sabbath to participate in sacred ritual. It is likely that Jews who gathered in sacred assembly on the Sabbath to read their holy texts perceived that they were entering a sacred realm. The nature of this sanctity may not have been permanent in the sense that it was associated with a sacred space per se. Rather, it was the holiness of the Torah that lent its sanctity to the synagogue, not as a physical building, but as an assembly of the people. Thus, on the continuum between the common and the holy, the early synagogue in the land of Israel may have had an emerging sanctity.

In summary, it seems probable that the early synagogue in the Diaspora and in the land of Israel was regarded, at least to some extent, as a sacred realm, but the nature of this sanctity varied according to geographic location. Jews in the Diaspora were more likely to have regarded their synagogues as inherently sacred. That is, they may have perceived a permanent holiness associated with both the liturgical and spatial aspects of the synagogue. In the land of Israel, however, the idea of the sanctity of the early synagogue was not as highly developed and may have been a temporary quality associated with the performance of Torah rituals. Finally, it is apparent that in both the Diaspora and the land of Israel the sanctity of the synagogue developed under the influence of a variety of social and cultural factors. Its holiness must therefore be considered independently of historical events such as the destruction of the Jerusalem temple.

Conclusion

In *Judaism: Practice and Belief,* Sanders convincingly establishes that there was a generalized concern with purity issues among Jews during the period under consideration. At the same time, he distinguishes between the purity practices of Jews living in the land of Israel and those who resided in the Diaspora. Our analysis takes this distinction one step further by considering the purity practices associated with the synagogue. As has been shown, the local-specific evidence pointing to the association of *miqwa'ot* with synagogues appears to be spatial rather than functional. While it is likely that Jews in the land of Israel immersed themselves in order to maintain a level of ritual purity on a regular basis, it is doubtful that they routinely purified themselves for the specific purpose of entering the synagogue. In contrast, Jews living in the Diaspora seemed to have been much more concerned with both ritual and moral impurity as it pertained to the synagogue. They likely performed ritual ablutions prior to entering the synagogue, utilizing water basins for the hand washing or sprinkling that removed ritual and moral impurity. Moreover, it seems as if they located their synagogues on "pure" land untainted by the moral pollution of Gentile idolatry and sin.

In the context of common Judaism, Sanders also considers the function of the synagogue in first-century Judaism. He contends, as do other scholars, that the synagogue was important to Jewish life and worship throughout Israel and the Diaspora. Most significantly, it was the place where Jews assembled on the Sabbath to hear the reading of the Torah and the exposition of the law. Sanders does not, however, address the issue of the sanctity of the synagogue during this period. The investigation of this question has offered some insight into perceptions of the holiness of the synagogue in both the Diaspora and the land of Israel. It has shown that the terminology used to describe synagogues in the Diaspora often alluded to their sacred status. In addition, the

Diaspora synagogue had architectural features similar to structures such as the Greco-Roman temple and the association building. In the latter two cases, access to sacred space required purification. Since similar purity practices were also connected to the synagogue, it is quite probable that Jews in the Diaspora considered their synagogues to be holy from both a spatial and a liturgical perspective.

In the land of Israel the situation was much more diverse. There is evidence to suggest that the synagogues of the Essenes were regarded as sacred in both their spatial and ritual aspects. For the most part, however, the synagogue sanctity in the land of Israel was less developed and derived from the Torah scrolls that were read and stored within its confines. On a local level, the presence of water basins inside the synagogue supports this position. Although we cannot determine the extent to which the synagogue would have been considered sacred in the first century, we can speculate that there was an impermanent sanctity associated with the liturgical function of the institution.

These observations remind us not to lose sight of the local context in our attempt to demonstrate the existence of a "common Judaism" and encourage us to see the synagogue as a locus that will allow us to elucidate both similarities and differences within and between Jewish practice in the Diaspora and in the land of Israel.

Part Two

Common Judaism/
Partisan Judaism

6. Pharisaic Authority: Prophecy and Power (*Antiquities* 17.41–45)

Albert I. Baumgarten

In Honor of Ed Sanders

*Those who simply settle questions
take a back seat to those
who open up ways of doing
further intellectual work.*
—Randall Collins[1]

The Pharisees stand at a crucial crossroads. Heirs of the Pharisees, according to the usual received narrative, played a critical role in the reconstruction of Jewish life after the destruction of the temple in 70 c.e., and the Pharisees had a large part in the self-definition of Christianity, as that story was told in the Gospels. Yet writing a history of the Pharisees is not a simple task due to the problematic nature of the primary sources.[2]

Further complicating this task, attitudes toward the Pharisees are an important marker for both Jews and Christians through the ages. Jews traditionally attribute to the Pharisees and their heirs a key place in the emergence of rabbinic Judaism.[3] The picture drawn of the historical Pharisees by a Jew may therefore say more about that author's Jewish loyalties than about the ancient sect. Christians, on the other hand, often perceive the Pharisees as self-righteous hypocrites who led the opposition to Jesus.[4] Their posture toward the Pharisees is often significant in determining the attitude of any particular

Christian author toward Jews and their religion.[5] All this is true also of scholars of first-century Judaism and Christianity. Down to the present, the Pharisees remain a lightning rod for attracting comment that defines not only the scholarly judgment but also the identity of the commentator.[6]

The challenge is to develop a way of studying the ancient Pharisees that will enable one to transcend particular loyalties. In this chapter, I will attempt to show that a contextual reading of the primary sources, that is, a consideration of the contents of those sources by the standards of the ancient world, will help sidestep some of the consequences of later Jewish or Christian loyalties. This approach focuses on clarifying the ways in which people argued, debated with each other, and were found convincing (hence achieving authority) in the ancient Mediterranean world, and then views the Pharisees against that background. This study takes Sanders's work on the Pharisees as its point of departure and adopts Sanders's conclusions concerning the moderate stature of the Pharisees and their position of influence, although not absolute authority.[7] The questions I wish to ask are the following: How did the Pharisees attain such a position of authority? What means did they employ to that end, and why did these means, as situated in their ancient Mediterranean context, have the desired effect?

I will test this approach on one passage in Josephus—*Ant.* 17.41–45. In doing so, I will draw on the work of James C. Scott, Clifford Geertz, and Edward Shils,[8] particularly their focus on the nature of charisma and how charisma is acquired and exercised, as well as on studies of holy men in antiquity. I will argue that *Ant.* 17.41–45 can help explain how the Pharisees played the card of foreknowledge, that is, claimed that their closeness to God endowed them with the ability to know what would happen, and hence entitled them to a special position in the Jewish world.

Antiquities 17.41–45: A First Reading

Although Josephus elsewhere shows the Pharisees' involvement in politics, including court intrigues of various sorts, the story in *Antiquities* 17 is the most explicit account of their trafficking in the supernatural as part of their political activity. The passage recounts that the Pharisees were proud of their adherence to ancestral custom and claimed to observe the laws of which God approved (17.41). Because God appeared to them (17.43), they had foreknowledge that they could have used to help the king, but which they instead employed to harm him (17.41). Out of gratitude to Pheroras's wife for her kindness to them (she paid a fine they were assessed as punishment for refusing to swear loyalty to Caesar and to Herod's government [17.42–43]), they announced that God had decreed an end to Herod's reign and the transfer of royal power to Herod's brother Pheroras and his children (17.43). Furthermore, the Pharisees corrupted other members of the court with their promises. They informed the eunuch Bagoas that a (presumably messianic) king would soon come in whose court Bagoas would enjoy the titles of "father" and "benefactor." Mocking Bagoas's eunuch status, they also promised that this future king would bestow upon him the ability to marry and beget children (17.45).[9]

This passage must first be seen in the larger context of the opening of book 17 of *Antiquities*. The subject of book 17 is Herod's dying days, a period filled with intrigue, betrayals, trials, and executions. Sons and grandsons were jockeying for position, with the backing of the women of the court. With an aging and ill king (likely paranoid by modern psychiatric standards), it is hard to make straightforward moral judgments on the participants in this drama. As narrated by Josephus, Antipater was responsible for the tragic consequences. Antipater had manipulated Herod into executing Antipater's brothers Alexander and Aristobulus and had continued to plot against Herod. One of his allies was Herod's brother Pheroras (17.33). Pheroras, in turn, was a pawn in the hands of his women—his wife, her mother, and her sister (17.34). Thus, when Herod directed Pheroras to divorce his wife, he refused (17.48–50). Pheroras's active role in the whole affair remains murky, but his wife was one of the many villains of the piece. Josephus repeats the rumor of a secret sexual connection between Antipater and Pheroras's wife, an affair supposedly encouraged by Antipater's mother (17.51). Perhaps the outrage to ordinary moral standards was intended to solidify the political alliance. Anyone associated with Pheroras's wife was tainted by murder and the suspicion of infidelity, and hence could be blamed for the domestic tragedy that would claim many victims. According to Josephus, the Pharisees were deeply implicated in this sordid business by prophesying a great and powerful future for Pheroras, his wife, and their children.

Thus, the Pharisees' introduction in as part of the retinue of Pheroras's wife implied their guilt by association (*Ant.* 17.41–45). Other elements of *Ant.* 17.41–45 also portray the Pharisees in an unfavorable light. In antiquity, methods of predicting the future, the sorts of questions asked, and those who provided answers were organized hierarchically. On the lowest rung were those associated with the common people: no man of reputation would consult dice oracles (Cicero, *Div.* 2.41, 86–87).[10] It was banal and boring to ask about prospects for a marriage. Rather, the elite could appropriately inquire about relief from a plague, or major political matters, such as impending dynastic changes.[11] Oracular questions on these topics were posed by exclusive (expensive) means.

Holy men, too, were classed hierarchically. Wandering holy men, often found in cities and military camps (cf. Celsus's parody [Origen, *Cels* 7.9]), served a lower-class clientele. By contrast, the holy man, not a Greek, was reached only after a long and expensive journey, spoke only once a year, knew many languages, and was consulted by potentates and their agents (Plutarch, *Def.* 421B).[12] Some holy men had close to official status in the retinue of the powerful. The hierarchies of holy men, methods, and clientele were linked to each other. For that reason, the best way to impugn the prestige of any expert was to suggest that only low-status questioners consulted him and took his pronouncements seriously, or that his methods of inquiry were low class.[13]

These same hierarchies are at play in Josephus's account of the Pharisees in Herod's court. In this light, the passage clearly takes them down a notch or two (compare the account of the activities of Manaemus the Essene, virtually an official figure at court; *Ant.* 15). Because the Pharisees were at court, assisting the king by prognosticating the future, their predictions concerned important matters of state. But contrary to popular perceptions, their audience, far from being prestigious, consisted of the women and a eunuch of the court (17.41). Thus, despite their presence in court, these Pharisees were not high-class holy men. They dabbled in exalted matters for an audience of gullible dupes.

The view that success among women was a sure indication of frivolity was widespread in antiquity.[14] Celsus's remarks (Origen, *Cels* 3.55) are especially telling. He declares that laundry workers, cobblers, and illiterate bucolic yokels, who would not dare speak in front of their elders and more intelligent masters, take advantage of children and stupid women to make astounding and ill-founded statements in private. When confronted, some have the decency to flee, but others up the ante with even more outrageous pronouncements. To Celsus's horror, these efforts sometimes succeed, but that very success demonstrates (for Celsus at least) the worthlessness of their teachings.

Similarly, the Pharisees' success with the eunuch Bagoas proved nothing. Eunuchs were universally useful, even indispensable, but were also despised as only half men, *hēmiandroi*. Because they had no biological stake in the future, their opinions had little value.[15] The implication is that the Pharisees would never have succeeded with serious (intelligent) people, such as the fully male narrator of the story and his circle, who would immediately have seen through their duplicity. Whether Josephus used a source unfriendly to the Pharisees for this episode, such as Herod's royal court historian, Nicolaus of Damascus, or wrote this passage entirely on his own, or some combination of these two possibilities, is unclear, but the intention to denounce the Pharisees could hardly be more explicit.[16] One must ask, however, whether Josephus simply fabricated these stories or whether there was some historical basis to his depictions of the Pharisees. Is *Ant.* 17.41–45 to be dismissed as nothing more than hostile imagination?[17]

As noted earlier, it is important that Josephus's negative evaluation of the Pharisees as prognosticators be evaluated in the context of his time and place: at a point of intersection between Jewish and Greco-Roman cultures, in the first centuries c.e. A useful parallel can be found in Lucian of Samosata's *Alexander*.[18] Human life, according to Lucian's Alexander, is swayed by two tyrants, fear and hope. These two tyrants combine to create anxiety about the future, an anxiety best allayed by prior knowledge (*Alex.* 8). As noted by Philostratus (*Vit. Apoll.* 8.7.9), "the gods perceive what lies in the future, and men what is going on before them, and wise men what is approaching."[19] Knowledge of the future is the mark of superhuman ability and, by extension, of authority. Few religious movements are able to resist appealing to this sort of foreknowledge based on special contact with the divine.

Among ancient Jews, this path to influence apparently worked in the case of the Essenes. Manaemus the Essene predicted Herod's rise to power and was consulted by him during his reign. Manaemus's prestige in Herod's eyes was sufficient to allow Herod to be satisfied with vague answers to urgent questions, such as how many years he would reign. The respect that Herod had for Manaemus extended to all Essenes, according to *Ant.* 15.373–79. Nevertheless, this example, and the fact that many religious groups claim special foreknowledge of events, cannot prove that the Pharisees did or did not do the things that Josephus attributes to them in our passage.

Yet in my view, *Ant.* 17:41–45 not only expresses Josephus's negative assessment of the Pharisees but also can be plausibly interpreted as evidence that the historical Pharisees may well have trafficked in foreknowledge. While the contextual readings that support this view are controversial, subject to challenge, and far from decisive, they are nevertheless suggestive. The argument of this chapter will be that Pharisaic authority was based, at least in part, on predicting the future, and that the Pharisees likely did the things attributed to them by Josephus in *Ant.* 17.41–45. It will be organized as a series of concentric circles, moving from our passage outward to the rest of Josephus's corpus, then to other ancient Jewish sources, notably the New Testament and Qumran, and finally to the most indirect evidence, namely, descriptions of the Pharisees as defending themselves against charges of maleficent magic. If one found only one such point concerning the Pharisees, it might be an accident. When one finds several such points, I suggest that these descriptions are pieces of a larger whole. They indicate that the charge of maleficent magic was a point on which the Pharisees felt the need for defense. I submit that, taken together, these four circles of evidence establish, to the greatest extent possible under the circumstances, that the description of the Pharisees in *Ant.* 17.41–45 is to be taken seriously and not dismissed as derogatory misinformation.

A Rereading of *Antiquities* 17.41–45

Steve Mason contends that the topic of foreknowledge or prophecy was one of special personal interest to Josephus; the theme appears a number of times in Josephus's works and has special connections to Josephus's own controversial life story.[20] Furthermore, Mason disagrees with the widespread conclusion that Josephus copied this passage from a source, such as Nicolaus of Damascus, on the grounds that Josephus regularly reworked his sources and that his hand is evident in the vocabulary and outlook of this passage.[21] Mason therefore concludes that although the account of the Pharisees in *Ant.* 17.41–45 may be based on the reworking of a source, that conclusion is not necessary, as "the description of the Pharisees [in *Ant.* 17.41–45] is wholly intelligible as Josephus's own considered formulation."[22] If Mason is correct, our passage can be read as the personal statement of a learned expert on the topic, but one who, like most learned experts, had a stake in the question.

Rebecca Gray has taken Mason's conclusions an important step further. She argues that in his account of his predictions to Vespasian after the fall of Jotapata, Josephus presented himself in the classical role of the biblical prophet. Perhaps Josephus felt justified in wrapping himself in a prophetic mantle because of his priestly pedigree: priests were the traditional interpreters of the Bible (for example, *Ag. Ap.* 2.187);[23] contemporary prophecy (such as it was in the Second Temple era) was closely connected with its biblical antecedents and therefore could also be claimed as the special province of priests.[24] If so, the Pharisees of *Ant.* 17.41–45 may have represented a double challenge to Josephus on his home turf. They were rivals at foreknowledge, and their claim to excellence in understanding the law contested priestly monopoly of that role. Accordingly, it is not surprising that Josephus dismissed both of these Pharisaic claims. Josephus discounted the Pharisees' prophetic prowess on account of the lowly status of their audience, as already noted. He cast doubt on their claim to observe ancestral custom and God's law by his choice of language (*prospoioumenon*; in the Latin translation *simulantium* [17.41]). Whether Josephus wrote *Ant.* 17.41–45 by himself or adapted it from some prior source, the final product suited his worldview quite well.

Josephus was therefore making two different kinds of arguments against the Pharisees. On foreknowledge, Josephus acknowledged the facts but put these facts in a less favorable context. On excellence in interpreting the law, he directly contradicted the Pharisees.

Josephus's negative comments on Pharisaic foreknowledge are not surprising by ancient standards. Trafficking in foreknowledge is prominently associated with the larger phenomenon of magic, itself a very elusive category. At one level, magic can be defined as someone else's religion. As Jonathan Z. Smith has argued, devil worship is a locative term,[25] and magic is no less locative.[26] Nevertheless, the ancients argued for more than a relativistic meaning and attempted to differentiate between beneficent and malevolent forms of magic. These arguments were often slippery, contradictory, and self-serving, yet the distinctions attempted were important for those making the case.[27] Andy M. Reimer, building on the work of Anitra Bingham Kolenkow, has argued that the ancients dealt with maleficent miracle workers by acknowledging the facts of their success but charging them with abusing their powers for the purposes of political subversion, the harming of others, or financial or other gain.[28]

All three of these standard denunciations are present in our passage. The Pharisees could have used their powers to help the king; indeed, political authorities cultivated "holy men" for this very purpose, sometimes even appointing an official court *magos* (Acts 13:8-12).[29] Highly placed Roman politicians, including Augustus (Herod's patron and role model[30]), regularly employed prognosticators of various sorts to help them plan their actions. It would be unrealistic to expect any different of Herod. Under those circumstances, the Pharisees could have expected a sympathetic ear at court, as they were able to help the king by their foreknowledge. But the Pharisees chose to harm Herod instead of help him (17:41). Furthermore, they did this for their own benefit, in order to repay Pheroras's wife for helping them. For this reason they got into trouble with the authorities.

As modern readers, we may wonder whether a description of negative behavior is true or a fiction invented by malicious opponents. Ancient standards were apparently different. Juvenal, a virtual contemporary of Josephus, noted ironically:

Nowadays no astrologer has credit unless he has been imprisoned in some distant camp, with chains clanking on either arm; none believe in his powers unless he has been condemned and all but put to death, having just contrived to get deported to a Cyclad, or to escape at last from the diminutive Seriphos. (*Sat.* 6.560–64)

Juvenal, of course, overstated the case to make his satirical point. Nevertheless, there was a sense in which charges of malevolent abuse of special powers and persecution by the authorities apparently served the interest of those who claimed these abilities. They were confirmation of the reality of these gifts and hence desirable assets. For this reason, according to Lucian (*Peregr.* 18), Peregrinus deliberately criticized the authorities in Rome in order to provoke their opposition. As a result, he benefited from prestige in the eyes of the masses. Charges of abuse of powers of foreknowledge were therefore just as likely to originate with the very people accused of malevolence as with their opponents. If so, one more reason not to dismiss what Josephus says about the Pharisees in *Ant.* 17.41–45 as defamatory fabrication.

If so, it is unlikely that an author less hostile to the Pharisees than Josephus or his source would have told the story much differently or denied that the Pharisees broadcast predictions and promises of the future in Herod's court. Yet this analysis of *Ant.* 17.41–45 by itself is not decisive, for the possibility of malevolent fabrication of the story cannot entirely be dismissed. We move, then, to evidence of Josephus's broader corpus.

Another Passage on Pharisaic Foreknowledge: *Antiquities* 15.4

The topic of Pharisaic foreknowledge occurs also in *Ant.* 15.4. Josephus has two slightly different accounts of Herod's trial before the Sanhedrin on charges of abusing power in governing the Galilee.[31] In *Ant.* 14.168–76, one member of the Sanhedrin, Samaias (a disciple of the Pharisee Pollion; cf. *Ant.* 15.370), was not overawed by Herod's appearance and troops. Nor was he moved by Hyrcanus's attempt to intervene on behalf of Herod. An upright man, Samaias warned the others that if they did not condemn Herod, they should "be assured, however, that God is great, and this man, whom you now wish to release for Hyrcanus's sake, will one day punish you and the king as well" (*Ant.* 14.174). Josephus noted that Samaias was right in both parts of his prediction. While one might have expected Herod to punish Samaias for having spoken against him, Herod respected his integrity. When Herod came to power, he killed Hyrcanus and all the other members of the Sanhedrin except Samaias. Samaias was thus a man of unusual political acumen, honest and not swayed by fear, but with no claim to prophetic prowess.[32]

The second version of Herod's trial appears in *Ant.* 15.4. In this passage, Pollion the Pharisee told the judges that "if Herod's life were spared, he would (one day) persecute them all. And in time it turned out to be so, for God fulfilled his words." It matters little whether Samaias or Pollion warned the judges.[33] Whether Samaias or Pollion, both versions agree that a Pharisee warned the judges what Herod would do if acquitted. The difference in the phrasing of the warning, however, requires attention. As opposed to the "you will live to rue this day" aspect of Samaias's warning in *Ant.* 14.168–76, in *Ant.* 15.4 Josephus wrote that Pollion's warning was fulfilled by God.

Foreknowledge was not unique to the Pharisees in Josephus's account of Jewish history. According to *Ant.* 15.373, Menaemus the Essene had prophetic powers and thus was able to greet Herod, when the latter was still a boy, as "king of the Jews."[34] The high priest Hyrcanus also enjoyed such encounters with the deity (*Ant.* 13.282–83). Whatever the source of Daniel's divine power, his prophecies had been fulfilled, and he therefore gained credit for his truthfulness and accuracy (*Ant.* 10.268–69). Even Josephus had prophetic powers—at least so Vespasian believed—when Josephus foretold that Vespasian would become emperor. Since Josephus had already proved a veracious prophet on other matters (*J. W.* 3.399–408),[35] Vespasian, unlike some of his officers, did not dismiss Josephus's prediction of Vespasian's glorious future as the desperate attempt of a captive to win favor in the eyes of his captor.

To ancient authors, more significant and prestigious than these prophetic achievements past and present was the ability to shape the future, to force the divine hand, so to speak.[36] This hierarchy of abilities is evident in the biblical story of Balaam. Balak of Moab hired Balaam to curse Israel because he believed that all those whom Balaam cursed were cursed and all those he blessed were blessed (Num 22:6). Balaam responded that he had no such power. Although he was a prophet, he depended on divine appearances to him. While he could increase the likelihood of such an appearance by sacrifice, divine manifestation was never guaranteed. Even when God appeared, Balaam reminded Balak, Balaam could not force God's hand and dictate the message. Balaam's only skill or power was to repeat what he was told (Num 22:38; 23:26). By way of contrast, the biblical patriarch Jacob, on his deathbed, uttered words that shaped the future (Genesis 49), as did Moses before his death (Deuteronomy 33). Honi the Circle Drawer, known from Josephus and rabbinic literature, could speak and God would act accordingly, answering Honi's requests as a father would those of his son. Had Honi been less favored by God, his insolence in demanding a divine response would have deserved punishment (*m. Ta'an* 3:8).[37] Perhaps this special connection with God and the power to shape the outcome were the reasons each side in the civil war wanted Honi to curse the other side, the circumstances that led to Honi's death (Josephus, *Ant.* 14.22–24).[38] Similar beliefs are attested for Jesus in the Gospels and the first generation of his disciples in Acts (Acts 5:1-11; 8:20-23; 13:9-11), as well as for Apollonius of Tyana, according to Philostratus (*Vit. Apoll.* 8.26).[39]

Yet it is precisely that higher power that was ascribed to the Pharisee Pollion in *Ant.* 15.4. God fulfilled (*teleiōsantos*) Pollion's words, using a term that echoes the fulfilling of other prophecies.[40] Herod persecuted those who spared him not because Pollion had foreknowledge of the outcome, but because his utterance had determined the outcome in Herod's favor.

Judged by the standards of antiquity, the power ascribed to Pollion was potentially problematic. When Apollonius of Tyana was charged with predicting the fall of Nero and the short reigns of Vitellius, Galba, and Otho, his defenders rejected the inference that Apollonius was a wizard (*goēta ton andra*; *Vit. Apoll.* 5.12).[41] Apollonius's admirers shared the widespread suspicion of wizards, suggesting that their loyalty to him was a further indication that he was not a wizard. They also defended their hero by arguing that

> wizards claim to alter the course of destiny by having recourse either to the torture of lost spirits or to barbaric sacrifices or to certain incantations or anointings. . . . But Apollonius submitted himself to the decrees of the Fates, and only foretold that things must come to pass; and his foreknowledge was gained not by wizardry but from what the gods revealed to him. And when among the Indians he beheld their tripods and their dumb waiters and other automata, which I described as entering the room of their own accord, he did not ask how they were contrived, nor did he ask to be informed; he only praised them but did not aspire to imitate them. (*Vit. Apoll.* 5.12)

The self-serving nature of this passage is patent. Elsewhere in Philostratus's *Life,* Apollonius was able to alter the course of destiny (8.26). Nevertheless, Apollonius's admirers argued, it was not appropriate to conclude that Apollonius was a wizard.[42]

What might Pollion's admirers have said to avert the charge of wizardry, in light of this defense of Apollonius? Perhaps they would have argued that Pollion only spoke; he did not torture lost spirits, perform any sacrifice, or indulge in any incantation or anointing. Perhaps they would also have appealed to the numerous biblical examples of the powerful speech of the man of God, or prophet, that can determine the course of events.

None of these issues is raised in *Ant.* 15.4. Yet in contrast to 17.41–45, 15.4 is not a hostile source, determined to denounce the Pharisees as thoroughly as possible. If anything, it seems mildly pro-Pharisaic. In predicting his eventual reign, Pollion's prophecy was a good act that was appreciated by Herod. The difference in attitude toward the Pharisees between *Ant.* 17.41–45 and 15.4 may perhaps be explained by the hypothesis that Josephus followed two different sources in these passages, one with a hostile attitude to the Pharisees and the other with a more positive perspective. Alternately, it may be argued that a single, pro-Herodian source was used. In the account in 17.41–45, the Pharisees sought to harm Herod—hence they were criticized. As they had proven useful to Herod in the events narrated in *Ant* 15.4, they enjoyed very mild praise.

In either case, the powers ascribed to the Pharisees in *Ant.* 15.4 exceeded foreknowledge. Foreknowledge due to regular contact with God would seem self-evident for a person/group able to compel God to act as one/they had spoken. The accusation that the Pharisees trafficked in foreknowledge in the hostile story in *Ant.* 17.41–45 seems to be confirmed and the ante raised higher by 15.4.

Four Other Ancient Jewish Sources

This conclusion is reinforced, if less directly, by four ancient Jewish sources on the Pharisees. None of these sources concerns Pharisaic foreknowledge, and, indeed, they have little to teach us about the Pharisees at all. Their relevance consists in their comments on magic and miracles more generally.

The Qumran pesharim comment extensively on events of the era in which they were composed. *Pesher Nahum* knows of the ultimately unsuccessful attack of Demetrius III on Jerusalem (88 B.C.E.) and, apparently, of the awful punishment inflicted by the "Lion of Wrath," Alexander Jannaeus, on his rebellious Jewish enemies when his rule was restored (4QpNah 3–4.i.1–8).[43] Throughout, the pesher denounces the "Seekers after Smooth Things," also known as Ephraim (4QpNah 3–4.ii.2). This group, which had all the organs of a fixed institution (council and congregation—*'etsah* and *keneset* [4QpNah 3–4.iii.7]), was likely the Pharisees.[44]

The reference to the Roman conquest of Jerusalem in 63 B.C.E. (4QpNah 3–4.i.3–4) indicates that the text postdates that event. The author is aware of the period of Pharisaic power during the reign of Salome Alexandra (76–67 B.C.E.), when the Pharisees had been the real rulers of the state, executing and exiling opponents, recalling others from exile almost at will (Josephus, *J.W.* 1.107–14; *Ant.* 13.408–18). In 4QpNah 3–4.ii.10, the author comments on this situation in elaborating the secret meaning of Nah. 3:1b–4:

> PREY DOES NOT CEASE. AND THE CRACK OF THE WHIP, THE RUMBLING SOUND OF THE WHEEL, THE DASHING HORSE AND THE BOUNDING CHARIOT, THE HORSEMAN CHARGING, THE FLASH (OF A SWORD) AND THE GLITTER OF A SPEAR, A MULTITUDE OF SLAIN AND A WEIGHT OF CORPSES. THERE IS NO END TO DEAD BODIES, AND THEY STUMBLE OVER THEIR CARCASSES. The interpretation of it concerns the dominion of the Seekers-After-Smooth-Things: the sword of the nations will not depart from the midst of their congregation. Captives, plunder, and heated strife (are) among them, and exile for fear of the enemy. A multitude of guilty corpses will fall in their days, and there will be no end to the sum-total of their slain. In fact, they will stumble over their decaying flesh because of their guilty counsel.
>
> (IT IS) BECAUSE OF THE MANY HARLOTRIES OF THE CHARMING HARLOT, THE WITCH OF SORCERIES, WHO TRADES(?) NATIONS

FOR HER HARLOTRY AND CLANS FOR HER [SORCER]IES. The interpretation [of it con]cerns those who lead Ephraim astray—with their false teaching, their lying tongue, and deceitful lip they lead many astray— [th]eir kings, princes, priests, and people, joined with the resident alien. Cities and clans will perish by their counsel; ho[no]red ones and ru[lers] will fall [on account of] their [inso]lent speech.[45]

From the perspective of issues discussed in this article, one phrase in Nah 3:4 deserves attention. While not elaborated in the pesher on the verse, one may ask whether the presence of these words in the text of the prophet played a role in generating the elaborate denunciation of the rule of the Seekers-After-Smooth-Things (= Pharisees), and their baleful influence over kings, princes, priests, ordinary Jews, and resident aliens (converts?[46]). The prophet portrays the opponent as employing harlotries (*zenuni zonah*) and as a sorceress (*ba'alat keshaphim*). She destroys nations with her harlotries (*biznotah*) and families with her sorceries (*bikshapeyah*).

The presence of two references to sorcery in the base verse of the pesher that laments wide-ranging Pharisaic political and religious power is potentially significant. The pesher may testify to the connection between the Pharisees' supremacy and their appeal to the supernatural. Pharisaic success at convincing a wide circle of Jews (including converts?) to follow their teachings is attributed implicitly to their invocation of supernatural proof, understood of course by the author of the pesher as the maleficent and forbidden sort of magic. Pharisaic miracle mongering is real, not illusory, but based on an alliance with the powers of evil.[47] Like *Ant.* 17.41–45, 4QpNah is a source hostile to the Pharisees; but as an independent source, it serves to confirm the hypothesis that the Pharisees were widely thought to wield superhuman powers.[48]

A similar conclusion may be drawn for Matt 12:22-29, esp. 12:27.[49] The context is the discussion of the powers by which Jesus drives out demons. Jesus responds to the charge of the Pharisees that he drives out demons by contact with Beelzebul, the prince of demons, by saying: "If it is by Beelzebul that I drive out demons, by whom do your own people drive them out? If this is your argument, they themselves will refute you." This passage suggests that the author of the Gospel of Matthew had access to a source that attributed to the Pharisees the ability to exorcise demons. It is not certain that Jesus' question "By whom do *your people* cast out demons?" refers to the Pharisees; the phrase "your people" could pertain to Jewish exorcists in general. Nevertheless, Matt 12:22-29 may provide indirect evidence that the Pharisees were known to be practitioners of magical arts. If so, we may suggest that both Jesus and the Pharisees were well known for their exorcisms. The debate between them concerned an aspect of these powers. Who drives out demons by contact with Beelzebul?

Yet another passage, more closely connected to foreknowledge but only making a weak claim for the Pharisees, is Luke 7:39. Jesus is at the home of a Pharisee, invited there for dinner,[50] when a woman of dubious reputation touches him. The Pharisaic host comments that Jesus cannot be a true prophet or else he would have known the character of this woman and not allowed her to touch him. One possible explanation of Jesus' special powers, raised twice in the Gospels, is that he is a prophet (Mark 6:14-16//Luke 9:7-8 and Mark 8:27-28//Matt 16:13-14//Luke 9:18-19). As a prophet, Jesus should have special knowledge beyond that of ordinary mortals (cf. John 4:17-19 and Mark 2:8). The Pharisee of this story believes that there are prophets in his day, but denies Jesus that status because he apparently lacks special insight into people he meets. It is not necessarily the case that this Pharisee perceived himself to be a rival prophet, disputing the claims of a competitor. But the fact that the Pharisees are chastised in the Gospels for restoring the tombs of the prophets (Matt 23:29-33//Luke 11:47-48) provides some support for this possible interpretation. Restorations of this sort were part of the standard *curriculum vitae* of a holy man, sage, sophist, and magician all rolled into one, such as Apollonius of Tyana (for example, Philostratus, *Vit. Apoll.* 1.23; on this point see further below).[51] Perhaps Pharisaic restoration of the tombs of the prophets was also a claim to prophetic powers. If so, the Pharisee's charge that Jesus lacked the special insight into people characteristic of a prophet could well have been motivated by a rivalry based on the claim that Pharisees too enjoyed such powers as a result of their own prophetic status.

Finally, we turn to the story of Paul's trial before the Sanhedrin in Acts 23:6-10. Recognizing that the court was divided between Pharisees and Sadducees, Paul attempted to deflect attention from himself by claiming to be a Pharisee and to be on trial for his Pharisaic belief in resurrection. Defending Paul as a fellow Pharisee, the Pharisees on the tribunal commented: "We find nothing wrong with this man. What if a spirit or an angel has spoken to him?" (Acts 23:9). For the story in Acts 23, the place of the Pharisees as recipients of special suprahuman knowledge is self-understood, almost proudly acknowledged by Pharisees about one of their own.

The Most Indirect of All: Responses to Charges of Maleficent Magic

How was one to defend oneself against the charge that one's abilities stemmed from evil beings and not benign ones? As noted above in the discussion of *Ant.* 17.41–45 charges of maleficence usually focused on three points: (1) politically subversive magic, (2) magic intended to harm, and (3) magic for financial or other gain. Accordingly, in response, those who needed to defend themselves usually stressed (1) their support of existing political institutions, (2) their goodwill toward the people, together with the help they extended to society at large through their wondrous works, and (3) their personal modesty and austere lifestyle.[52]

When seen in this context, a number of pieces of evidence on the Pharisees may take on additional significance. The Pharisees, as noted above, restored the tombs of the prophets. Implicit in this act may have been the claim that the members of their group were not subversive but rather were the legitimate heirs of the Jewish past. In addition, according to Josephus (*J. W.* 2.166), the Pharisees cultivated harmonious relations within the community. That is, they sought to reconcile people with each other and to resolve conflicts and thus promote good feeling. This was a standard part of the expectations of a sage, saint, or holy man, intended among other things to show that this holy man employed his powers to help, not to harm.[53]

The asceticism of the Pharisees is stressed by Josephus, *Ant.* 18.12. In a rabbinic text, *'Abot R. Nat.* 5, the moderation of the Pharisees is compared to the extravagance of the Sadducees. Indeed, the Sadducees chide the Pharisees for uselessly depriving themselves of the benefits of this world, as they will get no reward for their self-deprivation in the next (since, according to the Sadducees, there is no next world). Yet the moderation of the Pharisees, as opposed to the excesses of the Sadducees, is a point in favor of the former, as the two groups are described in *'Abot de Rabbi Nathan.*

The convergence of these claims may well be the final indication that the Pharisees trafficked in the supernatural and that the story in Josephus about their activities in Herod's court should not be dismissed as invented denunciation.

Our Story: Retold from a Pharisaic Point of View

How would the Pharisees themselves have narrated their actions in the court of Herod? I submit that the Pharisaic version of *Ant.* 17.41–45 would have acknowledged their predictions but tried to put them in a favorable light. The Pharisees would have portrayed the audience moved by their prophecies in more favorable terms, as a higher-class group than did Josephus or his hostile source. Perhaps they would have even suggested that their real audience was Herod himself—or, at the very least, Herod's brother Pheroras (not his wife).[54] The only cause for reticence would have been the outcome, so different than that predicted, although such "minor technical difficulties" did not crimp the style of professional oracle mongers such as Lucian's Alexander.[55] If pressed to defend themselves against charges of maleficent magic, they might have responded along the lines attributed to Apollonius in *Vit. Apoll.* 5.12. They were only predicting the future, not attempting to alter the course of destiny. That other stories about them indicated that they had the ability to shape the course of events (*Ant.* 15.4) was also a minor inconsistency, no more troubling for them than for the devotees of Philostratus's Apollonius. They indulged in none of the torture, sacrifice, incantations, or anointings that were characteristic of magicians. They communicated what God revealed to them only to the best people.

If these arguments are plausible, one further conclusion can be proposed. More than twenty years have passed since I argued that the literal meaning of the name of the Pharisees was "separatists," understood in a favorable sense as a designation the group took for itself. This interpretation of the name is now strengthened by a Qumran text formally published in 1994, 4QMMT. In the concluding section, C:7–8, the author explained with pride that his group separated from other Jews in order to preserve its version of purity. In addition to this layer of meaning, I proposed that the Pharisees took advantage of their name in order to suggest a play on words, according to which they were the "specifiers," the group that knew how to observe the law in all its details, as accurately and excellently as possible.[56]

The analysis above suggests yet another layer of meaning for the name of the Pharisees. As D. S. Potter notes, the agents from whom divine information was sought ought to have been, to some degree, set apart from the society of the inquirer.[57] In a similar vein, the idea that holy men derived their power from their marginal social location is fundamental to Reimer's analysis, which in turn derives from the work of Mary Douglas and Peter Brown.[58] Coming from the fringes endowed these holy men with power, and apparently insulated them from suspicion of abuse of power (see the discussion of austerity and modesty above). This sense of being apart from society was articulated as part of the self-conception of these holy men. The Syrian ascetics called themselves the "men of the mountains," or the "shepherds."[59] In light of the discussion above, I suggest that we understand the separatist meaning of the name of the Pharisees in a similar context. That name may have stood them in good stead as a means of asserting the reality and the legitimacy of their contact with the sacred. Their name may have served as a further argument that they had the power to predict the future and that these predictions were of the benign type.

Solo Virtuoso versus Holy Community: Similarities and Differences

In the examples discussed above, whether Jewish or Greco-Roman, I have relied on the description of the activities of individuals as well as groups. Apollonius of Tyana, for example, was an unusual holy man, but he was also a Pythagorean. Although he may not have founded a movement, he was an important link in a chain of tradition. Lucian's Alexander was supposedly a disciple of one of Apollonius's followers (Lucian, *Alexander*, 5). Apollonius was remembered centuries after his death, and the Pythagorean movement had a long history both before and after him. Honi the Circle Drawer was a solo virtuoso, but Pollion was a Pharisee, a member of a group with a distinguished past before Pollion's time and a future ahead until the years of the Great Revolt a century later. Nevertheless, the balance between the roles of individuals and groups was not the same in the Jewish world as in the classical context I have cited. Groups were much more prominent among Jews.[60]

Perhaps this was a consequence of the character of the biblical covenant, which was between God and a people. Individuals in that covenant community had a collective responsibility for one another, an accountability repeatedly emphasized by the prophets, but their role as individuals was usually seen as less significant. During the Second Temple era, when the national association of Jews no longer seemed to meet needs and Jews formed smaller organizations, they had a bias to form *communities* that claimed (each in its own way) to be Israel.[61] Thus, a solo virtuoso such as John the Baptist, who was probably not the founder of a real movement but was often followed by a crowd of people who came to hear him preach, stands at the beginning of a trajectory that will lead through his disciple Jesus to a *community*, the Christian church.

The Pharisees were, however, a bona fide movement within first-century Judaism. Their opponents in 4QpNah described them as having a council and congregation that would be disbanded in disgrace with their defeat at the end of days. What is the place of the appeal to the supernatural, the claim of foreknowledge in particular, in such a collective institutional context? To what extent are gifts of this sort purely individual, hence difficult to bequeath from one leader to another and to maintain in a community?

In answering this question we would do well to remember Rodney Stark's comment that the ability to transmit revelation is nearly universal among humans.[62] This gift should be compared to the ability to compose a tune. Everyone can do it, but there are also some geniuses with unequaled abilities, such as a Mozart or a Gershwin. So too the ability to predict the future. If the experience of Paul and that of the Dead Sea Scroll community are any indication, the problem among Jews of antiquity was not a dearth of prophets but an unruly surfeit thereof.[63] Thus, Pharisees could easily have had a steady stream of prognosticators from within their ranks. Some might have been better, others worse. Not every Pharisee was a Pollion with a royal clientele, but so long as they were adequate, with the occasional outstanding example of dramatic success, interest in Pharisaic foreknowledge should have remained reasonably high. Belief that Pharisees enjoyed special contact with the deity would have been maintained. This, in turn, would have been sufficient to maintain the claim that the Pharisees were somehow in touch with the vital layers of existence, proposed as the essence of charisma by Edward Shils, and therefore possessed of the special qualities that qualified them for a position of authority.

Conclusion

The argument above is based on an ancient contextual reading of the evidence. The connection of the Pharisees with the rabbis, or the old rivalries between Pharisees and gospel communities, have thus played as little a role as possible in the analysis. Shils, Geertz, and Scott have provided a modern set of filters through which to sift the ancient sources, revealing some of the dynamics of a claim to leadership, while Plutarch, Lucian, Celsus, and Philostratus have provided the ancient background. When viewed through this double set of lenses, religious loyalties that arose later in history interfere as little as possible with understanding the Pharisees and their part in ancient Jewish life.

I believe this argument shows that the account of the actions of the Pharisees in Herod's court in *Ant.* 17.41–45 should not be dismissed as hostile imagination. Prophecy and power regularly go hand in hand.[64] Lucian's Alexander became the leading man in Abonuteichos. At the simplest level his oracle cult was an important source of income for the town and its people. But Alexander's prestige was more broadly based, and he was influential on issues that had nothing to do with his oracle cult. Thus, in his capacity as a leading citizen, he petitioned the emperor to change the name of Abonuteichos to Ionopolis (*Alex.* 58).[65] The ancient Pharisees, as I see them, were no exception to this rule about the connection between power and prophecy.

Finally, in terms of the theme of this volume, the Pharisees were once viewed as equivalent to normative Judaism, plain and simple, for better or worse. If we are to adopt the perspective of "common Judaism" in understanding the complexities of Jewish life in the land of Israel before the destruction of the temple, the place of the Pharisees must be reassessed. We need to find a different way to evaluate the role of the Pharisees and the means they employed to reach the position they attained. This study is intended as a step in that direction.

7. From Where? To What? Common Judaism, Pharisees, and the Changing Socioreligious Location of the Matthean Community

Anders Runesson

Anyone interested in the religio-ethnic identity and social location of the community/communities that produced the Gospel of Matthew must contend not only with the multilayered composition of the Gospel but also with its complex reception history.[1] While the Gospel was used by groups identifying themselves as Jewish, it also served those of non-Jewish identity who actively opposed a Jewish understanding of "their" religion.[2] Interestingly, these two seemingly irreconcilable uses of the Gospel of Matthew are reflected in modern theories regarding the identity of the community behind the text: some scholars argue that Mattheans were well within the boundaries of "Judaism" (*intra muros*),[3] others that the author was a non-Jew writing for a community that had parted ways with the "synagogue" (*extra muros*).[4] Within and between these two positions, there are numerous interpretations varying in both methodological approaches and conclusions.[5]

The purpose of this chapter is to outline a social-scientific approach to the question of the nature and status of the group(s) that transmitted, redacted, and wrote down the traditions included in the Gospel. I begin by noting some problematic terms and categories that, in my opinion, confuse the discussion and may lead to inaccurate conclusions. After having identified the type of religion evidenced by the text and having related that religious type to the question of ethnic identity, I shall focus on tensions between the Mattheans and Jewish society, and then on Mattheans and Pharisees more specifically. In order to proceed, it will be necessary to reconstruct and analyze first-century institutions of importance to the Mattheans from a social-scientific perspective: we need a body to locate a soul.

I will argue that while the Mattheans were initially part of the Pharisaic association, the community that authored the Gospel was in the process of leaving the larger collectivity after the war of 66–70 C.E. Tensions between the Mattheans and Jewish society generally seem to have been comparatively low, both before and after 70; relations between the Mattheans and other Pharisees, however, were more complex and negative, with tensions increasing drastically after 70 C.E. Essential to the present interpretation of the social location of the Mattheans is Ed Sanders's well-argued case for the existence of a "common Judaism" in first-century Jewish society, as well as his insistence on the limited influence of the Pharisees in that society.[6]

The Religio-Ethnic Identity of the Matthean Community

Theories regarding the religio-ethnic identity of the Mattheans vary, from those who posit an exclusively Jewish community, to those who argue for an exclusively non-Jewish community, and several positions in between. Most often, Matthean scholars speak of Matthean identity in terms of binary opposites, whereby *Jesus and the disciples/ the Mattheans/Christianity/the church* are at one end of the spectrum, and *Jews/Israel/ Judaism/the synagogue* at the other.[7] A close reading of the Gospel, however, suggests that such distinctions are not found in the text but rather are imposed on it from other ancient or modern sources. Once such false oppositions are removed and authentic ones mapped, many of the traditional conclusions about the relationship between Mattheans and "others" in the Gospel are proved problematic.

Furthermore, the very terms "Jewish Christianity" and "Jewish Christians" tend to obscure what they intend to denote, namely, a belief in Jesus as the messiah embodied in communities existing within the religious system of Judaism.[8] Anthony Saldarini and others have argued that the general term indicating this religious type should rather be Christian Judaism(s).[9] However, even the term "Christian" as a name for Christ-believers in the first century is problematic, since it carries with it many meanings from later centuries. In a forthcoming study, Mark Nanos and I have therefore suggested "apostolic Judaism" as a designation for this type of Christ-belief.[10] Within the general category of apostolic Judaism, one might refer to distinct types of Christ-centered Judaisms, one of which is, it will be argued, Matthean Judaism.[11]

Christ-centered Judaisms should be distinguished from non-Jewish variants of Jesus-centered religion, which, while not part of the Jewish religious system, are nonetheless examples of "Adonayistic religion." This latter term functions well as a unifying category for all religious traditions, from antiquity until today, that focus their practice and belief around the metaphors of God that originate with the Hebrew Bible and the communities that produced these texts.[12]

These observations indicate that prior to addressing the identity of the community, it is essential to decide if the sacred texts of that community represent or describe a

Jewish or non-Jewish religious perspective. The first step is to discern the *pattern of religion* presupposed by the texts.[13] The pattern of religion includes not only theological aspects but also religious practices, such as the keeping of the Sabbath, purity laws, tithing, attendance of festivals, temple ritual, and so on.[14]

This procedure, however, defines only the texts, not the community. Jews in antiquity (as today) could and did choose different ways to worship—or not to worship at all—the God of Israel.[15] The same was true with regard to believers in Jesus, whether Jews or non-Jews. Thus, an individual or group of non-Jewish ethnic background may well have composed or redacted a text that we would identify as Jewish. A focus on the pattern of religion must therefore be supplemented by examining the Gospel's overall depiction and assessment of identifiable ethnic groups.[16]

The type of religion represented in Matthew's Gospel is located within the Jewish religious system. The pattern of religion, analyzed by focusing on one of the fundamental structures of patterns of religion, the theme of divine judgment,[17] indicates a Jewish understanding of divine retribution, punishment, and reward, as opposed to Greco-Roman ideas about judgment.[18] Furthermore, the text accepts most of the practices central to Jewish identity, such as prayer (6:5-7) and almsgiving (6:3-4); fasting (6:17-18); the Jewish law/the commandments (Matt 5:17-19; 19:17); dietary laws (15:1-20[19]) and other purity laws (8:4, 5-13;[20] 23:25-26); the Sabbath (12:1-14;[21] 24:20); festivals (Passover [26:2, 17-35]); tithing (23:23); the temple cult and practices connected with the temple, including the temple tax (5:23-24; 12:3-5; 17:24-27; 23:19-21);[22] and, most likely, circumcision.[23] As to religious type, then, we may locate Matthean religion in a table as follows.[24]

Type of Religion			
Adonayistic Religions			Non-Adonayistic Religions
Jewish Religious System		Non-Jewish Religious Systems	[Greco-Roman Religious Traditions]
"Common Judaism"	Parties: Apostolic Judaisms and non-Apostolic Judaisms[25]	Non-Jewish Christianities : Samaritan-ism[26] : Islam[27]	
["What the priests and the people agreed on"[28]]	Pharisaic Judaism; : Matthean Judaism; Enochic : Judaism; : Paul Judaism; Essene : Judaism	Ignatius; : Dositheanism : Shia; Irenaeus; : Sunni Valentinians	

Table 1. The religious system within which we find the Gospel of Matthew, compared to other variants of Adonayistic religions.

While non-Jewish characters such as the magi (2:1-12), the Roman centurion (8:5-13), and the Canaanite woman (15:21-28) are portrayed positively, these individuals are described as exceptions to a general rule according to which non-Jews are and do everything that Mattheans should avoid (5:47; 6:7, 32; 18:17). The non-Jewish nations are, furthermore, explicitly prophesied to hate and persecute the disciples/Mattheans (24:9). Jews are never generalized negatively in the same way (negative statements are limited to specific individuals and groups); all the good things that Mattheans should be and do are parts of Jewish life accepted by other Jews as well.[29] These and other features of the Gospel strongly suggest that the group in which the Gospel originated was ethnically Jewish.[30] The grid below includes some examples that may serve as a comparison to highlight the position of the Mattheans.

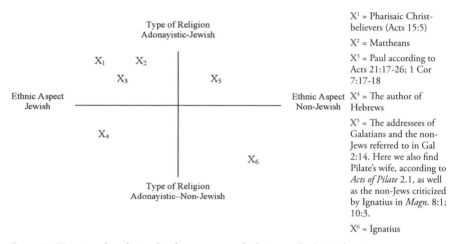

Figure 1. Mapping the relationship between type of religion and ethnic identity.

Place and Date

Evidence does not permit any firm conclusions with regard to the location of the transmission of traditions included in the Gospel of Matthew or the production of the text as we have it today. Jerusalem/Palestine, Caesarea Maritima, Phoenicia, Alexandria, east of the Jordan, Edessa, Syria, and Antioch have all been suggested in the last fifty years.[31] Recently, however, several scholars have argued convincingly for the land of Israel and, more narrowly, Galilee.[32] A larger city such as Tiberias or Sepphoris would have provided the socioreligious setting that we see reflected in Matthew's Gospel. Like the majority of Matthean scholars, I suggest the 80s or 90s for the final version of the Gospel.[33]

These conclusions, namely, that we are dealing with Jewish Christ-believers in a larger city in the Galilee in the latter half of the first century, will serve as a basic point of departure for the reconstruction of the institutional setting and, by implication, for the analysis of the interaction between Mattheans, the society in which they lived, and the groups that influenced the formation of their identity.

Social Tensions, Common Judaism, and the Problem of the "Jewish Majority"

Much research on the Mattheans builds on the assumption that there existed a dominant group in Jewish society—the Pharisees—in relation to which the Mattheans could be considered a sect.[34] On the basis of careful analysis, especially of Josephus, Sanders has argued convincingly that the Pharisees were not nearly as influential as many scholars have argued.[35] The discussion of Pharisaic influence has centered mostly on the pre-70 period. For the post-70 era, during which Matthew's Gospel was written down, Jacob Neusner's suggestion of a "formative Judaism," an emerging coalition of different groups and individuals, predominantly Pharisees, priests, and landowners, evolving after 70 C.E.,[36] has played an important role.[37]

Within Matthean studies, it is generally thought that the polemics of Matthew's Gospel must have played out against a dominant force in *society* against which the Mattheans competed for power or influence in the power vacuum created after the fall of the temple. The question is, of course, whether such a majority existed in the last quarter of the first century. In societies undergoing major turbulence, such as that created by the war of 66–70, there is a tendency for the people who enjoyed privileged positions and political power before the devastation to continue to exercise influence and power after it. Only rarely are political elites completely displaced.[38] This observation raises some questions concerning the general assumption of a meteoric rise to power of "formative Judaism" immediately after 70.

It is quite possible that the Pharisaic movement experienced an influx of sympathizers after the war and that, as a result, the group took off in a certain direction, negotiating and modifying certain Pharisaic traditions and customs to the new situation. Already before 70 the Pharisees seem to have been home to a number of subgroups, some of which, however, eventually left the movement.[39] Furthermore, it is probable that Pharisaism, as a result of these changes, eventually developed into what we know as rabbinic Judaism. What is not clear, however, is whether rabbinic Judaism, even in its fully developed form, had an influential position in Jewish society before the sixth century or even later.[40] In other words, we know very little about the late first century that would enable us to talk about a powerful formative/early rabbinic Judaism, from which Mattheans could be said to deviate.

Saldarini suggests that Matthew's Gospel should be seen not in the context of formative Judaism as such, but as a response to the *local* influence of formative Judaism in the Galilean city where the Mattheans lived.[41] It is not entirely clear whether he understands the Mattheans to be deviant in relation to a majority Judaism/Jewish society, or in relation to a specific leading group, which may or may not have had support among the majority of Jews. In any case, Saldarini defines the "leadership group" as a "reform/reformist movement." A quotation from his 1992 article on Matthew 23 sheds some light on our question:

> In the late first century the very early rabbinic coalition was, like Matthew's group, a reform movement. They and Matthew were rivals for influence and access to power in the assemblies and other institutions of the Jewish community. Each sought not to form a new sect, but to gather the disparate groups and forms of Judaism into one fold. At this stage of Judaism's development, neither group was dominant in the Jewish community as a whole, but in Matthew's city or area the rabbinic group's program was more influential than Matthew's Jesus-centered Judaism.[42]

Here it seems as if Saldarini equates the Mattheans and "early rabbis" regarding their relationship to society at large: he labels both "reform movements" (according to Bryan R. Wilson's sevenfold definition of "sect," they would be defined as "reformist sects"[43]), one being more successful locally—but not universally—than the other. If I understand Saldarini correctly, his conclusion is that the (reformist) sect of "very early rabbis"/formative Judaism is the *local* leadership group in Jewish society defining the parent body in relation to which the Matthean reformist sect deviated. There is no direct connection between the Mattheans and the Pharisees; the tensions are created in a struggle over influence in society. If this is correct, the obvious question would be: If the early rabbis were a reformist sect, in relation to whom did they, in turn, deviate? At this point we need to take into account common Judaism, as described by Sanders, before 70 C.E., as well as discuss the institutional framework of first-century Jewish society.

There is no indication that common Judaism ceased to exist immediately after 70 C.E., and the reason for this is connected with the role and function of public institutions beyond the Jerusalem temple. Figure 2 shows the relationship between the institutions relevant to our dicussion.[44]

In terms of the Mattheans' relation to society, the Gospel of Matthew indicates that they acknowledged the Jerusalem temple and its cult while the temple still stood, and continued to revere both Jerusalem and the temple after 70 C.E. (5:23-24; 12:3-5; 17:24-27). Jerusalem is the Holy City before as well as after the death of Jesus (Matt 4:5; 5:35; 27:53). Contrary to the view of Saldarini,[45] the destruction of Jerusalem and the temple, of which the final redactor was aware, does not affect the holiness of, or respect for, the temple itself. Rather, the destruction is used to blame the leaders who had been appointed by God but who had used their position in ways contrary to God's purposes.[46] The city receives its holiness from the temple. The holiness of the

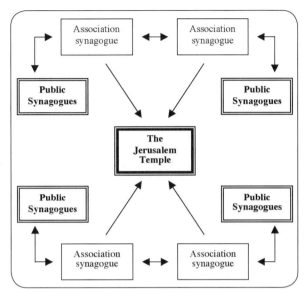

Figure 2. Reconstruction of the institutional framework of first-century Jewish society. Arrows indicate possible interaction between association synagogues and between associations and local as well as central public institutions.

city is thus connected with the God of Israel and the temple, not the leaders, who are also, however, related to the city and the temple but as the caretakers of things holy. Matthew's perspective is that some groups, which are connected with the temple and the city, were corrupt and acted as bad servants, or shepherds (cf., for example, Matt 9:36), or tenants (Matt 21:33, 45), and had thus caused the destruction of both temple and city.

In relation to the Jewish state and state religion as represented by the temple, and thus civil religion, it seems as if the Mattheans were not taking a sectarian stance. Indeed, by locating 23:37—24:2 directly after and thus in conjunction with the severe criticism of the Pharisees in chapter 23, the author in fact limits the responsibility of the Jerusalem leadership and attempts to transfer the guilt of the destruction of Jerusalem to the Pharisees, who, obviously, were not in charge of political affairs at the time. The same effect is aimed for when the Gospel of Matthew, alone among the Synoptics, introduces the Pharisees in the passion narrative after the death of Jesus. This creates the impression that the Pharisees were part of the leadership handing Jesus over to the Romans while, in fact, the "original" passion narrative lacks any references to the Pharisees.[47] In conclusion, the text indicates tensions between Jerusalem authorities (the chief priests as well as references to Jerusalem as a metaphor for religio-political leadership) and the Mattheans, but these tensions are less emphatic than those between the Mattheans and the Pharisees. The political establishment—and thus the state—is not the primary target of Matthean hostile rhetoric: the group referred to as Pharisees is.

Several scholars have pointed to the references to "their/your synagogue(s)," which have few parallels outside Matthew's Gospel,[48] arguing that this expression reflects a situation *extra muros*, or beyond the "synagogue"/"Judaism," on the part of the Mattheans. However, locating these statements in their "body," the institutional setting of first-century Palestine, will yield a very different, indeed opposite, conclusion. I shall first present a table sorting and summarizing the passages in question and then comment on each instance of the expression.

Activity	Verse	Text	"Their/Your Synagogue(s)"	Reference	Neutral/ Negative
Teaching	4:23	Jesus went throughout Galilee, teaching in their synagogues (*en tais synagōgais autōn*) and proclaiming the good news of the kingdom and curing every disease and every sickness among the people.	X	Location	Neutral
Teaching	9:35	Then Jesus went about all the cities and villages, teaching in their synagogues (*en tais synagōgais autōn*), and proclaiming the good news of the kingdom, and curing every disease and every sickness.	X	Location	Neutral
Teaching	13:54	He came to his hometown and began to teach the people in their synagogue (*en tē synagōgē autōn*), so that they were astounded and said, "Where did this man get this wisdom and these deeds of power?"	X	Specific single location	Neutral/ negative; mixed reaction
Worship and alms-giving	6:2	So whenever you give alms, do not sound a trumpet before you, as the hypocrites do in the synagogues (*en tais synagōgais*) and in the streets, so that they may be praised by others. Truly I tell you, they have received their reward.		General	Neutral

Activity	Verse	Text	"Their/Your Synagogue(s)"	Reference	Neutral/ Negative
Worship and alms-giving	6:5	And whenever you pray, do not be like the hypocrites; for they love to stand and pray in the synagogues (*en tais synagōgais*) and at the street corners, so that they may be seen by others. Truly I tell you, they have received their reward.		General	Neutral
Assembly (not specified)	23:6	They love to have the place of honor at banquets and the best seats in the synagogues (*en tais synagōgais*).		General	Neutral
Healing	12:9-10	He left that place and entered their synagogue (*eis tēn synagōgēn autōn*); a man was there with a withered hand, and they asked him, "Is it lawful to cure on the sabbath?" so that they might accuse him.	X	Group or location	Negative
Punish-ment	10:17	Beware of them, for they will hand you over to councils and flog you in their synagogues (*en tais synagōgais autōn*).	X	Group	Negative
Punish-ment	23:34	Therefore I send you prophets, sages, and scribes, some of whom you will kill and crucify, and some you will flog in your synagogues (*en tais synagōgais hymōn*) and pursue from town to town.	X	Group	Negative

Table 2. The portrayal of "synagogues" and events in "synagogues" in the Gospel of Matthew.

First, it is clear that we cannot generalize the meaning of *autōn* in relation to synagogues. It is sometimes used to indicate public institutions in specific places, which Jesus visited (4:23; 9:35; 13:54). That these institutions are public may be inferred from the fact that the reference is to large geographical areas or specific cities or villages: synagogues as public institutions represent the inhabitants of these places. When the reference is general, the evaluation is neutral; when the reference is specific (Jesus' hometown [13:54]), the evaluation is mixed or negative. The table indicates that the negative reaction is the exception and the neutral, nonhostile reaction is the rule. Second, supporting this conclusion is the fact that the general references to synagogues (without *autōn* [6:2, 5; 23:6]) indicate that the Mattheans regard the public synagogue as the normal or accepted place for worship in local public contexts.[49] These synagogues are public since the rhetorical point in all passages is the public or open nature of the space referred to, where "hypocrites" play out their religious devotion in order to enhance their status among the people (6:2: synagogues and streets; 6:5: synagogues and street corners). In 23:6 "the scribes and the Pharisees" are said to use public space to boost their status in the eyes of people not belonging to their own group, be they "ordinary Jews," Mattheans, or members of other parties.[50]

The references in Matthew's Gospel to public synagogues therefore support the point noted above, namely, that although tensions may exist in certain locations, the Mattheans recognized and interacted positively with public institutions. Indeed, the public synagogues provided an institutional and spatial setting in which the Mattheans carried out a mission to the people of the land. The "crowds" in the Gospel of Matthew play an important role in this regard, as a literary character representing the object of Matthean missionary activities, that is, people not belonging to any specific parties, people whom we would call "ordinary Jews," adhering to common Judaism.[52] A literary analysis of their function in the narrative shows that extreme tensions between them and Jesus/the disciples are lacking. "The crowds" are not among the groups being judged in Matthew's Gospel. They are sometimes portrayed positively, sometimes less positively, but they are never condemned.[53] To be sure, certain places are judged collectively (without references to "the crowds"), such as the cities of Chorazin and Bethsaida (Matt 11:21), and this would probably refer to encounters in public assemblies of these cities. The specificity in this case, however, should be compared to the general treatment of "the crowds" (and general references to public synagogues), which does not involve categorical rejection. Thus, as might be expected, depending on local context, certain places would be less favorable to the messianic proclamation, but this does not mean a general rejection by the people who represent Jewish practice and belief more broadly— ordinary Jews—who interacted positively with Mattheans in public assemblies and other public places.

Group Tensions: The Mattheans and the Pharisees

In sharp contrast to "ordinary Jews" and common Judaism, the Pharisees are repeatedly singled out for categorical condemnation in a way that leaves no room for exceptions.

The threat of divine judgment is applied to its fullest extent, including both their removal as leaders (21:33-45) and their exclusion from the world to come (5:20). For our purposes, it is important to locate this criticism in the institutional framework described above and apply insights from contemporary cross-culturally tested social-scientific and social-psychological theories. I begin with the former and then, distinguishing between pre- and post-70 periods in the life of the Matthean movement, identify their changing socioreligious location. As we shall see, in the words of L. Michael White, "The tension of the Matthean community with other Jewish groups (or to be more precise, the Pharisees and 'their synagogues') was born of proximity rather than distance, of similarity rather than difference."[54]

The expression "their/your synagogue(s)" (see table 2 above) will provide us with information often neglected because of the lack of a careful definition of "synagogue." Beginning with Matt 12:9, it is possible that we have here a reference to a Pharisaic association synagogue.[55] In 12:1-8, Jesus is debating with the Pharisees (v. 2), accusing them of not knowing the law (v. 5). He then enters "their synagogue" (v. 9) and heals a person. The people ("they") who ask Jesus whether it is right to heal on the Sabbath are clearly Pharisees, since (a) no other group has been introduced in the story since 12:2, (b) it is said to take place later the same day as the debate in 12:1-8, (c) the topic of discussion is the same (the definition of "work" on the Sabbath), and (d) the conclusion of the episode is that "the Pharisees went out and conspired against him, how to destroy him" (v. 14). "The crowds" join Jesus only after he has left the synagogue and the area (*anechōrēsen ekeithen kai ēkolouthēsan autō ochloi polloi* [v. 15]). This means that Jesus is said deliberately to seek out and relate to Pharisees in their own assembly building.[56] If this is correct, we have evidence of a specific association synagogue, belonging to a particular group, whose participants react negatively to Jesus.

The author of the Gospel provides two passages that deal with punishment of followers of Jesus/Mattheans in, or through,[57] synagogues. Interestingly, both texts specify these synagogues as "their" or "your" synagogues: *en tais synagōgais autōn* in 10:17[58] and *en tais synagōgais hymōn* in 23:34. Since these are the only passages that deal with punishment in synagogues, and since 23:29 states that *hymōn* in 23:34 refers to the Pharisees and their scribes,[59] 10:17 should be read from the perspective of 23:34, suggesting that *autōn* in 10:17 links the synagogues in question to Pharisees. There are, then, two possible interpretations of these passages: (a) the term "synagogues" refers to Pharisaic association synagogues generally, or (b) the term refers to public synagogues in specific places where the Pharisees were influential and had power to affect the decisions of the public assemblies (cf. above on Matt 11:21; however, no Pharisees are mentioned in relation to these places).

In favor of alternative (a) the following can be said with regard to 10:17. We know that public synagogues functioned as local courts (which is the meaning of *synedria* here).[60] Matthew does not further define these courts by calling them "their" courts, as in the case of the synagogues three words later, and so implies a common judicial institution for Mattheans and those who accuse them. These courts, then, refer to judicial activities taking place in public synagogues. The next thing to note is that people referred to as *anthrōpoi* will be handing over followers of disciples/Mattheans to these courts, which are public and not controlled by any specific group. These people are the same as those in charge of the synagogues mentioned: *autōn* refers to the nonspecific *tōn anthrōpōn*, as does the subject implied in *paradōsousin*. As we noted above, the parallel in 23:34 indicates that these people should be understood as Pharisees.[61] Once the reader has finished the whole Gospel and knows about 23:34, the interpretive result with regard to 10:17 is twofold: first, the Pharisees are said to hand Christ-believers/Mattheans over to be judged in Jewish courts. Second, the Pharisees are prophesied to flog Christ-believers/Mattheans in their own association synagogues. The latter point needs some elaboration.

Voluntary associations in the Greco-Roman world (including the land of Israel[62]) made up their own rules and had the right to impose punishment in case of disobedience to those rules.[63] It would have been a punishable offense for a member who had been attacked or beaten by another member of the association to turn to public courts and sue the offender. The victim was required first to consult the leaders of the association (in the case of the *Iobaccoi*, the priest or the arch-bacchus), who would then settle the case and prescribe appropriate punishment (cf. Matt 18:15-18). The punishments within an association would vary according to the character of the offense but would almost always range from fines and/or expulsion for certain time periods to permanent expulsion from the association.

Like the Qumranites, the Pharisees would have had their own penal codes within their association synagogues.[64] The question with regard to the passages under discussion, Matt 10:17 and 23:34, is whether flogging (the term used in both passages is *mastigoō*[65]) could be a punishment imposed by an association. No evidence in favor of such punishment exists with regard to any known voluntary association in the Greco-Roman world.[66] However, as Deut 25:1-3 indicates, it would be a type of punishment fitting the context of public courts.

Does this mean that Matt 10:17 and 23:34 refer to public institutions, despite everything said up to this point against this interpretation (and its sociopolitical implications)? I think not. Matthew uses hyperbole—and does so symmetrically. In 23:34 Matthew's Jesus promises to send prophets, sages, and scribes to the Pharisees and their scribes; the latter will "kill and crucify" some of these learned people. Others will be flogged "in their synagogues." We know that execution/crucifixion was a punishment that could be imposed only by the Roman imperial power. Yet Matthew, in order to increase the guilt of the Pharisees, turns them into the executioners, thus transforming them into the likeness of the (political) authorities in Israel's history who, according to the Hebrew Bible, executed prophets sent to them (23:29-33). In order to achieve this move, the author has to make use of images of Israel's past political authorities as well as of the current Roman authorities and their power to impose the capital punishment.

Then he has to transfer this power—not to Jewish political authorities of his own time (who would have been the chief priests), but to the nonofficial group he has selected as primary target, the Pharisees. The result, obviously, has nothing to do with sociohistorical or political realities in the late first century.

Step 2 is to transfer the power to impose a punishment that *was* possible in Jewish society (in the public courts), flogging,[67] to the same group—the Pharisees. In this way, Matthew achieves a connection, as complete as it can be on all levels of (unjust) punishment, between a contemporary group without judicial power in society and the prophet-killing political authorities of the Hebrew Bible. This allows the author to state in 23:35-36 that the Pharisees and their scribes shall be held responsible for all unjust punishment throughout Israelite history (including, by implication, punishments that may be imposed on Mattheans by Roman authorities!). Again, this carefully planned rewriting of history, fusing it with the present, has nothing to do with sociopolitical realities either before or immediately after 70 C.E.

If we return to Matt 10:17, the pattern becomes clear. "Their synagogues" indeed refers to Pharisaic associations, but the punishment mentioned is taken from another judicial context in order to increase the guilt of the Pharisees. The punishments that were considered possible in the past were distributed between two political bodies: the Jewish courts and Roman imperial legislation. The author of Matthew fuses these two judicial contexts, creating an image for his own time reflecting earlier Israelite society—and then substitutes the Pharisees for the political leaders of his time.

It would seem, therefore, that despite the author's creative use of Israelite history when interpreting his own time, the historical fact was that the Pharisaic synagogues ("their/your synagogue[s]" in 10:17 and 23:34) *did have judicial power* over the Mattheans, even if punishments were less severe than the Gospel wants us to believe. This situation created, and explains, the frustration the Mattheans—contrary to other groups in the Jesus movement who were not involved institutionally with the Pharisees—felt with the Pharisees, a frustration that permeates the Gospel from beginning to end and results in repeated and violent rhetorical attacks. Indeed, one of the keys to the origins of the Gospel of Matthew and the Matthean community lies in this observation. If the Mattheans did not belong within the Pharisaic associations, these extreme tensions would be difficult to explain sociologically. At the same time, however, some passages seem to indicate that a schism between some Mattheans and the Pharisaic associations had occurred when the Gospel was written down and redacted.

The hypothesis I am proposing unfolds as follows: The Mattheans were urban-based[68] Pharisees who became convinced, most likely after the death and resurrection of Jesus had been proclaimed to them by missionaries, that Jesus of Nazareth was Israel's messiah,[69] confirming their Pharisaic belief in the resurrection of the dead as well as their hope for a restored Israel.[70] Believing their hopes soon to be fulfilled, they formed a movement within Pharisaism that engaged in a mission to "ordinary Jews," proclaiming that the end of the present age—and the suffering it implied—was near.[71] Doing so, they constantly referred to Scripture, accepted as holy by the wider movement, but subjected it to a specific interpretation.[72]

Every reform movement causes tension to appear within the larger collectivity. The larger Pharisaic community remained unconvinced about the identification of this—now dead—individual as the messiah. Their lack of belief caused open conflicts in public synagogues as well as internal strife between messianic believers and the majority. With the destruction of the Jerusalem temple in 70 C.E., probably predicted by the historical Jesus, or, in any case, predicted by the earlier Markan community to whose Gospel the Mattheans had access, the majority of Mattheans experienced tremendous "real-life evidence" that the coming kingdom was within reach. This spurred missionary outreach on the part of the majority of the Matthean reform movement.[73] This activity ultimately expanded beyond the Jewish people, since, at the dawn of the new age, the Gentiles must come to Zion.[74] Previously, by contrast, more "theoretical" eschatological expectations had anticipated non-Jews coming to the people of God and their messiah of their own accord.[75]

This development within the Matthean reform movement happened coterminously with an increased influx of people to the wider Pharisaic denomination. These sympathizers and new members were most likely, as described by Neusner,[76] landlords and priests, who were of a relatively high status in Jewish society. As such, they had less interest in a radical movement proclaiming the imminent coming of the end; the Mattheans, on the other hand, at this stage likely recruited more people from the lower strata of society.[77] The result was increased tension within the Pharisaic associations, based on both ideological and social factors. Together these factors created a schism in which the majority, but not all,[78] of the Mattheans left the Pharisaic denomination and became, in relation to the Pharisees, a *sect*.[79] This group, whom we may call the separatists, authored and redacted the Gospel of Matthew as we have it today.[80] The reason they wrote a Gospel was twofold: to consolidate their own emerging association, providing a foundation for their particular identity, and to attempt to convince Mattheans who had remained within the Pharisaic association to join them.

These factors explain the hostile polemic and exaggeration regarding possible punishments Mattheans may suffer within the Pharisaic association, as discussed above. They also account for the relationship between Matt 23:1-3 and the rhetorical attacks that follow:[81] the author, a former member of the Pharisees with a modified self-understanding, takes as point of departure the shared and long-held conviction that the Pharisees sit on Moses' seat. This may have been an expression used by pre-70 Pharisees, including Mattheans. In the new situation experienced by the separatists, such acknowledgment of Pharisaic authority was probably meant to gain the sympathies of the Mattheans still within the Pharisaic association before introducing the complete and final delegitimation of the Pharisees themselves, using ad hominem arguments and accusing them of perverting rituals and customs that they all shared (for example, making use of/wearing phylacteries and fringes [23:5]; attending public synagogues [23:6]; tithing [23:23]; pronouncing oaths in relation to the temple [23:16-21; but cf.

5:33-37]). The reference to the "outside" that Pharisees are said to make look righteous (23:28) may also be an indication of halakhic positions shared by Mattheans and other Pharisees.[82]

The repeated assertions that the Pharisees are not going to be part of the coming kingdom (23:33, 36; cf. 5:20) are meant as a warning to those remaining within the denomination that they have nothing to gain and everything to lose by choosing to stay. Indeed, leaving means joining those who have the keys to the kingdom (Matt 16:18-19) and the power to exclude others from "what really matters."

These assertions show that the Matthean separatists had left the Pharisees and, in relation to them, constitute a *sect*. Joachim Wach has described the coexistence of conflicting orientations within the same collectivity—what he terms *ecclesiolae in ecclesia*—and identifies three basic types: *Collegium pietas*, *Fraternitas*, and the *Order*.[83] Common to all types, apart from the fact that they most often try to reform the larger collectivity, is the acceptance of a dual standard of religiosity, one for "the masses" and one for the virtuosi. While we find such a position in pre-70 Matthean tradition (Matt 19:16-22),[84] the denunciation of Pharisees combined with repeated condemnations resulting in their ultimate exclusion show that a schism had taken place at the time of final redaction.[85] Indeed, in the history of New Testament scholarship, the Pharisees are guilty of all innocent blood in the history of Israel; the implicit claim that they are to blame for the destruction of Jerusalem (Matt 23:35—24:2), their insertion into the passion narrative (Matt 27:62), and the institutional evidence of the first stages of a separate Matthean association (Matt 18; 21:33-46) strongly suggest that the separatists, while having belonged to the Pharisees, had, at the time of the final redaction of the Gospel,[86] parted ways with them.

On the basis of the above, however, one must recognize the diversity of traditions in the Gospel and distinguish between different Matthean communities, each displaying its own perspective and interpretation of the traditions.[87] In this regard, time is a crucial factor, and 70 C.E. is a watershed. Due to the socioeconomic changes brought about by the war,[88] the *sect* separating itself from the larger collectivity—and from Mattheans choosing not to follow them—would have been composed by a majority of people from nonelite lower stratum groups, partly explaining the egalitarian emphasis of the final redaction of the Gospel (cf. Matt 18:1-4; 23:8-11).[89] Apart from the increased intensity of eschatological expectations, the separatists brought about, as a result of the former, a change in missionary strategies, introducing an active Gentile mission.[90]

The post-70 changes, both social and theological, resulted in the fierce polemic in Matthew's Gospel against the Pharisees.[91] Taken out of its sociohistorical context and applied to the Jewish people as a whole, this polemic has had disastrous consequences in the history of Jewish-Christian relations. Originally, however, the denunciation of the Pharisees was meant for the ears of Mattheans and "ordinary Jews," whom the separatists hoped would join their community now when the end of time was nearer than it was when they had first embraced a faith in Jesus of Nazareth as the risen messiah.[92]

Conclusion

Few scholars have understood the Matthean communities as Pharisaic communities.[93] Indeed, a glance at any presentation of the history of scholarship of the New Testament will show that the Pharisees (often equated with "Judaism") have been presented as the absolute opposite of the Jesus movement (or "Christianity"), which, in turn, is most often understood as a homogeneous entity. Still, in addition to the evidence discussed above regarding Matthew's Gospel, there are clear indications in the ancient sources, supported by social-scientific theories based on contemporary empirical studies, that suggest a much more complex situation with considerable overlap between and within Jewish movements in the first century, including the Jesus movement and the Pharisees.

We know from Acts 15:5 that in the late first century, there were Pharisees who, without leaving their identity or institutional belonging behind, had accepted a belief in Jesus as the messiah.[94] Indeed, according to Acts, Paul never ceased to regard himself a Pharisee (Acts 23:6).[95] It seems that the earliest Jesus movement was rather loosely joined together institutionally. It included Christ-believers who retained their basic group identity and institutional affiliation, but related in different ways to an independent leadership body located in Jerusalem, which functioned as a centripetal force for the formation of a messianic identity (cf. Gal. 2:9). It is, of course, important to distinguish between the self-perception of the Christ-believers who remained within their original associations on the one hand and the perspective of those sharing institutional affiliation with them but who did not accept Jesus as the messiah. A Christ-believing Pharisee may or may not have been accepted as a Pharisee by other Pharisees, depending on which particular Pharisaic group we are dealing with. The tensions that would follow as Christ-believers established themselves as "subgroups" within larger groups, or associations, would lead to strife and, undoubtedly, suffering on the part of the minorities, eventually resulting in schisms between the parent body, in our case the Pharisees, and the reform movements.

The Pharisees themselves, in existence since the Hasmonean period (Jonathan [161–143 B.C.E]), had among them diverse groups that at times exhibited schismatic tendencies.[96] It was similar with the rabbinic movement. This diversity calls into question the tendency among many scholars to overemphasize the role of Christology in the divergence between Jews who believed Jesus to be the messiah and those who did not. Rabbi Akiva's support for Bar Kokhba as the messiah suggests that such beliefs were not decisive, whereas the story of Rabbi Eliezer's excommunication over a halakhic issue implies that halakhah may indeed have been more important than dogma (*b. B. Metzi'a* 59a–59b). If Christology is of prime importance in our own time, we must nevertheless acknowledge that social location and identity formation may have functioned quite differently within the institutional framework of Jewish society in the first centuries of the Common Era.

In conclusion, the Gospel of Matthew provides us with early evidence of an inner-Jewish parting of the ways, very different in character from the processes that much later would lead to the establishment of "Christianity" as a religion independent of "Judaism." Indeed, the use of the Gospel of Matthew by non-Jewish Christ-believers as a resource in that later process of identity formation is a fascinating and hermeneutically complex problem that deserves further study.

8. What Do Angels Have against the Blind and the Deaf? Rules of Exclusion in the Dead Sea Scrolls

Cecilia Wassen

Like other peoples of the Greco-Roman world, Jews in the Second Temple period believed in evil spirits and demons. One group that took the power of evil spirits very seriously was the Qumran sect. The Qumran community developed a system of protection against the demonic threat that included protective prayers, perfect Torah observance, exorcisms, and association with the angels. While not immune to the dangerous forces of evil spirits, the sect believed that, compared to the rest of the society, it had a superior ability to resist their deceptive powers.

The belief in evil spirits—Belial and his demon minions—made up a significant component of the construction of reality of the Qumran sect and impacted many areas of communal life.[1] In the Dead Sea Scrolls evil spirits appear as active, dangerous forces that cause damage to people. Most obviously, these evil forces were thought to be the root cause of illness and physical disability. At the same time, the Qumran texts devote some attention to categories of physically and mentally challenged individuals who are to be excluded from the communal meetings and from the eschatological war camp. In this essay, I argue that one important factor underlying rules of exclusion is the fear of evil spirits. The sectarian literature contains three lists of disabilities that exclude individuals from communal activities. These lists, found in the *Damascus Document* ("D": CD XV 15–17 / 4Q266 8 i 6–9 / 4Q270 6 ii 8–10), the *Rule of the Congregation* (1QSa II 3–9), and the *War Scroll* ("M": 1QM VII 4–6), include various categories of physical disabilities, and all refer to the presence of holy angels as the reason for the exclusion. Whereas D and 1QSa prohibit these categories of members from entering communal meetings, M bars them from participating in the final battle.[2] It is commonly accepted that these lists are based on Lev 21:17-23, which enumerates physical defects that render priests ineligible to serve in the temple.[3]

It is not clear why the sect applied rules for priests to its assemblies and in war. A common view is that the members of the Qumran sect identified themselves as a priestly community that embodied and even substituted the temple.[4] The association of the community with a sanctuary is apparent in several texts, for example, in the *Community Rule* ("S": 1QS) VIII 5–6: "the Council of the Community being established in truth— an eternal plant, the House of Holiness consisting of Israel, a most holy assembly for Aaron."[5] With little or no contact with the actual temple,[6] the sectarians developed a liturgy influenced by the temple service, ascribed leadership to the priests (for example, Sons of Zadok and Sons of Aaron),[7] and applied some specific priestly laws about purity and perfection to their gatherings.

Aaron Shemesh points out that the blemishes listed in Lev 21:17-23 that are said to "profane" the sanctuary in Lev 21:23 are related neither to the ability to carry out priestly duties nor to purity, but refer to aesthetics alone. Physical imperfection is opposed to holiness in Leviticus because the person offering in the temple is "seen" by God.[8] Accordingly, he argues, the sectarians adopted the concept of holiness as related to bodily perfection and applied it to their communal meetings and the war camp. Nevertheless, this explanation fails to account fully for the reference to the angels. As intermediaries between God and humans, why could they not look at human imperfections?[9] Saul Olyan, by contrast, understands the restrictions in the Qumran texts as examples of the general tendency to increase the severity of biblically based laws.[10]

Nevertheless, the association between the sect and the temple does not fully explain why the sectarians excluded "blemished" people from their assemblies. First, the lists conclude with a reference to angels, not priests or the temple. Second, additional categories of disability, such as mental disability and immoral character in D, have been added to the list in Leviticus 21. I would argue that in addition to the desire to imitate the priestly proceedings in the temple, we must add the fear of evil spirits as a factor influencing the categories of exclusion.

Protection and Combat against Demons in the Dead Sea Scrolls

The Qumran sect believed that demons led by Belial roamed the earth attacking victims and causing suffering during the time immediately preceding the final battle when all evil forces would be destroyed forever.[11] Living at the dawn of the eschaton, the sectarians were deeply aware of the evil forces' destructive and deceiving abilities and therefore developed coping strategies to protect themselves and join forces with the angels in the combat.

Many Dead Sea texts attribute illnesses to evil spirits and describe various means of protection.[12] *Genesis Apocryphon* (1QapGen ar; 1Q20), a nonsectarian text,[13] recounts that the patriarch Abraham expels an evil spirit that has caused a plague by praying—likely reciting a hymnic exorcism—and laying his hands on the afflicted pharaoh (XX 15–29).[14] The underlying logic is that by sinning—that is, taking Abraham's wife—the pharaoh had made himself vulnerable to demonic affliction. The same connection between sin and disease is made in the fragmentary text the *Prayer of Nabonidus* (4QPrAb ar; 4Q242), in which Nabonidus (Daniel 4)[15] prays, "I was afflicted [with an evil inflammation] for seven years and was banished from [men . . .] and an exorcist (*gzr*) pardoned my sins. He was a Jewish [man] of the [exiles . . .]" (4Q242 2b 2–4).[16]

The sectarian text known as the *Songs of the Maskil* (4Q510 and 4Q511) contains magical incantations to be recited as protection from evil spirits.[17] These fragmentary songs praise God, highlighting his majesty and power, but their purpose is apparent in lines such as these (4Q510 1 4–6):

> And as for me, I am a sage who makes known the splendor of his beauty, in order to frighten and ter[rify] all the spirits of the angels of destruction (*rwḥy ml'ky ḥbl*) and the bastard spirits (*wrwḥwt mmzrym*), demons (*šdym*), Lilith, howlers, and s[atyrs . . .] and those who strike unexpectedly to lead the spirit of understanding astray, and to appall their hearts and their so[uls].[18]

The document consists of several songs that have a protective function, as one introduction to a song reads, "[For the instructor:] the second [so]ng so as to frighten those who terrify," ([*lmskyl š*]*yr šny lpḥd myr'yw*) (4Q511 8 4). In addition to references to demons and angels, the text mentions "the demon possessed" (*hpgw'ym*) (11 8) and "those stricken by," (*ngw'*[*y*]) (10 4). The speaker is none other than the Maskil, the spiritual leader known from both D (CD XII 20–21; XIII 22)[19] and S, who is in charge of admitting new members (1QS IX 14–16) as well as instructing the Sons of Light about the two spirits (1QS III 13–15). The incantations are apotropaic, offering protection against future demonic attacks.[20] Bilhah Nitzan had noticed similarities between these texts and later incantations from amulets (for example, both address the evil spirits by name and command them to leave), but she clarifies that the songs do not invoke the name of God, as is done later. Instead, the songs use words about God's majesty as a magical power; thus, the hymn itself is magically powerful.[21] Philip Alexander adds that the references to angels (for example, 4Q511 2 i 8; 8 8–12; 10 11) may have functioned as protection as well: "Basically the Maskil warns the demons not to meddle with him and his community, because they have got 'protection.'"[22] These songs were likely recited by the Maskil at a public liturgy, since 4Q511 ends with "Amen, amen" (63–64 iv 1–3), normally a communal response (cf., for example, 1QS I 20; II 10, 18).[23]

Whether the fragmentary 11QApocryphal Psalms[a] (11QApPs[a]; 11Q11) should be classified as a sectarian composition is debated.[24] The document consists of four psalms that are similar to the *Songs of the Maskil*, except that they are exorcistic in nature; that is, they were to be recited in order to exorcise demons who had already afflicted persons.[25] Significantly, the text introduces one psalm as an "incantation": "[. . . An incanta]tion ([*l*]*ḥš*) in the name of YHW[H]" (V 4). The last of the four psalms is a variant form of Masoretic Text Psalm 91, a psalm that Talmudic tradition recognizes as a song for the stricken, that is, an incantation against demons (*y. 'Erub.* 10:10; *b. Šebu.* 15b).[26] The exorcistic character of the songs is clear in phrases such as in 11Q11 IV 4–8a:

> YHWH will strike you with a [grea]t b[low] to destroy you[. . .] And in his fury [he will send] against you a powerful angel[to carry out] his [entire comm]and, who [will not show] you mercy, wh[o . . .] over these, who [will bring] you [down] to the great abyss [and to] the deepest [Sheol].[27]

The promise of help from a "powerful angel" (possibly Raphael, mentioned in V 3) is one of several invocations to angels as protectors and warriors in the fight against demons. In the same vein, YHWH is presented as "Commander of the army" (V 8). There are also several references to evil powers, called "demons" (*ḥšdym*; I 9; II 3), "spirits" (*rwḥwt*; II 3, partly reconstructed), and "sons of Bel[ial]" (VI 3), and to Belial himself (V 5, partly reconstructed; possibly called "prince" *ś*[*r*] in II 4). The exorcist is supposed to recite the following segment on behalf of the stricken, or possessed, who in turn responds by saying, "Amen, amen" (V 5b–8a):

> Beli[al] (*bly*[*'l*]) shall come to you, [and] you shall [s]ay to him, "Who are you, [. . .] human(s) (*'dm*) and among the progeny of the Hol[y On]es?" Your presence (is) the presence of [emptin]ess and your horns (are) horns of a dre[a]m. Darkness (are) you and not light, [dece]it and not righteousness. [. . .] Commander of the Army. Yaweh [. . .] you [in] deepest [Sheo]l.[28]

The illnesses are not specified but are referred to in general terms in the text, parallel to Psalm 91, as pestilence and plague (VI 7). These songs were likely used for a variety of illnesses thought to have been caused by demonic affliction.

A short, fragmentary hymn, 8QHymn (8Q5), of which only parts of eight lines in two fragments have been preserved, appears to be of the same genre as 11QApPsᵃ. This hymn is presumably aimed at frightening evil spirits, as indicated by its beginning: "In Your name, [O M]ighty One, I intimidate (*'ny myr'*) and . . ."[29] One additional exorcistic incantation is likely found in 4QIncantation (4Q444), which is made up of six fragments.[30] The phrase "And strengthen yourself by the laws of God, and in order to fight against the spirits of wickedness" (*brwḥy rš'h*) (I 4), as well as the reference to evil spirits in line 8, "[. . . the b]astards and the spirit of uncleanness" ([*m*]*mzrym wrwḥ ḥtm'h*), points to a magical purpose. There are several linguistic and conceptual similarities between 4Q444 and the *Songs of the Maskil*, which strengthens the hypothesis of an intended magical function as well as a sectarian origin.[31]

A clearly magical manuscript is 4Q560 (4QExorcism ar), likely a nonsectarian composition since it is written in Aramaic.[32] Two columns of the text are preserved in one fragment. The first column lists a variety of diseases. The verb *ym* ("to adjure"), used for addressing evil spirits, occurs twice in column two, which indicates the genre, namely, an incantation composed for the exorcism of evil spirits. The main segment reads (4Q560 1 i 2–5):[33]

> 2 [ ] the midwife, the punishment of childbearers, and evil madness, a de[mon]
> 3 [I adjure all you who en]ter into the body, the male Wasting-demon and the female Wasting-demon
> 4 [I adjure you by the name of the YHWH, "*He Who re*]*moves iniquity and transgression*" (Exod 34:7), O Fever-demon and Chills-demon and Chest Pain-demon
> 5 [You are forbidden to disturb by night in dreams or by da]y during sleep, O male Shrine-spirit and female Shrine-spirit, O you demons who breach[34]

The text reflects fear of various diseases and makes little distinction between the demon and the illness it causes. It appears that these illnesses were literally understood as the damaging activities of a demon; the demon was in the fever, in the chills, and so on (a similar view is evident in D in a text about scale disease, as we will see below).[35] The actual possession is described in line 3 in the words "enter into the body" ('*ll bbśr*'), which also reveals the factual state of demon possession as an intrusion of a foreign entity. The reference to God's power to forgive transgressions (line 4) establishes the connection between sin and possession. The text also reflects fear in connection with childbirth. The reference to the midwife may express the worry that a demon (Lilith?) would possess her and thereby get to the baby.[36]

One text, 4Q184 (4QWiles of the Wicked Woman), may be focusing exclusively on a female demonic entity. This wisdom composition dwells on the trappings of Dame Folly, "the strange woman," the metaphor for foolishness in Proverbs 1–9. Highlighting her association with darkness and the underworld, and even references to her demonic physiognomy, Joseph M. Baumgarten perceptively identifies the seductress as a female demon.[37] In contrast to Proverbs, the wicked woman in this text specifically targets righteous men, whom she leads to Sheol.[38] The evil, deceptive powers of the "wicked woman" are remarkably similar to that of the "Angel of Darkness" in 1QS III 22–23.[39]

Although not "magical" per se, 4QHoroscope (4Q186) associates a person's spiritual character with bodily features and links physical imperfections to evil. 4QHoroscope explains how both astrology and physical characteristics reveal moral or spiritual qualities in a person.[40] Accordingly, a human's spirit (*rwḥ*) consists of nine parts, divided between "the House of Light" (*hbt h'wr*) and "the Pit of Darkness" (*hbwr hhwšk*). For example, certain types of thighs and toes are signs that such a person has "six (parts) spirit in the House of Light and three in the Pit of Darkness" (4Q186 1 ii 5–9).[41] The terminology and the idea of classifying individuals according to their affiliation with good or evil recall the discourse on the two spirits in S, which asserts that people *from birth* are influenced by the Spirit of Light or Deceit (1QS III 17–19).[42]

Given the similarities to S, it is likely that "the Pit of Darkness" or "House of Darkness" in 4Q186 refers to the domination of the Spirit of Darkness over humans (cf. 1QS III 20–21). In spite of its emphasis on predestination, 4Q186, like S, acknowledges that no person can be entirely good or entirely evil, since every person has parts belonging to each "house" within himself (or herself?).[43] Nevertheless, it is the dominant affiliation with good or evil that determines a person's nature.

In sum, these texts reveal a deep concern about demons among the sectarians. Indeed, as we will see, evil forces played a central role in the common sectarian ideology that divided both the human and the supernatural spheres into good and evil, light and darkness.

Rules of Exclusion and the Evil Forces

The three lists of exclusions occur in different contexts in the three Qumran documents. M provides instruction for the eschatological battle between the Sons of Light and the Sons of Darkness, a battle that will involve both humans and supernatural beings. In this context, the text prohibits blemished people from entering the war camp with the explanation that "holy angels are with their army" (1QM VII 6). The rules for the war camp in 1QM VII 3–7 are clearly inspired by the laws concerning the war camp in Deut 23:9-14, which, parallel to 1QM, includes rules for the exclusion of a person defiled by bodily discharge and rules for places to relieve oneself outside the camp. Deuteronomy 23 does not, however, mention blemished persons.[44]

The list of exclusions of physically disabled people in 1QSa appears immediately following a list of duties ascribed to members according to age. Although the introduction of 1QSa insists that "this is the rule for all in the Congregation of Israel at the end of days," the many detailed instructions about communal life indicate that the prescriptions for the future mirror a present reality.[45]

The third list appears in D, which reflects a community made up of men, women, and children.[46] Whereas both 1QSa and D bar "blemished" people from entering the assembly, it is noticeable that the list in D appears in the context of the initiation rules (CD XV 1–XVI 6) that regulate the formal entrance of both outsiders (XV 6–7) and children of members who reach maturity (XV 5–6).[47] The regulations about exclusion apparently have a dual function in D: they prohibit the initiation of the physically and mentally disabled (as well as other categories) into the covenant community as full members and also forbid full members, who later become disabled, from entering the meetings of the congregation.[48]

Scholars disagree on whether these categories of people were excluded completely or only partially.[49] It is evident in both D and 1QSa, however, that persons with mental and physical defects (and youth) were living within the community.[50]

The following chart compares the lists of excluded persons in D, 1QSa, and M:

Defects	CD XV 14–17/ 4Q266 8 i 6–9/ 4Q270 6 ii 8–10	1QSa II 3–9	1QM VII 3–6
mental disability	stupid, deranged[51]	tottering old man[52] (who cannot maintain himself)	—
moral inclination	simple minded, errant man[53]	—	—
physical defects	blind, limping, lame, deaf	afflicted in the flesh, crippled in legs or hands, lame, blind, deaf, dumb, stricken by visible blemish[54]	lame, blind, crippled, stricken by permanent blemish
age	youth	old man	youth
sex	—	—	woman[55]
purity	—	any human impurity	impurity in flesh, not purified from discharge
excluded from	entering into the midst of the congregation	taking a stand in the midst of the congregation; standing firm in the midst of the congregation of the men of renown	going into battle
rationale	for the holy angels are in their midst	for holy angels are in their council	for the holy angels are together with their armies

The three documents refer to the presence of "holy angels" as the rationale for excluding these persons. While the three lists include physical defects, only D specifically mentions transgressors and the mentally disabled. Curiously, 1QSa excludes the elderly who are suffering from dementia. While M and 1QSa refer specifically to impure people, D does not. In fact, the only category shared in common among the three documents, despite varying contents, is the list of physical defects. In each case, however, the disabilities are associated with demonic affliction.

Mental Disability[56]

Mental disability was generally seen as evidence of demonic possession.[57] A prime example is the Gerasene man, who was believed to have been possessed by many demons (Mark 5:1-20//Matt 8:28-34//Luke 8:26-39). In this case the man displays a variety of symptoms consistent with severe mental disorder—howling and acting so violent that he has to be chained.[58] A man who is shouting at Jesus in a synagogue and appears mentally unstable is also believed to be possessed by an "unclean spirit" (Mark 1:21-28//Luke 4:31-37). Both of these men are cured through Jesus' exorcism.[59] In the Beelzebul controversy (Mark 3:20-35//Matt 12:22-32//Luke 11:14-23), Jesus is accused of performing exorcism by the power of Beelzebul, "the ruler of the demons," and of being possessed by an unclean spirit himself (Mark 3:22, 30). The reason behind the accusation is that people believe that he is insane (Mark 3:21).[60] These passages show that mental disability was believed to be caused by demonic possession. Consequently, for the sectarians, who shared this worldview, it would have been inconceivable to allow any such individual into their meetings in which angels were present.

Moral Inclination

Several of the above texts suggest that sinning makes one vulnerable to demonic affliction (for example, 1QapGen XX 16–17; 4QPrAb ar; 4QExorcism 1 i 2–5). Similarly, *T. Asher* 1:8-9 describes how the mind of a sinner becomes possessed by Beliar:[61]

> But if the mind is disposed toward evil, all of his deeds are wicked; driving out the good, it accepts the evil and is overmastered by Beliar, who, even when good is undertaken, presses the struggle so as to make the aim of this action into evil, since the devil's storehouse is filled with venom of the evil spirit.

Demons were also widely known to deceive people and cause them to sin. The *Testaments of the Twelve Patriarchs* traces evil feelings to the works of evil spirits, who are named according to their function (for example, spirits of jealousy, envy, falsehood, fornication, anger, and ignorance). These spirits are presented as the root cause of the well-known sins of the patriarchs. So, for example, according to *T. Dan* 1:7, the brothers' murderous scheme against Joseph was due to an evil spirit at work within Dan, urging him to "take this sword, and with it kill Joseph."[62] These spirits, in turn, are in liaison with the Prince of Error, Beliar, who is locked in a cosmic battle with God and his spirits and angels.[63]

The Dead Sea Scrolls, too, indicate that Belial causes humans to sin through his evil spirits.[64] The *Songs of the Maskil* is aimed particularly at those demons who "strike unexpectedly to lead the spirit of understanding astray, and to appall their hearts and their so[ul]" (4Q510 1 4–6). Since the evil forces attempt to corrupt people, observing the "laws of God" serves as a defense in the fight against them. Esther Chazon highlights that in both 4QIncantation (4Q444) and the Songs of the Maskil (4Q511), observing the laws strengthens human beings to fight against the evil spirits.[65]

In the discourse on the two spirits in S, the Angel of Darkness—also called "the Spirit of Deceit" in IV 9—together with "all the spirits of his lot" (*kwl rwhy gwrlw*), cause the Sons of Light to stumble and sin (1QS III 24).[66] Were it not for the Angel of Truth, the Sons of Light would be lost in transgressions (1QS III 24–25). D insists that the majority has unwittingly been deceived by Belial and been caught in his three nets—fornication, arrogance/riches, and defilement of the sanctuary (CD IV 12–18). In addition, according to CD XII 2–3, apostasy is caused by demonic possession: "Each man who is ruled by the spirits of Belial and speaks apostasy, in accordance with the judgment of (one who communicates with) a ghost or a familiar spirit shall he be judged."[67] The text prescribes the death penalty for this type of demonic possession (Lev 20:27). Finally, in 4Q184 (4QWiles of the Wicked Woman), the demonic female entity attacks the righteous man, luring him into apostasy and committing transgressions.

It is, then, the strong link between sin and the evil forces that renders the transgressor ineligible to attend the communal meetings. By committing transgressions, a person reveals that he is under the influence of Belial and his minions and therefore cannot be allowed to enter the sacred meetings where angels are present. The same perspective surfaces in the penal code in D, which excludes transgressors from "the purity" (*hthrh*), for example, a person "who in]sults his fellow without consultation shall be [ex]cluded (from the purities) for one year" (4Q266 10 ii 2).[68] The term "purity" not only refers to a variety of things, such as pure food, but also refers to events considered sacred, particularly communal meetings.[69] In light of the penal code, one may assume that "the errant" person in the list of exclusions in D refers to someone who is temporarily disciplined, or anyone in the process of being expelled, who could thus be labeled "errant."[70]

Physical Defects

Physical disabilities and blemishes are at the core of the three lists. In a general way, S expresses the belief that demons not only cause moral corruption but also present afflictions and suffering: 1QS III 23-24 reads, "And all their physical afflictions (*ngw'yhm*) and the appointed times of their suffering (are caused) by the dominion of his [the Angel of Darkness's] hostility. And all the spirits of his lot cause to stumble the Sons of Light."[71] "Their afflictions" refers to physical ailments (cf. 1QSa II 4). This example from S confirms the centrality of this basic belief of the sect that demons cause illnesses and disabilities. In order to understand in more detail how people at the turn of the Common Era envisaged the connection between evil spirits and disease, we will revisit 4Q560 (4QExorcism), followed by an examination of possible connections between scale disease and demons in D, and end with general views about illness in the New Testament.

The "magical texts" provide a detailed glimpse into how demonic possession was understood. Noticeable is the explicit reference to illnesses as demons in 4Q560 (4QExorcism) in the phraseology "O Fever-demon, O Chills-demon" (4Q560 1 i 4), which illuminates the belief that the demons can enter the body and cause specific diseases and even be personified with the disease. A text on scale disease ("leprosy") in D (4Q266 6 i) sheds further light on the demonic aetiology of illnesses. The text prescribes how a priest should examine a person for scale disease, a diagnosis that had severe repercussions in terms of impurity for the sick person in the community (Leviticus 13). The examination concerns symptoms of the disease in the hair and the skin, and in this context the text refers to "the spirit," *hrwḥ* (4Q266 6 5b–8a):

> And the rule *vacat* for a scall of the head or the bea[rd . . . when the priest sees] that the spirit has entered (*b'h hrwḥ*) the head or the beard, taking hold of the blood vessels (*bgyd*) and [the malady has spro]uted from beneath under the hair, turning its appearance to fine yellowish; for it is like a plant which has a worm under it *vacat* which severs its root and makes its blossom wither.[72]

Baumgarten suggests that "the attribution of scale disease to the *rwḥ* in our text [involved] the intrusion of evil or demonic influences."[73] This view is supported by the frequent use of *rwḥ* with reference to evil spirits in other Qumran scrolls. Furthermore, evil spirits are associated with "blood vessels" (*tkmy bśr*) in 1QS, 4Q444 (4QIncantation), and 4Q511 (Songs of the Maskil).[74] Although a different term is used for "blood vessels" in these documents compared to 4Q266, the location of evil spirits in blood vessels strengthens the suggestion that *rwḥ* refers to an evil spirit in D (4Q266 6 i 6). Thus, the 4Q266 text on scale disease suggests that the evil spirit moved around in the body as it spread the disease.[75]

Illness is fused with the evil forces in the claim that Jesus "rebuked the fever" of Peter's mother-in-law.[76] Similar phraseology occurs in 1QapGen XX 29.[77] The evil spirits have not merely caused the illness and then departed, but in fact have remained within the body, controlling or "possessing" all or parts of the body.

Examples of total body possession include the Gerasene "demoniac" as well as the epileptic boy whom Jesus cures through exorcism. The symptoms of epilepsy, that is, convulsion and falling, were naturally taken in the ancient world as evidence of full demonic possession (cf. Mark 9:20-22). In other cases, the demon invades the body in part, as in the case of Peter's mother-in-law, in whom the spirit manifests itself through the fever (Luke 4:39). In the Gospels, blindness, deafness, and inability to speak are associated with spirit possession.[78] Matthew 12:22 refers to "a demoniac who was blind and mute" whom Jesus cures so that he can "speak and see." In Luke, Jesus cures a mute person by exorcising a "mute demon" (11:14). Consequently, there appear to be differences in degrees of "spirit possession." Ultimately, however, Satan is responsible for sickness. In Luke 13:10-17, Jesus refers to a crippled woman as "a daughter of Abraham whom Satan bound for eighteen long years."

The strong association of illnesses and disabilities with demonic activities, evident in these examples, helps explains why Qumran texts disqualify those suffering from disabilities such as blindness, dumbness, and deafness from entering into the sacred sphere of the community. In this context, 4Q186 (4QHoroscope) demonstrates the extent to which physical perfection is connected with light and physical imperfection with darkness. The explicit connection between physical imperfection and evil influence in 4Q186 strongly supports the main argument of this chapter, that the exclusion of blemished persons in the Qumran texts in part stems from a belief in demonic influence.

Impurity

Whereas D does not refer to the impure in its list of excluded categories of people, both 1QSa and M ban persons suffering from any kind of impurity.[79] Because the holy angels mark the space as sacrosanct, we may conclude that the exclusion of impure personas is taken for granted in D's rule. The exclusion of the impure from sacred space was deeply ingrained in the Jewish cultural universe. Impurity, like disability, was often connected with demonic activities in Jewish thought at the turn of the era. In the New Testament, the close link between demons and impurity is explicit in the common term "unclean spirit" (*pneuma akatharton*). The same expression, *rwḥ ṭm'h*, occurs several times in the scrolls, which suggests that demons, in addition to causing disease, have a polluting quality.[80] Todd Klutz points to the common interface between demonology and impurity in the Gospel stories. The Gerasene demoniac lived among the tombs, a highly impure space; his "unclean spirits" were transferred to a herd of swine, which are unclean animals.[81] For Klutz, the exorcism story of the Gerasene demoniac in Luke 8:33-37 is in effect a purification rite.[82]

Philip Alexander draws on Mary Douglas's definition of impurity to argue for a link between impurity and demonic presence in the Dead Sea Scrolls:

> One of the fundamental characteristics of polluting objects or beings is that they tend not to fit into society's categories: their classification is ambiguous. . . . This is certainly the case with demons. A demon which invades a human body is out of place: it should not be there, and as a result it pollutes and causes problems. Indeed, if we were to develop the Enochic aetiology of demons in a certain way, we could argue that the very existence of demons pollutes the world.[83]

In 4Q266 6 5b–8a, the evil spirit invades the body and causes scale disease, which results in the highest degree of ritual impurity for the afflicted person. 4QTohorot A (4Q274), which dictates rules of contact for different categories of impurity carriers, insists that a person suffering from scale disease should keep apart from other ritually impure persons.[84] The text reveals an intricate system of laws regulating how impurity spreads among *already impure persons*. Accordingly, impurity carriers of a higher level can transmit impurity by touch to impure persons of a lower level, thereby changing the impurity status of the latter. Highlighting the perceived power of impurity, Jacob Milgrom claims that for the Qumran community, the concept of impurity is demonic: "Clearly, at work here is a conception of impurity that is vital and active. Moreover, since Qumran espouses a cosmogenic doctrine akin to dualism—ascribing impurity to the forces of Belial—its concept of impurity is more than dynamic; it is demonic."[85] In this context, it is noteworthy that of the three nets of Belial, one concerns pollution (defilement of the sanctuary) (CD IV 17). Similarly, 1QS IV 10 attributes "unclean worship" to the Spirit of Deceit. More telling, however, is the reference to the general purification that comes with the destruction of everything evil at the end of the "dominion of deceit" in 1QS IV 20–22:[86]

> He will utterly destroy every spirit of deceit (*kwl rwḥ 'wlh*) from the veins
> of his (a human's) flesh. He will purify him (humanity) by the holy spirit
> from all ungodly acts and sprinkle upon him the spirit of truth like waters
> of purification, (to purify him) from all the abominations of falsehood and
> from being polluted by a spirit of impurity.

It has been widely recognized that concepts of sin and impurity are interconnected in the scrolls.[87] When illness causes impurity, all three fields—sin, impurity, and illness—converge, most obviously in the case of scale disease. Just as Miriam was punished by a scale disease (Deut 24:8) that made her impure, so the one suffering from scale disease is on a list of transgressors in D (4Q270 2 ii 12). The actual cause of the disease is identified in D as an evil spirit (4Q266 6 i). It is no surprise, then, that impurity excluded a person from the presence of the angels, and hence from communal meetings and the eschatological war camp.

Women and Youth

In M, women and youths form special subclasses that are not linked to demonic activities. Youths and women are differentiated from the other excluded categories in that they are prohibited from entering "their camps" (*mḥnwtm*; 1QM VII 3–4), while the disabled and the impure are not allowed to "go with them to battle" (*mlḥmh*; lines 5 and 6). The angels are associated with "the battle" and "the army" (line 6) and not the camp per se. Consequently, in this context the reference to the presence of the angels as a rationale for exclusion refers particularly to the impure and the impaired, but likely does not extend to the women and youths who are mentioned earlier.

Why were women and youths excluded from the camp? Traditionally, soldiers have been men, not women or children. By excluding women and youths from the war camp, M makes explicit what is implicit in the biblical accounts. Women are excluded because they constituted a threat to the purity of men by their very presence, corresponding to the traditional taboo against sex in connection with the holy war (for example, 2 Sam 11:11). The exclusion of boys from the war camp in M is related to the age requirements (1QM VI 13—VII 3) and may stem from a concern for the safety of children.

Unlike M, D does include youths in its list of excluded categories. This exclusion may reflect an underlying fear of demonic affiliation. A youth has not been formally initiated yet, according to the prescriptions in D. It is revealing that the angel Mastema (an alternative name for Belial or Satan) is said to turn from a person when he takes the oath at the entrance; as the ritual reads, "On the day when a man takes upon himself an oath to return to the Torah of Moses, the angel Mastema shall turn aside from him if he fulfills his words" (CD XVI 4–5).[88] Menahem Kister explains that the entrance ritual in itself was seen as a ritual of exorcism.[89] Hence, youths, as not full members, were viewed as potentially being under the influence, or possession, of evil powers until the moment of their entrance (CD XVI 4–5).

Because of the Angels . . .

The Dead Sea Scrolls reflect the widespread belief that the gap between the earthly and heavenly realms can be breached. Many documents envisage a communion between angels and humans, suggesting that the community members have in some respects joined the heavenly host. Thus, a segment from a hymn in 1QS reads:

> My eyes have gazed on that which is eternal, on wisdom concealed from men, on knowledge and wise design (hidden) from the sons of men; on the fountain of righteousness and on a storehouse of power, on a spring of glory (hidden) from the assembly of flesh. God has given them to His chosen ones as an everlasting possession, and has caused them to inherit the lot of the Holy Ones (*bgwrl qdwšym*). He has joined their assembly to the Sons of Heaven (*bny šmym*) to be a Council of the Community, a foundation of the Building of Holiness, and eternal Plantation throughout all ages to come. (1QS XI 5–8)[90]

This segment highlights the difference in status between ordinary humans ("the sons of men") and the community that has been elected to join the angels.[91] More specifically, the scrolls express the fellowship between humans and angels in the context of worship, in communal meetings, and, in the future, at the end-time war and the paradise-like life on earth that will follow when all the evil forces have been destroyed.[92]

The ability to praise God in communion with angels is a recurring theme in many liturgical texts; common worship is expressed most poignantly in the *Songs of the Sabbath Sacrifice*, which, in evocative, vivid language and in great detail, describe angelic worship in the heavenly sanctuary. Their function, according to Carol Newsom, "was to create and manipulate a virtual experience, the experience of being present in the heavenly temple and in the presence of angelic priests who serve there."[93] Baumgarten calls the literature "an early form of congregational mysticism."[94] Liturgical communion with angels could function as protection against evil forces, which we have seen with regard to the *Songs of the Maskil*. The explicit purpose of the songs is to frighten away evil spirits (4Q511 8 4). Lines 6–9 of fragment 8 refer to the protection the speaker finds with the angels:

> God has made me [dwell] in the shelter of the Almighty . . . [in the shadow of his ha]nds he has hidden me . . . [He has concea]led me among his holy ones . . . [in unis]on with his holy ones . . . [giving th]anks [to] God.[95]

In his thorough study of "liturgical communion with angels" in the scrolls, Björn Frennesson concludes that nearness to the heavenly world is possible because "men elected by grace . . . have been raised from the dust of nothingness and ignorance to share in divine mysteries and have a common lot with the angels in praise and continual newness."[96] In order to become companions of the angels, the sectarians had to imitate the angels in purity and perfection.[97] Examining a broad range of literature from Qumran, Devorah Dimant lists a number of characteristics that angels and community members share, including forming a special community, existing in perfect purity, having no sin in their midst, and possessing divine wisdom.[98] John J. Collins traces the alleged celibacy of (some) sectarians to their aspirations to an angelic life.[99]

The sectarians had already joined the angels in the struggle against the forces of Belial (the Angel of Darkness), which included demons and wicked people. The deep division and constant struggle between the forces of Light and Evil would escalate into a cataclysmic, final war, when human and angelic forces from both camps would fight side by side in a battle that would end with victory for the forces of Light. The sectarians interpreted their present realities from the perspective of this basic division between good and evil; in the words of Dimant:

> Seeing themselves as part of the hosts of Lights, the Qumranites viewed all their political conflicts and theological controversies in terms of this metaphysical struggle. . . . Moreover, in this struggle each human group was both supported by angels of the same camp, and opposed by angels of the rival one.[100]

In this apocalyptic climate, no trace of the opposite, evil camp could be accepted in those particular spheres—the council meeting, the final war, and perhaps particular worship services[101]—where the community would experience close encounter with the angels. Such a sentiment is clear in the words of 4Q511 1 5–7 (4QSongs of the Maskil): "Let them rejoice before the righteous God, with sho[uts of joy for] salvation *for the[re is no] destroyer within their borders nor do evil spirits walk among them.*"[102]

Conclusion

I have examined the prominence of the belief in demons and evil spirits within the Qumran sect and have proposed a link between the categories of excluded persons on the Qumran lists and the fear of demonic power. To exclude people who were directly or indirectly influenced by demonic forces became an important defense strategy for the sect in order to preserve its inner core pure and perfect, untouched by the outside forces of evil. Such a stance makes perfect sense in light of the Qumran community's symbolic universe, which divided human and angelic spheres into two diametrically opposite camps.

Although the sectarians belonged to the lot of Light, the evil forces presented a real, opposing force that threatened to penetrate their boundaries and influence the Sons of Light. The literature from Qumran testifies to the occasional success of the evil forces in this regard, which was manifested, as we have seen, primarily in transgressions by individual members, impurity, and physical afflictions. In addition, general beliefs about demons in the Second Temple period link mental disabilities closely with demonic affliction, which is a main concern in the list of exclusions in D.

In some regards, the Qumran sect identified itself as a pure and perfect sanctuary for worship; hence, the members naturally adopted Leviticus's laws concerning blemishes that disqualified priests from serving in the temple. An important aspect underlying this incorporation of priestly ideals was a real concern about demons, which the explicit reference to the angels indicates. As a pure sanctuary where humans and angels could meet, the community had to be vigilant about the threat posed by the forces of evil. Accordingly, in defense against the demonic forces and in order to continue enjoying the company of angels, the sectarians excluded from their most sacred spheres and activities all people who potentially had been affected by demons and evil spirits. The reference to the presence of angels that concludes each of the three lists of exclusions explains in just a few words the underlying metaphysical reality in which the forces of good and evil were locked in a battle. The sectarians, who saw themselves as the Sons of Light, took an active role in this cosmic battle as they endeavored to maintain purity and perfection in the presence of angels for the short time remaining before the final destruction of all the evil powers and the beginning of a new, glorious era.

9. The Search for the Common Judaic Understanding of God's Kingship

Anne Moore

Scholars of Second Temple Judaism and Christian origins have debated the meaning of the kingdom of God for over a century, and within this discussion, one axiom has remained constant. Since the kingdom of God is not explicitly defined or explained in any of the Jewish or early Christian texts, there must have been a shared understanding of God's kingship on which the various Jewish writers and the historical Jesus based their specific understandings or interpretations. Yet the primary sources testify to a diversity of meaning associated with the kingship or kingdom of God. This diversity includes both literary context and content. The diversity of literary context includes apocalyptic texts (*T. Mos.* 10) and sapiential compositions (Wis 6:4; *Sent. Sextus* 311); Hellenistic Jewish writings (*Sib. Or.* 3:97-161) and Aramaic Targumim (*Tg. Isa.* 24:23b); prophetic writings (Jer 46:18; 48:15) and psalmic literature (Psalm 145), as well as prayer verses (Eighteen Benedictions) and Qumran literature (4QShirSabb).[1] The kingdom is associated with (1) the pursuit of wisdom (Wis 10:10); (2) the acceptance of Torah (Philo, *Spec.* 4.164); (3) the eternal nature of God (Tob 13:2), and (4) the future acceptance of God's sovereignty among the nations (*Jub.* 1:28). Despite the diversity and variety of the literary contexts and the meanings of the kingship/kingdom of God, none of the texts engages in an explanation or redefinition. The texts assume there is a common or shared meaning on which they base their specific usage or view.

In this essay, I argue that the kingship/kingdom of God represents, in a microcosm, the dynamic of commonality and diversity that E. P. Sanders explored in his work on common Judaism. I propose that there was a common understanding of the kingship/ kingdom of God arising from the common Scripture of Second Temple Judaism—

the Hebrew Bible. The common understanding of the kingdom of God is associated with the metaphor "God is king" both explicitly, when Yahweh is linked with various permutations of *mlk* ("king"), and implicitly, when other attributes, actions, and trappings associated with human kingship are linked with God. Marc Zvi Brettler rightly observes that this association of God with human kingship results in "the predominate relational metaphor used of God in the Bible."[2] However, although this root metaphor does not have a single unified meaning, there is a "closed" set of meanings for understanding God in terms of relationship. This closed set permits a range of diverse meanings that is evident in specific usages of the metaphor in different literary contexts and contents. The diversity reflects shifts in understandings of the metaphor, or different ways groups understood or interpreted the metaphor. This diversity concerning the relationship of God as king is evident in three different ways: (1) Yahweh as the sovereign of Israel; (2) God as eternal suzerain of world, and (3) Lord as monarch of the disadvantaged and marginalized populace. These three different interpretations or versions of the metaphor are evident in the Hebrew Bible, and they are found in the diverse expressions represented in the Second Temple Jewish literature and early expressions of the Jesus and Christian movements.

"God Is King" as Symbol

There are two reasons why scholars of Second Temple Judaism and Christian origins have generally failed to acknowledge the dynamic of commonality and diversity regarding the kingship/kingdom of God. First, scholars of Christian origins have dominated the debate over the meaning of the kingship/kingdom of God, and in doing so, they have focused primarily on the New Testament and the texts deemed significant for understanding the historical Jesus, such as the prophetic writings in the Hebrew Bible or specific texts of the Old Testament Pseudepigrapha. Even for those who attempt to situate early Christianity within the broader spectrum of early Judaism, first-century Jewish sources tend to be mined for material useful for a reconstruction of the historical Jesus. The concept of the kingship/kingdom of God in Second Temple Judaism is rarely a focused topic for discussion, except for the revised dissertation by Odo Camponovo, *Königtum, Königsherrshaft und Reich Gottes in den frühjüdischen Schriften*. The dissertation employs Norman Perrin's understanding of symbol and myth as a means of understanding God's kingship, and therefore it arrives at conclusions that are similar to those of earlier scholars.[3] Typically, scholars of the Hebrew Bible have been more interested in the origins of the kingship of God than in its expressions in Second Temple Judaism.[4]

A second problem is methodological. Earlier studies categorized "the kingdom of God" as a symbol and hence adopted a methodological approach that obscured rather than revealed the diversity of the concept. This classification and its associated assumptions are intimately connected with the work of Perrin, particularly his book *Jesus and the Language of the Kingdom*. Perrin combined the literary analysis of Amos Wilder, the discussion of symbol by Phillip Wheelwright, and the semiotic work of Paul Ricoeur for his study.[5] Perrin advocated the use of literary-critical methods in the analysis of the texts pertaining to the kingdom of God and the reclassification of the kingship of God from concept or idea to symbol. Wheelwright's steno-symbol and tensive symbol became pivotal in Perrin's theory of the historical trajectory of the kingdom/kingship symbol. A steno-symbol has a one-to-one relationship with its referent. A tensive symbol has a "set of meanings that can neither be exhausted nor adequately expressed by any one referent."[6] According to Perrin, the kingdom of God was originally a tensive symbol that referred to "the myth of the activity of God as king on behalf of his people."[7] In Second Temple Judaism, however, the kingdom of God became a steno-symbol for God's future and final eschatological act of redemption on behalf of his people—the new ideal age. Perrin's historical trajectory of the kingdom of God symbol was based on theories associated with the development of the Hebrew Bible and the history-of-religions school's hypothesis about the transition from Israelite religion, with its affinities to the religions of the ancient Near East, to Second Temple Judaism, with its focus on eschatology. Therefore, according to the symbol-myth theory, the kingship/kingdom of God in Second Temple Judaism was viewed as a reference for the restoration of God's kingship over the world at the end of history.

This eschatological or apocalyptic designation of the kingdom of God is challenged by three observations. First, the kingdom of God is seldom found in the Second Temple Jewish texts that are concerned with the end of history.[8] Second, the Tanakh, the Pseudepigrapha, and the Apocrypha contain references to God's kingdom or kingship that are not eschatological (Pss 24:7-10; 29:1-10; 68:17; 145; *Jub.* 1:27-28; 12:19; 50:9; *Pss. Sol.* 2:18-37; 5:18; Wis 6:4; 10:10). Third, there were alternative interpretations of the kingship of God, such as those associated with the search for wisdom or adherence to Torah (Wis 6:4; 10:10; Philo, *Spec.* 4.164).

These sources cast some doubt on Perrin's theory about the kingdom of God symbol and its accompanying myth and history. The texts present varied and diverse expressions of God's kingdom and kingship, and hence this diversity works against the notion that the kingdom of God is a symbol. As noted by Wheelwright, a symbol is characterized by its stability, permanence, and frequency.[9] On the basis of Wheelwright's analysis, the kingdom or kingship of God does not function symbolically in Second Temple Judaism.

"God Is King" as Metaphor

I take a different approach by considering "the kingdom of God" as a metaphor rather than a symbol. This is not a unique approach. It has appeared, for example, in Dan O. Via's review of Perrin's *Jesus and the Language of the Kingdom*,[10] as well as in the work of James D. G. Dunn,[11] Gerd Theissen and Annette Merz,[12] and numerous others.[13]

Further, the shift from symbol to metaphor is not an issue of semantics.[14] The analysis of the kingdom of God as symbol uses methodology and paradigms from semiotics and literary criticism. The analysis of the kingdom of God as metaphor adopts paradigms, approaches, and insights from cognitive linguistics and literary analysis.

In *The Philosophy of Rhetoric*, I. A. Richards writes:

> In the simplest formulation, when we use metaphor we have two thoughts of different things active together, and supported by a single word or phrase, whose meaning is the resultant of their interaction.[15]

In other words, metaphors are not simply literal statements. The meaning of a metaphor rests with the interaction or "interillumination" between two systems of concepts or ideas connected with the literal words. The interpretation or meaning of the metaphor depends on the juxtaposition of or interaction between both the similarities and the dissimilarities between the vehicle field and the topic domain. In the metaphor "God is king," the topic domain, God, is viewed through the filter or lens of human kingship. Those aspects, attributes, or actions of God that may be understood in terms of human kingship will be highlighted, and the other aspects, attributes, or actions will be suppressed. The system of associated commonplaces focuses on semantics. It is recognized that words or a system of associated commonplaces may be part of a semantic field. A semantic field includes related words and concepts that are united by similar content.[16] Semantic fields explain how a metaphor may be extended and yet maintain a level of consistency in meaning. For example, kingship is part of several semantic fields that include law and judgment, palaces and thrones, and war and protection. Therefore, a full analysis of God's kingship would, for example, include occurrences of the divine throne or scepter and ideas of king as both lawgiver and judge.

The systems of meaning will include the connotations derived from the public discourse or culture.[17] This means that the system of associated commonplaces will change as there are shifts and alterations in the public discourse or culture due to historical events and experiences. Semantic fields involve a process of evolution. In other words, the system of associated commonplaces for God and king will draw upon the connotations of God and king as they are experienced, interpreted, discussed, and examined by the people of Israel. The system of commonplaces for "king" includes ideas about Israelite kings, historical experiences of various forms of kingship including non-Israelite, and ideal visions. Owing to various historical events regarded as pivotal and recorded in the Jewish texts, the system of commonplaces includes views of kings drawn from Israel's experience of the Egyptian, Assyrian, Babylonian, Persian, and Hellenistic empires. Experiences with the Hasmonean dynasty and the Roman imperial system would introduce other connotations of kingship into the system of commonplaces. Indeed, the semantic fields employed in some metaphors are highly conditioned by the history and religious mythology of the Israelites and Jews.

The final aspect of the cognitive theory of metaphor is pragmatics—that is, the relationship between words and their users. "Shared strategies" between the speaker and hearer are required in order to identify a statement as metaphorical and to establish the context for "deciphering" the metaphor. Simply stated, "The process of identifying metaphorical utterances is context-dependent."[18] In the case of the "kingdom of God" metaphor, the texts of the Hebrew Bible provide the context. Given the literary nature of these texts, the approach to the metaphor is informed by literary or poetic criticism.

Commonality within the "God Is King" Metaphor in the Hebrew Bible

Marc Zvi Brettler's exploration of the "God is king" metaphor focuses on the interaction of the semantic field of Israelite kingship as it was mapped onto God in the creation of the kingship metaphor. He concludes:

> The metaphor "God is king" was extremely productive in ancient Israel as evidenced by the large number of associated commonplaces between God as king and the Israelite king. They share the royal appellations, *mlk*, "king," *r'h*, "shepherd," *'dwn*, "master," *špṭ*, "judge," *nyr*, "lamp," *mgn*, "shield" and probably *mšl*, "ruler." . . . They are both depicted as wise, wealthy, and strong. God, like the human king sits on a throne and sets his feet on a footstool. Some of the same terminology is used to refer to the royal and divine palace; God's palace (the Temple) is called *byt yhwh*, "the house of the LORD" parallel to *byt hmlk*, "the house of the king," and the term *hykl*, "palace," used to refer to the Temple (or its parts), is borrowed from the human royal sphere.[19]

Brettler demonstrated that any full understanding of God's kingship requires moving beyond the use of *melek*. Owing to its nature as a metaphor, "God is king" drew selectively from the associated commonplaces of human kingship. There was a "closed" set of meanings due to several factors, including (1) the limited semantic field of human kingship; (2) the inappropriateness of associating specific human activities with God such as the acquisition of wealth, and (3) the focus on "the incomparability of God as divine king."[20] This third factor resulted in images such as Yahweh's eternal and cosmic kingship and the absolute nature of God's kingly judgment because of his role as the lawgiver; however, the idea of a "closed" set of meanings for the metaphor does not suggest that there is a single view of the "God is king" metaphor. There is a general set of understandings that results in a commonality, indeed, a limitation of the metaphor that expresses a common core of understandings. There is a framework or a common core to the "God is king" metaphor that emerges in the Hebrew Bible. It is quite likely that the various groups in Second Temple Judaism understood this common core, given the metaphor's status as the predominant relational metaphor. It is this common core that permitted them to employ the metaphor without engaging in a full process of explanation.

Based upon Brettler's study, this common core focused on the relationship demonstrated in Yahweh's actions as king and the human response to the divine monarch. It is a relationship evident in the kingly roles of judge, protector, and defender. These roles include (1) strong and mighty acts associated with war, (2) righteous and just deeds associated with maintenance of law, and (3) gentle and compassionate actions connected with roles of the shepherd. Finally, Yahweh's kingship is eternal.

The Diversity of the "God Is King" Metaphor

The interactive nature of the semantic fields within a metaphor permits and facilitates diversity, even while maintaining a common core or consistency. As noted by Brettler in reference to the "God is king" metaphor:

> Individual uses of the metaphor in different contexts and in different time-periods recall different specific entailments of God's kingship. Some of the changes are determined by shifts in the structure of the vehicle, human kingship, throughout time. For example, in the post-exilic period, when *mštym* "royal attendants" and royal spies joined the royal bureaucracy, the divine court changed correspondingly to incorporate these roles. Different ways the metaphor was unpacked may also have been determined by different perceptions that various groups in ancient Israel had about God. . . . Thus, one group may accept certain entailments of God's kingship while another may strongly reject them.[21]

The different ways that "God is king" is unpacked are vividly demonstrated in the various types of relationship Yahweh has with Israel, the nations, and the populace. First, the metaphor illustrates the relation between Yahweh as the "creator" and sovereign and his subject, Israel (Deut 33:5; Isa 43:15; Psalms 95; 99; 149). In terms of the interaction of the semantic fields, the vehicle field, as demonstrated by Brettler, is drawn from the semantic field of Israelite kingship. However, literary contexts narrow the topic domain to the semantic field associated with the God of the exodus. In other words, the metaphor is part of the covenantal language of the Hebrew Bible in which God acts as *Israel's sovereign*. Second, in other literary contexts, the metaphor draws on the semantic field associated with overlords or the great kings of Assyria, Egypt, and Babylon. In these occurrences, the focus on the relationship is between Yahweh as the *eternal suzerain* and the nations of the world. Third, specific literary contexts place the metaphor within the realm of a collective experience associated with the widow, orphan, and outcast. In these contexts, the semantic fields of judge and king are combined to present Yahweh as the *monarch of the people*, who is the protector of and provider for the prisoner and the oppressed. The common core of the metaphor possessed three views of the relationship aspect of the kingship metaphor: *Yahweh as Israel's sovereign*; *the Lord as eternal suzerain*; and *God as monarch of the people*.

Yahweh as Israel's Sovereign

The occurrences of the "God is king" metaphor in Exod 15:1b-18; 19:3-6; Deut 33:2-5; 1 Samuel 8–12; Jer 10:1-16; and Isaiah 41–44 clearly reveal the relational aspect of Yahweh as Israel's sovereignty. In these texts, Yahweh's sovereignty is intimately connected to the events of the exodus and the Sinai covenant. Yahweh, as divine sovereign, claims Israel's allegiance because, in the fulfillment of his kingly duties, he acted as Israel's warrior, lawmaker, judge, and creator. Israel, as the subject of the divine sovereign, demonstrates its allegiance through adherence to the Torah, through which Israel retains a unique status, separate from the other nations.

The declaration of Yahweh as king occurs for the first time, within the canonical order of the text, in the Song of the Sea, the poem in which Moses outlines God's actions in the exodus (Exod 15:1b-18).[22] God's sovereignty as well as God's covenantal relationship with Israel are based on this miraculous event. Yahweh's kingship is based on the anticipated guidance of Israel through the wilderness into the promised land, the establishment of a sanctuary, and the defeat of Pharaoh's army. All performed as part of God's redemption and acquisition of Israel. The Song of the Sea establishes the foundation of the "God is king" metaphor as it outlines the deeds on which Yahweh's sovereignty is based. Yahweh's deeds are only one aspect of the relationship; they are part of the informative function of the metaphor. The metaphor in Exod 15:1b-18 provides a specific perspective for visualizing the relationship between God and Israel. Metaphors also have a performative function intended to create new attitudes and actions.[23]

This performative function is specifically detailed in Exod 19:3-6 and Deut 33:2-5. Exod 19:3-6 is classified as a covenantal *Gattung*, or a proposal for entering into a covenant.[24] The text acknowledges that God's kingship extends over the whole world.[25] However, Israel has a special relationship with the universal divine suzerain as a result of the exodus. The relational aspect of the metaphor includes not only what Yahweh did in order to form a relationship with Israel; it includes Israel's obligation for maintaining this relationship (Exod 19:5). The "God is king" metaphor in Exod 19:3-6 evokes the performative aspect of metaphor. First, Exod 19:4 summarizes succinctly the events of Exod 15:1b-18: "You have seen what I did to the Egyptians, and how I bore you on eagles' wings and brought you to myself." Second, after establishing the basis for the relationship between the divine king and Israel, the subsequent two verses outline the obligations of the divine sovereign's subjects. Israel must adhere to God's voice and covenant to remain a possession of the divine king. The "righteous" and "holy" character of the people is emphasized. The topic domain for the metaphor remains the God of the exodus. However, there is a shift from the work of the divine king to the people's obligations and demonstrations of allegiance to their holy sovereign. In Deut 33:2-5, the obligation and allegiance are clearly associated with the adherence to Torah.[26]

God as Eternal Suzerain

In the Hebrew Bible, Yahweh appears not only as Israel's sovereign but also as the universal eternal suzerain.[27] As already noted, Yahweh's universal sovereignty is implied in Exod 19:3-6 with Israel's election over the other nations. It is explicitly stated in various prophetic and poetic writings (Jer 10:7; Dan 4:31; Pss 9:7-8; 22:26; 47; 96:10; 103:19). In these texts, Yahweh is called the "king of nations," or there is reference to his "kingly power over the world." The eternal nature of Yahweh's sovereignty is a major aspect of his kingship.[28] The image of Yahweh as suzerain is drawn from the use of specific language, the association of this language with claims of Yahweh's universal kingship, and specific actions associated with suzerains. The term that informs the use of the "God is king" metaphor is *gadol* ("great"). In the Hebrew Bible, this word is used predominantly in reference to the divine suzerain or foreign kings. The foreign kings are those who acted as overlords for the great empires such as Assyria (2 Kgs 18:19, 28; Isa 36:4, 13) or Egypt (Ezek 31:2, 7). It is only in the postexilic period that one finds *gadol* used for Israelite kings. More specifically, it is limited to Solomon (Ezra 5:11; 1 Chr 29:25; 2 Chr 1:1). The reference to Yahweh as a *melek gadol* ("great king") suggests that the vehicle field is the kingship associated with the overlords of empires. This is confirmed when the various literary contexts for the combination of *melek gadol* and *yhwh* (or other names of God) are taken into consideration. In Jeremiah 10, both the greatness of Yahweh's nation and his status as "king of the nations" are declared (vv. 6-7). In Ps 47:2, Yahweh is the "great king over all the earth," and in Ps 95:3, Yahweh is "a great King above all gods" (see also Mal 1:14; Pss 99:1-3; 145).

Yahweh's role as universal suzerain is evident in his ability to act as an overlord who establishes and removes kings or summons various human monarchs to do his bidding. In the "Oracles against the Nations" in Jeremiah (46:1—51:64), the "God is king" metaphor is employed three times (46:18; 48:1; 51:57). The basic theme of the section is Yahweh's use of King Nebuchadnezzar to defeat the Egyptians (46:13-28), Yahweh's judgment against Moab (48:1-47), and Yahweh's subsequent destruction of Babylon through the king of the Medes (51:11, 28). Yahweh's control of historical events is visualized through the metaphor of kingship. However, in this context, the vehicle field for the metaphor is the overlord or suzerain who rules through client kings. This image of the divine suzerain is found also in Deutero-Isaiah. In Isa 41:21-29, Yahweh, the "king of Jacob," validates his continuing relationship with Israel through the claim to control history. The specific example provided is the ascension of Cyrus (41:2-3, 25; 45:1).

The shift in the semantic field from Israelite kingship to suzerain results in an alteration in the relational aspect of the metaphor. Yahweh is not merely acting as a puppet master on the world stage as he employs kings in various war campaigns or deposes and raises monarchs. The relationship between the eternal suzerain and the nations is expressed through the nations' worship and praise of Yahweh. This response to Yahweh as eternal suzerain is found also in the Psalms (96; 97; 99) and in the prophetic literature, in particular the book of Daniel.[29]

The "God is king" metaphor shifts meaning in various literary contexts as the vehicle field draws from the ideas and concepts associated with suzerain. In these employments of the metaphor, Yahweh is the eternal universal suzerain who controls history and whose kingship is acknowledged through worship and praise from the nations.

Lord as Monarch of the People

The third set of literary contexts in which the "God is king" metaphor generally appears is in psalms spoken by individuals (Psalms 5; 9; 10; 22; 102; 103; 145; 146). This specific use of the kingship metaphor is best illustrated through a detailed analysis of Psalm 145.

Psalm 145 emphatically states its major theme, God's kingship. The first line of the psalm begins with the praise and exaltation of "my God, the king" (v. 1). Further, only Psalm 145 employs the definite article before the title *melek*. It is *the* king whom the psalm describes, *the* divine sovereign. Verses 11-13 are "the geographical and also thematic center of the psalm."[30] The major *Leitwort* in these verses is *malkut* ("kingdom"). In other words, the psalm centers on God's kingdom. Wilfred Watson's investigation of the psalm's literary techniques demonstrated a chiastic pattern that drew attention to the psalm's main theme, God's eternal and universal kingship.[31] These numerous and various literary devices focus one's attention on God's kingship.

In this psalm, Yahweh's kingship is not only praised (vv. 1-2); it is proclaimed. In response to Yahweh as *gadol* ("great") (v. 3), one is called on not only to praise but also to speak. There is a clustering of words drawn from a common semantic field that affirms the intensity of the proclamation. However, there is also variety in the proclamation of Yahweh's kingship, from spoken meditations to babbling to loud singing. In vv. 11-12, they will tell about the kingdom of God.

Verses 3 and 14 form an *inclusio*. Both Yahweh's kingdom and the proclamation of it will endure through the generations. The *inclusio* also indicates that the proclamation of Yahweh's kingship will include the attributes described in vv. 8-10. These attributes focus on Yahweh's compassion (vv. 8-9), which is evident in his "upholding all those who are falling and lifting up all who are bending low" (v. 14). God's actions demonstrate his "righteousness" and "faithfulness." These are some of the attributes that constitute Yahweh's kingdom.

Psalm 145 has a specific interpretation of the "God is king" metaphor that is based on ideas shared with psalms of individual complaint and thanksgiving (Psalms 5; 9; 10; 103). The divine king's "strength" and "glory" are woven together with the protection and care of the disadvantaged of Yahweh's community and the simple satisfaction of basic human needs. The metaphor includes the concepts of the relationship between Yahweh and Israel and the idea of the sovereign as protector of the people. Further, the vehicle field of the metaphor includes the idea of the king as the administrator of justice.[32] All of these contribute to the interpretation of the metaphor in Psalm 145. The unique aspect is that this view of the metaphor is to be proclaimed. The relationship between the divine king and the populace focuses on the interaction of the semantic fields of king as judge and protector who is acting on behalf of the prisoner and oppressed.

Conclusion

This examination of "God is king" as a metaphor reveals the employment of the metaphor in three relational spheres: (1) God as covenantal sovereign of Israel, (2) God as eternal suzerain of the world, and (3) God as just king of the disadvantaged. The "God is king" metaphor functions as a true metaphor with a range of expressions and meanings resulting from varying interactions within the semantic fields of the topic domain and vehicle field as created by the speakers and indicated to the audience through the pragmatics of the literary context. This range of expression is mirrored in the diversity of Second Temple Judaism, for example, in the prayers of Tobit (ch. 13) and Judith (Jdt 9:11-14) in which God is invoked as the king of Israel who provides protection of Israel. Yahweh as Israel's sovereign seems to be the metaphoric expression employed by Philo as he advocates the superior philosophy found in the Torah (*Spec.* 4.164). *Jubilees*, in its retelling of the commandments of the Sabbath, connects Yahweh's kingship with the Torah by referring to the Sabbath as "a day of the holy kingdom for all Israel" (*Jub.* 50:9).[33] The metaphoric expression of Yahweh as eternal suzerain is found in *T. Moses* 10; *Pss. Sol.* 17; *Sib. Or.* 3:46-47, 767-84, and various targumic passages such as *Tg. Zech.* 14:9a: "And the kingdom of the Lord will be revealed among the dwellers of the earth" (see also *Tg. Ezek.* 7:7, 10; *Tg. Obad.*). The issue in these texts is when and under what conditions the nations will recognize the eternal suzerain. This recognition of the eternal suzerain is often connected with peace, security, and justice for Israel and for the whole world. Yahweh as eternal suzerain occurs also in Wisdom of Solomon. In this text, the "God is king" metaphor seems to draw on some of the expressions found in Psalms 96; 97; and 99, in which the nations and kings of the world will recognize the eternal suzerain through his judgments (6:1-25). The figure of wisdom serves as a vehicle through which the client kings may understand the justice of the eternal suzerain, a justice required for the retention of their authority. The "God is king" metaphor within the framework of Yahweh as monarch of the populace is found also in *Psalms of Solomon* 5. The opening verses of the psalm refer to God as the "refuge of the poor" (vv. 2, 13); the one who answers the calls of the distressed (v. 6) and the cries of the hungry (v. 10; see also Jdt 9:11-12). Yahweh as monarch of the people, who assists the poor, the sick, and the hungry, may be represented in Gospel expressions associated with Jesus, such as "And cure the sick there, and say to them, God's kingship has reached unto you" (Q 10:9).

That the three relational expressions of the "God is king" metaphor of the Hebrew Bible appear also in texts from the Second Temple period suggests a trajectory of common sets of expressions for the metaphor of kingship and provides some indication of the understandings of these expressions. Consistent with the employment of metaphors, the texts have their own variation of the kingship metaphor. For example, the Wisdom of Solomon associates the kingdom with the search for wisdom. In the New Testament Gospels, "kingdom of God" is a primary expression over against the previous preferences for verbal, titular, or declarative statements of God's kingship.

The dynamic of commonality and diversity found in the "God is king" metaphor challenges the narrow emphasis of Perrin's symbol-myth theory. The symbol theory suggested that in Second Temple Judaism, the intellectual activity around the kingship of God narrowed to eschatological considerations. The focus was on the timing of the kingdom of God and the manner in which it would appear. However, a metaphoric approach reveals the continuing intellectual development of the idea of God's kingship, and it reveals a dynamic between commonality and diversity. *The issues are not temporal or formal; they are relational and responsive.* In Second Temple Judaism, there was a common set of semantic fields that focused on God's kingly relationship with three different groups, and these semantic fields drew on various semantic fields associated with kingly activities, roles, and attributes, as well as on human responses to the king. The specific variations or diverse interpretations of "God is king" reflect the normal usage of metaphor as a vehicle that responds to changes in the historical experience of a populace as represented in the evolution of semantic fields. The historical experiences associated with the Israelite kingships—the varying foreign kingdoms, the Hasmonean monarchy, the Roman Empire—combined with concepts formulated about the eternal suzerain, as reflected in the development of Jewish literature, influenced the semantic fields associated with the "God is king" metaphor. These changes in the semantic fields became part of the dynamic tension expressed in the commonality and diversity found in the Second Temple Jewish literature and the formative writings of Christian origins.

Part Three

Common Judaism and Hellenism

10. "Torah Shall Go Forth from Zion": Common Judaism and the Greek Bible

Tessa Rajak

When Ed Sanders chose to speak about those practices and conceptions that transcended the diverse currents and controversies of Second Temple Judaism, he brought us, along with "'common Judaism," a healthy dose of common sense. He gave us a model that is "good to think with" and that continues to be a healthy corrective to succeeding fads and fashions. I have found this to be so time and again. In *Judaism: Practice and Belief*, Sanders focused on the religious life of Jerusalem but made it clear that his "common Judaism" did not stop at the borders of Judea: there was much that crossed and indeed challenged the Palestine-Diaspora divide.[1] He grounded "common Judaism" in the life, rituals, and purity systems of the temple, as expressions of covenantal nomism, but by no means to the exclusion of other activities.

Here I wish to bring into the picture that other major phenomenon that lies at the heart of "common Judaism," in some way uniting all Jews in the period (and afterward)—the text of Scripture itself. How far can a common relationship with Scripture be seen as the common property of Jews across the language divide? I shall look particularly at the Diaspora, seeking to characterize the specific role of Scripture in Hellenistic Judaism, but also to map this within the wider picture. The biblical books were central to the whole of Jewish existence. Jewish communities were text-centered societies. But the uses they made of the texts, the genres of interpretation, and the relation of text to life were not identical for all Jewish communities. We shall discover a spectrum of textuality through the different types of communities, including here also the various early Christian groups. We shall observe differences but also commonalities. We owe to Ed Sanders our very ability to ask new questions of old material in a way that, it is hoped, will be productive of some new answers.

145

In the introduction to his classic study *Biblical Interpretation in Ancient Israel*, Michael Fishbane writes: "From the viewpoint of historical Judaism, the central task of exegetical tradition is to demonstrate the capacity of Scripture to regulate *all* areas of life and thought."[2] So it is not surprising that Moshe Halbertal found the concept of a text-centered society, developed in other fields, to work very well for rabbinic Judaism:[3] Torah, the five books of Moses, was still the fundamental text, but in time Mishnah and Talmud acquired their own very special kind of canonicity for the rabbis.

On the basis, no doubt, of a general sense of the importance of biblical interpretation in Jewish tradition, homage is regularly paid to the centrality of the Greek translation of the Bible in Hellenistic-Jewish culture. Much is made of the extraordinary status of the Bible (usually "Bible" is spoken of, rather than simply the Pentateuch) as a holy book, a feature that is believed to distinguish this culture sharply from its Greco-Roman milieu. The crucial role of the Homeric poems as identity-shaper is sometimes brought up by way of comparison, but there is also the sense of a gulf lying between the two.[4]

While many societies nurture fundamental texts, there are numerous different ways in which these texts can be embedded in those societies. "Centrality" covers a multitude of roles. Little has been said about the forms this text-dependence might have taken in the case of that particular world of Judaism as expressed in Greek, and about how this picture compares with what we see in the Judaism that was rooted in Hebrew and Aramaic, where the role of the biblical corpus is copiously studied. Rather, it is tacitly assumed that a specific pattern of relationships with the Scriptures can be taken as the common property of Jews across the language divide, across the Palestine-Diaspora divide, and over more than half a millennium.[5]

Here, I adopt the stance of a historian of culture as much as of religion, looking in from the outside and asking two large but important questions. First, I shall inquire into the sort of relationship we might envisage in this milieu between text and users. Then I shall move on to consider how this situation compares with that in other Jewish circles or communities of users. My focus, then, will be on Greek-speaking Judaism. In attempting to understand this particular tradition through its textuality, I shall propose the use of a pair of concepts, contrasting the kind of community that may simply be described as "text-based" with one whose level of engagement merits the name "textual." The distinction may help us grasp the range of possibilities. Further, to answer these questions, it will be necessary to give a reasonably precise sense to those elusive terms "traditions," "milieux," and "circles" or "communities" of users.

It has become a commonplace to say that Hellenistic-Jewish culture was dependent on the Greek translation of the Bible. By way of illustration, I can do no better than to quote the revised Schürer:[6] "The basis of all Jewish-Hellenistic culture is the old, anonymous Greek Bible translation known as the Septuagint. . . . [W]ithout it the religion of the Greek-speaking Jews was as unthinkable as the Church of England without the Authorized Version." The fourth German edition of Schürer's original work had spoken, as might be expected, of Luther's translation—whose role may not, in fact, have been the same for German literature as that of the King James Bible in English. We must conclude, in any case, that Schürer took that special "religion" (as he calls it) to have represented the essence of Jewish-Hellenistic culture. In a different spirit, Victor Tcherikover called the Greek translation of the Scriptures the "cornerstone on which the entire edifice of Jewish Alexandria rested."[7]

One large claim underlies all the others: that Greek-speaking Jews can be considered, for some purposes at least, in unitary terms. Is it justified? The term "Hellenistic Judaism" is conventionally applied not just to the Jews of the Hellenistic world proper but, for want of a better term, to the entire gamut of Greek-speaking Jewry from Alexandria to the Crimea, from 300 B.C.E. to 400 C.E. Arnaldo Momigliano wrote that "there was a distinctive brand of Hellenism which was Jewish Hellenism. Entire communities which considered themselves Jews and practised Judaism, spoke Greek, thought in Greek and hardly knew any Hebrew or Aramaic. For at least seven or eight centuries, Greek remained the alternative cultural language of the Jews."[8] The criterion is thus linguistic, and the focus is on Jews for whom Greek was the primary language. Most were in the Diaspora proper, but the description also applied to some of the Jewish inhabitants of Greek cities within and around Palestine. According to the view maintained by Martin Hengel in his epoch-making *Judaism and Hellenism*, Greek culture had penetrated Judea to such an extent by the turn of the third century B.C.E. that this might almost have been true for some residents of Jerusalem itself.[9] In broad terms, however, we are talking about the culture of the Jewish Diaspora and of the Christian communities that grew out of it.

So we are talking now about a long line of Jewish life lived through Greek, embodied in a long line of written self-expression in Greek. Writers in this line demonstrably built on the work of predecessors. This does not mean, of course, that all could possibly be conscious of all that had gone before; but it does legitimate the use of the term "tradition." The mainline has spurs. What has come down to us, moreover, is a line with many breaks. Entire texts have disappeared over time. As a notable instance, I mention here the Maccabean history of Jason of Cyrene in its unabridged form, of which the book we know as the Second Book of Maccabees is no more than a summary. There is no reason why there should not have existed some works now so irretrievably lost that we simply have no awareness of them.

If there is one unifying factor that suggests a continuing common culture, this lies precisely in the dependence on a text, the Greek version of the Hebrew Bible. We should note that what is in question is not simply Scripture, but Scripture in Greek. Conceivably, the biblical books in Hebrew may have been the ultimate ideal point of reference (and there are indications pointing that way), even for Jews who themselves were entirely ignorant of the language. But it is the distinctive Greek version that may claim to be the common heritage. So the first question to ask is whether and to what extent such a dependence can really be identified in Hellenistic Judaism, as expressed in its writing.

The Greek Bible and Jewish Literary Production

I have come to think that Schürer's separation of "works originally composed in Greek" from those written in Hebrew and Aramaic, nowadays criticized, was helpful and farsighted.[10] While assignations can be a good deal more arbitrary or hypothetical than they appear, this approach provides an immediate overview of the Jewish-Greek tradition and allows patterns to emerge. Our group contains diverse texts, and they are hooked into the Scriptures in different ways. But there is scarcely a single one that is not hooked into them. I can give just a brief sketch of the main kinds of relationship with Scripture to be found there.

The *Letter of Aristeas* is the earliest and in some ways the most remarkable piece of Hellenistic-Jewish writing. This is the foundation story of the Septuagint translation in the collective memory. It is noteworthy that the legend contained in the *Letter* is adopted by Philo and by Josephus, who include versions of it in their own works, for their own purposes. Josephus retells the narrative part of the *Letter*, sticking very close to the text, while Philo summarizes and embellishes, elaborating the miraculous dimension of the story. Another writer, Aristobulus, with more philosophical interests, also included the translation story, though we cannot be certain whether he wrote before or after the *Letter* as we have it was produced. If the "charter myth" was so crucial a document, the translation must itself have had a very high importance.

"Rewritten Bible" well describes much of the output of the Hellenistic-Jewish tradition. This term, brought originally into play by Geza Vermes, is now very widely adopted to cover adaptations of biblical material in a variety of styles, showing varying degrees of respect for the form and content of the original. The description is not without its problems, especially when we have to decide how to define its limits, but it serves very well to describe the Hellenistic-Jewish material that has reached us via Josephus, Clement of Alexandria, and Eusebius. There we see displayed a range of techniques for developing or embellishing the source. The scope is wider than the Torah—not only patriarchs but also kings and other figures of obvious interest such as Job and his daughters or Jeremiah; or, again, famous edifices (notably the temple and the Tower of Babel); and sometimes extensive chronological computations over the *longue durée*. Also quite characterisitic are elaborate genealogies linking the Hebrews to one another and to the rest of humankind. The approach ranges from close verbal analysis to simple allegorical readings in which the symbolic meaning is extracted from the stories. As Robert Doran has acutely observed, however, "since Eusebius was concerned with the earlier period of Jewish history and with the knowledge that non-Jews displayed of the biblical tradition, the preserved fragments necessarily deal with the Bible," which may give us a somewhat misleading impression as to the real range of interests of the diverse group of writers on which he drew.[11]

The description "rewritten Bible" also suits material that has reached us by other routes, such as the love story of Joseph and Aseneth, in which a strong romantic element and a religious conversion story are added to a bare theme from Genesis (chs. 41 and 46). Considerable freedom was often taken by the authors with the biblical subject matter, as Carl Holladay has stressed.[12] Eupolemus, for example, introduced an angel called Dianathan, who told David not to build the temple; added an exchange of letters between Solomon and Vaphres, king of Egypt, to the correspondence mentioned in Kings and Chronicles; and turned Eli into a high priest of the days of Solomon.[13] This fanciful but not frivolous technique is utterly at home in the genre of rewritten Bible in other languages, just as it is characteristic of the haggadic midrashim in later centuries.

The production of works in the "rewritten Bible mold" was closely intertwined with the translation process itself. This "work in progress" (as it has been well described) embodies a notable phenomenon whereby later translations demonstrably share vocabulary and phraseology with the pentateuchal books, with other translations that would seem to have been made in an early phase, especially, and understandably with Psalms. Emanuel Tov has made a beginning of gathering and analyzing such intertextual associations, suggesting how some Greek books served as a kind of master document and provided a repertoire of terms and concepts for other, presumably later translations.[14] These data are revealing, even if the direction and nature of particular dependencies may be less than certain.[15] A high degree of intimacy with the entire preexistent corpus in its Greek form is implied.

Copying, correcting, and improving the quality of the relationship between source and target texts are other activities included under the general rubric of translation. Particularly well known is the evidence of endeavors to make corrections in the light of the Hebrew text as early, it now seems, as the first century B.C.E., in the Minor Prophets scroll fragments found at Nahal Hever by the Dead Sea.[16]

A language for self-expression was forged by the Greek Bible. The translators supplied a vocabulary and with it a range of concepts that were not identical to their Hebrew prototypes. Greek words were deployed in specialized meanings, and neologisms were regularly created, some of them now very familiar: *diaspora, synagōgē, ekklēsia, laos* (for the people of Israel), *prosēlytos, thysiastērion* (for the Jewish altar, which is used even by 2 Maccabees), *hagiasma* (and cognate words, denoting sanctification), *eulogia* (for blessing), *diabolos*—the list is a long one and this is not the place to inspect it. Different Greek-Jewish authors used the vocabulary in different ways. Some terms had greater exposure than others; some a longer life than others. Their routes of transmission were not uniform. It is often when we explore that basic level of individual lexical units that we are above all struck by the pervasive influence of the Greek Bible on its communities of Jewish users.

Last but far from least, citations, whether precise or approximate, are an important vehicle for the diffusion of this special vocabulary and more broadly for asserting connections with the source text. Exact citation and close allusion to biblical material are found in nearly all the literary texts in my survey. Some are more dependent on these devices than others, but it is worth pointing out that biblical echoes or exempla have a special value as markers in works that do not follow traditional templates and are more or less Greek, in form and character. It is highly significant that we find them in 4 Maccabees. This is a work of quite elaborate Greek rhetoric, containing elements of philosophical dialogue in a mix characteristic of the second sophistic in the Roman Empire. It concludes with the martyred mother's remarkable exhortation, a veritable *derash torah*, in which she repeats the teachings of her late husband, offering paradigms of courage and also quoting familiar words of inspiration for those who suffer, drawn from Isaiah (43:2), Psalms (34:19), Proverbs (3:18), and Deuteronomy (32:39).

Text and Users

Adherence to an extensive sacred text of a particular kind, accessed in the form of a translation, must have major implications. Text-centeredness has its types and gradations, and the many different roles a key text might play within a society are conditioned at least as much by the character of the society as by the nature of the text—even if the users are prone to perceiving things differently and to attributing control to the unchanging dictates of the Scriptures that bind them. For Jews of the Greco-Roman Diaspora, not only is the literary legacy severely battered, but what remains relays little direct information about how they conducted their lives, either as groups or as individuals. Still, we will be able to develop this story, extrapolating from such reflections and comments as we find on Scripture operating in society. I shall move on to suggest that a comparative analysis in terms of broad typologies is an extra resource that offers a route to filling out the story and making sense of the evidence. If we cannot test our hypotheses, at least we can put them in perspective.

We have briefly surveyed a literary output that does indeed point to a highly privileged role for the Greek Bible among at least some groups of Greek-speaking Jews. In looking to confirm this picture, we need also to consider what limitations there may have been to that privileged position.

1. The physical Torah scrolls were an iconic object. The supreme importance of the scrolls themselves is attested in a historical episode such as the desperate efforts to rescue the scrolls from the communal conflict in Caesarea in 66 c.e. The crude figurative representations of what are evidently collections of scrolls lying on their sides in an *'aron* that decorate a number of the inscriptions of the Jewish catacombs of Rome support the case.

2. Moreover, the Pentateuch was for some Greek-speaking Jews—but not necessarily for all—an inspired or revealed text, vested with divine authority and containing ultimate truth requiring prophetic elucidation. This is a fundamental idea for Philo (*Mos.* 1.334).

3. Moses the lawgiver, as the author or transmitter of the Torah, was the ideal figure of the Hellenistic-Jewish imagination, the prophet who had seen God face-to-face and who had heard his voice. Philo called him an interpreter (*hermēneus*), but also, in the *Life of Moses*, a king.[17] Here Philo presents the roles of lawgiver, prophet, and high priest as the accompaniments of kingship (*Mos.* 1.344). In Josephus's narrative in *Antiquities*, Moses is king, statesman, and general.[18] If Greek-Jewish writers of a more universalizing bent, such as Artapanus (if indeed he should be regarded as a Jewish writer), preferred to stress Moses' role as a culture hero, inventor, and benefactor of humanity, this only increased his stature. In the *Exagogē*, the tragedy on the exodus ascribed to Ezekiel, there is a memorable and mysterious moment when God, a protagonist in the drama, vacates his throne temporarily in favor of Moses.[19] For the Alexandrian Jewish "extreme allegorizers" alluded to by Philo, Moses seems to have been quite simply the teacher who had revealed all wisdom.[20] Philo saw himself as a student of Moses. For the *therapeutai*, those Egyptian ascetics in their community beside Lake Mareotis, Moses was a choirmaster (*Contempl.* 87).

4. The Greek Bible was the source of the Greek-Jewish sense of history, a building block of identity.[21] This shines out in Josephus's writing, through his professions in *Against Apion* book 1, and equally through the structuring of the past in his *Jewish Antiquities*, where almost half of the twenty books are a rewriting of the biblical narrative.[22] The evidence suggests that Josephus used both Greek and Hebrew Bibles to assist him in this endeavor.

5. The mental furniture of literate Jews was biblical. One might think of the ready use of moral examples and helpful quotations even in unlikely places, for example, in the speeches Josephus ascribes to himself from the walls of Jerusalem to the besieged inhabitants. He is writing, of course, in Greek, and it is to be supposed that Greek-speaking Jews would be among the readers of his *Jewish War*. The picture must have had some plausibility. The Bible in their minds would have been the Septuagint.

6. For Greek-speaking Jews, the Greek Torah was the primary determinant of Jewish practice and observance, which were indeed probably determined by a perforce pragmatic interpretation of the requirements laid down in Exodus, Leviticus, and Deuteronomy. When a justification is offered of apparently trivial dietary and purity regulations in the *Letter of Aristeas*, this is done in terms of a broader moral purpose in the context of the pursuit of the higher virtues. But while the regulations may be purely symbolic, their starting point is one of respect for very precise requirements inscribed in Torah.

7. The Greek Bible was the source of Jewish practical ethics in the Diaspora. We might invoke those curious verses in archaic Greek that purport to be the work of the Greek gnomic poet Phocylides (and are therefore ascribed to a "Pseudo-Phocylides").[23] No mention is made there of Jews, Judaism, law, or Scripture. The

expected critique of idolatry is absent. But the influence of Jewish traditions on issues such as assistance of the poor, humility, treatment of the enemy, burial of the dead, and abhorrence of homosexuality (the latter given a rather prominent position) is clear. When it comes to details, there are propositions derived from the Septuagint in a straightforward way, such as the injunction to keep away from false witness[24] or to give just measure (*metra nemein ta dikaia*).[25] Some precepts are drawn from the wisdom literature and the prophets.[26] Since Jakob Bernays brought his detecting skills to this work in 1856, the author of Pseudo-Phocylides has generally been regarded as a Jew. If we are looking at a pagan Greek Judaizer who had become absorbed in the Jewish texts and fascinated by aspects of Jewish morality, then this individual has taken so much of Judaism on board that it comes to much the same thing. Similarly, the Wisdom of Solomon opens with an invocation to the mighty to pursue justice and love goodness, stressing the basic truth that wisdom cannot coexist with sin. Philo, too, while operating within a Platonic metaphysical framework, derives ethical imperatives from his exegesis of the Pentateuch.

8. The Greek Torah, most often translated *nomos*, may well at times have served as a law code employed in the jurisdiction of Jewish courts.[27] Even more recently, the editors of the dossier of twenty papyri from the organized Jewish community (*politeuma*) of Heracleopolis (*P. Colon.* 29) have noted the most surprising use there of the Septuagint term for a deed of divorce, *byblion apostasiou*, as well as an apparent smattering of other Septuagintal terms in the second half of the second century B.C.E.[28]

9. Torah reading was the focal point of the synagogue, contributing greatly to its communal prominence and powering its development. Josephus spells this out in relation to his own period, praising the regularity of the practice. Torah study as part of the activity that takes place in a pre-70, Greek-speaking Jerusalem synagogue is attested in the famous Theodotus inscription, as well as in the book of Acts.[29] Archaeology shows up the importance of the Torah shrine in the later synagogue.[30]

10. Devotion to the Torah is seen as the driving force of Judaism, and it was elevated to a supreme role—in some circumstances above life itself. Thus, for the end of the first century C.E., Josephus's insistence in *Against Apion* that Jews will die rather than transgress their *nomos* articulates the essence of the Jewish-Greek idea of martyrdom.

11. At the same time, analysis of the evidence encourages certain reservations. There is much that remains hazy, and we must remember that we see only a small part of the picture.

If easy access to the contents of the Bible in Greek or parts of it was the one thing that distinguished Jewish writing, the Bible may have been no more than an identifier, a badge of Jewishness, the way a person put him- or herself forward in order to be marked out as a Jewish writer in the eyes of the world. The recourse to the Bible, then, may in some cases be a question of style, a mark of a particular kind, a set of rhetorical devices, rather than a real and profound absorption. How are we to decide?

In any case, we cannot say that this Jewish identity was the sole or core identity of such Jews. Nor, therefore, can we accept what would be the correlate of this, that the Torah would have had corresponding preeminence in their thought world. The modern anthropological concept of "hybridity" well suits their situation.

It is clear that for the production of these works of Hellenistic-Jewish culture to be at all possible, study and interpretation of the Bible, or at least of Torah, would need to have figured somewhere in the life of an elite Jew. But we must allow that the very same Jewish urban elite could have had much in common with its Greek counterpart in the cities and may well have participated in the cultural life of the cities. So Scripture cannot have been the exclusive basis of this group's education and religio-cultural activity. In the case of Philo, Alan Mendelson draws not only on the content of the writings themselves but also on the philosopher's explicit statements about the "encyclical education" (*paideia*). He concludes that the upper crust of Alexandrian Jewry participated in a full Greek education centered on grammar, rhetoric, and philosophy and based in the gymnasium. Mendelson's study is concerned precisely with the complex process of "line-drawing" in which Philo was engaged: "His ruling passion was to make a grand synthesis between the two traditions he knew."[31]

Looking beyond the elite, can we be sure that knowledge of the Bible in Greek was the attribute to an equal extent of male Greek-speaking Jews of all classes, all the way down to a Jewish slave who had been one all his life? Josephus implies just this in the global language about the importance of the law to Jews that he adopts in *Against Apion,* but we might be inclined to discount his rhetoric. Admittedly, not all the Jewish-Greek literature belonged to high culture. *Joseph and Aseneth* has novelistic features, and the novel is often described as a middlebrow product. Inscriptions provide access to a wider sphere than the restricted world of high literature. Nevertheless, we have to admit that our grasp does not extend beyond the literate part of society.

One of the characteristics of a text-centered society is that the authority of the text conferred status on its interpreters—be they scribes, teachers, or even, as in this case, anonymous translators.[32] Without their labors, Scripture could not have remained relevant to changing circumstances.[33] Hermeneutics overcame "the cognitive dissonance, distance and tension between conceptions reflected in the old scriptures and present perceptions."[34] But who, apart from the translators, were the authoritative interpreters of Torah for Greek-speaking Jews? A sprinkling of personal titles that sound as though they denote scholars appears in the epigraphy, but not before late antiquity. We know about one *nomodidaskalos* (teacher of the law) and one *sophodidaskalos* (teacher of wisdom), for example. But had they had a major role in Diaspora life, we would perhaps have expected to hear more about them.

A Comparative Approach to Jewish Biblical Cultures

Always behind the texts lie communities, and we continue to grope toward them while remaining desperately dependent on literary evidence for generating information about these Jewish societies. This is where my model comes in, a proposed approach to text-centeredness in terms of two different types of Jewish textual culture. Perhaps, then, questioning the uses of the text might serve also to open a new window on the diversity of Diaspora Judaism.

What I want to highlight is the contrast between what I call simply a "text-based" society and one that has a more intense and intensive relationship with its writings, which I shall call "textual."[35] There may be some overlap between my categories and Fishbane's "two types of exegetical tradition," of which he writes that one is "dignified by its verbal origins in Scripture, the other dignified by the religious community which lives by Scripture and whose customs can therefore be regarded as a form of non-verbal exegesis."[36] Fishbane is evidently looking at trends, and it seems indeed that his two types of approach likely go together as often as they diverge. But it is clear that the second type of exegetical world produces an intensity that the first alone could never achieve. Fishbane's dichotomy can be developed by way of a three-part contrast among (1) the main Hellenistic-Jewish tradition that I have been discussing, (2) the Qumran sect, which created a Hebrew-based Jewish environment the remains of which contain a relatively small amount of Greek material; and (3) the New Testament groups, which for the purposes of this discussion may be regarded as part of the spectrum of Hellenistic-Jewish groups.

The producers of the literature of the Qumran community, who may also be deemed the users of its much broader nonsectarian library, offer a vivid example of a textual community, a group that saw itself as a "house of Torah" (CD VIII:10). Not only was the biblical corpus for them a "cherished inheritance," but their overriding preoccupation, as Fishbane well expresses it, was "with a vast labour of learning and elaboration . . . a living commitment to the truth and significance of Miqra."[37] Menahem Kister speaks of a postclassical world, in which the entire Bible was there to be "alluded to, interpreted, reworked and actualized."[38] He also points out that the material found at Qumran contains allusions to few works outside the Bible. Other interpreters, however, hold that the Qumran sectarians saw themselves as a special group to whom was given revelation on a par with that of the earlier prophets and thus the ability to produce new authoritative documents.[39] Either way, the guarantee of the inspired quality of sectarian interpretation lies in the direct exposition by God to the Teacher of Righteousness of the meaning of prophetic mysteries.[40] This "post-classicism," if that is what it is, still involves a sense of participating in the fulfillment of those mysteries.

When it comes to assessing the specific impact of the Bible in Greek on the New Testament writings, the study of the very numerous citations has naturally enough been at the forefront. In many cases, allusions, imprecise verbal echoes, combinations of phrases, and adaptations have been considered alongside precise quotations, and distinguishing between these different categories is in itself a never-ending challenge, necessary for students of textual history or of theology. As Krister Stendahl wrote: "The study of quotations of the OT standing in the NT can have many functions and the way in which it is handled is in part coloured by the purposes the various students had behind their studies."[41]

What is interesting for my quest is that each book or group of books in the New Testament displays its particular preferences and throws up its own distinctive and complex problems. Thus, in the Synoptic Gospels, eighteen of the forty-six distinct quotations are peculiar to Matthew (including the eleven special quotations preceded by a formula), but only three each to Mark and to Luke. None out of twelve quotations in John is unique to him. The twenty-three quotations in Acts fall almost entirely in the speeches. The Pauline letters have seventy-eight direct quotations, but of these seventy-one are in Romans, 1 and 2 Corinthians, and Galatians. The Pastoral Epistles scarcely quote at all. Revelation does not quote directly but has more septuagintal phraseology than any other book.[42] There are multiple explanations for these observed patterns, and often the root cause will be driven by theology or in some other way related to the subject matter.

The differences among New Testament communities are undeniably striking. For example, Luke is soaked in Septuagint language and terminology in a very special way, as demonstrated by A. Wifstrand.[43] However, Wifstrand explains the remarkable phenomenon of the "Septuagintisms" in vocabulary and syntax, once thought to be Semitisms, in terms of aspiration to the "dignity" of a "sacred text." Rather, one might look precisely to the Bible-soaked mind of someone formed by an intensely textual community. That is not to say that all Luke's readers would have been of this kind.

The fact remains that, of the New Testament books, most are suffused with Septuagint material. According to H. B. Swete's still invaluable Septuagint introduction,[44] we can find direct citations (under his definition) of every biblical book in the New Testament, except Ezra, Nehemiah, Esther, Ecclesiastes, Song of Songs, and a few Minor Prophets. At the same time, over half of these citations are from Isaiah and Psalms, and some New Testament texts, such as the Epistle to the Hebrews, are virtually fabrics woven of quotations. The absorption is such that we can justifiably describe the authors of these books and their core readers as members of textual communities, in the strong sense of the term. "The Bible was the touchstone not only of the New Testament writers' religious teachings but also of their total life and culture," not merely a "text-based" world.[45] Perhaps they did not always address groups or individuals who were all equally capable of participating in and responding to that textuality—as may well be the case with the recipients of most of Paul's epistles, many of whom probably lacked "hearer competence."[46] But still their authors were clearly formed in such a milieu: even the unique genius of Paul requires a context. In the New Testament, then, we have reflections of Greek-speaking communities of a special kind. Like the Qumran sectaries, they read the Bible through the filter of relevance to their own ideals and fortunes. Authoritative interpretations were offered by their teachers.

In this respect, therefore, the New Testament corpus is remarkably like the Qumran corpus. It is even the case that a comparable selectivity in preferred sources for citation or echo occurs among individual works in the Qumran corpus to a surprising extent, as explored by George Brooke.[47] Genesis, Deuteronomy, Isaiah, and Psalms are the texts found in the largest number of copies among the scrolls (followed by Exodus and then *Jubilees*), and the last three of these are indeed also often quoted. But, to take a couple of examples, in the *Hodayot* (hymns of thanksgiving), and similarly in the *Damascus Document*, the Minor Prophets are also notably influential. The latter also makes significant use of Numbers and Ezekiel, as well as of Hosea and Micah in the Admonition section. The *Hodayot*, on the other hand, have little from Numbers but draw on Jeremiah and Job. Diversity in the subject matter of the compositions may not provide the whole explanation. A pattern of pathways and preferences in the choice of reading and memorization within an extensive corpus known to all may well be characteristic of compositions emanating from groups that interact constantly and intensely with their texts. Where the central text for a community is not in fact one holy book but a large and unsystematic corpus, devotion to a selection of preferred texts within it could be more meaningful than a thinly spread attachment to the whole. We must imagine that the affections of individuals and of groups shifted over time.

Mapping

That most Hellenistic-Jewish writers manifested constant respect for biblical literature, through their choice of subject matter and the frequent display of intimate knowledge, is plain enough. This, too, is the technique by which the authors publicly defined themselves as Jewish writers. We can safely call them "text-based." There may have been some gap between the writers and readers. But the writers, at any rate, apparently knew some, if not all, of the Greek Bible well, and they used it inventively and creatively.

Hellenistic-Jewish writers may even be caught using the same kind of techniques as Qumran pesher does when they cite the Bible in Hebrew or weave allusions together in "exegetical systems." This is nicely illustrated by Devorah Dimant in relation to the theological application of phrases from the Song of Moses in Deuteronomy to the martyred brothers' prayer in 2 Macc 7:6.[48] Dimant's claim is that biblical allusions are used by authors writing in Greek in very much the same way as they are by Hebrew and Aramaic authors. That must to some extent be qualified, however, in the light of her own demonstration of a rather widespread tendency among the writers in Greek to avoid direct biblical citation, except in prayer (distinctly reminiscent of the practice of Acts).

There do exist, in any case, instructive parallels revealing common techniques of interpretation. But we remain with a clear sense that the creativity of the work produced in Greek is located somewhere else; and as a group, these books are distinct in the range they cover, not only of formal genres—many of which are, quite simply, accepted genres in Greek literature—but also of genres that are conspicuous by their scarcity: visions and apocalypses in particular. Furthermore, there are preferences among forms of interpretation. Even the most Hellenized of the writers are fond of typology. One thinks of the exodus motif threading its way through the *Letter of Aristeas*,[49] of the Deuteronomic models in the narratives of 1 Maccabees combined with those from Kings, or of the Esther paradigm underlying the persecution story in 3 Maccabees. As mentioned, Greek-Jewish writers use direct biblical citation surprisingly little, favoring rewritten Bible and the imaginative exploitation of biblical themes. There is, therefore, a marked difference in what we might call the dynamics of interaction with the original, at least if we are to use what survives as a sample.

In writing of Scripture as a model for language at Qumran, Fishbane aptly speaks of the creation of a "thick archaic texture" through the interweaving of Hebrew passages, and by means of the special resonance created by the richness of the intertextual associations.[50] Such density and interpretative complexity cannot be found even in the most "biblical" of surviving compositions in Greek.

The fundamental contrast between types of text-centered communities may be summarized, and in some measure explained, by saying that the main thrust in Hellenistic-Jewish literature is toward making connections, and the challenge for its authors is to generate new forms of fusion of their two received literary heritages, which are themselves subject to continual reinterpretation. The authors needed to be at home in both.[51] Carl Holladay has highlighted some pointers to the level of competence in and grasp of Greek literature evident in the fragments of the Hellenistic-Jewish writers,[52] notably the freedom of the biblical poet Theodotus with Homeric language and conceptualization, and Ezekiel the tragedian's awareness of dramatic technique.[53]

So we are looking at the making of bridges between those different worlds that combined in the minds and lives of Greek-speaking Jews and that made up their identities. The engagement with translation epitomizes the culture of Greek-speaking Jews. Their labors constitute no less important nor less impressive an enterprise than that which comes from the heart of one or the other of the traditions they lived with. Bridges suggest traffic in both directions—not only from Hebrew to Greek, but also from Greek to Hebrew. Hellenistic-Jewish writers and teachers were likely to have been a significant conduit of such Greek philosophical concepts and scholarly methods as were appropriated, consciously or unconsciously, by Jews who thought and worked in Hebrew or Aramaic. More directly to our purpose, it is a reasonable hypothesis that Greek-speaking Jews were responsible for transmitting patterns of textual behavior cultivated in Palestine (and preserved at Qumran) to the milieux in which the Jesus groups of the eastern Roman Empire operated. In Jewish memory, they have been greatly underestimated. I would contest the implicit disparagement by Chaim Rabin of the "essentially alien character of Hellenistic Judaism, receiving isolated principles, but without the attendant intellectual atmosphere."[54] In relation to the Jewish textual heartland, it might seem that the Jewish output in Greek was secondary and that its writers were the led rather than the leaders. But it is scarcely possible to assert this without falling into a circular argument about what is center and what is periphery. Rather, we can see Greek-speaking Jews as sharing honorably in "common Judaism" and as linked to those other Jewish worlds of Palestine and of the Diaspora through a common dedication to Scripture, albeit expressed in their own ways.

The constraints of living as a minority demand protection of traditions; self-imposed boundaries are sought and constantly redefined. Adherence to the Bible was a tool for this purpose for Greek-speaking Jews, from which other tools could be derived. Yet there is no reason to think that Diaspora Jews huddled around their Torah—or, rather, their *nomos*. Far from it. While the Greek Bible catered to the Jewish identity of "Hellenized" Jews, it also, and paradoxically, provided the intellectual route by which Mediterranean Jews became more "Hellenized," because it ensured that the entirety of their lives, including their religious lives, could be lived in Greek. The Greek language gave access to the world. Greek-speaking Jews perhaps lived *with* Torah, rather than fully *by* or *through* Torah. Paradoxically again, it was the spread of the Jesus movement that opened new opportunities in the Diaspora for a more totalizing brand of text-centered existence; yet this came now with a radical redefinition of what such an existence entailed.

11. *Aristeas* or Haggadah: Talmudic Legend and the Greek Bible in Palestinian Judaism

Eliezer Segal

Scholars of rabbinic literature from the Talmudic or late classical era have greatly valued E. P. Sanders's attempts to rescue rabbinic texts from abuse at the hands of theologians, New Testament scholars, and historians of Second Commonwealth politics and society. It is not simply a matter of calling attention to the negative presuppositions that are often attached to such terms as "Pharisees"[1] or "ritual."[2] His contributions extend to a more substantial scholarly recognition that the extant compendia of rabbinic teachings, all of which postdate the second century c.e., were not treatises on theology or chronicles of their authors' or protagonists' times. For that reason, they provide little if any evidence for the doctrines of the early church or the life of the historical Jesus. It is unfortunate that Talmudic Judaism has not left us a Paul or an Augustine, a Josephus or a Eusebius. Attempts to reconstruct historical narratives out of specialized works devoted to the minutiae of legal debate or rhetorical preaching can be undertaken only with extreme caution.[3]

The Rabbinic Septuagint Legend

By way of illustration of these methodological perils, I turn to a familiar passage from rabbinic literature that claims to preserve historical information about an important milestone in the development of Judaism in the third century B.C.E. I will argue that the failure to take into account the distinctive purposes and literary character of rabbinic traditions has led to fundamental errors in the historical conclusions that were drawn from this text.

The rabbinic text is a legend about the circumstances surrounding the translation of the Torah into Greek and the supposed emendations that were introduced into that document by the sages charged with that translation. The tradition is preserved in numerous versions, whether in the form of brief allusions or exhaustive lists of verses, in works emanating from the tannaitic, amoraic, and medieval eras.[4]

The tradition, in its various versions, was examined with characteristic thoroughness by Emanuel Tov in an article that appeared in 1984.[5] Tov undertook a detailed comparison of the rabbinic traditions and the extant Greek versions of the LXX. He classified the variants into different types and proposed reconstructions of the Greek text that underlay the rabbinic Hebrew versions. After noting the many disagreements between the rabbinic versions and the standard LXX, he arrived at a far-reaching conclusion:

> The surprising thing is that two-thirds of the biblical passages in the list were changed in the course of the textual tradition of the LXX, and if this is really so, then clearly the original text of the LXX completely differed from the translation known to us from the manuscripts.[6]

Tov's clear preference for the rabbinic tradition, which is contained in works redacted half a millennium or more after the composition of the LXX of the Pentateuch, over the manuscripts of LXX itself, was startling. The reasons for my surprise, and the objections I have to Tov's judgment on this matter, will form the basis for the present essay.

Let us begin with a presentation of the text under discussion, as it appears in *b. Megillah* 9a–b:

> King Ptolemy assembled seventy-two elders, and placed them inside seventy-two rooms without disclosing to them the reason why he had assembled them. He approached each one individually and said to them: Write for me the Torah of your master Moses.
> The Holy One instilled counsel into the hearts of each one, and they all arrived at a single consensus.
> They wrote for him:
> "God created in the beginning" (Genesis 1:1).
> "Let me make man in the image, after the likeness" (Genesis 1:26).
> "And on the sixth day God finished . . . and he rested on the seventh day" (Genesis 2:2).
> "Male and female he created him/it"[7] (Genesis 5:2).
> "Come, let me go down, and there confuse their language" (Genesis 11:7).
> "So Sarah laughed to her relations" (?; Genesis 18:12).[8]

"For in their anger they slayed men, and in their wantonness they hamstrung a stable" (Genesis 49:6).

"So Moses took his wife and his sons and set them on a carrier of persons" (Exodus 4:20).

"The time that the people of Israel dwelt in Egypt and in other lands was four hundred and thirty years" (Exodus 12:40).

"And he sent nobles [za'atutei] of the people of Israel" (Exodus 24:5).

"And against the nobles of the children of Israel he put not forth his hand" (Exodus 24:11).

"I have taken not one valuable [hmd] of theirs" (Numbers 16:15).

"Which the Lord thy God distributed to give light to all the peoples" (Deuteronomy 4:19).

"And he went and served other gods which I commanded should not be served" (Deuteronomy 17:3).

They also wrote for him "the beast with hairy legs" and they did not write "the hare" (Leviticus 11:6) because the name of Ptolemy's wife was "Hare"; lest he should say, The Jews have mocked me by putting the name of my wife in the Torah.

One important question raised by this list is whether it witnesses to the text of the LXX or the Hebrew on which it was based.

From the Parts to the Whole

It would seem that there is a strong propensity among scholars to attach greater credence to documents or editions that lie outside their strict domains of expertise. I personally used to envy the lot of scholars of the Qur'an, whose texts seemed to have been established much closer to the time of its revelation and hence were not subject to the complex issues of redaction and flexible transmission that plague the discipline of rabbinic philology. Such, at least, was my impression until I actually consulted with Qur'an experts and heard about the thorny challenges they face in trying to extrapolate the original text from the significant changes introduced during the era of the caliphs many generations after the time of Muhammad.[9]

The same problem applies to the present question. As Bible scholars examined the tradition about the seventy-two elders, their responses were marked by a credulous faith in traditions that professional rabbinists regarded with the utmost suspicion and skepticism.

The story of Ptolemy and the elders clearly and unequivocally belongs to the genre of rabbinic haggadah. In the discipline of Talmudic philology, there are established methodological approaches that guide our analyses of texts and traditions of the haggadic genre and that determine the appropriate ways for basing historical conclusions on them.

The most rudimentary literary analysis of this tradition will observe that it can be subdivided into two main parts:

1. A narrative framework that is similar in its main outline to the well-known story of the *Letter of Aristeas*[10]—or, to be precise, to the supplements provided by Philo (*Mos.* 2.25–44)[11] concerning the seventy-two elders who were assembled by the emperor Ptolemy, and who were given the supernatural inspiration that allowed them to produce identical Greek translations.[12]

2. Lists of biblical verses for which the translators' versions differed from the established Hebrew text.

The final product gives the impression that the two segments constitute a single unified entity, such that the miraculous status of the translation, as established by the narrative, is demonstrated by the existence of the variants. That is to say: if the translators had arrived at a unified translation only with respect to the verses that were translated literally from the Hebrew, then their achievement would not necessarily have been grasped as a supernatural one, since it might be argued that their agreement merely reflects their identical *Vorlage*. However, this cannot be argued about the cases when their translations constitute departures from the Hebrew original. For how would so many translators have arrived at the same translation if not through miraculous means? It therefore appears that the two components of the haggadah are interdependent and mutually complementary.[13]

The apparent integrity of the story, however, is called into question by the fact that the tradition about the miraculous concurrence of the seventy-two translators does not figure in any rabbinic tradition other than the Babylonian Talmud and works that derive from it. By contrast, lists of "things that our rabbis altered for King Ptolemy at the time that they wrote the Torah for him in Greek" (and similar formulations), or the identifications of particular verses that belong to those lists, are cited with some frequency in the literature, in such diverse collections as the *Mekhilta*,[14] the Palestinian Talmud, classic Palestinian midrashic compendia, and the Tanhumas—without any allusion whatsoever to the tale of the agreement between the translators.[15]

It should be noted that not all scholars would concur with my claim that the full story is limited to the Babylonian Talmud. Historians and biblicists are quick to cite additional works from the rabbinic corpus that provide independent corroboration of the tradition. In this connection, they are likely to bring support from Tractate *Soferim*, included among the "Minor Tractates" of the Talmud; the *Midrash Haggadol*; or the *Yalqut Shim'oni*. These collections, however, are not primary documents of rabbinic literature, but rather medieval anthologies whose compilers were striving to collect diverse material from the classical Talmudic era. In particular, the provenance and purposes of *Soferim* have recently been the topic of intense scholarly controversy. There is a growing tendency to date the tractate, or at least sections of it, as late as the eleventh century,[16] although the opening chapters, which include the tale of the seventy-two elders, evidently belong to the earlier stratum, perhaps from around the seventh century. The *Midrash Haggadol* and the *Yalqut Shim'oni*, while useful as textual witnesses to the documents that are anthologized therein, are nothing more than late compilations in which passages from the Talmud and Midrash are organized according to the sequence of the Hebrew Bible. They cannot under any circumstance be counted as rabbinic works in their own right. Although these observations might strike some readers as obvious, they have proven to be stumbling blocks to some distinguished scholars.[17]

When a tradition appears in diverse forms in different rabbinic collections, the versions found in the Babylonian Talmud are unlikely to represent the original or even an early form of that tradition. Of the various rabbinic compendia, the Babylonian Talmud is the most removed from the main wellspring of haggadic traditions, the land of Israel. It was also the last of the classical rabbinic works to undergo its final redaction, perhaps not until close to the Islamic age.[18] Despite the skepticism with which we customarily approach Babylonian haggadah, in the present specific instance there are good reasons not to dismiss its account of this story. First, it is introduced by the formula *tanya* ("it was taught"), thereby indicating its tannaitic provenance. Second, it is hard to find a reason to suspect that it was invented by the Talmud's redactors. Third, its agreement with the *Letter of Aristeas* and Philo further enhances the story's claims to authenticity.

Nevertheless, we would do well to reconsider the connection between the two parts of the Babylonian pericope, and to ask whether the two components are complementary, or even if they reflect a consistent approach. This question in and of itself will not necessarily spark a revolutionary change in the historiography of the Septuagint, or in the history of rabbinic thinking. Nonetheless, the separation of the text's two components has implications for several important issues.

One such topic concerns the rabbis' attitudes toward the Septuagint. Conventional wisdom in almost two centuries of historical writing would have it that the Jewish sages of the Talmudic era were moved by overt hostility to the Alexandrian Greek version of the Torah, whether because of its adoption by the Christian church or because it is not sufficiently faithful to the Hebrew syntax to allow for sophisticated midrashic interpretation.[19] At first glance, our Talmudic passage, taken in its entirety, would not support such a point of view, since its main point is to show that the elders were imbued with the Holy Spirit when performing their task; the activity of the Holy Spirit is evident particularly in their departures from the Hebrew.[20] If, on the other hand, the list of narratives is not seen as connected originally to the narrative about the translators, the passage upholds the conventional understanding of the rabbis' stance toward the Septuagint.[21] At the very least, the list of alterations can be described and characterized without imposing on it the assumptions of the preceding passage from the Babylonian Talmud.

A second issue concerns the homiletical point of the literary unit. Rabbinic haggadot are not usually known for their thematic complexity. Since they are frequently rooted in homilies that were delivered before synagogue congregations, they are likely to focus on a single issue, which is capable of being grasped by the folk who assemble for such occasions. Indeed, the presence of more than one homiletical topic is often an indication of the composite nature of a given passage, whether compiled in antiquity or from the marginal additions by medieval scribes and glossators that were copied into the main body of the manuscript. As we shall argue later on, the identification of multiple messages in the passage can assist us in reconstructing the pathways of the development of the Babylonian tradition regarding the writing of the Septuagint.

The need to identify the homiletical point of a rabbinic discourse, as a step toward unwrapping its "historical kernel" from its ancillary elements, is borne out by the fact that none of the lists of alterations comes close to being complete. We know of numerous variations between the Greek and Masoretic texts that find no mention whatsoever in the Talmudic traditions.[22]

It is undoubtedly difficult to use haggadic material for historical purposes, but it can be done. Though he was speaking about Palestinian Jewish history, the principle articulated by Saul Lieberman in his 1944 article "The Martyrs of Caesarea" holds for our material as well:

> The simple rule should be followed that the Talmud may serve as a good historic document when it deals in contemporary matters within its own locality. The legendary portions of the Talmud can hardly be utilized for this purpose. The Palestinian Talmud (and some of the early Midrashim) whose material was produced in the third and fourth centuries contains valuable information regarding Palestine during that period. . . . The evidence is all the more trustworthy since the facts are often recorded incidentally and casually.[23]

In other words, the historical credibility of rabbinic sources is in inverse proportion to their explicitly historical objectives.[24] Rabbinic sources are of greatest historical value when they are speaking unguardedly without consciously intending to provide historical information. This premise will serve us in good stead with respect to our tradition about the emendations introduced by the seventy-two Jewish elders: what they have to teach us relates more to the generations of the tannaitic and amoraic sages than to third-century B.C.E. Alexandria.

The Absence of Important Septuagint Variants

The historical nature of the list is further cast in doubt when we observe that the list of variants does not contain any halakhic passages and that the Jewish sages never cite the LXX variants in support of normative halakhic positions.[25] Indeed, there are at least two well-known examples of momentous translations that do *not* figure in the rabbinic list.

The first is the nonliteral rendering of Lev 23:11 as *tē epaurion tēs prōtēs* ("the morrow of the first day") rather than "the morrow of the Sabbath." This reading is consistent with the Pharisaic and rabbinic methods for dating the Feast of Weeks, a topic of deep sectarian controversy during the Second Temple era. Second, the LXX rendered Exod 21:22-23, dealing with causing a miscarriage to a pregnant woman (ruling that the difference between a civil and a capital offense depends on the state of the fetus's development): "If it be unformed, he shall be fined . . . but if it is formed, then thou shalt give life for life." This is drastically different from the conventional Jewish reading, according to which the difference hinges on the fate of the mother's life: "And if no harm follows [that is, to the woman], the one who hurt her shall be fined. . . . If any harm follows [to her], then you shall give life for life." The LXX, evidently reflecting an Alexandrian Greek tradition, became the basis for the normative Christian position on abortion.[26] If the list in our passage were the result of a serious, and real, attempt to collect significant variations in the LXX translation, it could not possibly have overlooked cases like this, which were at the center of Jewish exegetical concern.

The Talmudic List as a Hybrid

These omissions from the list suggest that its rabbinic compilers were motivated not by historical or halakhic concerns but by homiletics. On the basis of his detailed examinations of the respective verses, Giuseppe Veltri concluded that most of the examples can be justified as attempts to resolve exegetical difficulties that elsewhere in rabbinic works were discussed without explicit connection to the Greek translation. Emanuel Tov found this conclusion utterly bizarre: "It remains difficult, and actually unexplained, how and why difficulties in a biblical verse which one or more rabbis present according to some source should be ascribed to the translational activity of the seventy translators."[27] In the end, even Veltri does not call into question the basic historical reliability of the rabbinic tradition. All he proposes is that a distinction be made between the actual Greek translation and a separate interpretative midrash that the elders provided for Ptolemy. This conclusion seems arbitrary and motivated not so much by the evidence as by a prior commitment to the historicity of haggadic texts.

If one sets aside such prior commitments, a different picture emerges. A good starting point for an acceptable solution to our problem may be found in the approach adopted by Rashi to *b. Megillah*. Throughout his commentary on our story about the seventy-two elders, Rashi repeats the phrase "so that they should not say . . ." This formula is used to deflect a literal reading of the verse that would otherwise lead the naïve reader to conclusions that are unacceptable to Judaism.[28] In several instances, Rashi goes so far as to spell out the nature of the heresies that the elders were trying to avoid, principally, the belief that there are "Two Powers in Heaven," and the possibility of finding scriptural support for polytheistic beliefs.

Rashi's claim that the text was intended to counter such heresies can be borne out by a close look at some of the translations found in the list:

1. Genesis 1:1: "God created in the beginning"—The intention is evidently to avoid a reading such as "The beginning [bereshit] created God," which would have implied that God was the creature of a prior being. Note that the ambiguity allowed by the Hebrew could not really be replicated in Greek, where case structure very clearly designates grammatical subjects and objects.
2. Genesis 1:26: "Let me make man in the image, after the likeness"—The use of the first-person plural form has been a long-standing source of embarrassment for Jewish monotheists confronting dualists, pagans, or trinitarians.
3. Genesis 2:2: "And on the sixth day God finished . . . and he rested on the seventh day"—This version, which does in fact agree with the received text of the LXX, was evidently responding to a perceived contradiction in the Masoretic version: either God was finishing the work on the seventh day, or he rested, but not both! The Greek version makes it clear that the creation was completed by the end of the sixth day.
4. Genesis 11:7: "Come, let me go down, and there confuse their language"—As in 1:26, the Hebrew suggests a plurality in the divine.
5. Exodus 12:40: "The time that the people of Israel dwelt in Egypt and in other lands was four hundred and thirty years"—The Greek tradition removes a glaring incongruity between the claim of the verse and the chronology of events in Genesis and Exodus by allowing that the count does not refer strictly to the sojourn in Egypt but in fact begins during the patriarchal era.

This summary lends support to Veltri's thesis that what we have here is not an arbitrary collection of problematic verses but a selection of texts with common characteristics. Unfortunately, it is in the apologetic readings that we are least likely to find agreement with the Greek tradition of the LXX. The verses in which God is designated as a plural appear there unaltered. These discrepancies led Tov to question the authenticity of the manuscript tradition of the LXX.

A very different picture emerges if we treat the pericope as a standard haggadic passage rather than a historical record. There is considerable evidence in Talmudic and midrashic literature that the Jewish sages were sensitive to problematic biblical texts that could provide support for heretical or pagan positions. The rabbinic corpus contains several disputes between sages and sectarians or heretics, some of which revolve around similar lists of biblical texts that generated polemical arguments. Following are two examples:

1. *y. Berakhot* 9:1 (12d):[29]
The heretics [*minim*] asked Rabbi Simlai: How many deities created the universe?

He said to them: You ask me? Go and ask Adam, since it says (Deuteronomy 4:32) "For ask now of the days that are past. . . ." "Since the day that the gods created man upon the earth" is not what is written, but rather ". . . since the day that God created man upon the earth."

They said to him: But is it not written "In the beginning created God [*Elohim*, a plural noun form]"?

He said to them: Does it say *bar'u* [the plural verb form]? What is written is *bara* [the singular form].

Said Rabbi Simlai: In all instances where the heretics blasphemed, their refutation can be found right nearby.

They continued to challenge him: What is this verse that is written (Genesis 1:26) "Let us make man in our image, after our likeness"?

He answered them: It is not written here: "So the gods created man in their own image," but rather: "So God created man in his own image" (27).

His disciples said to him: These people you pushed aside with a reed. What will you reply to us?

He said to them: In the past, Adam was created out of dust and Eve was created out of Adam. From Adam onward, "in our image, after our likeness." Man cannot be without a woman and woman cannot be without a man, and the two of them cannot be without the divine presence.[30]

They continued to ask him: What is this text that is written (Joshua 22:22) "The Mighty One, God, the Lord! The Mighty One, God, the Lord! He knows"?

He answered them: It is not written here "they know," but rather "he knows."

They said to him: Rabbi, you could push those people aside with a reed, but what shall you reply to us?

He said to them: The three names refer to the same one, just as a person might say "King Caesar Augustus."

They continued to ask him: What is this that is written (Psalms 50:2): "The Mighty One, God the Lord, speaks and summons the earth"?

He said to them: Does it in fact say: "they spoke" or "and they summon." What is written is "speaks and summons the earth."

His disciples said to him: Rabbi, you could push those people aside with a reed, but what shall you reply to us?

He said to them: The three names refer to the same one, just as a person might say "a craftsman, builder, architect."

They continued to ask him: What is it that is written (Joshua 24:19) "for he is a holy God [*elohim qedoshim*]"?

He said to them: "They are holy gods" is not written, but rather "he is a jealous God."

His disciples said to him: Rabbi, you could push those people aside with a reed, but what shall you reply to us?

Rabbi Isaac said: Holy in all types of holiness. . . .

They continued to ask him: What is this that is written (Deuteronomy 4:7) "What great nation is there that has a God so near [*elohim qerovim*] to it?"

He said to them: It is not written here "as the Lord our God is to us, whenever we call upon them," but rather "whenever we call upon him."

His disciples said to him: Rabbi, you could push those people aside with a reed, but what shall you reply to us?

He said to them: Near in all manners of nearness . . .

2. *b. Sanhedrin* 38b:[31]

Rabbi Johanan said: Wherever the heretics blasphemed, their refutation is right nearby:

"Let us make man in our image, after our likeness"—"So God created man in his own image."

"Come, let us go down, and there confuse their language" (Genesis 11:7) — "And the Lord came down [sing.] to see the city and the tower" (verse 5).

"Because there God had revealed himself [literally: themselves] to him" (Genesis 35:7)—"to the God who answered [sing.] me in the day of my distress" (verse 3).

"What great nation is there that has a God so near [*elohim qerovim*] to it?" (2 Samuel 7:23)—"What other nation on earth is like thy people Israel?"

In light of these and similar passages (which may reflect the kinds of disputations that rabbis were involved in with some frequency),[32] it seems likely that at some stage in the evolution of the tradition about the alterations that were introduced before King Ptolemy, the narrators decided to graft the original list of variant readings in the Greek translation[33] onto a sequence of verses that were well-known subjects of religious debates. In the rabbis' historical imaginations, these verses *should* have been emended in the translation in order to avoid misrepresentations by actual or potential heretics. This reconstruction of the tradition's development follows a readily understandable ideological logic that is familiar to anyone with experience in tracing the development of haggadic traditions across the Talmudic era. Evidently, this grafting preceded all the extant versions in rabbinic literature.

Dwatted Wabbit

Of especial interest is the "hare" example, which is highlighted in the Babylonian Talmud by being moved to the end of the list, in contrast to the other examples, which are listed in the order of their appearance in the Pentateuch. A brief comparison of how this particular element is included in the various midrashic and Talmudic collections provides us with a textbook case for the evolution of haggadic traditions. In the *Mekhilta*, the list of the variants introduced for King Ptolemy includes the hare or rabbit (Lev 11:6 or Deut 14:7). This reading, like all the others in the passage, is presented without any additional explanation, and there is no mention of Ptolemy's wife and her problematic name.[34]

A discourse in *Leviticus Rabbah* in which various rabbis propose prophetic readings of some unlikely biblical passages contains the following pesher-like interpretation of the dietary laws (13:5):[35]

> Moses our master saw the empires in their activities: "the camel, and the hare, and the coney . . ." (Deuteronomy 14:7).
> "And the hare"—This is Greece. King Ptolemy's mother was named "Hare."

In this passage, the comment about Ptolemy's "mother" creates a link between the hare and Greece. However, it is not linked to any textual variants in the Bible, and certainly not to the legend of the seventy-two translators.

The Palestinian Talmud tractate *Megillah* (1:9 [71d])[36] is evidently the earliest source to incorporate the information about Ptolemy's mother as a gloss, in order to explain the significance of the variant in the Greek text. That it is a later gloss is indicated by the fact that it is cited partially in Aramaic, though the actual list of variants, presumably a *baraita*, is in Hebrew.[37] The Yerushalmi's version, like the *Mekhilta*'s and unlike the Bavli's, includes the verse in its proper sequential order; it is given no special prominence by being placed at the end of the list.[38]

Although there is no indisputable proof that the tradition evolved in precisely the order *Mekhilta* → *Leviticus Rabbah* → Yerushalmi → Babylonian Talmud, the hypothesis is an eminently plausible one, and it correlates nicely with the chronological order of the respective compendia. As has been noted, neither of the Palestinian traditions connects the list of Greek variants with the legend about the miraculous agreement of the translators. That decisive step was likely an innovation by the Babylonian redactors.[39] The "hare" variant is (to all appearances) not of a theological character. This fact supports the hypothesis that the theologically problematic examples were grafted on at a later stage in the tradition's evolution.

As many scholars have noted, the Talmud has got its history a bit garbled. Ptolemy II Philadelphus, in whose reign the Bible was translated into Greek, did not have a wife named "Hare," "Bunny," or anything of the sort. He did, however, have a grandfather who bore the epithet "Ptolemy *Lagos*," meaning "rabbit." The Talmudic story would have been just as effective if it had alluded to the correct historical information.[40] The fact that it did not do so is yet another indication of the unreliability of the historical traditions in the Babylonian Talmud. This unreliability applies also to the traditions that it claims to preserve of the textual variants in the old Greek Bible.

In fact, Talmudic and midrashic literature suggests that the Jewish sages of that era did not have firsthand familiarity with the Alexandrian Septuagint, which they knew merely as a legendary episode from the distant past. What is preserved in our list is a credible description of interreligious disputations that took place during the rabbis' own days. The tendency to conflate a list of textual variants with a list of apologetic interpretations was likely facilitated by the fact that there was an overlap between the two lists. Gen 2:2 and Exod 12:40 figure in both traditions.[41]

The methodologies that we adopted for this analysis dovetail neatly with the data presented by Tov, according to which it was precisely those verses that seemed to suggest duality or multiplicity in the godhead that remained unemended in the *textus receptus* of the Septuagint: that is, Gen 1:1, 26; 11:7; and Deut 4:19.

The LXX Translators Were Not Bothered about Theology

Furthermore, we have good reason to suspect that the LXX translators might have preferred *not* to draw too much attention to the Torah's severe condemnation of idolatry, at least insofar as it was extended to Gentiles. If the translators tended to avoid physical or anthropomorphic descriptions of God, they were not nearly as strict when it came to allusions to multiple deities.

This point is well illustrated by the LXX rendering of Exod 22:28 (LXX 22:27), "You shall not revile God," as *theous ou kakologēseis*. This reading provided Philo of Alexandria with a rationale for teaching (*Mos.* 2.205):

> No, clearly by "god" he is not here alluding to the Primal God, the Begetter of the Universe, but to the gods of the different cities who are falsely so called, being fashioned by the skill of painters and sculptors. For the world as we know it is full of idols of wood and stone, and suchlike images. We must refrain from speaking insultingly of these.[42]

In light of such an attitude, it is not surprising that the Alexandrian translators did not hasten to eliminate plural verbs such as "let us make man" or "let us go down."

Based on his survey of anthropomorphism-related passages in the Greek Bible, Charles T. Fritsch concluded that "for the most part, the LXX reveals no consistent method of avoiding the anthropomorphisms of the Hebrew."[43] Harry M. Orlinsky went even further. Based on his reexamination of the evidence, he declared that

> what have been regarded by virtually everyone as instances of an anti-anthropomorphic attitude on the part of the Septuagint translators are the result of nothing more tendentious than mere stylism, with theology and philosophy playing no direct role whatever in the matter. . . . Thus Fritsch made

nothing of the fact that the LXX translated the "face" of God literally 18 (!) times in the Pentateuch, and proceeded to create an anti-anthropomorphic fiction out of one (!) instance of this phenomenon—and an alleged one at that. . . . What is involved is not theology, but stylism and intelligibility.[44]

Although one can point to cases where the LXX translators probably did rephrase the Greek to avoid anthropomorphisms, the practice was not carried out with any consistency;[45] furthermore, such cases do not appear among the ones enumerated in the rabbinic traditions.

The LXX Was Not Known in Palestine

Even if the variants mentioned in the Talmudic accounts originated in a Greek text that was known to the rabbis—unlikely but possible—we would not need to accept the premise that the text they were referring to was an early edition of the LXX. There were, as we now know well, numerous Greek translations of the Bible circulating in ancient Palestine. Based on the nine fragments of Greek Bible translations that were unearthed at Qumran Caves 4 and 7 and at Nahal Hever, the present scholarly consensus[46] holds that during the Second Commonwealth era there existed Palestinian versions of the LXX that were emended by Hebrew speakers who were accustomed to a Masoretic-like text.[47] This phenomenon is normally understood as an attempt to produce a more literal adherence to the Hebrew. The resulting texts were neither LXX nor rabbinic but, as far as we can tell, merely the attempts of individual users, scholars, or communities to come up with the most faithful rendering they could of the Hebrew original.[48] It is conceivable that scholars might have used their linguistic proficiency in order to produce a revision of the LXX that was distinguished by its theological integrity, of the sort described in our rabbinic tradition. However, such a revision would not have been a witness to the original Alexandrian version. On the contrary, such a Greek text would have been yet another adaptation, whose distinctive readings cannot be credited to the original seventy-two sages.[49]

If the Septuagint text was not current in the Holy Land in their time, then we are forced to assume that the rabbis must have known of its use in Alexandria or some other Diaspora community. However, I am aware of no convincing evidence that the rabbis of the land of Israel during the tannaitic era possessed detailed knowledge about the Alexandrian synagogues or about Greek Bible versions in their times.[50]

Conclusion

Our analysis has demonstrated that the Talmudic version of the Aristeas legend is a composite that was assembled over several generations from numerous discrete sources.

When studied according to the methods of literary and philological analysis that are routinely applied to Talmudic and midrashic texts, the passage cannot be viewed as a reliable record of events that occurred centuries earlier than the compendia in which it is found. On the contrary, the exegetical attitudes that it ascribes to the Greek translators are inconsistent with what we do know about their theological concerns (or lack thereof); and more glaring disagreements between the LXX and the Masoretic Text find no place in the Talmudic lists of variants. The assumption that second- or third-century Palestinian rabbis would have preserved authentic memories of the original text of the Alexandrian Torah is contradicted by the literary and archaeological evidence.[51]

In light of these conclusions, it is hard to understand how scholarship ever treated the story with such respect. It is here, I believe, that we should remind ourselves of the tenacity of the outdated historiographic attitudes that E. P. Sanders has been instrumental in discrediting.[52]

It is not simply a matter of our having more information than previous generations of scholars, though one should not minimize the importance of the discoveries at Qumran and elsewhere in challenging conventional wisdoms about ancient Judaism. Rather, earlier generations often studied the lives, values, and literature of ancient Jews primarily from theological perspectives, which promoted the tendency to force the data—and the people—into rigid conceptual categories. After all, it is so much neater to divide the Jews of the late Second Commonwealth into Josephus's easily recognizable sects—Sadducees, Pharisees, and Essenes—and to accept the claim (which served the interests of both Jewish and Christian apologists) that a single, linear, and consistent tradition extended from the Pharisees through to the Babylonian Talmud as interpreted by its authoritative commentators. Only when speaking about rabbinic Jews as a theological category is it possible to imagine that they maintained a uniform Bible text, uniform observances, and uniform beliefs; and that they and their Pharisaic predecessors could impose them on all Jews. It is only by subscribing to those naïve beliefs that rabbinic literature can be used as the basis for reconstructions of Ptolemaic Alexandria or the age of Jesus. Compared to those neat classifications, the alternatives are just too . . . well, *messy*. Even if we could be persuaded that ancient Palestinian peasants were, for some reason, more consistent in their beliefs and practices than our own experience with human nature would suggest possible,[53] a faith in clearly defined sectarian divisions is much easier to deal with than the evidence of, say, an Essene-like community that honored the Zadokite priesthood, observed Sadducee halakhah, and yet maintained a belief in survival after death, perhaps even in bodily resurrection.[54] The tidy consistency of the older categories is unquestionably attractive, even if it is historically indefensible.

12. Whom Do You Follow? The Jewish *Politeia* and the Maccabean Background of Josephus's Sign Prophets

David M. Miller

Freedom, according to E. P. Sanders, was an ideal that was common to most Jews living in Roman Palestine despite considerable disagreement about what it entailed or how it should be realized.[1] Sanders envisions a spectrum of freedom seekers, with those who waited passively for divine intervention, willing to die rather than give up their own way of life, at one end, and those who promoted violent resistance to Roman rule at the other end. Both groups could appeal to role models from 1 Maccabees—the former to the pious individuals who refused to defend themselves on the Sabbath (1 Macc 2:29–38), the latter to Mattathias and his sons, who eventually secured both religious freedom and political independence. Even among those who opposed the later Hasmonean dynasty, Sanders suggests that memories of the successful Maccabean revolt encouraged a general desire for freedom.[2]

The popular prophets Josephus accused of inciting revolt against Rome are located toward the middle of the spectrum among freedom seekers who were "ready to fight, but hoping for miraculous intervention."[3] These "sign prophets"—so-called because of their association with miracles that were supposed to play a role in divine deliverance[4]—are often regarded as independent figures whose eschatological "signs of freedom" or "signs of salvation" distinguished them from their more politically minded contemporaries.[5] Such prophets are generally thought to have framed their activities not in terms of the Maccabees but in terms of the exodus and conquest,[6] if not also an expected prophet like Moses (Deut 18:15-18).[7]

Some of the sign prophets doubtless did evoke the distant biblical past, including the conquest of Canaan. According to Josephus's account in *Ant.* 20.169-72, an Egyptian prophet led his followers from the wilderness to the Mount of Olives, where he promised, like Joshua, that the walls of Jerusalem would collapse at his command. Josephus also reports that a prophet named Theudas claimed the ability to divide the Jordan River (*Ant.* 20.97–99). Whether this sign recalled the earlier Jordan crossing under Joshua, the passage through the Red Sea under Moses, or both at once, is debated.[8]

However, other arguments about the relationship between the sign prophets and the biblical exodus and conquest narratives fail to consider carefully Josephus's own portrayal of the sign prophets and neglect similarities between the sign prophets and events in the more recent past. For example, while the "signs" of the prophets are frequently connected to the "signs and wonders" associated with the departure from Egypt in the biblical text, Rebecca Gray has shown that Josephus diverges sharply from his scriptural source by carefully avoiding the use of either "sign" or "wonder" in reference to the miracles of deliverance from Egypt, such as the ten plagues and the crossing of the Red Sea.[9] According to Josephus, signs authenticate the words of prophets in much the same way that other omens signal divine approval or disapproval.[10] As a result, the mere performance of signs cannot be judged a particularly Mosaic quality from the perspective of Josephus's narrative. In addition, while the desert locale of several of the sign prophets[11] could recall the exodus from Egypt, it could also echo a variety of other traditions from Israel's past[12] or reflect contemporary use in the present. As the desert was a natural place to flee when in danger, it made a fitting location for the sign prophets, who faced the threat of swift Roman reprisal (cf. *J. W.* 4.407).[13] Since the desert could signify a variety of things, my initial concern will be with the function of departure into the desert in Josephus's own account. Finally, as it would be difficult for a first-century Jew to advocate freedom from oppression without in some way recalling Israel's deliverance from slavery in Egypt, the promise of "freedom" on its own connects the sign prophets to the exodus no more than it connected all freedom-seeking elements within Jewish society to the exodus.

Instead of moving directly from the sign prophets to the exodus, then, it is worth considering what else "freedom," "signs," and the "desert" would call to mind for readers familiar with the rest of Josephus's narrative. Such a literary analysis has the potential to highlight aspects of first-century Jewish thought that Josephus took for granted, and to clarify the place of the sign prophets within, and not simply on the margins of, first-century religious life. In this chapter, I argue that it is the Maccabean revolt, far more than the exodus or the conquest, that has shaped Josephus's portrayal of the sign prophets as impostors who incited rebellion against Rome. The framework of the Maccabean revolt allows Josephus to present himself as the one who faithfully defends the Jewish way of life in the face of the threat posed by the rebels. The latter, rather than being the inspired proponents of Jewish liberty from the Romans, correspond to the Hellenizers of an earlier era by their subversion of the national *politeia*. Josephus's polemical use of the Maccabean revolt depends for its effectiveness on—and as a result indirectly confirms—the importance of this event in the memory of first-century Jews.

The appropriation of the sign prophets as foils for his own prophetic role suggests, similarly, that the sign prophets were concerned about contemporary religious practice as well as future deliverance.

Signs of Freedom and the Revolt against Rome

Whatever their historical connection, Josephus clearly intends for the sign prophets to be viewed together with the rebel leaders as instigators of revolt who were responsible for Jerusalem's destruction.[14] In *J. W.* 2.258–60, Josephus claims that the "deceivers and impostors" who led their followers into the desert promising "signs of freedom" (*eleutherias*) had "purer hands but more impious intentions" than the *sicarii* and that they "no less than the assassins ruined the peace of the city." Then, immediately after mentioning the Egyptian "false prophet" (2.261–63), Josephus again links the rebels and the sign prophets together by their desire for freedom from Roman rule: "The impostors and brigands, banding together, incited numbers to revolt, exhorting them to assert their independence [*eleutherian*]" (2.264). The "false prophet" who had promised "signs of salvation" in the temple prompts another similar summary statement: "Numerous prophets . . . were at this period suborned by the tyrants to delude the people" (*J. W.* 6.286).[15] The same effect is produced in the *Antiquities*. Before his discussion of various "impostors and deceivers" who promised "wonders and signs" in the desert (20.167), Josephus mentions "bands of brigands and impostors who deceived the mob" as evidence of the worrisome political situation during Felix's rule (20.160–61). And immediately after describing the *sicarii*, he comments that "Festus also sent a force of cavalry and infantry against the dupes of a certain impostor who had promised them salvation and rest from troubles" (20.188). The violent suppression of Theudas's followers indicates that Theudas was also viewed as a threat to Roman rule (20.97).

The connection between the "deceivers and impostors" who promised "signs of freedom [*eleutherias*]" (*J. W.* 2.259) and the "impostors and brigands" who exhorted the people "to assert their independence [*eleutherian*]" (2.264) is especially telling, for it implies that the prophetic activity of the "impostors" offered inspired justification for those who sought freedom from Roman rule.[16] When the desire for freedom is considered in the context of Josephus as a whole, it appears as the leitmotif of the unrest that culminated in the Jewish revolt. Thus, Titus motivated his Roman troops by pitting their desire for glory against the renowned Jewish desire for liberty (*J. W.* 3.480). For his part, the high priest Ananus urged the people to drive the Zealots from the temple with the question:

> Have you then lost that most honourable, that most instinctive, of passions—the desire for liberty [*eleutherias*]? Have we fallen in love with slavery, in love with our masters, as though submission were a heritage from our forefathers?

> Nay, they sustained many a mighty struggle for independence and yielded neither to Egyptian nor to Median domination, in their determination to refuse obedience to a conqueror's behests. (*J. W.* 4.175–76)

Adding that liberty was the pretext for war against Rome, Ananus argued that it was even worse to submit to internal tyranny.[17]

Josephus not only juxtaposes references to the sign prophets and rebel leaders, and attributes to them the same desire for freedom that led to active revolt; he also accuses the prophets of actively turning the people from God. Within his narrative, the signs of the prophets contrast with the heavenly signs that portended Jerusalem's destruction, which he claims were tragically misunderstood by the inhabitants of the city. Commenting on the "signs of deliverance" promised by a "false prophet" (6.285), Josephus explains:

> Thus it was that the wretched people were deluded at that time by charlatans and pretended messengers of the deity; while they neither heeded nor believed in the manifest portents that foretold the coming desolation, but, as if thunderstruck and bereft of eyes and mind, disregarded the plain warnings of God. (*J. W.* 6.288)[18]

Freedom, the Jewish *Politeia*, and the Maccabees

Given the connection between "freedom" and the Jewish revolt against Rome, one may be forgiven for supposing that the concept would be tainted by its association with the rebel leaders. Yet "freedom" figures prominently in the *Antiquities* as part of Josephus's apologetic defense of the Jewish *politeia*, or constitution, and reappears at pivotal points in Josephus's narration of Israel's history—including, most notably, the Maccabean revolt.

Steve Mason has argued persuasively that "the *Antiquities/Life* was from start to finish about the Judean constitution."[19] The word *politeia* sometimes refers specifically to a form of government (*Ant.* 4.223)[20]—whether to priestly aristocracy, which was Josephus's preference, or to kingly rule, which he grudgingly acknowledged as a legitimate (albeit inferior) alternative, so long as the king observed the laws and acted in consultation with the high priest and his counsel.[21] But the term can also denote the wider code of religious and political laws summarized in *Ant.* 4.196–302, within which instructions about a particular form of government play a relatively minor role (*Ant.* 4.223–24).[22]

The relationship between this broader sense of the *politeia* and "freedom" is highlighted in the programmatic summary of the laws in *Antiquities* book 4. Before Moses takes leave of the Israelites, he commends the "moderation of the laws" and the "orderliness of the constitution" (*politeia*), obedience to which will result in divine protection (*Ant.* 4.184–85). Then, after Moses exhorts his audience to obey their leaders, Josephus, with the benefit of hindsight, has Moses add:

> Consider that freedom [*eleutherian*] is not to resent whatever the rulers demand that you do. For now you regard free speech to consist in this, to show insolence to your benefactors. If you are careful about this in the future, your situation will improve. Never show the same anger toward them that you have often ventured to display toward me. For you know that I have more frequently been in danger of death at your hands than from the enemy. (*Ant.* 4.187–88)

It is surely no accident that in his earlier work, Josephus focused so much attention on the internal dissent of the rebels and quotes Vespasian as saying that the Romans "owed their victory not to themselves but to sedition" (*J. W.* 4.376).[23]

Josephus argues that the freedom enjoyed so fully under Solomon (*Ant.* 8.38) was forfeited through disobedience to the law, resulting in the exile of both northern and southern kingdoms. At this narrative midpoint of the *Antiquities*,[24] Josephus goes out of his way to emphasize the prophetic parallels he uncovers between the destruction of Jerusalem by the Babylonians and the destruction of Jerusalem by the Romans.[25] He observes that Jeremiah not only predicted slavery in Babylon and release by the Persians (*Ant.* 10.112–13); he also "left behind writings concerning the recent capture of our city" (10.79). Josephus concludes his narration of events related to the exile with a summary of what he regards as Daniel's prediction of the sequence of world powers from the Persians to the Romans, to which he adds: "Daniel also wrote about the empire of the Romans and that Jerusalem would be taken by them and the temple laid waste" (10.276). By linking the prophets' predictions of Jerusalem's second demise to their predictions of the Babylonian exile, Josephus makes it obvious that the destruction of Jerusalem by the Romans resulted from a similar failure to adhere to the Mosaic laws.

In Josephus's account of postexilic history, the religious sense of the *politeia* first receives great emphasis in connection with the Maccabean revolt. Between the Tobiad romance and the beginning of his paraphrase of 1 Maccabees, Josephus appends a transitional section in which he notes that the high priest, Menelaus, and the Tobiads informed Antiochus IV "that they wished to abandon their country's laws [*tous patrious nomous*] and the way of life [*politeia*] prescribed by these, and to follow the king's laws and adopt the Greek way of life [*politeia*]" (12.240).[26]

Other passages in Josephus's narrative confirm the centrality of this challenge to the Jewish way of life by pointing forward to it and referring back to it. In *Ant.* 4.310, for example, the Israelites in the wilderness take an oath not only to observe the laws but also to exact vengeance on any of their kinsmen who would "undertake to confound and abolish the constitution [*politeia*] based upon them"—just as Mattathias eventually did (*Ant.* 12.268–71). According to *Ant.* 10.275, Daniel predicted the coming of Antiochus

Epiphanes, who "would make war on the nation and their laws, take away the *politeia* based on these laws, rob the temple, and forbid the sacrifices from being offered for three years."[27] Finally, the negative reaction to the athletic competitions Herod introduced into Jerusalem (*Ant.* 15.267–91) recalls the gymnasium built in Jerusalem by Menelaus and the Tobiads before the Maccabean revolt (12.241), and the eventual response by Mattathias and his family is similar to the response of Herod's opponents who believed it was "a sacred duty to undertake any risk rather than seem to be indifferent to Herod's forcible introduction of practices not in accord with custom, by which their way of life [*politeia*] would be totally altered" (*Ant.* 15.281).[28]

Though "freedom" is mentioned in connection with the return from exile (*Ant.* 11.60; cf. *J. W.* 5.389), and Josephus clearly views as a positive development the restoration of the land (*Ant.* 11.2), the rebuilding of the temple (11.2), cancellation of tribute (11.61), and the renewal of the traditional Jewish aristocratic system of government (11.111–13),[29] references to "freedom" are also much more prominent in connection with the exploits of the Maccabees.[30] Mattathias, for example, instructs his sons to "preserve our country's customs" (12.280) and to be prepared to die for the laws because "when the Deity sees you so disposed, He will not forget you, but in admiration of your heroism will give them [the laws] back to you again, and will restore to you your liberty [*eleutherian*], in which you shall live securely and in the enjoyment of your own customs" (*Ant.* 12.281). In this context, "liberty" refers first of all to freedom to observe the Jewish constitution outlawed by Antiochus IV. But Josephus refers more broadly to complete independence from foreign rule when he states that Judas Maccabeus "freed [*eleutherōsas*] his nation and rescued them from slavery to the Macedonians" (*Ant.* 12.434). Moreover, in his treatise *Against Apion*, Josephus contrasts the Egyptians, who were slaves "first of the Persians, and then of the Macedonians," with his own people, who "were not merely independent [*eleutheroi*], but had dominion over the surrounding states for about 120 years up to the time of Pompey the Great" (*Ag. Ap.* 2.133–34). Whatever the reason for this pattern, the early Hasmonean period is the era closest in time to the Roman period in which "freedom" is emphasized in Josephus's narrative.

Josephus states that the liberty enjoyed under the early Hasmoneans was finally lost at the time of Pompey's invasion because of internal dissension between Hyrcanus and Aristobulus (*Ant.* 14.77).[31] This point is repeatedly stressed as Josephus places his case for submission to Roman rule in the mouths of important characters. After drawing examples from the exodus to the exile, Josephus himself asks the inhabitants of Jerusalem, "Was it not from party strife among our forefathers, when the madness of Aristobulus and Hyrcanus and their mutual dissensions brought Pompey against the city, and God subjected to the Romans those who were unworthy of liberty [*eleutherias*]?" (*J. W.* 5.396). Since God was on the side of the Romans, and the Jews had passed up the opportunity to resist them when Pompey first invaded (5.365), Josephus claims that the only way of "salvation" was in repentance before God and surrender to the Romans (5.416). Agrippa similarly mentions Pompey and in the same breath claims that his audience will provoke

God's wrath by transgressing the laws they seek to defend if they go to war against the Romans (*J. W.* 2.355–57, 390–94).

Considering that Josephus goes out of his way to stress the legitimacy of the Maccabean revolt and the illegitimacy of the revolt against Rome, the concentration of terminology pertaining to freedom in his description of both revolts is surprising. Nevertheless, attempts to show that Josephus distinguishes between the freedom pursued by the Maccabees on the one hand and that pursued by the rebels against Rome on the other, are not convincing. Martin Hengel argues that Josephus adopts different attitudes toward "freedom" in his two major works, with "freedom" being evaluated negatively in *Jewish War* and positively in *Antiquities*.[32] But there is no sign that in his later work Josephus tries to disguise the desire for liberty among those who fomented revolt. Indeed, Josephus's comments in the *Antiquities* may presuppose his readers' familiarity with the more complete characterization of the rebel leaders in the *War*.[33] For those who had not read his earlier work, Josephus concludes his *Antiquities* by commending his account of the Jewish war as a logical sequel (*Ant.* 20.258–59). Since the *Antiquities* ends with the events leading up to the Jewish revolt against Rome, it is only to be expected that—in contrast to *War*—there are fewer references to "freedom" in connection with the revolt itself.

Nor does Josephus distinguish between the Maccabean pursuit of religious liberty and the purely political aims of the revolt against Rome, sanctioning the one and condemning the other,[34] for we have seen that Josephus presents the Maccabean quest in both religious and political terms. In addition, although Josephus attributes the basest of motivations to the rebel leaders, the speeches he records urging surrender to the Romans depend for their effectiveness on rebel claims to stand for God and to uphold the law. When Josephus blames the fall of the Hasmonean dynasty on the impiety of the people (*J. W.* 5.395) and claims that God is now on the side of the Romans (5.412), he employs "reverse polemic" to undercut the positions held by his opponents.[35] Acknowledging that his audience's "one aim is to preserve inviolate all the institutions of your fathers" (*J. W.* 2.393), Agrippa wonders how they can expect divine assistance when through war they will be "compelled to transgress the very principles on which [they] chiefly build [their] hopes of God's assistance" (*J. W.* 2.391).[36]

The apparent inconsistency between Josephus's portrayal of the Maccabees and his portrayal of the anti-Roman rebels vanishes when the central relationship between freedom and the Jewish *politeia* is recognized. According to Josephus, both religious freedom and political freedom are fundamentally good things that result from obedience to the laws established by Moses.[37] On this point both Josephus and the rebel leaders were in agreement. But although their quest for liberty was laudable, Josephus maintains that the rebels pursued it at the wrong time and in the wrong way,[38] in sharp contrast to the early Hasmoneans, who modeled the sort of fidelity to the *politeia* that results in true religious and political freedom.

As Josephus tells the story, the clearest example of freedom from foreign domination obtained through unswerving adherence to the Jewish *politeia* is the Maccabean revolt.

His narrative suggests, therefore, that references to freedom from Roman rule would recall the last period of independence from foreign rule under the Hasmoneans.

"Following" the Sign Prophets and the Maccabees

If in fact Josephus expects his readers to notice the similarities between the Maccabean revolt and the first Jewish revolt against Rome, and if Josephus portrays the sign prophets as providing inspired justification for the revolt, then it is already reasonable to suppose that the sign prophets should also be viewed in relation to the Maccabean revolt. But beyond this indirect evidence, an additional verbal parallel between Josephus's portrayal of the sign prophets and the Hasmonean patriarch points more directly to a relationship between the two groups.

In contrast to Josephus's account in the *War*, the verb *hepomai* is normally used in the *Antiquities* when the sign prophets persuade people to follow (*hepesthai*) them into the desert.[39] The verb is fairly common and is used in ways unrelated to our present concerns;[40] it is also used of Moses when he questions whether he can persuade the people to follow him where he leads them (*Ant.* 2.271), and when he commands the Israelites to follow him into the Red Sea (2.339). However, the closest parallel to the sign prophets, who persuaded the people to follow (*hepesthai*) them into the *desert*, is found in Josephus's account of the beginning of the Maccabean revolt. There Mattathias abandons his possessions in the city and flees with his family to the desert after crying: "Whoever is zealous for the ancestral customs [*patriōn ethōn*] and the worship of God [*tēs tou theou thrēskeias*], let him follow p*hepesthō*] me!" (*Ant.* 12.271).[41]

On its own, the juxtaposition of *hepomai* and "desert" would seem a tenuous connection between the sign prophets and the Maccabees, but the parallel takes on more significance when it is recognized that Josephus also uses the verb in connection with the Jewish *politeia*. In fact, the most important illustration of the use of *hepomai* in connection with following God and his commands occurs in Moses' programmatic exhortation to obey the constitution he recorded for the Israelites before his death. Stating that God will bless obedience, Moses warns against exchanging his constitution for another one: "Only obey those [rules] that God wishes you to follow [*hepesthai*], and do not value more highly another arrangement more than the present laws, and do not scorn the piety that you now have with regard to God and change it for another way" (*Ant.* 4.181).[42]

The word *hepomai* also carries religious connotations when it appears in contexts where following a human leader entails adopting their way of life. For example, the decision to follow Nimrod's advice to build the Tower of Babel is cast as rebellion against God: "The masses were eager to follow [*hepesthai*] the views [*tois dogmasi*] of Nebrodes, considering it slavery to submit to God" (*Ant.* 1.115). Moses' exhortation to obey his successors naturally appears in a more positive light. After encouraging obedience to the constitution (*politeia*) that he laid down (4.184), Moses adds: "The high priest Eleazar and Iesous, the council of elders, and the leading men of the tribes will propose to you the best counsels, by following [*hepomenoi*] which you will attain happiness" (4.186). In this context, following leaders necessarily involves heeding their counsel; their counsel, it is understood, will go hand in hand with the Mosaic constitution.

The close relationship established here between following a law code and following a human leader[43] finds clearest expression during the Maccabean revolt. Not only do Menelaus and the Tobiads—who "wished to abandon their country's laws [*tous patrious nomous katalipontes*] and the way of life [*politeia*] prescribed by these, and to follow [*hepesthai*] the king's laws and adopt the Greek way of life [*politeia*]" (*Ant.* 12.240)—provide a vivid illustration of the apostasy Moses warned against, but they also provide a foil for Mattathias, who, instead of abandoning his country's laws, chose to abandon (*katalipōn*) his possessions as he fled into the desert. While Menelaus and the Tobiads chose to follow the king's laws, Mattathias called all who were zealous for his "country's laws [*tōn patriōn ethōn*] and the worship of God [*tēs tou theou thrēskeias*]" to follow (*hepesthō*) him (*Ant.* 12.271).[44] In both passages the choice of a leader was bound up with a decision in favor of a specific *politeia* and its attendant laws. Those who chose to follow Mattathias into the desert were also pledging allegiance to their ancestral customs. Mattathias's son, Simon, echoed the same sentiments as his father when he urged the people to follow (*hepesthe*) him into battle as they had followed his brothers, and assured them that he would not "flee from or reject what seemed to [his brothers] the noblest thing of all, that is, to die for the laws and the worship of your God [*tēs tou theou thrēskeias*]" (13.199).

The verb *hepomai* is most likely used in the same way when it refers to following the sign prophets. Although adherence to the *politeia* is not made explicit when the sign prophets are depicted leading their followers into the desert, we have seen that Josephus allows that those who sought freedom from Roman rule believed they were zealous for the laws and that he regarded the sign prophets as ideological allies of the rebel movement.[45] Moreover, while he stresses the predictive ability of prophets in general, he also grants the legitimate role of prophets as defenders of the Jewish way of life.[46] Finally, we have observed how Josephus—who presents himself as an inspired figure modeled after Jeremiah and Daniel[47]—claimed to hold the correct interpretation of the signs and portents that were so tragically misunderstood by the inhabitants of the city. In his speeches urging the people to surrender to the Romans, Josephus pits his own predictions against the false messages of the sign prophets.[48] Although Josephus does not directly present the sign prophets as self-proclaimed guardians of Torah, the competing claims of Josephus suggest that the sign prophets did more than announce divine deliverance; they also claimed to represent God's will and to know the way to secure his favor. From Josephus's perspective, to be sure, the sign prophets led their followers *astray* from the way of life enjoined by Moses.

Conclusion

Those who accused Josephus of being a traitor may well have drawn the same conclusion as Per Bilde, who writes: "Josephus' position can and must be compared with the standpoint taken by the culturally liberal-minded Jews in Jerusalem before the year 170 B.C.E.; that is to say, with the group towards which the Hasmonean Revolt also directed its opposition."[49] Josephus's desire to defend himself against the accusation of being a traitor who betrayed the Jewish *politeia* helps explain the connections we have identified between the sign prophets and the Maccabean revolt. Instead of confessing his "liberal-minded" tendencies, Josephus meets his opponents head-on by presenting his argument in favor of submission to Roman rule in terms of the ideologically charged context of the Maccabean revolt. He allows that the rebels claimed zeal for the laws and that the sign prophets persuaded the people to follow them into the desert as Mattathias had done. But the signs of the prophets were not realized; those who claimed fidelity to the law were in fact its enemies (*J. W.* 4.184); and Jerusalem itself was destroyed by the internal dissent warned against by Moses. The competing claims of Josephus and the sign prophets to faithfully represent God and the Jewish *politeia* mirror the ideological opposition between Menelaus and Mattathias during the reign of Antiochus IV; but in a strange reversal it is Josephus—the one who found protection in a foreign ruler—who speaks on God's behalf and acts as the true heir of the early Hasmoneans, while the sign prophets and those who advocated freedom from Roman rule betrayed the Jewish *politeia* as the Hellenizers had done before them. Despite his contemporaries' criticisms, Josephus presents himself as a model of that common Judaism upon which the priests and the people agreed, a Judaism characterized by faithfulness to Torah and temple[50] or, as Josephus would put it, by faithfulness to the *politeia* and the "worship of God." The effect of this reversal is not simply to absolve Josephus from the charge of treachery; it also contributes to his apologetic defense of the *politeia*, fidelity to which results in freedom.

The importance of the Maccabean revolt in Josephus's own writing and the supposition that his polemic was comprehensible, if not necessarily convincing, point indirectly to the lasting influence of the Hasmoneans on first-century Jewish society. But what can be said about the sign prophets themselves? First, it is possible that some were motivated by memories of the Maccabean revolt even if they were also influenced by the exodus or conquest. Even though the Egyptian prophet is presented in *Ant.* 20.169–72 as a latter-day Joshua, anticipating the collapse of Jerusalem's walls, Josephus's earlier account explains that the Egyptian intended to enter the city by force, setting himself up as a tyrant after he had seized the Roman garrison (*J. W.* 2.261–63)—a plan that evokes Judas Maccabee's capture of the Macedonian garrison prior to the rededication of the Jerusalem temple (*J. W.* 1.39) much more than it recalls the conquest of Jericho. Presumably one of these two contradictory versions is more accurate than the other, but references to Joshua and Judas need not be seen as mutually exclusive in principle.

Second, the evidence from Josephus indicates what is otherwise inherently likely: the sign prophets were not preoccupied with eschatology to the neglect of other political and religious concerns. Thus, it is unhelpful to distinguish between sign prophets and rebel leaders solely on the basis of the eschatological motivations of the former and the political and religious aims of the latter. As Sanders rightly notes, "Those who hoped to trigger divine intervention in the cause of freedom were not, by the standards of the time, members of the lunatic fringe."[51] Even if the connections between sign prophets and rebel leaders are attributed to Josephus's own apologetic desire to blame the revolt on a few scoundrels, both rebels and sign prophets clearly shared a common desire to uphold the law and a common longing for liberty, which may have led, at times, to collaboration.

13. Memory in Josephus and the Culture of the Jews in the First Century

Seth Schwartz

Ed Sanders's account of nonelite, nonsectarian first-century Judaism was groundbreaking because it demonstrated the importance to the analyst of immersion in the details of practice, because of its constant and fruitful reference to the results of archaeological exploration, and because of its embrace of interrogation and hypothesis.[1] Sanders's decision to work outward from the ideological center I believe was correct; but it does raise questions. For example, how would an ethnography of the first-century Jews differ from Sanders's account of first-century Judaism? Such an ethnography, let us recall, would begin not with the institutional centers of Judaism but with such issues as kinship and land tenure patterns, networks of social relations, and domestic rituals. These are issues about which the Pentateuch had little, or at any rate little that was not utopian, to say, yet these elements were necessarily important components of the real-life experience of Jews in first-century Palestine.

Another way of framing the question is as follows: To what extent did *Judaism* constitute the *culture* of the Jews? And, to push our ethnographic investigation in a historical direction, was there a relation between Judaism and/or the culture of the Jews and the fact that as a group they proved unusually difficult to incorporate into the Roman state, or was this problem, as some have argued, essentially political? Rather than consider these issues on the theoretical level, in what follows, I would like to discuss a case: the Jewish reception of late Hellenistic and early Roman practices of benefaction and memorialization. This case was apparently peripheral in the Jewish literary/religious traditions (though a lot less peripheral if you know what you are looking for) but was arguably important as a component of ancient Jewish culture, and inarguably important in its political significance. My intention is not to undermine or displace Sanders's work, but to supplement it by approaching the remains of the ancient Jews from a different angle.

It has recently been argued that Roman culture of the early empire was unusually concerned with memorialization. In this view, the first century was characterized by a profound anxiety about the individual's place in the world—a consequence of the social upheavals produced by Roman expansion. People responded to this anxiety in two ways: first, with monumental construction, and, second, by more or less obsessively writing their names in public and semipublic spaces. The tombs of the citizenry and the writing that decorated them, the dedicatory and honorary inscriptions posted in temples and marketplaces, all reflect efforts by citizens and the communities they supported to mark their places in an alarmingly unstable world.

This is a rather reductive account of Greg Woolf's attempt to explain the rise of the epigraphic culture in the early Roman Empire.[2] It seems obvious in retrospect that one should be cautiously skeptical about the ascription of moods or states of mind—in this case, anxiety—to abstractions like society. Still, even if we think that large-scale cultural shifts are not so easy to explain, we can admit their reality and ask some questions of our own about them. Something did change under the early empire; the Mediterranean-wide spike in monumental construction and lapidary writing is real and meaningful. Finally, like so much writing from the ancient Mediterranean world starting sometime in the Iron Age, whether carved, painted on stone, or inscribed in books, it was meant at least in part to secure the memorialization of the people named.[3] The question I would like to ask is where the Jews of Palestine fit. Did they participate in the general early imperial culture of memorialization, did they reject it, or did they appropriate it?

Two complementary observations led me to these questions. First, first-century Jerusalem lacked public monumental construction aside from the temple and a theater and amphitheater allegedly built by Herod but not attested in the archaeological record.[4] The only other monumental construction in the city was private, consisting of houses and mausolea. Correspondingly, first-century Jerusalemite epigraphy consists almost entirely of names scratched or painted on ossuaries or on the walls of burial caves; there are next to none of the sort of building, dedicatory, or honorary inscriptions that was so prominent in the material culture of other cities of the early Roman Empire. Though one could always adduce accidents of preservation, it seems more reasonable to suppose that these archaeological anomalies reflect real cultural differences, that is, ways in which Jerusalem's practices of monumentalization and memory diverged from those of other Roman cities.[5]

This latter point seems to be confirmed by the many surprising and peculiar, though rarely noticed, passages about memory, building, and benefaction in Josephus's work (this is the second observation). In aggregate, these passages suggest that at least some Jews self-consciously opted out of a whole set of early Roman cultural norms or, more precisely, accepted them with significant adaptations, in ways that emphasized their subordination to norms of Jewish piety. The main goal of this larger investigation of the Jews' response to Roman-style benefaction and memory is to contribute to our understanding of the (larger) issue of the Jews' integration in the Roman world and the reasons for its eventual failure. The present discussion will be limited to the concept of *mnēmē*, memorialization, in Josephus.

Josephus's *Erga*[6]

I begin with a basic and at first glance trivial observation. There is reason to believe that Josephus's two main historical works, the *Jewish War* and the *Jewish Antiquities*, were written to memorialize the characters and events described in them. This is not meant to exclude the alternative view—that the works were written to advance certain arguments or prove certain points. Josephus claims that he wrote the *Jewish War* to display not only the might of the Romans but also the seriousness of the Jews' resistance and, despite this, to demonstrate that the Jewish nation was not actually hostile to the Romans. Rather, it was forced into revolt, and the Romans into response, by internal factional strife (*stasis*), a theme borrowed from Thucydides (see *J. W.* 1.1–16).[7] The *Antiquities*, for its part, was written to celebrate Moses, but also to show that when the Jews followed God's laws they prospered, and when they neglected them they suffered (*Ant.* 1.14–17).[8]

That these really were Josephus's concerns can be readily illustrated from the contents of the works, but a careful reading shows that he had many other concerns as well. Indeed, Josephus explicitly states that the *Jewish War* is meant to be a *mnēmē katorthōmaton*—a memorial of great achievements, presumably of both Jews and Romans.[9] But he evinces a certain cultural self-consciousness: Josephus says that he, "a foreigner, dedicates [*anatithēmi*] to the Greeks and Romans a memorial of great achievements, made with vast expense and great labors," and he continues by denouncing the "natives" (*gnēsioi*—apparently meaning both Greeks and Romans) for neglecting such labors for the pursuit of money and the conduct of lawsuits. In using language quite directly borrowed from that of honorary and dedicatory inscriptions, Josephus is obviously following the lead of Herodotus and Thucydides. He is also suggesting, however, that there is something paradoxical in an *allophylos* (alien, foreigner) producing such a piece of writing (and doing it better than the "natives"). Though this description of a piece of historiography as *mnēmē* (memory) is at first glance a tired commonplace,[10] there are elements of Josephus's account that make best sense if we take the commonplace seriously—that is, if we assume these elements to be aspects of a program of memorialization that, notwithstanding the self-consciousness of *Jewish War* 1.16, had been to some extent naturalized among the Jews of the first century.[11]

In the only discrete study of memory in Josephus of which I am aware, Gabriele Boccaccini argues that one of chief functions of *mnēmē* in Josephus's works, especially *Jewish Antiquities* and *Against Apion*, is closely related to the function of *zikkaron* (memory) in Josephus's biblical sources. What Josephus repeatedly calls on his readers to remember is the evidence of God's *euergesiai* (benefactions) to Israel, and Israel's obligation to reciprocate these benefactions with gratitude and loyalty.[12] Yet even in repeatedly stating matters in these terms, Josephus is tacitly updating the Bible's conception of memory as an element of a cultural system in which social reciprocity is institutionalized as vassalage or slavery. For Josephus, God is patron and *euergetēs* (benefactor (*Ant.* 4.213, 317; 6.211; 7.206) more than he is lord. Indeed, Josephus almost never uses the terms *despotēs* (master (*Ant.* 1.272; 4.40) or *kyrios* for God; unlike many of his Christian and rabbinic near contemporaries, he avoids characterizing Israel's relationship to God as one of *douleia* (Hebrew *'avdut*), that is, slavery or vassalage.

A more drastic innovation is Josephus's tendency to "humanize" *euergesia* and *aretē* (benefaction and virtuous deed) when he states or implies the desirability of remembering *people*, starting, in the introduction to *Antiquities*, with Moses. In his account of the binding of Isaac (paraphrasing Genesis 22), he has God assure Abraham that not only would he be the ancestor of many *genē* (nations, clan-groups), but that the *genarchai* (founders of these groups—apparently not Abraham alone) would enjoy *mnēmē aiōnios*—eternal memorialization (1.235). I would suggest that for Josephus, one of the means of securing such memorialization was inscription in the biblical text itself. That is, for Josephus, any character more or less favorably mentioned in the Hebrew Bible has ipso facto attained *mnēmē aiōnios*.

This point is evident in Josephus's remarkable excursus on King Saul and his sons in *Antiquities* (6.343–50). At 340, Josephus interrupts his narrative with two moralistic eulogies. In the first, he praises the witch of En-Dor for showing kindness to Saul without the hope of receiving anything in return, and he commends this behavior, which flies in the face of the natural human desire for reciprocation, as most noble. The second eulogy concerns Saul, who, though his death in battle had been foretold, nevertheless bravely faced up to his obligation as king to try to protect his nation. Josephus addresses "the kings of nations and the rulers of cities" about the virtue of facing "danger and even death on behalf of their countries" and of despising all terrors, as King Saul did. By forgoing the possibility of honor and loyalty in his lifetime, Saul secured *doxa* (glory) (perhaps more desirable than mere *timē* [honor]) and *mnēmē aiōnios* through his death. In other words, Saul, like the witch of En-Dor, admirably suppressed the natural desire to have his benefactions reciprocated. Indeed, he despised even another conventional route to *mnēmē*—male offspring, for he encouraged his sons to join him in his doomed defense of the Israelites, knowing that the *aretē* of his sons, much more than their survival, would truly secure his *epainos* (praise) and *agērōs* (ageless) *mnēmē*. Saul knew that this was the best course of action for anyone who desires to achieve *hē meta ton thanaton euphēmia* (good reputation after death).

Now in a speech addressed to the besieged rebels of Jerusalem in *Jewish War* (6.104–5), Josephus adduces the example of one of the last kings of Judah, Jehoiachin, to argue exactly the opposite point—the moral worth of timely surrender in a hopeless war—but in a conceptual framework similar to that of the encomium of Saul. Because of

Jehoiachin's surrender to the Babylonians (which we might have regarded as dishonorable but which preserved the temple and the city), Josephus continues, "a holy *logos* hymns him among all the Jews, and memory flowing ever new transmits him immortal to those coming after him" (*logos auton pros hapanton Ioudaion hieros hymnei kai mnēmē reousa di'aiōnos aei nea tois epiginomenois paradidosin athanaton* [6.105]). Of course, *hieros logos* (holy word) here is ambiguous, referring both to the actual biblical text and to oral storytelling (with orality perhaps suggested most strongly by *paradidosin* [hands down] as elsewhere in Josephus's works).[13] I would suggest that when Josephus speaks of the eternal memory of Saul and his family, he intends a similar ambiguity, and, further, that Josephus's narrative itself is a component of the flow of memorialization.

One way of understanding such passages is as a proposed solution to a kind of meta-exegetical problem: If we have been given the pentateuchal laws to live by, and the prophecies to serve as ever-meaningful oracles (as many Jews in the first century, including Josephus, thought), what is the purpose of the biblical histories? In the passages we have discussed, Josephus may well be providing his response: the biblical histories serve as monuments to the *euergesiai* and *aretai* of the founders of our nation.

If so, Josephus's approach to the biblical histories resembles that of Ben Sira, who almost three centuries earlier had written a poem memorializing precisely the *euergesiai* and *aretai* of (a selection of) the biblical heroes (chs. 44–49).[14] Both Ben Sira and Josephus brought the story down into their present (Ben Sira included his contemporary the high priest Simon as one of his protagonists [ch. 50]). By transforming the biblical histories into memorials of human *aretē* and *euergesia*, however heroic, both writers in effect obscured the boundary between the mythic past and the present.

In what follows, I turn to the role of memorialization in, as it were, Josephus's modern history, especially in the first book of the *Jewish War* and the last six books of *Antiquities*. The focus will be on the cases of Herod, his grandson Agrippa I, and the royal family of Adiabene, which converted to Judaism around the year 50 C.E. We have already seen that, for Josephus, though *mnēmē* may be secured by the materiality of written documents (in addition, perhaps, to speech), it is curiously unconnected to actual monuments—an important distinction between Josephus and the rest of the Greek historiographic tradition starting with Herodotus, in which *mnēmē* is often described as evoked by or embodied in places, buildings, and other objects.[15] In Josephus's postbiblical history, ambivalence about memorialization in the monumental form of public construction and lapidary writing is a running theme, an ambivalence interestingly manifested also in the remains of first-century Jerusalem. An additional peculiarity is Josephus's abstraction of *mnēmē* from its standard place, in a Greco-Roman context, in the discourse of *timē*, or honor. According to Woolf, monumental construction or writing is not infrequently meant to secure what Josephus called in the case of Saul *hē meta ton thanaton euphēmia*.[16] Just as frequently, however, it formed part of the culture of euergetism, that is, benefaction by the wealthy to their communities. Such benefaction was a way of advertising prosperity and superiority and, more to the point, of eliciting reciprocation, in the form of honor and loyalty, from their communities within their lifetimes. As his discussion of the witch of En-Dor and Saul indicates, it is for this type of memorialization that Josephus reserves his most articulate ambivalence.

There is, however, little sign of such ambivalence in the *Jewish War*. This is not surprising, given the *War*'s tendency to downplay the Jews' cultural distinctiveness. Josephus briefly lists Herod's construction projects before moving on to his central topic, the king's domestic/succession crises.[17] We may, however, note several peculiarities (*J. W.* 1.401–28). Josephus characterizes Herod's building projects in Palestine not in the language of *euergesia* but in that of memorialization. Thus, he views Herod's projects as attempts to perpetuate *tēn mnēmēn kai tas epiklēseis* ("the memory and the names") of his *philoi* (friends) (1.403), to offer honor to Caesar (1.407), and to provide memorials (*mnēmeia*) to his relatives (1.417) and *mnēmē* for himself (1.419). Only in the case of Herod's gifts to foreign cities does the *Jewish War* utilize the language of euergetism, characterizing them as *megalopsychia* (1.422), *charis* (1.426), and *euergesia* (1.428) (greatness of soul, grace, and benefaction), that is, as benefiting Herod's clients, not his patrons (including God).

This is the only passage in his works where Josephus associates monumental construction and *mnēmē* in a way that is not explicitly disapproving. Even so, he does not comment here on the success of Herod's memorialization project. In the next book of the *Jewish War*, however, Josephus describes the expulsion from Judea of both the Romans and the descendants of Herod. It may be suggested, then, that for Josephus, Herod's attempt to perpetuate among the Jews the memories of his Roman patrons and his own family ended in failure. But in the *War* this theme is at most implicit, lost in the flow of the narrative. Even if Josephus believes that Herod's attempt at memorialization was unsuccessful, he nevertheless seems to approve of Herod's efforts. This may be the reason that he neglects to mention those building projects that the Jews regarded as most problematic: the theater and amphitheater that Herod built in Jerusalem. In *Ant.* 15.267–79, Josephus claims that, though foreign visitors admired the buildings and the games and shows conducted in them, the *epichōrioi* (natives) disapproved, because they regarded the buildings themselves as alien to Jewish custom and *ou paradedotai* (have not been handed down) and the games performed and images displayed in them as outright violations of Jewish *ethē* (customs).[18]

Indeed, in *Antiquities* Josephus generally professes greater skepticism about Herod's motivations than he does in the *War* (15.330). The Jews, he says, generally regarded Herod's benefactions as illicit. Furthermore, Herod played both sides. To the Jews, Herod claimed that he had no choice; to his Roman patrons, by contrast, he said that his building projects demonstrated that he regarded their honor as more important than his native customs. In reality, says Josephus, "his entire aim was his own advantage; either that or he zealously strove to leave behind greater memorials of his rule to posterity" (*philotimoumenos meizō ta mnēmeia tēs archēs tois authis hypolipesthai*)—with the clear implication that this project was doomed to failure.

Even the two benefactions that Josephus describes in unambiguously favorable terms did nothing, in the historian's view, to perpetuate Herod's *mnēmē* among the Jews. Herod's devoted and self-sacrificing attempts to provide relief in a region-wide famine caused the Jews briefly to forget Herod's unlawful behavior (*Ant.* 15.299–316), and his magnificent reconstruction of the Jerusalem temple did secure the people's gratitude—but only to God, not the king (*Ant.* 15.421–23). Josephus's attitude is evident in the relatively scant attention he pays to the festival marking the dedication of Herod's temple, in contrast to the many pages he devotes to the dedication of Solomon's temple (*Ant.* 8.50–129).

Herod's desperate efforts to leave behind lasting *mnēmē* among the Jews is the subject of a remarkably explicit but infrequently discussed passage in *Antiquities* (16.150–59).[19] Josephus speculates that Herod was, above all, motivated by passionate *philotimia* (love of honor, ambition): his generosity was motivated by his desire to secure *mnēmē* for the future and a good reputation in the present. His constant drive for honor, however, made him exceedingly harsh to his relatives and his subjects; after all, someone had to pay for all his generosity. Herod's need to be honored was reflected in his intense deference to Augustus and his friends, and in his insistence that he be similarly deferred to by his own subjects, and he was enraged if disappointed. And he was constantly disappointed, because the very thing that he regarded as most beautiful, *therapeia*—in both senses, of courting and of being courted(16.157)—"was alien to the nation of the Jews, who were accustomed to love righteousness more than glory." So he disfavored the Jews, since they could not flatter him by making temples and statues in his honor.

These themes are taken up again with some modifications in Josephus's comparison of Herod and Agrippa I as benefactors (*Ant.* 19.328–31). This passage amplifies the rather surprising theme of book 16 that Herod never bestowed favors on the Jews, but only on the Greeks. Josephus praises his grandson Agrippa, though, as having had a kindly character and having bestowed benefits on all, but having been proportionately more beneficial to his Jewish *homophyloi* (compatriots). Now Josephus's account itself strongly contradicts the argument that Agrippa was more generous to the Jews than his grandfather had been. In fact, Josephus is here conflating *euergesia* with character (Herod was *ponēros* [wicked] and Agrippa *praüs* [mild or nice]) and, more strikingly, with piety. Herod neglected the laws, while Agrippa loved living in Jerusalem, observed the traditions *katharos* (whatever this means), and never let a day pass without a rite of purification or a sacrifice.

For Josephus, then, true *euergesia* consists in a combination of generosity, niceness, ethnic solidarity, and the appearance or reputation of careful legal observance. This is why he praises Agrippa, whose actual benefactions to the Jews were dwarfed by those of his grandfather, as genuinely *euergetikos* and as having rightly earned *euphēmia* (like King Saul), while depriving his grandfather Herod—and successfully so, it might be added!—of precisely what he most strove for—*mnēmē*.[20]

Our final example of Josephan *mnēmē* is provided by the royal family of Adiabene, whose conversion to Judaism in the middle of the first century is recounted at length in *Antiquities* (20.17–99).[21] Embedded in this narrative is the story (20.49) of how Queen Helena, thankful to God for having preserved her son Izates from the many dangers (political rather than medical) she thought to be attendant on his decision to be circumcised, decided to travel to Jerusalem in order to thank God in person. She arrived during a famine (20.51) and so dispatched her retinue to purchase food, which she then distributed. Her son Izates (20.53) also sent much money to the "leaders of the Jerusalemites" for distribution to the hungry. Queen Helena, unlike Herod in similar circumstances, "left behind the greatest *mnēmē* of her good deed to our entire nation." In sum, while famine relief is, on the face of it, a perfectly normal type of benefaction in a Greco-Roman context, it was also in this case a kind of pious practice. As Josephus implies in the passage just quoted, it was also an expression of ethnic solidarity, for through it Queen Helena celebrated her recently acquired Jewishness. Furthermore, popular reciprocation took initially an oral rather than a material form—no publicly built statues, no monuments, no honorary inscriptions, but rather *mnēmē*, even, according to one odd manuscript reading, *mnēmē eis aei diaboomenē* ("memory energetically recounted for all eternity"; this is odd because Josephus was writing only a generation after the gift). Here, too, Josephus's story was meant to serve as memorialization.

Josephus, Archaeology, Mnēmē

As we have seen, Josephus presented *mnēmē* in distinctive ways: he abstracted it from its standard Greco-Roman situation in the cultural complex of honor, benefaction, and monumental construction; he asserted that it is secured mainly through piety and through types of public generosity assimilable to norms of Jewish piety, and that it is perpetuated orally, or through inscription, not on stones but in texts. This is true especially of biblical texts, which Josephus sometimes presents as if they themselves were meant to be monuments to the benefactions and heroic deeds of the Jews' ancestors. He presented even his own historiography as an act of commemoration.

This presentation of *mnēmē* is explicable in terms of Josephus's countercultural description of Judaism especially in his later works. In the *Antiquities* and *Against Apion*, Josephus repeatedly emphasized that the Jews reject honor and everything associated with it;[22] they do not erect statues for their benefactors, since these so little confer honor that the Greeks make them even of their favorite slaves (*Ag. Ap.* 2.71–78); they pay no attention to wealth and inherited rank (*Ag. Ap.* 2.186); they do not value athletic competition or artistic innovation, though these are commonly supposed to confer honor. Instead, they believe that the victor's wreath is awarded by God to the righteous in the next life (*Ag. Ap.* 2.217–19); they have no aristocracy in the conventional sense but rather live under what Josephus was the first to call a "theocracy," which is to say that they are ruled by a group of men distinguished not by wealth and rank but only by wisdom and obedience to God (*Ant.* 4.223).[23] In *Against Apion* (2.157–63), Josephus described their lawgiver Moses as an ideal *euergetēs*, who used his influence over the people not to enhance his own power or establish a tyranny, but only to provide them with *eunomia*—good legislation[24] —expecting for this favor no reciprocation from the Israelites. In sum, for Josephus, the Jews utterly reject the social, political, and cultural norms of the Greco-Roman city, preferring instead to conduct their entire lives according to norms of piety. In his account, Jews lived in a perpetual state of purity and religious dedication, a condition that the Greeks struggle to maintain only a few days a year (*Ag. Ap.* 2.188). In other words, Josephus argues that Judaism is a *religion*, though strikingly he lacked the language to say so.

Josephus's comments about *mnēmē* largely (and rather surprisingly) conform to his summary and idealizing accounts of the Jewish "constitution," but not completely. In the *Jewish War*, the Jews do not seem entirely resistant to Herod's benefactions and memorialization projects, even if their descendants ultimately rejected them. Indeed, one could say that in his historical works, Josephus in general moderated the extreme presentation of *Against Apion* by describing the Jews' response to the cultures of euergetism and memorialization not as simple rejection but as thorough adaptation: the Jews did have benefactors and did reciprocate their generosity, provided that generosity took an acceptable form, such as famine relief (as opposed to, for example, gladiatorial shows) or the provision of sacrifices or votive gifts to the temple (as opposed to monumental public construction). Jews reciprocated not with statues and inscriptions, but orally and textually, with *mnēmē*.

Matters look more different still if we look outside of Josephus's writing. In fact, on the whole the material culture of first-century Jerusalem more or less conforms to Josephus's countercultural presentation of the Jews. Jerusalem did not look like a standard city of the early Roman imperial East. Aside from the temple, no public buildings, no statues, no honorary or dedicatory inscriptions have yet been discovered.

Yet the material remains also suggest that Jerusalem's culture of memorialization, while not normatively Greco-Roman, sometimes strayed from Josephus's characterization. An inscription of the first century marking the (undiscovered) burial place of the eighth-century Judahite king Uzziah implies that the memorialization of, in this case, mythic benefactors might sometimes take material form and not be restricted to storytelling and Bible reading.[25] Indeed, Josephus's claim that the Jews, because of their rejection of honor, also rejected lavish funerals and grand tombs (*Ag. Ap.* 2.205) is contradicted repeatedly not only in his own works, which often mention in passing conspicuous mausolea[26]—and on one occasion denounce the obligatory practice of providing excessively expensive public funerary feasts (*J. W.* 2.1)—but also by the archaeological record. The mausolea of first-century Jerusalemite grandees are prominent components of the Jerusalem landscape even today. Even modest burial caves, thousands of which have been found in the vicinity of Jerusalem, generally display architectural traces of monumentalization.[27] For some Jews, at least, it seems to have been legitimate to secure memorialization through the construction of monumental tombs, which occasionally (though not often) were inscribed with the names of the deceased, and the provision of public feasts.

At this juncture, our study could follow several directions. One could consider why rabbinic stories about the Second Temple period tend to focus precisely on the people Josephus said had earned *mnēmē* among the Jews, a group that includes not only King Agrippa and Queen Helena, but even such obscure figures as Nicanor, maker of the temple gates, and Alexas of Syrian Apamaea. Alternatively, one could set the whole inquiry in the context of a study of institutionalized relationships of social reciprocity, observing the structural need for such social institutions in a premodern agrarian economy, and the Torah's quite adamant rejection of them, and then examine how the Jews coped with the tension. In other words, one could ask how socioeconomic necessity in general produced cultural adaptations among the Jews, and try to see their peculiar culture of memory as an example of such adaptation. It would also be possible to approach the issue from the (related) angle of the Jews' integration in the Roman Empire, or rather its stunning failure, at least initially. Did the Jews' partial rejection of honor, euergetism, and patronage and their embrace of a quite different set of norms contribute to their unassimilability in an empire that depended for its integration at least in part on cultural practices that otherwise were widely embraced in the Mediterranean world? The very fact that the results of this investigation point in so many different directions is suggestive for showing how much profit we can derive from the assumption of the role and mind-set of the ethnographer. This is not, of course, to deny the immense importance of Sanders's center-out model. Indeed, one of the great strengths of "common Judaism" was its relentless exploration of the implications for actual cultural practice of every detail of its normative system: Sanders has himself been a kind of ethnographer. But I hope to have demonstrated at least that there remains work to be done, and that practices that appear to be peripheral may turn out to be in both cultural and political terms unexpectedly important.

14. Epistemology and Social Conflict in *Jubilees* and *Aristeas*

Ian W. Scott

Introduction

When we think about diversity within the "common Judaism" of the Second Temple period, our thoughts do not usually go to issues of epistemology, that is, how early Jews understood the process of knowing. Often it is simply presumed that Jews had no epistemology, that they did not reflect on how they could attain knowledge. It is true, of course, that most Jews did not engage in the kind of analysis that was common among Platonists and Stoics, or for that matter in contemporary departments of philosophy. Yet a close reading of early Jewish texts often reveals a great deal about how the authors understood human knowing in general and religious knowing in particular. Moreover, when we read these documents with an eye to epistemology, we find evidence that different Jewish groups endorsed very different ways of knowing. This epistemological diversity is illustrated well by a comparison between the *Book of Jubilees* and the *Letter of Aristeas*. Although these two Jewish texts were composed around the same time, they reflect very different approaches to religious knowledge. At the same time, this diversity also points to a deeper commonality among Second Temple Jewish groups. For the epistemological approach of each text has, in its own way, been shaped by the social anxieties and ambitions of its author, and in each case these social factors revolve around the marginalization of Jews in a Mediterranean world that was increasingly governed by elite Hellenists. A comparison of *Jubilees* with *Aristeas* will thus illustrate the way in which widely divergent trends in early Jewish thinking often arose from the common struggle of educated Jews to cope with the dominance of Hellenistic culture in the elite circles that such Jews often longed to join.

Two Ways of Knowing

Knowing in *Jubilees*: A Moral Struggle

Composed in the latter second century B.C.E.,[1] the *Book of Jubilees* is cast as a speech delivered to Moses by an angel of the Presence on Mount Sinai, spoken during the forty days when Israel's leader received the Torah (see *Jub.* 33:13).[2] In these speeches, the angel surveys human history from creation to Moses' own day, and the bulk of the document is a creative retelling of the biblical narrative from Genesis 1 to Exodus 20. Along the way, a few key passages offer glimpses of the future that extends to the second-century world of the actual author and beyond.

In *Jubilees*, knowledge of God or of the divine will is never the product of reasoned thought or human inquiry. Most often in *Jubilees* knowledge comes as direct verbal revelation from God. Since the whole book purports to be a transcript of an angelic speech, the interpretation it offers of history and cosmology is represented as immediate revelation.[3] The history surveyed by the angel provides several examples of this kind of revelation. Enoch receives his knowledge of proper times in a dream vision (4:19) and a tour of the heavens (4:21). Noah is taught methods of healing by angelic tutors (10:10-13). God appears to Abraham at the oak of Mamre, "talks" with him, and "causes him to know" that Sarah will have a son (16:1).[4] God speaks directly to Isaac (24:9-11, 22) and communicates with Jacob at Bethel in a dream (27:21-24).[5] Even Laban is given a dream, in which God instructs him not to deal cruelly with Jacob when the patriarch leaves (29:6).[6] The standard model for divine communication is not the prophetic speech but rather a verbal communication from God, whether spoken directly, carried by an angel, or revealed in a dream.[7] Even in dreams, this communication is direct and explicit, without the symbolic encoding that requires special interpretation.[8] Whatever the medium of revelation, these encounters are treated as immediate and self-authenticating. The question of how to distinguish, for example, genuine dreams from spurious ones is not even recognized. The basic mode of acquiring knowledge is, rather, a direct and self-authenticating encounter with God's message.

The author of *Jubilees*, of course, does not expect everyone, or even every righteous person, to receive direct revelation of this sort—hence the emphasis in *Jubilees* on the reliable transmission of revelation in written documents. Moses is told at the outset: "Set your mind on every thing which I shall tell you on this mountain, and write it in a book so that their descendants might see that I have not abandoned them on account of all of the evil which they have done to instigate transgression of the covenant" (1:5). It is through the written document that the readers of *Jubilees* are to encounter the angelic revelation. Enoch is set up as the first to "testify" in this way to human beings, first repeating verbally and then writing down the knowledge of the proper times "just as we [the angels] made it known to him" (4:18). Noah's knowledge of healing and the wiles of satanic forces is likewise written by the patriarch in a book, out of which he teaches his son Shem (10:13-14). Some of these written records of revelation to the patriarchs even seem to correspond to other pseudepigrapha that circulated at the time.[9] The author of *Jubilees* depicts the formation of an unbroken literary tradition that carries revealed knowledge through the generations from Israel's first patriarch through to Joseph. Knowledge that adultery is wrong, for example, is passed down to Joseph, along with "the words which Jacob, his father, used to read, which were from the words of Abraham" (39:6).

Yet even with this written codification of the divine words, questions of hermeneutics or of authentication never arise. Such texts are treated, rather, as if they re-present for the reader the original revelatory encounter. We see the intimate connection between this written tradition and direct revelation in the experience of Abraham. After praying for guidance and protection, Abram is miraculously given a knowledge of Hebrew, "the tongue of creation," which had "ceased from the mouth of all of the sons of men from the day of the Fall" (12:25-26). With this knowledge, he can then understand the traditional books of his father (Terah), which were unreadable before. Moreover, God "caused him to know everything which he was unable (to understand)" (12:27). The ordinary vicissitudes of textual interpretation are thus overcome by virtue of God's direct revelatory involvement in the process of reading. The text carries all of the self-authentication and clarity that characterize a divine epiphany; reading a textual record of revelation is the equivalent of encountering God's voice directly.

Direct revelation by supernatural agents is not, however, the only source of knowledge in *Jubilees*. Some religious knowledge is available innately to human beings. This kind of innate knowledge is implied in the text's assumption that the patriarchs observe God's righteous requirements long before explicit commands are given. Abram, for example, does not receive any revelation and yet comes to understand that idolatry is wrong (11:14-17). Lot and his daughters should have known that incest was wrong, even though that sin had not yet been committed or forbidden (16:7-9).[10] Esau's violation of his oath of love for Jacob is evil (37:11—38:14), even though the obligation to keep one's oaths has never been laid down explicitly. Humanity is also expected to recognize that the astrological lore revealed illegitimately by the fallen Watchers is forbidden and should not be practiced.[11] All of this suggests that although human beings are sometimes given the aid of direct revelation from God, they all possess an innate knowledge (or at least potential for knowledge) of God's moral demands.

Although *Jubilees* does not specify how this innate knowledge of God's will manifests itself to the individual, there is little to suggest that it is the product of rational inquiry. Indeed, the narrative appears to discount the utility of rational inquiry. One night, soon after his initial awakening to God's will, Abram stays up late, intending to predict the coming year's rainfall by the stars (12:16). The author tells us that before he could carry out his plan, a "word came into his heart" telling him to stop (12:17-18). Now this "word" seems most likely to be Abram's own thought, particularly since its content is reported as Abram's own speech ("Why am I seeking?" [12:17]). Moreover, the word does not come as a simple declaration that such astrological inquiry is wrong. Instead, Abram presents himself with reasons why his meteorology is unnecessary:

> All of the signs of the stars and the signs of the sun and the moon are all in the hand of the LORD. Why am I seeking? If he desires, he will make it rain morning and evening, and if he desires he will not send (it) down; and everything is in his hand. (12:17-18)

This transcript of Abram's thought does not provide sufficient grounds for Abram's ethical conclusion. Abram declares that God is in control of both the heavenly bodies and the weather. Yet this fact does not obviously render astrological prediction unnecessary. Still less do these insights suggest that it is morally *wrong* to try to predict the weather. This is clearly what Abram is thinking, however, when he goes on to pray for deliverance from "the hands of evil spirits which rule over the thought of the heart of man" (12:20). Abram's thought therefore does not represent a reasoned argument against meteorology. Instead, it is the fruit of some innate understanding that human beings must not attempt to usurp the control that belongs to God.[12] At the end of this incident, we still do not know how or why human beings have access to this innate knowledge, but it is clearly not imagined by the author as the product of rational inquiry.

We usually assume that *access* to knowledge is the primary problem in human knowing. In *Jubilees*, on the other hand, access is not a problem; knowledge is freely given to human beings, whether in direct revelation or by way of an innate awareness. Rather, the epistemic issue for the author is a moral one: will human beings *acknowledge* what has been revealed? In Abraham's vision of Israel's history, he is shown a long period of apostasy. Apostasy, however, results not from the loss of access to religious knowledge but from the mass refusal to acknowledge it. The land is filled with Israelite sin "because they have forgotten the commandments." This "forgetting" is a willful act, a symptom of their "evils" (23:19, 21). Hence, Abraham is told, the apostasy will come to an end when people "begin to search the law, and to search the commandments and to return to the way of righteousness" (23:26). The revealed law, it seems, remains all along in Israel's possession. Her struggle concerns whether or not to acknowledge it and respond with obedience.

The parallel review of Israel's history provided at the outset of the book provides an identical picture of apostasy and return. Those who "forget" God's covenant in 1:9 are morally culpable for that "forgetting" (1:8). Likewise, the same ones who "neglect everything and begin to do evil in my sight" are also said to "forget all of my laws and all of my commandments" and so "err concerning new moons, Sabbaths, festivals, jubilees, and ordinances" (1:12-14). The willfulness of this "forgetting" is underlined by the fact that these rebellious Israelites persecute and kill the witnesses sent by God to remind them of the commandments (1:12). If the loss of religious knowledge is a result of moral corruption, the return to knowledge is equally a matter of moral restoration. In the opening review of Israel's history the people "remember" the covenant and the commandments only when they repent, "turn" to God, and "seek" God "with all their heart and with all their soul" (1:15). For Israel, at least, knowledge is a moral matter. The righteous accept God's revealed truth, while those who reject it do so because of their sinful heart.[13]

Although Israel has the benefit of God's explicit revelation to the patriarchs and to Moses, this epistemic situation applies more or less universally. Non-Jews have (or at least had) the testimony of Enoch and Noah as vehicles of explicit revelation.[14] Likewise, they share the potential for the innate knowledge of God that guides Abraham. Hence pre-Israelite humanity stands in an epistemic position analogous to that of Israel. Adam and Eve are held morally responsible for their decision to believe the serpent's words instead of God's (3:17-25). Enoch stands as a witness against pre-deluvian humanity, implying that their wickedness results not from innocent ignorance but from culpable rejection of God's demand (4:24). When Cainan finds writings containing the Watchers' astrological lore, he "sinned because of what was in it" (8:3). Yet this, again, is not treated as an innocent misstep. Cainan knew that the practices were wrong: "He did not tell about it [the Watchers' books] because he feared to tell Noah about it lest he be angry with him because of it" (8:4).

Nor does this situation of responsibility change after the flood and the confusion of languages at Babel. After the flood, God makes "for all his works a new and righteous nature so that they might not sin in all their nature forever, and so that they might all be righteous, each in his kind, always" (5:12). This confirms that the problem prior to the flood was not access to knowledge but the moral will to act on it. Furthermore, the point in this passage is not that human beings after the flood (and so in the reader's present) no longer face such a moral struggle, but rather that they are now, more than ever, fully responsible to keep God's commands. The human beings involved in the Babel incident are morally culpable (they are "evil") for following such "perverse counsel" (10:18). This is, again, due not to a lack of access to moral guidance but to a free decision to reject the awareness of God's will.[15] Indeed, Enoch is said to remain in heaven "writing condemnation and judgment of the world" (4:23). Hence, long after Babel, Abraham tells Jacob that the Gentiles "have no heart to perceive, and they have no eyes to see what their deeds are, and where they wander astray, saying to the tree 'you are my god,' and to a stone 'you are my lord, and you are my savior'; and they have no heart" (22:18). The Gentiles are deceived about idols, not because they have no opportunity to learn the truth, but because of the corruption of their "heart" and "eyes."

Nor is the Gentile world responsible only for a limited set of nonritual requirements, such as the "Noachian commandments" of the later rabbis. The Enochic testimony to humanity concerned, primarily, the observance of the proper "times." Thus, a prominent part of the Gentiles' sin is their lack of obedience to these calendrical observances. Moses is told, at one point, that Israel must keep the feasts in the proper days "lest they forget the feasts of the covenant and walk in the feasts of the gentiles, after their errors and after their ignorance" (6:35). Yet not only Israel but also others are implicated in this requirement. It is not clear whether the author of *Jubilees* imagines the Gentiles to have access to the Enochic calendrical works, or whether the author presumes that God would reveal such knowledge were the Gentiles responsive to the innate knowledge they have already received. What is plain, however, is that the knowledge to which all humanity has access, and hence for which all humanity is responsible, includes at least some of the calendrical and festal regulations of Israel's law.[16]

The prominent interference of demons in the lives of human beings in *Jubilees* does not attenuate this moral responsibility to respond to God's revelation. In 10:1-2, for example, the wickedness of Noah's sons is attributed to the corrupting influence of demons who "lead them to folly" and "blind" them (10:2). Yet this same passage reasserts the freedom (and hence responsibility) of human beings in the reader's present. For at Noah's request God intervenes and binds nine-tenths of the demons. Mastema, lord of the demons, is still allowed to retain some spirits to help him "corrupt and lead astray" human beings (10:8) because "the evil of the sons of men is great" (10:8). On the other hand, Noah's prayer asks specifically that God help "the children of the righteous" (10:6; cf. 10:3). In this post-deluvian world, humanity is no longer overwhelmed by irresistible demonic forces. Rather, human beings are now, because of God's intervention, free to choose a righteous life. Should they reject God's way, some demons remain to reinforce and deepen their corruption.[17] Those who reject righteousness can still be called the "sons of Beliar" in that they choose the way of evil and place themselves under the influence of the demonic (15:33-34). Yet the frequent prayers for God to deliver the righteous from such demonic influence testify to a confidence that the deity will allow human beings to choose and live a righteous life (1:20; 19:28).[18]

If Jews and Gentiles have equal access to or potential for knowledge of God and his moral will, why does Israel alone seem to follow this will? *Jubilees*' answer is that Israel's leaders (and hence, by extension, the people as a whole) were more virtuous than the surrounding peoples.[19] Abraham is a righteous man who responds to revelation when others around him do not, and who is able to respond precisely because he has a stronger moral will. When Abram comes to reason with his father about the uselessness of worshiping idols, Terah replies:

> I also know (that), my son, but what shall I do to the people who have made me minister before them? And if I speak to them in righteousness, they will kill me because their souls cleave to them so that they might worship them and praise them. Be silent, my son, lest they kill you. (12:6-7)

The issue is not that Terah is unaware of the truth but that he refuses to dwell on and live by that truth because of what it would cost him.[20] On the other hand, it is after Abram's righteous rejection of idolatry that he is provided with a wealth of further revelation in the form of the Hebrew books. Hence, it is Abraham's superior moral character that allows him to respond to his innate knowledge of God's commands.

Given the way Abraham's unusual knowledge of God is attributed to his moral fiber, it is no surprise that *Jubilees* places so much emphasis on Abraham's righteous acts. The whole cycle of Abraham stories stresses his virtue, particularly in the *Aqedah* (17:15—18:19) and in his self-restraint after the death of his wife (19:3-9). At the end of his life, Abraham was "perfect in all of his actions with the Lord and was pleasing through righteousness all of the days of his life" (23:10).[21] Some events in the Genesis account that call the patriarch's character into question are simply omitted. Abraham does not lose faith and declare to God that since he is childless his servant Eliezer will be his heir (cf. Gen 15:2-3). Nor does he try to pass Sarai off to Abimelech as his sister (cf. Gen 20:1-18). When Abram does go down to Egypt and Sarai is taken into Pharaoh's court, we hear nothing of the patriarch's deceptiveness about his actual relationship with his wife. Rather, Pharaoh is depicted as a sexual aggressor (13:13-15; cf. Gen 12:10-20). *Jubilees*, in contrast to Genesis, portrays Abraham as a flawless moral hero.

The later patriarchs too are portrayed as morally pure. Isaac's own attempt to pass off his wife as his sister is omitted (cf. Gen 26:6-11). Jacob, a dubious character in Genesis, is entirely virtuous in *Jubilees*. When Rebecca instructs Jacob to honor his family, the patriarch is affronted that she would think the instruction necessary. Jacob insists that he has never done anything unkind or wrong, and his mother is quick to agree: "My son, all my days I have never seen against you anything perverse but only uprightness" (35:6). Esau's pursuit of Jacob is no longer the just action of a cheated older brother, but rather the madness of a man whose inclination "has been evil since his youth" (35:9; cf. 35:13). Isaac's blessing of Jacob in his older brother's place is justified on the basis that, unlike Esau, "he has no evil but only goodness" (35:12). Because Jacob does no wrong, the incidents in Genesis that focus on his repentance are dropped from the *Jubilees* account (cf. Genesis 32–33). The author even has Esau voluntarily yield his larger inheritance to Jacob, admitting that the sale of his inheritance was just and binding (36:14).[22] Finally, while Joseph's virtue is already a part of the biblical cycle, it is emphasized even more by the author of *Jubilees*. After his elevation to power in Egypt, all loved Joseph "because he walked uprightly and he had no pompousness or arrogance or partiality, and there was no bribery because he ruled all the people of the land uprightly" (40:4). There may well be other reasons for this sanitization of the patriarchal narratives, but one of its effects is to help explain why Israel alone, among all the nations of the world, enjoys the knowledge of God. At the same time, this portrayal also explains why the post-patriarchal generations have so much trouble acknowledging this revelation. The patriarchs, beginning with Abraham, were able to acknowledge God's will only because of their superior moral will.[23] When the Israelites wander from this pattern of righteous receptiveness, they descend into the same willful "forgetting" in which the Gentiles are mired.

The nature of this moral struggle in *Jubilees* to accept and appropriate the knowledge that God makes available becomes even clearer in the author's treatment of astrology. When Abram is told not to employ the stars as a guide to future weather, the patriarch's inner voice observes, as we have seen, that the weather is in God's control and hence is not a proper object for independent inquiry (12:16-18). Human beings, as creatures, must recognize and accept their dependence on the creator. Any attempt to establish one's own security independent of God is a kind of rebellion. This calls to mind Isaac's exhortation to his sons, where he tells them to avoid idols "because they are full of error for those who worship and bow down to them" (36:5). In both of these passages the key moral corruption is idolatry, the refusal to acknowledge the reality of God's being and the subordinate, dependent role that human beings ought to play. Religious knowing is thus, for the author of *Jubilees*, rooted in a moral struggle to accept one's own createdness, to give up idolatrous bids for independence, and to embrace a life of reliance on the good and sovereign God. This is the only existential stance that allows one to accept the knowledge that God makes available, whether in the innate awareness of God's demand or in direct revelation. This is not to say that *Jubilees* is utterly consistent on this point; isolated passages suggest conflicting lines of approach.[24] As is evident to students of the book's eschatology, however, absolute consistency seems not to have been the author's concern. The document as a whole presents religious knowing as a moral struggle to accept the knowledge that God gives.

Knowing in *Aristeas*: An Intellectual Quest

The *Letter of Aristeas* presents an entirely different epistemological approach. Although it is often called a letter, the book is actually a narrative account of the translation of the Pentateuch into Greek under Ptolemy II Philadelphus of Egypt (283–247 b.c.e.). The text was almost certainly written by an Alexandrian Jew,[25] most likely in the mid to late second century b.c.e.[26] It purports, however, to be penned by a certain Aristeas, a Gentile minister in Ptolemy's court, and is addressed to his brother Philocrates.[27]

In *Aristeas*, the epistemological emphasis falls on the importance of human reason in distinguishing truth from falsehood. In the opening line of the book, Aristeas claims to have compiled "a trustworthy narrative" (*axiologou diēgēseōs*) (1).[28] Here the claim to present a "trustworthy" account presumes the possibility that some accounts are *not* trustworthy. But how to distinguish between the two?

Aristeas explains that he assembled this narrative because his reader, Philoctetes, attaches "great importance to hearing a personal account of our mission" (1). The allusion here is to the emphasis in Greek historiography on autopsy and eyewitness testimony.[29] One must employ reason to make an independent judgment as to the credibility of any testimony about the past, and this credibility is (naturally) greater when the witness has been directly involved in the events. Aristeas connects such concern for autopsy with Philoctetes' "scholarly disposition" (*philomathē diathesin*) (1). Aristeas calls this "love of learning" a "supreme quality" (*megiston*) and describes it as a man's attempt "continually to increase his learning and understanding, whether from the accounts (of others) or by actual experience" (2). Where the epistemic problem in *Jubilees* is the moral struggle to respond to revelation, here in *Aristeas* the problem is precisely one of access. Human beings must accumulate as much information as possible, using their rational powers to assess the credibility of various potential sources of knowledge.[30]

The concept of revelation, however, is not entirely absent from *Aristeas*. At the end of the narrative, Demetrius affirms that the law is "holy" (*semnēn*) and has "come from God" (313). Yet the immediate, self-authenticating encounters with the divine voice that predominate in *Jubilees* are nowhere to be found in *Aristeas*. Instead, the books of Moses are treated as a traditional text that contains wise ideas. Notice that the context for King Ptolemy's sponsorship of the law's translation is his attempt to collect all of the world's learned texts in a library. From the outset, *Aristeas* views the Jewish law as one text among many.[31] Whatever claim the Jews make that this text is divinely revealed and hence distinctive must be justified and evaluated by rational arguments. So, while Demetrius, the court librarian, recognizes that the law is "divine" (*theian*), he accepts the special status of this text only because of his own evaluation of its contents as "very philosophical and genuine" (*philosophōteron . . . kai akeraion*) (31).

The high priest Eleazar's explanation of the law in 130–71 provides the reader with rational arguments of just this kind, demonstrating that even the most bizarre-seeming portions of Israel's law can, on closer inspection, be recognized by thoughtful people as true and wise. Eleazar begins by "demonstrating [*proüpedeixe*] that God is one," offering a rational justification of the biblical portrait of God in Hellenistic philosophical parlance (132).[32] The high priest then offers a series of arguments against idolatry, against polytheism, and in particular against the deification of human beings.[33] The body of Eleazar's speech, however, is devoted to a justification of the Jewish dietary regulations, one of the portions of Torah that seemed most strange and irrational to educated Hellenists. Eleazar explains that the distinctions between clean and unclean foods have a didactic purpose. They represent differences in virtue between different kinds of people (130), and they are intended to remind Jews of the virtue toward which they ought to strive. The food regulations thus encourage "unblemished investigation [*hagnēn episkepsin*] and amendment of life for the sake of righteousness [*dikaiosynēs heneken*]" (144).[34] Aristeas is then able to evaluate the justification that the high priest has offered for the law's teaching. He concludes: "In my view, he habitually made out a good case [*kalōs . . . apologeisthai*] for each separate category" (170). On the other hand, Eleazar also provides a second purpose for these strange laws, explaining that they provide "unbroken palisades and iron walls to prevent our mixing with any of the other peoples in any matter" and so the Jews are "preserved from false beliefs" (139; cf. 142).

Eleazar's speech thus displays a conviction that the truth of Israel's law can (and should) be confirmed by means of human reason. Not only is the law recognized as true and "divine" by rational argument, however, but its substantial contents can be learned through philosophical reasoning alone. Notice, again, how Eleazar justifies Jewish monotheism not by claiming a special authority for the scriptural text, but by providing an independent argument for the idea. This prepares the reader for Eleazar's claim that the regulations of Torah, even the dietary restrictions, are codified in keeping with "natural reasoning" (*ton physikon logon*) (143).[35] If the truth of Scripture is apparent to human reason, then intelligent people anywhere can, at least in theory, come to the same understanding. Eleazar describes Moses as a man "endowed by God for the knowledge of universal truths" (139). Torah itself thus appears to be "divine," not because it records divine speech or actions, but because it contains the insight into divine things achieved by a human philosopher, albeit one who was gifted by God for the task.[36]

The emphasis on reasoned inquiry as the source of knowledge is confirmed in the seven-day banquet that Ptolemy holds for the Jewish translators when they arrive in Alexandria (172–300). In the tradition of the philosophical "symposia" of Plato and Xenophon, Aristeas has each of the translators take a turn giving wise answers to the king's questions. The range of questions is broad, but most revolve around the issues of attaining virtue, living a wise life, and governing a kingdom effectively. The answers given are typically very brief and most lack any argumentative justification. Yet they all reflect the kind of ideas that would have been acceptable to anyone familiar with popular Hellenistic philosophy.[37] Moreover, it is clear that the men are able to give appropriate answers because they reason correctly. At the end of the first day of questioning, Aristeas observes that "all the assembled company acclaimed and applauded loudly," and he points out that this crowd included many philosophers who approved of the Jews' answers because they reflected good reasoning. The king himself remarks to the listening philosophers that the Jews "have a fuller understanding" (*synienai pleion*). He goes on, however, to point out *why* they are able to answer so well: they all "make God the basis of their argument" (*apo theou tou logou tēn katarchēn poioumenoi*). In other words, the translators can answer well (on short notice) not because they have memorized traditional wisdom but because they reason on the basis of appropriate first principles. This emphasis on God as a necessary presupposition for proper reasoning is not peculiar to the Jews, for Aristeas has the philosopher Menedemus of Eritrea concur: "Yes, indeed, O King, for since the whole universe is governed by providence, and on the correct assumption [*hypeilēphotōn orthōs*] that man is a creature of God, it follows that all power and beauty of argument has its origin in God." Not only is the wisdom of the Jewish translators a product of their skill in reasoning, but even their first principles are ones with which many Hellenistic philosophers would agree (200–201; cf. 235).

Aristeas does not define the reason from which all knowledge springs, but he is working with the basic Hellenistic understanding of reason (or *logos*). In a brief discussion of the nature of sleep, one of the translators says that when human beings dream of impossible things, "we are irrational" (*alogistoumen*) (214). This shows that, for Aristeas, reason is an activity of the conscious mind that involves distinguishing the real from the unreal, the possible from the impossible. The emphasis is on *practical* reasoning. When one of the translators is asked what "sound judgment" (*euboulia*) is, one guest says it is

> doing everything well . . . with due consultation [*meta dialogismou*], in your deliberation [*kata tēn boulēn*] taking into account as well the harmful

features of the opposite side of the argument [*tou logou*], in order that after paying attention to each detail our deliberations may be good [*ōmen eu bebouleumenoi*] and our objective achieved. (255)

Similarly, when the king asks another translator what philosophy (*philosophia*) is, the guest replies:

> To have a well-reasoned assessment of [*to kalōs dialogizesthai*] each occurrence . . . and not to be carried away by impulses but to study carefully the harmful consequences of the passions, and by exercising proper and necessary restraint in carrying out what the occasion demands. (256)

These are not highly technical definitions. They do, however, make it clear that the author of *Aristeas* values a weighing of various arguments that aims not just to distinguish truth from falsehood but also to distinguish the best way of acting. While the author may differ with many Hellenistic philosophers (as they differed among themselves) over precisely how one ought to weigh different arguments, his basic conception of reason was one that was widely shared in educated circles around the Hellenized Mediterranean. It is this mental activity of argumentation and weighing of arguments that the book holds up as the sole source of genuine knowledge.

This is not to deny the presence of a moral dimension in the epistemology of *Aristeas*. The achievement of religious knowledge is repeatedly connected with virtue, and especially the virtue of piety (*eusebeia*). In his introduction, Aristeas explains that a "pure disposition of mind" (*kathara diathesis*) is reached by one who, "turning to piety [*tēn eusebeian*], the highest of all ends, lives by adopting a rule which does not err" (2). In other words, proper rationality is not possible until one attains a virtuous life, which prominently includes proper worship of the deity. This initial statement is placed on the lips of the (imagined) Gentile author, but the Jewish translators say strikingly similar things. When one translator defines practical reasoning for Ptolemy, he concludes: "What is most important, by the power of God your every purpose will be accomplished if you practice piety [*tēn eusebeian*]" (255). Later, he stresses that "in order to have due care for these things, it is necessary to serve God [*theratheuein . . . ton theon*]" (256). All of these statements go beyond the general observation discussed above that a proper understanding of the deity is the necessary first principle for right reasoning about life. Each case suggests that theoretical understanding *is impossible* unless one practices a life of pious virtue.[38]

Morality does not, however, play the same role in the epistemology of *Aristeas* that it does in *Jubilees*. In the latter text, moral response eclipses reasoned thought as the path to knowledge, but in *Aristeas* virtue emerges as a *necessary prerequisite* to proper rationality. In their negotiations, the translators "rose above conceit and contempt of other people, and instead engaged in discourse and listening to and answering each and every one, as is meet and right" (122). The virtue of the translators facilitates their reasoning by reducing the influence of personal bias and allowing them to consider all of the arguments fairly. Rather than competing with reason as a means of gaining knowledge, virtue thus appears in *Aristeas* as a necessary component in the reasoning process itself.

Social Conflict

We have arrived now at a sharp distinction between the ways of knowing endorsed by these two texts. In *Jubilees*, the human reasoning faculty is assigned no role at all in the knowing process. Access to knowledge is not a problem, since God reveals his nature and will to all. The epistemic question is instead a moral one, whether human beings can exercise the moral effort required to respond to this revelation with affirmation and obedience. In *Aristeas*, in contrast, the question of virtue arises only insofar as such virtue facilitates free and proper reasoning. Access to knowledge *is* treated by Aristeas as a real problem, and one that can be solved only by an essentially intellectual quest. As we shift our focus now to the social conflicts that formed the contexts for the composition of these texts, we find that in each case the author's epistemology has been definitively shaped by the Jewish confrontation with elite Hellenistic society.

Aristeas: Joining the Elite

Both *Aristeas* and *Jubilees* were written at a time when Jewish communities were still trying to establish a new equilibrium after the sudden appearance in the late fourth century of a Greek ruling class around the eastern Mediterranean. This elite brought with it not only a new political and social hierarchy but also a new Hellenistic culture, which quickly became a prerequisite for social and political advancement. Not surprisingly, deep divisions grew up within the Jewish community about how far Jews should try to establish status and prominence within this new Hellenistic elite, and to what extent they should reject the transformation of Jewish life and tradition that such social prominence would require. The authors of *Jubilees* and *Aristeas* assume very different stances toward aristocratic Hellenism. What they share is a concern to establish a place for Jews within the redrawn social landscape of the Hellenistic kingdoms.

Aristeas reflects a community that does not want to be left out. Whether directed toward a Gentile readership or (as is more likely) the Jewish community's own membership,[39] *Aristeas* pictures the Jews as members of the Hellenistic elite, at the top of the second-century Egyptian social scale, enjoying political influence, high status, and the physical security that tends to accompany both. The price for entry into this social stratosphere, a price that *Aristeas* believes his community should accept, is the adoption of the language and thought forms of that elite Hellenistic circle. There is no reason to think, however, that this vision corresponds in any way to actual Jewish-Gentile relations in second-century Alexandria.[40]

Aristeas's agenda is obvious in its depictions of Jewish-Gentile relations. What Gentiles say about Jews is overwhelmingly positive. After all, the book as a whole describes a Gentile initiative to learn from the Jewish people. Indeed, at the outset of the book, Aristeas (a Gentile character) refers to a glowing account of the Jews penned by "the most renowned high priests" of Egypt (6), and Aristeas presumes that, as a learned and pious man, Philocrates will be "favourably inclined toward the piety and disposition of those who live by the sacred Law" (5). Moreover, the author seems eager to show that (at least in Egypt) the Gentile leadership has never been hostile to Jews as such and is anxious to redress any past wrongs. Although a previous monarch enslaved Jews in Egypt, this was not "so much out of any personal predilection for such a course, but because he was prevailed upon by his troops on account of the services which they had given" (14).[41] When Aristeas points out this injustice to the king (12–16), Ptolemy not only releases the prisoners at great personal cost (20), but also decries their enslavement as "entirely inequitable" (23) and makes significant extra reparations.[42] He goes so far as to employ some of these released Jews as ministers in his own court, since they are "worthy of confidence in our household" (37). The ruler even tells Eleazar that he wishes "to grant favors to them and to all the Jews throughout the world, including future generations" (38). To demonstrate the king's sincerity, Aristeas describes in detail the lavish gifts that Ptolemy sent, along with his embassy asking for translators, to the temple in Jerusalem (40, 51–82). The Hellenistic ruler speaks of "friendship" with the high priest (40). When the Jewish delegation arrives, the king dispenses with the usual four-day waiting period and has them ushered directly into his presence because of the "greater honor" that they deserve on account of their sender, Eleazar (175). Even the strange customs that tend to isolate Jews are treated by Ptolemy with great delicacy. Not only is the king's banquet prepared according to Jewish customs, but the sovereign himself joins in this kosher meal (180–81).[43]

This overwhelming embrace of Jews by elite Gentiles is matched by the Jews' own remarkable openness to Gentiles and to Hellenistic culture in general. It is significant that Eleazar was able to find, on relatively short notice, seventy-two Jews in Jerusalem who "had not only mastered the Jewish literature, but had made a serious study of that of the Greeks as well" (121). Eleazar, accepting Ptolemy's overtures, addresses the king as his "dear friend" and says he "rejoiced greatly" on hearing of the Egyptian ruler's plan to translate Israel's law (42).[44] At the start of the royal banquet, Eleazar offers an expansive prayer for the blessing of the king and his family (185). There is certainly no expectation of judgment on Gentiles as a group, either as individual punishment or as political subjugation. Gentiles in *Aristeas* are not sinful enemies but learned friends.

We must notice, however, that *Aristeas* only depicts such close relations between Jews and the most elite, Hellenized Gentiles. This aspect of the document can easily go unnoticed precisely because the *only* Gentiles who appear in the text are cultural elites— kings and courtiers, philosophers and priests. The author would likely not have been so favorable toward ordinary or lower-class Gentiles. For the very aspects of Hellenistic thought in which he finds points of contact with Judaism—monotheism and a rigorous conception of virtue—were not characteristic of the lower classes, that is, the vast majority of non-Jews. When, for example, Eleazar launches his polemic against idolatry and cults of the dead, he is in fact siding with elite philosophical elements of Hellenistic society against the religious activity of the masses. His desire is to establish a place for Jews not simply within the Gentile world but within that elite governing class who were most heavily Hellenized.[45]

Elite Hellenistic thought tended to look down not only on the religion of the masses, but also on the less Hellenized groups whom they ruled. Educated writers might flirt with the mystique of Egypt, for example, but whatever was not consonant with educated "Greek" sensibilities was quickly castigated as "barbarous." Here again the author of *Aristeas* attempts to position his Jewish community within the Hellenized elite by joining in the ridicule of the Egyptian populace. Notice how, once Eleazar has finished siding with Hellenistic elites against the silliness of the popular Greek cults, he points to even greater ridiculousness of non-Greek forms of worship. "There is surely no need to mention," he says, "the rest of the very foolish people [*polymataiōn*], the Egyptians and those like them, who have put their confidence in beasts and most of the serpents and monsters, worship them, and sacrifice to them both while alive and dead" (138). True, such objects of worship are derided already by Israel's prophets.[46] Here, however, the author of *Aristeas* is not simply restating traditional Israelite polemics. He is establishing himself and other Jews as insiders within the elite Hellenistic cultural circle. By beginning Eleazar's speech with the phrase "There is surely no need to mention . . . ," he is claiming that Jews and educated Hellenists both share the same special understanding. In sociological terms, such an appeal to shared assumptions functions like a badge of membership in the same restricted social group, a shared membership that is established by joining in the elite ridicule and marginalization of the non-Hellenized world in general.

In this social power game the epistemology of *Aristeas* plays a significant role. It hardly needs repeating at this point that the epistemological outlook espoused by the protagonists in *Aristeas* is the same kind of rationalism that was prevalent among the Hellenistic elites who consumed most philosophy. As much as anything else, it is the rationality of the Jews that gains them the respect of the elite Gentiles in the text. Eleazar's long speech displays not so much his piety as his impressive ability to justify apparently foolish Jewish customs using the kind of argument admired by his elite audience. Likewise, at the king's banquet the Jewish translators are praised by their elite host and his other guests because they can participate so skillfully in the forms of intellectual discourse respected by Hellenistic elites. Hence, *Aristeas* suggests that Jews may participate in the highest circles of Hellenistic society *if* they embrace a Greek approach to knowledge and argument. For *Aristeas*, elite Hellenistic rationalism has become social currency.

Yet this rationalism is not merely a form of argument. It brings with it a whole tradition of thought about what constitutes a plausible conclusion. After all, the vast majority of the Hellenistic elite were not skilled philosophers, capable of evaluating the rationality of a truly novel argument. For most educated Hellenists, rationality would consist of repeating and adapting the arguments of others, arguments that arrived at familiar and expected conclusions. Hence, if the author of *Aristeas* wants to assume a place in the Hellenistic elite as a wise rationalist, he must also show that his substantive ideas accord with the views of a Hellenistic rationalist. This is, as we noted above, precisely what happens at the king's banquet, where the translators are commended for their reasoning *on the basis of their conclusions*. Since they offer the correct answers, they are recognized as wise within the terms of the Hellenistic tradition.[47] The consequence is, however, that Israel's law must be treated not as the unique repository of revelation, but rather as one (albeit extraordinary) voice in the general body of religious wisdom.[48] If the Jews were to claim that their own teaching is unique and different from all others, they could no longer expect to be recognized as rational within the Hellenistic tradition. The substance of their ideas would no longer allow elite Hellenists to identify them as wise, rational thinkers.

Even Jewish piety must be shown to concord with Hellenistic conceptions of piety; any exclusivist or distinctive elements are relativized. Hence, in *Aristeas* piety is treated as a constant across Jewish and Greek cultures.[49] One Jewish translator tells Ptolemy that the evils that stem from bad conduct will not befall him, "God fearing as you are" (233). It is simply assumed that these pious pagans and Jews worship the same God. Aristeas himself assures the king that the Jews worship "God the overseer and creator of all, whom all men worship [*sebonta*] including ourselves, O King, except that we name him differently as Zeus and Dis [*ēmeis de . . . prosonomazontes heterōs Zēna kai Dia*]" (16).[50] Eleazar writes in his response to Ptolemy that he had the king's letter read publicly, "that they might know your piety [*eusebeian*] toward our God" (42). *Aristeas* raises no objection to statements like that of Sosibus, the king's adviser, who suggests that the oppressed Jews' release is a "thank offering [*charistērion*] to the Most High God" (19; cf. 37). Such Gentile offerings are treated as entirely acceptable, and Ptolemy is even allowed to provide furnishings and implements for the Jerusalem temple cult (51–82). What is more, the Jews downplay the necessity for distinctive Jewish practices in the pursuit of piety. As noted above, Eleazar explains Jewish food and ritual regulations as symbolic tools, intended merely to train Israelites in virtue. When one guest at the king's banquet is asked about the highest form of glory, he answers, "Honouring God," and explains that "this is not done with gifts or sacrifices, but with purity of heart and of devout disposition." The guest assures the king: "This is also your attitude, evidence of which can be seen by all from your past and present accomplishments" (234). In other words, this Gentile king does not suffer at all from his non-Jewish status. Because Jewish piety and Gentile piety are, in their essence, identical, the worship of such Gentiles is every bit as acceptable as that of their Jewish neighbors.[51]

The radical acceptance of elite Hellenistic culture and religion is not a necessary corollary of a rationalist approach to knowledge. Rather, out of a desire to have his rationalism validated by a specific social group, the author reinterprets his Jewish tradition in terms of that group's *Weltanschauung*. *Aristeas* imagines a social reality in which the members of his Jewish community are accepted as full participants in the elite world of the Hellenistic ruling class. His narrative suggests, moreover, that such acceptance can be gained if those elites can recognize Jews as wise, learned, and able to reason superbly. Yet in order to appear wise to a heavily Hellenized social group, they will need to show that they too have accepted a basically Hellenistic perspective on the nature of the world.

Jubilees: The Great Reversal

The very choice to compose *Jubilees* in Hebrew rather than Greek reflects the author's rejection of the kind of Hellenized elite that *Aristeas* seeks to join.[52] After all, the first sign of being a "Hellenist" was the ability to speak and write good Greek. Moreover, as has often been observed, the injunctions of *Jubilees* seem specifically geared to resist the influence of Hellenistic culture on the Jewish community.[53] Exhortations against nakedness (3:31), uncircumcision (15:34), and use of a lunar calendar (6:35) all explicitly mention the Gentiles as those whose practice is wicked. Repeated warnings against idolatry (20:7-9; 22:16-18) and eating blood (6:12-14; 7:30-33; 21:6) seem to be aimed at the practices of Hellenized Gentiles and/or assimilating Jews. Likewise, the polemic against intermarriage reflects a period of anxiety about the distinctiveness and integrity of the author's Jewish community.[54] The cause of this anxiety was almost certainly the deliberate program of Hellenization that the Jerusalem aristocracy pursued in the years leading up to the anti-Jewish decrees of Antiochus IV and the Maccabean revolt (ca. 180–167 B.C.E.).[55] Under the leadership of the high priests Jason and Menelaus, Jerusalem was converted for a time into a Greek-style *polis*, complete with cultural institutions such as a gymnasium and an ephebate.[56] Although much remains obscure about this chapter in Jewish history, it is clear that the Jerusalem Hellenists were making a bid to end the cultural and economic isolation of Judea by gaining entry to the circle of Hellenized *poleis* and their aristocratic citizens.[57] The strategy employed by the upper-class Jerusalemites was to minimize their distinctiveness in relation to common Hellenistic ideals. Some even discarded circumcision as a mark of their Jewishness.[58] Since the author of *Jubilees* seems himself to have been part of the priestly aristocracy, he would almost certainly have felt the aftereffects of this Hellenizing movement.[59] He may even have lived through its heyday in the Holy City. Yet he has roundly rejected its aims. If the "evil generation" of 23:16-21 is intended to represent these aristocratic citizens of Jerusalem who have downplayed Jewish distinctives and adopted badges of Hellenistic identity,[60] it is clear that the author of *Jubilees* perceived this whole attempt to enter the broader Hellenistic elite as a grave mistake.[61] Since *Jubilees* probably dates from the early stages of the Maccabean dynasty, the Hellenizing movement in Jerusalem was not likely a live option in the author's day. Yet the Seleucid campaign against the observance of

Torah that traumatized Judea in 167 B.C.E. would have underscored the terrible danger that that assimilationist course held, and the vehemence of the anti-Hellenizing rhetoric in *Jubilees* suggests that the author still senses the appeal that the elite Hellenistic world holds for many of his contemporaries.[62]

Would the author of *Jubilees* have included *Aristeas* among the expressions of this evil, assimilationist generation? One mitigating factor would be the attempt in *Aristeas* to insist that there is value in the observance of distinctive Jewish practices, and to suggest that these customs should lead to a degree of social isolation from Gentile society (139). As George W. E. Nickelsburg puts it, the author of *Aristeas* "is counseling rapprochement without assimilation."[63] Yet the author of *Jubilees* would be very unhappy with the radical reinterpretation of Torah that *Aristeas* promotes. Instead of relativizing the more obscure of these commandments and minimizing their importance, the author of *Jubilees* claims they are written on "heavenly tablets" that are eternal and unchanging.[64] Even the feasts of Israel and the ritual codes are retrojected back into the time of Enoch and Noah and seen as binding on all humanity. The very marks of Jewish differentness that the author of *Aristeas* takes pains to minimize are the aspects of Israel's tradition that are deliberately emphasized and intensified in *Jubilees*.

Jubilees, then, reflects a very different strategy for coping with the Jews' marginal position vis-à-vis the Hellenistic elite of the eastern Mediterranean. The author of *Aristeas* wants to join this elite by showing that in fact Jews are *not* outsiders. The author of *Jubilees* clearly believes that such a strategy will betray Israel's covenant. As in *Aristeas*, so too in *Jubilees* we find the author presuming at the outset that Hellenistic elites judge Jews to be culturally alien and so inferior. Unlike the writer of *Aristeas*, however, the author of *Jubilees* reverses the scale of values that is attached to that judgment of differentness. In *Jubilees*, it seems that whatever is judged different (and so inferior) by Hellenistic elites is promoted as *superior*, precisely because of its difference. Instead of the Hellenists representing the center and the "barbarians" the margin, *Jubilees* depicts Israel as the center and the Hellenistic elites as inferior and marginal. From this point of view, the Gentiles are the sinners in the text; the eschatology of *Jubilees* leaves no room for anything but their destruction.[65] It is through this total reversal of the value structure employed by the elites that the author hopes to maintain a viable Jewish community, despite being marginalized on the broader social stage.

This is not a particularly novel insight. Yet the reaction to Hellenistic pressures in *Jubilees* may help to explain why the document's epistemology is so intensely anti-rational. We have already seen how a particular kind of rationalist argumentation plays such a prominent role in *Aristeas* as a badge of membership in the Hellenistic circle. What few indications we have of the ideology shared by the Jerusalem Hellenizers suggests that they too sought to appear "reasonable" in elite Hellenistic eyes by relativizing and discarding practices that were not thought to fit the model of a "rational" life.[66] If, in contrast, the author of *Jubilees* is determined to affirm these same "irrational" practices, it would stand to reason that he would also reject *all* rational inquiry that (at least rhetorically) grounded the judgments of elite Hellenistic society. This rejection would be all the more necessary given that, as we saw above in *Aristeas*, the validity of one's reasoning was often judged purely on the basis of one's conclusions. Writing in reaction to a Hellenistic elite that identifies its own beliefs and practices with rationality per se, the author of *Jubilees* can accept the label "irrational" precisely in order to challenge that elite's system of evaluation and, ultimately, its claim to represent the social and cultural center. If this explanation of the anti-rationalism of *Jubilees* is correct, it would seem that even the epistemology of *Jubilees* is, in its own way, a product of Hellenism. The author's approach to knowing represents a deliberate mirror-image of the same Hellenistic way of knowing embraced by *Aristeas*.

Conclusion: Moral Struggle, Intellectual Quest, and Social Conflict

The epistemologies reflected in *Aristeas* and *Jubilees* offer a textbook example of the diversity that could flourish within the compass of "common Judaism." Though written at roughly the same juncture in Jewish history, these two texts reflect opposite ways of understanding religious knowing. In *Jubilees*, knowledge is always already available because of God's revelatory activity and the innate awareness that (presumably) God has placed within each human being. The epistemic problem is thus the moral struggle to accept and obey the knowledge that is given. Human reason has no role in justifying or extending this revelatory deposit. On the contrary, such independent human investigation is an idolatrous bid for self-sufficiency. In *Aristeas*, on the other hand, knowledge is primarily an achievement of the human intellect. Far from being freely accessible, such knowledge must be gleaned from the world by diligent consideration of competing arguments. While virtue is a necessary prerequisite for the full and proper exercise of rational thought, it is itself merely an aspect of rational inquiry. Even the contents of Torah (or at least what is essential) can be discovered by philosophically minded people anywhere. One can hardly imagine two more diametrically opposed epistemological approaches.

At the same time, these two epistemologies are both products of the social conflict that resulted when Jewish communities were confronted with a Hellenistic ruling class. The author of *Aristeas* wants his Jewish community to gain entry into that exclusive circle, to which his Hellenistic rationalism is presented as a badge of membership. In order to be perceived as truly rational and wise, however, the author must also transform his Jewish heritage so that it accords with the Hellenistic view of the world, that set of conclusions which the Hellenized elites presume will issue from any properly rational inquiry. The writer of *Jubilees*, in contrast, rejects any attempt to join that elite Hellenistic circle by reinterpreting Judaism. Instead, he attempts to turn the judgments of such Hellenists on their head, insisting that what these elites perceive as foolish is in fact the heart of wisdom. This strategy of value reversal may well be the root of the opposition in *Jubilees* to any kind of rationalism, as the author attempts to valorize precisely the irrationality that the Hellenistic elites would have perceived in traditional Jewish practices. Thus, even the widely divergent ways of knowing endorsed by *Aristeas* and *Jubilees* remind us of a shared reality that was a part of the "common Jewish" experience: the social and cultural pressures of life in a world dominated by Hellenistic elites who regarded the traditional Jewish way of life with at best an ambivalent eye. This comparison reminds us that even the diversity we find among Second Temple Jewish groups often points to more fundamental features that all of these communities shared.

Conclusion

Wayne O. McCready and Adele Reinhartz

This book has been guided by two principal questions: Did the common Judaism that characterized Jewish practice and belief in Judea also describe Jewish life in the Roman Diaspora? How does the concept of common Judaism intersect with the diversity that is known to have existed in Second Temple Judaism?

Through explorations of a variety of topics, including the synagogue, purity, Bible translation, and numerous other issues, the essays in this volume demonstrate the productive tension between diversity on the one hand and common belief and practice on the other. In doing so, they also show the fundamental role of Hellenism as Greek language, concepts, and practices are adopted in some cases and rejected in others. In this final essay, we briefly review the contribution of each article to the guiding questions and then step back to consider the contribution of the volume to our understanding of common Judaism and suggest directions for future examination.

Common Judaism in Its Local Settings

Lee I. Levine's study of synagogues in the period both before and after the first revolt against Rome affirms the presence of a common Judaism throughout the Roman Empire. The material and literary evidence, however, points to a tension between shared Jewish practices, beliefs, values, and modes of expression on the one hand and the significant differences and divergent tendencies within Palestine and Diaspora Judaism and between them on the other. In this context, we must not underestimate the freedom exercised by each community to determine how to negotiate the tension between unity and diversity, as well as to mediate between the differing perspectives of the synagogue leaders and the ordinary participants.

The tension between unity and diversity is evident also with regard to ritual purity. On the one hand, ritual purity was widely practiced in Palestine and in the Diaspora, by all levels of society. Yet the archaeological record testifies to the wide variety of ritual baths in the Second Temple period, as well as to their different environmental and functional contexts. As Boaz Zissu and David Amit point out, a ritual bath designed for the residents of a private farmstead will differ from a public bath on the road to Jerusalem, designed to serve many people simultaneously. Both of these examples in turn will differ from a bath associated with a wine press or an olive press, which served the handful of laborers who engaged in ritual purification before processing the agricultural produce.

A similar dynamic can be seen in the more specific association of purity with the synagogue. While this association seems to have been widespread in Palestine and the Diaspora, Susan Haber notes that it functioned differently in these two geographical areas. Diaspora Jews considered their synagogues to be holy from both a spatial and a liturgical perspective, a view likely shared by the Essenes in Palestine. Among the general population of Palestine, however, this perception was far less developed. Sanctity was likely derived primarily from the presence of the Torah scrolls and therefore would not have been associated with the synagogue building as such.

Several observations emerge from these studies. First, the practice of ritual purity and the institution of the synagogue were integral elements of common Judaism in both Palestine and the Diaspora. At the same time, there are local variations as well as differences that can be accounted for by specific functions and needs. Furthermore, these practices were not exclusive to one particular social or other Jewish group but spanned all strata and groups. They seem not to have been imposed or controlled by authorities but were part and parcel of the everyday life and practice of the ordinary people.

Common Judaism/Partisan Judaism

As noted in the introduction, some scholars argued that E. P. Sanders's *Judaism: Practice and Belief* downplayed the authority and influence of the Pharisees in Second Temple Judaism. Indeed, the role of the Pharisees in the period before the first revolt against Rome is one of the most difficult issues facing contemporary scholarship on Judaism in this era. Determining how the Pharisees were viewed by the common people is especially challenging.

Albert I. Baumgarten's essay acknowledges this difficulty and supports Sanders's view. Without emphasizing the actual power of the Pharisees, Baumgarten looks at how the Pharisees legitimated their authority, namely, by claiming prophetic power. In doing so, the Pharisees were by no means unique. Indeed, they were drawing on the well-established connection between prophecy and power that can be seen elsewhere in Hellenistic literature. Whether or not Josephus exaggerated the Pharisees' overall power, his account of their actions in Herod's court (*Ant.* 17.41–45) should by no means be dismissed as hostile imagination.

Another difficult issue pertains to the process by which the different Jewish groups separated from one another. Anders Runesson examines in detail one particular instance of this separation, namely, the process by which the Mattheans, whom he understands to have been a group of Pharisees who accepted belief in Jesus as the messiah, separated themselves from the mainstream of the Pharisaic group. His analysis supports the view that there was considerable overlap between and within Jewish movements in the first century, including the Jesus movement and the Pharisees. The same may well have been true of "ordinary Jews" and the movements that are known from the extant literature.

The divisions within known groups or parties are also the subject of Cecilia Wassen's analysis, which focuses on the categories of persons that certain Qumran texts consider to be excluded from certain activities or places within their community. In Wassen's view, the exclusions testify to a profound belief in demons and evil spirits in the Qumran sect. Although the study focuses on the inner workings of one specific group, it also points to a belief in exclusion that, she argues, was shared with Judaism more broadly and hence constituted part of "common Judaism." Wassen's chapter demonstrates that even extreme groups such as Qumran take common Judaism as their point of departure.

Alongside a belief in the demonic, Jews shared a belief in the kingship of God. According to Anne Moore, this concept was developed during the period of the Babylonian exile. It was based on the covenantal relationship between God and Israel, and it incorporated aspects of Assyrian, Babylonian, and Persian ideas of king as suzerain. The interplay of God as covenantal sovereign, eternal suzerain, and just king in the "God as king" metaphor demonstrates how diversity and commonality were inherent in the religious ideas in common Judaism.

Although these essays do not directly address the question of the relationship between common Judaism and partisan Judaism, they do remind us of the complexity of Second Temple Judaism by exploring the tensions within various Jewish groups. This complexity should warn against imagining Second Temple Judaism as multiple and discrete "Judaisms" or as a large entity called Judaism consisting of three or four homogeneous groups alongside a large group of unaffiliated "common" Jews. The tension between unity and diversity characterized not only the relationship between Palestinian and Diaspora Judaism and among the groups for which we have evidence (Sadducees, Pharisees, Essenes, proto-Christians), but the relationships within those groups as well. Furthermore, it is likely, as Runesson's study suggests, that the boundaries between these groups were fluid and that people may well have moved between or among these groups over the course of a lifetime.

Common Judaism and Hellenism

Through the Second Temple period, Hellenism shaped the worldview, politics, social organization, law, philosophy, and religion(s) of Greco-Roman society. For Judaism, Hellenism was a force to be reckoned with both in Palestine and in the Diaspora.

The impact of Hellenization is most obvious with regard to Diaspora Judaism, for which Greek became the lingua franca. The Greek translations of the Bible may at first glance look like evidence of diversity, for they mark the explicit acknowledgment that the Jewish Scriptures circulated in multiple forms. At the same time, however, the fact of Bible translation and role of the Greek translation in the lives of Diaspora Jews was arguably both testimony to and a factor in maintaining significant commonality between Palestinian and Diaspora Judaism. As Eliezer Segal notes, legends surrounding the translation of the Bible into Greek emphasized its sanctity. These legends demonstrate the desire to emphasize the continuity between Palestinian and Diaspora Judaism rather than a desire to transmit historically accurate information.

Tessa Rajak contends, however, that the translation of the Bible likely happened in both directions—not only from Hebrew to Greek, but also from Greek to Hebrew. The latter can be seen in the many Greek philosophical concepts and scholarly methods that were absorbed into the work of Jews who thought and wrote in Hebrew or Aramaic. While it is often portrayed in a negative way in our primary and secondary sources, Hellenism may well have served as a vehicle for binding Palestinian and Diaspora Judaism and as a conduit for common Judaism. It is important to note, however, that despite the common belief in the centrality of Scripture, the biblical books may have functioned differently for Diaspora Jews and Palestinian Jews. Rajak suggests that unlike many of their Palestinian compatriots, Greek-speaking Jews may have lived *with* Torah but not completely *by* or *through* the Torah.

While it cannot be denied that Jews, both in Palestine and in the Diaspora, were open to Greek language and Greco-Roman ideas, they did not always take on new practices and beliefs whole cloth. Seth Schwartz's analysis of memorialization practices as reflected in Josephus, and the archaeological and epigraphical remains of pre-destruction Judaism, shows that in contrast to Roman practice, the Jewish culture of memorialization, at least in Judea, tended, with some exceptions, to take an oral and textual rather than an artifactual form. In Schwartz's view, the Jewish adaptation of memorialization practices contributed to the distinctiveness of Jewish public life and material culture and may have been at least partially responsible for Rome's persistent failure fully to integrate Jews into Roman society.

Sanders's idea of common Judaism underscores the degree to which politics and religion were intertwined in Second Temple Judaism. The Maccabean war had settled certain issues and inspired others, and these issues were likely formative for religious parties. Although all Jews agreed that "extreme" Hellenism was to be rejected and that Jews should have freedom to practice and believe according to their own traditions, the continuing presence of Hellenism demanded that Judaism deal with questions relating to its interactions with the larger Gentile world. David Miller's chapter focuses on a specific question facing Judaism in the first century C.E.: Who should be held responsible for the destruction of Jerusalem in the Jewish revolt against Rome? He argues that Josephus responds to that question through a portrayal of the "sign prophets" as instigators of the revolt. Josephus defends himself against accusations of treason by claiming, through his commitment to temple and Torah, to be a model of the common Judaism on which the priests and people agree. Josephus's accounts of the Maccabean revolt and his characterization of the sign prophets illustrate Sanders's observation that a common Jewish desire for freedom was nurtured by memories of the Maccabean revolt.

The push and pull of Hellenization emerge also in Ian W. Scott's discussion of epistemology in *Aristeas* and *Jubilees*. Their different ways of understanding what it meant to "know" testifies to the diversity within common Judaism. Nevertheless, both epistemologies reflect the social conflict that resulted when Jewish communities were confronted with a Hellenistic ruling class. If the author of *Aristeas* sought entrée for his Jewish community into the Hellenistic elite, the writer of *Jubilees* disdained such aspirations. Scott concludes that these widely divergent ways of knowing endorsed by *Aristeas* and *Jubilees* remind us of a shared reality that was a part of the "common Jewish" experience: "the social and cultural pressures of life in a world dominated by Hellenistic elites who regarded the traditional Jewish way of life with at best an ambivalent eye."

We may now return to the initial questions with which the authors of this volume began their investigations. It is clear that common Judaism was not limited to Judea and Palestine more generally. It also extended in large measure to the Diaspora. Diaspora Jews read the Bible and considered it to be their sacred Scripture; they attended synagogue, observed purity laws, and in numerous other ways endeavored to maintain a distinct identity and also to see themselves as part of the Jewish people alongside their Palestinian counterparts.

The evidence, therefore, strongly points in the direction of a set of common practices and beliefs, as well as shared identification, both within Palestinian Judaism and between Palestine and the Diaspora. At the same time, the push and pull, within Palestinian Judaism and between Palestine and the Diaspora, are evident at every turn.

Within Palestinian Judaism, groups differentiated themselves from others by virtue of their interpretation of texts (for example, the Pharisees), their liturgical calendar (the Essenes), or the functions of at least some of their members within Jewish ritual life (for example, the Sadducees). All of our primary sources testify to the struggle for power, authority, and ascendancy. Even within specific groups, differentiation occurred. The Dead Sea community, for example, had elaborate rules for inclusion and exclusion of their membership from particular locations, events, and privileges; the Pharisees may have had a more stringent group within them entitled the Chaverim, whose purity practices limited their social contacts with other Jews.

Common Judaism, as defined by Sanders, was alive and well in Diaspora Judaism. Jews from Italy, Egypt, Mesopotamia, and Jerusalem believed that God had given the Torah to Israel, rescued Israel from Egyptian bondage, and would in some fashion free Israel in the future yet again. Included within common Judaism was a commitment to the sacrificial system, the temple, observance of Sabbath and festivals, circumcision, purity, dietary laws, and charity. True, profound differences existed. While Torah, synagogue, and purity were important for all Jews, their language, function, and significance differed. Although Palestinian Jews were by no means immune to Hellenistic influence, Diaspora Jews confronted and dealt with Greek language, culture, and social structures in a much more direct and widespread way than did Palestinian Jews. Yet Palestinian and Diaspora Jews identified themselves and each other as members of the same people, just as Israeli Jews and North American Jews do today.

Sanders's work was a corrective to the scholarly tendency to focus on the distinct sects and parties mentioned in our extant sources. In addition to affirming Sanders's insights about the existence of a common Judaism that characterized the ordinary people as well as the diverse groups, the essays in this volume support Segal's call to overcome an intellectual preference for neat and circumscribed categories and to acknowledge that Second Temple Judaism, like Judaism of our own era, was replete with indeterminacies, contradictions, and messiness. Second Temple Judaism was in fact an untidy, complex, and contradictory reality that fused widespread adherence to a set of beliefs and practices with fierce controversy and contradiction, the tussle for power, and the impulse to exclude others on one basis or another.

The essays in this volume help to add detail and texture to Sanders's exposition of common Judaism by considering its place within the larger fabric of Jewish society in Palestine and the Diaspora in the Second Temple period. They also adumbrate some of the questions that remain to be answered. For example, what was the impact of the first Jewish revolt on common Judaism? Popular treatments of prerabbinic Judaism state that the destruction of the temple also reconfigured Jewish society and eliminated some of the diversity that had existed before 70 c.e. Can the areas that have been identified as "common" help us to analyze the changes and transitions in the immediate post-70 period?

A second set of questions pertains to the role of common Judaism in the formation of nascent Christianity. Although the "parting of the ways" is dated anywhere from the first to the fourth century c.e. or even later, it is reasonable to consider the ways in which the Jesus movement and even Paul's teachings fit, or do not fit, within the paradigm of unity and diversity that we have traced with regard to Palestinian and Diaspora Judaism more generally. Indeed, any treatment of the "parting of the ways" must make some assumptions regarding the nature of the "Judaism" from which "Christianity" may or may not have parted. It can therefore be instructive to look at common Judaism as we think about when, why, and how Christianity came to take on an identity separate from Judaism. Which aspects were still held in common? Did the common aspects act as an irritant to the point of propelling the group outside? Or was there a dynamic at work similar to that which we have seen with regard to the exclusion of some from the Dead Sea community?[1]

The work begun by Sanders with the publication of *Judaism: Practice and Belief* has provided the stimulus for the essays presented in this volume, and it will without a doubt continue to stimulate and inform scholars' exploration of early Judaism not only in the Second Temple period but beyond to the early rabbinic and early patristic eras.

Abbreviations

Ancient Works

Cicero
    Div.   *De divinatione*
    Flac.   *Pro Flacco*
Ignatius
    Magn.   *Letter to the Magnesians*
Josephus
    Ag. Ap.   *Against Apion*
    Ant.   *Jewish Antiquities*
    J.W.   *Jewish War*
Juvenal
    Let. Aris.   *Letter of Aristeas*
    Sat.   *Satirae*
Lucian of Samosata
    Alex.   *Alexander*
    Demon.   *Demonax*
    Peregr.   *De morte Peregrini*
LXX   Septuagint
Origen
    Cels.   *Contra Celsum*
Philo
    Cher.   *De cherubim*
    Contempl.   *De vita contemplativa*
    Det.   *Quod deterius potiori insidari soleat*
    Embassy   *On the Embassy to Gaius* (see also *Leg.*)
    Flacc.   *In Flaccum*
    Good Person   *That Every Good Person Is Free* (see also *Prob.*)
    Hypoth.   *Hypothetica*
    Legat.   *Legatio ad Gaium*

Mos.	*De vita Mosis*
Prob.	*Quod omnis probus liber sit* (see also *Good Person*)
Spec.	*De specialibus legibus*

Philostratus

Vit. Apoll.	*Life of Apollonius*

Plutarch

Def.	*De defectu oraculorum*

Qumran

CD	*Damascus Document*
1QH	*Hodayot*
1QM	*War Scroll*
1QS	*Rule of the Community*
1QSa	*Rule of the Congregation*

Sib. Or.	*Sibylline Oracles*

Rabbinic Writings

Babylonian Talmud

b. B. Metzi'a	*Baba Metzi'a*
b. B. Qam.	*Baba Qamma*
b. Meg.	*Megillah*
b. Mo'ed Qat.	*Mo'ed Qatan*
b. Pesaḥ	*Pesaḥim*
b. Roš Haš.	*Roš Haššanah*
b. Šabb.	*Šabbat*

Jerusalem Talmud

y. Hag.	*Ḥagigah*
y. Meg.	*Megillah*

Mishnah

m. 'Abod. Zar.	*'Abodah Zarah*
m. 'Abot	*'Abot*
m. Ber.	*Berakot*
m. Makš.	*Makširin*
m. Sanh.	*Sanhedrin*
m. Šeqal.	*Šeqalim*
m. Ta'an.	*Ta'anit*
m. Tehar.	*Teharot*

Tosefta

t. Ber.	*Berakot*
t. Šeqal.	*Šeqalim*
t. Sukkah	*Sukkah*

'Abot R. Nat.	*'Abot de Rabbi Nathan*
Esth. Rab.	*Esther Rabbah*
Gen. Rab.	*Genesis Rabbah*

Secondary Sources

AB	Anchor Bible
AGJU	Arbeiten zur Geschichte des antiken Judentums und de Urchristentums
AJA	*American Journal of Archaeology*
AJP	*American Journal of Philology*
ALGHJ	Arbeiten zur Literatur und Geschichte des hellenistischen Judentums
ANRW	*Aufstieg und Niedergang der römischen Welt: Geschichte und Kultur Roms im Spiegel der neueren Forschung.* Edited by H. Temporini and W. Haase. Berlin: Walter de Gruyter, 1972–.
ATDan	Acta theologica danica
BAG	Walter Bauer, W. F. Arndt, and F. W. Gingrich. *Greek-English Lexicon of the New Testament and Other Early Christian Literature.* 2nd ed. Chicago: University of Chicago Press, 1979.
BAR	British Archaeological Reports
BASORSup	Supplements to *Bulletin of the American Schools of Oriental Research*
BETL	Bibliotheca ephemeridum theologicarum lovaniensium
BJS	Brown Judaic Studies
BZNW	Beihefte zur Zeitschrift für die neutestamentliche Wissenschaft
CBQ	*Catholic Biblical Quarterly*
CBQMS	Catholic Biblical Quarterly Monograph Series
CCWJCW	Cambridge Commentaries on Writings of the Jewish and Christian World
ConBNT	Coniectanea biblica: New Testament Series
ConBOT	Coniectanea biblica: Old Testament Series
CPJ	*Corpus papyrorum judaicorum.* Edited by Victor Tcherikover et al. 3 vols. Cambridge, Mass.: Harvard University Press, 1957–64.
CRINT	Compendia rerum iudaicarum ad Novum Testamentum
CSHJ	Chicago Studies in the History of Judaism
DJD	Discoveries in the Judaean Desert
DSD	*Dead Sea Discoveries*
EKKNT	Evangelisch-katholischer Kommentar zum Neuen Testament

ESI	*Excavations and Surveys in Israel*
FRLANT	Forschungen zur Religion und Literatur des Alten und Neuen Testaments
HA-ESI	*Hadashot Arkheologiyot—Excavations and Surveys in Israel*
HeyJ	*Heythrop Journal*
HSS	Harvard Semitic Studies
HTR	*Harvard Theological Review*
HUCA	*Hebrew Union College Annual*
IAAR	Israel Antiquities Authority Reports
IBS	*Irish Biblical Studies*
ICC	Internationa Critical Commentary
IEJ	*Israel Exploration Journal*
Int	*Interpretation*
IRT	Issues in Religion and Theology
JBL	*Journal of Biblical Literature*
JIGRE	*Jewish Inscriptions of Graeco-Roman Egypt.* Edited by William Horbury and David Noy. Cambridge: Cambridge University Press, 1992.
JJS	*Journal of Jewish Studies*
JQR	*Jewish Quarterly Review*
JRA	*Journal of Roman Archaeology*
JRS	*Journal of Roman Studies*
JSJ	*Journal for the Study of Judaism*
JSJSup	Supplements to the *Journal for the Study of Judaism*
JSNT	*Journal for the Study of the New Testament*
JSNTSup	Supplements to the *Journal for the Study of the New Testament*
JSOTSup	Supplements to the *Journal for the Study of the Old Testament*
JSPSup	Supplements to the *Journal for the Study of the Pseudepigrapha*
JSQ	*Jewish Studies Quarterly*
JTS	*Journal of Theological Studies*
LSJ	H. G. Liddell, R. Scott, H. S. Jones. *A Greek-English Lexicon.* 9th ed. Oxford: Clarendon, 1996.
NovT	*Novum Testamentum*
NovTSup	Supplements to *Novum Testamentum*
NTS	*New Testament Studies*
NTTS	New Testament Tools and Studies
OBO	Orbis biblicus et orientalis
Qad	*Qadmoniot*
RB	*Revue biblique*
RevQ	*Revue de Qumran*
SBLDS	Society of Biblical Literature Dissertation Series

SBLEJL	Society of Biblical Literature Early Judaism and Its Literature
SBLMS	Society of Biblical Literature Monograph Series
SBLSymS	Society of Biblical Literature Symposium Series
ScEs	*Science et esprit*
SEÅ	*Svensk exegetisk årsbok*
SHR	Study in the History of Religions
SIG	*Sylloge inscriptionum graecarum.* Edited by W. Dittenberger. 4 vols. 3rd ed. Leipzig: Hirzelium, 1915–24.
SJLA	Studies in Judaism in Late Antiquity
SNTSMS	Society for New Testament Studies Monograph Series
SP	Sacra pagina
SR	*Studies in Religion*
STDJ	Studies on the Texts of the Desert of Judah
STK	*Svensk teologisk Kvartalskrift*
StPB	Studia post-biblica
SVTP	Studia in Veteris Testamenti pseudepigraphica
SwJT	*Southwestern Journal of Theology*
TDNT	*Theological Dictionary of the New Testament.* Edited by Gerhard Kittel and Gerhard Friedrich. Translated by Geoffrey W. Bromiley. 10 vols. Grand Rapids: Eerdmans, 1964–76.
TDOT	*Theological Dictionary of the Old Testament.* Edited by G. Johannes Botterweck, Helmer Ringgren, and Heinz-Josef Fabry. Translated by Douglas W. Stott et al. Grand Rapids: Eerdmans, 1974–.
TJ	*Trinity Journal*
TSAJ	Texte und Studien zum antiken Judentum
TUGAL	Texte und Untersuchungen zur Geschichte der altchristlichen Literatur
VT	*Vetus Testamentum*
VTSup	Supplements to *Vetus Testamentum*
WUNT	Wissenschaftliche Untersuchungen zum Neuen Testament
ZDPV	*Zeitschrift des deutschen Palästina-Vereins*

Notes

Chapter 1: Common Judaism and Diversity within Judaism

1. E. P. Sanders, *Judaism: Practice and Belief, 63 BCE–66 CE* (1992; corrected ed., London: SCM; Philadelphia: Trinity Press International, 1994), 494.

2. Ibid., 47–48. For a detailed study of the *'am hā-āareṣ*, see Aharon Oppenheimer, *The 'Am Ha-Aretz: A Study in the Social History of the Jewish People in the Hellenistic-Roman Period*, ALGHJ 8 (Leiden: Brill, 1977).

3. Morton Smith, "The Dead Sea Sect in Relation to Ancient Judaism," *NTS* 7 (1960–61): 353.

4. See p. 18.

5. On the academic study of "lived religion," see David H. Hall, ed., *Lived Religion in America: Toward a History of Practice* (Princeton: Princeton University Press, 1997); Robert Anthony Orsi, *The Madonna of 115th Street: Faith and Community in Italian Harlem, 1880–1950*, 2nd ed. (New Haven, Conn.: Yale University Press, 2002).

6. Martin Hengel and Roland Deines, "E. P. Sanders' 'Common Judaism,' Jesus, and the Pharisees," trans. Daniel P. Bailey, *JTS* 46 (1995): 1–70, here 68 (review of *Jewish Law: From Jesus to the Mishnah* and *Judaism: Practice and Belief*).

7. Roland Deines, "The Pharisees between 'Judaisms' and 'Common Judaism,'" in *Justification and Variegated Nomism*, vol. 1, *The Complexities of Second Temple Judaism*, ed. D. A. Carson, Peter T. O'Brien, and Mark A. Seifrid, WUNT 2.140 (Tübingen: Mohr Siebeck; Grand Rapids: Baker Academic, 2001), 444–46.

8. Lester L. Grabbe, *Judaic Religion in the Second Temple Period: Belief and Practice from the Exile to Yavneh* (London and New York: Routledge, 2000), 2.

9. See the discussion in Günter Stemberger, "Was There a 'Mainstream Judaism' in the Late Second Temple Period?" *Review of Rabbinic Judaism* 4, no. 2 (2001): 189–207.

10. See also E. P. Sanders, "Common Judaism and the Synagogue in the First Century," in *Jews, Christians, and Polytheists in the Ancient Synagogue: Cultural Interaction during the Greco-Roman Period*, ed. Steven Fine (New York: Routledge, 1999), 1–17.

11. Stemberger, "Was There a 'Mainstream Judaism'?" 194.

12. Ibid., 191.

13. See Catherine Hezser, *Jewish Literacy in Roman Palestine*, TSAJ 81 (Tübingen: Mohr Siebeck, 2001).

Chapter 2: Common Judaism Explored

This chapter is a revision of a paper given at a conference entitled "'Common Judaism' or a Plurality of 'Judaisms' in Late Antiquity: The State of the Debate," held at the Institute for Advanced Studies, the Hebrew University, the Thirteenth School in Jewish Studies, Jerusalem, May 13–16, 2003. I am very grateful to Isaiah Gafni for the invitation and to Martin Goodman and Albert Baumgarten for suggesting improvements.

1. *Judaism: Practice and Belief, 63 BCE–66 CE* (1992; corrected ed., London: SCM; Philadelphia: Trinity Press International, 1994).

2. There is a more comprehensive account in my "Intellectual Autobiography" in *Redefining First-Century Jewish and Christian Identities: Essays in Honor of Ed P. Sanders*, ed. Fabian Udoh et al. (South Bend: University of Notre Dame Press, 2008), 11–41.

3. Walter Bauer, *Rechtgläubigkeit und Ketzerei im ältesten Christentum*, 2nd ed., ed. Georg Strecker (1934; reprint, Tübingen: J. C. B. Mohr [Paul Siebeck], 1964); Eng. trans., *Orthodoxy and Heresy in Earliest Christianity*, ed. Robert Kraft and Gerhard Krodel (Philadelphia: Fortress Press, 1971).

4. Josephus, *J.W.* 2.119–66; *Ant.* 13.171–73; 18.12–25.

5. See the discussion in my *Paul and Palestinian Judaism: A Comparison of Patterns of Religion* (Philadelphia: Fortress Press, 1977), 287–98, esp. 291.

6. Ibid., 16–18.

7. "I continue to regard 'covenantal nomism' as the common denominator which underlay all sorts and varieties of Judaism" (*Jesus and Judaism* [Philadelphia: Fortress Press, 1985], 336).

8. In *Paul and Palestinian Judaism*, note the following terms and phrases: "general understanding of religion and religious life" (69); "common pattern . . . which underlies . . ." (70); "basic religious principles" (71); "what principles lie behind" (71); not a "system" (73f.); "underlying agreement" (85); "the same underlying pattern" (424); "basic common ground . . . in the various bodies of literature" (424). In rereading Erwin Goodenough's *Jewish Symbols in the Greco-Roman Period* (13 vols., Bollingen Series 37 [New York: Pantheon, 1953–68]) in the spring of 2004, I discovered that he had written that Jews were loyal to "some common Jewish denominator," which consisted of loyalty to the Jewish people and belief in the Bible. He also referred to this as "minimal Judaism." Philo "still believed with all his heart that Jews had a special revelation of God in the Torah, and a peculiar relationship with him" (12:6–9). These pages, which I had read in 1964 or 1965, contained no pencil marks indicating that I had regarded the terms or the proposal as important. I nevertheless wonder whether they lodged in my subconscious mind, to surface ten years later. I wish that I had remembered these pages, since I would have been delighted to have Goodenough's support on both Philo and Judaism in general.

9. The original intention was to write on Paul and Judaism; the restriction to literature stemming from Palestine was forced entirely by issues of space. I separately argued that Philo

shared at least major aspects of covenantal nomism ("The Covenant as a Soteriological Category and the Nature of Salvation in Palestinian and Hellenistic Judaism," in *Jews, Greeks and Christians: Religious Cultures in Late Antiquity; Essays in Honor of William David Davies*, ed. Robert Hamerton-Kelly and Robin Scroggs, SJLA 21 [Leiden: Brill, 1976], 11–44).

10. I shall soon publish an essay called "Covenantal Nomism Revisited," in which I defend some of the main arguments of *Paul and Palestinian Judaism*. The essay will appear in a volume of the *Jewish Studies Quarterly*, to be guest-edited by Dana Hollander and Joel Kaminsky.

11. Neusner's review is reprinted in his *Ancient Judaism: Debates and Disputes*, BJS 64 (Chico, Calif.: Scholars Press, 1984), 127–41, here 128.

12. A related criticism appears in the review by Martin McNamara in *JSNT* 5 (1979): 67–73: "The 'pattern of religion' in fact may be so basic as to have little effect on the working of religion in practice" (72). This review is one of the best of the early reactions to *Paul and Palestinian Judaism*, since the author described my own efforts very fairly, without misstating or caricaturing them, and then presented fair and useful criticisms. If I understand the point of McNamara's paragraph on the present point (71–72) it is not that "covenantal nomism" is so obvious as to be irrelevant, but that it may not succeed in defining how different varieties of Judaism functioned *in practice*. And that, of course, is true. "Covenantal nomism" was intended to describe how getting in and staying in were *understood*. No *theology*—whether covenantal nomism or the theology of Aquinas or of Luther—tells us how people actually practiced their religion. I have tried to come a little nearer to this in *Practice and Belief*: it is the best I can do toward describing how people lived their religion. There is a brief but good summary of criticisms in Petri Luomanen, *Entering the Kingdom of Heaven: A Study on the Structure of Matthew's View of Salvation*, WUNT 2.101 (Tübingen: Mohr Siebeck, 1998), 41–42.

13. See, for example, D. A. Carson, "Summaries and Conclusions," in *Justification and Variegated Nomism*, vol. 1, *The Complexities of Second Temple Judaism*, ed. D. A. Carson, Peter T. O'Brien, and Mark A. Seifrid, WUNT 2.140 (Tübingen: Mohr Siebeck, 2001), 544–45.

14. Jonathan Z. Smith, "Fences and Neighbors: Some Contours of Early Judaism," in *Approaches to Ancient Judaism*, ed. William Scott Greed, vol. 2, BJS 9 (Chico, Calif.: Scholars Press, 1980), 1–25, here 1. Smith attributed the suggested comparison to Francis Ponge. The essay also appears in Smith, *Imagining Religion: From Babylon to Jonestown* (Chicago: University Press, 1982), 1–18.

15. For example, *Paul and Palestinian Judaism*, 12, on the inadequacy of "one-line essences" or "reduced essences," such as faith versus works or liberty versus law.

16. See below at n. 35.

17. We were assisted greatly by the presence of several scholars for one or two years each. The list above names participants for the entire five-year period.

18. Lawrence Schiffman, *Who Was a Jew? Rabbinic and Halakhic Perspectives on the Jewish–Christian Schism* (Hoboken, N.J.: KTAV, 1985).

19. "The research project takes as its starting point the observation that in the first century both Jews and Christians had numerous options before them, including that of retaining a great deal of diversity. By the early part of the third century, however, both Judaism and Christianity had decisively narrowed their options" (E. P. Sanders, Albert I. Baumgarten, and Alan Mendelson,

eds., *Jewish and Christian Self-Definition*, vol. 2, *Aspects of Judaism in the Graeco-Roman Period* (London: SCM, 1981), ix.

20. Jacob Neusner, *Judaism: The Evidence of the Mishnah* (Chicago: University of Chicago Press, 1981), 24.

21. Ibid., 37.

22. Jacob Neusner, "Parsing the Rabbinic Canon with the History of an Idea: The Messiah," in *Formative Judaism: Religious, Historical and Literary Studies*, 3rd ser., *Torah, Pharisees, and Rabbis*, BJS 46 (Chicago: University of Chicago Press, 1983), 173.

23. Jacob Neusner, *Messiah in Context: Israel's History and Destiny in Formative Judaism* (Philadelphia: Fortress Press, 1984), 6.

24. Ibid., 7.

25. Ibid., 14.

26. In addition to the works cited in nn. 20, 22, and 23 above, see also Neusner, *Midrash in Context: Exegesis in Formative Judaism* (Philadelphia: Fortress Press, 1983); idem, *Torah: From Scroll to Symbol in Formative Judaism* (Philadelphia: Fortress Press, 1985).

27. E. P. Sanders, "Jacob Neusner and the Philosophy of the Mishnah," in *Jewish Law from Jesus to the Mishnah: Five Studies* (London: SCM; Philadelphia: Trinity Press International, 1990), 309–31.

28. Menahem Stern, *Greek and Latin Authors on Jews and Judaism*, 3 vols. (Jerusalem: Israel Academy of Sciences and Humanities, 1976–84).

29. Against the concept of "Judaisms," see, for example, J. M. G. Barclay, *Jews in the Mediterranean Diaspora: From Alexander to Trajan (323 BCE–117 CE)* (Edinburgh: T&T Clark, 1996), 400. According to Giorgio Jossa's recent book, *Jews or Christians? The Followers of Jesus in Search of Their Own Identity*, WUNT 202 (Tübingen: Mohr Siebeck, 2006), the majority of scholars now tend to speak of "a plurality of different Judaisms" (23), though he takes the other side (see also 22–29). My own view is that if one included Jewish scholars in the survey, the plural "Judaisms" would not be in the majority.

30. "Intellectual Autobiography" (n. 2 above).

31. Morton Smith, "Palestinian Judaism in the First Century," in *Israel: Its Role in Civilization*, ed. Moshe Davis (New York: Israel Institute of the Jewish Theological Seminary, 1956), 67–81, here 68, 73, 81; reprinted in *Essays in Greco-Roman and Related Talmudic Literature*, ed. Henry A. Fischel (New York: KTAV, 1977), 183–97.

32. Morton Smith, "The Dead Sea Sect in Relation to Ancient Judaism," *NTS* 7 (1960–61), 347–60, here 356.

33. See, for example, 236–37. See further my "Covenantal Nomism Revisited" (n. 10 above).

34. A lecture given at a conference entitled "'Common Judaism' or a Plurality of 'Judaisms' in Late Antiquity: The State of the Debate," held at the Hebrew University, Jerusalem, May 13–16, 2003.

35. E. P. Sanders, "The Dead Sea Sect and Other Jews," in *The Dead Sea Scrolls in Their Historical Context*, ed. Timothy H. Lim et al. (Edinburgh: T&T Clark, 2000), 7–43. The paper was written in 1998.

36. Jonathan Z. Smith has more than once used taxonomy (often called "systematics") in discussing religion. See recently his "A Matter of Class: Taxonomies of Religion," *HTR* 89 (1996): 387–403.

37. I wish that I had written "some aspects"; cf. "general conformity" in the last sentence of this paragraph.

38. Families, clans, and tribes are much more ancient than nations. The tendency to form groups and clubs may reflect the need to revert to relatively small groupings. Students of baboons and chimpanzees have noted that these primates can relate without enmity to a small number of other animals.

39. See Albert I. Baumgarten, *The Flourishing of Jewish Sects in the Maccabean Era: An Interpretation*, JSJSup 55 (Leiden: Brill, 1997), 34, 55–58.

40. On Augustus's support of Jewish rights, see also Philo, *Leg.* 156–57, 291, 311–16.

41. For a fuller analysis of the decrees in Josephus's *Antiquities*, see my *Practice and Belief*, 212 (n. 1 above).

42. See my *Practice and Belief*, 52.

43. Besides relating stories of theft of the temple tax en route to Jerusalem, Cicero writes this in favor of Flaccus: "When every year it was customary to send gold to Jerusalem on the order of the Jews from Italy and from all our provinces, Flaccus forbade by an edict its exportation from Asia" (*Flac.* 28.67).

44. For stories of plunder, see *Practice and Belief*, 83–84, 161–62.

45. According to Cicero, *Flac.* 28.68, Flaccus's decree to stop the exportation of gold from his province (Asia) to Jerusalem led to the confiscation of more than 220 pounds of gold. It would have taken the farmers and merchants of Jewish Palestine a long time to contribute that much money to the temple.

46. Josephus, *J. W.* 7.218; Cassius Dio *History of Rome* 66.7.

47. In the Greco-Roman period, Jews paid one-half sheqel (two drachmas) annually. This combines the half-sheqel tax of Exod 30.13 (which was apparently a one-time-only tax) with the regular tax of Neh 10.32 (which specifies one-third sheqel).

48. See, for example, Josephus, *Ant.* 12.125–27. This dispute also involved Nicolaus as advocate for the Jews and Marcus V. Agrippa as judge.

49. There is a convenient collection of Gentile sources in Molly Whittaker, *Jews and Christians: Graeco-Roman Views* (Cambridge: Cambridge University Press, 1984), 80–85. The sources, with translation, will be found in Stern, *Greek and Latin Authors on Jews and Judaism* (n. 28 above).

50. In *Practice and Belief*, 236–37. I listed five common practices. In the present summary, I have left out purification, since everyone in the ancient world purified themselves for sacred occasions. Thus, periodic purification was common to Jews, but it was also common to everyone else. In the Diaspora, Jewish purification (especially hand washing and the use of basins for sprinkling, called *perirrantēria*) agreed with pagan practice. On Jewish purity laws and practices, see *Practice and Belief*, 214–30. On hand washing and *perirrantēria* in the Diaspora and in paganism, see my *Jewish Law from Jesus to the Mishnah* (n. 27 above), 260–70. For further references to hand washing, see the index in ibid., s.v. "Purity laws: sub-topics."

51. See, for example, *Paul and Palestinian Judaism*, ch. 13.

52. One example in addition to the lecture by Jonathan Z. Smith cited above (n. 36) is Philip Alexander, "'The Parting of the Ways' from the Perspective of Rabbinic Judaism," in *Jews and Christians: The Parting of the Ways, A.D. 70 to 135*, ed. James D. G. Dunn (Tübingen: Mohr Siebeck, 1992), 2.

53. "The Christian religion is something simple and sublime; it means one thing and one thing only: eternal life in the midst of time, by the strength and under the eyes of God" (Adolf von Harnack, *Das Wesen des Christentums* [Leipzig: J. C. Hinrichs, 1929], 8).

54. I am indebted to a conversation with Hans Hillerbrand, who explained the context of von Harnack's *Wesen des Christentums*.

Chapter 3: "Common Judaism": The Contribution of the Ancient Synagogue

1. George Foot Moore, *Judaism in the First Centuries of the Christian Era: The Age of the Tannaim*, 3 vols. (Cambridge, Mass.: Harvard University Press, 1927), 1:3.

2. Erwin R. Goodenough (*Jewish Symbols in the Greco-Roman Period*, 13 vols., Bollingen Series 37 [New York: Pantheon, 1953–68]) nevertheless assumed that the Pharisees maintained control over Jewish religious life in the Second Temple period.

3. Morton Smith, "Palestinian Judaism in the First Century," in *Israel: Its Role in Civilization*, ed. Moshe Davis (New York: Jewish Theological Seminary, 1956), 67–81.

4. See, for example, Jacob Neusner, *Introduction to Rabbinic Literature* (New York: Doubleday, 1994), 633–49.

5. E. P. Sanders, *Jewish Law from Jesus to the Mishnah: Five Studies* (London: SCM, 1990); idem, *Judaism: Practice and Belief, 63 BCE–66 CE* (London: SCM, 1992; corrected ed., 1994).

6. Sanders, *Judaism*, 3.

7. Lee I. Levine, *The Ancient Synagogue: The First Thousand Years*, rev. ed. (New Haven. Conn.: Yale University Press, 2005), ch. 10.

8. Ibid., chs. 7, 8, and 9.

9. Ibid., 567–87.

10. Smith, "Palestinian Judaism," 81.

11. See Levine, *Ancient Synagogue*, 215–20.

12. Jaś Elsner, *Art and the Roman Viewer: The Transformation of Art from the Pagan World to Christianity* (Cambridge: Cambridge University Press, 1995), 1.

13. Henry Maguire, *The Earth and Ocean: The Terrestrial World in Early Byzantine Art* (University Park: Pennsylvania State University Press, 1987), 8.

14. On the limits of rabbinic involvement in the aspects of synagogue life, see Levine, *Ancient Synagogue*, ch. 13.

15. On local autonomy and diversity in village life and organization, the functions of village assemblies, and the variety in the titles of local officials in Roman Arabia at this time, see Henry I. MacAdam, *Studies in the History of the Roman Province of Arabia: The Northern Sector*, BAR International Series 295 (Oxford: BAR, 1986), 147–90; Maurice Sartre, "Villes et villages du

Hauran (Syrie) au IVe siècle," in *Sociétés urbaines, sociétés rurales dans l'Asie Mineure et la Syrie hellénistiques et romaines*, ed. Edmond Frézouls (Strasbourg: AECR, 1987), 239–57; John D. Grainger, " 'Village Government' in Roman Syria and Arabia," *Berytus* 27 (1995): 179–95.

16. This phenomenon is the subject of the author's forthcoming *Visual Judaism: History, Art, and Identity in Late Antiquity* (New Haven, Conn.: Yale University Press).

17. Levine, *Ancient Synagogue*, 146–53.

18. Three verses for each of the seven people called to the Torah (*b. Meg.* 23a).

19. Levine, *Ancient Synagogue*, 583–88. The issue of comprehension is of major importance. Even today, when studying *piyyut* and utilizing the various available apparatuses, it is often very difficult to understand the language of these poems or their allusions, metaphors, and nuances. If the intended audience were the ordinary synagogue congregant, then comprehension of this genre speaks wonders for the cultural and Hebraic level of the average Jewish worshiper! Perhaps, however, *piyyutim* were to be enjoyed primarily for their aesthetic value, for example, the melodies in which they were sung. Are we to assume that these compositions were recited when only a very few (if any) in attendance could understand their language? Alternatively, were the *piyyutim* intended primarily for certain types of audiences in which the participation of the learned was more pronounced (for example, an academy setting)? Or, perhaps, a particular congregation included the recitation of *piyyutim* composed by one of its members. Whatever the case, the contrast between the attempt to make the Torah reading and sermon comprehensible to a wider audience, on the one hand, and the complexity of most *piyyutim*, on the other, is puzzling. Regrettably, we are not in a position at present to answer the above questions. While the *piyyut* has led to a new understanding of the variety of components in Jewish worship of late antiquity, it has also left us with a series of intriguing questions.

20. Joseph Naveh, *On Stone and Mosaic: The Aramaic and Hebrew Inscriptions from Ancient Synagogues* (Jerusalem: Israel Exploration Society and Carta, 1978), nos. 16, 26, 60, 64, 65 (Hebrew); Lea Roth-Gerson, *The Greek Inscriptions from the Synagogues in Eretz-Israel* (Jerusalem: Yad Izhak Ben-Zvi, 1987), nos. 3, 10, 17, 21, 23 (Hebrew).

21. Naveh, *On Stone and Mosaic*, nos. 46, 69, 84.

22. Avigdor Shinan, "The Aramaic Targum as a Mirror of Galilean Jewry," in *The Galilee in Late Antiquity*, ed. Lee I. Levine (New York and Jerusalem: Jewish Theological Seminary, 1992), 248–49.

23. *Theodosian Code* 7, 8, 2 (Amnon Linder, *The Jews in Roman Imperial Legislation* [Detroit: Wayne State University Press, 1987], 161–63).

24. Levine, *Ancient Synagogue*, 236–49.

25. It goes without saying that within this commonality of religious expression, the ways it was expressed in each particular setting might differ considerably.

26. There are three possible ways to define orientation: (1) the external direction of a building, indicated by its facade, doors, or adjacent atrium, following pagan models; (2) the internal design of the main hall, indicated by the placement of columns, benches, *bima*, and Torah shrine; and (3) the direction of prayer for the *ʿAmidah*, which, with rare exception (see below), requires facing Jerusalem. Scholars have often used the direction of synagogue facades and doors to determine synagogue orientation. However, the positioning of these external architectural elements, which

was often a matter of style or topographical necessity, seems to have been a consideration of secondary importance. More decisive are the internal design and the activities within the main hall. The focus inside all synagogue buildings was likely both the center of the hall and the Jerusalem wall, where a Torah shrine, apse, or *bima* might be found. This conclusion is supported by the fact that seating was arranged along the walls. Exceptionally, in Galilean buildings, the exterior of a building reflected this internal orientation as well. Thus, it can be assumed that the direction of prayer followed (or perhaps determined) the building's internal design.

27. This rule, too, has its exceptions. See Levine, *Ancient Synagogue*, 327–29.

28. 1 Kgs 8:44; 2 Chr 6:34, 38; Dan 6:11. See also *m. Ber.* 4, 5.

29. For further discussion, see Steven Fine, *This Holy Place: On the Sanctity of Synagogues during the Greco-Roman Period*, Christianity and Judaism in Antiquity 11 (Notre Dame: University of Notre Dame Press, 1997), 105–11; Levine, *Ancient Synagogue*, 351–56.

30. See Levine, *Ancient Synagogue*, 230–36.

31. Rachel Hachlili, *The Menorah, the Ancient Seven-Armed Candelabrum: Origin, Form, and Significance* (Leiden: Brill, 2001), 204–9.

32. Roth-Gerson, *Greek Inscriptions*, 46–48. For a highly speculative suggestion that the synagogue in Ḥammam Lif (Naro) in Tunisia bore scenes representing the Creation and Paradise, see Edward Bleiberg, *Tree of Paradise: Jewish Mosaics from the Roman Empire* (Brooklyn: Brooklyn Museum, 2005), 24–46.

33. For the above sites, see the relevant entries in Ephraim Stern, ed., *The New Encyclopedia of Archaeological Excavations in the Holy Land*, 4 vols. (Jerusalem: Israel Exploration Society and Carta, 1993); and Zeev Weiss, *The Sepphoris Synagogue: Deciphering an Ancient Message through Its Archaeological and Socio-historical Contexts* (Jerusalem: Israel Exploration Society, 2005), 77–104. Mention should be made of the 'En Gedi inscription, where the following are noted: the thirteen ancestors of the world per 1 Chr 1:1–4 (including Noah and his three sons); the three biblical patriarchs; the three friends of Daniel—Hananiah, Mishael, and Azariah. See Lee I. Levine, "The Inscription in the 'En Gedi Synagogue," in *Ancient Synagogues Revealed*, ed. Lee I. Levine (Jerusalem: Israel Exploration Society, 1981), 140–45.

34. See Rachel Hachlili, "The Zodiac in Ancient Synagogal Art: A Review," *JSQ* 9 (2002): 219–58.

35. In addition, as noted, the 'En Gedi community registered the zodiac signs by name and with no figural representation.

36. Diklah Zohar, "The Iconography of the Zodiac and the Months in the Synagogue of Sepphoris: A Study in Diffusion of Artistic Models," *Mo'ed* 16 (2006): 1–26.

37. A caveat is in order here. The above categories of artistic expression (Jewish symbols, biblical figures and scenes, and the zodiac) are not divided equally between the Diaspora and Byzantine Palestine. In each of these categories, the representations are more (or exclusively) apparent in the latter. The concentration of Jewish symbols is greater, more biblical figures and scenes are depicted (Dura aside), and the zodiac appears only in late antique Palestine. Surprisingly, Diaspora synagogues, far from being more syncretistic and Hellenized in this regard, were by and large more conservative than their Palestinian counterparts. Perhaps the security of living in

their land amid a greater concentration of Jews allowed some communities to indulge in artistic expressions that their fellow Jews in the Diaspora might have found objectionable.

38. Relatively few urban buildings have been discovered (undoubtedly owing to the destruction activity in such settings), but even those discovered in cities do not all seem to have been particularly impressive structures on their exterior (for example, the fourth-century Ḥammat Tiberias building).

39. See, for example, Mordechai Aviam, "Christian Galilee in the Byzantine Period," in *Galilee through the Centuries: Confluence of Cultures: Proceedings of the Second International Conference in Galilee*, ed. Eric M. Meyers (Winona Lake, Ind.: Eisenbrauns, 1999), 281–300.

40. Levine, *Ancient Synagogue*, 242–48. Regarding Jewish symbols and, more particularly, the menorah, see Lee I. Levine, "The History and Significance of the Menorah in Antiquity," in *From Dura to Sepphoris: Studies in Jewish Art and Society in Late Antiquity*, ed. Lee I. Levine and Zeev Weiss, JRA Supplementary Series 40 (Ann Arbor, Mich.: Journal of Roman Archaeology, 2000), 145–53; a more detailed discussion will appear in the author's forthcoming *Visual Judaism*. See also Seth Schwartz, *Imperialism and Jewish Society: 200 BCE to 640 CE* (Princeton: Princeton University Press, 2001), 179–202.

41. On the Patriarchate and the synagogue, see Levine, *Ancient Synagogue*, ch. 12, and the bibliography listed there, 454 n. 1.

42. Ḥorvat 'Etri, south of Bet Shemesh, may also be a first-century synagogue. The building is clearly of a different order from those in the vicinity, and the entranceway is a further indication of its public nature. Our main reservations involve the meager finds within the building itself. In contrast to the two other Judean village synagogues from this time, the building has no benches or stone-paved floor, nor is the deployment of its columns (three in a single row in the middle of the hall) evidenced elsewhere, where two to four columns surround an open space in the middle. See Boaz Zissu and Amir Ganor, "Horvat 'Ethri—A Jewish Village from the Second Temple in the Judaean Foothills" (in Hebrew), *Qad* 123 (2002): 18–27 (Hebrew).

43. See also Shaye J. D. Cohen, *From the Maccabees to the Mishnah* (Philadelphia: Westminster, 1987), 24–26.

44. See Levine, *Ancient Synagogue*, 616; as well as the articles by Yigael Yadin ("The Synagogue at Masada," 19–23), Gideon Foerster ("The Synagogues at Masada and Herodium," 24–29), and Zvi U. Ma'oz ("The Synagogue at Gamla and the Typology of Second Temple Synagogues," 35–41) in *Ancient Synagogues Revealed*, ed. Lee I. Levine (Jerusalem: Israel Exploration Society, 1981).

45. Levine, *Ancient Synagogue*, 52–54, 66–68.

46. For references and a discussion of the material cited in this paragraph, see my *Ancient Synagogue*, ch. 4.

47. *Ant.* 19.299–305; *J. W.* 2.285–92; Philo, *Embassy* 132–34.

48. For the above, see William Horbury and David Noy, eds., *Jewish Inscriptions of Graeco-Roman Egypt* (Cambridge: Cambridge University Press, 1992), nos. 22, 24, 25, 27, 28, 117; Philo, *Embassy* 133; Harry J. Leon, *The Jews of Ancient Rome* (Philadelphia: Jewish Publication Society, 1960), 140–42; Levine, *Ancient Synagogue*, 100–102, 118–20.

49. John S. Kloppenborg Verbin, "Dating Theodotos (*CIJ* II 1404)," *JJS* 51 (2000): 243–80; Lee I. Levine, *Jerusalem: Portrait of the City in the Second Temple Period (538 B.C.E.–70 C.E.)* (Philadelphia: Jewish Publication Society, 2002), 95–97.

50. Levine, *Ancient Synagogue*, 103.

51. Donald D. Binder, *Into the Temple Courts: The Place of the Synagogues in the Second Temple Period*, SBLDS 169 (Atlanta: Society of Biblical Literature, 1999), 348–52. On the many communal functions that took place in synagogues everywhere, see Levine, *Ancient Synagogue*, 139–45.

52. Levine, *Ancient Synagogue*, 119; Horbury and Noy, *Jewish Inscriptions*, no. 26.

53. Philo also describes Essene practice on the Sabbath: "They use these laws [of the Torah] to learn from at all times, but especially each seventh day, since the seventh day is regarded as sacred. On that day they abstain from other work and betake themselves to the sacred places which are called synagogues. They are seated according to age in fixed places, the young below the old, holding themselves ready to listen with the proper good manners. Then one of them takes the books and reads. Another, from among those with most experience, comes forward and explains anything that is not easy to understand" (*Good Person* 81–82).

54. Levine, *Ancient Synagogue*, 57–59.

55. *Moses* 2.215–16; *Special Laws* 2.62–64, and *Hypoth.* 7.13.

56. Levine, *Ancient Synagogue*, 159–62.

57. Arthur D. Nock, *Conversion: The Old and the New in Religion from Alexander the Great to Augustine of Hippo* (1933; reprint, Oxford: Oxford University Press, 1965), 26–32.

58. See Arnaldo Momigliano, *On Pagans, Jews and Christians* (Middletown, Conn.: Wesleyan University Press, 1987), 89–91.

59. Levine, *Ancient Synagogue*, 38–41; Shaye J. D. Cohen, "Were Pharisees and Rabbis the Leaders of Communal Prayer and Torah Study in Antiquity? The Evidence of the New Testament, Josephus, and the Church Fathers," in *Evolution of the Synagogue: Problems and Progress*, ed. Howard Clark Kee and Lynn H. Cohick (Harrisburg, Pa.: Trinity Press International, 1999), 89–105; Binder, *Into the Temple Courts*, 399–404; Anders Runesson, *The Origins of the Synagogue: A Socio-historical Study* (Stockholm: Almqvist & Wiksell International, 2001), 259–303.

60. Levine, *Ancient Synagogue*, 162–69.

61. Lee I. Levine, "The Second Temple Synagogue: The Formative Years," in *The Synagogue in Late Antiquity*, ed. Lee I. Levine (Philadelphia: Jewish Theological Seminary and American Schools of Oriental Research, 1987), 20–22.

62. Other terms being used in the first century: *hierōn* ("holy place"), *eucheīon* ("place of prayer"), *sabbateion* ("Sabbath meeting-place"), and *didaskaleīon* ("place of instruction"). More unusual terms, such as *amphitheater* and *templum*, were also invoked, as was the word *oīkos*. The synagogues of Rome—some early, others late—are of a unique order, having been named after famous people, professions, or places of origin.

63. See generally Martin Goodman, "Sacred Space in Diaspora Judaism," in *Studies on the Jewish Diaspora in the Hellenistic and Roman Periods*, ed. Benjamin Isaac and Aharon Oppenheimer, Te'uda 12 (Tel Aviv: Ramot, 1996), 1–16.

64. Horbury and Noy, *Jewish Inscriptions*, nos. 16, 17, 127. Although the term *proseuchē* does not appear in these fragmentary inscriptions, there can be little doubt that such a building was intended.

65. Horbury and Noy, *Jewish Inscriptions*, nos. 27 and 105.

66. Ibid., no. 125. See also Victor Tcherikover, Alexander Fuks, and Menahem Stern, *Corpus Papyrorum Judaicarum*, 3 vols. (Cambridge, Mass.: Harvard University Press, 1957–64), vol. 1, no. 125.

67. Ibid., vol. 1, no. 129.

68. Horbury and Noy, *Jewish Inscriptions*, nos. 9 and 129; Jean-Baptiste Frey, ed., *Corpus Inscriptionum Judaicarum*, 2 vols. (Rome: Pontificio Istituto di Archeologia Cristiana, 1936–52; vol. 2 reprint, New York: KTAV, 1975), 2:1433; Baruch Lifshitz, *Donateurs et fondateurs dans les synagogues juives* (Paris: Gabalda, 1967), no. 87.

69. Tcherikover et al., *Corpus Papyrorum Judaicarum*, vol. 1, no. 134.

70. Levine, *Ancient Synagogue*, 89–91. Another indication of the holiness of a *proseuchē* is reflected in 3 Macc 7:19–20: "And when they finished their voyage in peace with appropriate thanksgivings, there, too, in like manner they determined to celebrate these days also as festive for the duration of their community. They inscribed them as holy on a pillar and dedicated a house of prayer [*tōpon proseuchēs*] at the site of the banquet." That a *proseuchē* was built as a memorial to the miraculous salvation of a community is noteworthy. Although the historicity of much of this book's narrative is questionable, the fact that the *proseuchē* is mentioned in such a context indicates some sort of reality in Jewish Hellenistic Egypt.

71. See Levine, *Ancient Synagogue*, ch. 4.

72. A. Thomas Kraabel, "Social Systems of Six Diaspora Synagogues," in *Diaspora Jews and Judaism: Essays in Honor of, and in Dialogue with, A. Thomas Kraabel*, ed. J. Andrew Overman and Robert S. MacLennan, South Florida Studies in the History of Judaism 41 (Atlanta: Scholars Press, 1992), 257–67.

73. Gert Lüderitz, "What Is the *Politeuma*?" in *Studies in Early Jewish Epigraphy*, ed. Jan W. van Henten and Pieter W. van der Horst, AGJU 21 (Leiden: Brill, 1994), 219–22.

74. Paul-Eugène Dion, "Synagogues et temples dans l'Egypte hellénistique," *ScEs* 29 (1977): 45–75.

Chapter 4: Common Judaism, Common Purity, and the Second Temple Period Judean *Miqwa'ot* (Ritual Immersion Baths)

1. Gedalia Alon, *The Jews in Their Land in the Talmudic Age (70–640 CE)*, trans. and ed. Gershon Levi (Cambridge, Mass.: Harvard University Press, 1996), 259–60.

2. E. P. Sanders, *Jewish Law from Jesus to the Mishnah: Five Studies* (London: SCM; Philadelphia: Trinity Press International, 1990); idem, *Judaism: Practice and Belief 63 BCE–66 CE* (London: SCM; Philadelphia: Trinity Press International, 1992; corrected ed., 1994).

3. Ronny Reich, "Mishnah Sheqalim 8:2 and the Archaeological Evidence," in *Perakim be-toldot Yerushalayim bi-yeme Bayit Sheni: sefer zikaron le-Avraham Shalit* (*Jerusalem in the Second Temple Period: Abraham Schalit Memorial Volume*), ed. A. Oppenheimer et al., Sifriyah le-toldot

ha-yishuv ha-Yehudi be-Erets-Yisrael (Jerusalem: Yad Yitzhak Ben-Tsvi, 1980), 225–56; idem, "Archaeological Evidence of the Jewish Population at Hasmonean Gezer," *IEJ* 31 (1981): 48–52; idem, "A Miqweh at 'Isawiya Near Jerusalem," *IEJ* 34 (1984): 220–23.

4.   Eyal Regev, "Ritual Baths of Jewish Groups and Sects in the Second Temple Period" (in Hebrew) *The Jerusalem Cathedra* 79 (1996): 3–21; idem, "More on Ritual Baths of Jewish Groups and Sects: On Research Methods and Archaeological Evidence—A Reply to A. Grossberg" (in Hebrew), *The Jerusalem Cathedra* 83 (1996): 169–76.

5.   Asher Grossberg, "Ritual Baths in Second Temple Period Jerusalem and How They Were Ritually Prepared" (in Hebrew), *The Jerusalem Cathedra* 83 (1996): 151–68; idem, "How Were the Mikva'ot of Masada Made Ritually Fit?" (in Hebrew), *The Jerusalem Cathedra* 85 (1997): 33–44.

6.   Yoel Elitzur, "Ritual Pools for Immersion of Hands" (in Hebrew), *The Jerusalem Cathedra* 91 (1999): 169–72. But see Asher Grossberg, "Ritual Pools for Immersion of Hands at Masada" (in Hebrew), *The Jerusalem Cathedra* 95 (2000): 165–71.

7.   Interestingly, the Talmudic sources suggest that the baths continued to exist and remained in use during the Mishnaic and Talmudic periods (late Roman–early Byzantine period). We believe that further research and excavation of sites will show that purity concerns remained central during this period. Excavations of private houses at Sepphoris clearly attest to the continuation of the custom during the Roman and Byzantine periods. See Eric M. Meyers, "Aspects of Everyday Life in Roman Palestine with Special Reference to Private Domiciles and Ritual Baths," in *Jews in the Hellenistic and Roman Cities*, ed. J. R. Bartlett (London: Routledge, 2002), 211–20; H. Eshel, "A Note on Miqva'ot at Sepphoris," in *Archaeology and the Galilee: Texts and Contexts in the Greco-Roman and Byzantine Periods*, ed. D. R. Edwards and C. T. McCollough, South Florida Studies in the History of Judaism 143 (Atlanta: Scholars Press, 1997), 131–33.

8.   An up-to-date classification based on the size, architectural features such as double entrances, separation arrangements, and relations between baths and neighboring water cisterns is desirable. The ritual immersion bath's typology, its possible halakhic implications, and sociohistorical conclusions will be undertaken in our future publication (Amit and Zissu, in preparation).

9.   *Discoveries at St. John's, 'Ein Karim, 1941–1942* (Jerusalem: Franciscan Press, 1946), 64–77, pl. 5:1.

10.   This type is quite rare among the baths known from that period. Only an "optical illusion" caused it to be considered for many years the definitive representative of the ritual baths of the period. As Reich expressed it in the introduction to his study, "Although the installations on Masada that were published by Yadin made researchers aware of the existence of such installations, they also created a tremendous stumbling block in that the researchers perceived the ritual baths on Masada, from the standpoint of their structure and shape as well as the manner of their operation, as the characteristic type of ritual bath in the Second Temple period, and believed that similar ones should be sought elsewhere" (*Miqva'ot*, 7). Indeed, the first step in Reich's breakthrough was to identify as ritual baths dozens of stepped water installations found in extensive excavations in Jerusalem. The picture that arises from our study stresses just how rare and anomalous ritual baths with a storage tank were.

11. The Mishnah (*m. Miqw.* 4:1–3; 6:8–11) describes various connections between the cistern and the bath, mostly through pipes made of lead and other materials, but up to the present none has been found by archaeologists.

12. However, the Roman style bathhouses are almost absent in the late Second Temple period archaeological record outside the Herodian palaces. Reich suggested that because of halakhic difficulties, the Jews resented the appearance of the Roman bathhouse when it was first introduced, apparently in the days of Herod ("The Hot-Bath House [Balneum], the Miqweh and the Jewish Community in the Second Temple Period," *JJS* 39 [1988]: 102–7). Yaron Z. Eliav reexamined the written sources and argued that the Roman-style bathhouses became an integral part of Jewish life ("Did the Jews at First Abstain from Using the Roman Bath-House?" *The Jerusalem Cathedra* 75 [1995]: 3–35).

13. Ehud Netzer, "Ancient Ritual Baths (*Miqwāʾot*) in Jericho," *The Jerusalem Cathedra* 2 (1982): 113–15.

14. Ehud Netzer, "Herodian Bath-Houses," in *Roman Baths and Bathing: Proceedings of the First International Conference on Roman Baths Held at Bath, England, 30 March–4 April 1992*, ed. J. DeLaine and D. E. Johnston, JRA Supplementary Series 37 (Portsmouth, R.I.: Journal of Roman Arcaeology, 1999), 47–50.

15. Ehud Netzer, *The Palaces of the Hasmoneans and Herod the Great* (Jerusalem: Yad Ben-Zvi, 1999), 107–13.

16. Nahman Avigad, *Ha ʿIr ha-ʿelyonah Shel Yerushalayim* (Jerusalem: Shikoma, 1980), 139–43; translated as *Discovering Jerusalem: Recent Archaeological Excavations in the Upper City* (Nashville: Thomas Nelson, 1983).

17. Reich, "Miqvaʾot," 171–252, 266–70.

18. Y. Magen, Y. Tzionit, and O. Sirkis, "Kirbet BaddʾIsa—Qiryat Sefer," in *The Land of Benjamin*, ed. Noga Haimovich-Carmin, trans. Tsipi Kuper-Blau, Michael Guggenheimer, and Robert Amoils, Judea and Samaria Publications 3 (Jerusalem: Israel Antiquities Authority, 2004), 179–218.

19. B. Zissu and A. Ganor, "Horbat ʿEthri," *HA-ESI* 113 (2001): 101–4; B. Zissu and A. Ganor, "Horvat ʿEthri—A Jewish Village from the Second Temple in the Judaean Foothills" (in Hebrew), *Qad* 123 (2002): 18–25.

20. E. Eisenberg, "Nahal Yarmut," *HA-ESI* 112 (2000): 91–93.

21. D. Amit and B. Zissu, "Jewish Sites from the Second Temple Period Near Masuʾot Itzhak" (in Hebrew), in *Yad le-Yair, Eretz-Israel: Researches in the Memory of Yair Bashan*, ed. M. Livneh and R. Yehezkeli (Tel-Aviv: Society for the Protection of Nature in Israel, 1999), 116–21.

22. Y. Magen, "Qalandia—A Second Temple Period Viticulture and Wine-Manufacturing Agricultural Settlement," in *The Land of Benjamin*, ed. Noga Haimovich-Carmin, trans. Tsipi Kuper-Blau, Michael Guggenheimer, and Robert Amoils, Judea and Samaria Publications 3 (Jerusalem: Israel Antiquities Authority, 2004), 54–65.

23. Zissu and Ganor, "Horbat ʿEthri."

24. B. Zissu, "Rural Settlement in the Judaean Hills and Foothills from the Late Second Temple Period to the Bar-Kokhba Revolt" (in Hebrew) (Ph.D. diss., Hebrew University, Jerusalem, 2001), 218–19.

25. A. Strobel, "Die Wasserversorgung der Hirbet Qumran," *ZDPV* 88 (1972): 55–86; K. Galor, "Plastered Pools: A New Perspective," in *Fouilles de Khirbet Qumrân et de 'Aïn Feshkha*, vol. 2, ed. J. -B. Humbert and J. Gunneweg (Göttingen: Vandenhoeck & Ruprecht, 2003), 291–320; Jodi Magness, *The Archaeology of Qumran and the Dead Sea Scrolls* (Grand Rapids: Eerdmans, 2002), 134–58; Yizhar Hirschfeld, *Qumran in Context: Reassessing the Archaeological Evidence* (Peabody, Mass.: Hendrickson, 2004), 120–28.

26. Reich, "Miqva'ot," 306–18; idem, "Miqwa'ot at Khirbet Qumran and the Jerusalem Connection," in *The Dead Sea Scrolls: Fifty Years after Their Discovery: Proceedings of the Jerusalem Congress, July 20–25, 1997*, ed. Lawrence H. Schiffman, Emanuel Tov, and James C. VanderKam (Jerusalem: Israel Exploration Society, in collaboration with The Shrine of the Book, Israel Museum, 2000), 728–31; Ehud Netzer, "A Proposal Concerning the Utilization of the Ritual Baths at Qumran" (in Hebrew), *Qad* 124 (2002): 116–17.

27. Ronny Reich, "The Synagogue and the Miqweh in Eretz-Israel in the Second-Temple, Mishnaic and Talmudic Periods," in *Ancient Synagogues: Historical Analysis and Archaeological Discovery*, ed. Dan Urman and Paul V. M. Flesher, 2 vols., StPB 47 (Leiden: Brill, 1995), 1:289–97.

28. Magen, Tzionit, and Sirkis, "Kirbet," 200–205.

29. Zissu and Ganor, "Horbat 'Ethri."

30. A. Onn et al., "Umm el-'Umdan," *HA-ESI* 114 (2002): 64–68.

31. Ehud Netzer, "A Synagogue from the Hasmonean Period Recently Exposed in the Western Plain of Jericho," *IEJ* 49 (1999): 203–21; but see Lee I. Levine's critique in "The First Century Synagogue: Critical Reassessments and Assessments of the Critical," in *Religion and Society in Roman Palestine: Old Questions, New Approaches*, ed. Douglas R. Edwards (London: Routledge, 2004), 90–94.

32. John S. Kloppenborg-Verbin, "Dating Theodotos (*CIJ* II 1404)," *JJS* 51 (2000): 243–80.

33. Reich, "Synagogue," 290–92; see also discussion in Lee I. Levine, *The Ancient Synagogue: The First Thousand Years* (New Haven, Conn.: Yale University Press, 2000), 310–11.

34. Levine, *Ancient Synagogue*, 70, 308–11.

35. David Amit, "Miqwa'ot at Gamla," in *Gamla II—The Architecture*, ed. D. Syon (forthcoming).

36. Y. Adler, "The Ancient Synagogue and the Ritual Bath: The Archaeological Evidence and Its Relevance to an Extinct Rabbinic Enactment Requiring Ablutions after Seminal Emission" (in Hebrew), *The Jerusalem Cathedra* 128 (2008), 51–72.

37. Reich, "Miqva'ot," 122–25.

38. Magen "Qalandia," 29–45.

39. Amit, "Ritual Baths" (1996), 30–31.

40. Zissu, "Rural Settlement," 101.

41. B. Zissu, Y. Tepper, and D. Amit, "*Miqwa'ot* at Kefar 'Othnai Near Legio," *IEJ* 56 (2006): 61–63.

42. Reich, *Miqva'ot*, 122–25.

43. Sanders, *Jewish Law*, 36; idem, *Judaism*, 228, 522 n. 31.

44. B. Zissu, G. Solimany, and D. Weiss, "Sha'ar Ha-Gay: Survey," *ESI* 19 (1999): 72.

45. Amos Kloner and Y. Tepper, *The Hiding Complexes in the Judean Shephelah* (in Hebrew) (Tel Aviv: Ha-Kibuts ha-meuhad: ha-Hevrah la-hakirat Erets-Yisrael ve-atikoteha, 1987), 115–27; G. Avni and S. Gudovitz, "Underground Olive Presses and Storage Systems at Ahuzat Hazzan," in *Olive Oil in Antiquity: Israel and Neighbouring Countries from the Neolithic to the Early Arab Period*, ed. D. Eitam and M. Heltzer (Padua: Sargon, 1996), 137–47.

46. Amit, "Ritual Baths" (1996), 21–23.

47. D. Syon and Z. Yavor, "Gamla—Old and New," *Qad* 34 (2001): 13–24; Amit, "Miqwa'ot at Gamla."

48. Magen, Tzionit, and Sirkis, "Kirbet," 188–93.

49. See discussion and references in Magen, "Qalandia," 44–45.

50. For example, B. Mazar, *The Mountain of the Lord: Excavating in Jerusalem* (Garden City, N.Y.: Doubleday, 1975), 146; Meyer Ben-Dov, *In the Shadow of the Temple: The Discovery of Ancient Jerusalem* (Jerusalem: Keter, 1982), 150–53; E. Mazar, *The Complete Guide to the Temple Mount Excavations* (in Hebrew) (Jerusalem: Shoham Academic Research and Publication, 2000), 51.

51. Reich, "Miqva'ot," 89–90.

52. E. Regev, "The Ritual Baths Near the Temple Mount and Extra-purification before Entering the Temple Courts," *IEJ* 55 (2005): 194–204; but see reply by Y. Adler, "The Ancient Synagogue and the Ritual Bath: The Archaeological Evidence and Its Relevance to an Extinct Rabbinic Enactment Requiring Ablutions after Seminal Emission" (in Hebrew), *The Jerusalem Cathedra* 128 (2008), 51–72.

53. Ronny Reich and Ely Shukron, "The Shiloah Pool during the Second Temple Period" (in Hebrew), *Qad* 130 (2005): 91–96.

54. S. Gibson, "The Pool of Bethesda in Jerusalem and Jewish Purification Practices of the Second Temple Period," *Proche-Orient Chrétien* 55 (2005): 270–93.

55. D. Amit, "A Miqveh Complex Near Alon Shevut," *'Atiqot* 38 (1999): 75–84; Y. Peleg and D. Amit, "Another *Miqveh* Near Alon Shevut," *'Atiqot* 48 (2004): 95–98.

56. Amit, "Ritual Baths" (1996), 37–45.

57. Reich, "Mishnah, Sheqalim 8:2"; idem, "Miqva'ot," 34–39.

58. Amit, "Ritual Baths" (1994); idem, "Ritual Baths" (1996).

59. Saul Lieberman, "Notes," in *P'raqim: Yearbook of the Schocken Institute for Jewish Research of the Jewish Theological Seminary of America*, ed. E. S. Rosenthal (Jerusalem: Schocken Institute, 1968), 1:97–98.

60. "Letter of Aristeas," in *The Apocrypha and Pseudepigrapha of the Old Testament in English*, ed. R. H. Charles, 2 vols. (Oxford: Clarendon, 1913), line 106.

61. Reich, "Miqva'ot," 284.

62. M. Fischer, "The Jerusalem-Emmaus Road in Light of the Excavations at Hurvat Metzad" (in Hebrew), in *Greece and Rome in Eretz-Israel: Collected Essays*, ed. A. Kasher, G. Fuks, and U. Rappaport (Jerusalem: Yad Izhak Ben-Zvi, 1989), 198–99; M. L. Fischer, B. H. Isaac, and I. Roll, *Roman Roads in Judaea II: The Jaffa–Jerusalem Roads*, BAR International Series 628 (Oxford: BAR, 1996), 212–16.

63. Amos Kloner and Boaz Zissu, *The Necropolis of Jerusalem in the Second Temple Period* (Jerusalem: Yad Izhak Ben-Zvi and the Israel Exploration Society, 2003), 16.

64. M. Kon and O. Schneid, *The Tombs of the Kings* (Tel Aviv: Dvir, 1947), 28–38; Reich, "Miqva'ot," 119–20.

65. Ehud Netzer, *Greater Herodium*, Qedem 13 (Jerusalem: Institute of Archaeology, Hebrew University of Jerusalem, 1981), 35–45.

66. Amit, "Ritual Baths" (1996), 37–45.

67. R. Hachlili and A. E. Killebrew, eds., *Jericho: The Jewish Cemetery of the Second Temple Period*, IAAR 7 (Jerusalem: Israel Antiquities Authority, Civil Administration in Judea and Samaria—Staff Officer of Archaeology, 1999), 37–44; E. Netzer, "Mourning Enclosure of Tomb H (Goliath Tomb) in ibid., 45–50.

68. I. Zilberbod and D. Amit, "Mazor (Elad), Sites 50 and 62," *Hadashot Arkheologiyot— Excavations and Surveys in Israel* 113 (2001): 60–61.

69. Esther Eshel, "4Q414 Fragment 2: Purification of a Corpse-Contaminated Person," in *Legal Texts and Legal Issues: Proceedings of the Second Meeting of the International Organization for Qumran Studies, Cambridge, 1995, Published in Honour of Joseph M. Baumgarten*, ed. M. Bernstein, F. García Martínez, and J. Kampen, STDJ 23 (Leiden: Brill, 1997), 3–10.

70. Ze'ev Safrai and Chanah Safrai, "Were the Rabbis a Dominant Elite?" in *The Path of Peace: Studies in Honor of Israel Friedman Ben-Shalom*, ed. D. Gera and M. Ben-Zeev (Be'er Sheva: Ben Gurion University of the Negev, 2005), 414–16.

71. Reich, "Miqva'ot," 121.

72. Sanders, *Jewish Law*, 29–36.

Chapter 5: Common Judaism, Common Synagogue? Purity, Holiness, and Sacred Space at the Turn of the Common Era

I would like to acknowledge the gracious assistance of Anders Runesson, who read and critiqued successive drafts of this chapter.

1. E. P. Sanders, *Judaism: Practice and Belief, 63 BCE–66 CE* (1992; corrected ed., London: SCM; Philadelphia: Trinity Press International, 1994).

2. Ibid., 198.

3. Lee I. Levine, "The First-Century CE Synagogue in Historical Perspective," in *The Ancient Synagogue from Its Origins until 200 CE: Papers Presented at an International Conference at Lund University, October 14–17, 2001*, ed. B. Olsson and M. Zetterholm, ConBNT 39 (Stockholm: Almqvist & Wiksell International, 2003), 3.

4. For an overview of synagogue research, see Anders Runesson, *The Origins of the Synagogue: A Socio-historical Study*, ConBNT 37 (Stockholm: Almqvist & Wiksell International, 2001), 67–168.

5. On the holiness of the synagogue, see especially Steven Fine, *This Holy Place: On the Sanctity of the Synagogue during the Greco-Roman Period*, Christianity and Judaism in Antiquity 11 (Notre Dame: University of Notre Dame Press, 1997); cf. idem, "From Meeting House to Sacred Realm: Holiness and the Ancient Synagogue," in *Sacred Realm: The Emergence of the Synagogue in the Ancient World*, ed. Steven Fine (New York: Oxford University Press, 1996), 27–49.

6. Runesson, *Origins*, 34–35.

7. Jonathan Klawans, *Impurity and Sin in Ancient Judaism* (New York: Oxford University Press, 2000), 23–31.

8. Ibid.

9. One exception would be the Day of Atonement rites, which involve the purgation of the altar and shrine from the effects of sin (Lev 16:11-19), as well as atonement for the transgressions of the people (Lev 16:20-22).

10. Sanders, *Judaism*, 229; cf. Donald D. Binder, *Into the Temple Courts: The Place of the Synagogues in the Second Temple Period*, SBLDS 169 (Atlanta: Society of Biblical Literature, 1999), 394.

11. Remains of *miqwa'ot* have been found throughout the land of Israel, attesting to widespread purity practices throughout the Second Temple period. These pools were cut into bedrock, had steps leading to the bottom, and were deep enough for full immersion of the body. Most often the pools were filled by channels that carried rain- or springwater. Alternatively, the water from a nearby reservoir or *otsar* ("treasury") was released through a conduit that connected the two pools. See Ronny Reich, "The Synagogue and the Miqweh in Eretz-Israel in the Second-Temple, Mishnaic, and Talmudic Periods," in *Ancient Synagogues: Historical Analysis and Archaeological Discovery*, ed. Dan Urman and Paul V. M. Flesher, 2 vols., StPB 47 (Leiden: Brill, 1995), 1:289–97; Sanders, *Judaism*, 223; Binder, *Into the Temple Courts*, 393–94. See chapter 4 in this volume.

12. As of this time, there have been no *miqwa'ot* found in the Diaspora (Binder, *Into the Temple Courts*, 395). The only possible *miqweh* was at the Delos synagogue, but this has been ruled out in Monika Trümper's thorough study of the edifice ("The Oldest Original Synagogue Building in the Diaspora: The Delos Synagogue Reconsidered," *Hesperia* 73 [2004]: 513–98). The *Letter of Aristeas* and the *Sibylline Oracles* mention hand washing but not immersion (*Let. Aris.* 304–6; *Sib. Or.* 3:591–93), whereas Philo refers to *perirranamenoi kai apolousamenoi*, which may be translated as "aspersions and ablutions" or "sprinkling and bathing" (*Spec.* 3:205–6). On purity in the Diaspora, see the detailed discussion in E. P. Sanders, *Jewish Law from Jesus to the Mishnah: Five Studies* (London: SCM, 1990), 258–71; cf. idem, *Judaism*, 223–24.

13. Against Jacob Neusner, who emphasizes the association between purity and the temple in Second Temple period Judaism. He contends that a community's interpretation of biblical purity law is inextricably linked to its relationship to the temple (Jacob Neusner, *The Idea of Purity in Ancient Judaism*, SJLA 1 [Leiden: Brill, 1973], 33). This "minimalist" view of purity was recently contested by John C. Poirier, who views the temple-oriented view of purity as "a scholarly construct with little basis in reality" ("Purity beyond the Temple in the Second Temple Era," *JBL* 122 [2003]: 247–65).

14. Jacob Milgrom, *Leviticus 1–16: A New Translation with Introduction and Commentary*, AB 3 (New York: Doubleday, 1991), 730.

15. See Christine E. Hayes, *Gentile Impurities and Jewish Identities: Intermarriage and Conversion from the Bible to the Talmud* (New York: Oxford University Press, 2002), 34–37, 59–63.

16. It is commonly held that women's access to the temple was restricted on the grounds of impurity. Yet the law makes no distinction between the level of purity of a pure Jewish female and a pure Jewish male. See Hayes, *Gentile Impurities*, 60–61.

17. Milgrom, *Leviticus 1–16*, 732.

18. On the dating of these and other ancient synagogues, see the helpful chart in Peter Richardson, "An Architectural Case for Synagogues and Associations," in Olsson and Zetterholm, *Ancient Synagogue*, 92–93. Commenting on this table, Binder suggests that the structures at Jericho, Qiryat Sefer, and Modi'in should be moved to the "uncertain" category, pending further investigation and argumentation. Levine, however, seems quite clear about the synagogues at Qiryat Sefer and Modi'in, although he does express some reservations about the building at Jericho. See Donald D. Binder, "The Origins of the Synagogue: An Evaluation," in Olsson and Zetterholm, *Ancient Synagogue*, 124 n. 15; Lee I. Levine, "The First-Century Synagogue: Critical Reassessments and Assessment of the Critical," in *Religion and Society in Roman Palestine: Old Questions, New Approaches*, ed. Douglas R. Edwards (London: Routledge, 2004), 84–89. Also worthy of mention is a building in Khirbet Qana that may possibly be a synagogue dating to the first or second century c.e. According to Richardson, no water installation has yet been discovered near the synagogue. One excavated house (dating to the Byzantine period) did, however, have a courtyard with a large cistern and a *miqweh* dating to the early Roman period. Moreover, there are two or three other installations that could be *miqwa'ot*, but further investigation is required to be certain. This information was conveyed in a private communication with Peter Richardson, April 28, 2005. For a preliminary description of some of the archaeological discoveries at Khirbet Qana, see Peter Richardson, *Building Jewish in the Roman East* (Waco: Baylor University Press, 2004), 103–5.

19. For a description of the buildings in Qiryat Sefer and Modi'in, see Levine, "First-Century Synagogue," 84–87. Although Levine does not refer to the *miqwa'ot* found in Qiryat Sefer, they are mentioned in an online publication of the Israel Ministry of Foreign Affairs: "Kiryat Sefer: A Synagogue in a Jewish Village of the Second Temple Period," *Archaeological Sites in Israel* 8, http://www.israel-mfa.gov.il/MFA/History/Early+History+-+Archaeology/.

20. On the dating of the Theodotus inscription to the early first century, see John S. Kloppenborg, "Dating Theodotos (*CIJ* II 1404)," *JJS* 51 (2000): 243–80.

21. On the Jericho synagogue, see Ehud Netzer, "A Synagogue from the Hasmonean Period Recently Exposed in the Western Plain of Jericho," *IEJ* 49 (1999): 203–21. The identification of this building as a synagogue is not entirely certain. Levine (*The Ancient Synagogue: The First Thousand Years* [New Haven, Conn.: Yale University Press, 2000], 69), for example, is cautious in his assessment, suggesting that future excavations may enable Netzer to solidify his contention. See also the discussion between Ehud Netzer and David Stacey in the online journal *Bible and Interpretation*: Ehud Netzer, "A Synagogue from the Hasmonean Period Exposed at Jericho," http://www.bibleinterp.com/articles/Synagogue.htm; David Stacey, "Was There a Synagogue in Hasmonean Jericho?" http://www.bibleinterp.com/articles/Hasmonean_Jericho.htm. Commenting on the location of the synagogue, Netzer speculates that it was used by the king's employees, some of whom may have lived in the adjacent houses. Runesson also calls attention to the fact that the building is near the Hasmonean palace complex but disconnected from any formal village structure. He suggests that the organization of the people would be best described as a guild, and that their synagogue was used for semipublic assemblies, both social and religious. See Netzer, "Synagogue" (*IEJ*), 217; Runesson, *Origins*, 357–59.

22. Netzer estimates 50 centimeters as the average space for one person ("Synagogue" [*IEJ*], 220 n. 29).

23. For a description of the synagogue at Gamla (Gamala), see, for example, Shmaryahu Gutman, "Gamala," in *The New Encyclopedia of Archaeological Excavations in the Holy Land*, ed. Ephraim Stern, 4 vols. (Jerusalem: Israel Exploration Society, 1993), 2:459–63; Binder, *Into the Temple Courts*, 162–72.

24. Netzer, "Synagogue" (*IEJ*), 220.

25. So Gutman, "Gamala," 461. Binder indicates that a separate bench was placed along the northeastern wall of the synagogue near the water basin. Commenting on the prominent location of this bench overlooking the rest of the hall, he speculates that the leaders of the assembly sat there and that they used the water basin before handling the sacred scrolls (Binder, *Into the Temple Courts*, 170–71).

26. Levine, *Ancient Synagogue*, 52.

27. See Gutman, "Gamala," 462–63; Danny Syon, "Gamla: Portrait of a Rebellion," *BAR* 18, no. 1 (1992): 21–37.

28. Ehud Netzer, *Masada: The Yigael Yadin Excavations, 1963–1965: Final Reports*, 6 vols. (Jerusalem: Israel Exploration Society, 1989), 3:402–13; Binder, *Into the Temple Courts*, 172–79.

29. Gideon Foerster, "The Synagogues at Masada and Herodium," in *Ancient Synagogues Revealed*, ed. Lee I. Levine (Jerusalem: Israel Exploration Society, 1981), 24–29; Binder, *Into the Temple Courts*, 180–85.

30. Binder, *Into the Temple Courts*, 184–85.

31. Foerster, "Masada and Herodium," 26.

32. Jodi Magness, *The Archaeology of Qumran and the Dead Sea Scrolls* (Grand Rapids: Eerdmans, 2002), 127. Magness suggests that a second dining room in the secondary building of the complex also had two *miqwaʾot* (loci 117–18) in proximity.

33. So Matthias Klinghardt, "The Manual of Discipline in the Light of Statutes of Hellenistic Associations," in *Methods of Investigation of the Dead Sea Scrolls and the Khirbet Qumran Site: Present Realities and Future Prospects*, ed. John J. Collins et al., Annals of the New York Academy of Sciences 722 (New York: New York Academy of Sciences, 1994), 251–70; cf. Moshe Weinfeld, *The Organizational Pattern and the Penal Code of the Qumran Sect* (Göttingen: Vandenhoeck & Ruprecht, 1986). Klinghardt's comparison of 1QS to a statute of an association offers some insight, but I think that he goes too far when he suggests that the Qumran community should not be characterized as a sect.

34. As translated by Kloppenborg, "Dating Theodotos," 244.

35. See Kloppenborg, "Dating Theodotos," 244 n. 5.

36. On the sanctity of the Torah, see Martin Goodman, "Sacred Scripture and 'Defiling the Hands,'" *JTS* 41 (1990): 103–4; cf. Shamma Friedman, "The Holy Scriptures Defile the Hands— The Transformation of a Biblical Concept in Rabbinic Theology," in *Minhah le-Nahum: Biblical and Other Studies Presented to Nahum M. Sarna in Honour of His 70th Birthday*, ed. M. Brettler and M. Fishbane, JSOTSup 154 (Sheffield: JSOT Press, 1993), 117–32; Chaim Milikowsky, "Reflections on Hand-Washing, Hand Purity and Holy Scripture in Rabbinic Literature," in

Purity and Holiness: The Heritage of Leviticus, ed. M. Porthuis and J. Schwartz (Leiden: Brill, 2000), 149–62; Fine, *This Holy Place*, 30.

37.   See, for example, *J.W.* 5.194, 227; 6.426–27; Philo *Cher.* 94–95; *Det.* 20; CD XI:19–21; XII:1–2; 1QM XLV:11–12.

38.   One exception would be the large *miqwa'ot* found at Qumran, which resemble the "Jerusalem type" *miqweh* identified by Reich. This type of *miqweh* can be used by several people simultaneously and is characterized by (1) its relatively large entrance on the broad side of the structure, (2) steps that alternate with wider and narrower treads, and (3) a double entrance and/or a small partition built down the center of the stairway. See Ronny Reich, "They Are Ritual Baths: Immerse Yourself in the Ongoing Sepphoris *Mikveh* Debate," *BAR* 28, no. 2 (2002): 50–55.

39.   Richardson, "Architectural Case," 92–93.

40.   Trümper, "Oldest Original Synagogue," 513–14.

41.   Anders Runesson, "The Synagogue at Ancient Ostia: The Building and Its History," in *The Synagogue of Ancient Ostia and the Jews of Rome: Interdisciplinary Studies*, ed. Birger Olsson, Olof Brandt, and Dieter Mitternacht, Acta Instituti Romani Regni Sueciae, Series 4, 57 (Stockholm: Paul Åströms, 2001), 31, 37.

42.   Victor Tcherikover, A. Fuks, and M. Stern, eds., *Corpus Papyrorum Judaicarum* [*CPJ*], 3 vols. (Cambridge, Mass.: Harvard University Press, 1957–64), vol. 1, no. 134. It should be noted that the original editors of the text indicate that the synagogue was outside the town. See B. P. Grenfell, A. S. Hunt, and J. G. Smyly, eds., *The Tebtunis Papyri*, 4 vols. (London: Oxford University Press, 1902), vol. 4, no. 86.

43.   Ralph Marcus, *Jewish Antiquities, Books XII–XIV*, vol. 7 of *Josephus with an English Translation*, LCL (Cambridge, Mass.: Harvard University Press, 1986), 587.

44.   Ismar Elbogen, *Jewish Liturgy: A Comprehensive History*, trans R. P. Scheindlin (Philadelphia: Jewish Publication Society, 1993), 340; translation of *Der jüdische Gottesdienst in seiner geschichtlichen Entwicklung* (Leipzig: G. Fock, 1913).

45.   Translation from F. H. Colson and G. H. Whitaker, *Philo, with an English Translation by F. H. Colson and G. H. Whitaker*, 10 vols., LCL (reprint, Cambridge, Mass.: Harvard University Press, 1962).

46.   Cf. LSJ, s.v. *katharos*, 850–51.

47.   Contra Runesson, who contends that the purity of the location is at least partially defined by its proximity to the water ("Water and Worship: Ostia and the Ritual Bath in the Diaspora Synagogue," in Olsson, Brandt, and Mitternacht, *Synagogue of Ancient Ostia*, 119–23).

48.   Leonard Victor Rutgers, "Diaspora Synagogues: Synagogue Archaeology in the Greco-Roman World," in Fine, *Sacred Realm*, 74–75.

49.   Levine, *Ancient Synagogue*, 308.

50.   Levine also cites 'En Gedi, Dura Europos, Sardis, Philadelphia in Lydia, Priene, and Gerasa, thereby covering a time period from the second century B.C.E to the fifth century C.E. (*Ancient Synagogue*, 308–9).

51.   Binder, *Into the Temple Courts*, 297–317; Trümper, "Oldest Original Synagogue," 513–98. Cf. White, whose analyses are, however, disputed by Binder and Trümper (L. Michael White,

"The Delos Synagogue Revisited: Recent Fieldwork in the Graeco-Roman Diaspora," *HTR* 80 [1987]: 133–60).

52. Trümper, "Oldest Original Synagogue," 577.

53. Levine, *Ancient Synagogue*, 101; Runesson, "Water and Worship," 124 n. 84. On human access to the cistern, see Binder, *Into the Temple Courts*, 306–7 n. 153.

54. Trümper, "Oldest Original Synagogue," 575–77.

55. L. Michael White, "Synagogue and Society in Imperial Ostia: Archaeological and Epigraphic Evidence," *HTR* 90 (1997): 23–58; Anders Runesson, "The Oldest Synagogue Building in the Diaspora: A Response to L. Michael White," *HTR* 92 (1999): 409–33. White responded to Runesson in "Reading the Ostia Synagogue: A Reply to A. Runesson," *HTR* 92 (1999): 435–64, and Runesson offered a subsequent response in "A Monumental Synagogue from the First Century: The Case of Ostia," *JSJ* 33 (2002): 171–220; cf. Runesson, "Synagogue of Ancient Ostia," 29–99. An important contribution is also made by Binder, *Into the Temple Courts*, 322–36.

56. Richardson, "Architectural Case," 97–105.

57. Runesson, "Synagogue of Ancient Ostia," 69–71; cf. idem, "Water and Worship," 125.

58. The notion that ritual ablutions were associated with synagogues in the Diaspora may be substantiated by epigraphic evidence. A papyrus from Egypt, dated to 113 B.C.E., records the expenses incurred to supply two synagogues with water. The sums of money reflect the usage of considerable quantities of water, which may have been used for both ritual and nonritual activities (*CPJ* 2, no. 432; cf. Rutgers, "Diaspora Synagogues," 74–75).

59. Walter Burkert, *Greek Religion*, trans. J. Raffan (Cambridge, Mass.: Harvard University Press, 1985), 75–84.

60. Roman sanctuaries also provided basins for ritual ablutions. When the worshiper entered the shrine, he would wash his hands in the basin and pray facing the image (John E. Stambaugh, "The Functions of Roman Temples," *ANRW* 2.16.1 [1978]: 579).

61. William Horbury and David Noy, eds., *Jewish Inscriptions of Graeco-Roman Egypt* (Cambridge: Cambridge University Press, 1992), nos. 22, 24, 25, 27, 28, 125.

62. *JIGRE*, nos. 9, 129. For a full discussion of epigraphical and papyrological evidence in relation to the Egyptian synagogue, see Levine, *Ancient Synagogue*, 75–84.

63. *CPJ* 1, no. 134.

64. Binder, *Into the Temple Courts*, 123.

65. As cited by Robert A. Wild, *Water in the Cultic Worship of Isis and Sarapis* (Leiden: Brill, 1981), 130.

66. For a discussion of the communion of angels, see, for example, Carol Newsom, *Songs of the Sabbath Sacrifice: A Critical Edition*, HSS 27 (Atlanta: Scholars Press, 1985), 17–19; Esther Chazon, "Prayers from Qumran and Their Historical Implications," *DSD* 1 (1994): 265–84; idem, "The Function of the Qumran Prayer Texts: An Analysis of the Daily Prayers (4Q503)," in *The Dead Sea Scrolls Fifty Years after their Discovery: Proceedings of the Jerusalem Congress, July 20–25, 1997*, ed. Lawrence H. Schiffman, Emanuel Tov, and James C. VanderKam (Jerusalem: Israel Exploration Society, 2000), 217–25.

67. Fine, "From Meeting House to Sacred Realm," 24.

68. See Lee I. Levine, "The Nature and Origin of the Palestinian Synagogue Reconsidered," *JBL* 115, no. 3 (1996): 425–48. For a discussion of the public reading of the Torah during the Persian period, see Runesson, *Origins*, 278–99; James W. Watts, ed., *Persia and Torah: The Theory of Imperial Authorization of the Pentateuch*, SBLSymS 17 (Atlanta: Society of Biblical Literature, 2001).

69. See Goodman, "Sacred Scripture," 103–4.

Chapter 6: Pharisaic Authority: Prophecy and Power (*Antiquities* 17:41-45)

This chapter is the first piece to appear in print of a larger project tentatively titled "The Pharisees: A Comparative Multi-disciplinary Portrait." The principal research on the Pharisees on which this study is based was undertaken while I was Jacob and Hilda Blaustein Visiting Fellow in Jewish Studies, Yale University, New Haven, Connecticut, in 2003–2004. I would like to thank my colleagues in the Judaic Studies Program at Yale for the opportunity to spend a sabbatical there, and for the chance to think, read, write, and then present these ideas to a wider audience.

1.   Randall Collins, "On the Acrimoniousness of Intellectual Disputes," *Common Knowledge* 8 (2002): 50.

2.   See especially Steve Mason, *Flavius Josephus on the Pharisees: A Composition-Critical Study*, StPB 39 (Leiden: Brill, 1991), 274–80. Mason demolished the source-critical theory proposed by Morton Smith, yet I do not find Mason's alternative convincing. I cannot accept Mason's conclusions that, aside from the school passages, where his motives are different, Josephus was consistently hostile to the Pharisees, always presenting them and their claims in an unfavorable light (Mason, *Josephus*, 373–75). This characterization of Josephus's attitude does not fit well in all places, especially not in *Life* 191–98. I read *Life* 191–98 as the most successful example of the strategy for reading Josephus on the Pharisees proposed by Smith: that Josephus modified his view of the group in light of political developments in the years after the destruction of the temple, and the emergence of a Jewish leadership under the aegis of R. Gamaliel II (son of the Simon of *Life* 191–98) at Yavneh. Josephus, who never seems to have forgotten or forgiven a slight, should simply have denounced Simon for his friendship with John of Gischala and their sordid dealings intended to harm Josephus, not praised him. With one eye on the present, however, Josephus wrote an encomium on Simon but also noted his misdeeds, then connected these two contradictory evaluations with the comment that Simon was "then, at that time, at variance with me" (*Life* 192). As I read that comment, it suggests that Josephus intended to imply that although he and Simon were on opposite sides of the fence then, there was nothing preventing their cooperation now, that is, Josephus's reasonable relations with Simon's son, R. Gamaliel II of Yavneh. On that reading, the encomium on Simon (and by extension on the Pharisees) stands and is not undermined by the dubious deeds related immediately afterward. On these points, see further A. I. Baumgarten, "Rivkin and Neusner on the Pharisees," in *Law in Religious Communities of the Roman Period: The Debate over Torah and Nomos in Post-biblical Judaism and Early Christianity*, ed. G. P. Richardson, Studies in Christianity and Judaism 4 (Waterloo, Ont.: Canadian Corporation for Studies in Religion, 1991), 109–26.

3.   Compare Peter Schäfer, "Der vorrabinische Pharisäismus," in *Paulus und das antike Judentum: Tübingen-Durham-Symposium im Gedenken an den 50. Todestag Adolf Schlatters (19. Mai 1938)*, ed. M. Hengel and U. Heckel, WUNT 58 (Tübingen: J. C. B. Mohr [Paul Siebeck], 1991), 125–72, who has challenged the conventional account.

4.   See, for example, the denunciation of the Pharisees in Matthew 23.

5.   See A. I. Baumgarten, "Marcel Simon's *Verus Israel* as a Contribution to Jewish History," *HTR* 92 (1999): 465–78.

6.   George Foot Moore, "Christian Writers on Judaism," *HTR* 14 (1921): 197–254.

7.   E. P. Sanders, *Judaism: Practice and Belief, 63 BCE–66 CE* (1992; corrected ed., London: SCM; Philadephia: Trinity Press International, 1994), 380–451. See also Martin Hengel and Roland Deines, "E. P. Sanders' 'Common Judaism,' Jesus and the Pharisees: Review Article of *Jewish Law: From Jesus to the Mishnah* and *Judaism: Practice and Belief*," *JTS* 46 (1995): 1–70. See also Roland Deines, "The Pharisees between 'Judaisms' and 'Common Judaism,'" in *Justification and Variegated Nomism*, vol. 1, *The Complexities of Second Temple Judaism*, ed. D. A. Carson, Peter T. O'Brien, and Mark A. Seifrid, WUNT 2.140 (Grand Rapids: Baker Academic, 2001), 443–504. The Hengel-Deines attack on Sanders inspired a resounding rejoinder by Jacob Neusner. See J. Neusner, "Debunking the German Anti-Judaic Caricature," *National Jewish Post and Opinion* 69, no. 8 (October 16, 2002): 8–9, 15. As should be clear from the formulation, my view is much closer to that of Sanders.

8.   See James C. Scott, *Domination and the Arts of Resistance: Hidden Transcripts* (New Haven, Conn.: Yale University Press, 1990), 202–27, esp. 221–24; and Clifford Geertz, "Centers, Kings, and Charisma: Reflections on the Symbolics of Power," in idem, *Local Knowledge: Further Essays in Interpretive Anthropology* (New York: Basic Books, 1983), 121–46. Geertz, in turn, acknowledges his debt to the essays of Edward Shils, now collected in *Center and Periphery: Essays in Macrosociology* (Chicago: University of Chicago Press, 1975), in particular "The Meaning of Coronation" (135–52) and "Charisma, Order and Status" (256–75).

9.   For one indication of the superhuman powers the messiah was expected by some to enjoy, see the rabbinic explanation of why Bar Kokhba was *not* the messiah. He could not judge by smell alone (*b. B. Qam.* 93b). I take this obscure phrase to mean that Bar Kokhba did not have the special insight into individuals, perceiving things beyond ordinary human knowledge, that was typical of holy men. For convenient examples of this sort of knowledge from the Gospels, see Mark 2:8; Luke 7:39; John 4:17-19.

10.   For the various lower-class forms of oracular consultation, see D. S. Potter, *Prophets and Emperors: Human and Divine Authority from Augustus to Theodosius*, Revealing Antiquity 7 (Cambridge, Mass.: Harvard University Press, 1994), 22–29.

11.   Ibid., 38.

12.   As Potter notes (*Prophets*, 33–35), not all holy men conformed to the type parodied by Celsus. Paul came from a respectable family and was a Roman citizen. Apollonius of Tyana was a Pythagorean and came to be appreciated in ever-higher strata of Roman society. Even Lucian's Alexander had a senatorial patron, thanks to whom Alexander gained access to the highest ranks of the Roman aristocracy.

Some Pharisees were apparently from the higher classes of Jewish society. Josephus, a Jerusalem priest, described himself as a Pharisee (*Life* 12), and Simon b. Gamaliel (*Life* 191) was from a distinguished aristocratic family. Of the three Pharisees on the delegation to depose Josephus, two were from the lower ranks, but one, Joazar, was a priest (*Life* 197). Some of the Pharisees who predicted the future at the court of Herod may also have been of higher social standing, like Simon b. Gamaliel and Joazar. Thus, the Pharisees of *Ant.* 17.41–45 need not have been the type of holy men parodied by Celsus.

13. Potter, *Prophets*, 181.

14. From among many examples, see Celsus (Origen, *Cels.* 2.55 and 2.70 [in the name of the Jew quoted by Celsus] and 3.44 [in Celsus's own name]). In *J. W.* 2.560–61, Josephus reported the plot of the men of Damascus to massacre the Jews. He noted that the allegiance of Damascene women to Judaism (with few exceptions many had become converts) was an obstacle to this plot. Accordingly the men had to keep their intentions secret from the women. At first sight, this passage would seem to contradict the usual bias against women. The interest of the Damascene women in Judaism was, for Josephus, a good thing, not an instance of female gullibility. Nevertheless, Josephus was writing here from the perspective of the Damascene men. As the latter saw things, the dedication of their wives to Judaism was not laudable. Presumably, if asked, they would have employed the usual misogynistic arguments to explain the interest of their women in Judaism. For Josephus's own attitude toward women, see, for example, *J. W.* 7.399.

15. Pheroras, according to Josephus, was also not much of a man—almost a eunuch. He was manipulated by his women, and rumor told that his wife cheated on him with Antipater, his political ally. Bagoas was therefore not the only eunuch in this story. To the extent that Pheroras was involved, he would have done nothing to bolster the reputation of the Pharisees, only undermined it in much the same way as Bagoas.

16. This is not the only passage in Josephus in which Pharisees are described as doing unsavory things. In *Life* 196, Simon b. Gamaliel, a high-ranking Pharisee and one of the leaders of the revolution, joined John of Gischala in bribing the high priest Ananus to expel Josephus from his command in the Galilee. As this piece of sordid business has nothing to do with predictions of the future, I have not brought it into the discussion of *Ant.* 17.41–45 in this chapter.

17. Cf. Rebecca Gray, *Prophetic Figures in Late Second Temple Jewish Palestine: The Evidence from Josephus* (New York: Oxford University Press, 1993), 152–58, who assumes the incident took place as described.

18. Lucian was born ca. 120 C.E.; hence, he was two to three generations younger than Josephus. His satires on contemporary mores are an important source for the religious and intellectual atmosphere of the time. On the unending (that is, long unresolved) debate concerning the reliability of Lucian's description of Alexander, see the summary in James A. Francis, *Subversive Virtue: Asceticism and Authority in the Second-Century Pagan World* (University Park, Pa.: Pennsylvania State University Press, 1995), 54–55 nn. 3–5. But see now Louis Robert, "Lucien et son temps," À *travers l'Asie Mineure: Poètes et prosateurs, monnaies grecque, voyageurs et géographie*, Bibliothèque des écoles françaises d'Athènes et de Rome 239 (Athens: École française d'Athènes, 1980), 393–421. Francis ventures the guess that Philostratus's description of the career

of Apollonius will one day benefit from a similar reappraisal as a result of which the prejudice concerning its factual reliability will be lifted (89 n. 18).

19. Philostratus, who lived in the early third century c.e., wrote the life of Apollonius of Tyana, a famous holy man, who had lived some two centuries earlier. Many scholars see Philostratus's *Vita Apollonii* as an attempt to create a story of a pagan holy man to rival the Gospel accounts of Jesus.

20. Mason, *Josephus*, 274–80.

21. Ibid., 278–80.

22. Ibid., 279.

23. Ibid., 92–96.

24. Gray, *Prophetic Figures*, 35–79.

25. Jonathan Z. Smith, "Towards Interpreting Demonic Powers in Hellenistic and Roman Antiquity," *ANRW* 2.16.1 (1979): 427.

26. Andy M. Reimer, *Miracle and Magic: A Study in the Acts of the Apostles and the Life of Apollonius of Tyana*, JSNTSup 235 (London: Sheffield Academic Press, 2002), 8.

27. Thus, to cite one typical argument discussed in greater detail below, moderation or asceticism was proof that one was not an evil wizard. At the same time, excessive asceticism could be construed as grounds for suspicion that someone was a wizard. See, on the one hand, Philostratus, *Vit. Apoll.* 6.10–11; 8.7, but compare Epictetus, *Ench.* 3.12.1—if philosophers perform aberrant acts of asceticism contrary to nature, then all distinction between them and wonder-workers will be erased.

28. Reimer, *Miracle and Magic*, 12.

29. See Graham Anderson, *Sage, Saint and Sophist: Holy Men and Their Associates in the Early Roman Empire* (London: Routledge, 1994), 153–57. Servicing the needs of politicians was a specialty of Apollonius of Tyana or of Lucian's Alexander. See also Reimer, *Miracle and Magic*, 189–201.

30. Potter, *Prophets*, 146–70.

31. For my purposes, the version in *J.W.* 1.210–11 is not relevant, as there is no Pharisaic intervention or prediction in that account.

32. Compare, for example, the comment of Winston Churchill at the time of the Munich accords: "We seem to be very near the bleak choice between War and Shame. My feeling is that we shall choose Shame, and then have War thrown in a little later" (M. Gilbert, *Winston Churchill: The Wilderness Years* [London: Macmillan, 1981], 227). Churchill's prediction is a case of political prescience. We would not call Churchill a prophet in the biblical sense of the term. Nor would we go so far as to claim that Churchill's words were a cause of World War II, by analogy with Josephus's implication in the case of Pollion, as discussed below.

33. Some manuscripts read Samaias instead of Pollion at *Ant.* 15.4, thereby making the stories consistent with each other.

34. As Josephus presents them in *J.W.* 2.159, the Essenes' ability to predict the future was based on their familiarity with holy books, purifications, and sayings of the prophets. The latter sort of prophecy, based on knowledge of the sayings of the prophets, looks more like exegetical prophecy, based on the thrill of discovery of a new understanding (prophetic message) in an

old prophetic text. Perhaps this is the sort of prophecy that is the province of priests, the usual experts in interpreting biblical sources. Without intending to encourage the identification of the Qumran group with the Essenes, I should nevertheless note that this description is equally valid for Qumran pesher texts. See further Potter, *Prophets*, 58–59 and 215–16.

35. Josephus told the people of Jotapata that their city would fall after a siege of forty-seven days, as well as that he would be taken alive by the Romans. Vespasian questioned prisoners and found that Josephus had, indeed, made these predictions.

36. This higher power to which I refer should not be confused with the ability to command the demons. As the debate concerning the source of Jesus' power shows, it was widely believed that demons could be forced to do things, for example, to submit to exorcism, by contact with the evil powers.

37. Was Honi a Pharisee? In the strict sense, of course not. No legal opinion of his is ever cited in rabbinic sources. In another sense, however, he was no less a Pharisee than Elijah (with whom he was linked in a tradition from *Gen. Rab.* 117) or than Moses himself (who heads the Pharisaic list of links of the tradition in *m. 'Abot* 1). Given the Pharisaic construction of the Jewish past, any favorable character from that past could be claimed as a Pharisee. On the rabbinization of Honi in *b. Ta'an.* 23a, where he has disciples who call him Rabbi and he explains all difficulties to the rabbis when he comes to the house of study, see W. S. Green, "Palestinian Holy Men: Charismatic Leadership and Rabbinic Tradition," *ANRW* 2.19.2 (1979), 619–47.

38. As Josephus tells the story, Honi was much less insolent than in the rabbinic account. Josephus's Honi *prayed* for rain. Since he was a *righteous man*, his *prayers* were answered. Josephus's Honi did not threaten that he would not leave the circle until it rained.

39. See further Reimer, *Magic and Miracle*, 113–14. In the age of Julian, the power to alter the future by means of the material rites of theurgy was made more intellectually respectable through the Chaldean Oracles. See further Potter, *Prophets*, 203–6.

40. Thus Philo, commenting on the dying "blessings" of Moses, noted that Moses' parting words had the power to shape the future. One should have full confidence in the truth of these predictions because of the fulfillment of other predictions in the past (*Mos.* 2.288). See also Luke 1:45 and BAG, s.v. *teleioō* and *teleiōsis*.

41. As Francis (*Subversive Virtue*, xviii) comments, perhaps the best English translation for Greek *goēs* that captures the sense of charlatanism in the original is "mountebank." Unfortunately, that term is archaic in English. "Wizard" will have to do.

42. Compare the Egyptian naked sophists encountered by Apollonius, who denigrated the wonders of the Indian miracle workers, but hastened to add that they, of course, were also capable of performing such fantastic deeds, but chose not to do so (*Vit. Apoll.* 6.10).

43. See Yigael Yadin, "Pesher Nahum (4QpNahum) Reconsidered," *IEJ* 21 (1971): 1–12.

44. See David Flusser, "Pharisäer, Sadducäer und Essener im Pescher Nahum," in *Qumran*, ed. K. Grözinger et al., Wege der Forschung 410 (Darmstadt: Wissenschaftliche Buchgesellschaft, 1981), 121–66; Lawrence H. Schiffman, "Pharisees and Sadducees in Pesher Nahum," *Minḥah le-Naḥum: Biblical and Other Studies Presented to Nahum M. Sarna in Honour of His 70th Birthday*, ed. Marc Zvi Brettler and Michael A. Fishbane, JSOTSup 154 (Sheffield: JSOT Press, 1993) 272–90.

45. Text and translation from Maurya P. Horgan, *Pesharim: Qumran Interpretations of Biblical Books*, CBQMS 8 (Washington, D.C.: Catholic Biblical Association of America, 1979), 163–64.

46. Some translations render the term *ger nilweh* as "proselyte." See, for example, Florentino García Martínez, *The Dead Sea Scrolls Translated: The Qumran Texts in English*, trans. Wilfred G. E. Watson (Leiden: Brill, 1996), 196. If this translation is adopted, this passage in 4QpNah should be compared to Matt 23:15, where Pharisaic zeal to proselytize is denounced. It is notable that this possible combination of testimonies is never mentioned, to the best of my knowledge, by Edouard Will and Claude Orrieux, *"Prosélytisme Juif"? Histoire d'une erreur* (Paris: Les Belles Lettres, 1992).

47. Compare the Pharisaic critique of the miracles performed by Jesus, to be discussed immediately below. Note that here too the reality of these cures or exorcisms is not disputed. The only issue at stake is whether these actions are to be understood as confirmation of alliance with the beneficent powers or with the malevolent ones.

48. When the rabbis remembered that the Pharisee Simeon b. Shetah executed witches in Ashkelon by hanging (crucifixion? *m. Sanh.* 6:1 and *y. Hag.* 2.2.77d), was Simeon so uncompromising and harsh in putting down witchcraft because he saw these witches as rivals of his own Pharisees? Certainty is impossible, but the possibility should be noted.

49. In the parallel in Mark 3:22-27, the question "By whom do your people cast out demons?" is missing. In the parallel in Luke 11:14-22, the question "By whom do you cast out demons?" is present, but the opponents of Jesus are not specified as Pharisees.

50. In Luke, incidents occur when Pharisees invite Jesus home for meals. See Luke 7:36; 11:37; 14:1-14. Note that in parallels to Luke 7:36 (Matt 26:6 and Mark 14:3-9) the host is not specified as a Pharisee. There are numerous ancient accounts of disputes that erupted at meals that provide a context for the disagreements between Jesus and his hosts related in Luke. In the contemporary world, invitations to one's home are a standard tactic to promote friendship as part of efforts to missionize. See further Rodney Stark and William Sims Bainbridge, "Networks of Faith: Interpersonal Bonds and Recruitment to Cults and Sects," *American Journal of Sociology* 85 (1980): 1376–95. I wonder if these passages in Luke are to be understood in this latter sense. Are they evidence for a Pharisaic attempt to encourage other Jews to become Pharisees? If so, might these verses in Luke be connected with Matt 23:15 and suggest that the Pharisaic mission of Matt 23:15 was directed toward Jews (outreach, in contemporary parlance)? See further Martin Goodman, *Mission and Conversion: Proselytizing in the Religious History of the Roman Empire* (Oxford: Clarendon, 1994), 69–74.

51. See further L. Bieler, *THEIOS ANER: Das Bild des "göttlichen Menschen" in Spätantike und Frühchristentum* (Vienna: O. Höfels, 1935), 119ff.; Anderson, *Sage, Saint, and Sophist*, 104–5.

52. See, for example, Philostratus, *Vit. Apoll.* 6.10–11; 8.7 (I can't be a bad type of wizard. Proof: I am not rich). For discussions in the secondary literature, see Bieler, *THEIOS ANER*, 87–94, and especially Reimer, *Magic and Miracle*, 212–44.

53. Note Philostratus's account of the behavior of Apollonius of Tyana: "These years of silence he spent partially in Pamphylia and partially in Cilicia; and though his paths lay through such effeminate races as these, he never spoke nor was even induced to murmur. Whenever, however,

he came on a city engaged in civil conflict (and many were divided into factions over spectacles of a low kind) he would advance and show himself, and by indicating something of his intended rebuke by manual gesture or by look on his face, he would put an end to all the disorder, and people hushed their voices, as if they were engaged in the mysteries" (*Vit. Apoll.* 1.15).

See also Lucian, *Demon.* 8. For Lucian, Demonax is the parade example of a "good" holy man, as opposed to Peregrinus or Alexander, "bad" holy men.

54. As noted at the outset, Pheroras's role in the whole account is murky. Was he really an ineffective pawn in the hands of the women, as Josephus portrayed him?

55. According to Lucian, Alexander kept a written record of the oracular replies of his god as proof of the excellence of his answers. Other oracular centers did likewise. The instances of apparent failure of prediction apparently did not trouble the proprietors of these centers. Thoroughgoing skeptics, who had become disillusioned by oracles, such as Oenomaus of Gadara, were rare. See further Potter, *Prophets*, 45–46.

In the contemporary world, we continue to rely on the advice of economic pundits and the knowledge of weather forecasters, in spite of the malfeasance (often criminal) of the economic advisers and the frequent errors of the weather forecasters. Inaccurate prediction is no hindrance to these modern prophets. If pressed, we focus on the times they were right and easily overlook the times they were wrong.

56. See A. I. Baumgarten, "The Name of the Pharisees," *JBL* 102 (1983): 411–28. If I were rewriting this article today, I would stress that Pharisees were not the only group to make this claim. While they tried to appropriate the favorable quality of specifying for themselves, there were other contestants to that title. What group would have boasted that it observed the law in a slipshod and inexact manner?

57. Potter, *Prophets*, 22.

58. Reimer, *Magic and Miracle*, 35–41; Mary Douglas, *Purity and Danger: An Analysis of the Concepts of Pollution and Taboo* (London: Routledge and Kegan Paul, 1966), 109–10; Peter Brown, *The Making of Late Antiquity* (Cambridge, Mass.: Harvard University Press, 1978), 84–94; idem, *Society and the Holy in Late Antiquity* (Berkeley: University of California Press, 1982), 103–65.

59. Brown, *Society*, 112. It is difficult to determine whether these figures really came from the fringes or only claimed to do so.

60. On the alternation between corporate and personal manifestations of holiness in Christianity, see Brown, *Society*, 151–52.

61. A. I. Baumgarten, *The Flourishing of Jewish Sects in the Maccabean Era: An Interpretation*, JSJSup 55 (Leiden: Brill, 1997), 81–91. Scholars disagree whether these groups claimed the status of the true Israel in the here and now or expected that claim to be fulfilled only in the end of days. See E. P. Sanders, *Paul and Palestinian Judaism: A Comparison of Patterns of Religion* (Philadelphia: Fortress Press, 1977), 244–57. In either case, ancient Jewish sects exhibited a typical mixture of rejection of their fellow Jews for inadequate loyalty to the law, combined with an unwillingness to sever ties with the larger community. At the very least, even the most introverted expected matters to be set right at the end of days. On this aspect of sects, see Shils, "Introduction," in *Center and Periphery*, xxiii.

62. Rodney Stark, "How Sane People Talk to the Gods: A Rational Theory of Revelation," in *Innovation in Religious Traditions: Essays in the Interpretation of Religious Change*, ed. M. Williams, C. Cox, and M. Jaffee (Berlin: Mouton de Gruyter, 1992), 19–34, esp. 28–29.

63. A. I. Baumgarten, "The Zadokite Priests at Qumran: A Reconsideration," *DSD* 4 (1997): 137–56.

64. See Potter's concluding remarks (*Prophets*, 213–16).

65. For a discussion of the meaning and purpose of the name change in the context of the era, see Robert, "Lucien et son temps," 408–14, esp. 412.

Chapter 7: From Where? To What? Common Judaism, Pharisees, and the Changing Socioreligious Location of the Matthean Community

I would like to thank the participants of the Calgary conference entitled "Common Judaism Explored: Second Temple Judaism in Context," especially Ed Sanders, for sharing several observations that have helped improve the text. I am also grateful to my colleagues at McMaster, Stephen Westerholm and Michael Knowles, for reading and commenting on the penultimate draft. I alone am responsible, of course, for the conclusions drawn and any remaining errors.

A longer version of the essay appeared in the *Journal of Biblical Literature* 127, no. 1 (2008: 95–132, under the title "Rethinking Early Jewish-Christian Relations: Matthean Community History as Pharisaic Intragroup Conflict."

1. See the introductory statement regarding the early reception of Matthew by Graham Stanton, "Introduction: Matthew's Gospel in Recent Scholarship," in *The Interpretation of Matthew*, ed. G. Stanton, 2nd ed., Studies in New Testament Interpretation (Edinburgh: T&T Clark, 1995), 1: "Matthew's Gospel was more widely used and more influential in the early Church than any of the other Gospels." Stanton does not, however, discuss the fact that this reception meant widely different uses and interpretations of Matthew.

2. For a discussion of the use of Matthew by Jewish Christ-believers, see James Carleton Paget, "Jewish Christianity," in *The Cambridge History of Judaism*, ed. W. D. Davies and Louis Finkelstein, vol. 3, *The Early Roman Period*, ed. William Horbury et al. (Cambridge: Cambridge University Press, 1999). The early reception of Matthew before Irenaeus is treated by Édouard Massaux, *Influence de l'évangile de saint Matthieu sur la littérature chrétienne avant saint Irénée*, Universitas Catholica Lovaniensis, Dissertationes, ser. 2, 42 (Louvain: Publications Universitaires de Louvain, 1950). Cf. Helmut Koester, *Synoptische Überlieferung bei den Apostolischen Vätern*, TUGAL 65 (Berlin: Akademie-Verlag, 1957); Wolf-Dietrich Köhler, *Die Rezeption des Matthäusevangeliums in der Zeit vor Irenäus*, WUNT 24 (Tübingen: Mohr Siebeck, 1987); H. Benedict Green, "Matthew, Clement, and Luke: Their Sequence and Relationship," *JTS* 40 (1989): 1–25. Among New Testament scholars, Ulrich Luz has been among the pioneers in his emphasis on the reception history of Matthew in his interpretation of the Gospel; see his multivolume commentary on Matthew (*Das Evangelium nach Matthäus*, 4 vols., EKKNT 1 [Neukirchen-Vluyn: Neukirchener Verlag, 1985–2006]), as well as his *Matthew in History: Interpretation, Influence, and Effects* (Minneapolis: Fortress Press, 1994).

3. We find a range of opinions in the literature, from Mattheans being well within the confines of first-century Judaism (*intra muros*) to scholars arguing that the community had parted

ways with the larger Jewish community, still, however, being a Jewish sect (*extra muros*). For *intra muros*, see, for example, Günther Bornkamm, "End-Expectation and Church in Matthew," in *Tradition and Interpretation in Matthew*, ed. Günther Bornkamm, Gerhard Barth, and Heinz Joachim Held, NTL (Philadelphia: Westminster, 1963), 15–51 (though he seems to have changed his mind in 1970: see "The Authority to 'Bind' and 'Loose' in the Church in Matthew's Gospel," reprinted in Stanton, *Interpretation of Matthew*, 101–14; commented on by Donald Hagner, "The Sitz im Leben of the Gospel of Matthew," in *Treasures New and Old: Contributions to Matthean Studies*, ed. David R Bauer and Mark Allan Powell [Atlanta: Scholars Press, 1996], 27–68, esp. 35); Gerhard Barth, "Matthew's Understanding of the Law," in Bornkamm, Barth, and Held, *Tradition*, 58–164; W. D. Davies, *The Setting of the Sermon on the Mount* (Cambridge: Cambridge University Press, 1963); Schuyler Brown, "The Matthean Community and the Gentile Mission," *NovT* 22 (1980): 193–221; Alan F. Segal, "Matthew's Jewish Voice," in *Social History of the Matthean Community: Cross-Disciplinary Approaches*, ed. David L. Balch (Minneapolis: Fortress Press, 1991), 3–37, esp. 37: "But there was no uniformity in Judaism. . . . Thus we cannot say that Judaism uniformly dismissed Matthean Christians from their midst"; J. Andrew Overman, *Matthew's Gospel and Formative Judaism: The Social World of the Matthean Community* (Minneapolis: Fortress Press, 1990); idem, *Church and Community in Crisis: The Gospel According to Matthew*, New Testament in Context (Valley Forge, Pa.: Trinity Press International, 1996); Anthony Saldarini, *Matthew's Christian-Jewish Community*, CSHJ (Chicago: University of Chicago Press, 1994); David Sim, *Apocalyptic Eschatology in the Gospel of Matthew*, SNTSMS 88 (Cambridge: Cambridge University Press, 1996); idem, *The Gospel of Matthew and Christian Judaism: The History and Social Setting of the Matthean Community*, Studies of the New Testament and Its World (Edinburgh: T&T Clark, 1998). For *extra muros*, see Ulrich Luz, *Matthew 1–7: A Commentary* (Minneapolis: Augsburg, 1989); idem, *The Theology of the Gospel of Matthew*, New Testament Theology (Cambridge: Cambridge University Press, 1995); Petri Luomanen, *Entering the Kingdom of Heaven: A Study on the Structure of Matthew's View of Salvation*, WUNT 2.101 (Tübingen: Mohr Siebeck, 1998); Graham Stanton, "5 Ezra and Matthean Christianity in the Second Century," *JTS* 28 (1977): 67–83; idem, *A Gospel for a New People: Studies in Matthew* (Edinburgh: T&T Clark, 1992); Wayne A. Meeks, "Breaking Away," in "*To See Ourselves as Others See Us": Christians, Jews, "Others" in Late Antiquity*, ed. Jacob Neusner, Caroline McCracken-Flesher, and Ernest S. Frerichs, Scholars Press Studies in the Humanities (Chico, Calif.: Scholars Press, 1985), 93–115; Sean Freyne, "Vilifying the Other and Defining the Self," in Neusner, McCracken-Flesher, and Frerichs, "*To See Ourselves as Others See Us,*" 117–43; Benno Przybylski, "The Setting of Matthean Anti-Judaism," in *Anti-Judaism in Early Christianity*, vol. 1, *Paul and the Gospels*, ed. Peter Richardson, S. G. Wilson, and David M. Granskow, Studies in Christianity and Judaism 2 (Waterloo, Ont.: Wilfrid Laurier University Press, 1986). Amy-Jill Levine, *The Social and Ethnic Dimensions of Matthean Salvation History*, Studies in the Bible and Early Christianity 14 (Lewiston, N.Y.: Edwin Mellen, 1988); cf. her recent contribution "Matthew's Advice to a Divided Readership," in *The Gospel of Matthew in Current Study: Studies in Memory of William G. Thompson*, ed. David Aune (Grand Rapids: Eerdmans, 2001), 30: "The Gospel is, finally, a Christian, not a Jewish, text." It is not always easy to categorize scholars in either of these groups, *intra* or *extra muros* (I apologize to anyone who feels that he or she should have been placed in the other category). This difficulty probably has something to do with a not infrequent neglect among researchers to distinguish between the perspective of the Matthean community and that of the parent body (whether called "formative Judaism" or "early rabbinic Judaism" or just referred to as "mainstream Judaism" or the like), as has been pointed out by Boris Repschinski, *The Controversy Stories in the Gospel of Matthew: Their Redaction, Form and Relevance for the Relationship between the Matthean Community and Formative Judaism*, FRLANT 189 (Göttingen: Vandenhoek & Ruprecht, 2000), 346–47. To this we shall return below.

4.   See, for example, K. W. Clarke, "The Gentile Bias in Matthew," *JBL* 66 (1947): 165–72; Samuel Sandmel, *A Jewish Understanding of the New Testament* (1956; reprint, with a new preface, Woodstock: SkyLight Paths Publications, 2004); Poul Nepper-Christensen, *Das Matthäusevangelium: Ein judenchristliches Evangelium,* ATDan 1 (Aarhus: Universitetsforlaget, 1958); Georg Strecker, *Der Weg der Gerechtigkeit: Untersuchung zur Theologie des Matthäus*, 3rd rev. and enl. ed., FRLANT 82 (Göttingen: Vandenhoeck & Ruprecht, 1971); Sjef van Tilborg, *The Jewish Leaders in Matthew* (Leiden: Brill, 1972); David Flusser, "Two Anti-Jewish Montages in Matthew," *Immanuel* 5 (1975): 37–45; Lloyd Gaston, "The Messiah of Israel as Teacher of the Gentiles: The Setting of Matthew's Christology," *Interpretation* 21 (1975): 24–40; John P. Meier, *The Vision of Matthew: Christ, Church, and Morality in the First Gospel* (New York: Paulist, 1979); Michael J. Cook, "Interpreting 'Pro-Jewish' Passages in Matthew," *HUCA* 54 (1983): 135–46.

5.   Owing to divergent uses of terminology and different interpretations of how to apply social-scientific terminology and theories, it is often difficult to define where scholars stand in relation to each other.

6.   E. P. Sanders, *Judaism: Practice and Belief, 63 BCE–66 CE* (London: SCM; Philadelphia: Trinity Press International, 1992; corrected ed., 1994). Common Judaism is described generally as "what the priests and the people agreed on" (47). The concept thus refers to beliefs and practices of individuals, "ordinary Jews," who did not belong to any specific party. This does not mean, however, that there would not have been considerable overlap between what ordinary Jews and people belonging to parties believed and practiced: these similarities include the Pharisees (415–16, 451). Cf. Jacob Neusner, "The Formation of Rabbinic Judaism: Yavneh (Jamnia) from A.D. 70 to 100," *ANRW* 2.19.2 (1979): 3–42, who similarly talks about a common Judaism, defining it by referring to three main elements: Torah, temple, and the "common and accepted practices of the ordinary folk—their calendar, their mode of living, their everyday practices and rites, based on these first two" (21). For a critical discussion of common Judaism, see Martin Hengel and Roland Dienes, "E. P. Sanders' 'Common Judaism,' Jesus, and the Pharisees," *JTS* 46, no. 1 (1995): 1–70. On Pharisaic (lack of) influence, see Sanders, *Judaism*, 388–412, 448–51. Sanders refers to Morton Smith, Jacob Nesuner, Shaye Cohen, and Martin Goodman as scholars sharing his "'low' view of the authority of the Pharisees" (401). We may add the part of the entry on Pharisees by Rudolf Meyer ("Pharisees," *TDNT* 9 [Grand Rapids: Eerdmans, 1974], 11–35); see esp. 31, and note the emphasis on the heterogeneity of the Pharisaic movement (26–28, 35).

7.   "Synagogue" is usually treated as a phenomenon in the singular and as being in opposition to the "church." The "church," in turn, is often understood as an institution replacing "Israel," and

so "Israel," third, is presented as something other than, and opposed to, Jesus and the disciples, with implications for the analysis of the community/ies behind the text. Fourth, "Christianity" is often treated as if it were a homogeneous phenomenon and, as such, something that can be compared to and contrasted with "Judaism," which, fifth, is also understood in the singular.

8. This was noted already by Johannes Munck, "Jewish Christianity in Post-apostolic Times," *NTS* 6 (1960): 103–16. See also Brown, "Matthean Community," 208–9; Sim, *Christian Judaism*, 25 n. 67. "Religious system" refers to thought patterns and rituals within what can be defined as a "religion" (the term has nothing to do with "systematic theology"). "Type of religion" refers to a larger "family" of religions (cf. the concept of language families) that display important similarities. The relationship between "religious system" and "religious type" is defined in table 1 below.

9. Saldarini, *Matthew's Christian-Jewish Community*. Before him, Gabriele Boccaccini made the same point (*Middle Judaism: Jewish Thought, 300 B.C.E. to 200 C.E.* [Minneapolis: Fortress Press, 1991]).

10. Mark Nanos and Anders Runesson, *Paul and Apostolic Judaism* (in progress). As will be discussed in detail in the book, there are several advantages to using this term, which, terminologically, parallels "Pharisaic Judaism," "Enochic Judaism" (cf. the recent study by David R. Jackson, *Enochic Judaism: Three Defining Paradigm Exemplars*, Library of Second Temple Studies 49 [London: T&T Clark, 2004]; see also Gabriele Boccaccini, *Beyond the Essene Hypothesis: The Parting of the Ways between Qumran and Enochic Judaism* [Grand Rapids: Eerdmans, 1998]), "rabbinic Judaism," and the like. It should be noted that "apostolic Judaism" as a term, like "Pharisaic Judaism," is *not* meant to indicate uniformity in beliefs, nor a developed supralocal authority structure among "apostolic Jewish" communities. Rather, it denotes a variant of Jewish religion within which Jesus is accepted—in different ways and with different implications—as the messiah. See further below.

11. This would solve the problem that Sim (*Christian Judaism*) perceives in Overman's insistence on "Matthean Judaism" as the preferred term. It would also take seriously the specifics of the type of religion that is evidenced in Matthew, which should not be generalized to apply to all variants of apostolic Judaism.

12. See Anders Runesson, *The Origins of the Synagogue: A Socio-historical Study*, ConBNT 37 (Stockholm: Almqvist & Wiksell International, 2001), 63, where I used the term "Yahwistic" in the same sense; cf. the use of "Yahwistic" by Gary Knoppers, "Mt. Gerizim and Mt. Zion: A Study in the Early History of the Samaritans and Jews," *SR* 34, nos. 3–4 (2005): 309–38.

13. See E. P. Sanders, *Paul and Palestinian Judaism: A Comparison of Patterns of Religion* (London: SCM, 1979), 12–18.

14. See Magnus Zetterholm, *The Formation of Christianity in Antioch: A Social-Scientific Approach to the Separation between Judaism and Christianity* (London: Routledge, 2003). In his criticism of James D. G. Dunn's approach to the problem of the so-called parting(s) of the ways, Zetterholm writes: "While ideological aspects certainly played a vital part in the process, it seems more correct to assume that what Dunn describes as *the cause* of the separation process actually represents *the result* of the separation defined in ideological terms. The reason for this assumption

is that *concrete cultural resources* (for example, church architecture, symbolic practices, liturgical forms) are more likely to be the object of contention, while *abstract resources* (for example, ideas, ideologies, values) are easier to manipulate and often function as strategically mobilized resources in conflicts over other kind of resources" (4). Zetterholm refers to F. Kniss, "Ideas and Symbols as Resources in Intrareligious Conflict: The Case of American Mennonites," *Sociology of Religion* 57, no. 1 (1996): 7–23. Cf also the emphasis on practice in Sanders, *Judaism.*

15. For examples, see John M. G. Barclay, *Jews in the Mediterranean Diaspora: From Alexander to Trajan (323 BCE–117 CE)* (Berkeley: University of California Press, 1996).

16. The construction of ethnic identity is a complex process. For a general discussion, see Thomas H. Eriksen, *Ethnicity and Nationalism: Anthropological Perspectives* (London: Pluto, 1993). See also Jonathan M. Hall, *Ethnic Identity in Greek Antiquity* (Cambridge: Cambridge University Press, 1997). A recent collection of essays relating the question of ethnicity to biblical texts is found in Mark G. Brett, ed., *Ethnicity and the Bible*, Biblical Interpretation Series 19 (Leiden: Brill, 1996). For the purposes of the present study, see the articles by David Sim, "Christianity and Ethnicity in the Gospel of Matthew," 171–96; and Philip Esler, "Group Boundaries and Intergroup Conflict in Galatians: A New Reading of Galatians 5:13—6:10," especially the methodological discussion on pp. 220–31. See also the discussion of ethnicity by Esler in *Conflict and Identity in Romans: The Social Setting of Paul's Letter* (Minneapolis: Fortress Press, 2003), 40–76. One of the most recent contributions to the discussion of ethnicity in relation to the claims of early Christ-believers is Denise Kimber Buell, *Why This New Race: Ethnic Reasoning in Early Christianity*, Gender, Theory, Religion (New York: Columbia University Press, 2005). Space does not allow a full discussion applying this procedure to the Gospel of Matthew and the Mattheans: for this I will have to refer the reader to a forthcoming study: Anders Runesson, *The Gospel of Matthew and the Myth of Christian Origins: Rethinking the So-Called Parting(s) of the Ways between Judaism and Christianity* (in preparation). This study gives a detailed analysis of the elaboration of divine judgment in the Gospel (as it relates to beliefs and practices) as well as the treatment of ethnic groups in the world of the text and the implications of both of these parameters for the ethnic identity of the community. For studies on Matthew and aspects of covenantal nomism, see, for example, Benno Przybylski, *Righteousness in Matthew and His World of Thought*, SNTSMS 41 (Cambridge: Cambridge University Press, 1980); Kari Syreeni, *The Making of the Sermon on the Mount: A Procedural Analysis of Matthew's Redactoral Activity*, part 1, *Methodology and Compositional Analysis* (Helsinki: Suomalainen Tiedeakatemia, 1987). See also more recently, Luomanen, *Entering the Kingdom of Heaven.*

17. As is commonly acknowledged, in the New Testament the Gospel of Matthew emphasizes divine judgment more than any other text. In the author's perspective, the story of Jesus is understood only if and when God's judgment permeates and explains the teaching, events, and conflicts described.

18. For a study of Greco-Roman thinking on divine judgment, see David Kuck, *Judgment and Community Conflict: Paul's Use of Apocalyptic Judgment Language in 1 Corinthians 3:5—4:5*, NovTSup 66 (Leiden: Brill, 1992), 96–149. See also J. Gwyn Griffiths's wide-ranging study of divine judgment, arranged thematically with regard to ideas about judgment occurring in history

and after death respectively, discussing, apart from Israel, Greek, Roman, Egyptian, Hittite, Babylonian, Iranian, and Indian traditions: *The Divine Verdict: A Study of Divine Judgment in the Ancient Religions*, SHR 52 (Leiden: Brill, 1991). For an overview and discussion of judgment discourse in the Hebrew Bible and the New Testament, see Anders Runesson, "Judgment," in *New Interpreters Dictionary of the Bible*, vol. 3, ed. Katharine Doob Sakenfeld et al. (Nashville: Abingdon Press, 2008) 457–66. Recent studies on the judgment in Matthew include Daniel Marguerat, *Le jugement dans l'évangile de Matthieu*, 2nd ed., Le Monde de la Bible (Geneva: Labor et Fides, 1995); Blaine Charette, *The Theme of Recompense in Matthew's Gospel*, JSNTSup 79 (Sheffield: JSOT Press, 1992); Sim, *Apocalyptic Eschatology*.

19.   Jewish food regulations are not rejected in Matt 15:1-20, which represents the author's reworked version of Markan material, where such regulations are explicitly rejected (Mark 7:19). This suggests that the Mattheans kept the dietary laws.

20.   Note that Jesus never enters the house of the Roman centurion. *Kai legei autō egō elthōn therapeusō auton* may be translated as a question: "Should I come and cure him?"—so the Swedish translation of 1981, but not, for example, NRSV, KJV, ASV. W. D. Davies and Dale C. Allison Jr. (*A Critical and Exegetical Commentary on the Gospel According to Saint Matthew*, 3 vols., ICC [London: T&T Clark, 1988–97], 2:21–22) read it as a question, comparing the story to Matt 15:21-28.

21.   Far from abolishing the Sabbath, this passage is a clear example of a discussion of the weightier things in the law: see esp. vv. 5, 7, 12. The inviolability of the Sabbath is confirmed in Matt 24:20.

22.   The recognition of the temple is related to Matthew's view of Jerusalem as the Holy City (Matt 4:5; 5:35; 27:53): the city receives its holiness from the temple. The holiness of the city is thus connected to the God of Israel and the temple, not the leadership, which is also, however, related to the city and the temple but as the caretaker of holy things. Indeed, Matthew's perspective is that some groups, which he connects with the temple and the city, were corrupt and were bad servants, or shepherds (cf., for example, Matt 9:36), or tenants (Matt 21:33, 45), and have thus caused the destruction of both. Note the location of Matt 23:37—24:2 following directly after the criticism of the "scribes and Pharisees." See further below.

23.   Circumcision is not explicitly mentioned in the Gospel, but probably would have been if the Mattheans had rejected this custom, as they did with hand washing before meals (Matt 15:1-20), the use of oaths (Matt 5:33-37; 23:16-22), and divorce (except in the case of *porneia*: Matt 5:31-32; 19:1-12). Scholars arguing that circumcision was part of Matthean practice include Brown, "Matthean Community," 218; Roger Mohrlang, *Matthew and Paul: A Comparison of Ethical Perspectives* (Cambridge: Cambridge University Press, 1984), 44–45; Levine, *Social and Ethnic Dimensions*, 183–85; L. Michael White, "Crisis Management and Boundary Maintenance: The Social Location of the Matthean Community," in *Social History of the Matthean Community: Cross Disciplinary Approaches*, ed. David L. Balch (Minneapolis: Fortress Press, 1991), 211–47, 241–42 n. 100; Anthony Saldarini, "The Gospel of Matthew and Jewish-Christian Conflict in Galilee," in *The Galilee in Late Antiquity*, ed. Lee I. Levine (New York: Jewish Theological Seminary of America, 1992), 23–38, esp. 25–26. (In his study *Matthew's Christian-Jewish Community*, however, Saldarini modifies his position somewhat, stating that "some [Gentiles] may have been

circumcised, and some not" [160]); Sim, *Apocalyptic Eschatology*, 208–9; idem, *Gospel of Matthew and Christian Judaism*, 251–55; idem, "Christianity and Ethnicity." See also the discussion in Davies and Allison, *Matthew*, 1:7–58.

24. This categorization differs from several previous attempts at defining, especially varieties of Christianity, as, for example, Raymond E. Brown, "Not Jewish Christianity and Gentile Christianity but Types of Jewish/Gentile Christianity," *CBQ* 45 (1983): 74–79. While this study is thought provoking, it suffers from not emphasizing the distinction between the Jewish and the non-Jewish religious systems.

25. Of course, this general distinction between Jewish believers in Jesus and "other parties" is adapted to the present study and is unsatisfactory as a general categorization, since it gives the impression that these other parties had things in common, which they did not necessarily have. More important, however, is that there were no neat divisions between these movements and parties, and considerable overlap could exist between these groups. See further below.

26. Samaritans should be regarded not as a Jewish sect but as an independent interpretation of Israelite religion: see Runesson, *Origins*, 388–94, and references there, especially the studies by J. D. Purvis and R. J. Coggins. See also Oskar Skarsaune, *In the Shadow of the Temple: Jewish Influences on Early Christianity* (Leicester: Inter-Varsity Press, 2002), 128: "Samaritanism was not Judaism, for the simple reason that the Samaritans did not recognize the true center." Cf. the conclusion of Martin S. Jaffee, *Early Judaism* (Upper Saddle River, N.J.: Prentice Hall, 1997), 138: "These parallels and contrasts lead to an unavoidable conclusion; *the Samaritan's religious world is an example of a Judaic world that, in its own view as well as in the eyes of the Jews, is not part of Judaism*" (emphasis original). Jaffee discusses Samaritans under the heading "Israel but not Jews."

27. I have included Islam here since current debate on "the parting(s) of the ways" extends into the seventh century and beyond. Thus, according to some scholars, Judaism and Christianity had, in fact, not fully parted ways when Islam emerged on the historical scene. See Adam H. Becker and Annette Yoshiko Reed, eds., *The Ways That Never Parted: Jews and Christians in Late Antiquity and the Early Middle Ages* (Tübingen: Mohr Siebeck, 2003). This conclusion is, of course, dependent on how the metaphor parting(s) is defined. See, for example, Judith Lieu, *Neither Jew nor Greek? Constructing Early Christianity* (London: T&T Clark, 2002), 11–29.

28. Sanders, *Judaism*, 47.

29. I have listed some such practices above.

30. Cf. the discussion and conclusion in Davies and Allison, *Matthew*, 1:7–58. See also David Sim, "The Gospel of Matthew and the Gentiles," *JSNT* 57 (1995): 19–48; idem, "The 'Confession' of the Soldiers in Matthew 27:54," *HeyJ* 34 (1993): 401–24.

31. For a discussion of possible locations, see Davies and Allison, *Matthew*, 1:138–47. Davies and Allison end up favoring Antioch, though being careful to point out the lack of evidence supporting this position. See also Graham Stanton, "The Origin and Purpose of Matthew's Gospel," *ANRW* 2.25.3 (1987): 1891–92. Several scholars reckon with two distinct stages in the life of the community, the first being located in Palestine and the second in Antioch, after the community moved there (after the Jewish war). These two stages serve an explanatory purpose meant to solve assumed tensions within the Gospel, which, it is argued, occurred as a result of the change of location.

See, for example, Brown, "Matthean Community." In my opinion, this is an unnecessary hypothesis and the tensions within the Gospel can be explained more easily in other ways, as we shall see.

32. Overman (*Church and Community*, 16–19) suggests Sepphoris or Tiberias. Eduard Schweizer ("Matthew's Church," in Stanton, *Interpretation of Matthew*, 149–77) suggests "Syria, or perhaps the neighbouring areas of Galilee" as the most probable supposition. Saldarini ("Jewish-Christian Conflict," 26–27), concludes, "Galilee, with its complex and cosmopolitan society and its tightly woven cultural network, could easily have supported the nascent rabbinic Jewish and Christian Jewish movements, as well as the other apocalyptic, priestly, messianic, revivalist, and revolutionary currents running through society"; see also Segal, "Matthew's Jewish Voice," 26–29; Daniel J. Harrington, *The Gospel of Matthew*, SP (Collegeville, Minn.: Liturgical Press, Michael Glazier, 1991); Ekkehard W. Stegemann and Wolfgang Stegemann, *The Jesus Movement: A Social History of Its First Century* (Minneapolis: Fortress Press, 1999), 223–29. Aaron M. Gale (*Redefining Ancient Borders: The Jewish Scribal Framework of Matthew's Gospel* [New York: T&T Clark, 2005], 41–63) concludes that Sepphoris is the best candidate.

33. This is the position of the overwhelming majority of Matthean scholars, and any commentary may be consulted for detailed arguments (see, for example, Davies and Allison, *Matthew*, 1:127–38, who list scholarly views since Grotius [!]). In the discussion of internal evidence, the Synoptic problem, of course, has a primary place. If we do not accept Q (see Mark Goodacre, *The Case against Q: Studies in Markan Priority and the Synoptic Problem* [Harrisburg, Pa.: Trinity Press International, 2002]), Matthew would have to predate Luke, who would be using Matthew and Mark (this solution is, in my opinion, the only real competitor to the Q hypothesis). Cf. the recent study by Benedict Viviano ("John's Use of Matthew: Beyond Tweaking," *RB* 111 [2004]: 209–37), in which he argues that the author of the Gospel of John knew Matthew, which would place Matthew in the 80s at the latest, if we accept a date for John in the 90s. Be that as it may, there are, in any case, several good arguments for placing Matthew in the late first century. One of the key passages always referred to is Matt 22:7, which is argued to convey knowledge of the destruction of Jerusalem. As to external evidence, quotations of or allusions to Matthew in early-second-century church fathers serve as a *terminus ante quem*. The following texts are listed by Davies and Allison and are usually part of the discussion: Ignatius, the *Didache*, Polycarp, the *Epistle of Barnabas*, the *Gospel of Peter*, and Justin Martyr. See also the discussion provided by scholars listed in n. 2 above.

34. Proponents of a high level of influence of the Pharisees include Emil Schürer, Kaufman Kohler, Gedaliah Alon, and Louis Finkelstein, all mentioned by Steve Mason, "Pharisaic Dominance before 70 CE and the Gospel's Hypocrisy Charge (Matt 23:2-3)," *HTR* 83 (1990): 363–81, esp. 363–64. Mason's article itself provides a renewed attempt at arguing for a pre-70 dominance of the Pharisees. See also Peter J. Tomson, *"If This Be from Heaven": Jesus and the New Testament Authors in Their Relationship to Judaism*, Biblical Seminar 76 (Sheffield: Sheffield Academic Press, 2001), 50–55.

35. See Steve Mason, "Pharisaic Dominance," 363–67. See also A. I. Baumgarten's chapter in this volume. There are basically three source groups available on the basis of which conclusions may be drawn: Josephus, the New Testament, and early rabbinic writings.

36. Jacob Nesuner has discussed formative Judaism in several publications. See, for example, "Formation of Rabbinic Judaism" and *Judaism: The Evidence of the Mishnah* (Chicago: University of Chicago Press, 1981).

37. Cf. Saldarini ("Jewish-Christian Conflict," 30–31 n. 22), who states that Matthew is "probably responding to the leaders of an early form of rabbinic Judaism who were competing with him for the loyalties of the local Jewish Community." See also Overman (*Formative Judaism*, 2), who defines formative Judaism as a precursor to rabbinic Judaism, which came to dominate Judaism in late antiquity. Sim (*Christian Judaism*, 113–15) concludes that formative Judaism "was certainly cohesive enough and sufficiently influential in *the society* of the Matthean community . . . to stand as the parent body with which the evangelist and his group were in dispute" (115; my emphasis).

38. Cf., for example, how Josephus managed to arrange not only for his survival after the war but also for a position from which he could continue to exercise influence. The same is true for Josephus's enemy Justus of Tiberias, who after the war became the secretary/historian of Agrippa II: see Tessa Rajak, *Josephus: The Historian and His Society* (Philadelphia: Fortress Press, 1984), 146.

39. See Meyer, "Pharisees," 16–31. The basic point Meyer makes is well taken; however, some of his reconstructions display an overly optimistic approach to the many problems of the source material.

40. See Shaye J. D. Cohen, *From the Maccabees to the Mishnah* (Philadelphia: Westminster, 1987), 221–24; idem, "The Place of the Rabbi in Jewish Society of the Second Century," in *The Galilee in Late Antiquity*, ed. Lee I. Levine (New York: Jewish Theological Seminary of America, 1992), 157–83; Lee I. Levine, "The Sages and the Synagogue in Late Antiquity: The Evidence of the Galilee," in idem, *Galilee in Late Antiquity*, 201–22. Seth Schwartz (*Imperialism and Jewish Society: 200 BCE to 640 CE* [Princeton: Princeton University Press, 2001]) makes a convincing case for understanding the (re-)construction of Jewish identity as partly a result of the Christianization of the Roman Empire in late antiquity. Schwartz, however, does not see the rabbis as particularly influential in this process, and he dates their rise to prominence in the early Middle Ages. See also my "From Integration to Marginalization: Archaeology as Text and the Analysis of Early Diaspora Judaism" (in Swedish), *SEÅ* 67 (2002): 121–44, esp. 125–26, discussing the fact that the lack of rabbinic influence prior to this date is further evidenced in the art of several fourth-century and later synagogue buildings.

41. Cf. Sim (*Christian Judaism*, 115), who addresses the same difficulty, but in relation to Antioch, where he believes the Mattheans belonged.

42. Anthony Saldarini, "Delegitimation of Leaders in Matthew 23," *CBQ* (1992): 663–64.

43. Cf. Saldarini, "Jewish-Christian Conflict," 114.

44. For a full discussion of the institutional realities of first-century Judaism, with a focus on the two types of synagogue institution—the public village assembly and the semipublic, or private, association synagogue, see Runesson, *Origins*, esp. ch. 3 (169–235).

45. Saldarini, "Jewish-Christian Conflict," 33.

46. This is why the temple needed to be cleansed (Matt 21:12-13). The fact that Jesus is regarded as something greater than the temple (12:6) is not meant to reduce the significance of the temple, but to enhance and emphasize the status and position of Jesus as God's messiah.

47. In Matthew, the Pharisees disappear in 23:29 and reappear together with the chief priests in 27:62; Mark and Luke do not mention them at all after Mark 12:13 and Luke 19:39.

48. The references in Mark 1:23, 39 are sometimes explained as non-Markan insertions, possibly by a copyist influenced by the Gospel of Matthew. Cf. George Dunbar Kilpatrick, *The Origins of the Gospel According to St. Matthew* (Oxford: Oxford University Press, 1946), 111. Although this is a possibility, it is an unnecessary hypothesis since the meaning of "their" may shift both within Matthew and between Matthew and Mark. Cf. the one instance in Luke 4:15, and see further below.

49. The fact that Mattheans are admonished to perform their *private* prayer at home does not invalidate this conclusion. On *public* prayer in synagogues, a disputed issue, see my *Origins*.

50. "Pharisees" are thus not said to operate the public synagogues, but to use them for promoting their own status in society.

51. For a recent, in-depth study of the crowds in Matthew, see J. R. C. Cousland, *The Crowds in the Gospel of Matthew*, NovTSup 102 (Leiden: Brill, 2002).

52. Great crowds followed Jesus (4:25; 8:1); Jesus has compassion on them, since they lack proper leadership (9:36; cf. 14:14); he preaches to them and heals them (5:1; 12:15; 19:2); they are astonished and praise the God of Israel for Jesus' ministry (7:28; 9:8, 33; 15:31; cf. 22:33), wondering whether he could be the messiah ("the son of David," 12:23 [in contrast to the reaction of the Pharisees, 12:24]; 21:9). The chief priests and the Pharisees are said to want to arrest Jesus, but they hesitate because they fear the crowds, who regarded Jesus as a prophet (21:46; cf. 21:11), just as they had John the Baptist (21:26, exchanging Pharisees for elders; cf. 14:5). The sometimes ambivalent reactions of the crowds, as well as their suffering, are blamed on the lack of proper leadership (9:36). The accusations against the Pharisees and their scribes are framed as warnings directed to both the disciples and the crowds (23:1). It is sometimes argued that "the crowds" are portrayed as shifting their allegiance in the passion narrative, on account of their role in the arrest and trial of Jesus. However, the chief priests and the elders are said to plan to arrest Jesus in a way that would avoid upsetting the crowds (26:1-5), and "the crowds" arresting Jesus are specifically mentioned as being sent by the chief priests and elders (26:47), avoiding generalization. Indeed, the crowds in the passion narrative seem to be representative of people in the capital rather than the land as a whole, acting together with the leaders in a way that, in the author's eyes, condemns them both—the people of Jerusalem and the leaders together (switching to the inclusive *ho laos* [27:25]). In other words, what the passion narrative shows are tensions between different areas of the land and the populations of those areas: whereas Galilee is home of and supports the prophet and would-be messiah Jesus (with the exception of some specified towns; cf. Matt 11:20-24; 13:55-58), Jerusalem, from where the messiah must rule the restored Israel, rejects him as the chosen one in order to protect its own—according to the author—corrupt leadership. These tensions between a Galilean popular leader and the political establishment of the capital are most likely historical with regard to Jesus' times. By inserting the Pharisees into the passion narrative (27:62) and in other ways connecting the Pharisees with the political leadership in Jerusalem, the Gospel of Matthew transfers the conflict—and the guilt—to apply also (and therefore more) to the Pharisees, thus extending, symbolically, the reach of Jerusalem's power and

corruption geographically and chronologically to apply to Pharisees of the Galilee in the post-70 period of the Mattheans. A further piece of evidence supporting this hypothesis is the reference to *Ioudaioi* in Matt 28:15, which should here be translated not "Jews" but "Judeans," referring to the geographical area. This may be a general reference, but since the Pharisees are introduced together with the chief priests in 27:62, it may well be that the author refers to Judean Pharisees, as opposed to his own Galilean community. For the presence of Pharisees in Galilee, see, for example, Richard A. Horsley, "Conquest and Social Conflict in Galilee," in *Recruitment, Conquest, and Conflict: Strategies in Judaism, Early Christianity, and the Greco-Roman World*, ed. Peder Borgen et al., Emory Studies in Early Christianity 6 (Atlanta: Scholars Press, 1998), 157; Segal, "Matthew's Jewish Voice," 27. See further below.

53. White, "Crisis Management," 241.

54. See Runesson, *Origins*, 355–57.

55. This may be compared to the practice recorded in Matthew's Gospel to send "prophets, sages, and scribes" to the Pharisees, as witnessed by Matt 23:34, a passage to which we shall return. Cf. Luke 7:36, where Jesus accepts an invitation to the home of a Pharisee who wants to eat together with him. In Matthew's Gospel, however, the initiative comes from Jesus.

56. If *en* is taken as instrumental; see Davies and Allison, *Matthew*, 2:183.

57. The mention of "Gentiles" in Matt 10:18 has sometimes been taken to indicate that this verse refers to a Diaspora situation. It is more likely, however, that the text is patterned on the passion of Jesus, who was first delivered to a Jewish council and then handed over to the governor (that is, the Gentiles): see Davies and Allison, *Matthew*, 2:183. In addition, Matt 10:5-6 clearly sets the context for the passage: "Go nowhere among the Gentiles, and enter no town of the Samaritans, but go rather to the lost sheep of the house of Israel."

58. While not all scribes would have been Pharisees, some would. I understand the combination of "scribes and Pharisees" in the Gospel of Matthew to refer to scribes who belonged to the Pharisaic party; this does not exclude the existence of scribes outside of that community. (On scribes, see Sanders, *Judaism*, esp. 179–82. See also Neusner, "Formation of Rabbinic Judaism," 39, referred to also by Petri Luomanen, "The 'Sociology of Sectarianism' in Matthew; Modeling the Genesis of Early Jewish and Christian Communities," in *Fair Play: Diversity and Conflicts in Early Christianity; Essays in Honor of Heikki Räisänen*, ed. Ismo Dunderberg, Christopher Tuckett, and Kari Syreeni. NovTSup 103 (Leiden/Boston: Brill, 2002), 119–24)

59. Donald D. Binder, *Into the Temple Courts: The Place of the Synagogue in the Second Temple Period*, SBLDS 169 (Atlanta: Society of Biblical Literature, 1999), 445–49. Lee I. Levine, *The Ancient Synagogue: The First Thousand Years*, 2nd ed. (New Haven, Conn.: Yale University Press, 2005), 131–32, 370–72.

60. The general warning *Prosechete de apo tōn anthrōpōn*, rather than a specific warning against the Pharisees, is motivated by the fact that the passage begins within the Jewish people but extends beyond it to the non-Jews. The warning cannot, then, be limited to a specific group or people.

61. It is somewhat ironic that one of the groups that isolated itself most from outside influences, the sect at the Dead Sea, shows very clear signs of outside influences in its organizational pattern; see further below.

62. The most famous and fullest description of penal codes in associations is the statutes of the *Iobaccoi* (Athens, 176 c.e.), translated by Wilhelm Dittenberger, *Sylloge Inscriptionum Graecarum*, 3rd ed. (Leipzig: Hirzelium, 1915–24); translation provided in Moshe Weinfeld, *The Organizational Pattern and the Penal Code of the Qumran Sect* (Göttingen: Vandenhoeck & Ruprecht, 1978), 51–54.

63. So Matthias Klinghardt, "The Manual of Discipline in the Light of Statutes of Hellenistic Associations," in *Methods of Investigation of the Dead Sea Scrolls and the Khirbet Qumran Site: Present Realities and Future Prospects*, ed. John J. Collins et al., Annals of the New York Academy of Sciences 722 (New York: New York Academy of Sciences, 1994). Cf. Weinfeld, *Organizational Pattern*, especially his response to Lawrence Schiffman (*Sectarian Law in the Dead Sea Scrolls: Courts, Testimony, and the Penal Code*, BJS 33 [Chico, Calif.: Scholars Press, 1983]), app, E, 71–76. Unfortunately, Klinghardt argues that the identification of the Qumranites as an association contradicts their categorization as a sect. Associations could have different views of society; some of them would qualify as sects, others as denominations. The designation "association" does not dictate the "content," but rather the (organizational) "form." This is further evidenced in Roman imperial treatment of different *collegia*, some of which were banished while others, old enough to have proven their loyalty to the empire, were allowed to continue business as usual.

64. Cf. LXX Deut 25:1-3.

65. I am grateful to Philip Harland for discussions of this issue.

66. Cf. Davies and Allison, *Matthew*, 2:182-83.

67. Cf. Stegemann and Stegemann, *Jesus Movement*, 227–28. I would, however, think of an urban context of somewhat larger size than they suggest for several reasons, among which are language and evidence of mixed population.

68. Even if there may have been people within the movement who had met Jesus, the urban setting suggests a lack of direct continuity since Jesus focused his ministry and missionary activity on rural areas.

69. This was before the consolidation of believers of Jesus in a single group with a supralocal leadership organization: at this time, many Christ-believers belonged to other parties and did not interpret their new beliefs as necessitating the creation of a new association. People previously not belonging to an association, however, most likely joined together forming new associations in an early stage of the history of the Jesus movement (cf. the Jerusalem-based group referred to by Paul in Galatians, and by the author of Acts, which seems to have achieved a leading position by the middle of the first century).

70. Rituals specific to the Christ-believers, such as the Eucharist (Matt 26:26-29—regardless of whether this was celebrated on a weekly or an annual cycle), would have been performed in meetings that did not involve non–Christ-believers. It is not uncommon for subgroups within larger groups to develop or maintain rituals not practiced by the majority; for different types of subgroups and possible relationships between subgroup and larger collectivity, see further below. We find a similar phenomenon when Pharisees and other groups—but not the Qumranites—develop rituals practiced only by their own group (in their associations) but not to the exclusion of participation in the Jerusalem temple cult. The same pattern develops for Christ-believers in Acts

2:46, where the distinction between temple worship and worship in private homes is described as not mutually exclusive but rather complementary.

71. In this way, one could say that the reform movement was "conservative" in that it focused on traditions, of which they claimed they had the true interpretations, as opposed to wholly new phenomena that would override shared traditions. In the same way, Jesus becomes a teacher, like those of the Pharisees and their scribes, with the difference that he would be the only one. In Matthew's Gospel, the emphasis is on knowing the traditions and interpreting them correctly: see Matt 9:13; 12:3-7; 21:16, 42; 22:29, 31. Cf. Freyne, "Vilifying," 120–21. Jesus' teaching takes on the same importance, since these teachings are indispensable both for interpreting the sacred texts and for knowing the truth about what was happening in the Mattheans' own time (cf. Matt 7:24-29 [cf. Prov 10:25]; 24:35): two aspects, past and present, old and new, that are inseparably interwoven. Indeed, a Matthean is best identified as a scribe combining new and old (Matt 13:52: "Therefore every scribe who has been trained for the kingdom of heaven is like the master of a household who brings out of his treasure what is new and what is old"). Of course, one must also note that, for the Mattheans, acknowledging Jesus' teaching in and of itself will help no one: "only the one who does the will of my Father in heaven" will enter the kingdom (Matt 7:21; cf. 7:24).

72. Thus, the common assumption that the missionary zeal and eschatological expectations were intense in the beginning of the movement and then faded is turned on its head.

73. See Terrence Donaldson, "Proselytes or 'Righteous Gentiles'? The Status of Gentiles in Eschatological Pilgrimage Patterns of Thought," *JSP* 7 (1990): 3–27.

74. Matt 2:1-12; 8:5-13; 15:21-28. These passages display a consistent centripetal movement toward the people of Israel and its messiah, Jesus, as opposed to the centrifugal force of the so-called Great Commission in Matt 28:19-20.

75. Neusner, "Formation of Rabbinic Judaism."

76. Cf. Stegemann and Stegemann, *Jesus Movement*, 227–29, 230, and the social pyramid chart, 232.

77. When a reform movement within a denomination parts from the parent body, those who leave will not be able to convince all members of the movement to leave with them. See the example where 10 percent of the members of a reform movement remained within the parent body as the others left, referred to by Philip Esler, *Community and Gospel in Luke-Acts: The Social and Political Motivations of Lucan Theology*, SNTSMS 57 (Cambridge: Cambridge University Press, 1987), and the discussion in Brent Holmberg, *Sociology and the New Testament: An Appraisal*, (Minneapolis: Fortress Press, 1990), 102–103. A main reason for the schism could be indicated in Matt 23:13, where Pharisees and the scribes are said to "lock people out of the kingdom of heaven": this may refer to an active attempt by leading Pharisees to prevent people—including other Pharisees and sympathizers—from joining the Matthean reform movement.

78. Thus the focus on community building and the establishment of rules for the new association (Matthew 18; cf. the transfer of leadership in Matthew's version of the parable of the vineyard, including the concluding comments, adding the Pharisees [21:33-46]). See Dennis Duling, "The Matthean Brotherhood and Marginal Scribal Leadership," in *Modelling Early Christianity: Social Scientific Studies of the New Testament in Its Context*, ed. Philip Esler (London: Routledge, 1995),

159–82; and Richard Ascough, "Matthew and Community Formation," in Aune, *Gospel of Matthew in Current Study*, 96–126. I would, however, emphasize that the Matthean association, *pace* Ascough (125), is, at the time of the writing of the Gospel, still in the process of formation. Important to note regarding the definition of "sect" is that the more traditional understanding going back to Troeltsch, focusing on relationships between (religious) groups rather than between groups and society at large, is, *pace* Overman and Saldarini, better suited for the analysis of the Matthean community. See the similar position in Luomanen, "Sociology of Sectarianism," based on Rodney Stark and William Sims Bainbridge, *A Theory of Religion* (New York: Peter Lang, 1987). I do not, however, agree with Luomanen on the characterization of the Mattheans as a cult movement [129–30]. Cf. the discussion in Esler, *Community and Gospel*, 46–70.

79. Meaning that within our Gospel there are preserved not only non-Matthean traditions from before 70 c.e. (from Mark and Q, if Q is accepted), but also Matthean traditions antedating the war.

80. There is an almost endless flow of articles and sections in books that attempts to solve this problem. One of the best studies, including a comprehensive discussion of most theories, is Mark Alan Powell, "Do and Keep What Moses Says (Matthew 23:2-7)," *JBL* 114 (1995): 419–35.

81. The lawlessness of the inside is the opposite of the law-abiding of the outside; that is, there is agreement on the basic halakhic requirements that take the form of external signs of identity. This does not mean acceptance of all Pharisaic customs by the separatists. For example, Matt 15:1-9 keeps the basic criticism of Mark's Gospel (7:1-13), even though disagreeing with Mark's conclusion (Mark 7:23; Matt 15:20).

82. Joachim Wach, *Sociology of Religion* (Chicago: University of Chicago Press, 1944), 173–86. Cf. Meredith B. McGuire, *Religion: The Social Context*, 2nd ed. (Belmont: Calif.: Wadsworth, 1987), 127–29. These groups may be described as sectarian or cultic dissent within a *church* or *denomination*.

83. Other passages indicating an intra-Pharisaic location include, for example, Matt 13:52 (identifying the Mattheans as scribes) and 23:34 (showing signs of their being actively involved in trying to reform the Pharisaic denomination). To this should be added the evidence of shared institutional context discussed above. In terms of virtuoso religion in Matthew's Gospel, see the comments on celibacy (19:10-12) and perfection (5:38). The author's attitude to "sinners and righteous" is also stated as avoiding premature judgment and allowing for a *corpus mixtum* (13:24-30; cf. 22:11-14). Contrary to the example of 19:16-22, however, the sinners are, ultimately, not going to enter the kingdom.

84. I take the inclusivity of Matt 5:17-19 to be addressed to Mattheans still remaining within the Pharisaic association, expressing willingness to modify their religious outlook. The exclusion of Pharisees from the kingdom in 5:20 serves as a warning aimed at preventing such adjustment. Moreover, it assures them that the separatists uphold a strict law observance, despite the type of Gentile mission the latter are now involved in (28:19-20).

85. A Pharisaic origin for the Mattheans has been suggested by, for example, Freyne, "Vilifying," 138. Cf. Reinhart Hummel, *Die Auseinandersetzung zwischen Kirche und Judentum in Matthäusevangelium*, 2nd ed. (Munich: Kaiser, 1966).

86. On the plurality of Matthean communities—but without the conclusions drawn here—see Graham Stanton, "The Communities of Matthew," *Int* 46 (1992): 379–91. See also Elaine Wainwright, *Shall We Look for Another? A Feminist Rereading of the Matthean Jesus* (Maryknoll, N.Y.: Orbis Books, 1998), 41–45. Although my conclusions differ from Wainwright's in many regards, her insistence on and sensitivity to different voices in Matthew's Gospel is a valuable contribution to the interpretation of the Matthean community and its text. I have emphasized two basic communities, the split occurring after 70, constituting the institutional frames within which interpretations of Jesus traditions were made. However, we must not overlook the fact that *within* these two communities we must reckon with some diversity. Of course, this does not mean that every tradition would have come from a separate (Matthean) community, only that the Matthean material is best explained by not theorizing about too homogeneous a setting in which it was kept, transmitted, and redacted. Other communities, consisting mainly of non-Jews, would soon adopt Matthew's Gospel as their preferred text, a fact that should make us even more cautious about postulating too much regarding possible readers of Matthew.

87. Regarding socioeconomic changes as reasons for sects to emerge, see the discussion in McGuire, *Social Context*, 131.

88. For characterization of the social status of sect members, see Rodney Stark, *The Rise of Christianity: How the Obscure, Marginal Jesus Movement Became the Dominant Religious Force in the Western World in a Few Centuries* (Princeton: Princeton University Press, 1996), 33; cf. McGuire, *Social Context*. See discussion of egalitarianism among the Mattheans in Ascough, "Matthew and Community Formation," 99; cf. Duling, "Matthean Brotherhood."

89. On the question whether this mission included the circumcision of male converts, affirming that this was likely the case, see Brown, "Matthean Community," 218; A.-J. Levine, *Social and Ethnic Dimensions*; Saldarini, "Jewish-Christian Conflict"; idem, *Matthew's Christian-Jewish Community*; Sim, *Apocalyptic Eschatology*; idem, *Christian Judaism*.

90. The negative stereotyping and slander of the "Pharisees" in Matthew have been analyzed by several scholars. One important insight is that the offensive language used by the author was not unusual in antiquity and may thus have been regarded as less offensive by the ancients than it seems to us today. See, for example, Luke Timothy Johnson, "The New Testament's Anti-Jewish Slander and the Conventions of Ancient Polemic," *JBL* 108 (1989): 419–41; Moshe Weinfeld, "The Charge of Hypocrisy in Matthew 23 and in Jewish Sources," *Immanuel* 24/25 (1990): 52–58; Benedict Viviano, "Social World and Community Leadership: The Case of Matthew 23:1-12, 34," *JSNT* 39 (1990): 3–21; Saldarini, "Delegitimation"; Margaret Davies, "Stereotyping the Other: The 'Pharisees' in the Gospel According to Matthew," in *Biblical Studies/ Cultural Studies: The Third Sheffield Colloquium*, ed. J. Cheryl Exum and Stephen D. Moore, JSOTSup 226 (Sheffield: Sheffield Academic Press, 1998), 415–32. Cf. James D. G. Dunn, "Pharisees, Sinners, Jesus," in *The Social World of Formative Christianity and Judaism*, ed. Howard Clark Kee and Jacob Neusner (Philadelphia: Fortress Press, 1988), 264–89. However, regardless of the level of offensiveness, it is clear that the author of the Gospel targets the Pharisees as the enemy par excellence, even above the political establishment, which, historically, decided to hand Jesus over to the Romans.

91. Sociologically, this phenomenon is similar to what we see in John Chrysostom's extreme polemic against the Jews. It is quite clear that this polemic is meant to be heard by Christ-believers, who did not perceive their identity as Christians to exclude participation in activities provided by the synagogue. By delegitimizing the group that attracted members of his church, Chrysostom hoped to establish his own institution as the only viable alternative for Christ-believers and to prevent any "dual memberships." See Robert L. Wilken, *John Chrysostom and the Jews: Rhetoric and Reality in the Late Fourth Century* (Berkeley: University of California Press, 1983). See also Leonard V. Rutgers, "Archaeological Evidence for the Interaction of Jews and Non-Jews in Late Antiquity," *AJA* 96 (1992): 115–16.

92. Cf., however, the conclusion by Wolfgang Roth, "To Invert or Not to Invert: The Pharisaic Canon in the Gospels," in *Early Christian Interpretation of the Scriptures of Israel: Investigations and Proposals*, ed. Craig A. Evans and James A. Sanders (Sheffield: Sheffield Academic Press, 1997), 76: "One seeks Matthew among Jesus-affirming Pharisees, much like Saul of Tarsus or Nicodemus of Jerusalem. His (still intra-Pharisaic) polemic is at times stinging, betraying a passionate involvement." Cf. Freyne, "Vilifying," 138, who suggests a Pharisaic origin for the Mattheans.

93. Acts:15:5: *exanestēsan de tines tōn apo tēs haireseōs tōn Pharisaiōn pepisteukotes legontes hoti dei peritemnein autous parangellein te tērein ton nomon Mōyseōs*. Although the passage recounts an event taking place in the middle of the first century, the author, writing in the late first century, seems to have no problem with the fact that some Pharisees were believers in Jesus, remaining within a group in which the majority would not share that belief.

94. Note the present tense: *egō Pharisaios eimi, huios Pharisaiōn, peri elpidos kai anastaseōs nekrōn [egō] krinomai*. I believe that this self-understanding attributed to Paul reflects his own and, consequently, that Phil 3:5-11 should not be read as contradicting a Pharisaic identity, but rather as emphasizing the importance of Jesus as Christ transcending specific group identities, without necessarily abolishing them.

95. See the discussion above and Meyer, "Pharisees."

Chapter 8: What Do Angels Have Against the Blind and the Deaf? Rules of Exclusion in the Dead Sea Scrolls

1. For the belief that Satan is in charge of the demons, see, for example, *Jub.* 10:7-12; 4QBerakhot^a (4Q286) 10 ii 1–13; 1QM XIII 10–12; 1QS III 20–24 ("Angel of Darkness"); 4QFlorilegium (4Q174) 1–2 i 7–9; 11Q11 V 13 ("sons of Belial"); possibly 1QH^a X 22. See also Matt 25:41.

2. In addition, there are lists restricting people from entering the temple that are primarily based on ethnicity and descent: 4QFlor (4Q174) excludes an Ammonite, a Moabite, a *mamzer*, an alien, and a proselyte from entering the temple (4QFlor 1–2 i 3–5); see also the fragmentary text of 4QMMT B 39–41, which excludes the Ammonite, the Moabite, the *mamzer*, the eunuch; 11QT XLV 12–14 excludes the blind from entering the temple.

3. The influence of the text of Leviticus is evident in several parallel categories of physical defects and in the use of the word *mwm* ("blemish") in 1QSa and M.

4. There are many variations on this theme; see, for example, Elisha Qimron, "Celibacy in the Dead Sea Scrolls and the Two Kinds of Sectarians," in *The Madrid Qumran Congress:*

Proceedings of the International Congress on the Dead Sea Scrolls, Madrid, 18–21 March 1991, ed. Julio C. Trebolle Barrera and Luis Vegas Montaner, STDJ 11 (Leiden: Brill, 1992), 1:291; E. P. Sanders, *Judaism: Practice and Belief, 63 BCE–66 CE* (London: SCM; Philadelphia: Trinity Press International, 1992), 376–77. The issue is complex and there are dissenting voices; for example, John Kampen argues that "no spiritualisation" of the temple took place; instead, the community prepared itself for the eschatological temple ("The Significance of the Temple in the Manuscripts of the Damascus Document," in *The Dead Sea Scrolls at Fifty: Proceedings of the 1997 Society of Biblical Literature Qumran Section Meetings*, ed. Robert Kugler and Eileen Schuller; SBLEJL 15 [Atlanta: Society of Biblical Literature, 1999], 2:185–97).

5. See also, for example, 1QS IX 5–6; translation from Elisha Qimron and James Charlesworth, "Rule of the Community," in *The Dead Sea Scrolls: Hebrew, Aramaic, and Greek Texts with English Translations*, ed. James Charlesworth et al., vol. 1, *Rule of the Community and Related Documents*, Princeton Theological Seminary Dead Sea Scrolls Project 1 (Tübingen: J. C. B. Mohr; Louisville, Ky.: Westminster John Knox, 1995), 35.

6. Several passages in D provide evidence of continuous association with the temple. CD XI 18–21 assumes that gifts were sent to the temple. There are laws in D concerning purity in connection with entering the temple (for example, CD XI 21–23; 4Q266 6 ii 3–10) and laws disqualifying priests who have lived abroad from serving in the temple (4Q266 5 ii).

7. "The Sons of Zadok" likely refers to the priestly leaders of the present community; see, for example, CD III 21–22; CD IV 3–4: "'The Sons of Zadok' are the chosen ones of Israel, those called by name, who stand in the end of days"; cf. 1QS V 8–10; IX 7; 1QSb III 22–28; 1QSa I 1–3.

8. See Aaron Shemesh, "'The Holy Angels Are in Their Council': The Exclusion of Deformed Persons from Holy Places in Qumranic and Rabbinic Literature," *DSD* 4 (1997): 179–206. Writing long before the publication of the 4QD fragments, Jerome Murphy-O'Connor argued that the bodily defects listed in 1QSa and 1QM were believed to offend the sight of the angels (*Paul and Qumran* [London: Geoffrey Chapman, 1968], 41–42).

9. The intercessory role of angels is stressed in *1 En.* 15:2-3.

10. Saul M. Olyan, "The Exegetical Dimensions of Restrictions of the Blind and the Lame in Texts from Qumran," *DSD* 8 (2001): 38–50.

11. See, for example, 1QS III 21–24; IV 16–23; 1QM XIII 11–18; 4Q266 1 a–b 1–5 (that is, the introduction to D); CD IV 12–13 (cf. VII 9–10; VIII 2–4); 4Q510 1 6–7; 4Q511 35 6–8; 1QHa XIII 32–36; 1Q27 1 i 5–7; 4Q444 I 4–7 ("until the completion of its dominion").

12. For an overview of the means of defense against evil in the Dead Sea Scrolls, see Armin Lange, "The Essene Position on Magic and Divination," in *Legal Texts and Legal Issues: Proceedings of the Second Meeting of the International Organization for Qumran Studies, Cambridge, 1995: Published in Honour of Joseph M. Baumgarten*, ed. Moshe J. Bernstein, Florentino García Martínez, and John Kampen, STDJ 23 (Leiden: Brill, 1997), 377–435; Philip S. Alexander, "The Demonology of the Dead Sea Scrolls," in *The Dead Sea Scrolls after Fifty Years*, ed. Peter W. Flint and James C. VanderKam, 2 vols. (Leiden: Brill, 1999), 2:331–52; idem, "'Wrestling against Wickedness in High Places': Magic in the Worldview of the Qumran Community," in *The Scrolls and the Scriptures: Qumran Fifty Years After*, ed. Stanely E. Porter and Craig A. Evans, JSPSup

26 (Sheffield: Sheffield Academic Press, 1997), 318–37; John Lyons and Andy Reimer, "The Demonic Virus and Qumran Studies: Some Preventive Measures," *DSD* 5 (1998): 16–32.

13. By "sectarian literature," I refer to those documents that are generally viewed as being composed within the sect behind the Scrolls; see Carol Newsom, "'Sectually Explicit' Literature from Qumran," in *The Hebrew Bible and Its Interpreters*, ed. William Propp, Baruch Halpern, and David Noel Freedman (Winona Lake, Ind.: Eisenbrauns, 1990), 167–87.

14. As Lange explains, prayer is the principal means of exorcism, whereas the laying on of hands is of secondary importance. He compares the description with *Jub.* 10:3-5 and 12:19-20, which are prayers for help against evil sprits ("Essene Position," 383).

15. The text may build on a version of Daniel 4 that featured Nabonidus rather than Nebuchadnezzar (Frank M. Cross, "Fragments of the Prayer of Nabonidas," *IEJ* 34 [1984]: 260–64). The text was first published by J. T. Milik in "'Prière de Nabonide' et autres écrits d'un cycle Daniel: Fragments Araméen de Qumrân 4," *RB* 63 (1956): 407–15.

16. Translation by Florentino García Martínez, *Qumran and Apocalyptic: Studies on the Aramaic Texts from Qumran* (Leiden: Brill, 1992), 121.

17. See Bilah Nitzan, "Hymns from Qumran—4Q510–511," in *Dead Sea Scrolls: Forty Years of Research*, ed. D. Dimant and U. Rappaport (Leiden: Brill, 1992), 53. Menahem Kister ("Demons, Theology and Abraham's Covenant [CD 16:4–6] and Related Texts," in Kugler and Schuller, *Dead Sea Scrolls at Fifty*, 167–84) proposes that this text as well as 4Q444 (see below) were used at the entrance rituals to expel evil spirits from those joining the sect.

18. Translation by Carol A. Newsom, "The Sage in the Literature of Qumran: The Functions of the Maśkîl," in *The Sage in Israel and the Ancient Near East*, ed. John G. Gammie and Leo G. Perdue (Winona Lake, Ind.: Eisenbrauns, 1990), 381.

19. In addition, Joseph M. Baumgarten suggests the reconstruction [*prwš hmšptym lmśkyl lb*] *ny 'wr*, "[The elaboration of the laws by the Sage for the s]ons of light," for the introduction to D (4Q266 1 a–b 1); see *The Damascus Document (4Q266–273): Qumran Cave 4, XIII*, DJD 18 (Oxford: Clarendon, 1996), 31.

20. See Alexander, "Wrestling," 320–21.

21. Nitzan, "Hymns," 54–63. The comparison is based on Aramaic incantations from amulets in J. Naveh and S. Shaked, *Amulets and Magic Bowls: Aramaic Incantations of Late Antiquity* (Jerusalem: Magnes Press, Hebrew University, 1985), 222–23, 237. Alexander also highlights the lack of "*materia magica*," such as magical formulae ("Wrestling," 323).

22. Alexander, "Wrestling," 323.

23. Ibid., 321.

24. Whereas Émile Puech ("11QPsApª: Un ritual d'exorcismes: Essai de reconstruction," *RevQ* 14 [1999]: 402) and Alexander ("Wrestling," 328) are in favor of sectarian origin, Lange argues against such identification ("Essene Position," 380).

25. As suggested by the original editor, J. van der Ploeg ("Le Psaume XCI dans une recension de Qumran," *RevQ* 72 [1965]: 210–17), these songs should possibly be identified with the four songs to be played for the "stricken" (*hpgw'ym*) that David composed (among his 4,050 compositions), according to 11QPsª (11Q5) XXVII 9–10.

26. The psalm is cited also in Jewish amulets; see Alexander, "Wrestling," 325; James A. Sanders, "A Liturgy for Healing the Stricken (11QPsAp^a = 11Q11)," in *The Dead Sea Scrolls: Hebrew, Aramaic, and Greek Texts with English Translations*, ed. James Charlesworth et al., *Pseudepigraphic and Non-Masoretic Psalms and Prayers*, Princeton Theological Seminary Dead Sea Scrolls Project 4A (Tübingen: J. C. B. Mohr; Louisville, Ky.: Westminster John Knox, 1997), 217.

27. Translation by García Martínez et al., *The Dead Sea Scrolls Reader*, ed. Donald W. Parry and Emanuel Tov (Leiden: Brill, 2005), 6:219. I am following their numbering of the columns, which differs from the numbering of J. A. Sanders.

28. Translation by J. A. Sanders, "Liturgy," 227. García Martínéz offers a different translation of lines 5–6 by reconstructing *bly*[*lh*] instead of *bly*['*l*]: "when] he comes to you in the nig[ht,] you will [s]ay to him . . ." (Parry and Tov, *Dead Sea Scrolls Reader*, 6:219).

29. Translation by M. Wise, M. Abegg, and E. Cook (Parry and Tov, *Dead Sea Scrolls Reader*, 6:215).

30. The text is published by Esther Chazon, "444. 4QIncantation," in *Qumran Cave 4, XX: Political and Liturgical Texts, Part 2*, ed. E. Chazon et al., DJD 29 (Oxford: Clarendon, 1999), 365–78.

31. Chazon lists six parallels between this short document and the *Songs of the Maskil*. Note particularly the unique phrase *w'ny myr'y 'l*, "And as for me, because of my fearing God" (alternatively, "terrifier of God"), which is also found in 4Q511 35 6. Reminiscent of 1QS IV 23, 4Q444 I 2–3 alludes to a struggle of spirits within a person (Chazon, "444. 4QIncantation," 370–71, 374).

32. Already J. T. Milik highlighted its character as a magic text ("Écrits préesséniens de Qumran: d'Hénoch à Amram," in *Qumran: sa piété, sa théologie et son milieu*, ed. M. Delcor, BETL 46 (Paris: Duculot, 1978], 91–106). See also Lange ("Essene Position," 386) and Alexander ("Demonology," 345; "Wrestling," 329).

33. Translation by D. Penney and M. Wise (Parry and Tov, *Dead Sea Scrolls Reader*, 6:227). For a critique of this reading and translation, see Joseph Naveh ("Fragments of an Aramaic Magic Book from Qumran," *IEJ* 4 [1998]: 252–61), who offers a slightly different reading and a new translation of the text.

34. The exact meaning of the male and female diseases/evil entities in line 5 is elusive; Naveh translates the line ". . . male and female crushing [ente]rs into the tooth, the blow of [the han]ds (?) of" ("Fragments," 256–57).

35. Similarly, Naveh holds that references to the two pairs of male and female evil entities show that the illnesses have been "demonized" ("Fragments," 260).

36. For a discussion of the widespread fears of demonic attacks in connection with childbirth, see Michael Wise and Douglas Penney, "By the Power of Beelzebub: An Aramaic Incantation Formula from Qumran (4Q560)," *JBL* 113 (1994): 634–35.

37. Noting that underworld creatures in Near Eastern mythology are represented as having wings, Joseph M. Baumgarten ("On the Nature of the Seductress in 4Q184," *RevQ* 15, nos. 57–58, special issue Mémorial Jean Starky [1991]: 140–41) argues that *bknpyh* (1 i 4) should be translated according to its literal meaning "in her wings" rather than "in her skirt" (so J. M. Allegro, *Qumrân*

Cave 4, 1 [4Q158–4Q186], DJD 5 [Oxford: Clarendon, 1968], 82); similarly Baumgarten (ibid.) suggests "horns" for *tw'pwt* (cf. Num 23:22; 24:8) instead of "depths" as Allegro translated the word.

38. In agreement with Baumgarten, Sidnie White Crawford points out that the female figure in 4Q184 appears to be more cosmic in scope than the simple "loose woman" of Proverbs 1–9 ("Lady Wisdom and Dame Folly at Qumran," in *Wisdom and Psalms: A Feminist Companion to the Bible*, ed. Athalya Brenner and Carole R. Fontaine [Sheffield: Sheffield Academic Press, 1998], 211).

39. Both Baumgarten ("On the Nature," 142) and White Crawford ("Lady Wisdom," 212) make this connection.

40. For a detailed discussion of this document, see Philip S. Alexander, "Incantations and Books of Magic," in Emil Schürer, *The History of the Jewish People in the Age of Jesus Christ (175 BC–AD 135)*, rev. and ed. Geza Vermes, Fergus Millar, and Martin Goodman, 3 vols. (Edinburgh: T&T Clark, 1986), 3.1:364–65; idem, "Physiognomy, Initiation, and Rank in the Qumran Community," in *Geschichte–Tradition–Reflexion: Festschrift für Martin Hengel*, ed. Hubert Cancik, Hermann Lichtenberger, and Peter Schäfer, 3 vols. (Tübingen: Mohr Siebeck, 1996), 1:385–94.

41. Translation by J. M Allegro and N. Gordon (Parry and Tov, *Dead Sea Scrolls Reader*, 6:223).

42. See, for example, 1QS III 17–19.

43. Alexander states, "I assume . . . that the scale did not include zero, and that, consequently, no one could be totally good or totally bad" ("Physiognomy," 387). This corresponds to 1QS IV 15–16, where the sharp dualistic division of humankind into two camps of good and evil in the previous is softened by the explanations that humans have "a portion of their [good and evil] divisions and walk in (both) their ways."

44. Deut 23:14 emphasizes the divine presence in the war camp: "Because the LORD your God travels along with your camp . . . therefore your camp must be holy, so that he may not see anything indecent among you and turn away from you."

45. Lawrence Schiffman states, "The description of the eschatological congregation in the *Rule of the Congregation* repeatedly mirrors the regulations of the sect for the present age found in other Qumran texts" (*The Eschatological Community of the Dead Sea Scrolls: A Study of the Rule of the Congregation*, SBLMS 38 [Atlanta: Scholars Press, 1989], 68).

46. D does not appear to reflect an isolated desert community. It refers to members living in camps (CD VII 6; IX 11; X 23; XII 23) and towns (CD XII 19) who are involved in trade (CD XII 8–11; XIII 15–16); own property, including slaves (CD XII 10; XIV 12–13); and have extensive contact with Gentiles (CD XII 8–11).

47. Although most translators render *hbnyhm* as "their sons," a good case can be made for a gender-inclusive translation, "their children" (see Cecilia Wassen, *Women in the Damascus Document*, Society of Biblical Literature Academia Biblica 21 [Atlanta: Society of Biblical Literature; Leiden: Brill, 2005], 134–38). The bottom of CD XV is heavily damaged. Nevertheless, the rules of exclusion in lines 15–17 can be restored on the basis of two copies of D from Cave 4, 4Q266 and 4Q270 (Baumgarten, *Damascus Document*, 178).

48. The summary statement at the end of the list explains that "none of these shall [come] into the midst of the congregation" (4Q266 8 i 8–9) (*'[l ybw] 'yš [m] 'lh 'l twk h'dh*). A comparison with the expressions in 1QSa indicates that the phrase pertains to a council meeting: see 1QSa II 5 (*btwk hdh*, "in the midst of congregation") and II 8 ([*b*]*twk 'dt* [*n*]*wšy hšm*, "[in] the midst of the congregation of the m[e]n of renown").

49. Scholars who argue that exclusion from the community is at stake include Florentino García Martínez and Julio Trebolle Barrera (*The People of the Dead Sea Scrolls* [Leiden: Brill, 1995], 156) and Michael Newton (*The Concept of Purity at Qumran and in the Letters of Paul* [Cambridge: Cambridge University Press, 1985], 50). In contrast, Schiffman (*Eschatological Community*, 38; "Purity and Perfection: Exclusion from the Council of the Community in the *Serekh Ha-'Edah*," in *Biblical Archaeology Today: Proceedings of the International Congress of Biblical Archaeology, April 1984* [Jerusalem: Israel Exploration Society 1985], 373–89) and Shemesh ("'Holy Angels,'" 180) claim that the exclusion concerns taking part in the assembly.

50. See CD XIII 6; XIV 15; 1QSa I 19–22; II 9b–10.

51. The words *'wyl wmšwg'* ("stupid and deranged") concern general madness or insanity that is expressed in deviant behavior, or "raving" (see Deut 28:28, where the root *šg'* refers to panic behavior, and 1 Sam 21:16, where David's deviant behavior—feigning madness by scratching marks on a door and letting his saliva run down his beard—is compared to that of "madmen" [*mšg'ym*] and is described as raving [*lhštg'*]). The word *'wyl*, "fool" or "foolish" (Prov 29:9), often refers to moral foolishness. In Hos 9:7, the adjective stands as parallelism to *mšwg'* ("mad").

52. 1QSa II 7 reads: *'yš zqn kwšl lblty hthzq btwk h'dh*, "a tottering old man who cannot maintain himself within the congregation." Translation from James Charlesworth and Loren Stuckenbruck, "Rule of the Congregation," in *The Dead Sea Scrolls: Hebrew, Aramaic, and Greek Texts with English Translations*, ed. James Charlesworth et al., vol. 1 (Tübingen: J. C. B. Mohr; Louisville, Ky.: Westminster John Knox, 1994). The issue is likely related to dementia or reduced cognitive abilities associated with age. The fragmentary text of the list in a copy of D, 4Q270 6 ii 10, adds three words in the middle of the line after the ending of the list in the line above: *m*] *'t wšny h' d*[*m*, "the years of man have been diminish[ed." In CD X 9, the same expression *m'tw ymw*, "his days have been diminished," is part of an explanation of why judges should not be older than sixty years. Perhaps 4Q270 6 ii 10 was part of an explanation of why some people became senile and physically impaired with old age and unfit to attend congregational meetings (Baumgarten, *Damascus Document*, 157). The category is thus closer to "mental disability" than age. Although elderly men are not part of the list in M, the previous segment specifies that sixty years is the upper age for anyone involved in the war (namely, "the inspectors of the camps").

53. In the Hebrew Bible, the word *pty* ("simpleminded") refers to a person who is easily enticed or deceived (for example, Prov 25:15; Jer 20:7, 10); *wšwgh*(from *šgh*, "to go astray") together with the word *pty* here alludes to someone who is easily misled and consequently takes the wrong path, that of sins and transgressions (cf. Prov 1:22). Elsewhere in D, the term is used primarily with regard to reduced cognitive ability; CD XIII 6 prescribes that a priest who is *pty* must be instructed by the Examiner; in CD XV 11, *pty* refers to someone who cannot answer questions at the entrance ritual. This meaning is evident also in 1QSa I 19b–22, which excludes

the "simpleminded" (*'yš pyty*) from full service in the congregation; a simple-minded person cannot "enter the lot to take his firm stand over the congregation of Israel" (*'l ybw' bgwrl lhtysb 'l 'dt yśr'l*) nor participate in deciding legal cases or other matters of the congregation or in battle. Instead, "he shall perform his service according to his ability."

54. A visible blemish refers to skin disease that does not cause impurity (Shemesh, "'Holy Angels,'" 196). For an in-depth analysis of each term of the list in 1QSa, see Schiffman, "Purity and Perfection," 373–89.

55. It is questionable whether the categories women and youths should be included in the list of excluded persons in 1QM (see discussion below).

56. "Mental disability" is here used in a wide sense to include those who are *mentally challenged* from birth, who in addition to reduced cognitive ability may also display abnormal behavior, as well as those who through severe *mental disorder*, such as schizophrenia, become "insane" (at one level, while maintaining their intelligence) and may also act in socially deviant ways. In ancient times, these types of mental disabilities were likely not distinguished. For specific meaning of the terms *'wyl wmšwg'* and *pty*, see above.

57. For this general belief, see Norman Cohn, *Cosmos, Chaos and That World to Come: The Ancient Roots of Apocalyptic Faith* (New Haven, Conn.: Yale University Press, 1993), 196.

58. The story as a whole has similarities to an exorcism story involving Apollonius of Tyana; see Todd Klutz, *The Exorcism Stories in Luke-Acts: A Socio-Stylistic Reading*, SNTSMS 129 (Cambridge: Cambridge University Press, 2004), 122–25.

59. Mark 3:11 gives a general description of unclean spirits causing people to act strangely (notice that the persons are not even mentioned; that is, they are fully possessed): "Whenever the unclean spirits saw him, they fell down before him and shouted, 'You are the Son of God!' But he [Jesus] sternly ordered them not to make him known."

60. See Mark 3:20-35; it is highly unlikely that the church would have made up such negative traditions about Jesus (for in-depth discussion about the authenticity of the passage, see Graham H. Twelftree, *Jesus the Exorcist: A Contribution to the Study of the Historical Jesus*, WUNT 2.54 [Tübingen: Mohr Siebeck, 1993], 99–113, 177).

61. All citations from the *Testaments of the Twelve Patriarchs* are from Howard Clark Kee, "Testaments of the Twelve Patriarchs," in *The Old Testament Pseudepigrapha*, ed. James H. Charlesworth, 2 vols. (Garden City, N.Y.: Doubleday, 1983), 1:782–828. See also *T. Reu.* 4:7, "For promiscuity has destroyed many. Whether a man is old, well born, rich, or poor, he brings on himself disgrace among mankind and provides Beliar with an opportunity to cause him to stumble" (cf. *T. Naph.* 3:1-2). I am very grateful to Anne Moore (University of Calgary) for sharing her unpublished work on demonic possession with me, in which she discusses the *Testaments of the Twelve Patriarchs*.

62. See, for example, *T. Jud.* 19:4—20:5; *T. Dan* 1:6; 2:1; *T. Sim.* 3:1. The spirits are collectively called "spirits of error" and interchangeably called "evil spirits" (*T. Sim.* 6:6-7). Frequently, specific spirits "overcome," "take over" a person, expressions that suggest possession (e.g., *T. Reu.* 5:3; cf. *T. Sim.* 3:2). At the same time, a struggle between the spirits takes place within each person (*T. Reu.* 2:1—3:9), and humans have a choice (*T. Jud.* 20:1; *T. Levi* 19:1-2). The concept of a struggle

between good and evil forces on a cosmic scale as well as within a person—who can be persuaded either way and has a choice—is remarkably similar to the dualistic worldview and anthropological reflections in 1QS III–IV.

63. See *T. Reu.* 4:11; *T. Sim.* 2:7; 5:3; *T. Levi* 3:3; 18:11-12; *T. Jud.* 19:4; *T. Dan* 3:6; 5:1, 6.

64. See, for example, 4QFlor (4Q174 1–2 i 7b–9).

65. Chazon refers to 4Q444 I 2, 4 and 4Q511 48–49+51 ii 4–5; in the context of frightening spirits, the latter reads, "The statutes of God are in my heart, and I prof[it] from all the wonders of man" ("444. 4QIncantation," 370–71, 374).

66. See also 1QS III 22–23; cf. the promise to "not keep Belial in my heart" in 1QS X 21.

67. Translation from Joseph Baumgarten and Daniel Schwartz, "Damascus Document (CD)," in *The Dead Sea Scrolls: Hebrew, Aramaic, and Greek Texts with English Translations*, ed. James Charlesworth et al., vol. 2, *Damascus Document, War Scroll, and Related Documents*, Princeton Theological Seminary Dead Sea Scrolls Project 2 (Tübingen: J. C. B. Mohr; Louisville, Ky.: Westminster John Knox, 1995).

68. Parts of the penal code are preserved in CD XIV 20–23; 4Q266 10 i 14–15; ii 1–15; 4Q269 11 i 4–8; ii 1–2; 4Q270 7 i 1–15. Penal codes appear also in S and the fragmentary text 4QMiscellaneous Rules (4Q265).

69. The term *hthrh* ("the purity") carries a wide range of meanings; see Friederich Avemarie, "'Tohorat Ha-rabbim' and 'Mashqeh Ha-rabbim': Jacob Licht Reconsidered," in Bernstein, García Martínez, and Kampen, *Legal Texts*, 215–29.

70. D imposes expulsion as the most severe penalty for offenses such as murmuring against the fathers (4Q270 7 i 13–14), despising the "law of the Many" (4Q270 7 i 11), and the enigmatic crime of fornicating with a wife (4Q270 7 i 12–13).

71. Translation from Qimron and Charlesworth, *Rule of the Community*.

72. Translation from Baumgarten, *Damascus Document*.

73. Baumgarten also points to a connection between this disease and transgressions ("The 4Q Zadokite Fragments on Skin Disease," *JJS* 41 [1990]: 162). See also discussion of Lyons and Reimer, "Demonic Virus," 30.

74. 4Q444 I 3. 1QS IV 20–21 states that God will destroy the spirit of deceit (*rwḥ 'wlh*) from a part in the body called *tkmy bśr*, which Elisha Qimron interprets as "blood vessels." Qimron clarifies that "*tkmym* is the part of the flesh invaded by the evil spirit" ("Notes on the 4Q Zadokite Fragments on Skin Disease," *JJS* 42 [1991]: 258). Similarly, 4Q511 18–19 4 locates *'wlh* (preceded by a lacuna) in *tkmy bśry* (cf. 4Q511 48–49+51 3–4). As Chazon explains ("444. 4QIncantation," 376), the association between something evil and *tkmy bśr/tkmy* is apparent also in 1QHᵃ XV 4; XIII 28; and likely 4QHᵇ 10 8; 1Q36 (1QHymns) 14 2.

75. Conversely, *rwḥ ḥḥyym* ("the spirit of life") restores the skin to life, which likely refers to the flow of blood that pulsates; the view that connects blood with life-giving spirit is consistent with Gen 9:3-4; see Baumgarten, "4Q Zadokite Fragments," 163.

76. Luke 4:39 (the parallels in Matt 8:15 and Mark 1:31 instead read "the fever left her"). The similarity between 4Q560 and Luke is highlighted by Wise and Penney ("By the Power of Beelzebub," 642) as well as by Klutz (*Exorcism Stories*, 76–77).

77. 1QapGen XX 29 equates the evil spirit with the disease: "The plague was removed from him; the evil [spirit] was banished [from him] and he recovered" (translation by Florentino García Martínez and Eibert J. C. Tigchelaar, *The Dead Sea Scrolls Study Edition* [Leiden: Brill, 1997], 1:43).

78. Cf. Jesus' command in Mark 9:25: "You spirit that keeps this boy from speaking and hearing, I command you, come out of him, and never enter him again!"

79. See 1QSa II 3–4; 1QM VII 5–6. In addition, M specifically prohibits a man who has a nocturnal emission from taking part in the battle (line 6).

80. For example, 11QPs^a XIX 5; 4Q444 I 8. A variation is *rwḥ ndh*, "spirit of impurity" (1QS IV 22).

81. Klutz also highlights the immediate context of impurity (the hemorrhaging woman and the corpse in Luke 8:40-56). Other examples of the demonology-impurity interface include Jesus' expelling an "impure spirit" from the daughter of a Gentile woman (Mark 7:24-30) after a segment on ritual purity (7:1-23); see Klutz, *Exorcism Stories*, 125–37.

82. Ibid., 135–36.

83. Alexander, "Demonology," 350; Mary Douglas, *Purity and Danger: An Analysis of the Concepts of Pollution and Taboo* (London: Ark, 1988).

84. Jacob Milgrom, "4QTohora^a: An Unpublished Qumran Text on Purities," in *Time to Prepare the Way in the Wilderness: Papers on the Qumran Scrolls*, ed. Lawrence Schiffman and Devorah Dimant (Leiden: Brill, 1995), 59–68.

85. Ibid., 66.

86. Translation (with minor alterations) from Qimron and Charlesworth, "Rule of the Community," 19.

87. For example, 1QS IV 18-23; V 13–14, 19; 1QH^a XIX 10–11; it is also revealing that transgressors are penalized by exclusion from "the purity/ies" in the penal codes in S (1QS VI 24–VII 25), D (4Q266 10 i 14–ii 1–15; 4Q270 7 i), and possibly in 4QMiscellanous Rules (4Q265 4 i 1–12; ii 1–2; a reference to "the purity" is reconstructed in 4 i 7). For a discussion of the association between sin and impurity, see, for example, Jonathan Klawans, *Impurity and Sin in Ancient Judaism* (New York: Oxford University Press, 2000), 67–91; Baumgarten, "4Q Zadokite Fragments"; García Martínez and Trebolle Barrera, *People*, 152–57.

88. The oath to return to the Torah of Moses clearly refers to the oath taken at the entrance ritual, which is referred to as "the oath of the covenant which Moses made with Israel, the cove[na]nt to re[turn t]o the Torah of Moses" (CD XVI 4–5).

89. Kister ("Demons," 167–84) points out that a member who fails to live according to the laws, to "fulfill his word" (CD XVI 5), will likely come under Belial's sway again, as CD XII 1–6 indicates.

90. Translation by Geza Vermes, *The Complete Dead Sea Scrolls in English* (New York: Penguin, 1997), 115.

91. Cf. 1QH^a XI 21–22: "The depraved spirit you have purified from great offence so that he can take a place with the host of the holy ones, and can enter in communion with the congregation of the sons of heaven" (translation by García Martínez, *Dead Sea Scrolls Study Edition*, 1:165). For an analysis of this hymn, see James Davila, "The Hodayot Hymnist and the Four Who Entered

Paradise," *RevQ* 17, nos. 65–68, special issue, J. T. Milik Festschrift (1996), 457–78. The very real presence of angels in the community is expressed elsewhere in the sectarian literature; for example, 1QM VII 6; IX 10b–11a ("hearers of glorious voices, seers of holy angels"); 1QH^a XIV 13; XIX 11–12; 4QH^a (4Q427) 7 i 6–13; 4Q181 1 3–4 (4QAges of Creation B). The topic of human and angelic communion has been thoroughly explored; see, for example, Björn Frennesson, *"In a Common Rejoicing": Liturgical Communion with Angels in Qumran*, Studia Semitica Upsaliensia 14 (Uppsala: University of Uppsala Press, 1999).

92. Frennesson emphasizes liturgy, the assembly, and the final war as three recurring contexts for the fellowship between humans and angels (*"In a Common Rejoicing,"* 39). The future union between angels and humans is apparent in 11QSefer ha-Milhamah (11Q14) 1 ii 14–15: "and there will be no plag]ue in your land, for God is with you and [his holy] angels [ar]e [standing] in your congregation and his holy name is invoked over you" (translation by F. García Martínez, E. J. C. Tigchelaar, and A. S. van der Woude, *Qumran Cave 11, II: [11Q2–18, 11Q20–31]*, DJD 23 [Oxford: Clarendon, 1998], 248). I am indebted to Jonathan Norton (Oxford University) for bringing this passage to my attention.

93. Carol Newsom, "He Has Established for Himself Priests," in *Archaeology and History in the Dead Sea Scrolls: The New York Conference in Memory of Yigael Yadin*, ed. Lawrence H. Schiffman, JSPSup 8 (Sheffield: JSOT Press, 1990), 115.

94. Joseph M. Baumgarten, "The Qumran Sabbath Shirot and Rabbinic Merkabah Traditions," *RevQ* 13 (1988): 201.

95. Translation by Bilhah Nitzan, *Qumran Prayer and Religious Poetry*, STDJ 12 (Leiden: Brill, 1994), 270.

96. Frennesson, *"In a Common Rejoicing,"* 54. His overview of liturgical texts includes *Hodayot* (1QH, 4QH), the *Community Rule* (1QS), 4Q503 (4QDaily Prayers), 4Q510–511 (4QSongs of the Maskil), 4Q504–506 (4QWords of the Luminaries^{a-c}), 4Q286–290 (4QBlessings), 1QSb (*Rule of the Blessings*), 1QM (*War Scroll*), and *Songs of the Sabbath Sacrifice* (4Q400–407).

97. Related to this view is the belief that a few, elect persons such as Moses (evident in 4Q374 [4QDiscourse on the Exodus/Conquest Tradition] 2 ii) and the high priest (1QSb IV 24–28) have actually been elevated to the same status as angels. On this theme, see John J. Collins, "Powers in Heaven: God, Gods, and Angels in the Dead Sea Scrolls," in *Religion in the Dead Sea Scrolls*, ed. John J. Collins and Robert Kugler, Studies in the Dead Sea Scrolls and Related Literature (Grand Rapids: Eerdmans, 2000), 22–23; Crispin Fletcher-Louis, "Some Reflections on Angelomorphic Humanity Texts among the Dead Sea Scrolls," *DSD* 7 (2000): 292–312.

98. Devorah Dimant, "Men as Angels: The Self-Image of the Qumran Community," in *Religion and Politics in the Ancient Near East*, ed. Adele Berlin, Studies and Texts in Jewish History and Culture (Bethesda: University Press of Maryland, 1996), 93–103.

99. Collins, "Powers in Heaven," 24. Daniel J. Harrington notes that the community's aspiration of living an angelic life is reflected in the wisdom text 4QSapiential Work A (4Q416–4Q418) ("Wisdom at Qumran," in *The Community of the Renewed Covenant: The Notre Dame Symposium on the Dead Sea Scrolls*, ed. Eugene Ulrich and James C. VanderKam (Notre Dame: University of Notre Dame Press, 1994], 57–58).

100. Dimant, "Men as Angels," 96.

101. Since some liturgical texts clearly assume the presence of angels, it is not inconceivable that the impure and blemished would be prohibited from attending certain forms of worship services.

102. Parry and Tov, *Dead Sea Scrolls Reader*.

Chapter 9: The Search for the Common Judaic Understanding of God's Kingship

1.   This list is only representative of the possible references to kingdom and kingship found in association with God.

2.   Marc Zvi Brettler, *God Is King: Understanding an Israelite Metaphor*, JSOTSup 76 (Sheffield: JSOT Press, 1989), 160.

3.   Odo Camponovo, *Königtum, Königsherrschaft und Reich Gottes in den früjüdischen Schiften*, OBO 58 (Göttingen: Vandenhoeck & Ruprecht, 1984).

4.   Brettler's *God Is King* is the most extensive. It focuses on how concepts and ideas connected with the Israelite monarchy were transferred onto God to create the metaphor "God is king." Marco Treves suggests that the kingdom of God is an alternative form of leadership advocated in reaction to the abuses associated with the human dynasties of the Israelites and foreign monarchs ("The Reign of God in the O.T.," *VT* 19 [1969]: 230–43). There are several studies that assume that the kingship of God was a common idea in the ancient Near East that was ritualized through various practices, including the Babylonian Marduk feast. The assumption is that Israelites adopted both the ritual and the mythology, adapting it—to a small degree—for Yahweh. Sigmund Mowinckel, *The Psalms in Israel's Worship*, trans. D. R. Ap-Thomas, 2 vols. (Oxford: Blackwell, 1961), 1:130–36; A. R. Johnson, *Sacral Kingship in Ancient Israel*, 2nd ed. (Cardiff: University of Wales, 1967), 35–53.

5.   Norman Perrin, *Jesus and the Language of the Kingdom: Symbol and Metaphor in the New Testament Interpretation* (Philadelphia: Fortress Press, 1976), 29.

6.   Ibid., 30.

7.   Ibid.

8.   T. Francis Glasson, "What Is Apocalyptic?" *NTS* 27 (1980–81): 103; David Hill, "Towards an Understanding of the 'Kingdom of God,'" *IBS* 3 (1981): 64; Günter Klein, "The Biblical Understanding of the 'Kingdom of God,'" *Int* 26 (1972): 397; Michael Lattke, "On the Jewish Background of the Synoptic Concept, 'Kingdom of God,'" in *The Kingdom of God in the Teaching of Jesus*, ed. Bruce Chilton, IRT 5 (Philadelphia: Fortress Press, 1984), 78–88.

9.   Philip Wheelwright, *Metaphor and Reality* (Bloomington: Indiana University Press, 1962), 93.

10. Dan O. Via, "Kingdom and Parable: The Search for a New Grasp of Symbol, Metaphor and Myth," review of *Jesus and the Language of the Kingdom of God in New Testament Interpretation*, by Norman Perrin, *Int* 31 (1977): 183.

11. James D. G. Dunn, *Christianity in the Making*, vol. 1, *Jesus Remembered* (Grand Rapids: Eerdmans, 2003), 401–4, 484–87.

12. Gerd Theissen and Annette Merz, *The Historical Jesus: A Comprehensive Guide*, trans. John

Bowden (Philadelphia: Fortress Press, 1998), 245. Theissen and Merz refer to the kingdom of God as a metaphor throughout their book.

13. Jerome F. D. Creach, *Yahweh as Refuge and the Editing of the Hebrew Psalter*, JSOTSup 217 (Sheffield: Sheffield Academic Press, 1996), 55–56; James Luther Mays, "The Language of the Reign of God," *Int* 47 (1993): 118; Tryggve N. D. Mettinger, *In Search of God: The Meaning and Message of the Everlasting Names*, trans. Frederick H. Cryer (Philadelphia: Fortress Press, 1987), 92–93; Gary V. Smith, "The Concept of God/Gods as Kings in the Ancient Near East and the Bible," *TJ* 3 (1982): 33–37; Janet Martin Soskice, *Metaphor and Religious Language* (Oxford: Clarendon, 1985), 43–61; Nelly Stienstra, *YHWH Is the Husband of His People: Analysis of a Biblical Metaphor with Special Reference to Translation* (Kampen: Kok Pharos, 1993), 67–69; Michael Wolter, "Was heisst nun Gottes Reich?" *ZNW* 86 (1995): 5; John D. W. Watts, "Images of Yahweh: God in the Prophets," in *Studies in Old Testament Theology*, ed. Robert L. Hubbard Jr., Robert K. Johnston, and Robert P. Meye (Dallas: Word, 1992), 135; Hans Weder, *Die Gleichnisse Jesu als Metaphern: Traditions- und redaktionsgeschichtliche Analysen und Interpretationen* (Göttingen: Vandenhoeck & Ruprecht, 1978).

14. Bruce D. Chilton rejects the classification of the kingdom of God as either a symbol or a metaphor, because each category carries with it "assumptions in regard to accomplished speech, and particularly the creativity of the speakers." See "The Kingdom of God in Recent Discussion," in *Studying the Historical Jesus: Evaluations of the State of Current Research*, ed. Bruce Chilton and Craig A. Evans (Leiden: Brill, 1994), 271. Chilton seems to be referring to the idea of metaphor as a decorative or rhetorical form of speech.

15. I. A. Richards, *The Philosophy of Rhetoric* (Oxford: Oxford University Press, 1936), 93.

16. Max Black, *Models and Metaphors: Studies in Language and Philosophy* (Ithaca, N.Y.: Cornell University Press), 33.

17. Ibid., 40.

18. Gören Eidevall, *Grapes in the Desert: Metaphors, Models and Themes in Hosea 4–14* ConBOT 43 (Stockholm: Almqvist & Wiksell International, 1996), 29. Eidevall makes direct reference to Brettler's work and criticizes Brettler's tendency to remove the "God is king" metaphor from its literary context. David Aaron has a similar criticism (*Biblical Ambiguities: Metaphor, Semantics and Divine Imagery*, Brill Reference Library of Ancient Judaism 4 (Leiden: Brill, 2001), 35–41.

19. Brettler, *God Is King*, 160–61.

20. Ibid., 162.

21. Ibid., 165.

22. The significant role of Exod 15:1b-18 in the discussion of the kingship of God is evident in several studies, including Martin Buber, *The Kingship of God*, trans. Richard Scheimann (1956; reprint, New York: Harper & Row, 1967), 108–35; Susan M. Piggot, "The Kingdom of the Warrior God: The Old Testament and the Kingdom of Yahweh," *SwJT* 40 (1998): 7–8; Perrin, *Jesus and the Language*, 21–22.

23. Theorists propose that metaphors have both an informative function, which presents a new conceptual framework for understanding reality, and a performative function, which influences

the audience's attitude and results (if successful) in particular action based on this new framework. Kirsten Nielsen, *There Is Hope for a Tree: The Tree as Metaphor in Isaiah*, trans. Christine Crowley and Frederick Crowley, JSOTSup 65 (Sheffield: JSOT Press, 1989), 47.

24. Thomas B. Dozeman, *God on the Mountain: A Study of the Redaction, Theology and Canon in Exodus 19–24*, SBLMS 37 (Atlanta: Scholars Press, 1989), 39.

25. Ibid., 94–95.

26. The association of the Torah with Yahweh's sovereignty over Israel is *not* due to the judicial semantic field associated with kings. One of the major roles of kings in the ancient Near East was as judge; however, the creation of a law code was a divine task. Keith W. Whitelam, *The Just King: Monarchical Judicial Authority in Ancient Israel*, JSOTSup 12 (Sheffield: JSOT Press, 1979), 217–18. Therefore, the inclusion of the Torah derives from the semantic field associated with the God of the exodus.

27. Jon D. Levenson (*Sinai and Zion: An Entry into the Jewish Bible* [Minneapolis: Winston, 1985], 70–75) suggests that the people of the ancient Near East would have been very familiar with two types of kings. The first would be their city-state or national king, and the second would be an overlord or "suzerain" to whom the other kings were subservient.

28. Brettler, *God Is King*, 52–53.

29. Ibid., 146–47. These psalms were once classified as Enthronement Psalms and situated within a cultic performance of Yahweh's kingship. However, this classification has been challenged on numerous points. For a review of the discussion, see Brettler, *God Is King*, 123–56; Allan Rosengren Petersen, *The Royal God: Enthronement Festivals in Ancient Israel and Ugarit?* JSOTSup 259 (Sheffield: Sheffield Academic Press, 1998). Further, this study concurs with Brettler that the absence of eschatological language and events and the *yaqtul* form of the verbs prevent an eschatological reading of the psalms (*God Is King*, 150).

30. Jonathan Magonet, "Some Concentric Structures in Psalms," *HeyJ* 23 (1982): 367.

31. Wilfred G. E. Watson, "Reversed Rootplay in Ps 145," *Bib* 62 (1981): 101–2.

32. Whitelam (*Just King*) noted that care for the underprivileged was one of the ideas associated with the ancient Near Eastern view of a king's justice.

33. This passage is extant only in the Ethiopic version of *Jubilees*.

Chapter 10: "Torah Shall Go Forth from Zion": Common Judaism and the Greek Bible

1. E. P. Sanders, *Judaism: Practice and Belief, 63 BCE–66 CE* (London: SCM; Philadelphia: Trinity Press International, 1992; corrected ed., 1994).

2. Michael A. Fishbane, *Biblical Interpretation in Ancient Israel* (Oxford: Clarendon, 1985), 3.

3. As developed in M. Halbertal, *People of the Book: Canon, Meaning, and Authority* (Cambridge, Mass.: Harvard University Press, 1997), esp. 1–10.

4. For contrasting views, see M. Finkelberg, "Homer as a Foundation Text," in *Homer, the Bible, and Beyond: Literary and Religious Canons in the Ancient World*, ed. M. Finkelberg and Guy G. Stroumsa, Jerusalem Studies in Religion and Culture 2 (Leiden: Brill, 2003); and Philip S. Alexander, "'Homer the Prophet of All' and 'Moses Our Teacher': Late Antique Exegesis of the

Homeric Epics and of the Torah of Moses," in *The Use of Sacred Books in the Ancient World*, ed. L. V. Rutgers et al., Contributions to Biblical Exegesis and Theology 22 (Leuven: Peeters, 1998), 127–42.

5.   But for a carefully nuanced brief sketch of the picture in the Greco-Roman Diaspora, see J. M. G. Barclay, *Jews in the Mediterranean Diaspora: From Alexander to Trajan (323 BCE–117 CE)* (Edinburgh: T&T Clark, 1996), 424–26.

6.   Emil Schürer, *The History of the Jewish People in the Age of Jesus Christ (175 B.C.–A.D. 135): A New English Version*, rev. and ed. Fergus Millar, Geza Vermes, and Martin Goodman (Edinburgh: T&T Clark, 1986), 3.1:474.

7.   Victor Tcherikover, *Hellenistic Civilization and the Jews* (Philadelphia: Jewish Publication Society; Jerusalem: Magnes Press, Hebrew University, 1959), 348.

8.   Arnaldo Momigliano, *The Classical Foundations of Modern Historiography*, Sather Classical Lectures 54 (Berkeley: University of California Press, 1990), 25.

9.   Martin Hengel, *Judaism and Hellenism: Studies in Their Encounter in Palestine during the Early Hellenistic Period*, trans. J. Bowden, 2 vols. (London: SCM, 1974).

10.   The structure emerges clearly through perusal of the table of contents of Schürer, *History*.

11.   Robert Doran, "The Jewish Hellenistic Historians before Josephus," *ANRW* 2.20.1 (1986): 248.

12.   Carl Holladay, "Hellenism in the Fragmentary Hellenistic Jewish Authors: Resonance and Resistance," in *Shem in the Tents of Japhet: Essays on the Encounter of Judaism and Hellenism*, ed. J. L. Kugel, JSJSup 74 (Leiden: Brill, 2002), 66–91; P. W. van der Horst, "The Interpretation of the Bible by the Minor Hellenistic Jewish Writers," in *Mikra: Text, Translation, Reading and Interpretation of the Hebrew Bible in Ancient Judaism and Early Christianity*, CRINT, Section 2, Literature of the Jewish People in the Period of the Second Temple and the Talmud (Assen: Van Gorcum, 1988), 519–46; reprinted in P. W. van der Horst, *Essays on the Jewish World of Early Christianity* (Freiburg, Schweiz: Universitätsverlag; Göttingen: Vandenhoeck & Ruprecht, 1990), 187–219.

13.   See B. Z. Wacholder, *Eupolemus: A Study of Judaeo-Greek Literature* (Cincinnati: Hebrew Union College, Jewish Institute of Religion, 1974).

14.   Emanuel Tov, *The Greek and Hebrew Bible: Collected Essays on the Septuagint*, VTSup 72 (Leiden: Brill, 1999), 183–94.

15.   As James Barr pointed out. See Barr's critique of Tov: J. Barr, "Did the Greek Pentateuch Really Serve as a Dictionary for the Translation of the Later Books?" in *Hamlet on a Hill: Semitic and Greek Studies Presented to Professor T. Muraoka on the Occasion of His Sixty-fifth Birthday*, ed. M. F. J. Baasten and W. T. van Peursen, Orientalia Lovaniensia Analecta 118 (Leuven: Peeters, 2003), 523–44; see ch. 5, n. 94.

16.   As revealed by Dominique Barthélemy (*Les devanciers d'Aquila: première publication intégrale du texte des fragments du Dodécaprophéton*, VTSup 10 [Leiden: Brill, 1963]), whose central conclusion on the scribal activity involved is still widely accepted, although with an earlier date for the documents than he proposed. For the authoritative publication, see P. J. Parsons, "The Scripts

and Their Date," in *The Greek Minor Prophets Scroll from Nahal Hever (8HeXIIgr)*, ed. Emanuel Tov, Robert A. Kraft, and P. J. Parsons, DJD 8 (Oxford: Clarendon, 1990), 19–26. The succinct account of J. M. Dines is a good guide (*The Septuagint*, Understanding the Bible and Its World [London: T&T Clark, 2004], 3–4, 81–84).

17. S. J. K. Pearce, "King Moses: Notes on Philo's Portrait of Moses as an Ideal Leader in the Life of Moses," in *The Greek Strand in Islamic Political Thought: Proceedings of the Conference Held at the Institute for Advanced Study, Princeton, 16–27 June, 2003*, ed. P. Crone, D. Gutras, and E. Shütrumpf, Mélanges de l'Université Saint-Joseph 57 (Beirut: L'Université Saint-Joseph, 2004), 37–40; F. Calabi, *The Language and the Law of God: Interpretation and Politics in Philo of Alexandria*, South Florida Studies in the History of Judaism 188; Studies in Philo of Alexandria and Mediterranean Antiquity (Atlanta: Scholars Press, 1998), 2–9.

18. On the figure of Moses in general: J. G. Gager, *Moses in Greco-Roman Paganism*, SBLMS 16 (Nashville: Abingdon, 1972); on Josephus's representation of Moses, see the chapter on Josephus's Moses in Tessa Rajak, "Flavius Josephus: Jewish History and the Greek World" (Ph.D. diss., University of Oxford, 1975), available online at http://pace.cns.yorku.ca/York/york/tei/jewish_history?id=50; and Louis H. Feldman, *Jew and Gentile in the Ancient World: Attitudes and Interactions from Alexander to Justinian* (Princeton: Princeton University Press, 1993), 374–442.

19. Discussion by van der Horst, "Interpretation," 519–46 (= idem, *Essays*, 187–219).

20. For an extensive and original study of this community, see J. E. Taylor, *Jewish Women Philosophers of First-Century Alexandria: Philo's 'Therapeutae' Reconsidered* (Oxford: Oxford University Press, 2003).

21. Discussion in Tessa Rajak, *The Jewish Dialogue with Greece and Rome: Studies in Cultural and Social Interaction*, AGJU 48 (Leiden: Brill, 2000), 11–37.

22. On what is implied by the Greek name for the work *Archaiologia*, see Rajak, *Jewish Dialogue*, 241–55.

23. Text and commentary in P. W. van der Horst, *The Sentences of Pseudo-Phocylides*, SVTP 4 (Leiden: Brill, 1978). The best short discussion is John J. Collins, *Between Athens and Jerusalem: Jewish Identity in the Hellenistic Diaspora*, 2nd ed. (Grand Rapids: Eerdmans, 2000), 168–74, built around Collins's conception of the "common ethic."

24. Pseudo-Phocylides v. 12, *martyrien pseudē*; cf. Exod 20:16; Deut 19:13-19; Prov 21:28.

25. Pseudo-Phocylides v. 13; cf. Deut 25:14; Lev 19:35.

26. See van der Horst (*Sentences*, 122), who writes, "The LXX origin of these verses is very clear."

27. This line of interpretation has been intriguingly developed by J. Mélèze-Modrzejewski ("Jewish Law and Hellenistic Practice in the Light of Greek Papyri from Egypt," in *An Introduction to the History and Sources of Jewish Law*, ed. N. Hecht [Oxford: Clarendon, 1996], 75–99; idem, "La Septante comme Nomos: Comment la Torah est devenue une 'loi civique' pour les Juifs d'Egypte," *Annali di Science Religiose* 2 [1997]: 143–58) on the basis of papyrological material and parallels from Hellenistic Egypt.

28. M. S. Cowey and K. Maresch, *Urkunden des Politeuma der Juden von Herakleopolis (144/3–133/2 V. Chr.) (P. Polit. Iud.): Papyrus aus den Sammlungen von Heidelberg, Köln, München*

und Wien, Abhandlungen der Nordrhein-Westfälischen Akademie der Wissenschaften, Sonderreihe Papyrologica Coloniensia 29 (Wiesbaden: Westdeutscher Verlag, 2001), together with the long review by Sylvie Honigman, "The Jewish 'Politeuma' at Heracleopolis," *Scripta Classica Israelica* 21 (2003): 251–66.

29. For a comprehensive reassessment of the inscription, see John S. Kloppenborg, "Dating Theodotos (*CIJ* II 1404)," *JJS* 51 (2000): 243–80.

30. See P. W. van der Horst, "Was the Synagogue a Place of Sabbath Worship before 70 CE?" in *Japheth in the Tents of Shem: Studies on Jewish Hellenism in Antiquity* (Leuven: Peeters, 2002), 55–82, arguing against Heather McKay, *Sabbath and the Synagogue: The Question of Sabbath Worship in Ancient Juaism* (Leiden: Brill, 1994), on the interpretation of the early evidence for Sabbath Torah reading. On synagogue shrines as a unifying (if not ubiquitous) feature and on the commonalities of ancient synagogues in general, see L. V. Rutgers, *The Hidden Heritage of Diaspora Judaism*, Contributions to Biblical Exegesis and Theology 20 (Leuven: Peeters, 1998), chs. 4 and 5.

31. Alan Mendelson, *Secular Education in Philo of Alexandria*, Monographs of the Hebrew Union College 7 (Cincinnati: Hebrew Union College Press, 1982), xx.

32. See Halbertal, *People of the Book*, 6–8.

33. Fishbane (*Biblical Interpretation*) offers the classic close reading of how this operated.

34. Guy G. Stroumsa, "The Christian Hermeneutical Revolution and Its Double Helix," in *The Use of Sacred Books in the Ancient World*, ed L. V. Rutgers, Contributions to Biblical Exegesis and Theology 22 (Leuven: Peeters, 1998), 10; and cf. his "Early Christianity—A Religion of the Book?" in *Homer, the Bible, and Beyond: Literary and Religious Canons in the Ancient World*, ed. M. Finkelberg and Guy G. Stroumsa, Jerusalem Studies in Religion and Culture 2 (Leiden: Brill, 2003), 53–73.

35. I do not intend by either of these terms to refer to what Robert Alter (*Canon and Creativity: Modern Writing and the Authority of Scripture* [New Haven, Conn.: Yale University Press, 2000], 5) means by a "textual community," applying the term not to any group located in one place at one moment in time, but to a transhistorical community united by its high valuation and use—whatever sort of use—of a particular text or texts.

36. Fishbane, *Biblical Interpretation*, 3.

37. Michael A. Fishbane, "Use, Authority and Interpretation of Mikra at Qumran," in *Mikra: Text, Translation, Reading and Interpretation of the Hebrew Bible in Ancient Judaism and Early Christianity*, ed. M. J. Mulder and H. Sysling, CRINT, Section 2: Literature of the Jewish People in the Period of the Second Temple and the Talmud 1 (Assen: Van Gorcum, 1988), 340.

38. Menahem Kister, "A Common Heritage: Biblical Interpretation at Qumran and Its Implications," in *Biblical Perspectives: Early Use and Interpretation of the Bible in Light of the Dead Sea Scrolls: Proceedings of the First International Symposium of the Orion Center for the Study of the Dead Sea Scrolls and Associated Literature, 12–14 May 1996*, ed. M. E. Stone and E. G. Chazon, STDJ 28 (Leiden: Brill, 1998), 101–11.

39. For a strong formulation of this position, see now J. G. Campbell, "4QMMT(d) and the Tripartite Canon," *JJS* 51 (2000): 181–90.

40. See, for example, the Habakkuk commentary, 1QpHab 7:4–5.

41. Krister Stendahl, *The School of St. Matthew and Its Use of the Old Testament*, 2nd ed. (Philadelphia: Fortress Press, 1968), 40.

42. H. B. Swete, *An Introduction to the Old Testament in Greek*, rev. R. R. Otley (Cambridge: Cambridge University Press, 1914), 391–92.

43. A. Wifstrand, "Luke and the Septuagint" (in Swedish), *STK* 6 (1940): 243–62; translated in A. Wifstrand, *Epochs and Style: Selected Writings on the New Testament, Greek Language and Greek Culture in the Post-Classical Era*, ed. L. Rydbeck and S. E. Porter, trans. D. Searby. WUNT 2.179 (Tübingen: Mohr Siebeck, 2005). See also Loveday C. A. Alexander, "Septuaginta, Fachprosa, Imitatio: Albert Wifstrand and the Language of Luke-Acts," in idem, *Acts in Its Ancient Literary Context: A Classicist Looks at the Acts of the Apostles*, Library of New Testament Studies 298 (London: T&T Clark International, 2005), 231–52.

44. Swete, *Introduction*, 26.

45. E. E. Ellis, "Biblical Interpretation in the New Testament Church," in *Mikra: Text, Translation, Reading and Interpretation of the Hebrew Bible in Ancient Judaism and Early Christianity*, ed. M. J. Mulder and H. Sysling, CRINT, Section 2: Literature of the Jewish People in the Period of the Second Temple and the Talmud 1 (Assen: Van Gorcum, 1988), 692.

46. This was pointed out to me by Ed Sanders. Cf. J. R. Wagner, *Heralds of the Good News: Isaiah and Paul "in Concert" in the Letter to the Romans*, NovTSup 101 (Leiden: Brill, 2002), 33–39, on the "hearer competence" of Paul's Roman recipients.

47. George J. Brooke, "The Canon within the Canon at Qumran and in the New Testament," in *The Scrolls and the Scriptures: Qumran Fifty Years After*, ed. Stanley E. Porter and Craig A. Evans, JSPSup 26 (Sheffield: Sheffield Academic Press, 1997), 242–66.

48. Devorah Dimant, "The Problem of Non-translated Biblical Greek," in *VI Congress of the International Organization for Septuagint and Cognate Studies, Jerusalem, 1986*, ed. C. E. Cox, SBLSCS 23 (Atlanta: Scholars Press, 1987), 3–6.

49. Recently explored in a new and fruitful way by N. Hacham, "The Letter of Aristeas: A New Exodus Story?" *JSJ* 36 (2005): 1–20.

50. Fishbane, "Use, Authority and Interpretation," 356.

51. A point effectively demonstrated throughout Barclay, *Jews in the Mediterranean Diaspora.*

52. Holladay, "Hellenism."

53. Cf. the remarks of van der Horst ("Interpretation") and Doran ("Jewish Hellenistic Historians").

54. Chaim Rabin, "The Translation Process and the Character of the Septuagint," *Textus* 6, (1968): 21.

Chapter 11: Aristeas or Haggadah: Talmudic Legend and the Greek Bible in Palestinian Judaism

1. E. P. Sanders, *Judaism: Practice and Belief, 63 BCE–66 CE* (1992; corrected ed., London: SCM; Philadelphia: Trinity Press International, 1994), 400.

2. Ibid., 329–30.

3.   Ibid., 10–11.

4.   An excellent analytical survey of the development of this legend may be found in Abraham Wasserstein and David Wasserstein, *The Legend of the Septuagint: From Classical Antiquity to Today* (Cambridge: Cambridge University Press, 2006).

5.   Emanuel Tov, "The Rabbinic Tradition Concerning the 'Alterations' Inserted into the Greek Pentateuch and Their Relation to the Original Text of the LXX," *JSJ* 15 (1984): 65–89.

6.   Ibid., 76. This section underwent considerable revision in the reissue of the article in Emanuel Tov, *The Greek and Hebrew Bible: Collected Essays on the Septuagint*, VTSup 72 (Leiden, Boston, and Cologne: Brill, 1999), 10.

7.   Some texts add the gloss: "And they did not write 'created them.'"

8.   An interesting attempt to interpret this variant in terms of an attested LXX reading may be found in Abraham Geiger, *Urschrift und Übersetzungen der Bibel, in ihrer Abhängigkeit von der innern Entwicklung des Judentums*, 2nd ed. (Frankfurt am Main: Verlag Madda, 1928), 415–19 (Heb.: 267–68). According to Geiger's conjecture, the original allusion was to the fact that the LXX altered *beloti* ("worn out"), which the translators regarded as too crude. Most recent scholarship ascribes the variation to a different Hebrew *Vorlage*. See Tov, "Alterations," 78–79.

9.   For example, John Wansbrough, *Quranic Studies: Sources and Methods of Scriptural Interpretation*, London Oriental Series 31 (Oxford: Oxford University Press, 1977).

10.   Moses Hadas, ed., *Aristeas to Philocrates (Letter of Aristeas)*, Jewish Apocryphal Literature (New York: Harper & Brothers, 1951).

11.   F. H. Colson and G. H. Whitaker, eds., *Philo with an English Translation*, ed. T. E. Page, E. Capps, and W. H. D. Rouse, 10 vols., LCL (London: William Heinemann; Cambridge, Mass.: Harvard University Press, 1935), 6:460–70.

12.   See Wasserstein and Wasserstein, *LXX Legend*, 51–54.

13.   Ibid., 59; see also 65: "The story . . . is clearly intended to commend the changes to the reader as being worthy of attention precisely because they are the direct outcome of a miraculous event." Many scholars have unjustifiably twisted the meaning of the passage in order to support their presupposition that the rabbis were out to discredit the LXX by accusing it of tampering with the biblical text.

14.   *Pisha* 14 (H. S. Horovitz and I. A. Rabin, eds., *Mechilta D'Rabbi Ismael*, 2nd ed. [Jerusalem: Wahrmann, 1970], 50–51; Jacob Z. Lauterbach, ed., *Mekilta de-Rabbi Ishmael*, 3 vols., Jewish Classics, paper ed. [Philadelphia: Jewish Publication Society of America, 1961], 111–12). The (lack of) distribution among the tannaitic midrashic collections deserves some mention. Given that the alterations cover all five books of the Pentateuch (if we count the "hare" example as referring to Lev 11:6, and not only Deut 14:7), we should have expected the respective midrashic works to mention them, if only cursorily, as they were encountered. This is not the case, and the single reference in *Mekhilta* remains the only attestation in the literature of tannaitic midrash. The general situation remains the same in tannaitic midrashim that were not known to earlier scholars. J. N. Epstein and E. Z. Melamed (*Mekhilta d'Rabbi Sim'on b. Jochai* [Jerusalem: Mekize Nirdamim, 1955]) do not mention Ptolemy or the alterations in the commentaries on Exod 12:40 (34), transcribed from ms. Firkovitch, or on 24:5 (220), based on *Midrash Haggadol*. The same

holds true for Menahem I. Kahana, *Sifre Zuta on Deuteronomy: Citations from a New Tannaitic Midrash* (in Hebrew) (Jerusalem: Magnes Press, Hebrew University, 2003), where the surviving quotations contain no such references.

15. A methodical comparison of the rabbinic versions was already conducted by Geiger (*Urschrift*, 439–47; Heb. 282–87). Geiger was substantially correct in noting that the earliest and most reliable traditions are those contained in the *Mekhilta*, where the miracle story is not mentioned. He also noted the composite nature of the Babylonian version, while dismissing the medieval *Masekhet Soferim* as irrelevant to the ancient reality. Cf. Tov, "Alterations," 66–67, and Wasserstein and Wasserstein, *LXX Legend*, 60.

16. Ezra Fleischer, *Eretz-Israel Prayer and Prayer Rituals as Portrayed in the Geniza Documents*, Publications of the Perry Foundation (Jerusalem: Magnes, 1988), 199–202; Debra Reed Blank, "It's Time to Take Another Look at 'Our Little Sister' Soferim: A Bibliographical Essay," *JQR* 90 (1999): 20–21.

17. A rare and notable exception to this pattern is Giuseppe Veltri, *Eine Tora für den König Talmai: Untersuchungen zum Übersetzungsverständnis in der jüdisch-hellenistischen und rabbinischen Literatur*, TSAJ 41 (Tübingen: Mohr Siebeck, 1994). In his review of Veltri's book, Tov was compelled to concede the point; see Emanuel Tov, "Review of G. Veltri, *Eine Tora für den König Talmai*," *Scripta Classica Israelica* 14 (1995): 178–83.

18. Günter Stemberger, *Introduction to the Talmud and Mishnah*, (Edinburgh: TBT Clark, 1996), 204–208; cf. Wasserstein and Wasserstein, *LXX Legend*, 54.

19. The conventional view is expressed in Tov's chapter on the LXX in the collection *Mikra*: "This negative approach is visible also in the view of the Rabbis who explained the differences between the MT and LXX as alterations of the latter." See Emanuel Tov, "The Septuagint," in *Mikra: Text, Translation, Reading and Interpretation of the Hebrew Bible in Ancient Judaism and Early Christianity*, ed. M. J. Mulder and H. Sysling, CRINT Section 2: Literature of the Jewish People in the Period of the Second Temple and the Talmud 1 (Assen: Van Gorcum; Philadelphia: Fortress Press, 1988), 162.

20. This simple understanding of the passage is found in Rashi's standard commentary.

21. Nevertheless, I am convinced that they are fundamentally incorrect. See also Abraham Wasserstein, "On Donkeys, Wine and the Uses of Textual Criticism: Septuagintal Variants in Jewish Palestine," in *The Jews in the Hellenistic-Roman World: Studies in Memory of Menahem Stern*, ed. Isaiah Gafni, Aharon Oppenheimer, and Daniel Schwartz (Jerusalem, Zalman Shazar Center for Jewish History and the Historical Society of Israel, 1996), 122–23.

22. This fact was noted by Tov, "Review of G. Veltri."

23. Saul Lieberman, "The Martyrs of Caesarea," *Annuaire de l'Institut de Philologie et d'Histoire Orientales et Slaves* 7 (1939–44): 395. See also idem, *Texts and Studies* (New York: KTAV, 1974), 182.

24. Lieberman's caveats have been followed with judicious results by most scholars of Talmudic philology and literature, to the point where the historical value of texts is often treated as virtually irrelevant to their study. See Shamma Friedman, "La-Aggadah Ha-Historit Ba-Talmud Ha-Bavli," in *Saul Lieberman Memorial Volume*, ed. Shamma Friedman (New York and Jerusalem: Jewish

Theological Seminary of America, 1993). Friedman warns that "in light of the Bavli's propensity for embellishing and expanding the tales about sages with formulas and motifs borrowed from other contexts, it is crucial to identify the original literary kernel of the passage before we determine the historical kernel" (119).

25. See Zacharias Frankel, *Über den Einfluss der palästinischen Exegese auf die alexandrinische Hermeneutik* (Westmead: Gregg International Publishers, 1972); Hanoch Albeck, *Introduction to the Mishna* (Jerusalem: Mosad Bialik; Tel-Aviv: Dvir, 1959), 10–14.

26. See Viktor Aptowitzer, "Observations on the Criminal Law of the Jews," *JQR* 15 (1924–25): 55–118; David Michael Feldman, *Birth Control in Jewish Law: Marital Relations, Contraception, and Abortion as Set Forth in the Classic Texts of Jewish Law with Comparative Reference to the Christian Exegetical Tradition* (Westport, Conn.: Greenwood, 1980), 257–62.

27. Tov, "Review of G. Veltri," 183.

28. Cf. Wasserstein and Wasserstein, *LXX Legend*, 59.

29. For additional texts and discussion of the theological issues, see Alan F. Segal, *Two Powers in Heaven: Early Rabbinic Reports about Christianity and Gnosticism*, SJLA (Leiden: Brill, 1977), 121–22, 124–34.

30. See also *Gen. Rab.* 8:8-11 (J. Theodor and C. Albeck, *Bereschit Rabba: Mit kritischem Apparat und Kommentar* [in Hebrew], 3 vols. [Berlin: H. Itzkowski, 1903–23], 64). On the passage, see Veltri, *Eine Tora*, 39–41, 106.

31. Mentioned by Tov, "Rabbinic Tradition," 85; Veltri, *Eine Tora*, 38–39, 106; Segal, *Two Powers*, 122–24.

32. Segal, *Two Powers*, 128: "Thus, we can derive a list of scriptural passages which were viewed as dangerous in the third century, contemporary with R. Simlai or R. Yohanan."

33. See Wasserstein, "Donkeys," 126–36 (dealing with Exod 4:20 and Num 16:15); Wasserstein and Wasserstein, *LXX Legend*, 64; and Tov, "Alterations."

34. Cf. Veltri, *Eine Tora*, 222.

35. Mordecai Margulies, ed., *Midrash Wayyikra Rabbah*, 4 vols. (Jerusalem: Wahrmann, 1972), 290 (see his notes to line 7). Cf. Veltri, *Eine Tora*, 226, 232–33.

36. Veltri, *Eine Tora*, 233.

37. The sentence is, in fact, formulated in a mixture of Hebrew and Aramaic. Given the poor state of the Yerushalmi text, we should probably not attach too much importance to these nuances, which can easily get obscured by copyists. At any rate, it should be made clear that the Aramaisms in the Yerushalmi version cannot be explained on the same literary grounds as in the Babylonian version (as speech by a "foreigner"; see below). The fact that allusions to Ptolemy's mother/wife are entirely absent from the *Mekhilta* version should remove any reasonable doubt about its being an explanatory gloss introduced during the amoraic era. The fact that this last sentence is worded in Aramaic, in contrast to the rest of the source, which is in Hebrew, as expected from a tannatic text (*baraita*), should not of itself be regarded as evidence that the story (or that part of it) is not original to the *baraita* in the Babylonian Talmud. In its current setting, it appears as if Aramaic is being used here as a literary device to suggest the foreignness of the speaker. This would be consistent with the use of the term "Jews" in the quotation, rather than

"Israel," which is the normal manner for Jews to refer to themselves in rabbinic usage. "Jews," on the other hand, usually appears in speech that is being ascribed to foreign speakers. In the Talmud, the use of the form *Yehuda'ei* (Jews) rather than "Israel" is almost exclusively confined to speech by or to Gentiles. This pattern holds true generally, though not as consistently, in the Yerushalmi and Palestinian midrashim as well.

38. This is true, as well, of the *Mekhilta*. The unit would be out of sequence even if it were based on Deut 14:7, since it should be followed by Deut 17:3.

39. See Friedman ("La-Aggadah," 162), who argues for the primacy of Palestinian over Babylonian versions of historical *haggadot*. The question of whether the Yerushalmi made use of *Leviticus Rabbah* or vice versa is a long-standing controversy in Talmudic scholarship. Albeck ("*Midrash Vayikra Rabba*," in *Louis Ginzberg Jubilee Volume on the Occasion of His Seventieth Birthday*, ed. Saul Lieberman et al. [New York: American Academy for Jewish Research, 1945], 30–31) insisted that *Leviticus Rabbah* utilized the Yerushalmi. Margulies (*Midrash Wayyikra Rabbah*, Introduction XVII–XXII) refuted Albeck's arguments, suggesting that similarities between the two collections could more profitably be ascribed to their both drawing from common sources. See also Leib Moskovitz, "The Relationship between the Yerushalmi and Leviticus Rabbah: A Re-examination," in *Eleventh World Congress of Jewish Studies*, ed. World Union of Jewish Studies (Jerusalem: World Union of Jewish Studies, 1993), 31–38. None of these studies cites our example in connection with the debates over the direction of borrowing between *Leviticus Rabbah* and the Palestinian Talmud.

40. Wasserstein, "Donkeys," 139–41; cf. Tov, "Alterations," 73–74, 89.

41. A useful summary of the relevant facts and scholarly discussions may be found in Segal, *Two Powers*, 129–30 n. 13.

42. Similarly, in *Leg.* 153, Philo states that the law of Moses prohibits unrestrained affronts to pagan deities because their worshipers do not know any better. See also Josephus, *Ag. Ap.* 2.237, who justifies this prohibition by the Hebrew legislator out of reverence for the very word "god." See Robert Goldenberg, "The Septuagint Ban on Cursing the Gods," *JSJ* 28 (1997): 381–89.

43. Charles T. Fritsch, *Anti-Anthropomorphisms of the Greek Pentateuch* (Princeton: Princeton University Press, 1943).

44. Harry Meyer Orlinsky, "The Hebrew Vorlage of the Septuagint of the Book of Joshua," in *Congress Volume: Rome 1968*, ed. G. W. Anderson et al., VTSup 17 (Leiden: Brill, 1969), 187–95; idem, "The Septuagint as Holy Writ and the Philosophy of the Translators," *HUCA* 46 (1975): 89–114; Emanuel Tov, "Theologically Motivated Exegesis Embedded in the Septuagint," in *Translation of Scripture: Proceedings of a Conference at the Annenberg Research Institute, May 15–16, 1989*, ed. Annenberg Research Institute, JQR Supplements (Philadelphia: Annenberg Institute, 1989), 215–33.

45. See also Tov ("Theologically Motivated Exegesis"), who mentions Num 12:8; Exod 4:24; 24:10.

46. As formulated by Leonard J. Greenspoon, "The Dead Sea Scrolls and the Greek Bible," in *The Dead Sea Scrolls after Fifty Years: A Comprehensive Assessment*, ed. Peter W. Flint and James C. VanderKam (Leiden: Brill, 1998), 101–27.

47. There remains much that is unclear about the target audience of the Palestinian Greek Bible texts. See Greenspoon, "Dead Sea Scrolls," 101; Wasserstein, "Donkeys," 121–25.

48. The Greek Minor Prophets scroll from Nahal Hever provides an object lesson in the pitfalls facing those who would try to pigeonhole the data into a theory of authoritarian centralization. Recognizing that the scroll fits the paradigm of "*kaige*" translations, on account of its propensity to translate all the occurrences of the Hebrew particle *gam* (sometimes termed "proto-Theodotion" because they anticipate the literal approaches that would later typify the translations of Achilles and Theodotion), the first editor, Dominique Barthélemy, was compelled to date the scroll to the mid-first century, on the assumption that translations of this sort were "rabbinic" in character, reflecting the hermeneutical methods of Rabbi Akiva and his school, which attached midrashic importance to such minutiae (Barthélemy, "Redécouverte d'un chaînon manquant de l'histoire de la LXX," *RB* 60 [1953]: 18–29). The link between Aquila's translation and Rabbi Akiva's hermeneutics is itself problematic, since rabbinic sources connect Aquila primarily to Rabbis Joshua and Eliezer, who belonged to an earlier generation and were not associated with Rabbi Akiva's methods. This assumption underlies the conventional wisdom that "the rabbis" rejected the Septuagint because of its inadequacies for their new exegetical methods and sponsored Aquila's new version to replace it. Unfortunately, the paleographical analysis of Barthélemy's scroll produced a date in the first century B.C.E. or earlier, long before the alleged emergence of those rabbinic hermeneutical methods—and, for that matter, before the actual existence of "rabbis" as such. See Emanuel Tov, Robert A. Kraft, and P. J. Parsons, eds., *The Greek Minor Prophets Scroll from Nahal Hever (8Ḥ evXIIgr): The Seiyâl Collection I*, DJD 8 (Oxford: Clarendon, 1990).

49. Another important testimony to the use of the Septuagint in first-century Palestine comes from Josephus. H. St. J. Thackeray observed that Josephus generally cited the Pentateuch from a Semitic original, whereas his quotations for the historical books derive from the Greek (*Josephus: The Man and the Historian*, The Hilda Stich Strook Lectures [New York: Jewish Institute of Religion Press, 1929], 81–89; Eugene Ulrich, *The Qumran Text of Samuel and Josephus*, HSM 19 [Missoula, Mont.: Scholars Press, 1978], 223–59). Josephus's reliance on the Septuagint is evident not only in the biblical text that he brings but in his citations of apocryphal texts such as the *Letter of Aristeas* or the Additions to Esther. Most significant is the fact that Josephus's Greek Bible has been identified as consistently "proto-Lucianic" in its textual tradition, reflecting a revision of the LXX and not a pure version of the Alexandrian text. Ulrich concluded that Josephus "used a text intimately related to 4QSamᵃ. His text was a biblical text in a tradition not aberrant but apparently more widely influential in the Second Temple period than that of the MT."

50. References to Alexandria in the Talmud and Midrash tend either to imbue it with the legendary aura of bygone Jewish magnificence (as in the descriptions of the great Alexandrian synagogue, in *y. Sukkah* 5:1 (55a–b); *b. Sukkah* 51b) or to portray it as a stereotypical metropolis in which were blended worldly sophistication and moral corruption. See, for example, *Esth. Rab.* 1:17. The rabbinic sources do not indicate much firsthand familiarity with the city; see *b. Sanh.* 67b.

51. See Wasserstein and Wasserstein, *LXX Legend*, 64–65.

52. E. P. Sanders, "Jesus and the Kingdom: The Restoration of Israel and the New People of God," in *Jesus, the Gospels and the Church: Essays in Honor of William R. Farmer*, ed. E. P. Sanders

(Macon, Ga.: Mercer University Press, 1987), 225–39; idem, "Defending the Indefensible," *JBL* 111 (1991): 463–77.

53. And, for that matter, more consistent than those fickle mobs that are so easily swayed back and forth in Josephus's accounts of the Jewish wars.

54. For a summary of these issues, see James C. VanderKam, "Identity and History of the Community," in *The Dead Sea Scrolls after Fifty Years*, ed. Peter W. Flint and James C. VanderKam (Leiden, Boston, and Cologne: Brill, 1999), 487–533; Émile Puech, "Immortality and Life after Death," in *The Dead Sea Scrolls: Fifty Years after Their Discovery: Proceedings of the Jerusalem Congress, July 20–25, 1997*, ed. Lawrence H. Schiffman, Emanuel Tov, and James C. VanderKam (Jerusalem: Israel Exploration Society in cooperation with The Shrine of the Book, Israel Museum, 2000), 512–20.

Chapter 12: Whom Do You Follow? The Jewish *Politeia* and the Maccabean Background of Josephus's Sign Prophets

1. E. P. Sanders, *Judaism: Practice and Belief, 63 BCE– 66 CE* (1992; corrected ed., London: SCM; Philadelphia: Trinity Press International, 1994), 279.

2. Ibid., 41, 493. Cf. William Reuben Farmer, *Maccabees, Zealots, and Josephus: An Inquiry into Jewish Nationalism in the Greco-Roman Period* (Westport, Conn.: Greenwood, 1956), 203; S. G. F. Brandon, *Jesus and the Zealots: A Study of the Political Factor in Primitive Christianity* (New York: Charles Scribner's Sons, 1967), 63; Morton Smith, "Zealots and Sicarii, Their Origins and Relation," *HTR* 64 (1971): 2; David M. Rhoads, *Israel in Revolution, 6–74 CE: A Political History Based on the Writings of Josephus* (Philadelphia: Fortress Press, 1976), 22–23.

3. Sanders, *Practice and Belief*, 288.

4. The term was coined by P. W. Barnett, "The Jewish Sign Prophets—AD 40–70—Their Intentions and Origin," *NTS* 27 (1981): 679, and includes Theudas (*Ant.* 20.97–99), an unnamed Egyptian (*Ant.* 20.169–72; *J.W.* 2.261–63), other anonymous prophets (*Ant.* 20.167–68, 188; *J.W.* 2.258–60; 6.285–86), and possibly Jonathan the Weaver, active in Cyrene after the Jewish revolt (*J.W.* 7.438; cf. 437–50; *Life* 424–25). Although these individuals are introduced in various ways—the promised actions of Theudas and the Egyptian are not called "signs"; the impostors who pledged "wonders and signs" are usually not labeled "prophets"—*J.W.* 2.258–63 indicates that Josephus viewed them together. Cf. Rebecca Gray, *Prophetic Figures in Late Second Temple Jewish Palestine: The Evidence from Josephus* (Oxford: Oxford University Press, 1993), 198–99 n. 2.

5. *J.W.* 2.259; 6.285; cf. *Ant.* 20.188. On the sign prophets as independent figures, see Smith, "Zealots," 14; Rhoads, *Israel in Revolution*, 163–64; Richard A. Horsley, "'Like One of the Prophets of Old': Two Types of Popular Prophets at the Time of Jesus," *CBQ* 47 (1985): 460. On the sign prophets as eschatological figures, see E. P. Sanders, *Jesus and Judaism* (Philadelphia: Fortress Press, 1985), 171; Gray, *Prophetic Figures*, 137, 141; Rhoads, *Israel in Revolution*, 83; Horsley, "Two Types," 454.

6. Cf. Barnett, "Jewish Sign Prophets," 685; Horsley, "Two Types," 454.

7. Cf. Joachim Jeremias, "*Mōusēs*," *TDNT* 4:863; Howard M. Teeple, *The Mosaic Eschatological Prophet* (Philadelphia: Society of Biblical Literature, 1957), 65, 109; Ferdinand Hahn, *The Titles*

of Jesus in Christology: Their History in Early Christianity (London: Lutterworth, 1969), 358–59, 364–65; Martin Hengel, *The Zealots: Investigations into the Jewish Freedom Movement in the Period from Herod I until 70 AD*, trans. David Smith (Edinburgh: T&T Clark, 1989), 230; Dale C. Allison, *The New Moses: A Matthean Typology* (Minneapolis: Fortress Press, 1993), 83.

8.   The Jordan River location most naturally recalls Joshua. The strongest reason for connecting Theudas to the exodus from Egypt is the description of his followers taking their possessions with them into the desert (*Ant.* 20.97; cf. Exod 12:31-39; cf. Hengel, *Zealots*, 229–30).

9.   Gray, *Prophetic Figures*, 125–33. In contrast to Josephus, the phrase "signs and wonders" is used frequently in the Septuagint for God's mighty acts of deliverance at the exodus from Egypt. The three authenticating "signs" given to Moses at the burning bush, Josephus observes, were intended to confirm Moses as Israel's deliverer (*Ant.* 2.272–84); the ten plagues, on the other hand, are attributed solely to God.

10.   Cf. *Ant.* 6.110; 18.211; 19.9, 94; *J.W.* 3.404; 4.623; and esp. *J.W.* 1.377. For other prophetic *sēmeia* in Josephus, see *Ant.* 6.54, 57, 91; 8.232, 236, 347; 10.28–29.

11.   *J.W.* 2.259 and *Ant.* 20.167 (the Egyptian); *Ant.* 20.188 (a certain impostor); cf. Theudas, who persuaded the people to follow him to the Jordan (*Ant.* 20.97), as well as Jonathan the Weaver (*J.W.* 7.438).

12.   Gray, *Prophetic Figures*, 137: "As a religious motif, the wilderness had wider associations than the exodus and conquest events alone." Cf. Daniel R. Schwartz, "Temple and Desert: On Religion and State in Second Temple Period Judaea," in idem, *Studies in the Jewish Background of Christianity*, WUNT 60 (Tübingen: Mohr Siebeck, 1992), 34–38, for examples.

13.   The most likely reason why the rebels asked permission "to retire to the desert" (*J.W.* 6.351) was because the desert surrounding Jerusalem afforded a natural escape route, not because they believed God would there provide salvation (contra Gerhard Kittel, "*erēmos*," *TDNT* 2:659; Farmer, *Maccabees*, 116; Hengel, *Zealots*, 255).

14.   Cf. Gray, *Prophetic Figures*, 117; Klaus-Stefan Krieger, "Die Zeichenpropheten: eine Hilfe zum Verständnis des Wirkens Jesu?" in *Von Jesus zum Christus: christologische Studien: Festgabe für Paul Hoffmann zum 65. Geburtstag*, ed. Rudolf Hoppe and Ulrich Busse (Berlin: Walter de Gruyter, 1998), 186.

15.   Unless otherwise noted, all quotations of Josephus are taken from H. St. J. Thackeray, Ralph Marcus, Allen Wikgren, and L. H. Feldman, *Josephus*, 10 vols., LCL (Cambridge, Mass.: Harvard University Press, 1926–65), except quotations of *Antiquities* books 1–4, which are taken from Louis H. Feldman, *Judean Antiquities 1–4*, vol. 3 of *Flavius Josephus: Translation and Commentary*, ed. Steve Mason (Leiden: Brill, 2000).

16.   Cf. Krieger, "Zeichenpropheten," 184; *J.W.* 6.286. Hengel (*Zealots*, 114–15) and Barnett ("Sign Prophets," 688; cf. 682–83) suggest that "signs of freedom" (*sēmeia eleutherias*) (*J.W.* 2.259) recalls a related expression (*tōn . . . pros tēn eleutherian autois sēmeiōn gegonotōn*) applied to Moses in *Ant.* 2.327. This suggestion overlooks the fact that the word "sign" is combined with "freedom" most frequently in a context that anticipates the Jewish revolt, but has no relation to the exodus at all. In Josephus's lengthy account concerning the assassination of the emperor Gaius, a password of freedom (*sēmeion eleutherias*) ironically portends Gaius's murder (*Ant.* 19.54, 186, 188).

17. Cf. *Ant.* 17.267; 18.4; 20.120; *J. W.* 2.264; 3.367, 480; 4.146, 159, 228, 234, 246, 272–73, 276, 282, 508; 5.28, 321, 406; 7.255.

18. Cf. *J. W.* 6.295–96, 315. The "wonders and signs" promised by the "impostors" in *Ant.* 20.168 are a recognized collocation for portents in Hellenistic Greek (cf. Karl Heinrich Rengstorf, "*Sēmeion*," *TDNT* 7:206–7). In the only other occurrence of this phrase (*J. W.* 1.28), "signs and wonders" presage the destruction of the temple.

19. Steve Mason, "'Should Any Wish to Enquire Further' (*Ant.* 1.25): The Aim and Audience of Josephus's *Judean Antiquities/Life*," in *Understanding Josephus: Seven Perspectives*, ed. Steve Mason (Sheffield: Sheffield Academic Press, 1998), 81; cf. 80–87. Cf. Yehoshua Amir, "Josephus on the Mosaic 'Constitution,'" in *Politics and Theopolitics in the Bible and Postbiblical Literature*, ed. Henning Graf Reventlow, Yair Hoffman, and Benjamin Uffenheimer, JSOTSup 171 (Sheffield: Sheffield Academic Press, 1994), 13–27; Tessa Rajak, "The *Against Apion* and the Continuities in Josephus's Political Thought," in Mason, *Understanding Josephus*, 222–46.

20. Cf. *Ant.* 6.83–85, 268; 11.111; 20.229, 251; *J. W.* 1.169, 178. Cf. *politeuma* in *Ag. Ap.* 2.165, 184, 188.

21. In *Ag. Ap.* 2.165, 184, 188, Josephus presents a priestly aristocracy as the only divinely instituted mode of government, but this statement must be qualified by Josephus's earlier account. In the *Antiquities*, Josephus depicts the eventual demand for a king as a terrible mistake and an expression of impiety against God (6.35–42, 60–61, 88–94), yet there remained the possibility of continued "salvation and continued felicity under their king" should they remember the law of Moses (6.93). Significantly, Josephus notes that God chose Saul (6.66), David (6.165), and Solomon (7.372) as kings, and he portrays both David and Solomon (at least initially) in a positive light. Cf. Rajak, "Continuities," 237.

22. Cf. Lucio Troiani, "The ΠΟΛΙΤΕΙΑ of Israel in the Graeco-Roman Age," in *Josephus and the History of the Greco-Roman Period: Essays in Memory of Morton Smith*, ed. Fausto Parente and Joseph Sievers, StPB 41 (Leiden: Brill, 1994), 11; Rajak, "Continuities," 228. Although references to the *politeia* are largely absent from Josephus's review of the period between Samuel and the exile, King Manasseh's repentance and subsequent piety were prompted by the realization of "how close he had been to disaster because of following the opposite way of life [*politeia*]" (*Ant.* 10.43).

23. Cf. Rajak, "Continuities," 239–40. For similar statements about internal dissent during the revolt, see *J. W.* 4.388; 5.3–4, 28, 71, 254–74; 7.410. The concept of freedom expressed by Moses' opponent, Zambrias (*Ant.* 4.146), also anticipates the Zealots' claim to admit no master but God (*J. W.* 2.118; 7.410). Cf. Feldman, *Antiquities 1–4*, 382.

24. Cf. Steve Mason, "Introduction to the *Judean Antiquities*," in idem, *Flavius Josephus: Translation and Commentary*, 3:xx–xxii.

25. Cf. Per Bilde, *Flavius Josephus between Jerusalem and Rome: His Life, His Works, and Their Importance*, JSPSup 2 (Sheffield: JSOT Press, 1988), 90.

26. Judas and his brothers are later distinguished from the "godless, and the transgressors against their country's manner of life" (*tēn patrion politeian*) (*Ant.* 13.2). In *Ant.* 13.245 and 15.254 the religious aspects of the Jewish constitution are distinguished from the practices of Gentiles. Cf. *Ant.* 11.140, 157.

27. My translation.

28. Josephus's introduction to his account of the athletic contests is telling: "For this reason Herod went still farther in departing from the native customs [*tōn patriōn ethōn*], and through foreign practices he gradually corrupted the ancient way of life [*tēn palai katastasin*], which had hitherto been inviolable" (*Ant.* 15.267).

29. Josephus also records the changing fortunes of the Jews after the return from exile. Despite the claim that Darius canceled tribute (*Ant.* 11.61), *Ant.* 11.214 and 297 imply that tribute was imposed on Jews during the Persian period, and in *Ant.* 12.5, Josephus reports Agatharchides' claim that the Jews lost their freedom when Ptolemy Soter entered Jerusalem on the Sabbath. For a discussion of the complex realities that lie behind JosephusΛ's account of the Ptolemaic era, see Seth Schwartz, "On the Autonomy of Judaea in the Fourth and Third Centuries BCE," *JJS* 45 (1994): 157–68.

30. Cf. *Ant.* 12.281, 302, 304, 312, 315, 433–34; 13.1, 5, 51–53, 198, 213. Only *Ant.* 13.51–53 and 13.213 are paralleled in 1 Maccabees (cf. 1 Macc 10:33; 14:26).

31. It is true that Josephus speaks positively of the temporary return of aristocratic rule that resulted from Pompey's invasion. He notes that the nation opposed both Hyrcanus and Aristobulus before Pompey, asking "not to be ruled by a king" (*Ant.* 14.41; cf. 17.227). According to *J.W.* 1.170, "The Jews welcomed their release [*eleutherōthentes*] from the rule of an individual and were from that time forward governed by an aristocracy." However, Josephus also celebrated the "freedom" enjoyed under David and Solomon (*Ant.* 7.258; 8.38) even when it did not coincide with aristocratic rule. Despite the return of the "correct" form of government, Josephus as well as many other Jews (cf. *Ant.* 17.267; 18.4, 23; 20.120; *Life* 185) regretted their loss of freedom under Roman rule. Cf. Rajak, "Continuities," 240: "It is perhaps unexpected that Josephus was always ready to label foreign rule enslavement and to take for granted the positive value of national liberation."

32. Cf. Hengel, *Zealots*, 113. It is true that *eleutheria* and its cognates are not applied to the Hasmoneans in the short account of the Maccabean revolt in *J.W.* 1.31–69. Josephus does, however, mention that Simon "liberated [*apallattei*] the Jews from the Macedonian supremacy which had lasted for 170 years" (*J.W.* 1.53; cf. 1.37).

33. Cf. Mason, "Aim and Audience," 72, for the possibility that Josephus assumed "his readers' knowledge of *War*."

34. Cf. Sidney B. Hoenig, "Maccabees, Zealots and Josephus: Second Commonwealth Parallelisms; Review of William Reuben Farmer *Maccabees, Zealots and Josephus*," *JQR* 49 (1958–59): 77; Louis H. Feldman, "Josephus' Portrayal of the Hasmoneans Compared with 1 Maccabees," in Parente and Sievers, *Josephus and the History of the Greco-Roman Period*, 46, 48 n. 9.

35. Cf. Hengel, *Zealots*, 185–86, and Rhoads, *Israel in Revolution*, 166–73, for discussions of reverse polemic in Josephus's speeches.

36. The later speeches of Agrippa, Josephus, and Eleazar also indicate that the rebels believed God was on their side (*J.W.* 5.376–78, 413–14; 7.327–29). Cf. Farmer, *Maccabees*, 107.

37. Cf. Rajak, "Continuities," 242; idem, "Friends, Romans, Subjects: Agrippa II's Speech in Josephus' *Jewish War*," in idem, *The Jewish Dialogue with Greece and Rome: Studies in Cultural and Social Interaction* (Leiden: Brill, 2002), 154–58. Eleazar's lengthy speech in *J.W.* 7.323–88 also illustrates Josephus's consistently positive evaluation of "freedom," even when it is advocated by those he opposed.

38. Cf. *J. W.* 4.385; 6.99–102; Rhoads, *Israel in Revolution*, 166–67.

39. Theudas (*Ant.* 20.97: *peithei ton pleiston ochlon . . . hepesthai pros ton Iordanēn potamon autō*); impostors and deceivers during Felix's rule (*Ant.* 20.167: *ton ochlon epeithon autois eis tēn erēmian hepesthai*; cf. *proagō* in *J. W.* 2.259); a certain impostor during Festus's rule (*Ant.* 20.188: *ei boulētheien hepesthai mechri tēs erēmias autō*). The verb is not used of the Egyptian (*Ant.* 20.169–70), nor is it used in the LXX, in the Greek text of 1 Maccabees, or in connection with sign prophets in *War*.

40. For example, the word may mean to pursue an enemy (e.g., *Ant.* 1.178; 2.324; 5.60; 13.343; *J. W.* 5.119); to follow in sequence (e.g., *Ant.* 2.136; 7.249; 14.69); to follow a master (e.g., *Ant.* 6.171; 8.354; 11.234; *J. W.* 1.340); or to follow a military leader (e.g., *Ant.* 6.122, 299; 7.283; *J. W.* 1.304).

41. *Ant.* 12.271: *ei tis zēlōtēs estin tōn patriōn ethōn kai tēs tou theou thrēskeias hepesthō phēsin emoi* (my translation). The parallel is admittedly less exact in the case of Theudas, for his followers accompany him to the Jordan rather than to the desert. They also take their possessions with them, whereas Josephus implies that Mattathias's followers abandoned their possessions as he had done (contrast 1 Macc 2:30, which mentions the cattle of Mattathias's followers).

42. Cf. *Ant.* 1.20; 3.88; 4.50, 181; 8.337.

43. There are additional examples: In *Ant.* 7.212, Ahithophel tells Absalom "that one ought to follow [*hepesthai*] God and the entire people." In *Ant.* 9.115, Jehu, anointed as king "to avenge the blood of the prophets" (9.108), instructs King Joram's horsemen to follow him—both literally and figuratively—as leader. The word is also used of following the Sadducees (*Ant.* 13.298) and the Pharisees (18.12).

44. The "ancestral customs" (*patriōn ethōn*) are here synonymous with the Jewish *politeia*. Cf. *Ant.* 5.90, 101; 8.192; 9.95, 137; 11.339.

45. Cf. *War* 2.391–94; 4.184

46. See, for example, the role of Huldah the prophet in Josiah's reform (*Ant.* 10.59–65). On the role of the prophets as God's spokespersons to their contemporaries, see Louis H. Feldman, "Prophets and Prophecy in Josephus," *JJS* 41 (1990): 395–96.

47. Cf. Steve Mason, "Josephus, Daniel, and the Flavian House," in Parente and Sievers, *Josephus and the History of the Greco-Roman Period*, 177; Shaye J. D. Cohen, "Josephus, Jeremiah, and Polybius," *History and Theory* 21 (1982): 367–68.

48. Cf. Rhoads, *Israel in Revolution*, 171; Cohen, "Josephus," 376–77; Gray, *Prophetic Figures*, 144.

49. Bilde, *Josephus*, 181.

50. Sanders, *Practice and Belief*, 47–48.

51. Ibid., 287.

Chapter 13: Memory in Josephus and the Culture of the Jews in the First Century

1. E. P. Sanders, *Judaism: Practice and Belief, 63 BCE–66 CE* (London: SCM; Philadelphia: Trinity Press International, 1992; corrected ed., 1994).

2.   Greg Woolf, "Monumental Writing and the Expansion of Roman Society in the Early Empire," *JRS* 86 (1996): 22–39.

3.   See Mary Beard, "Writing and Religion: Ancient Literacy and the Function of the Written Word in Roman Religion, in *Literacy in the Roman World*, ed. Mary Beard et al., JRA Supplementary Series 3 (Ann Arbor: Journal of Roman Archaeology, 1991), 133–43; H. Mouritsen, "Freedmen and Decurions: Epitaphs and Social History in Imperial Italy," *JRS* 95 (2005): 38–63.

4.   See Josephus, *Ant.* 15.267–79. On the theater, see most recently J. Patrich, "Herod's Theatre in Jerusalem: A New Proposal," *IEJ* 52 (2002): 231–39. Lee I. Levine (*Jerusalem: Portrait of the City in the Second Temple Period [538 BCE to 70 CE]* [Philadelphia: Jewish Publication Society, 2002], 201–6) discusses these buildings and Herod's games but contradicts Josephus by situating the events described in the amphitheater rather than the theater; see A. Schalit, *König Herodes: der Mann und sein Werk* (Berlin: Walter de Gruyter, 1969), 370–71.

5.   The above summarizes part of the argument of the companion piece to this chapter, Seth Schwartz, "Euergetism in Josephus and the Epigraphical Culture of First-Century Jerusalem," in *From Hellenism to Islam: Cultural and Linguistic Change in the Roman Near East*, ed. H. Cotton et al. (Cambridge: Cambridge University Press, forthcoming), which surveys the epigraphy of first-century Jerusalem. In brief, the main publications are *CIJ* 2; L. Y. Rahmani, *A Catalogue of Jewish Ossuaries in the Collections of the State of Israel* (Jerusalem: Israel Antiquities Authority, 1994); and H. Misgav, "The Epigraphic Sources (Hebrew and Aramaic) in Comparison with the Traditions Reflected in Talmudic Literature" (Ph.D. diss., Hebrew University, 1999). The exceptional building inscriptions (which are also exceptional *as* building inscriptions) are *CIJ* 2.1404 (with discussion of John S. Kloppenborg-Verbin, "Dating Theodotos [*CIJ* II 1404]," *JJS* 51 [2000]: 243–80); and Benjamin H. Isaac, "A Donation for Herod's Temple in Jerusalem," *IEJ* 33 (1983): 86–92, reprinted in idem, *The Near East under Roman Rule: Selected Papers* (Leiden: Brill, 1998), 21–28.

6.   Cf. Herodotus, *Histories* 1.1.1.

7.   On Josephus's appropriation—and subversion—of Thucydidean tropes in the preface to *Jewish War*, see J. Price, "Josephus's First Sentence and the Preface to BJ," in *For Uriel: Studies in the History of Israel in Antiquity, Presented to Professor Uriel Rappaport*, ed. M. Mor et al. (Jerusalem: Merkaz Shazar, 2005), 131–44.

8.   The most compelling discussion of the aims of *Jewish War*, *Antiquities*, and *Life* remains Shaye J. D. Cohen, *Josephus in Galilee and Rome: His Vita and Development as a Historian*, Columbia Studies in the Classical Tradition 8 (Leiden: Brill, 1979), 67–180. On the "Deuteronomic" character of *Antiquities*, see Seth Schwartz, *Josephus and Judaean Politics* (Leiden: Brill, 1990). For a different approach to *Antiquities* and *Life*, see Steve Mason, "'Should Any Wish to Enquire Further' (*Ant.* 1.25): The Aim and Audience of Josephus's *Judean* [*sic*] *Antiquities/Life*," in *Understanding Josephus: Seven Perspectives*, ed. Steve Mason (Sheffield: Sheffield Academic Press, 1998), 64–103; and Louis H. Feldman, *Judean Antiquities 1–4*, vol. 3 of *Flavius Josephus: Translation and Commentary*, ed. Steve Mason (Leiden: Brill, 2000); see especially the introduction by Mason, xiii–xxxvi. For a less single-minded account, see Per Bilde, *Flavius Josephus between Jerusalem and Rome: His Life, His Works, and Their Importance*, JSJSup 2 (Sheffield: JSOT Press, 1988), 75–79; 99–103.

9.   This theme is borrowed from Herodotus, who claimed to have presented the results of his investigation (*apodexis historias*) to ensure that "the great and marvelous *erga* of both Greeks and barbarians" not lack *kleos* (fame).

10.   See already H. Immerwahr, "Ergon: History as a Monument in Herodotus and Thucydides," *AJP* 81 (1960): 261–90; D. Lateiner, *The Historical Method of Herodotus* (Toronto: University of Toronto Press, 1989), 13–51.

11.   This may explain a feature of *War*'s account of the Great Revolt, which, as far as I know, has not been explained and is unparalleled in Greek and Roman historiography (even Livy features no such lists, even though his reliance on the annalistic tradition predisposed him to include many lists), namely, Josephus's tendency to list the bravest fighters of both sides at the conclusion of accounts of battle. This issue would benefit from fuller investigation.

12.   Gabriele Boccaccini, "Il tema della memoria in Giuseppe Flavio," *Henoch* 6 (1984): 147–63. Cf. R. Hendel, *Remembering Abraham: Culture, Memory, and History in the Hebrew Bible* (New York: Oxford University Press, 2005), 32–33; Marc Zvi Brettler, "Memory in Ancient Israel," in *Memory and History in Christianity and Judaism*, ed. Michael A. Signer (Notre Dame: Notre Dame University Press, 2001), 1–17; R. Clements, "ZKR," *TDOT* 4:64–86.

13.   On the oral *paradosis* of the Pharisees, see A. I. Baumgarten, "The Pharisaic Paradosis," *HTR* 80 (1987): 63–77; more recently and controversially, Martin Goodman, "A Note on Josephus, the Pharisees and the Ancestral Tradition," *JJS* 50 (1999): 17–20.

14.   See Burton L. Mack, *Wisdom and the Hebrew Epic: Ben Sira's Hymn in Praise of the Fathers* (Chicago: University of Chicago Press, 1985).

15.   See Immerwahr, "Ergon."

16.   Woolf, "Monumental Writing."

17.   On Herod's building projects—the most prominent but not the only component of his benefactions—see Peter Richardson, *Herod: King of the Jews and Friend of the Romans* (Columbia: University of South Carolina Press, 1996), 174–215; Schalit, *König Herodes*, 328–403; and W. Otto, *Herodes: Beiträge zur Geschichte des letzten jüdischen Königshauses* (Stuttgart: Metzler, 1913), 77–85.

18.   Josephus frequently noted the Jews' abhorrence of images; see, in greatest detail, J.-B. Frey, "La question des images chez les juifs à la lumière des récentes découvertes," *Biblica* 15 (1934): 265–300, esp. 273–82 (cf., more recently, in less detail but with more special pleading Y. [S.] Stern, "Figurative Art and Halakhah in the Mishnaic-Talmudic Period," *Zion* 61 [1996]: 397–419, at 419). On statues in particular, see *Ag. Ap.* 2.71–78: statues are forbidden because they are a practice useless to God and humans; they so little convey honor on their subjects that the Greeks make them even of their favorite slaves. Our Jewish practice of honoring the emperor by sacrificing on his behalf is more effective.

19.   This is a passage that B. Shaw's review of Goodman, *JRS* 79 (1989): 246–47, was right to call "startling," though it has received little scholarly attention; for Shaw, this passage provides the background for Goodman's claim that euergetism was of little importance in first-century Jerusalem, an argument I am trying here to complicate. Shaw's observation is clearly the inspiration for his own (stimulating but not unproblematic) attempt to account for the failure of Roman rule in Judea ("Josephus—Roman Power and Responses to it," *Athenaeum* 83 [1995]: 357–90).

20. Cf. *Megillat Taanit*, 7 Kislev—one of the two festivals not given a rationale in the scroll itself is said in the scholion to commemorate Herod's death—so, a kind of *damnatio memoriae*. The other, 2 Shevat, is said to commemorate the death of Alexander Jannaeus (!); see V. Noam, *Megillat Ta'anit: Versions, Interpretation, History, with a Critical Edition* (Jerusalem: Yad Ben-Zvi, 2003), 99, 109.

21. The great majority of the scholarship on this episode concerns the family's conversion and neglects its subsequent activities in Jerusalem. For some recent discussion, see Daniel R. Schwartz, "God, Gentiles and Jewish Law: On Acts 15 and Josephus's Adiabene Narrative," in *Geschichte-Tradition-Reflexion: Festschrift für Martin Hengel zum 70. Geburtstag*, ed. Hubert Cancik, Hermann Lichtenberger, and Peter Schäfer, 3 vols. (Tübingen: Mohr Siebeck, 1996), 1:263–83.

22. On the surprisingly similar attitudes expressed in these two works, see Tessa Rajak, "The *Against Apion* and the Continuities in Josephus's Political Thought," in idem, *The Jewish Dialogue with Greece and Rome: Studies in Cultural and Social Interaction*, AGJU 48 (Leiden: Brill, 2001), 195–217; along similar lines, see S. Castelli, "*Antiquities 3–4* and *Against Apion* 2.145ff.: Different Approaches to the Law," in *Internationales Josephus-Kolloquium Amsterdam 2000*, ed. J. Kalms (Münster: LIT, 2001), 151–69.

23. On *aristokratia*, see Daniel R. Schwartz, "Josephus on the Jewish Constitution and Community," *Scripta Classica Israelica* 7 (1983): 30–52; in this passage it clearly does not mean what Schwartz claims it means in general—rule by council. On *theokratia*, see Hubert Cancik, "Theokratia und Priesterherrschaft," in *Theokratie*, ed. Jacob Taubes, Religionstheorie und Politische Theologie 3 (Munich: W. Fink and F. Schöningh, 1987), 65–77 (exercising due skepticism about the argument that Josephus's conception was influenced by developments in Flavian politics); P. Spilsbury, "Contra Apionem and Antiquitates Judaicae: Points of Contact," in *Josephus' Contra Apionem*, ed. Louis H. Feldman and J. Levison (Leiden: Brill, 1996), 348–68, esp. 362–67.

24. Cf. Solon Apud, fragment 4.39 (G. S. Kirk, J. E. Raven, and Malcolm Schofield, *Presocratic Philosophers: A Critical History with a Selection of Texts* [Cambridge: Cambridge University Press, 1983]).

25. See E. L. Sukenik, "An Epitaph of Uzziahu King of Judah," *Tarbiz* 2 (1931): 288–92, with the additional comments of E. Ben-Eliahu, "The Source of the Tombstone Inscription of Uziah," *The Jerusalem Cathedra* 98 (2000): 157–58, curiously unaware of A. Schremer, "Comments Concerning King Uziahu's Burial Place," *The Jerusalem Cathedra* 46 (1987): 188–90.

26. For example, *J. W.* 4.567; 5.55, 119, 147, 252; 6.355.

27. Mausolea: on the Tomb of the Kings, see M. Kon and O. Schneid, *The Tombs of the Kings* (Tel Aviv: Dvir, 1947); on the Kidron Valley monuments, see now D. Barag, "The 2000–2001 Exploration of the Tombs of Benei Hezir and Zechariah," *IEJ* 53 (2003): 78–110. On monumentalized tombs, see A. Kloner and B. Zissu, *The Necropolis of Jerusalem in the Second Temple Period* (Jerusalem: Yad Ben Zvi and the Israel Exploration Society, 2003), 16–22.

Chapter 14: Epistemology and Social Conflict in *Jubilees* and *Aristeas*

1. See O. S. Wintermute, "Jubilees," in *The Old Testament Pseudepigrapha*, ed. James H. Charlesworth, 2 vols. (New York: Doubleday, 1985), 1:43–44; George W. E. Nickelsburg, "The Bible Re-written and Expanded," in *Jewish Writings of the Second Temple Period*, ed. M. E. Stone

(Assen: Van Gorcum; Phildadelphia: Fortress Press, 1984), 101–3; James C. VanderKam, *Textual and Historical Studies in the Book of Jubilees*, HSM 14 (Missoula, Mont.: Scholars Press, 1977), 207–85, esp. 283–85.

2.   It would seem from the reference to "the book of the first law" in *Jub.* 6:22 that *Jubilees* presumes both the existence and the inspired authority of the Pentateuch (so Philip S. Alexander, "Retelling the Old Testament," in *It Is Written: Scripture Citing Scripture*, ed. D. A. Carson and H. G. M. Williamson [Cambridge: Cambridge University Press, 1988], 100).

3.   It is, of course, difficult to know how seriously this fictional setting was originally intended to be taken. It is clear from the reception of *Jubilees* at Qumran, however, that at least some readers quickly assumed its authenticity. Alexander ("Retelling," 101) suggests that the author was heir to esoteric priestly traditions that he honestly believed stemmed from this encounter on Sinai.

4.   See also *Jub.* 17:6-7; 18:9-16. Quotations from *Jubilees* in English translation are from Wintermute, "Jubilees."

5.   A heavy emphasis is placed on Jacob's vision at Bethel (31:26) and the vow he made in association with it. See, for example, 44:5-6; 45:4.

6.   There are several other instances of dream revelations in *Jubilees*. See, for example, 32:16-26; 35:6; 39–40.

7.   The divine inspiration of the blessings in 25:14-23 and 31:12 is probably geared to avoid any suggestion that the biblical blessings are magically effective.

8.   See Armin Lange, "Divinatorische Träume und Apokalyptic im Jubiläenbuch," in *Studies in the Book of Jubilees*, ed. M. Albani, J. Frey, and A. Lange, TSAJ 65 (Tübingen: Mohr Siebeck, 1997), 28–29.

9.   The writers of such traditions in *Jubilees*, Enoch and Noah, are the same figures who appear as pseudepigraphal authors in apocalyptic literature of the third century B.C.E. and following. The references in *Jub.* 4:21-22 to Enoch's heavenly tours and testimony against the watchers seem to be drawn from the Enochic Book of the Watchers (*1 Enoch* 1–36). Nickelsburg ("Bible Re-written," 103 n. 76) points to the parallel between *Jub.* 23:16, 26 and *1 En.* 90:6-7; 93:10. *Jubilees* 4:19 may also allude to *1 Enoch* 83–90. See further James C. VanderKam, "Enoch Traditions in Jubilees and Other Second-Century Sources," in *SBL 1978 Seminar Papers*, ed. Paul Achtemeier (Missoula, Mont.: Scholars Press, 1978), 1:228–51. *Jub.* 10:1-14 (and perhaps 7:20-39) has often been taken as a citation from a (no longer extant) *Book of Noah* (Alexander, "Retelling," 103; R. H. Charles, *The Book of Jubilees, or, The Little Genesis* (Jerusalem: Makor, 1971), 78; Geza Vermes in Emil Schürer, *History of the Jewish People in the Age of Jesus Christ (175 BC to AD 135)*, rev. and ed. Geza Vermes, Fergus Millar, and Martin Goodman [Edinburgh: T&T Clark, 1973–87], 3:332–33).

10.   There is some inconsistency between this passage and 33:15-16, where the incest of Reuben and Bilhah was excused on the basis that "the ordinance and judgment and law had not been revealed till then (as) completed for everyone."

11.   See, for example, 11:8, where Nahor is taught astrology by Serug in Ur (cf. 8:3).

12.   Note how Abram begins his prayer: "My God, the Most High God, you alone are God to me" (12:19). The emphasis here seems to fall on Abram's submission to God's sovereignty as creator.

13. Notice in 1:22 how Israel's "forgetting" is treated as a matter of "contrariness" and "stubbornness," and how they must "acknowledge their sin and the sins of their fathers" before they can return to God. See also 2:29; 15:33-34.

14. True, in the Abraham story we are told that the pre-deluvian writings are in a language that none can understand any longer. Yet in that same story we see God gifting Abram with an understanding of those books after he shows a willingness to respond to his innate knowledge concerning idolatry. Thus, at least in theory, other Gentiles could gain the same access to that lost lore if they were sufficiently righteous. Hence, the writings of Enoch are said to be a "testimony" against "all the children of men and their generations" (4:19), apparently including those living after the flood.

15. See also 3:31, where we are told that the commandment to cover one's "shame" is directed "to all *who will know* the judgment of the Law."

16. See 2:1, 18-19, 25 (on Sabbath); 6:17-19 (on Shavuot); 6:23-24 (on the first days of the first, fourth, seventh, and tenth months); 7:34-39 (on the offering of first fruits); 7:37-39 (on the land's rest in the seventh year). In each case the festivals and rituals of Torah are universally binding before Israel even exists. The sun itself is created "as a great sign upon the earth for days, sabbaths, months, feast(days), years, sabbaths of years, jubilees, and for all of the (appointed) times of the years" (2:9). More ambiguous are the Feast of Booths (see 16:20-31) and the festival commemorating the *Aqedah* (see 18:19).

17. See, for example, 11:1-6; 48:16.

18. Note, too, how God has Mastema "shut up" in 48:15.

19. At one point, it seems to be suggested that Israel is uniquely protected from demonic oppression, while other nations are assigned deceiving spirits (15:31-32). Yet elsewhere Israel also suffers demonic delusion, and this protection is never mentioned again. If 15:31-32 reflects a systematized idea in *Jubilees*, then Abraham represents a Gentile who *is* able to overcome the demonic control of his nation. It is more likely, however, that 15:31-32 is a theological fragment sitting in tension with the thought of *Jubilees* as a whole.

20. See also the anger of Abram's brothers in 12:8, which suggests that they are far from ignorant.

21. This is, we are told, why he was allowed to live longer than other human beings (23:10).

22. Esau himself tries to stop his sons from attacking Jacob, saying that he sold his right fairly (37:1-8). Only after they force him to lead their army does Esau become hostile toward his brother (37:11-13).

23. Judah's incest with Tamar cannot be excused so easily, but even here the author of *Jubilees* attempts to redeem the flawed patriarch by displaying his earnest repentance (see 41:24).

24. Abraham is told by the angelic mediator that as human life spans shorten, "their knowledge will forsake them because of their old age" (23:11). On the other hand, he is also told that the world will degrade like this because of "the evil generation which sins in the land" (23:14). Both statements add further dimensions to the document's epistemology, but here again they are not integrated into the narrative as a whole.

25. So George W. E. Nickelsburg, "Stories of Biblical and Early Post-biblical Times," in Stone, *Jewish Writings*, 78.

26. So John R. Bartlett, *Jews in the Hellenistic World*, CCWJCW (Cambridge: Cambridge University Press, 1985), 16–17; Nickelsburg, "Stories," 77.

27. In what follows, "Aristeas" (not italicized) designates the character in the book, while *Aristeas* (italicized) designates the book itself. The Gentile identity of the character Aristeas is made clear in 16, where he identifies himself with King Ptolemy over against the Jews, who call God by a different name. The same assumption is evident in 3 and 6 (so, for example, Bartlett, *Jews*, 13; Victor Tcherikover, "The Ideology of the Letter of Aristeas," *HTR* 51 [1958]: 63). R. J. H. Schutt treats Aristeas as an Alexandrian Jew ("Letter of Aristeas," in Charlesworth, *Old Testament Pseudepigrapha*, 1:7; idem, *The Anchor Bible Dictionary*, ed. David Noel Freedman, 6 vols. [New York: Doubleday, 1992], s.v. "Aristeas, Letter of"), but his evidence demonstrates only that the actual author is Jewish. The author of the work and the character Aristeas must be distinguished from one another.

28. Citations of the Greek text of *Aristeas* are from K. M. Penner, ed., "Letter of Aristeas," in *The Online Critical Pseudepigrapha*, ed. D. M. Miller, K. M. Penner, and I. W. Scott (Atlanta: Society of Biblical Literature, 2006), http://www.purl.org/net/ocp/Aristeas.html). English translations are from Shutt, "Letter of Aristeas."

29. So Bartlett, *Jews*, 18. This concern for autopsy dates back at least to Herodotus. Cf. Luke 1:2.

30. Since access to knowledge is the main problem in *Aristeas*, we also see an emphasis on human care in *preserving* knowledge in 30–32 and 39.

31. The translation of the law is driven by the devotion of Aristeas and Philocrates to "the things of God" in general (3–4), suggesting that the law is one text among many that convey knowledge of the divine.

32. See also Aristeas's reference to "primitive men" (Jews?) who "demonstrated [*diesēmanan*] that the one by whom all live and are created is the master and Lord of all" (16).

33. Eleazar's argument is probably not intended to show that the gods were overglorified human beings (contra Bartlett, *Jews*, 31). Rather, he criticizes the self-conscious worship of divinized humans such as Hercules and Aesclepius, who were often portrayed as cultural pioneers (136). Eleazar then adds that it is even more foolish to worship animals as the Egyptians do (138).

34. Eleazar says that food legislation was not laid down for its own sake, but only in order to promote devotion to the "sovereignty of God" (141). "All the regulations have been made with righteousness [*dikaiosynēn*] in mind," he insists, and none has been laid down "without purpose or fancifully." The law's purpose is "that through the whole of our lives we may also practice justice [*diakaiosynēn*] to all mankind in our acts, remembering the all-sovereign God" (168). For specific interpretations, see 145–57, 163–66. Eleazar's speech also extends beyond the food laws to touch on other peculiar requirements of Torah, such as distinctive clothing, *mezuzot* (158), and *tephillin* (159).

35. See also 161 regarding the "truth" (*alētheian*) and "right reason" (*orthou logou*) behind these laws.

36. Later accounts of the birth of the LXX culminate in the comparison of seventy(-two?) complete translations, each produced in isolation, which are found miraculously to agree (see, for example, Philo, *Mos.* 2.25–44 [esp. 36–37, 40]). In *Aristeas*, though, the translation remains a collaborative human achievement.

37. So Bartlett, *Jews*, 14–15; Tcherikover, "Ideology," 65–66; Nickelsburg, "Stories," 77; Moses Hadas, *Aristeas to Philocrates (Letter of Aristeas)*, Jewish Apocryphal Literature (New York: Harper, 1951), 40–43.

38. See also the king's remark to the philosophers that "these men excel in virtue [*diapherein tous andras aretē*] and have a fuller understanding" (200).

39. So Bartlett, *Jews*, 12.

40. For the history of the Jewish community in Alexandria, see Victor Tcherikover, *Hellenistic Civilization and the Jews* (1959; reprint, Philadelphia: Jewish Publication Society, 1999), 284–85, 320–28; Aryeh Kasher, *The Jews in Hellenistic and Roman Egypt*, TSAJ 7 (Tübingen: Mohr Siebeck, 1985), passim; J. M. G. Barclay, *Jews in the Mediterranean Diaspora: From Alexander to Trajan (323 BCE–117 CE)* (Edinburgh: T&T Clark; Berkeley: University of California Press, 1996), 19–81. Josephus records an edict of Claudius that addresses the question of Jewish civic rights in Alexandria (see Josephus, *Ant.* 19.278–85; cf. *Ag. Ap.* 2.38–64). Some understand *Aristeas* to be an intra-Jewish polemic concerning some translation of Israel's Scriptures or the sanctuary at Leontopolis (so S. Jellicoe, "The Occasion and Purpose of the Book of Aristeas," *NTS* 12 [1966]: 144–50). As Bartlett rightly observes, though, such readings "lose sight of the undoubtedly pro-Hellenistic attitude of Aristeas" (*Jews*, 13).

41. Even here, the best Jews were made soldiers rather than serfs (14) and were given "generous pay" (35).

42. Ptolemy releases (and pays for) nursing children and their mothers (27), and he promises to "make amends for any damage caused by mob violence" (37).

43. Notice how at the banquet Ptolemy's seating plan assures that all the visitors are honored (183), while Eleazar's prayer preempts the usual sacred heralds, sacrificial ministers, and so forth (184).

44. Ptolemy refers to Andreas and Aristeas as "men held in high esteem" by Eleazar (40).

45. In fact, there is some suggestion that the law should not be read by ordinary pagans. God is said to have prevented pagan authors from broadcasting the law "to common man" (see 313–15; so Bartlett, *Jews*, 22). Hence, the Jews who possess this law are by implication already part of the cultural elite.

46. See, for example, Isa 44:9-20.

47. Notice, too, Aristeas's conspicuous mention of Greek cultural figures such as Demetrius of Phalerum (9–11), Hecataeus of Abdera (31), Theopompus (314), and Theodectes (316). The author of *Aristeas* also displays his facility with several Greek literary genres: the travel narrative (83–120), the symposium (182–294), allegorical interpretation of an ancient text, and so forth. He even quotes from a Greek poet in 2 (so Bartlett, *Jews*, 19; Nickelsburg, "Stories," 78; Hadas, *Aristeas*, 55; Tcherikover, "Ideology," 64).

48.   So, for example, Aristeas knows that Philocrates will be interested in the law of the Jews because of his general interest in "matters pertaining to the edification of the soul" (5; cf. 171). Similarly, Ptolemy's interest in the law is an expression of his general "love of culture" (124). So the king shows emotional reverence for the law (177–78) because it is an excellent specimen of that broader class of wise and pious books. Along the same lines, cf. Demetrius's reaction in 31. The annual festival that Ptolemy says will mark the translators' arrival is a preexisting celebration of the king's victory against Antigonus (180).

49.   The "piety" (*eusebeia*) for which Ptolemy strives (24) is praised by the Jewish translators (229), and the Jews are in turn recognized as pious by Gentiles (e.g., 140).

50.   This is the one God to whom Aristeas prays for the Jews' release (17). I have departed here from Shutt's translation, which treats "Zeus" and "Dis" as the names that *Jews* give the one God. In the Greek, it is clearly Aristeas's Gentile "we" (*hēmeis*) that is the subject of the verb of naming.

51.   Notice, too, how the prosperity of Ptolemy's kingdom is attributed to God's blessing (see 15, 37).

52.   For Hebrew as the original language of the text, see Charles, *Jubilees*, xxvi–xxxiii; VanderKam, *Studies*, 1–18; Wintermute, "Jubilees," 43. This has been confirmed by the discovery of Hebrew fragments of *Jubilees* at Qumran from the first century B.C.E.

53.   So Nickelsburg, "Bible Re-written," 103.

54.   See, for example, ch. 25 (cf. 27:8-11), along with 20:4; 22:20; 30:1-15.

55.   On the date of *Jubilees*, see above, n. 1.

56.   The classic treatments of this period are found in Martin Hengel, *Judaism and Hellenism: Studies in Their Encounter in Palestine during the Early Hellenistic Period*, 2 vols., 2nd ed., trans. J. Bowden (London: SCM, 1974), 1:277–309; Tcherikover, *Hellenistic Civilization*, 152–203; Elias Bickerman, *The God of the Maccabees*, trans. H. R. Moehring, SJLA 32 (Leiden: Brill, 1979), 34–42; Schürer, *History*, 1:143–50. See also 1 Macc 1:12-15; 2 Macc 4:7-20; Josephus, *Ant.* 12.237–41. The aristocratic elements of Jerusalem seem to have been moving in a Hellenizing direction for at least two generations prior to Jason's official establishment of a Hellenistic constitution in the city. The prominence of the highly Hellenized Tobiad family suggests a general openness toward the wider Hellenistic world (see Tcherikover, *Hellenistic Civilization*, 117–51; Hengel, *Judaism and Hellenism*, 1:267–77; Josephus, *Ant.* 12.154–222, 224, 228–36; *CPJ* 1:125-127 no. 4 [= *P. Cair. Zen.* 59076]). Shortly after 200 B.C.E., Ben Sira seems to be resisting some of the innovations of this earlier aristocratic Hellenism (see Hengel, *Judaism and Hellenism*, 1:131–53; Tcherikover, *Hellenistic Civilization*, 143–51). We even see signs of significant Hellenism (and even religious syncretism) among the aristocratic opponents of Jason's reform (see Hengel, *Judaism and Hellenism*, 1.277 on 2 Macc 4:33; though cf. Tcherikover, *Hellenistic Civilization*, 469 n. 39).

57.   In 1 Maccabees, the Hellenizers want to "make a covenant with the Gentiles around us, for since we separated from them many disasters have come upon us" (1:11). See further 2 Macc 4:15-16, 18-20. On the other hand, Ben Sira bears witness to a "shame" of Torah that has led some to abandon it (Sir 41:8; 42:2).

58.   1 Macc 1:15; cf. Josephus, *Ant.* 12.241.

59. On the priestly background of *Jubilees*, see J. C. VanderKam, "Jubilees," in *The Anchor Bible Dictionary*, ed. D. N. Freedman (New York: Doubleday, 1986), 3.1030–32. Wintermute, "Jubilees," 45.

60. So Nickelsburg, "Bible Re-written," 102–3.

61. Of course, *Jubilees* has not escaped all Hellenistic influence in, for example, its understanding of geography (see Alexander, "Retelling," 102).

62. Indeed, it does not take many decades for the Hasmonean rulers of a "purified" Jewish state to begin imitating the habits of neighboring Hellenistic princes. Aristobulus I (104–103 B.C.E.) seems to have been known as *Philellēn* (Josephus, *Ant.* 13.318), and it is not clear whether his forced conversion of the Ituraeans to Judaism (*Ant.* 13.318) should be taken as a sign of his personal commitment to Torah or rather as a political move. As high priests, Aristobulus and his successors continued to observe Torah and administer the temple cult, but their adoption of Greek names and willingness to make alliances with foreign rulers may reflect a pragmatic and cosmopolitan attitude as much akin to the Jason's Hellenism as it was to the militant Torah devotion of Judas the Maccabee. See further Schürer, *History*, 1:216–32.

63. Nickelsburg, "Stories," 79.

64. See, for example, the commands regarding nakedness (3:31), murder (4:5), retaliation for murder (4:32), Shavuot (6:17, 21), the four sacred days in the calendar (6:23-31), circumcision (15:25), and adultery (39:6), all of which are said to be written in the "heavenly tablets." Laban also says that giving the younger daughter in marriage before the older will be written down "as a sin in heaven" (28:6). Other commands are said to be "eternal," such as those concerning Sabbath (2:33), purification after childbirth (3:14), tithing to temple servants (13:25-27), and (once again) circumcision (15:11-15, 28). The position of Levi and his family as priests is also said to be written in the heavenly tablets (30:18-20).

65. See, for example, 23:30-31.

66. This reading of the situation presumes that the Jerusalem Hellenizers thought of what they were doing in part as embracing a more "rational" view of the world. The emphasis on such rationality in *Aristeas* confirms both that this kind of rhetoric was used by Hellenistic elites to dismiss the traditional cultures of those they ruled, and that educated Jews outside Judea were sensitive to this critique. Note, too, Ben Sira's opposition to an intellectual "conceit" that has "led many astray" (Sir 3:21-24). Hengel, following Bickerman, suggests that the Hellenistic reformers under Jason and Menelaus discarded circumcision, food restrictions, and so forth, as "superstitious" corruptions of Moses' pure, "philosophical" doctrine (*Judaism and Hellenism*, 1:259; Bickerman, *God of the Maccabees*, 84–88; cf. Strabo, *Geogr.* 16.2.37). Although Hengel produces little positive evidence for this attitude among the Jerusalemites, it would explain well how eager young Jews under Jason could justify effacing their circumcision (1 Macc 1:15). The establishment of an ephebate in Jerusalem under Jason suggests at least that the pre-Maccabean Hellenizing movement would have provided its younger members some exposure to Hellenistic philosophy, with its rhetoric of living in accordance with "reason" (*logos*) and its derision of "superstition" (see *Oxford Classical Dictionary*, 3rd ed., s.v. "*ephēboi*." Tcherikover may well be right that the initial motives of the leaders of the movement were much more pragmatic (economic and political), but even

he recognizes that "changes in the spheres of religion and culture" were a by-product of the push toward Hellenism in Jerusalem (*Hellenistic Civilization*, 169).

Chapter 15: Conclusion

1.   For an attempt to use the hypothesis of Common Judaism to discuss the Gospel of John in relation to the parting of the ways, see Adele Reinhartz, "Common Judaism, the Parting of the Ways, and the Johannine Community," in *Coping with Change: Orthodoxy and Liberalism as Religious Reflexes to Societal Change*, ed. Bob Becking, Studies in Theology and Religion (Leiden: Brill, forthcoming).

Bibliography

Aaron, David. *Biblical Ambiquities: Metaphor, Semantics and Divine Imagery*. Brill Reference Library of Ancient Judaism 4. Leiden and Boston: Brill, 2001.

Achtemeier, Paul J., ed. *SBL 1978 Seminar Papers*. Missoula, Mont.: Scholars Press, 1978.

Adler, Y. "The Ancient Synagogue and the Ritual Bath: The Archaeological Evidence and Its Relevance to an Extinct Rabbinic Enactment Requiring Ablutions after Seminal Emission," (in Hebrew). *The Jerusalem Cathedra* 128 (2008) 51–72.

Albani, M., J. Frey, and A. Lange, eds. *Studies in the Book of Jubilees*. TSAJ 65. Tübingen: Mohr Siebeck, 1997.

Albeck, Chanoch. "*Midrash Vayikra Rabba*." In *Louis Ginzberg Jubilee Volume on the Occasion of His Seventieth Birthday, Hebrew Section*, edited by Saul Lieberman, Shalom Spiegel, Solomon Zeitlin, and Alexander Marx, 25–44. Jerusalem and New York: American Academy for Jewish Research, 1945.

———. See also Albeck, Hanoch.

Albeck, Hanoch. *Introduction to the Mishna*. Jerusalem: Mosad Bialik; Tel-Aviv: Dvir, 1959.

———. See also Albeck, Chanoch.

Alexander, Loveday C. A. *Acts in Its Ancient Literary Context: A Classicist Looks at the Acts of the Apostles*. Library of New Testament Studies 298. London: T&T Clark International, 2005.

———. "Septuaginta, Fachprosa, Imitatio: Albert Wifstrand and the Language of Luke-Acts." In idem, *Acts in Its Ancient Literary Context: A Classicist Looks at the Acts of the Apostles*, 231–52. Library of New Testament Studies 298. London: T&T Clark International, 2005.

Alexander, Philip S. "The Demonology of the Dead Sea Scrolls." In *The Dead Sea Scrolls after Fifty Years: A Comprehensive Assessment*, edited by Peter W. Flint and James C. VanderKam, 331–52. Leiden: Brill, 1999.

———. "'Homer the Prophet of All' and 'Moses Our Teacher': Late Antique Exegesis of the Homeric Epics and of the Torah of Moses." In *The Use of Sacred Books in the Ancient World*, edited by L. V. Rutgers, 127–42. Contributions to Biblical Exegesis and Theology 22. Leuven: Peeters, 1998.

————. "Incantations and Books of Magic." In Emil Schürer, *The History of the Jewish People in the Age of Jesus Christ (175 BC—AD 135)*, rev. and ed. Geza Vermes, Fergus Millar, and Martin Goodman, 3.1:364–65. 3 vols. Edinburgh: T&T Clark, 1986.

————. "'The Parting of the Ways' from the Perspective of Rabbinic Judaism." In *Jews and Christians: The Parting of the Ways AD 70 to 135*, edited by James D. G. Dunn, 1–25. Tübingen: Mohr Siebeck, 1992.

————. "Physiognomy, Initiation, and Rank in the Qumran Community." In *Geschichte—Tradition—Reflexion: Festschrift für Martin Hengel zum 70. Geburtstag*, edited by Hubert Cancik, Hermann Lichtenberger, and Peter Schäfer, 1:385–94. 3 vols. Tübingen: Mohr Siebeck, 1996.

————. "Retelling the Old Testament." In *It Is Written: Scripture Citing Scripture*, edited by D. A. Carson and H. G. M. Williamson, 99–121. Cambridge: Cambridge University Press, 1988.

————. "'Wrestling against Wickedness in High Places': Magic in the Worldview of the Qumran Community." In *The Scrolls and the Scriptures: Qumran Fifty Years After*, edited by Stanley E. Porter and Craig A. Evans, 318–37. JSPSup 26. Sheffield: Sheffield Academic Press, 1997.

Allegro, J. M. *Qumrân Cave 4, I [4Q158–4Q186]*. DJD 5. Oxford: Clarendon, 1968.

Allison, Dale C. *The New Moses: A Matthean Typology*. Minneapolis: Fortress Press, 1993.

Alon, Gedalia. "The Bounds of the Laws of Purity" (in Hebrew). *Studies in Jewish History 1* (1967): 148–76.

————. *The Jews in Their Land in the Talmudic Age (70–640 CE)*. Translated and edited by Gershon Levi. Cambridge, Mass.: Harvard University Press, 1996.

Alter, Robert. *Canon and Creativity: Modern Writing and the Authority of Scripture*. New Haven, Conn.: Yale University Press, 2000.

American Ethnological Society, ed. *The Proceedings of the American Ethnological Society: Symposium on New Approaches to the Study of Religion*. Seattle: American Ethnological Society, 1964.

Amir, Yehoshua. "Josephus on the Mosaic 'Constitution.'" In *Politics and Theopolitics in the Bible and Postbiblical Literature*, edited by Henning Graf Reventlow, Yair Hoffman, and Benjamin Uffenheimer, 13–27. JSOTSup 171. Sheffield: JSOT Press, 1994.

Amit, David. "Baths (*Miqva'ot*) of the 'Jerusalem Type' from the Second Temple Period in the Hebron Hills" (in Hebrew). In *Hikrei Eretz: Studies in the History of the Land of Israel (Dedicated to Prof. Yehuda Feliks)*, edited by Y. Friedman, Z. Safrai, and J. Schwartz, 35–48. Ramat Gan: Bar Ilan University Press, 1997.

————. "A Miqveh Complex near Alon Shevut." *'Atiqot* 38 (1999): 75–84.

————. "Miqwa'ot at Gamla." In *Gamla II—The Architecture*, edited by D. Syon. Forthcoming.

————. "Ritual Baths (*Mikva'ot*) from the Second Temple Period in the Hebron Mountains" (in Hebrew). In *Judea and Samaria Research Studies: Proceedings of the Third Annual Meeting 1993*, 157–89. Kedumim–Ariel: The College of Judea and Samaria, 1994.

————. "Ritual Baths (*Mikva'ot*) from the Second Temple Period in the Hebron Mountains" (in Hebrew). M.A. thesis, Hebrew University, Jerusalem, 1996.

Amit, David, and Boaz Zissu. "Jewish Sites from the Second Temple Period near Masu'ot Itzhak" (in Hebrew). In *Yad le-Yair, Eretz-Israel: Researches in the Memory of Yair Bashan*, edited by M. Livneh and R. Yehezkeli, 114–29. Tel-Aviv: Society for the Protection of Nature, 1999.

Anderson, G. W., P. A. H. de Boer, G. R. Castellino, Henri Cazelles, E. Hammershaimb, H. G. May, and W. Zimmerli, eds. *Congress Volume: Rome 1968*. VTSup 17. Leiden: Brill, 1969.

Anderson, Graham. *Sage, Saint, and Sophist: Holy Men and Their Associates in the Early Roman Empire*. London: Routledge, 1994.

Annenberg Research Institute, ed. *Translation of Scripture: Proceedings of a Conference at the Annenberg Research Institute, May 15–16, 1989*. JQR Supplements. Philadelphia: Annenberg Institute, 1989.

Aptowitzer, Viktor. "Observations on the Criminal Law of the Jews." *JQR* 15 (1924–25): 55–118.

Ascough, Richard. "Matthew and Community Formation." In *The Gospel of Matthew in Current Study: Studies in Memory of William G. Thompson*, edited by David Aune, 96–126. Grand Rapids: Eerdmans, 2001.

Aune, David, ed. *The Gospel of Matthew in Current Study: Studies in Memory of William G. Thompson*. Grand Rapids: Eerdmans, 2001.

Avemarie, Friedrich. "'Tohorat Ha-rabbim' and 'Mashqeh Ha-rabbim': Jacob Licht Reconsidered." In *Legal Texts and Legal Issues: Proceedings of the Second Meeting of the International Organization for Qumran Studies, Cambridge, 1995: Published in Honour of Joseph M. Baumgarten*, edited by Moshe J. Bernstein, Florentino García Martínez, and John Kampen, 215–29. STDJ 23. Leiden: Brill, 1997.

Aviam, M. "Christian Galilee in the Byzantine Period." In *Galilee through the Centuries: Confluence of Cultures: Proceedings of the Second International Conference in Galilee*, edited by Eric M. Meyers, 281–300. Winona Lake, Ind.: Eisenbrauns, 1999.

Avigad, Nahman. *Ha 'Ir ha-'elyonah Shel Yerushalayim*. Jerusalem: Shikoma, 1980. Translated as *Discovering Jerusalem: Recent Archaeological Excavations in the Upper City*. Nashville: Thomas Nelson, 1983.

Avni G., and S. Gudovitz. "Underground Olive Presses and Storage Systems at Ahuzat Hazzan." In *Olive Oil in Antiquity: Israel and Neighbouring Countries from the Neolithic to the Early Arab Period*, edited by D. Eitam and M. Heltzer, 137–47. Padua: Sargon, 1996.

Baasten, M. F. J., and W. T. van Peursen, eds. *Hamlet on a Hill: Semitic and Greek Studies Presented to Professor T. Muraoka on the Occasion of His Sixty-fifth Birthday*. Orientalia Lovaniensia Analecta 118. Leuven: Peeters, 2003.

Balch, David L., ed. *Social History of the Matthean Community: Cross-Disciplinary Approaches*. Minneapolis: Fortress Press, 1991.

Barag, D. "The 2000–2001 Exploration of the Tombs of Benei Hezir and Zechariah." *IEJ* 53 (2003): 78–110.

Barclay, J. M. G. *Jews in the Mediterranean Diaspora: From Alexander to Trajan (323 BCE–117 CE)*. Edinburgh: T&T Clark; Berkeley: University of California Press, 1996.

Barnett, P. W. "The Jewish Sign Prophets—AD 40–70: Their Intentions and Origin." *NTS* 27 (1981): 679–97.

Barr, James. "Did the Greek Pentateuch Really Serve as a Dictionary for the Translation of the Later Books?" In *Hamlet on a Hill: Semitic and Greek Studies Presented to Professor T. Muraoka on the Occasion of His Sixty-fifth Birthday*, edited by M. F. J. Baasten and W. T. van Peursen, 523–44. Orientalia Lovaniensia Analecta 118. Leuven: Peeters, 2003.

Barth, Gerhard. "Matthew's Understanding of the Law." In *Tradition and Interpretation in Matthew*, edited by Günther Bornkamm, Gerhard Barth, and Heinz Joachim Held, 58–164. New Testament Library. Philadelphia: Westminster, 1963.

Barthélemy, Dominique. *Les devanciers d'Aquila: première publication intégrale du texte des fragments du Dodécaprophéton*. VTSup 10. Leiden: Brill, 1963.

———. "Redécouverte d'un chaînon manquant de l'histoire de la LXX." *RB* 60 (1953): 18–29.

Bartlett, John R., ed. *Jews in the Hellenistic and Roman Cities*. London: Routledge, 2002.

———. *Jews in the Hellenistic World*. CCWJCW 1. Cambridge: Cambridge University Press, 1985.

Bauer, David R., and Mark Allan Powell, eds. *Treasures New and Old: Recent Contributions to Matthean Studies*. SBLSymS 1. Atlanta: Scholars Press, 1996.

Bauer, Walter. *Rechtgläubigkeit und Ketzerei im ältesten Christentum*. 2nd ed. Edited by Georg Strecker. 1934. Reprint, Tübingen: J. C. B. Mohr (Paul Siebeck), 1964.

Bauer, Walter, William F. Arndt, Frederick W. Danker, and F. Wilbur Gingrich. *Greek-English Lexicon of the New Testament and Other Early Literature: A Translation and Adaptation of the Fourth Revised and Augmented Edition of Walter Bauer's Griechisch-deutsches Wörterbuch zu den Schriften des Neuen Testaments und der übrigen urchristlichen Literatur*. Chicago: University of Chicago Press, 1979.

Baumgarten, A. I. *The Flourishing of Jewish Sects in the Maccabean Era: An Interpretation*. JSJSup 55. Leiden: Brill, 1997.

———. "Marcel Simon's *Verus Israel* as a Contribution to Jewish History." *HTR* 92 (1999): 465–78.

———. "The Name of the Pharisees." *JBL* 102 (1983): 411–28.

———. "The Pharisaic Paradosis." *HTR* 80 (1987): 63–77.

———. "Rivkin and Neusner on the Pharisees." In *Law in Religious Communities of the Roman Period: The Debate over Torah and Nomos in Post-biblical Judaism and Early Christianity*, edited by G. P. Richardson, 109–26. Studies in Christianity and Judaism 4. Waterloo, Ont.: Canadian Corporation for Studies in Religion, 1991.

———. "The Rule of the Martian as Applied to Qumran." *Israel Oriental Studies* 14 (1994): 179–200.

———. "The Zadokite Priests at Qumran: A Reconsideration." *DSD* 4 (1997): 137–56.

Baumgarten, Joseph M. *The Damascus Document (4Q266–273): Qumran Cave 4, XIII*. DJD 18. Oxford: Clarendon, 1996.

———. "The 4Q Zadokite Fragments on Skin Disease." *JJS* 41 (1990): 153–65.

———. "On the Nature of the Seductress in 4Q184." *RevQ* 15, nos. 57–58, special issue, *Mémorial Jean Starky* (1991): 133–43.

———. "The Qumran Sabbath Shirot and Rabbinic Merkabah Traditions," *RevQ* 13 (1988): 199–213.

Baumgarten, Joseph M., and Daniel R. Schwartz. "Damascus Document (CD)." In *The Dead Sea Scrolls: Hebrew, Aramaic, and Greek Texts with English Translations*, edited by James H.

Charlesworth et al., vol. 2, *Damascus Document, War Scroll, and Related Documents*, 4–58. Princeton Theological Seminary Dead Sea Scrolls Project. Tübingen: J. C. B Mohr; Louisville, Ky.: Westminster John Knox, 1995.

Beard, Mary. "Writing and Religion: Ancient Literacy and the Function of the Written Word in Roman Religion." In *Literacy in the Roman World*, edited by Mary Beard et al., 133–43. JRA Supplementary Series 3. Ann Arbor: Journal of Roman Archaeology, 1991.

Beard, Mary, et al., eds. *Literacy in the Roman World*. JRA Supplementary Series 3. Ann Arbor: Journal of Roman Archaeology, 1991.

Becker, Adam H., and Annette Yoshiko Reed, eds. *The Ways That Never Parted: Jews and Christians in Late Antiquity and the Early Middle Ages*. TSAJ 95. Tübingen: Mohr Siebeck, 2003.

Ben-Dov, Meyer. *In the Shadow of the Temple: The Discovery of Ancient Jerusalem*. Translated by Ina Friedman. Jerusalem: Keter, 1982.

Ben-Eliahu, E. "The Source of the Tombstone Inscription of Uziah." *The Jerusalem Cathedra* 98 (2000): 157–58.

Berlin, Adele, ed. *Religion and Politics in the Ancient Near East*. Studies and Texts in Jewish History and Culture. Bethesda, Md.: University Press of Maryland, 1996.

Bernstein, Moshe J., Florentino García Martínez, and John Kampen, eds. *Legal Texts and Legal Issues: Proceedings of the Second Meeting of the International Organization for Qumran Studies, Cambridge, 1995: Published in Honour of Joseph M. Baumgarten*. STDJ 23. Leiden: Brill, 1997.

Bickerman, Elias. *The God of the Maccabees*. Translated by H. R. Moehring. SJLA 32. Leiden: Brill, 1979.

Bieler, L. THEOS ANER: *Das Bild des "göttlichen Menschen" in Spätantike und Frühchristentum*. Vienna: O. Höfels, 1935.

Bilde, Per. *Flavius Josephus between Jerusalem and Rome: His Life, His Works, and Their Importance*. JSPSup 2. Sheffield: JSOT Press, 1988.

Binder, Donald D. *Into the Temple Courts: The Place of the Synagogues in the Second Temple Period*. SBLDS 169. Atlanta: Society of Biblical Literature, 1999.

———. "The Origins of the Synagogue: An Evaluation." In *The Ancient Synagogue from Its Origins until 200 CE: Papers Presented at an International Conference at Lund University, October 14–17, 2001*, edited by Birger Olsson and Magnus Zetterholm, 118–31. ConBNT 39. Stockholm: Almqvist & Wiksell International, 2003.

Black, Max. *Models and Metaphors: Studies in Language and Philosophy*. Ithaca, N.Y.: Cornell University Press, 1963.

Blank, Debra Reed. "It's Time to Take Another Look at 'Our Little Sister' Soferim: A Bibliographical Essay." *JQR* 90, nos. 1–2 (1999): 1–26.

Bleiberg, E. *Tree of Paradise: Jewish Mosaics from the Roman Empire*. Brooklyn: Brooklyn Museum, 2005.

Boccaccini, Gabriele. *Beyond the Essene Hypothesis: The Parting of the Ways between Qumran and Enochic Judaism*. Grand Rapids: Eerdmans, 1998.

———. "Il tema della memoria in Giuseppe Flavio." *Henoch* 6 (1984): 147–63.

———. *Middle Judaism: Jewish Thought, 300 BCE to 200 CE* Minneapolis: Fortress Press, 1991.

Bockmuehl, Marcus. "1QS and Salvation at Qumran." In *Justification and Variegated Nomism*, vol. 1, *The Complexities of Second Temple Judaism*, edited by D. A. Carson, Peter T. O'Brien, and Mark A. Seifrid, 381–414. WUNT 2.140. Tübingen: Mohr Siebeck, 2001.

Borgen, Peder, Vernon K. Robbins, and David B. Gowler, eds. *Recruitment, Conquest, and Conflict: Strategies in Judaism, Early Christianity, and the Greco-Roman World.* Emory Studies in Early Christianity 6. Atlanta: Scholars Press, 1998.

Bornkamm, Günther. "The Authority to 'Bind' and 'Loose' in the Church in Matthew's Gospel." In *The Interpretation of Matthew*, edited by Graham Stanton, 101–14. 2nd ed. Edinburgh: T&T Clark, 1995. Previously published in *Perspective* [Pittsburgh] 11, nos. 1–2 (1970): 37–50.

———. "End-Expectation and Church in Matthew." In *Tradition and Interpretation in Matthew*, edited by Günther Bornkamm, Gerhard Barth, and Heinz Joachim Held, 15–51. New Testament Library. Philadelphia: Westminster, 1963.

Bornkamm, Günther, Gerhard Barth, and Heinz Joachim Held, eds. *Tradition and Interpretation in Matthew.* New Testament Library. Philadelphia: Westminster, 1963.

Botterweck, G. Johannes, Helmer Ringgren, and Heinz-Josef Fabry, eds. *Theological Dictionary of the Old Testament.* Translated by John T. Willis. 14 vols. Grand Rapids: Eerdmans, 1980.

Brandon, S. G. F. *Jesus and the Zealots: A Study of the Political Factor in Primitive Christianity.* New York: Charles Scribner's Sons, 1967.

Brenner, Athalya, and Carole R. Fontaine, eds. *Wisdom and Psalms: A Feminist Companion to the Bible.* Sheffield: Sheffield Academic Press, 1998.

Brett, Mark G., ed. *Ethnicity and the Bible.* Biblical Interpretation Series 19. Leiden: Brill, 2002.

Brettler, Marc Zvi. *God Is King: Understanding an Israelite Metaphor.* JSOTSup 76. Sheffield: JSOT Press, 1989.

———. "Memory in Ancient Israel." In *Memory and History in Christianity and Judaism*, edited by Michael A. Signer, 1–17. Notre Dame: Notre Dame University Press, 2001.

Brettler, Marc Zvi, and Michael A. Fishbane, eds. *Minḥah le-Naḥum: Biblical and Other Studies Presented to Nahum M. Sarna in Honour of His 70th Birthday.* JSOTSup 154. Sheffield: JSOT Press, 1993.

Brooke, George J. "The Canon within the Canon at Qumran and in the New Testament." In *The Scrolls and the Scriptures: Qumran Fifty Years After*, edited by Stanley E. Porter and Craig A. Evans, 242–66. JSPSup 26. Sheffield: Sheffield Academic Press, 1997.

———. "Isaiah 40:3 and the Wilderness Community." In *New Qumran Texts and Studies: Proceedings of the First Meeting of the International Organization for Qumran Studies: Paris 1992*, edited by George J. Brooke and Florentino García Martínez, 117–32. STDJ 15. Leiden: Brill, 1994.

Brooke, George J., and Florentino García Martínez, eds. *New Qumran Texts and Studies: Proceedings of the First Meeting of the International Organization for Qumran Studies: Paris 1992.* STDJ 15. Leiden: Brill, 1994.

Brown, Peter. *The Making of Late Antiquity.* Cambridge, Mass.: Harvard University Press, 1978.

———. *Society and the Holy in Late Antiquity.* Berkeley: University of California Press, 1982.

Brown, Raymond E. "Not Jewish Christianity and Gentile Christianity but Types of Jewish/

Gentile Christianity." *CBQ* 45 (1983): 74–79.

Brown, Schuyler. "The Matthean Community and the Gentile Mission." *NovT* 22, no. 3 (1980): 193–221.

Brownlee, William Hugh. *The Dead Sea Manual of Discipline: Translation and Notes.* BASORSup 10–12. New Haven, Conn.: American Schools of Oriental Research, 1951.

Bruce, F. F. *Biblical Exegesis in the Qumran Texts.* London: Tyndale, 1960.

Buber, Martin. *The Kingship of God.* Translated by Richard Scheimann. 1956. Reprint, New York: Harper & Row, 1967.

Buell, Denise Kimber. *Why This New Race: Ethnic Reasoning in Early Christianity.* New York: Columbia University Press, 2005.

Burkert, Walter. *Greek Religion.* Translated by J. Raffan. Cambridge, Mass.: Harvard University Press, 1985.

Calabi, F. *The Language and the Law of God: Interpretation and Politics in Philo of Alexandria.* South Florida Studies in the History of Judaism 188; Studies in Philo of Alexandria and Mediterranean Antiquity. Atlanta: Scholars Press, 1998.

Campbell, J. G. "4QMMT(d) and the Tripartite Canon." *JJS* 51, no. 2 (2000): 181–90.

Camponovo, Odo. *Königtum, Königsherrschaft und Reich Gottes in den frühjüdischen Schriften.* OBO 58. Göttingen: Vandenhoeck & Ruprecht, 1984.

Cancik, Hubert. "Theokratia und Priesterherrschaft." In *Theokratie,* edited by Jacob Taubes, 65–77. Religionstheorie und Politische Theologie 3. Munich: W. Fink and F. Schöningh, 1987.

Cancik, Hubert, Hermann Lichtenberger, and Peter Schäfer, eds. *Geschichte—Tradition—Reflexion: Festschrift für Martin Hengel zum 70. Geburtstag.* 3 vols. Tübingen: Mohr Siebeck, 1996.

Carson, D. A. "Summaries and Conclusions." In *Justification and Variegated Nomism,* vol. 1, *The Complexities of Second Temple Judaism,* edited by D. A. Carson, Peter T. O'Brien, and Mark A. Seifrid. WUNT 2.140. Tübingen: Mohr Siebeck, 2001.

Carson, D. A., Peter T. O'Brien, and Mark A. Seifrid, eds. *Justification and Variegated Nomism,* vol. 1, *The Complexities of Second Temple Judaism.* WUNT 2.140. Tübingen: Mohr Siebeck, 2001.

Carson, D. A., and H. G. M. Williamson, eds. *It Is Written: Scripture Citing Scripture.* Cambridge: Cambridge University Press, 1988.

Castelli, S. "*Antiquities* 3–4 and *Against Apion* 2.145ff.: Different Approaches to the Law." In *Internationales Josephus-Kolloquium Amsterdam 2000,* edited by J. Kalms, 151–69. Münster: LIT, 2001.

Charette, Blaine. *The Theme of Recompense in Matthew's Gospel.* JSNTSup 79. Sheffield: Sheffield Academic Press, 1992.

Charles, R. H., ed. *The Apocrypha and Pseudepigrapha of the Old Testament in English.* 2 vols. Oxford: Clarendon, 1913.

———. *The Book of Jubilees, or, The Little Genesis.* Jerusalem: Makor, 1971.

Charlesworth, James H. "Intertextuality: Isaiah 40:3 and the Serek Ha-Yahad." In *The Quest for Context and Meaning: Studies in Biblical Intertextuality in Honor of James A. Sanders,* edited by Craig A. Evans and Shemaryahu Talmon, 271–83. Biblical Interpretation Series 28. Leiden: Brill, 1994.

———, ed. *The Old Testament Pseudepigrapha*. 2 vols. Garden City, N.Y.: Doubleday, 1983.

Charlesworth, James H., et al., eds. *The Dead Sea Scrolls: Hebrew, Aramaic, and Greek Texts with English Translations*. Princeton Theological Seminary Dead Sea Scrolls Project. Tübingen: J. C. B Mohr; Louisville, Ky.: Westminster John Knox, 1995–.

Chazon, Esther. "444. 4QIncantation." In *Qumran Cave 4, XX: Political and Liturgical Texts, Part 2*, edited by E. Chazon et al., 365–78. DJD 29. Oxford: Clarendon, 1999.

———. "The Function of the Qumran Prayer Texts: An Analysis of the Daily Prayers (4Q503)." In *The Dead Sea Scrolls Fifty Years after Their Discovery: Proceedings of the Jerusalem Congress July 20–25, 1997*, edited by Lawrence H. Schiffman, Emanuel Tov, and James C. VanderKam, 217–25. Jerusalem: Israel Exploration Society, 2000.

———. "Prayers from Qumran and Their Historical Implications." *DSD* 1 (1994): 265–84.

Chazon, Esther, et al., eds. *Qumran Cave 4, XX: Political and Liturgical Texts, Part 2*. DJD 29. Oxford: Clarendon, 1999.

Chilton, Bruce. "The Kingdom of God in Recent Discussion." In *Studying the Historical Jesus: Evaluations of the State of Current Research*, ed. Bruce Chilton and Craig A. Evans, 225–80. NTTS 19. Leiden: Brill, 1994.

———, ed. *The Kingdom of God in the Teaching of Jesus*. IRT 5. Philadelphia: Fortress Press, 1984.

Chilton, Bruce, and Craig A. Evans, eds. *Studying the Historical Jesus: Evaluations of the State of Current Research*. NTTS 19. Leiden: Brill, 1994.

Clarke, K. W. "The Gentile Bias in Matthew." *JBL* 66 (1947): 165–72.

Clements, R. "ZKR." In *Theological Dictionary of the Old Testament*, edited by G. Botterweck, H. Ringgren, and Heinz-Josef Fabry, translated by Douglas W. Stott, 4:64–86. Grand Rapids: Eerdmans, 1980.

Cohen, Shaye J. D. *From the Maccabees to the Mishnah*. Philadelphia: Westminster, 1987.

———. *Josephus in Galilee and Rome: His Vita and Development as a Historian*. Columbia Studies in the Classical Tradition. Leiden: Brill, 1979.

———. "Josephus, Jeremiah, and Polybius." *History and Theory* 21 (1982): 366–81.

———. "The Place of the Rabbi in Jewish Society of the Second Century." In *The Galilee in Late Antiquity*, edited by Lee I. Levine, 157–83. New York: Jewish Theological Seminary of America, 1992.

———. "Were Pharisees and Rabbis the Leaders of Communal Prayer and Torah Study in Antiquity? The Evidence of the New Testament, Josephus, and the Church Fathers." In *Evolution of the Synagogue: Problems and Progress*, ed. Howard Clark Kee and Lynn H. Cohick, 89–105. Harrisburg, Pa.: Trinity Press International, 1999.

Cohn, Norman. *Cosmos, Chaos and That World to Come: The Ancient Roots of Apocalyptic Faith*. New Haven, Conn.: Yale University Press, 1993.

Cohn, Robert L. *The Shape of Sacred Space: Four Biblical Studies*. AAR Studies in Religion 23. Ann Arbor, Mich.: Scholars Press, 1981.

Collins, John Joseph. *Between Athens and Jerusalem: Jewish Identity in the Hellenistic Diaspora*. 2nd ed. Grand Rapids: Eerdmans, 2000.

————. "Forms of the Community in the Dead Sea Scrolls." In *Emanuel: Studies in Hebrew Bible, Septuagint, and Dead Sea Scrolls in Honour of Emanuel Tov*, edited by Shalom M. Paul and Eva Ben-David, 97–111. VTSup 94. Leiden: Brill, 2003.

————. "Powers in Heaven: God, Gods, and Angels in the Dead Sea Scrolls." In *Religion in the Dead Sea Scrolls*, edited by John Joseph Collins and Robert Kugler, 9–28. Studies in the Dead Sea Scrolls and Related Literature. Grand Rapids: Eerdmans, 2000.

Collins, John Joseph, and Robert A. Kugler, eds. *Religion in the Dead Sea Scrolls*. Studies in the Dead Sea Scrolls and Related Literature. Grand Rapids: Eerdmans, 2000.

Collins, John Joseph, Michael Owen Wise, Norman Golb, and Dennis Pardee, eds. *Methods of Investigation of the Dead Sea Scrolls and the Khirbet Qumran Site: Present Realities and Future Prospects*. Annals of the New York Academy of Sciences 722. New York: New York Academy of Sciences, 1994.

Collins, Randall. "On the Acrimoniousness of Intellectual Disputes." *Common Knowledge* 8 (2002): 47–70.

Colson, F. H., and George Herbert Whitaker. *Philo, with an English Translation*. 10 vols. LCL. 1935. Reprint, Cambridge, Mass.: Harvard University Press, 1962.

Cook, Michael J. "Interpreting 'Pro-Jewish' Passages in Matthew." *HUCA* 54 (1983): 135–46.

Cotton, H., R. Hoyland, J. Price, and D. Wasserstein, eds. *From Hellenism to Islam: Cultural and Linguistic Change in the Roman Near East*. Cambridge: Cambridge University Press, forthcoming.

Cousland, J. R. C. *The Crowds in the Gospel of Matthew*. NovTSup 102. Leiden: Brill, 2002.

Cowey, M. S., and K. Maresch. *Urkunden des Politeuma der Juden von Herakleopolis (144/3–133/2 V. Chr.) (P. Polit. Iud.): Papyri aus den Sammlungen von Heidelberg, Köln, München und Wien*. Abhandlungen der Nordrhein-Westfälischen Akademie der Wissenschaften. Sonderreihe Papyrologica Coloniensia 29. Wiesbaden: Westdeutscher Verlag, 2001.

Cox, C. E., ed. *VI Congress of the International Organization for Septuagint and Cognate Studies, Jerusalem, 1986*. SBL Septuagint and Cognate Studies 23. Atlanta: Scholars Press, 1987.

Crawford, Sidnie White. "Lady Wisdom and Dame Folly at Qumran." In *Wisdom and Psalms: A Feminist Companion to the Bible*, edited by Athalya Brenner and Carole R. Fontaine, 205–17. Sheffield: Sheffield Academic Press, 1998.

Creach, Jerome F. D. *Yahweh as Refuge and the Editing of the Hebrew Psalter*. JSOTSup 217. Sheffield: Sheffield Academic Press, 1996.

Cross, Frank Moore. "Fragments of the Prayer of Nabonidas." *IEJ* 34 (1984): 260–64.

David, H., ed. *Lived Religion in America: Toward a History of Practice*. Princeton: Princeton University Press, 1997.

Davies, Margaret. "Stereotyping the Other: The 'Pharisees' in the Gospel According to Matthew." In *Biblical Studies/Cultural Studies: The Third Sheffield Colloquium*, edited by J. Cheryl Exum and Stephen D. Moore, 415–32. JSOTSup 226. Sheffield: Sheffield Academic Press, 1998.

Davies, Philip. "Redaction and Sectarianism in the Qumran Scrolls." In *The Scriptures and the Scrolls: Studies in Honour of A. S. van der Woude on the Occasion of His 65th Birthday*, edited by C. J. Labuschagne, A. Hilhorst, and F. García Martínez. VTSup 49. Leiden: Brill, 1992.

Davies, W. D. *The Setting of the Sermon on the Mount.* Cambridge: Cambridge University Press, 1963.

Davies, W. D., and Dale C. Allison. *A Critical and Exegetical Commentary on the Gospel According to Saint Matthew.* 3 vols. ICC. London: T&T Clark, 1988–97.

Davies, W. D., and Louis Finkelstein, eds. *The Cambridge History of Judaism.* 4 vols. Cambridge: Cambridge University Press, 1999.

Davila, James. "The Hodayot Hymnist and the Four Who Entered Paradise." *RevQ* 17, nos. 65–68, special issue, *Milik Festschrift* (1996): 457–78.

Davis, Moshe, ed. *Israel: Its Role in Civilization.* New York: Israel Institute of the Jewish Theological Seminary, 1956.

Deines, R. "The Pharisees between 'Judaisms' and 'Common Judaism.'" In *Justification and Variegated Nomism,* vol. 1, *The Complexities of Second Temple Judaism,* edited by D. A. Carson, Peter T. O'Brien, and Mark A. Seifrid, 443–504. WUNT 2.140. Tübingen: Mohr Siebeck, 2001.

DeLaine, J., and D. E. Johnston, eds. *Roman Baths and Bathing: Proceedings of the First International Conference on Roman Baths Held at Bath, England, 30 March–4 April 1992.* JRA Supplementary Series 37. Portsmouth, R.I.: Journal of Roman Archaeology, 1999.

Delcor, M., ed. *Qumran: sa piété, sa théologie et son milieu.* BETL 46. Paris: Duculot, 1978.

Dimant, Devorah. "Men as Angels: The Self-Image of the Qumran Community." In *Religion and Politics in the Ancient Near East,* edited by Adele Berlin, 93–103. Studies and Texts in Jewish History and Culture. Bethesda, Md.: University Press of Maryland, 1996.

———. "The Problem of Non-translated Biblical Greek." In *VI Congress of the International Organization for Septuagint and Cognate Studies, Jerusalem, 1986,* edited by C. E. Cox, 1–19. SBL Septuagint and Cognate Studies 23. Atlanta: Scholars Press, 1987.

Dimant, Devorah, and Uriel Rappaport, eds. *Dead Sea Scrolls: Forty Years of Research.* STDJ 10. Leiden: Brill, 1992.

Dines, J. M. *The Septuagint.* Understanding the Bible and Its World. London: T&T Clark, 2004.

Dion, P.-E. "Synagogues et temples dans l'Egypte hellénistique." *ScEs* 29 (1977): 45–75.

Dittenberger, Wilhelm. *Sylloge Inscriptionum Graecarum.* 3rd ed. Leipzig: Hirzelium, 1915–24.

Donaldson, Terrence. *Judaism and the Gentiles: Jewish Patterns of Universalism (to 135 CE).* Waco: Baylor University Press, 2007.

———. "Proselytes or 'Righteous Gentiles'? The Status of Gentiles in Eschatological Pilgrimage Patterns of Thought." *JSP* 7 (1990): 3–27.

Doran, Robert. "The Jewish Hellenistic Historians before Josephus," *ANRW* 2.20.1 (1986), 246–97. Douglas, Mary. *Purity and Danger: An Analysis of the Concepts of Pollution and Taboo.* London: Ark, 1988.

Dozeman, Thomas. *God on the Mountain: A Study of the Redaction, Theology, and Canon in Exodus 19–24.* SBLMS 37. Atlanta: Scholars Press, 1989.

Duling, Dennis. "The Matthean Brotherhood and Marginal Scribal Leadership." In *Modelling Early Christianity: Social Scientific Studies of the New Testament in Its Context,* edited by Philip Esler, 159–82. London: Routledge, 1995.

Dunn, James D. G. *Christianity in the Making*, vol. 1, *Jesus Remembered*. Grand Rapids: Eerdmans, 2003.

———. "Pharisees, Sinners, Jesus." In *The Social World of Formative Christianity and Judaism*, edited by Howard Clark Kee and Jacob Neusner, 264–89. Philadelphia: Fortress Press, 1988.

———, ed. *Jews and Christians: The Parting of the Ways AD 70 to 135*. Tübingen: Mohr Siebeck, 1992.

Edwards, Douglas R., ed. *Religion and Society in Roman Palestine: Old Questions, New Approaches*. London: Routledge, 2004.

Eidevall, Gören. *Grapes in the Desert: Metaphors, Models and Themes in Hosea 4–14*. ConBOT 43. Stockholm; Almqvist & Wiksell International, 1996.

Eisenberg, E. "Nahal Yarmut.'" *HA-ESI* 112 (2000): 91–93.

Eitam, D., and M. Heltzer, eds. *Olive Oil in Antiquity: Israel and Neighbouring Countries from the Neolithic to the Early Arab Period*. Padua: Sargon, 1996.

Elbogen, Ismar. *Jewish Liturgy: A Comprehensive History*. Translated by R. P. Scheindlin. Philadelphia: Jewish Publication Society, 1993. Originally published as *Der jüdische Gottesdienst in seiner geschichtlichen Entwicklung*. Leipzig: G. Fock, 1913.

Eliav, Yaron Z. "Did the Jews at First Abstain from Using the Roman Bath-House?" *The Jerusalem Cathedra* 75 (1995): 3–35.

Elitzur, Yoel. "Ritual Pools for Immersion of Hands" (in Hebrew). *The Jerusalem Cathedra* 91 (1999): 169–72.

Ellis, E. Earle. "Biblical Interpretation in the New Testament Church." In *Mikra: Text, Translation, Reading and Interpretation of the Hebrew Bible in Ancient Judaism and Early Christianity*, edited by M. J. Mulder and H. Sysling, 691–725. CRINT, Section 2: Literature of the Jewish People in the Period of the Second Temple and the Talmud 1. Assen: Van Gorcum, 1988.

Elsner, Jaś. *Art and the Roman Viewer: The Transformation of Art from the Pagan World to Christianity*. Cambridge: Cambridge University Press, 1995.

Epstein, J. N., and E. Z. Melamed, eds. *Mekhilta d'Rabbi Shim'on b. Jochai*. Jerusalem: Mekize Nirdamim, 1955.

Eriksen, Thomas H. *Ethnicity and Nationalism: Anthropological Perspectives*. London: Pluto, 1993.

Eshel, Esther. "4Q414 Fragment 2: Purification of a Corpse-Contaminated Person." In *Legal Texts and Legal Issues: Proceedings of the Second Meeting of the International Organization for Qumran Studies, Cambridge, 1995, Published in Honour of Joseph M. Baumgarten*, edited by Moshe J. Bernstein, Florentino García Martínez, and John Kampen, 3–10. STDJ 23. Leiden: Brill, 1997.

Eshel, H. "A Note on Miqva'ot at Sepphoris." In *Archaeology and the Galilee: Texts and Contexts in the Greco-Roman and Byzantine Periods*, edited by Douglas R. Edwards and C. Thomas McCollough, 131–33. South Florida Studies in the History of Judaism 143. Atlanta: Scholars Press, 1997.

Esler, Philip. *Community and Gospel in Luke-Acts: The Social and Political Motivations of Lucan Theology*. SNTSMS 57. Cambridge: Cambridge University Press, 1987.

———. *Conflict and Identity in Romans: The Social Setting of Paul's Letter*. Minneapolis: Fortress Press, 2003.

———. "Group Boundaries and Intergroup Conflict in Galatians: A New Reading of Galatians 5:13—6:10." In *Ethnicity and the Bible*, edited by Mark G. Brett, 215–40. Biblical Interpretation Series 19. Leiden: Brill, 1996.

———, ed. *Modelling Early Christianity: Social Scientific Studies of the New Testament in Its Context*. London: Routledge, 1995.

Evans, Craig A., and James A. Sanders, eds. *Early Christian Interpretation of the Scriptures of Israel: Investigations and Proposals*. JSNTSup 148. Sheffield: Sheffield Academic Press, 1997.

Evans, Craig A., and Shemaryahu Talmon, eds. *The Quest for Context and Meaning: Studies in Biblical Intertextuality in Honor of James A. Sanders*. Biblical Interpretation Series 28. Leiden: Brill, 1994.

Exum, J. Cheryl, and Stephen D. Moore, eds. *Biblical Studies/Cultural Studies: The Third Sheffield Colloquium*. JSOTSup 226. Sheffield: Sheffield Academic Press, 1998.

Farmer, William Reuben. *Maccabees, Zealots, and Josephus: An Inquiry into Jewish Nationalism in the Greco-Roman Period*. Westport, Conn.: Greenwood, 1956.

Feldman, David Michael. *Birth Control in Jewish Law: Marital Relations, Contraception, and Abortion as Set Forth in the Classic Texts of Jewish Law with Comparative Reference to the Christian Exegetical Tradition*. Westport, Conn.: Greenwood, 1980.

Feldman, Louis H. *Jew and Gentile in the Ancient World: Attitudes and Interactions from Alexander to Justinian*. Princeton: Princeton University Press, 1993.

———. "Josephus' Portrayal of the Hasmoneans Compared with 1 Maccabees." In *Josephus and the History of the Greco-Roman Period: Essays in Memory of Morton Smith*, edited by Fausto Parente and Joseph Sievers, 41–68. StPB 41. Leiden: Brill, 1994.

———. *Judean Antiquities 1–4*. Vol. 3 of *Flavius Josephus: Translation and Commentary*, edited by Louis H. Feldman and Steve Mason. Leiden: Brill, 2000.

———. "Prophets and Prophecy in Josephus." *JJS* 41 (1990): 386–422.

Feldman, Louis H., and John R. Levison, eds. *Josephus' Contra Apionem: Studies in Its Character and Context with a Latin Concordance to the Portion Missing in Greek*. AGJU 34. Leiden: Brill, 1996.

Feldman, Louis H., and Steve Mason, eds. *Josephus: Translation and Commentary*. 10 vols. Leiden: Brill, 2000.

Fine, Steven. "From Meeting House to Sacred Realm: Holiness and the Ancient Synagogue." In *Sacred Realm: The Emergence of the Synagogue in the Ancient World*, edited by Steven Fine, 27–49. New York: Oxford University Press, 1996.

———. *This Holy Place: On the Sanctity of the Synagogue during the Greco-Roman Period*. Christianity and Judaism in Antiquity 11. Notre Dame: University of Notre Dame Press, 1997.

———, ed. *Jews, Christians, and Polytheists in the Ancient Synagogue: Cultural Interaction during the Greco-Roman Period*. New York: Routledge, 1999.

———, ed. *Sacred Realm: The Emergence of the Synagogue in the Ancient World*. New York: Oxford University Press, 1996.

Finkelberg, M. "Homer as a Foundation Text." In *Homer, the Bible, and Beyond: Literary and Religious Canons in the Ancient World*, edited by M. Finkelberg and Guy G. Stroumsa, 75–96. Jerusalem Studies in Religion and Culture 2. Leiden: Brill, 2003.

Finkelberg M., and Guy G. Stroumsa. *Homer, the Bible, and Beyond: Literary and Religious Canons in the Ancient World*. Jerusalem Studies in Religion and Culture 2. Leiden: Brill, 2003.

Fischel, Henry A., ed. *Essays in Greco-Roman and Related Talmudic Literature*. New York: KTAV, 1977.

Fischer, M. "The Jerusalem-Emmaus Road in Light of the Excavations at Hurvat Metzad" (in Hebrew). In *Greece and Rome in Eretz-Israel: Collected Essays*, edited by A. Kasher, G. Fuks, and U. Rappaport, 185–206. Jerusalem: Yad Izhak Ben-Zvi, 1989.

Fischer, Moshe L., Benjamin H. Isaac, and Israel Roll. *Roman Roads in Judaea II: The Jaffa–Jerusalem Roads*. BAR International Series 628. Oxford: BAR, 1996.

Fishbane, Michael A. *Biblical Interpretation in Ancient Israel*. Oxford: Clarendon, 1985.

———. "Use, Authority and Interpretation of Mikra at Qumran." In *Mikra: Text, Translation, Reading and Interpretation of the Hebrew Bible in Ancient Judaism and Early Christianity*, edited by M. J. Mulder and H. Sysling, 339–77. CRINT, Section 2: Literature of the Jewish People in the Period of the Second Temple and the Talmud 1. Assen: Van Gorcum, 1988.

Fleischer, Ezra. *Eretz-Israel Prayer and Prayer Rituals as Portrayed in the Geniza Documents*. Publications of the Perry Foundation. Jerusalem: Magnes, 1988.

Flint, Peter W., and James C. VanderKam, eds. *The Dead Sea Scrolls after Fifty Years: A Comprehensive Assessment*. Leiden: Brill, 1999.

Flusser, David. "Pharisäer, Sadducäer und Essener im Pescher Nahum." In *Qumran*, edited by K. Grözinger et al., 121–66. Wege der Forschung 410. Darmstadt: Wissenschaftliche Buchgesellschaft, 1981.

———. "Two Anti-Jewish Montages in Matthew." *Immanuel* 5 (1975): 37–45.

Foerster, Gideon. "The Synagogues at Masada and Herodium." In *Ancient Synagogues Revealed*, edited by Lee I. Levine, 24–29. Jerusalem: Israel Exploration Society, 1981.

Francis, James A. *Subversive Virtue: Asceticism and Authority in the Second-Century Pagan World*. University Park, Pa.: Pennsylvania State University Press, 1995.

Frankel, Zacharias. *Über den Einfluss der palästinischen Exegese auf die alexandrinische Hermeneutik*. Westmead: Gregg International Publishers, 1972.

Frennesson, Björn. *"In a Common Rejoicing": Liturgical Communion with Angels in Qumran*. Studia Semitica Upsaliensia 14. Uppsala: University of Uppsala Press, 1999.

Frey, J.-B., ed. *Corpus Inscriptionum Judaicarum*. 2 vols. Rome: Pontificio Istituto di Archeologia Cristiana, 1936–52. Vol. 2 reprint, New York: KTAV, 1975.

———. "La question des images chez les juifs à la lumière des récentes découvertes." *Biblica* 15 (1934): 265–300.

Freyne, Sean. "Vilifying the Other and Defining the Self." In *"To See Ourselves as Others See Us": Christians, Jews, "Others" in Late Antiquity*, edited by Jacob Neusner, Caroline McCracken-Flesher, and Ernest S. Frerichs, 117–43. Scholars Press Studies in the Humanities. Chico, Calif.: Scholars Press, 1985.

Friedman, Shamma. "The Holy Scriptures Defile the Hands—The Transformation of a Biblical Concept in Rabbinic Theology." In *Minḥah le-Naḥum: Biblical and Other Studies Presented to Nahum M. Sarna in Honour of His 70th Birthday*, edited by Marc Zvi Brettler and Michael A. Fishbane, 117–32. JSOTSup 154. Sheffield: JSOT Press, 1993.

————. "La-Aggadah Ha-Historit Ba-Talmud Ha-Bavli." In *Saul Lieberman Memorial Volume*, edited by Shamma Friedman. New York and Jerusalem: Jewish Theological Seminary of America, 1993.

————, ed. *Saul Lieberman Memorial Volume*. New York and Jerusalem: Jewish Theological Seminary of America, 1993.

Friedman, Y., Z. Safrai, and J. Schwartz, eds. *Hikrei Eretz: Studies in the History of the Land of Israel (Dedicated to Prof. Yehuda Feliks)*. Ramat Gan: Bar Ilan University Press, 1997.

Fritsch, Charles T. *Anti-Anthropomorphisms of the Greek Pentateuch*. Princeton: Princeton University Press, 1943.

Gafni, Isaiah, Aharon Oppenheimer, and Daniel Schwartz, eds. *The Jews in the Hellenistic-Roman World: Studies in Memory of Menahem Stern*. Jerusalem: Zalman Shazar Center for Jewish History and the Historical Society of Israel, 1996.

Gager, J. G. *Moses in Greco-Roman Paganism*. SBLMS 16. Nashville: Abingdon, 1972.

Gale, Aaron M. *Redefining Ancient Borders: The Jewish Scribal Framework of Matthew's Gospel*. New York: T&T Clark, 2005.

Galor, K. "Plastered Pools: A New Perspective." In vol. 2 of *Fouilles de Khirbet Qumrân et 'Aïn Feshkha*, edited by Jean-Baptiste Humbert and Jan Gunneweg, 291–320. Göttingen: Vandenhoeck & Ruprecht, 2003.

Gammie, John G., and Leo G. Perdue, eds. *The Sage in Israel and the Ancient Near East*. Winona Lake, Ind.: Eisenbrauns, 1990.

García Martínez, Florentino. *The Dead Sea Scrolls Translated: The Qumran Texts in English*. Translated by Wilfred G. E. Watson. Leiden: Brill, 1996.

————. *Qumran and Apocalyptic: Studies on the Aramaic Texts from Qumran*. Leiden: Brill, 1992.

García Martínez, Florentino, Eibert J. C. Tigchelaar, and A. S. van der Woude. *Qumran Cave 11, II: [11Q2–18, 11Q20–31]*. DJD 23. Oxford: Clarendon, 1998.

García Martínez, Florentino, and Julio Trebolle Barrera. *The People of the Dead Sea Scrolls*. Leiden: Brill, 1995.

Gaston, Lloyd. "The Messiah of Israel as Teacher of the Gentiles: The Setting of Matthew's Christology." *Int* 21 (1975): 24–40.

Geertz, Clifford. "Centers, Kings, and Charisma: Reflections on the Symbolics of Power." In idem, *Local Knowledge: Further Essays in Interpretive Anthropology*, 121–46. New York: Basic Books, 1983.

————. *Local Knowledge: Further Essays in Interpretive Anthropology*. New York: Basic Books, 1983.

Geiger, Abraham. *Urschrift und Übersetzungen der Bibel, in ihrer Abhängigkeit von der innern Entwicklung des Judentums*. 2nd ed. Frankfurt am Main: Madda, 1928.

Gennep, Arnold van. *The Rites of Passage*. Translated by Monika B. Vizedom and Gabrielle L. Caffee. Chicago: University of Chicago Press, 1960.

Gera, Dov, and Miriam Ben-Zeev, eds. *The Path of Peace, Studies in Honor of Israel Friedman Ben-Shalom*. Be'er Sheva: Ben Gurion University of the Negev, 2005.

Gibson, S. "The Pool of Bethesda in Jerusalem and Jewish Purification Practices of the Second Temple Period." *Proche-Orient Chrétien* 55 (2005): 270–93.

Gilbert, M. *Winston Churchill: The Wilderness Years.* London: Macmillan, 1981.

Glasson, T. Francis. "What Is Apocalyptic?" *NTS* 27 (1980): 98–105.

Golb, Norm. *Who Wrote the Dead Sea Scrolls: The Search for the Secret of Qumran.* New York: Scribner, 1995.

Goldenberg, Robert. "The Septuagint Ban on Cursing the Gods." *JSJ* 28, no. 4 (1997): 381–89.

Goodacre, Mark. *The Case against Q: Studies in Markan Priority and the Synoptic Problem.* Harrisburg, Pa.: Trinity Press International, 2002.

Goodenough, Erwin R. *Jewish Symbols in the Greco-Roman Period.* 13 vols. Bollingen Series 37. New York: Pantheon Books, 1953–68.

Goodman, Martin. *Mission and Conversion: Proselytizing in the Religious History of the Roman Empire.* Oxford: Clarendon, 1994.

———. "A Note on Josephus, the Pharisees and the Ancestral Tradition." *JJS* 50 (1999): 17–20.

———. *The Ruling Class of Judaea: The Origins of the Jewish Revolt against Rome, A.D. 66–70.* Cambridge: Cambridge University Press, 1987.

———. "Sacred Scripture and 'Defiling the Hands.'" *JTS* 41 (1990): 98–107.

———. "Sacred Space in Diaspora Judaism." In *Studies on the Jewish Diaspora in the Hellenistic and Roman Periods*, ed. B. Isaac and A. Oppenheimer, 1–16. Teʻuda 12. Tel Aviv: Ramot, 1996.

———. *State and Society in Roman Galilee, A.D. 132–212.* Totowa, N.J.: Rowman & Allan, 1983.

Grabbe, Lester L. *Judaic Religion in the Second Temple Period: Belief and Practice from the Exile to Yavneh.* London and New York: Routledge, 2000.

Grainger, J. D. " 'Village Government' in Roman Syria and Arabia." *Berytus* 27 (1995): 179–95.

Gray, Rebecca. *Prophetic Figures in Late Second Temple Jewish Palestine: The Evidence from Josephus.* Oxford: Oxford University Press, 1993.

Green, H. Benedict. "Matthew, Clement, and Luke: Their Sequence and Relationship." *JTS* 40 (1989): 1–25.

Green, W. S. "Palestinian Holy Men: Charismatic Leadership and Rabbinic Tradition." *ANRW* 2.19.2 (1979): 619–47.

Greenspoon, Leonard J. "The Dead Sea Scrolls and the Greek Bible." In *The Dead Sea Scrolls after Fifty Years: A Comprehensive Assessment*, edited by Peter W. Flint and James C. VanderKam, 101–27. Leiden: Brill, 1998.

Grenfell, B. P., A. S. Hunt, and J. G. Smyly, eds. *The Tebtunis Papyri.* 4 vols. London: Oxford University Press, 1902.

Griffiths, J. Gwyn. *The Divine Verdict: A Study of Divine Judgment in the Ancient Religions.* SHR 52. Leiden: Brill, 1991.

Grossberg, Asher. "How Were the Mikvaʾot of Masada Made Ritually Fit?" (in Hebrew). *The Jerusalem Cathedra* 85 (1997): 33–44.

———. "Ritual Baths in Second Temple Period Jerusalem and How They Were Ritually Prepared" (in Hebrew). *The Jerusalem Cathedra* 83 (1996): 151–68.

————. "Ritual Pools for Immersion of Hands at Masada" (in Hebrew). *The Jerusalem Cathedra* 95 (2000): 165–71.

Grözinger, K., et al., eds. *Qumran*. Wege der Forschung 410. Darmstadt: Wissenschaftliche Buchgesellschaft, 1981.

Gutman, Shmaryahu. "Gamala." In *The New Encyclopedia of Archaeological Excavations in the Holy Land*, edited by Ephraim Stern, 2:459–63. 4 vols. Jerusalem: Israel Exploration Society, 1993.

Hacham, N. "The Letter of Aristeas: A New Exodus Story?" *JSJ* 36, no. 1 (2005): 1–20.

Hachlili, R. *The Menorah, the Ancient Seven-Armed Candelabrum: Origin, Form, and Significance*. Leiden: Brill, 2001.

————. "The Zodiac in Ancient Synagogal Art: A Review," *JSQ* 9 (2002): 219–58.

Hachlili, R., and A. E. Killebrew, eds. *Jericho, The Jewish Cemetery of the Second Temple Period*. IAAR 7. Jerusalem: Israel Antiquities Authority, Civil Administration in Judea and Samaria— Staff Officer of Archaeology, 1999.

Hadas, Moses. *Aristeas to Philocrates (Letter of Aristeas)*. Jewish Apocryphal Literature. New York: Harper, 1951.

Hagner, Donald. "The Sitz im Leben of the Gospel of Matthew." In *Treasures New and Old: Recent Contributions to Matthean Studies*, edited by David R. Bauer and Mark Allan Powell, 27–68. SBLSymS 1. Atlanta: Scholars Press, 1996.

Hahn, Ferdinand. *The Titles of Jesus in Christology: Their History in Early Christianity*. London: Lutterworth, 1969.

Haimovich-Carmin, Noga, ed. *The Land of Benjamin*. Translated by Tsipi Kuper-Blau, Michael Guggenheimer, and Robert Amoils. Judea and Samaria Publications 3. Jerusalem: Israel Antiquities Authority, 2004.

Halbertal, M. *People of the Book: Canon, Meaning, and Authority*. Cambridge, Mass.: Harvard University Press, 1997.

Hall, Jonathan M. *Ethnic Identity in Greek Antiquity*. Cambridge: Cambridge University Press, 1997.

Hamerton-Kelly, Robert, and Robin Scroggs, eds. *Jews, Greeks and Christians: Religious Cultures in Late Antiquity; Essays in Honor of William David Davies*. SJLA 21. Leiden: Brill, 1976.

Harnack, Adolf von. *Das Wesen des Christentums*. Leipzig: J. C. Hinrichs, 1929.

Harrington, Daniel J. *The Gospel of Matthew*. SP. Collegeville, Minn.: Liturgical Press, Michael Glazier, 1991.

————. "Wisdom at Qumran." In *The Community of the Renewed Covenant: The Notre Dame Symposium on the Dead Sea Scrolls*, edited by Eugene Ulrich and James C. VanderKam, 137–52. Notre Dame: University of Notre Dame Press, 1994.

Hawkins, Peter S., ed. *Civitas: Religious Interpretations of the City*. Atlanta: Scholars Press, 1986.

Hayes, Christine E. *Gentile Impurities and Jewish Identities: Intermarriage and Conversion from the Bible to the Talmud*. New York: Oxford University Press, 2002.

Hecht, N., ed. *An Introduction to the History and Sources of Jewish Law*. Oxford: Clarendon, 1996.

Hendel, R. *Remembering Abraham: Culture, Memory, and History in the Hebrew Bible*. New York: Oxford University Press, 2005.

Hengel, Martin. *Judaism and Hellenism: Studies in Their Encounter in Palestine during the Early Hellenistic Period.* 2 vols. 2nd ed. Translated by J. Bowden. London: SCM, 1974.

———. *The Zealots: Investigations into the Jewish Freedom Movement in the Period from Herod I until 70 A.D.* Translated by David Smith. Edinburgh: T&T Clark, 1989.

Hengel, Martin, and Roland Deines. "E. P. Sanders' 'Common Judaism,' Jesus and the Pharisees: Review Article of *Jewish Law: From Jesus to the Mishnah* and *Judaism: Practice and Belief.*" Translated by Daniel P. Bailey. *JTS* 46 (1995): 1–70.

Hengel, Martin, and U. Heckel, eds. *Paulus und das antike Judentum: Tübingen-Durham-Symposium im Gedenken an den 50. Todestag Adolf Schlatters (19. Mai 1938).* WUNT 58. Tübingen: Mohr Siebeck, 1991.

Henten, J. W. van, and P. W. van der Horst, eds. *Studies in Early Jewish Epigraphy.* Leiden: Brill, 1994.

Hezser, Catherine. *Jewish Literacy in Roman Palestine.* Tübingen: Mohr Siebeck, 2001.

Hill, David. "Towards an Understanding of the 'Kingdom of God.'" *IBS* 3 (1981): 62–76.

Hirschfeld, Y. *Qumran in Context: Reassessing the Archaeological Evidence.* Peabody, Mass.: Hendrickson, 2004.

Hoenig, Sidney B. "Maccabees, Zealots and Josephus: Second Commonwealth Parallelisms; Review of William Reuben Farmer *Maccabees, Zealots and Josephus,*" *JQR* 49 (1958–59): 75–80.

Holladay, Carl. "Hellenism in the Fragmentary Hellenistic Jewish Authors: Resonance and Resistance." In *Shem in the Tents of Japhet: Essays on the Encounter of Judaism and Hellenism,* edited by J. L. Kugel, 66–91. JSJSup 74. Leiden: Brill, 2002.

Holmberg, Bengt. *Sociology and the New Testament: An Appraisal.* Minneapolis: Fortress, 1990.

Honigman, Sylvie. "The Jewish 'Politeuma' at Heracleopolis." *Scripta Classica Israelica* 21 (2003): 251–66.

Hoppe, Rudolf, and Ulrich Busse, eds. *Von Jesus zum Christus: Christologische Studien: Festgabe für Paul Hoffmann zum 65. Geburtstag.* Berlin: Walter de Gruyter, 1998.

Horbury, William, W. D. Davies, and John Sturdy, eds. *The Early Roman Period.* Vol. 3 of *The Cambridge History of Judaism,* edited by W. D. Davies and Louis Finkelstein. Cambridge: Cambridge University Press, 1999.

Horbury, William, and David Noy, eds. *Jewish Inscriptions of Graeco-Roman Egypt.* Cambridge: Cambridge University Press, 1992.

Horgan, Maurya P. *Pesharim: Qumran Interpretations of Biblical Books.* CBQMS 8. Washington: Catholic Biblical Association of America, 1979.

Horovitz, H. S., and I. A. Rabin, eds. *Mechilta D'Rabbi Ismael.* 2nd ed. Jerusalem: Wahrmann, 1970.

Horsley, Richard A. "Conquest and Social Conflict in Galilee." In *Recruitment, Conquest, and Conflict: Strategies in Judaism, Early Christianity, and the Greco-Roman World,* edited by Peder Borgen, Vernon K. Robbins, and David B. Gowler, 129–68. Emory Studies in Early Christianity 6. Atlanta: Scholars Press, 1998.

———. "'Like One of the Prophets of Old': Two Types of Popular Prophets at the Time of Jesus." *CBQ* 47 (1985): 425–63.

Horst, P. W. van der. *Essays on the Jewish World of Early Christianity*. Freiburg, Schweiz: Universitätsverlag; Göttingen: Vandenhoeck & Ruprecht, 1990.

———. *Hellenism, Judaism, Christianity: Essays on Their Interaction*. Contributions to Biblical Exegesis and Theology 8. Kampen: Kok Pharos, 1994.

———. "The Interpretation of the Bible by the Minor Hellenistic Jewish Writers." In *Mikra: Text, Translation, Reading and Interpretation of the Hebrew Bible in Ancient Judaism and Early Christianity*, edited by M. J. Mulder and H. Sysling, 519–46. CRINT, Section 2: Literature of the Jewish People in the Period of the Second Temple and the Talmud 1. Assen: Van Gorcum, 1988. Reprinted in P. W. van der Horst, *Essays on the Jewish World of Early Christianity*, 187–219. Freiburg, Schweiz: Universitätsverlag; Göttingen: Vandenhoeck & Ruprecht, 1990.

———. *The Sentences of Pseudo-Phocylides*. Studia in Veteris Testamenti Pseudepigrapha 4. Leiden: Brill, 1978.

———. "Was the Synagogue a Place of Sabbath Worship before 70 CE?" In *Japheth in the Tents of Shem: Studies on Jewish Hellenism in Antiquity*, 55–82. Leuven: Peeters, 2002.

Hubbard, Robert L., Jr., Robert K. Johnston, and Robert P. Meye, eds. *Studies in Old Testament Theology*. Dallas: Word, 1992.

Humbert, Jean-Baptiste, and Jan Gunneweg, eds. *Khirbet Qumrân et 'Aïn Feshkha*. Göttingen: Vandenhoeck & Ruprecht, 2003.

Hummel, Reinhart. *Die Auseinandersetzung zwischen Kirche und Judentum in Matthäusevangelium*. 2nd ed. Munich: Kaiser, 1966.

Immerwahr, H. "Ergon: History as a Monument in Herodotus and Thucydides," *AJP* 81 (1960): 261–90.

Isaac, Benjamin H. "A Donation for Herod's Temple in Jerusalem." *IEJ* 33 (1983): 86–92. Reprinted in Benjamin H. Isaac, *The Near East under Roman Rule: Selected Papers*, 21–28. Leiden: Brill, 1998.

———. *The Near East under Roman Rule: Selected Papers*. Leiden: Brill, 1998.

Isaac, Benjamin H., and A. Oppenheimer, eds. *Studies on the Jewish Diaspora in the Hellenistic and Roman Periods*. Te'uda 12. Tel Aviv: Ramot, 1996.

Israel Exploration Society, ed. *Biblical Archaeology Today: Proceedings of the International Congress of Biblical Archaeology, April 1984*. Jerusalem: Israel Exploration Society, 1985.

Israel Ministry of Foreign Affairs. "Kiryat Sefer: A Synagogue in a Jewish Village of the Second Temple Period." Archaeological Sites in Israel 8. http://www.israel-mfa.gov.il/MFA/History/Early+History+-+Archaeology/.

Jackson, David R. *Enochic Judaism: Three Defining Paradigm Exemplars*. Library of Second Temple Studies 49. London: T&T Clark, 2004.

Jaffee, Martin S. *Early Judaism*. Upper Saddle River, N.J.: Prentice Hall, 1997.

Jellicoe, S. "The Occasion and Purpose of the Book of Aristeas." *NTS* 12 (1966): 144–50.

Johnson, A. R. *Sacral Kingship in Ancient Israel*. 2nd ed. Cardiff: University of Wales, 1967.

Johnson, Luke Timothy. "The New Testament's Anti-Jewish Slander and the Conventions of Ancient Polemic." *JBL* 108, no. 3 (1989): 419–41.

Jossa, Giorgio. *Jews or Christians? The Followers of Jesus in Search of Their Own Identity*. WUNT 202. Tübingen: Mohr Siebeck, 2006.

Judea and Samaria Research Studies, ed. *Judea and Samaria Research Studies: Proceedings of the Third Annual Meeting 1993*. Kedumim–Ariel: Mekhon ha-meḥkhar, 1994.

Kahana, Menahem I. *Sifre Zuta on Deuteronomy: Citations from a New Tannaitic Midrash*. Jerusalem: Magnes, 2003.

Kalms, J., ed. *Internationales Josephus-Kolloquium Amsterdam 2000*. Münster: LIT, 2001.

Kampen, John. "The Significance of the Temple in the Manuscripts of the Damascus Document." In *The Dead Sea Scrolls at Fifty: Proceedings of the 1997 Society of Biblical Literature Qumran Section Meetings*, edited by Robert Kugler and Eileen Schuller, 185–97. SBLEJL 15. Atlanta: Society of Biblical Literature, 1999.

Kasher, Aryeh. *The Jews in Hellenistic and Roman Egypt*. TSAJ 7. Tübingen: Mohr Siebeck, 1985.

Kasher, Aryeh, G. Fuks, and U. Rappaport, eds. *Greece and Rome in Eretz-Israel: Collected Essays*. Jerusalem: Yad Izhak Ben-Zvi, 1989.

Kee, Howard Clark. "Testaments of the Twelve Patriarchs." In *The Old Testament Pseudepigrapha*, edited by James H. Charlesworth, 1:782–828. Garden City, N.Y.: Doubleday, 1983.

Kee, Howard Clark, L. H. Cohick, eds. *Evolution of the Synagogue: Problems and Progress*. Harrisburg, Pa.: Trinity Press International, 1999.

Kee, Howard Clark, and Jacob Neusner, eds. *The Social World of Formative Christianity and Judaism*. Philadelphia: Fortress Press, 1988.

Kilpatrick, George Dunbar. *The Origins of the Gospel According to St. Matthew*. Oxford: Oxford University Press, 1946.

Kirk, G. S., J. E. Raven, and Malcolm Schofield. *Presocratic Philosophers: A Critical History with a Selection of Texts*. Cambridge: Cambridge University Press, 1983.

Kister, Menahem. "A Common Heritage: Biblical Interpretation at Qumran and Its Implications." In *Biblical Perspectives: Early Use and Interpretation of the Bible in Light of the Dead Sea Scrolls: Proceedings of the First International Symposium of the Orion Center for the Study of the Dead Sea Scrolls and Associated Literature, 12–14 May 1996*, edited by M. E. Stone and E. G. Chazon, 101–11. STDJ 28. Leiden: Brill, 1998.

———. "Demons, Theology and Abraham's Covenant (CD 16:4–6) and Related Texts." In *The Dead Sea Scrolls at Fifty: Proceedings of the 1997 Society of Biblical Literature Qumran Section Meetings*, edited by Robert Kugler and Eileen Schuller, 167–84. SBLEJL 15. Atlanta: Society of Biblical Literature, 1999.

Kittel, Gerhard, Gerhard Friedrich, and Geoffrey William Bromiley, eds. *Theological Dictionary of the New Testament*. Translated by Geoffrey William Bromiley. Grand Rapids: Eerdmans, 1964–76.

Klawans, Jonathan. *Impurity and Sin in Ancient Judaism*. New York: Oxford University Press, 2000.

Klein, Günter. "The Biblical Understanding of the 'Kingdom of God.'" *Int* 26, no. 4 (1972): 387–418.

Klinghardt, Matthias. "The Manual of Discipline in the Light of Statutes of Hellenistic Associations." In *Methods of Investigation of the Dead Sea Scrolls and the Khirbet Qumran Site: Present Realities and Future Prospects*, edited by John Joseph Collins, Michael Owen Wise, Norman Golb, and Dennis Pardee, 251–70. Annals of the New York Academy of Sciences 722. New York: New York Academy of Sciences, 1994.

Kloner, Amos, and Y. Tepper. *The Hiding Complexes in the Judean Shephelah* (in Hebrew). Tel Aviv: Ha-Kibuts ha-meuhad: ha-Hevrah la-hakirat Erets-Yisrael ve-atikoteha, 1987.

Kloner, Amos, and Boaz Zissu. *The Necropolis of Jerusalem in the Second Temple Period*. Jerusalem: Yad Ben Zvi and the Israel Exploration Society, 2003.

Kloppenborg, John S. "Dating Theodotos (*CIJ* II 1404)." *JJS* 51, no. 2 (2000): 243–80.

Kloppenborg-Verbin, John S. See Kloppenborg, John S.

Klutz, Todd. *The Exorcism Stories in Luke-Acts: A Socio-Stylistic Reading*. SNTSMS 129. Cambridge: Cambridge University Press, 2004.

Kniss, F. "Ideas and Symbols as Resources in Intrareligious Conflict: The Case of American Mennonites." *Sociology of Religion* 57, no. 1 (1996): 7–23.

Knoppers, Gary. "Mt Gerizim and Mt. Zion: A Study in the Early History of the Samaritans and Jews." *SR* 34, nos. 3–4 (2005): 309–38.

Koester, Helmut. *Synoptische Überlieferung bei den Apostolischen Vätern*. TUGAL 65. Berlin: Akademie-Verlag, 1957.

Köhler, Wolf-Dietrich. *Die Rezeption des Matthäusevangeliums in der Zeit vor Irenäus*. WUNT 24. Tübingen: Mohr Siebeck, 1987.

Kollmann, Bernd, Wolfgang Reinbold, and Annette Steudel, eds. *Antikes Judentum und frühes Christentum: Festgabe für Hartmut Stegemann zum 65*. BZNW 97. Berlin and New York: Walter de Gruyter, 1999.

Kon, M., and O. Schneid. *The Tombs of the Kings*. Tel Aviv: Dvir, 1947.

Kraabel, A. T. "Social Systems of Six Diaspora Synagogues." In *Diaspora Jews and Judaism: Essays in Honor of, and in Dialogue with, A. Thomas Kraabel*, ed. J. A. Overman and R. S. McLennan, 257–67. South Florida Studies in the History of Judaism 41. Atlanta: Scholars Press, 1992.

Kraft, Robert A., and Gerhard Krodel, eds. *Orthodoxy and Heresy in Earliest Christianity*. Philadelphia: Fortress Press, 1971.

Krieger, Klaus-Stefan. "Die Zeichenpropheten: Eine Hilfe zum Verständnis des Wirkens Jesu?" in *Von Jesus zum Christus: Christologische Studien: Festgabe für Paul Hoffmann zum 65. Geburtstag*, edited by Rudolf Hoppe and Ulrich Busse. Berlin: Walter de Gruyter, 1998.

Kuck, David. *Judgment and Community Conflict: Paul's Use of Apocalyptic Judgment Language in 1 Corinthians 3:5—4:5*. NovTSup 66. Leiden: Brill, 1992.

Kugel, J. L., ed. *Shem in the Tents of Japhet: Essays on the Encounter of Judaism and Hellenism*. JSJSup 74. Leiden: Brill, 2002.

Kugler, Robert. "Priesthood at Qumran." In *The Dead Sea Scrolls after Fifty Years: A Comprehensive Assessment*, edited by Peter W. Flint and James C. VanderKam. Leiden: Brill, 1999.

Kugler, Robert, and Eileen Schuller, eds. *The Dead Sea Scrolls at Fifty: Proceedings of the 1997*

Society of Biblical Literature Qumran Section Meetings. SBLEJL 15. Atlanta: Society of Biblical Literature, 1999.

Labuschagne, C. J., A. Hilhorst, and F. García Martínez, eds. *The Scriptures and the Scrolls: Studies in Honour of A. S. van der Woude on the Occasion of His 65th Birthday*. VTSup 49. Leiden: Brill, 1992.

Lange, Armin. "Divinatorische Träume und Apokalyptic im Jubiläenbuch." In *Studies in the Book of Jubilees*, edited by M. Albani, J. Frey, and A. Lange, 25–38. TSAJ 65. Tübingen: Mohr Siebeck, 1997.

———. "The Essene Position on Magic and Divination." In *Legal Texts and Legal Issues: Proceedings of the Second Meeting of the International Organization for Qumran Studies, Cambridge, 1995: Published in Honour of Joseph M. Baumgarten*, edited by Moshe J. Bernstein, Florentino García Martínez, and John Kampen, 377–435. STDJ 23. Leiden: Brill, 1997.

Lateiner, D. *The Historical Method of Herodotus*. Toronto: University of Toronto Press, 1989.

Lattke, Michael. "On the Jewish Background of the Synoptic Concept, 'Kingdom of God.'" In *The Kingdom of God in the Teaching of Jesus*, edited by Bruce Chilton, 78–88. IRT 5. Philadelphia: Fortress Press, 1984.

Lauterbach, Jacob Z., ed. *Mekilta de-Rabbi Ishmael*. 3 vols. Jewish Classics. Paper ed. Philadelphia: Jewish Publication Society of America, 1961.

Leon, H. *The Jews of Ancient Rome*. Philadelphia: Jewish Publication Society, 1960.

Levenson, Jon D. *Sinai and Zion: An Entry into the Jewish Bible*. Minneapolis: Winston, 1985.

Levine, Amy-Jill. "Matthew's Advice to a Divided Readership." In *The Gospel of Matthew in Current Study: Studies in Memory of William G. Thompson*, edited by David Aune, 22–41. Grand Rapids: Eerdmans, 2001.

———. *The Social and Ethnic Dimensions of Matthean Social History: Go Nowhere among the Gentiles (Matt. 10:5b)*. Lewiston, N.Y.: Edwin Mellen, 1988.

Levine, Lee I. *The Ancient Synagogue: The First Thousand Years*. 2nd ed. New Haven, Conn.: Yale University Press, 2005.

———. "The First-Century CE Synagogue in Historical Perspective." In *The Ancient Synagogue from Its Origins until 200 CE: Papers Presented at an International Conference at Lund University, October 14–17, 2001*, edited by Birger Olsson and Magnus Zetterholm, 613–41. ConBNT 39. Stockholm: Almqvist & Wiksell International, 2003.

———. "The First-Century Synagogue: Critical Reassessments and Assessments of the Critical." In *Religion and Society in Roman Palestine: Old Questions, New Approaches*, edited by Douglas R. Edwards, 70–102. London: Routledge, 2004.

———. "The History and Significance of the Menorah in Antiquity." In *From Dura to Sepphoris: Studies in Jewish Art and Society in Late Antiquity*, edited by Lee I. Levine and Z. Weiss, 145–53. JRA Supplementary Series 40. Ann Arbor, Mich: Journal of Roman Archaeology, 2000.

———. "The Inscription in the 'En Gedi Synagogue." In *Ancient Synagogues Revealed*, edited by Lee I. Levine, 140–45. Jerusalem: Israel Exploration Society, 1981.

————. *Jerusalem: Portrait of the City in the Second Temple Period (538 BCE to 70 CE.)*. Philadelphia: Jewish Publication Society, 2002.

————. "The Nature and Origin of the Palestinian Synagogue Reconsidered." *JBL* 115, no. 3 (1996): 425–48.

————. "The Sages and the Synagogue in Late Antiquity: The Evidence of the Galilee." In *The Galilee in Late Antiquity*, edited by Lee I. Levine, 201–22. New York: Jewish Theological Seminary of America, 1992.

————. "The Second Temple Synagogue: The Formative Years." In *The Synagogue in Late Antiquity*, edited by Lee I. Levine, 20–22. Philadelphia: Jewish Theological Seminary and American Schools of Oriental Research, 1987.

————. *Visual Judaism: History, Art, and Identity in Late Antiquity*. New Haven, Conn.: Yale University Press, forthcoming.

————, ed. *Ancient Synagogues Revealed*. Jerusalem: Israel Exploration Society, 1981.

————, ed. *The Galilee in Late Antiquity*. New York: Jewish Theological Seminary of America, 1992.

————, ed. *The Synagogue in Late Antiquity*. Philadelphia: Jewish Theological Seminary and American Schools of Oriental Research, 1987.

Levine, Lee I., and Z. Weiss, eds. *From Dura to Sepphoris: Studies in Jewish Art and Society in Late Antiquity*. JRA Supplementary Series 40. Ann Arbor, Mich.: Journal of Roman Archaeology, 2000.

Lieberman, Saul. "The Martyrs of Caesarea." *Annuaire de l'Institut de Philologie et d'Histoire Orientales et Slaves* 7 (1939–44): 395–466.

————. "Notes." In *P'raqim: Yearbook of the Schocken Institute for Jewish Research of the Jewish Theological Seminary of America*, edited by E. S. Rosenthal, 1:97–98. Jerusalem: *Schocken Institute*, 1968.

————. *Texts and Studies*. New York: KTAV, 1974.

Lieberman, Saul, Shalom Spiegel, Solomon Zeitlin, and Alexander Marx, eds. *Louis Ginzberg Jubilee Volume on the Occasion of His Seventieth Birthday, Hebrew Section*. Jerusalem and New York: American Academy for Jewish Research, 1945.

Lieu, Judith. *Neither Jew nor Greek? Constructing Early Christianity*. London: T&T Clark, 2002.

Lifshitz, B. *Donateurs et fondateurs dans les synagogues juives*. Paris: Gabalda, 1967.

Lim, Timothy H., Larry W. Hurtado, A. Graham Auld, and Alison M. Jack, eds. *The Dead Sea Scrolls in Their Historical Context*. Edinburgh: T&T Clark, 2000.

Linder, A. *The Jews in Roman Imperial Legislation*. Detroit: Wayne State University Press, 1987.

Livneh M., and R. Yehezkeli, eds. *Yad le-Yair, Eretz-Israel: Researches in the Memory of Yair Bashan*. Tel-Aviv: Society for the Protection of Nature, 1999.

Loew, Cornelius. *Myth, Sacred History, and Philosophy: The Pre-Christian Religious Heritage of the West*. New York: Harcourt, 1967.

Lüderitz, G. "What Is the *Politeuma*?" In *Studies in Early Jewish Epigraphy*, edited by J. W. van Henten and P. W. van der Horst, 219–22. AGJU 21. Leiden: Brill, 1994.

Luomanen, Petri. *Entering the Kingdom of Heaven: A Study on the Structure of Matthew's View of Salvation.* WUNT 2.101. Tübingen: Mohr Siebeck, 1998.

———. "The 'Sociology of Sectarianism' in Matthew: Modelling the Genesis of Early Jewish and Christian Communities." In *Fair Play: Diversity and Conflicts in Early Christianity; Essays in Honour of Heikki Räisänen,* edited by Ismo Dunderberg, Christopher Tuckett, and Kari Syreeni, 109–14. NovTSup 103. Leiden/Boston: Brill, 2002.

Luz, Ulrich. *Das Evangelium nach Matthäus.* 4 vols. EKKNT 1. Neukirchen-Vluyn: Neukirchener Verlag, 1985–2006.

———. *Matthew 1–7: A Commentary.* Minneapolis: Augsburg, 1989.

———. *Matthew in History: Interpretation, Influence, and Effects.* Minneapolis: Fortress Press, 1994.

———. *The Theology of the Gospel of Matthew.* New Testament Theology. Cambridge: Cambridge University Press, 1995.

Lyons, John, and Andy Reimer. "The Demonic Virus and Qumran Studies: Some Preventive Measures." *DSD* 5, no. 1 (1998): 16–32.

MacAdam, H. I. *Studies in the History of the Roman Province of Arabia: The Northern Sector.* BAR International Series 295. Oxford: BAR, 1986.

MacDonald, Mary N., ed. *Experiences of Place.* Cambridge, Mass.: Harvard University Press, 2003.

———. "Place and the Study of Religions." In *Experiences of Place,* edited by Mary N. MacDonald, 1–20. Cambridge, Mass.: Harvard University Press, 2003.

Mack, Burton L. *Wisdom and the Hebrew Epic: Ben Sira's Hymn in Praise of the Fathers.* Chicago: University of Chicago Press, 1985.

Magen, Y. "Qalandia—A Second Temple Period Viticulture and Wine-Manufacturing Agricultural Settlement." In *The Land of Benjamin,* edited by Noga Haimovich-Carmin, translated by Tsipi Kuper-Blau, Michael Guggenheimer, and Robert Amoils, 29–144. Judea and Samaria Publications 3. Jerusalem: Israel Antiquities Authority, 2004.

Magen, Y., Y. Tzionit, and O. Sirkis. "Kirbet Badd'Isa—Qiryat Sefer." In *The Land of Benjamin,* edited by Noga Haimovich-Carmin, translated by Tsipi Kuper-Blau, Michael Guggenheimer, and Robert Amoils, 179–241. Judea and Samaria Publications 3. Jerusalem: Israel Antiquities Authority, 2004.

Magness, Jodi. *The Archaeology of Qumran and the Dead Sea Scrolls.* Grand Rapids: Eerdmans, 2002.

Magonet, Jonathan. "Some Concentric Structures in Psalms." *HeyJ* 23 (1982): 365–76.

Maguire, Henry. *The Earth and Ocean: The Terrestrial World in Early Byzantine Art.* University Park: Pennsylvania State University Press, 1987.

Marcus, Ralph. *Jewish Antiquities, Books XII–XIV.* Vol. 7 of *Josephus, with an English Translation.* LCL. Cambridge, Mass.: Harvard University Press, 1986.

Marguerat, Daniel. *Le jugement dans l'évangile de Matthieu.* 2nd ed. Le Monde de la Bible. Geneva: Labor et Fides, 1995.

Margulies, Mordecai, ed. *Midrash Wayyikra Rabbah.* 4 vols. Jerusalem: Wahrmann, 1972.

Ma'oz, Z. "The Synagogue at Gamla and the Typology of Second Temple Synagogues." In *Ancient Synagogues Revealed*, edited by Lee I. Levine, 35–41. Jerusalem: Israel Exploration Society, 1981.

Mason, Steve. *Flavius Josephus on the Pharisees: A Composition-Critical Study*. StPB 39. Leiden: Brill, 1991.

———. "Josephus, Daniel, and the Flavian House." In *Josephus and the History of the Greco-Roman Period: Essays in Memory of Morton Smith*, edited by Fausto Parente and Joseph Sievers, 161–91. StPB 41. Leiden: Brill, 1994.

———. "Pharisaic Dominance before 70 CE and the Gospel's Hypocrisy Charge (Matt 23:2-3)." *HTR* 83, no. 4 (1990): 363–81.

———. "'Should Any Wish to Enquire Further' (*Ant.* 1.25): The Aim and Audience of Josephus's *Judean Antiquities/Life*." In *Understanding Josephus: Seven Perspectives*, edited by Steve Mason, 64–103. Sheffield: Sheffield Academic Press, 1998.

———, ed. *Understanding Josephus: Seven Perspectives*. Sheffield: Sheffield Academic Press, 1998.

Massaux, Édouard. *Influence de l'évangile de saint Matthieu sur la littérature chrétienne avant saint Irénée*. Universitas Catholica Lovaniensis, Dissertationes, ser. 2, 42. Louvain: Publications Universitaires de Louvain, 1950.

Mays, James Luther. "The Language of the Reign of God." *Int* 47 (1993): 117–26.

Mazar, B. *The Mountain of the Lord: Excavating in Jerusalem*. Garden City, N.Y.: Doubleday, 1975.

Mazar, E. *The Complete Guide to the Temple Mount Excavations* (in Hebrew). Jerusalem: Shoham Academic Research and Publication, 2000.

———. *The Complete Guide to the Temple Mount Excavations*. Translated by D. Glick and N. Panitz-Cohen. Jerusalem: Old City Press, 2002.

McGuire, Meredith B. *Religion: The Social Context*. 2nd ed. Belmont, Calif.: Wadsworth, 1987.

McKay, Heather. *Sabbath and the Synagogue: The Question of Sabbath Worship in Ancient Judaism*. Leiden: Brill, 1994.

McLaren, James S. *Power and Politics in Palestine. The Jews and the Governing of Their Land 100 BC–AD 70*. Sheffield: JSOT Press, 1991.

McNamara, Martin. "Paul and Palestinian Judaism: A Comparison in Patterns of Religion." *JSNT* 5 (1979): 67–73.

Meeks, Wayne A. "Breaking Away." In *"To See Ourselves as Others See Us": Christians, Jews, "Others" in Late Antiquity*, edited by Jacob Neusner, Caroline McCracken-Flesher, and Ernest S. Frerichs, 93–115. Scholars Press Studies in the Humanities. Chico, Calif.: Scholars Press, 1985.

Meier, John P. *The Vision of Matthew: Christ, Church, and Morality in the First Gospel*. New York: Paulist, 1979.

Mélèze-Modrzejewski, J. "Jewish Law and Hellenistic Practice in the Light of Greek Papyri from Egypt." In *An Introduction to the History and Sources of Jewish Law*, edited by N. Hecht, 75–99. Oxford: Clarendon, 1996.

——— "La Septante comme Nomos: Comment la Torah est devenue une 'loi civique' pour les Juifs d'Egypte." *Annali di Science Religiose* 2 (1997): 143–58.

Mendelson, Alan. *Secular Education in Philo of Alexandria*. Monographs of the Hebrew Union

College 7. Cincinnati: Hebrew Union College Press, 1982.

Metso, Sarianna. "Methodological Problems in Reconstructing History from Rule Texts Found at Qumran." *DSD* 11, no. 3 (2004): 315–34.

———. *The Textual Development of the Community Rule*. Leiden: Brill, 1997.

Mettinger, Tryggve N. D. *In Search of God: The Meaning and Message of the Everlasting Names*. Translated by Frederick H. Cryer. Philadelphia: Fortress Press, 1987.

Meyer, Rudolf. "Pharisees." In *Theological Dictionary of the New Testament*, edited by Gerhard Kittel, Gerhard Friedrich, and Geoffrey William Bromiley, translated by Geoffrey William Bromiley, 9:11–35. Grand Rapids: Eerdmans, 1964–76.

Meyers, Eric M. "Aspects of Everyday Life in Roman Palestine with Special Reference to Private Domiciles and Ritual Baths." In *Jews in the Hellenistic and Roman Cities*, edited by John R. Bartlett, 193–220. London: Routledge, 2002.

———, ed. *Galilee through the Centuries: Confluence of Cultures: Proceedings of the Second International Conference in Galilee*. Winona Lake, Ind.: Eisenbrauns, 1999.

Milgrom, Jacob. "4QTohora\u1d43: An Unpublished Qumran Text on Purities." In *Time to Prepare the Way in the Wilderness: Papers on the Qumran Scrolls*, edited by Lawrence Schiffman and Devorah Dimant, 59–68. Leiden: Brill, 1995.

———. *Leviticus 1–16: A New Translation with Introduction and Commentary*. AB 3. New York: Doubleday, 1991.

Milik, J. T. "Écrits préésséniens de Qumran: d'Hénoch à Amram." In *Qumran: sa piété, sa théologie et son milieu*, edited by M. Delcor, 91–106. BETL 46. Paris: Duculot, 1978.

———. "'Prière de Nabonide' et autres écrits d'un cycle Daniel: Fragments Araméen de Qumrân 4," *RB* 63 (1956): 407–15.

Milikowsky, Chaim. "Reflections on Hand-Washing, Hand Purity and Holy Scripture in Rabbinic Literature." In *Purity and Holiness: The Heritage of Leviticus*, edited by M. Porthuis and J. Schwartz, 149–62. Leiden: Brill, 2000.

Misgav, H. "The Epigraphic Sources (Hebrew and Aramaic) in Comparison with the Traditions Reflected in Talmudic Literature." Ph.D. diss., Hebrew University, 1999.

Mohrlang, Roger. *Matthew and Paul: A Comparison of Ethical Perspectives*. Cambridge: Cambridge University Press, 1984.

Momigliano, Arnaldo. *The Classical Foundations of Modern Historiography*. Sather Classical Lectures 54. Berkeley: University of California Press, 1990.

———. *On Pagans, Jews and Christians*. Middletown, Conn.: Wesleyan University Press, 1987.

Moore, George Foot. "Christian Writers on Judaism." *HTR* 14 (1921): 197–254.

———. *Judaism in the First Centuries of the Christian Era: The Age of the Tannaim*. 3 vols. Cambridge, Mass.: Harvard University Press, 1927.

Mor, M., et al., eds. *For Uriel: Studies in the History of Israel in Antiquity, Presented to Professor Uriel Rappaport*. Jerusalem: Merkaz Shazar, 2005.

Moskovitz, Leib. "The Relationship between the Yerushalmi and Leviticus Rabbah: A Re-examination." In *Eleventh World Congress of Jewish Studies*, edited by the World Union of Jewish Studies, 31–38. Jerusalem: World Union of Jewish Studies, 1993.

Mouritsen, H. "Freedmen and Decurions: Epitaphs and Social History in Imperial Italy." *JRS* 95 (2005): 38–63.

Mowinckel, Sigmund. *The Psalms in Israel's Worship*. Translated by D. R. Ap-Thomas. 2 vols. Oxford: Blackwell, 1961.

Mulder, M. J., and H. Sysling, eds. *Mikra: Text, Translation, Reading and Interpretation of the Hebrew Bible in Ancient Judaism and Early Christianity*. CRINT, Section 2: Literature of the Jewish People in the Period of the Second Temple and the Talmud 1. Assen: Van Gorcum, 1988.

Munck, Johannes. "Jewish Christianity in Post-apostolic Times." *NTS* 6 (1960): 103–16.

Murphy-O'Connor, Jerome. *Paul and Qumran*. London: Geoffrey Chapman, 1968.

Najman, Hindy. "Towards a Study of the Uses of the Concept of Wilderness in Ancient Judaism." *DSD* 13, no. 1 (2006): 99–113.

Nanos, Mark, and Anders Runesson. *Paul and Apostolic Judaism*. Forthcoming.

Naveh, Joseph. "Fragments of an Aramaic Magic Book from Qumran." *IEJ* 4 (1998): 252–61.

———. *On Stone and Mosaic: The Aramaic and Hebrew Inscriptions from Ancient Synagogues*. Jerusalem: Israel Exploration Society and Carta, 1978.

Naveh, Joseph, and S. Shaked. *Amulets and Magic Bowls: Aramaic Incantations of Late Antiquity*. Jerusalem: Magnes Press, Hebrew University, 1985.

Nepper-Christensen, Poul. *Das Matthäusevangelium: Ein judenchristliches Evangelium?* ATDan 1. Aarhus: Universitetsforlaget, 1958.

Netzer, Ehud. "Ancient Ritual Baths (*Miqwa'ot*) in Jericho." *The Jerusalem Cathedra* 2 (1982): 106–19.

———. *Greater Herodium*. Qedem 13. Jerusalem: Institute of Archaeology, Hebrew University of Jerusalem, 1981.

———. "Herodian Bath-Houses." In *Roman Baths and Bathing: Proceedings of the First International Conference on Roman Baths Held at Bath, England, 30 March–4 April 1992*, edited by J. DeLaine and D. E. Johnston, 45–55. JRA Supplementary Series 37. Portsmouth, R.I.: Journal of Roman Arcaeology, 1999.

———. *Masada: The Yigael Yadin Excavations, 1963–1965: Final Reports*. 6 vols. Jerusalem: Israel Exploration Society, 1989.

———. "Mourning Enclosure of Tomb H (Goliath Tomb)." In *Jericho: The Jewish Cemetery of the Second Temple Period*, edited by R. Hachlili and A. E. Killebrew, 45–50. IAAR 7. Jerusalem: Israel Antiquities Authority, Civil Administration in Judea and Samaria—Staff Officer of Archaeology, 1999.

———. *The Palaces of the Hasmoneans and Herod the Great*. Jerusalem: Yad Ben-Zvi, 1999.

———. "A Proposal Concerning the Utilization of the Ritual Baths at Qumran" (in Hebrew). *Qad* 124 (2002): 116–17.

———. "A Synagogue from the Hasmonean Period Exposed at Jericho." *Bible and Interpretation*. http://www.bibleinterp.com/articles/Synagogue.htm.

———. "A Synagogue from the Hasmonean Period Recently Exposed in the Western Plain of Jericho." *IEJ* 49 (1999): 203–21.

Neusner, Jacob. *Ancient Judaism: Debates and Disputes.* BJS 64. Chico, Calif.: Scholars Press, 1984.

———. "Debunking the German anti-Judaic Caricature." *National Jewish Post and Opinion* 69, no. 8 (October 16, 2002).

———. "The Formation of Rabbinic Judaism: Yavneh (Jamnia) from AD 70 to 100." *ANRW* 2.19.2 (1979): 3–42.

———. *Formative Judaism: Religious, Historical, and Literary Studies: Third Series: Torah, Pharisees, and Rabbis.* BJS 46. Chicago: University of Chicago Press, 1983.

———. *Introduction to Rabbinic Literature.* New York: Doubleday, 1994.

———. *Judaism: The Evidence of the Mishnah.* Chicago: University of Chicago, 1981.

———. *Messiah in Context: Israel's History and Destiny in Formative Judaism.* Philadelphia: Fortress Press, 1984.

———. *Midrash in Context: Exegesis in Formative Judaism.* Philadelphia: Fortress Press, 1983.

———. "Parsing the Rabbinic Canon with the History of an Idea: The Messiah." In idem, *Formative Judaism: Religious, Historical, and Literary Studies: Third Series: Torah, Pharisees, and Rabbis,* 173–98. BJS 46. Chicago: University of Chicago Press, 1983.

———. "Paul and Palestinian Judaism." In *Ancient Judaism: Debates and Disputes,* 127–41. BJS 64. Chico, Calif.: Scholars Press, 1984.

———. *Torah: From Scroll to Symbol in Formative Judaism.* Philadelphia: Fortress Press, 1985.

Neusner, Jacob, Caroline McCracken-Flesher, and Ernest S. Frerichs, eds. *"To See Ourselves as Others See Us": Christians, Jews, "Others" in Late Antiquity.* Scholars Press Studies in the Humanities. Chico, Calif.: Scholars Press, 1985.

Newsom, Carol. "He Has Established for Himself Priests." In *Archaeology and History in the Dead Sea Scrolls: The New York Conference in Memory of Yigael Yadin,* edited by Lawrence H. Schiffman, 101–20. JSPSup 8. Sheffield: JSOT Press, 1990.

———. "The Sage in the Literature of Qumran: The Functions of the Maśkîl." In *The Sage in Israel and the Ancient Near East,* edited by John G. Gammie and Leo G. Perdue, 373–82. Winona Lake, Ind.: Eisenbrauns, 1990.

———. "'Sectually Explicit' Literature from Qumran." In *The Hebrew Bible and Its Interpreters,* edited by William Propp, Baruch Halpern, and David Noel Freedman, 167–87. Winona Lake: Eisenbrauns, 1990.

———. *The Self as Symbolic Space: Constructing Community and Identity at Qumran.* Leiden: Brill, 2004.

———. *Songs of the Sabbath Sacrifice: A Critical Edition.* HSS 27. Atlanta: Scholars Press, 1985.

Newton, Michael. *The Concept of Purity at Qumran and in the Letters of Paul.* Cambridge: Cambridge University Press, 1985.

Nickelsburg, George W. E. "The Bible Re-written and Expanded." In *Jewish Writings of the Second Temple Period,* edited by M. E. Stone. Assen: Van Gorcum; Phildadelphia: Fortress Press, 1984.

———. *Resurrection, Immortality and Eternal Life in Intertestamental Judaism.* HTS 26. Cambridge, Mass.: Harvard University Press, 1972.

———. "Stories of Biblical and Early Post-biblical Times." In *Jewish Writings of the Second Temple Period,* edited by M. E. Stone. Assen: Van Gorcum; Phildadelphia: Fortress Press, 1984.

Nielsen, Kirsten. *There Is Hope for a Tree: The Tree as Metaphor in Isaiah.* Translated by Christine Crowley and Frederick Crowley. JSOTSup 65. Sheffield: JSOT Press, 1989.

Nitzan, Bilah. "Hymns from Qumran—4Q510–511." In *The Dead Sea Scrolls: Forty Years of Research,* edited by Devorah Dimant and Uriel Rappaport. STDJ 10. Leiden: Brill, 1992.

———. *Qumran Prayer and Religious Poetry.* STDJ 12. Leiden: Brill, 1994.

Noam, V. *Megillat Ta'anit: Versions, Interpretation, History, with a Critical Edition.* Jerusalem: Yad Ben-Zvi, 2003.

Nock, A. D. *Conversion: The Old and the New in Religion from Alexander the Great to Augustine of Hippo.* 1933. Reprint, Oxford: Oxford University Press, 1965.

Olsson, Birger, Olof Brandt, and Dieter Mitternacht, eds. *The Synagogue of Ancient Ostia and the Jews of Rome: Interdisciplinary Studies.* Acta Instituti Romani Regni Sueciae, Series in 4, 57. Stockholm: Paul Åströms Förlag, 2001.

Olsson, Birger, and Magnus Zetterholm, eds. *The Ancient Synagogue from Its Origins until 200 CE: Papers Presented at an International Conference at Lund University, October 14–17, 2001.* ConBNT 39. Stockholm: Almqvist & Wiksell International, 2003.

Onn, A., et al. "Umm el-'Umdan." *HA-ESI* 114 (2002): 64–68.

Oppenheimer, Aharon. *The 'Am Ha-Aretz: A Study in the Social History of the Jewish People in the Hellenistic-Roman Period.* ALGHJ 8. Leiden: Brill, 1977.

Oppenheimer, Aharon, et al., eds. *Perakim be-toldot Yerushalayim bi-yeme Bayit Sheni: Sefer zikaron le-Avraham Shalit (Jerusalem in the Second Temple Period: Abraham Schalit Memorial Volume).* Sifriyah le-toldot ha-yishuv ha-Yehudi be-Erets-Yisrael. Jerusalem: Yad Yitzhak Ben-Tsvi, 1980.

Orlinsky, Harry Meyer. "The Hebrew Vorlage of the Septuagint of the Book of Joshua." In *Congress Volume: Rome 1968,* edited by G. W. Anderson, P. A. H. de Boer, G. R. Castellino, Henri Cazelles, E. Hammershaimb, H. G. May, and W. Zimmerli, 187–95. VTSup 17. Leiden: Brill, 1969.

———. "The Septuagint as Holy Writ and the Philosophy of the Translators," *HUCA* 46 (1975): 89–114.

Orsi, Robert Anthony. *The Madonna of 115th Street: Faith and Community in Italian Harlem, 1880–1950.* 2nd ed. New Haven, Conn.: Yale University Press, 2002.

Otto, W. *Herodes: Beiträge zur Geschichte des letzten jüdischen Königshauses.* Stuttgart: Metzler, 1913.

Overman, J. Andrew. *Church and Community in Crisis: The Gospel According to Matthew.* New Testament in Context. Valley Forge, Pa.: Trinity Press International, 1996.

———. *Matthew's Gospel and Formative Judaism: The Social World of the Matthean Community.* Minneapolis: Fortress Press, 1990.

Overman, J. Andrew, and R. S. McLennan, eds. *Diaspora Jews and Judaism: Essays in Honor of, and in Dialogue with, A. Thomas Kraabel.* South Florida Studies in the History of Judaism 41. Atlanta: Scholars Press, 1992.

Paget, James Carleton. "Jewish Christianity." In *The Early Roman Period,* edited by William Horbury, W. D. Davies, and John Sturdy, 731–75. Vol. 3 of *The Cambridge History of Judaism,* edited by W. D. Davies and Louis Finkelstein. Cambridge: Cambridge University Press, 1999.

Parente, Fausto, and Joseph Sievers, eds. *Josephus and the History of the Greco-Roman Period: Essays in Memory of Morton Smith*. StPB 41. Leiden: Brill, 1994.

Parry, Donald W., and Emanuel Tov, eds. *Additional Genres and Unclassified Texts*. Vol. 6 of *The Dead Sea Scrolls Reader*. Leiden: Brill, 2005.

———. *The Dead Sea Scrolls Reader*. 6 vols. Leiden: Brill, 2004.

Parsons, P. J. "The Scripts and Their Date." In *The Greek Minor Prophets Scroll from Nahal Hever (8HeXIIgr)*, edited by Emanuel Tov, Robert A. Kraft, and P. J. Parsons, 19–26. DJD 8. Oxford: Clarendon, 1990.

Patrich, J. "Herod's Theatre in Jerusalem: A New Proposal." *IEJ* 52 (2002): 231–39.

Paul, Shalom M., and Eva Ben-David, eds. *Emanuel: Studies in Hebrew Bible, Septuagint, and Dead Sea Scrolls in Honor of Emanuel Tov*. VTSup 94. Leiden: Brill, 2003.

Pearce, S. J. K. "King Moses: Notes on Philo's Portrait of Moses as an Ideal Leader in the Life of Moses." In *The Greek Strand in Islamic Political Thought: Proceedings of the Conference Held at the Institute for Advanced Study, Princeton, 16–27 June 2003*, edited by P. Crone, D. Gutras, and E. Shütrumpf, 37–74. Mélanges de l'Université Saint-Joseph 57. Beirut: L'Université Saint-Joseph, 2004.

Peleg, Y., and D. Amit. "Another *Miqveh* Near Alon Shevut." *'Atiqot* 48 (2004): 95–98.

Penner, K. M., ed., "Letter of Aristeas." In *The Online Critical Pseudepigrapha*, edited by D. M. Miller, K. M. Penner, and I. W. Scott (Atlanta: Society of Biblical Literature, 2006), http://www.purl.org/net/ocp/Aristeas.html.

Perrin, Norman. *Jesus and the Language of the Kingdom: Symbol and Metaphor in the New Testament Interpretation*. Philadelphia: Fortress Press, 1976.

Petersen, Allan Rosengren. *The Royal God: Enthronement Festivals in Ancient Israel and Ugarit?* JSOTSup 259. Sheffield: Sheffield Academic Press, 1998.

Piggot, Susan M. "The Kingdom of the Warrior God: The Old Testament and the Kingdom of Yahweh." *SwJT* 40, no. 2 (1998): 5–20.

Ploeg, J. van der. "Le Psaume XCI dans une recension de Qumran." *RevQ* 72 (1965): 210–17.

Poirier, John C. "Purity beyond the Temple in the Second Temple Era." *JBL* 122 (2003): 247–65.

Poorthuis, M., and Ch. Safrai, eds. *The Centrality of Jerusalem: Historical Perspectives*. Kampen: Kok Pharos, 1996.

Poorthuis, M., and J. Schwartz, eds. *Purity and Holiness: The Heritage of Leviticus*. Jewish and Christian Perspectives 2. Leiden: Brill, 2000.

Porter, Stanley E., and Craig A. Evans, eds. *The Scrolls and the Scriptures: Qumran Fifty Years After*. JSPSup 26. Sheffield: Sheffield Academic Press, 1997.

Potter, D. S. *Prophets and Emperors: Human and Divine Authority from Augustus to Theodosius*. Revealing Antiquity 7. Cambridge, Mass.: Harvard University Press, 1994.

Powell, Mark Alan. "Do and Keep What Moses Says (Matthew 23:2-7)." *JBL* 114 (1995): 419–35.

Price, J. "Josephus's First Sentence and the Preface to BJ." In *For Uriel: Studies in the History of Israel in Antiquity, Presented to Professor Uriel Rappaport*, edited by M. Mor et al., 131–44. Jerusalem: Merkaz Shazar, 2005.

Propp, William, Baruch Halpern, and David Noel Freedman, eds. *The Hebrew Bible and Its Interpreters*. Winona Lake, Ind.: Eisenbrauns, 1990.

Przybylski, Benno. *Righteousness in Matthew and His World of Thought*. SNTSMS 41. Cambridge: Cambridge University Press, 1980.

———. "The Setting of Matthean Anti-Judaism." In *Anti-Judaism in Early Christianity*, vol. 1, *Paul and the Gospels*, edited by Peter Richardson, S. G. Wilson, and David M. Granskow. Studies in Christianity and Judaism 2. Waterloo, Ont.: Wilfrid Laurier University Press, 1986.

Puech, Émile. "11QPsAp^a: Un ritual d'exorcismes: Essai de reconstruction." *RevQ* 14 (1999): 377–403.

———. "Immortality and Life after Death." In *The Dead Sea Scrolls: Fifty Years after Their Discovery; Proceedings of the Jerusalem Congress, July 20–25, 1997*, edited by Lawrence H. Schiffman, Emanuel Tov, and James C. VanderKam, 512–20. Jerusalem: Israel Exploration Society in cooperation with The Shrine of the Book, Israel Museum, 2000.

Qimron, Elisha. "Celibacy in the Dead Sea Scrolls and the Two Kinds of Sectarians." In *The Madrid Qumran Congress: Proceedings of the International Congress on the Dead Sea Scrolls, Madrid, 18–21 March 1991*, edited by Julio C. Trebolle Barrera and Luis Vegas Montaner, 287–94. STDJ 11. Leiden: Brill, 1992.

———. "Notes on the 4Q Zadokite Fragments on Skin Disease." *JJS* 42 (1991): 256–59.

Qimron, Elisha, and James Charlesworth. "Rule of the Community." In *The Dead Sea Scrolls: Hebrew, Aramaic, and Greek Texts with English Translations*, edited by James Charlesworth et al., vol. 1, *Rule of the Community and Related Documents*, 1–52. Princeton Theological Seminary Dead Sea Scrolls Project 1. Tübingen: J. C. B. Mohr; Louisville, Ky.: Westminster John Knox, 1995.

Rabin, Chaim. "The Translation Process and the Character of the Septuagint." *Textus* 6 (1968): 1–26.

Rahmani, L. Y. *A Catalogue of Jewish Ossuaries in the Collections of the State of Israel*. Jerusalem: Israel Antiquities Authority, 1994.

Rajak, Tessa. "The *Against Apion* and the Continuities in Josephus's Political Thought." In *Understanding Josephus: Seven Perspectives*, edited by Steve Mason, 222–46. Sheffield: Sheffield Academic Press, 1998.

———. "The *Against Apion* and the Continuities in Josephus' Political Thought." In idem, *The Jewish Dialogue with Greece and Rome: Studies in Cultural and Social Interaction*, 195–217. AGJU 48. Leiden: Brill, 2001.

———. "Flavius Josephus: Jewish History and the Greek World." Ph.D. diss., University of Oxford, 1975. Available at http://pace.cns.yorku.ca/York/york/tei/jewish_history?id=50.

———. "Friends, Romans, Subjects: Agrippa II's Speech in Josephus' *Jewish War*." In *The Jewish Dialogue with Greece and Rome: Studies in Cultural and Social Interaction*. AGJU 48. Leiden: Brill, 2002.

————. *The Jewish Dialogue with Greece and Rome: Studies in Cultural and Social Interaction.* AGJU 48. Leiden: Brill, 2000.

————. *Josephus: The Historian and His Society.* Philadelphia: Fortress Press, 1984.

Regev, Eyal. "More on Ritual Baths of Jewish Groups and Sects: On Research Methods and Archaeological Evidence—A Reply to A. Grossberg" (in Hebrew). *The Jerusalem Cathedra* 83 (1996): 169–76.

————. "The Ritual Baths Near the Temple Mount and Extra-Purification before Entering the Temple Courts." *IEJ* 55 (2005): 194–204.

————. "Ritual Baths of Jewish Groups and Sects in the Second Temple Period" (in Hebrew). *The Jerusalem Cathedra* 79 (1996): 3–21.

Reich, Ronny. "Archaeological Evidence of the Jewish Population at Hasmonean Gezer." *IEJ* 31 (1981): 48–52.

————. "The Hot-Bath House (Balneum), the Miqweh and the Jewish Community in the Second Temple Period." *JJS* 39 (1988): 102–7.

————. "Miqva'ot (Jewish Ritual Immersion Baths) in Eretz Israel in the Second Temple and Mishnah and Talmud Periods" (in Hebrew). Ph.D. diss., Hebrew University, Jerusalem, 1990.

————. "Miqwa'ot at Khirbet Qumran and the Jerusalem Connection." In *The Dead Sea Scrolls: Fifty Years after Their Discovery; Proceedings of the Jerusalem Congress, July 20–25, 1997,* edited by Lawrence H. Schiffman, Emanuel Tov, and James C. VanderKam, 728–31. Jerusalem: Israel Exploration Society in collaboration with The Shrine of the Book, Israel Museum, 2000.

————. 'A Miqweh at 'Isawiya Near Jerusalem.' *IEJ* 34 (1984): 220–23.

————. "Mishnah, Sheqalim 8:2 and the Archaeological Evidence." In *Perakim be-toldot Yerushalayim bi-yeme Bayit Sheni: Sefer zikaron le-Avraham Shalit (Jerusalem in the Second Temple Period: Abraham Schalit Memorial Volume),* edited by A. Oppenheimer et al., 225–56. Sifriyah le-toldot ha-yishuv ha-Yehudi be-Erets-Yisrael. Jerusalem: Yad Yitzhak Ben-Tsvi, 1980.

————. "The Synagogue and the Miqweh in Eretz-Israel in the Second-Temple, Mishnaic, and Talmudic Periods." In *Ancient Synagogues: Historical Analysis and Archaeological Discovery,* edited by Dan Urman and Paul V. M. Flesher, 1:289–97. Leiden: Brill, 1995.

————. "They Are Ritual Baths: Immerse Yourself in the Ongoing Sepphoris *mikveh* Debate." *BAR* 28, no. 2 (2002): 50–55.

Reich, Ronny, and Ely Shukron. "The Shiloah Pool during the Second Temple Period" (in Hebrew). *Qad* 130 (2005): 91–96.

Reimer, Andy M. *Miracle and Magic: A Study in the Acts of the Apostles and the Life of Apollonius of Tyana.* JSNTSup 235. London: Sheffield Academic Press, 2002.

Reinhartz, Adele. "Common Judaism, the Parting of the Ways, and the Johannine Community." In *Coping with the Changed/Changing Reality,* edited by Bob Becking. Leiden: Van Gorcum, forthcoming.

Rengstorf, Karl Heinrich. "*Sēmeion*." In *Theological Dictionary of the Old Testament,* edited by G. Johannes Botterweck, G. H. Ringgren, and Heinz-Josef Fabry, translated by John T. Willis, 7:206–7. Grand Rapids: Eerdmans, 1980.

Repschinski, Boris. *The Controversy Stories in Matthew: Their Redaction, Form and Relevance for the Relationship between the Matthean Community and Formative Judaism*. Göttingen: Vandenhoeck & Ruprecht, 2000.

Reventlow, Henning Graf, Yair Hoffman, and Benjamin Uffenheimer, eds. *Politics and Theopolitics in the Bible and Postbiblical Literature*. JSOTSup 171. Sheffield: JSOT Press, 1994.

Rhoads, David M. *Israel in Revolution, 6–74 CE: A Political History Based on the Writings of Josephus*. Philadelphia: Fortress Press, 1976.

Richards, I. A. *The Philosophy of Rhetoric*. Oxford: Oxford University Press, 1936.

Richardson, G. P., ed. *Law in Religious Communities of the Roman Period: The Debate over Torah and Nomos in Post-biblical Judaism and Early Christianity*. Studies in Christianity and Judaism 4. Waterloo, Ont.: Canadian Corporation for Studies in Religion, 1991.

Richardson, Peter. "An Architectural Case for Synagogues and Associations." In *The Ancient Synagogue from Its Origins until 200 CE: Papers Presented at an International Conference at Lund University, October 14–17, 2001*, edited by Birger Olsson and Magnus Zetterholm, 90–117. ConBNT 39. Stockholm: Almqvist & Wiksell International, 2003.

———. *Building Jewish in the Roman East*. Waco: Baylor University Press, 2004.

———. *Herod: King of the Jews and Friend of the Romans*. Columbia: University of South Carolina Press, 1996.

Richardson, Peter, S. G. Wilson, and David M. Granskow, eds. *Anti-Judaism in Early Christianity*. Waterloo, Ont.: Wilfrid Laurier University Press, 1986.

Robert, Louis. "Lucien et son temps." In *À travers l'Asie Mineure: Poètes et prosateurs, monnaies grecque, voyageurs et géographie*, 393–421. Bibliothèque des écoles françaises d'Athènes et de Rome 239. Athens: École française d'Athènes, 1980.

———. *À travers l'Asie Mineure: Poètes et prosateurs, monnaies grecque, voyageurs et géographie*. Bibliothèque des écoles françaises d'Athènes et de Rome 239. Athens: École française d'Athènes, 1980.

Roth, Wolfgang. "To Invert or Not to Invert: The Pharisaic Canon in the Gospels." In *Early Christian Interpretation of the Scriptures of Israel: Investigations and Proposals*, edited by Craig A. Evans and James A. Sanders, 59–78. JSNTSup 148. Sheffield: Sheffield Academic Press, 1997.

Roth-Gerson, L. *The Greek Inscriptions from the Synagogues in Eretz-Israel*. Jerusalem: Yad Izhak Ben-Zvi, 1987.

Runesson, Anders. "From Integration to Marginalization: Archaeology as Text and the Analysis of Early Diaspora Judaism" (in Swedish.) *SEÅ* 67 (2002): 121–44.

———. *The Gospel of Matthew and the Myth of Christian Origins: Rethinking the So-Called Parting(s) of the Ways between Judaism and Christianity*. Forthcoming.

———. "Judgment." In *The New Interpreters Dictionary of the Bible*, vol. 3, edited by Katharine Doob Sakenfeld et al., 457–66. Nashville: Abingdon, 2008.

———. "A Monumental Synagogue from the First Century: The Case of Ostia." *JSJ* 33 (2002): 171–220.

———. "The Oldest Synagogue Building in the Diaspora: A Response to L. Michael White." *HTR* 92 (1999): 409–33.

————. *The Origins of the Synagogue: A Socio-historical Study.* Stockholm: Almqvist & Wiksell International, 2001.

————. "The Synagogue at Ancient Ostia: The Building and Its History." In *The Synagogue of Ancient Ostia and the Jews of Rome: Interdisciplinary Studies*, edited by Birger Olsson, Dieter Mitternacht, and Olof Brandt, 29–99. Acta Instituti Romani Regni Sueciae, Series in 4, 57. Stockholm: Paul Åströms Förlag, 2001.

————. "Water and Worship: Ostia and the Ritual Bath in the Diaspora Synagogue." In *The Synagogue of Ancient Ostia and the Jews of Rome: Interdisciplinary Studies*, edited by Birger Olsson, Dieter Mitternacht, and Olof Brandt, 115–29. Acta Instituti Romani Regni Sueciae, Series in 4, 57. Stockholm: Paul Åströms Förlag, 2001.

Rutgers, Leonard Victor. "Archaeological Evidence for the Interaction of Jews and Non-Jews in Late Antiquity." *AJA* 96 (1992): 101–18.

————. "Diaspora Synagogues: Synagogue Archaeology in the Greco-Roman World." In *Sacred Realm: The Emergence of the Synagogue in the Ancient World*, edited by Steven Fine. New York: Oxford University Press, 1996.

————. *The Hidden Heritage of Diaspora Judaism.* Contributions to Biblical Exegesis and Theology 20. Leuven: Peeters, 1998.

————, ed. *The Use of Sacred Books in the Ancient World.* Contributions to Biblical Exegesis and Theology 22. Leuven: Peeters, 1998.

Safrai, Ze'ev, and Chanah Safrai. "Were the Rabbis a Dominant Elite?" In *The Path of Peace: Studies in Honor of Israel Friedman Ben-Shalom*, edited by D. Gera and M. Ben-Zeev, 373–440. Be'er Sheva: Ben Gurion University of the Negev, 2005.

Saldarini, Anthony. "Delegitimation of Leaders in Matthew 23." *CBQ* (1992): 659–80.

————. "The Gospel of Matthew and Jewish-Christian Conflict in Galilee." In *The Galilee in Late Antiquity*, edited by Lee I. Levine, 23–38. New York: Jewish Theological Seminary of America, 1992.

————. *Matthew's Christian-Jewish Community.* CSHJ. Chicago: University of Chicago Press, 1994.

Saller, Sylvester John. *Discoveries at St. John's, 'Ein Karim, 1941–1942.* Jerusalem: Franciscan Press, 1946.

Sanders, E. P. "Common Judaism and the Synagogue in the First Century." In *Jews, Christians, and Polytheists in the Ancient Synagogue: Cultural Interaction during the Greco-Roman Period*, edited by Steven Fine, 1–17. New York: Routledge, 1999.

————. "The Covenant as a Soteriological Category and the Nature of Salvation in Palestinian and Hellenistic Judaism." In *Jews, Greeks and Christians: Religious Cultures in Late Antiquity: Essays in Honor of William David Davies*, edited by Robert Hamerton-Kelly and Robin Scroggs, 11–44. SJLA 21. Leiden: Brill, 1976.

————. "Covenantal Nomism Revisited." In *Jewish Studies Quarterly*, guest-edited by Dana Hollander and Joel Kaminsky. Forthcoming.

————. "The Dead Sea Sect and Other Jews." In *The Dead Sea Scrolls in Their Historical Context*, edited by Timothy H. Lim, Larry W. Hurtado, A. Graham Auld, and Alison M. Jack, 7–43. Edinburgh: T&T Clark, 2000.

———. "Defending the Indefensible," *JBL* 111, no. 3 (1991): 463–77.

———. "Jacob Neusner and the Philosophy of the Mishnah." In *Jewish Law from Jesus to the Mishnah: Five Studies*, 309–31. London: SCM; Philadelphia: Trinity Press International, 1990.

———. *Jesus and Judaism*. Philadelphia: Fortress Press, 1985.

———. "Jesus and the Kingdom: The Restoration of Israel and the New People of God." In *Jesus, the Gospels and the Church: Essays in Honor of William R. Farmer*, edited by E. P. Sanders, 225–39. Macon, Ga.: Mercer University Press, 1987.

———. *Jewish Law from Jesus to the Mishnah: Five Studies*. London: SCM; Philadelphia: Trinity Press International, 1990.

———. *Judaism: Practice and Belief, 63 BCE–66 CE*. 1992. Corrected ed., London: SCM; Philadelphia: Trinity Press International, 1994.

———. *Paul and Palestinian Judaism: A Comparison of Patterns of Religion*. Philadelphia: Fortress Press, 1977.

———, ed. *Jesus, the Gospels and the Church: Essays in Honor of William R. Farmer*. Macon, Ga.: Mercer University Press, 1987.

Sanders, E. P., A. I. Baumgarten, and Alan Mendelson, eds. *Jewish and Christian Self-Definition II: Aspects of Judaism in the Graeco-Roman Period*. London: SCM, 1981.

Sanders, James A. "A Liturgy for Healing the Stricken (11QPsAp^a = 11Q11)." In *The Dead Sea Scrolls: Hebrew, Aramaic, and Greek Texts with English Translations*, edited by James Charlesworth et al., vol. 4A, *Pseudepigraphic and Non-Masoretic Psalms and Prayers*, 216–34. Princeton Theological Seminary Dead Sea Scrolls Project 4A. Tübingen: J. C. B. Mohr; Louisville, Ky.: Westminster John Knox, 1995.

Sandmel, Samuel. *A Jewish Understanding of the New Testament*. 1956. Reprint, with a new preface, Woodstock: SkyLight Paths Publications, 2004.

Sartre, M. "Villes et villages du Hauran (Syrie) au IVe siècle." In *Sociétés urbaines, sociétés rurales dans l'Asie Mineure et la Syrie hellénistiques et romaines*, edited by E. Frézouls, 239–57. Strasbourg: AECR, 1987.

Schäfer, Peter. "Der vorrabbinische Pharisäismus." In *Paulus und das antike Judentum: Tübingen-Durham-Symposium im Gedenken an den 50. Todestag Adolf Schlatters (19. Mai 1938)*, edited by M. Hengel and U. Heckel, 125–72. WUNT 58. Tübingen: Mohr Siebeck, 1991.

Schalit, A. *König Herodes: Der Mann und sein Werk*. Berlin: Walter de Gruyter, 1969.

Schiffman, Lawrence. *The Eschatological Community of the Dead Sea Scrolls: A Study of the Rule of the Congregation*. SBLMS 38. Atlanta: Scholars Press, 1989.

———. "Jerusalem in the Dead Sea Scrolls." In *The Centrality of Jerusalem: Historical Perspectives*, edited by M. Poorthuis and Ch. Safrai, 73–88. Kampen: Kok Pharos, 1996.

———. "Pharisees and Sadducees in Pesher Nahum." In *Minḥah le-Naḥum: Biblical and Other Studies Presented to Nahum M. Sarna in Honour of His 70th Birthday*, edited by Marc Zvi Brettler and Michael A. Fishbane, 272–90. JSOTSup 154. Sheffield: JSOT Press, 1993.

———. "Purity and Perfection: Exclusion from the Council of the Community in the *Serekh Ha-'Edah*." In *Biblical Archaeology Today: Proceedings of the International Congress of Biblical*

Archaeology, April 1984, edited by the Israel Exploration Society, 373–89. Jerusalem: Israel Exploration Society, 1985.

———. *Sectarian Law in the Dead Sea Scrolls: Courts, Testimony, and the Penal Code.* BJS 33. Chico, Calif.: Scholars Press, 1983.

———. *Who Was a Jew? Rabbinic and Halakhic Perspectives on the Jewish-Christian Schism.* Hoboken, N.J.: KTAV, 1985.

Schiffman, Lawrence, and Devorah Dimant, eds. *Time to Prepare the Way in the Wilderness: Papers on the Qumran Scrolls.* Leiden: Brill, 1995.

Schiffman, Lawrence H., Emanuel Tov, and James C. VanderKam, eds. *The Dead Sea Scrolls: Fifty Years after Their Discovery: Proceedings of the Jerusalem Congress, July 20–25, 1997.* Jerusalem: Israel Exploration Society in cooperation with The Shrine of the Book, Israel Museum, 2000.

Schremer, A. "Comments Concerning King Uziahu's Burial Place." *The Jerusalem Cathedra* 46 (1987): 188–90.

Schürer, Emil. *The History of the Jewish People in the Age of Jesus Christ (175 BC—AD 135): A New English Version.* Revised and edited by Fergus Millar, Geza Vermes, and Martin Goodman. 3 vols. Edinburgh: T&T Clark, 1986.

Schutt, R. J. H. "Letter of Aristeas." In *The Old Testament Pseudepigrapha*, edited by James H. Charlesworth, 2:7–34. 2 vols. Garden City, N.Y.: Doubleday, 1983.

Schwartz, Daniel R. "God, Gentiles and Jewish Law: On Acts 15 and Josephus's Adiabene Narrative." In *Geschichte—Tradition—Reflexion: Festschrift für Martin Hengel zum 70. Geburtstag*, edited by Hubert Cancik, Hermann Lichtenberger, and Peter Schäfer, 263–83. Tübingen: Mohr Siebeck, 1996.

———. "Josephus on the Jewish Constitution and Community." *Scripta Classica Israelica* 7 (1983): 30–52.

———. *Studies in the Jewish Background of Christianity.* WUNT 60. Tübingen: Mohr Siebeck, 1992.

———. "Temple and Desert: On Religion and State in Second Temple Period Judaea." In idem, *Studies in the Jewish Background of Christianity*, 29–43. WUNT 60. Tübingen: Mohr Siebeck, 1992.

———. "Temple or City: What Did Hellenistic Jews See in Jerusalem?" *The Centrality of Jerusalem: Historical Perspectives*, edited by M. Poorthuis and Ch. Safrai. Kampen: Kok Pharos, 1996.

Schwartz, Seth. "Euergetism in Josephus and the Epigraphical Culture of First-Century Jerusalem." In *From Hellenism to Islam: Cultural and Linguistic Change in the Roman Near East*, edited by H. Cotton, R. Hoyland, J. Price, and D. Wasserstein. Cambridge: Cambridge University Press, forthcoming.

———. *Imperialism and Jewish Society: 200 BCE to 640 CE.* Princeton: Princeton University Press, 2001.

———. *Josephus and Judaean Politics.* Leiden: Brill, 1990.

———. "On the Autonomy of Judaea in the Fourth and Third Centuries BCE." *JJS* 45 (1994): 157–68.

Schweizer, Eduard. "Matthew's Church." In *The Interpretation of Matthew*, edited by Graham Stanton, 149–77. Studies in New Testament Interpretation. Edinburgh: T&T Clark, 1995.

Scott, James C. *Domination and the Arts of Resistance—Hidden Transcripts*. New Haven, Conn.: Yale University Press, 1990.

Segal, Alan F. "Matthew's Jewish Voice." In *Social History of the Matthean Community: Cross-Disciplinary Approaches*, edited by David Balch, 3–37. Minneapolis: Fortress Press, 1991.

———. *Two Powers in Heaven: Early Rabbinic Reports about Christianity and Gnosticism*. SJLA. Leiden: Brill, 1977.

Shaw, B. "Josephus—Roman Power and Responses to It." *Athenaeum* 83 (1995): 357–90.

Shemesh, Aaron. "'The Holy Angels Are in Their Council': The Exclusion of Deformed Persons from Holy Places in Qumranic and Rabbinic Literature." *DSD* 4 (1997): 179–206.

Shils, Edward. *Center and Periphery: Essays in Macrosociology*. Chicago: University of Chicago Press, 1975.

Shinan, A. "The Aramaic Targum as a Mirror of Galilean Jewry." In *The Galilee in Late Antiquity*, edited by Lee I. Levine, 248–49. New York and Jerusalem: Jewish Theological Seminary, 1992.

Signer, M., ed. *Memory and History in Christianity and Judaism*. Notre Dame: Notre Dame University Press, 2001.

Sim, David. *Apocalyptic Eschatology in the Gospel of Matthew*. SNTSMS 88. Cambridge: Cambridge University Press, 1996.

———. "Christianity and Ethnicity in the Gospel of Matthew." In *Ethnicity and the Bible*, edited by Mark G. Brett, 171–96. Biblical Interpretation Series 19. Leiden: Brill, 2002.

———. "The 'Confession' of the Soldiers in Matthew 27:54." *HeyJ* 34 (1993): 401–24.

———. *The Gospel of Matthew and Christian Judaism: The History and Social Setting of the Matthean Community*. Studies of the New Testament and Its World. Edinburgh: T&T Clark, 1998.

———. "The Gospel of Matthew and the Gentiles." *JSNT* 57 (1995): 19–48.

Skarsaune, Oskar. *In the Shadow of the Temple: Jewish Influences on Early Christianity*. Leicester: Inter-Varsity Press, 2002.

Smith, Gary V. "The Concept of God/Gods as Kings in the Ancient Near East and the Bible." *TJ* 3 (1982): 33–37.

Smith, Jonathan Z. "Earth and Gods." In idem, *Map Is Not Territory: Studies in the History of Religions*. Leiden: Brill, 1978.

———. "The Influence of Symbols on Social Change: A Place on Which to Stand." In idem, *Map Is Not Territory: Studies in the History of Religions*, 129–46. Leiden: Brill, 1978.

———. "Jerusalem: The City as Place." In *Civitas: Religious Interpretations of the City*, edited by Peter S. Hawkins, 25–38. Scholars Press Studies in the Humanities. Atlanta: Scholars Press, 1986.

———. *Map Is Not Territory: Studies in the History of Religions*. Leiden: Brill, 1978.

———. "A Matter of Class: Taxonomies of Religion." *HTR* 89 (1996): 387–403.

———. "Towards Interpreting Demonic Powers in Hellenistic and Roman Antiquity." *ANRW* 2.16.1 (1979), 425–39.

Smith, Morton. "The Dead Sea Sect in Relation to Ancient Judaism." *NTS* 7 (1960–61): 347–60.

———. "Palestinian Judaism in the First Century." In *Israel: Its Role in Civilization*, edited by Moshe Davis, 67–81. New York: Israel Institute of the Jewish Theological Seminary, 1956. Reprinted in *Essays in Greco-Roman and Related Talmudic Literature*, edited by Henry A. Fischel, 183–97. New York: KTAV, 1977.

———. "Zealots and Sicarii, Their Origins and Relation." *HTR* 64 (1971): 1–19.

Soskice, Janet Martin. *Metaphor and Religious Language*. Oxford: Clarendon, 1985.

Spilsbury, P. "Contra Apionem and Antiquitates Judaicae: Points of Contact." In *Josephus' Contra Apionem*, edited by Louis H. Feldman and John R. Levison, 348–68. Leiden: Brill, 1996.

Stacey, David. "Was There a Synagogue in Hasmonean Jericho?" *Bible and Interpretation*. http://www.bibleinterp.com/articles/Hasmonean_Jericho.htm.

Stambaugh, John E. "The Functions of Roman Temples." *ANRW* 2.16.1 (1978): 554–608.

Stanton, Graham. "The Communities of Matthew." *Int* 46 (1992): 379–91.

———. "5 Ezra and Matthean Christianity in the Second Century." *JTS* 28 (1977): 67–83.

———. *A Gospel for a New People: Studies in Matthew*. Edinburgh: T&T Clark, 1992.

———. "Introduction: Matthew's Gospel in Recent Scholarship." In *The Interpretation of Matthew*, edited by Graham Stanton, 1–26. 2nd ed. Studies in New Testament Interpretation. Edinburgh: T&T Clark, 1995.

———. "The Origin and Purpose of Matthew's Gospel." *ANRW* 2.25.3 (1987): 181–92.

———, ed. *The Interpretation of Matthew*. 2nd ed. Studies in New Testament Interpretation. Edinburgh: T&T Clark, 1995.

Stark, Rodney. "How Sane People Talk to the Gods: A Rational Theory of Revelation." In *Innovation in Religious Traditions: Essays in the Interpretation of Religious Change*, edited by M. Williams, C. Cox, and M. Jaffee, 19–34. Berlin: Walter de Gruyter, 1992.

———. *The Rise of Christianity: How the Obscure, Marginal Jesus Movement Became the Dominant Religious Force in the Western World in a Few Centuries*. Princeton: Princeton University Press, 1996.

———. *A Theory of Religion*. New York: Peter Lang, 1987.

Stark, Rodney, and William Sims Bainbridge. "Networks of Faith: Interpersonal Bonds and Recruitment to Cults and Sects." *American Journal of Sociology* 85 (1980): 1376–95.

Stegemann, Ekkehard W., and Wolfgang Stegemann. *The Jesus Movement: A Social History of Its First Century*. Minneapolis: Fortress Press, 1999.

Stegemann, Harmut. *The Library at Qumran: On the Essenes, Qumran, John the Baptist and Jesus*. Leiden: Brill, 1998.

Stemberger, Günter. *Introduction to the Talmud and Midrash*. Edinburgh: T & T Clark, 1996.

———. "Was There a 'Mainstream Judaism' in the Late Second Temple Period?" *Review of Rabbinic Judaism* 4, no. 2 (2001): 189–207.

Stendahl, Krister. *The School of St. Matthew and Its Use of the Old Testament*. 2nd ed. Philadelphia: Fortress Press, 1968.

Stern, Ephraim, ed. *The New Encyclopedia of Archaeological Excavations in the Holy Land*. 4 vols. Jerusalem: Israel Exploration Society and Carta, 1993.

Stern, Menahem. *Greek and Latin Authors on Jews and Judaism*. 3 vols. Jerusalem: Israel Academy of Sciences and Humanities, 1976–84.

Stern, Y. S. "Figurative Art and Halakhah in the Mishnaic-Talmudic Period." *Zion* 61 (1996): 397–419.

Stienstra, Nelly. *YHWH Is the Husband of His People: Analysis of a Biblical Metaphor with Special Reference to Translation*. Kampen: Kok Pharos, 1993.

Stone, M. E., ed. *Jewish Writings of the Second Temple Period*. Assen: Van Gorcum; Phildadelphia: Fortress Press, 1984.

Stone, M. E., and E. G. Chazon, eds. *Biblical Perspectives: Early Use and Interpretation of the Bible in Light of the Dead Sea Scrolls: Proceedings of the First International Symposium of the Orion Center for the Study of the Dead Sea Scrolls and Associated Literature, 12–14 May 1996*. STDJ 28. Leiden: Brill, 1998.

Strecker, Georg. *Der Weg der Gerechtigkeit: Untersuchung zur Theologie des Matthäus*. 3rd rev. and enl. ed. FRLANT 82. Göttingen: Vandenhoeck & Ruprecht, 1971.

Strobel, A. "Die Wasserversorgung der Hirbet Qumran." *ZDPV* 88 (1972): 55–86.

Stroumsa, Guy G. "The Christian Hermeneutical Revolution and Its Double Helix." In *The Use of Sacred Books in the Ancient World*, edited by L. V. Rutgers, 9–28. Contributions to Biblical Exegesis and Theology 22. Leuven: Peeters, 1998.

———. "Early Christianity—A Religion of the Book?" In *Homer, the Bible, and Beyond: Literary and Religious Canons in the Ancient World*, edited by M. Finkelberg and Guy G. Stroumsa, 153–73. Jerusalem Studies in Religion and Culture 2. Leiden: Brill, 2003.

Sukenik, E. L. "An Epitaph of Uzziahu King of Judah." *Tarbiz* 2 (1931): 288–92.

Swete, H. B. *An Introduction to the Old Testament in Greek*. Revised by R. R. Otley. Cambridge: Cambridge University Press, 1914.

Syon, Danny. "Gamla: Portrait of a Rebellion." *BAR* 18, no. 1 (1992): 21–37.

Syon, Danny, and Z. Yavor. "Gamla—Old and New." *Qad* 34 (2001): 2–33.

Syreeni, Kari. *The Making of the Sermon on the Mount: A Procedural Analysis of Matthew's Redactoral Activity*. Part 1, *Methodology and Compositional Analysis*. Helsinki: Suomalainen Tiedeakatemia, 1987.

Talmon, Shemaryahu. "The Desert Motif in the Bible and in Qumran Literature." In idem, *Literary Studies in the Hebrew Bible: Form and Content—Collected Studies*, 216–54. Jerusalem: Magnes Press, 1993.

———. *Literary Studies in the Hebrew Bible: Form and Content—Collected Studies*. Jerusalem: Magnes Press, 1993.

Taubes, Jacob, ed. *Theokratie*. Religionstheorie und Politische Theologie 3. Munich: W. Fink and F. Schöningh, 1987.

Taylor, J. E. *Jewish Women Philosophers of First-Century Alexandria: Philo's 'Therapeutae' Reconsidered*. Oxford: Oxford University Press, 2003.

Tcherikover, Victor. *Hellenistic Civilization and the Jews*. Jerusalem: Magnes Press, Hebrew University, 1959. Reprint, Philadelphia: Jewish Publication Society, 1999.

———. "The Ideology of the Letter of Aristeas." *HTR* 51 (1958): 59–86.

Tcherikover, Victor, A. Fuks, and M. Stern, eds. *Corpus papyrorum judaicarum.* 3 vols. Cambridge, Mass.: Harvard University Press, 1957–64.

Teeple, Howard M. *The Mosaic Eschatological Prophet.* Philadelphia: Society of Biblical Literature, 1957.

Temporini H., ed. *Aufstieg und Niedergang der römischen Welt: Geschichte und Kultur Roms im Spiegel der neueren Forschung.* Part 1: vols. 1–8. Berlin: Walter de Gruyter, 1972–73.

Temporini H., and W. Haase, eds. *Aufstieg und Niedergang der römischen Welt: Geschichte und Kultur Roms im Spiegel der neueren Forschung.* Part 2: vols. 9–37. Berlin: Walter de Gruyter, 1975–94.

Thackeray, H. St. John. *Josephus: The Man and the Historian.* The Hilda Stich Strook Lectures. New York: Jewish Institute of Religion Press, 1929.

Thackeray, H. St. John, Ralph Marcus, Allen Wikgren, and Louis H. Feldman, trans. *Josephus.* 10 vols. LCL. Cambridge, Mass.: Harvard University Press, 1926–65.

Theissen, Gerd, and Annette Merz. *The Historical Jesus: A Comprehensive Guide.* Translated by John Bowden. Philadelphia: Fortress Press, 1998.

Theodor, Julius, and Chanoch Albeck. *Bereschit Rabba: Mit kritischem Apparat und Kommentar* (in Hebrew). 3 vols. Berlin: H. Itzkowski, 1903–23.

Tilborg, Sjef van. *The Jewish Leaders in Matthew.* Leiden: Brill, 1972.

Tomson, Peter J. *"If This Be from Heaven": Jesus and the New Testament Authors in Their Relationship to Judaism.* Biblical Seminar 76. Sheffield: Sheffield Academic Press, 2001.

Tov, Emanuel. *The Greek and Hebrew Bible: Collected Essays on the Septuagint.* VTSup 72. Leiden: Brill, 1999.

———. "The Rabbinic Tradition Concerning the 'Alterations' Inserted into the Greek Pentateuch and Their Relation to the Original Text of the LXX." *JSJ* 15 (1984): 65–89.

———. Review of G. Veltri, *Eine Tora für den König Talmai. Scripta Classica Israelica* 14 (1995): 178–83.

———. "The Septuagint." In *Mikra: Text, Translation, Reading and Interpretation of the Hebrew Bible in Ancient Judaism and Early Christianity,* edited by M. J. Mulder and H. Sysling, 161–88. CRINT, Section 2: Literature of the Jewish People in the Period of the Second Temple and the Talmud 1. Assen: Van Gorcum, 1988.

———. "Theologically Motivated Exegesis Embedded in the Septuagint." In *Translation of Scripture: Proceedings of a Conference at the Annenberg Research Institute, May 15–16, 1989,* edited by Annenberg Research Institute, 215–33. JQR Supplements. Philadelphia: Annenberg Institute, 1989. Reprinted in idem, *The Greek and Hebrew Bible: Collected Essays.* VTSup 72. Brill: Leiden, 1999.

Tov, Emanuel, Robert A. Kraft, and P. J. Parsons, eds. *The Greek Minor Prophets Scroll from Nahal Hever (8HeXIIgr): The Seiyâl Collection I.* DJD 8. Oxford: Clarendon, 1990.

Trebolle Barrera, Julio C., and Luis Vegas Montaner, eds. *The Madrid Qumran Congress: Proceedings of the International Congress on the Dead Sea Scrolls, Madrid, 18–21 March 1991.* STDJ 11. Leiden: Brill, 1992.

Treves, Marco. "The Reign of God in the O.T." *VT* 19, no. 2 (1969): 230–43.

Troiani, Lucio. "The ΠΟΛΙΤΕΙΑ of Israel in the Graeco-Roman Age." In *Josephus and the History of the Greco-Roman Period: Essays in Memory of Morton Smith*, edited by Fausto Parente and Joseph Sievers. StPB 41. Leiden: Brill, 1994, 11–22.

Trümper, Monika. "The Oldest Original Synagogue Building in the Diaspora: The Delos Synagogue Reconsidered." *Hesperia* 73 (2004): 513–98.

Tuan, Yi-Fu. *Topophilia: A Study of Environmental Perceptions, Attitudes and Values*. Englewood Cliffs, N.J.: Prentice-Hall, 1974.

Turner, Victor. "Betwixt and Between: The Liminal Period in Rites de Passage." In *The Proceedings of the American Ethnological Society: Symposium on New Approaches to the Study of Religion*, edited by the American Ethnological Society, 4–20. Seattle: American Ethnological Society, 1964.

———. *The Ritual Process: Structure and Anti-Structure*. Chicago: Aldin, 1969.

Twelftree, Graham H. *Jesus the Exorcist: A Contribution to the Study of the Historical Jesus*. WUNT 2.54. Tübingen: Mohr Siebeck, 1993.

Udoh, Fabian, et al., eds. *Redefining First-Century Jewish and Christian Identities: Essays in Honor of Ed P. Sanders*. South Bend: University of Notre Dame Press, 2007.

Ulrich, Eugene. *The Qumran Text of Samuel and Josephus*. HSM 19. Missoula, Mont.: Scholars Press, 1978.

Ulrich, Eugene, and James C. VanderKam, eds. *The Community of the Renewed Covenant: The Notre Dame Symposium on the Dead Sea Scrolls*. Notre Dame: University of Notre Dame Press, 1994.

VanderKam, James C. "Enoch Traditions in Jubilees and Other Second-Century Sources." In *SBL 1978 Seminar Papers*, edited by Paul J. Achtemeier, 1.228–51. Missoula, Mont.: Scholars Press, 1978.

———. "Identity and History of the Community." In *The Dead Sea Scrolls after Fifty Years: A Comprehensive Assessment*, edited by Peter W. Flint and James C. VanderKam, 487–533. Leiden: Brill, 1999.

———. "Jubilees." In *The Anchor Bible Dictionary*, edited by D. N. Freedman, 3.1030–32. New York: Doubleday, 1986.

———. "The Judean Desert and the Community of the Dead Sea Scrolls." In *Antikes Judentum und frühes Christentum: Festschrift für Hartmut Stegemann zum 65*, edited by Bernd Kollmann, Wolfgang Reinbold, and Annette Steudel, 159–71. BZNW 97. Berlin and New York: Walter de Gruyter, 1999.

———. *Textual and Historical Studies in the Book of Jubilees*. HSM 14. Missoula, Mont.: Scholars Press, 1977.

Veltri, Giuseppe. *Eine Tora für den König Talmai: Untersuchungen zum Übersetzungsverständnis in der jüdisch-hellenistischen und rabbinischen Literatur*. TSAJ 41. Tübingen: Mohr Siebeck, 1994.

Vermes, Geza. *The Complete Dead Sea Scrolls in English*. New York: Penguin, 1997.

Via, Dan O., Jr. "Kingdom and Parable: The Search for a New Grasp of Symbol, Metaphor and Myth." Review of *Jesus and the Language of the Kingdom of God: Symbol and Metaphor in New Testament Interpretation*, by Norman Perrin. *Int* 31 (1977): 181–83.

Viviano, Benedict. "John's Use of Matthew: Beyond Tweaking." *RB* 111, no. 2 (2004): 209–37.

———. "Social World and Community Leadership: The Case of Matthew 23:1-12, 34." *JSNT* 39 (1990): 3–21.

Wach, Joachim. *Sociology of Religion.* Chicago: University of Chicago Press, 1944.

Wacholder, B. Z. *Eupolemus: A Study of Judaeo-Greek Literature.* Cincinnati: Hebrew Union College, Jewish Institute of Religion, 1974.

Wagner, J. R. *Heralds of the Good News: Isaiah and Paul "in Concert" in the Letter to the Romans.* NovTSup 101. Leiden: Brill, 2002.

Wainwright, Elaine. *Shall We Look for Another? A Feminist Rereading of the Matthean Jesus.* Maryknoll, N.Y.: Orbis Books, 1998.

Wansbrough, John. *Quranic Studies: Sources and Methods of Scriptural Interpretation.* London Oriental Series 31. Oxford: Oxford University Press, 1977.

Wassen, Cecilia. *Women in the Damascus Document.* SBL Academia Biblica 21. Atlanta: Society of Biblical Literature; Leiden: Brill, 2005.

Wasserstein, Abraham. "On Donkeys, Wine and the Uses of Textual Criticism: Septuagintal Variants in Jewish Palestine." In *The Jews in the Hellenistic-Roman World: Studies in Memory of Menahem Stern*, edited by Isaiah Gafni, Aharon Oppenheimer, and Daniel Schwartz, 119–42. Jerusalem: Zalman Shazar Center for Jewish History and the Historical Society of Israel, 1996.

Wasserstein, Abraham, and David Wasserstein. *The Legend of the Septuagint: From Classical Antiquity to Today.* Cambridge: Cambridge University Press, 2006.

Watson, Wilfred G. E. "Reversed Rootplay in Ps 145." *Biblica* 62 (1981): 101–2.

Watts, James W., ed. *Persia and Torah: The Theory of Imperial Authorization of the Pentateuch.* SBLSymS 17. Atlanta: Society of Biblical Literature, 2001.

Watts, John D. W. "Images of Yahweh: God in the Prophets." In *Studies in Old Testament Theology*, edited by Robert L. Hubbard Jr., Robert K. Johnston, and Robert P. Meye, 135–47. Dallas: Word, 1992.

Weder, Hans. *Die Gleichnisse Jesu als Metaphern: Traditions- und redaktionsgeschichtliche Analysen und Interpretationen.* Göttingen: Vandenhoeck & Ruprecht, 1978.

Weinfeld, Moshe. "The Charge of Hypocrisy in Matthew 23 and in Jewish Sources." *Immanuel* 24/25 (1990): 52–58.

———. *The Organizational Pattern and the Penal Code of the Qumran Sect.* Göttingen: Vandenhoeck & Ruprecht, 1986.

Weiss, Z. *The Sepphoris Synagogue: Deciphering an Ancient Message through Its Archaeological and Socio-historical Contexts.* Jerusalem: Israel Exploration Society, 2005.

Wheelwright, Philip. *Metaphor and Reality.* Bloomington: Indiana University Press, 1962.

White, L. Michael. "Crisis Management and Boundary Maintenance: The Social Location of the Matthean Community." In *Social History of the Matthean Community: Cross-Disciplinary Approaches*, edited by David L. Balch, 211–47. Minneapolis: Fortress Press, 1991.

———. "The Delos Synagogue Revisited: Recent Fieldwork in the Graeco-Roman Diaspora." *HTR* 80 (1987): 133–60.

———. "Reading the Ostia Synagogue: A Reply to A. Runesson." *HTR* 92 (1999): 435–64.

———. "Synagogue and Society in Imperial Ostia: Archaeological and Epigraphic Evidence." *HTR* 90 (1997): 23–58.

Whitelam, Keith W. *The Just King: Monarchical Judicial Authority in Ancient Israel*. JSOTSup 12. Sheffield: JSOT Press, 1979.

Whittaker, Molly. *Jews and Christians: Graeco-Roman Views*. Cambridge: Cambridge University Press, 1984.

Wifstrand, A. "Luke and the Septuagint" (in Swedish). *STK* 6 (1940): 243–62.

Wild, Robert A. *Water in the Cultic Worship of Isis and Sarapis*. Leiden: Brill, 1981.

Wilken, Robert L. *John Chrysostom and the Jews: Rhetoric and Reality in the Late Fourth Century*. Berkeley: University of California Press, 1983.

Will, Edouard, and Claude Orrieux. *"Prosélytisme Juif"? Histoire d'une erreur*. Paris: Les Belles Lettres, 1992.

Williams, M., C. Cox, and M. Jaffee, eds. *Innovation in Religious Traditions: Essays in the Interpretation of Religious Change*. Berlin: Walter de Gruyter, 1992.

Wintermute, O. S. "Jubilees." In *The Old Testament Pseudepigrapha*, edited by James H. Charlesworth, 2:35–142. 2 vols. New York: Doubleday, 1985.

Wise, Michael Owen, Martin G. Abegg, and Edward M. Cook. "Charter of a Jewish Sectarian Association." In *The Dead Sea Scrolls: A New Translation*, 123–42. San Francisco: HarperSanFrancisco, 1996.

———. *The Dead Sea Scrolls: A New Translation*. San Francisco: HarperSanFrancisco, 1996.

Wise, Michael Owen, and Douglas Penney. "By the Power of Beelzebub: An Aramaic Incantation Formula from Qumran (4Q560)." *JBL* 113, no. 4 (1994): 627–50.

Wolter, Michael. "Was heisst nun Gottes Reich?" *ZNW* 86 (1995): 5–19.

Woolf, Greg. "Monumental Writing and the Expansion of Roman Society in the Early Empire." *JRS* 86 (1996): 22–39.

World Union of Jewish Studies. *Eleventh World Congress of Jewish Studies*, 31–38. Jerusalem: World Union of Jewish Studies, 1993.

Yadin, Yigael. "Pesher Nahum (4QpNahum) Reconsidered." *IEJ* 21 (1971): 1–12.

———. "The Synagogue at Masada." In *Ancient Synagogues Revealed*, edited by Lee I. Levine, 19–23. Jerusalem: Israel Exploration Society, 1981.

Zetterholm, Magnus. *The Formation of Christianity in Antioch: A Social-Scientific Approach to the Separation between Judaism and Christianity*. London: Routledge, 2003.

Zilberbod, I., and D. Amit, "Mazor (Elad), Sites 50 and 62." *HA-ESI* 113 (2001): 60–61.

Zissu, Boaz. "Rural Settlement in the Judaean Hills and Foothills from the Late Second Temple Period to the Bar-Kokhba Revolt" (in Hebrew). Ph.D. diss., Hebrew University, Jerusalem, 2001.

Zissu, Boaz, and A. Ganor. "Horbat 'Ethri." *HA-ESI* 113 (2001): 101–4.

———. "Horvat 'Ethri—A Jewish Village from the Second Temple in the Judaean Foothills" (in Hebrew). *Qad* 123 (2002): 18–27.

Zissu, Boaz, G. Solimany, and D. Weiss. "Sha'ar Ha-Gay, Survey." *ESI 19* (1999): 71–72.

Zissu, Boaz, Y. Tepper, and D. Amit. "*Miqwa'ot* at Kefar 'Othnai Near Legio." *IEJ* 56 (2006): 57–66.

Zohar, D. "The Iconography of the Zodiac and the Months in the Synagogue of Sepphoris: A Study in Diffusion of Artistic Models." *Mo'ed* 16 (2006): 1–26.

Index of Ancient Sources

New Testament

Index of Modern Authors

Index of Subjects